BOOKS BY EDWARD HOAGLAND

Cat Man

The Circle Home

The Peacock's Tail

Notes from the Century Before: A Journal from British Columbia

The Courage of Turtles

Walking the Dead Diamond River

The Moose on the Wall

Red Wolves and Black Bears

African Calliope: A Journey to the Sudan

The Edward Hoagland Reader

The Tugman's Passage

City Tales

Seven Rivers West

Heart's Desire

The Final Fate of the Alligators

Balancing Acts

Tigers & Ice

Compass Points

HOAGLAND ON NATURE

Essays

Edward Hoagland

THE LYONS PRESS
Guilford, Connecticut
An imprint of The Globe Pequot Press

The Lyons Press is an imprint of The Globe Pequot Press.

10 9 8 7 6 5 4 3 2 1

Printed in the United States of America

ISBN 1-58574-652-5

Library of Congress Cataloging-in-Publication data is available on file.

Contents

Contents

III

People

Foreword

To read an essay by Ted Hoagland is to travel on an uncertain path, pitching and tilting as if on a wild sea, then slamming down hard on bedrock. It is to track the peregrinations of a mind so keen-nosed and acute, so yeasty, restless, and digressive that the reader has to catch herself from a descent into emotional vertigo. Yet, after the free fall, an uncanny sense of balance radiates from his words—not from any strict structural logic, but from a yearning to shine light on the hidden bends and bights of life and, in the process, to unveil whatever truths are to be had.

Hoagland's essays are supple and intimate. He's swift-footed but has an all-seeing eye and a loner's vulnerability. In these twenty-six written essays gathered over a period of thirty-five years, no other writer has so exuberantly juxtaposed and interlarded the natural history of mammals, birds, reptiles, bugs, and fish—with human history, autobiography, social commentary, and opinion. It all works because Hoagland's sympathies are ecumenical: the deeper the current and the more flotsam and jetsam along the way, the better. Though he can seem jittery and brusque, he is a staunch man of values, a true New Englander who does not suffer fools gladly. Always, under the opposing currents, is a voice of sanity, a durable optimism, and an effortless appreciation of the world that makes us feel welcome inside his mind.

Like his late friend, the poet, John Barryman, Hoagland is a man for whom memory and unstinting curiosity is genius. Daily, he ransacks his mind and follows his heart's desire to all kinds of places, inside and out. He gives us alligators, tigers, snakes, lovers, circus people, tugboat captains, and backwoods families; he gives us the torment of his shattered marriages, the joy of his one child, of his Vermont cabin, and the astonishment of being able to see again after a bout of blindness. Every essay is a call to attention, a caution against apathy, an ardent love letter to life.

"A writer's work is to witness things," he says. Hoagland not only witnesses the world but sponges it up, stares down detail with a microscopic intensity, dives in and lets the rapids carry him willy-nilly, then climbs out to tell us what he has seen. An essayist is, by necessity, a generalist and, like all brilliant generalists, Hoagland depends on the particular, the arresting detail, the mind-boggling variety, to remind us of our commonality, of the complexity of the ways in which we all belong. We know from reading these essays that we do not have domination over the world but more simply, we are part of the wolf pack.

I began reading Ted Hoagland's books, *The Courage of Turtles, Red Wolves, and Black Bears,* and *Walking the Dead Diamond River,* in the 1970s and was so moved by his words that I thanked him in a letter for the gift of his books. He wrote back within the week and invited me to visit him in New York.

We walked the streets of the West Village with his dog on a leash, ate lunch, did errands, picked up his daughter, Molly, from school. At that time, Ted's stutter was so bad it sometimes took minutes for a single word to come out and, inevitably, a bus would roar by at just that moment and, to my embarassment, I would fail to hear him.

Later he and his daughter went on a pack trip with my husband and me to the interior of Yellowstone Park. He was legally blind at the time and despondent. He became fond of disappearing from camp. We found him lying on the trail where a few hours before we'd seen fresh grizzly tracks, apparently hoping to be eaten by a bear. Perhaps it was not so much that he wanted to die as to live in the presence of death. How else do we learn to live fully? His daughter and I conjectured that rubbing elbows with a silver-tipped grizzly would have been enough. He once described the life of a writer: "Time is short. By covering his ears with his forearms he hears the roar of his own living body, and, by touching the hollows of his cheeks, foresees the feel of the dead skull." For Ted, every rub of the elbow counted, whether it was with a salamander or a red-haired female beauty.

Thoreau said: "A lover of Nature is pre-eminently a lover of man. If I have no friend, what is nature to me?" What's unusual about Hoagland, compared to many other contemporary "nature writers," is that humans are never precluded from the scene. We might be despoilers, but we are still part of nature, we are animals, after all. While the "eco-elite" try desperately to "get things back to their pristine state"—an obvious impossibility—Hoagland starts with things as they are and goes from there.

The key to anyone's humanity has to do with how large an accommodation can be made, how much can be let in. In Hoagland's work, the margins are wide. He's as awed by the extraordinary abilities of the human, the human-like bear, the circus high diver, and the ridge-slope fox as he is dismayed, no, crushed, by the pointless destruction by humans of biological diversity. He is, after all, a dedicated "biophiliac," one who readily acknowledges what E. O. Wilson describes as our innate affiliation with other creatures.

Hoagland agonizes over the current state of the world: not the foibles of so-called civilization, but the holocaust of species extinctions, and wonders why more scientists have not dedicated themselves to fighting it. He writes: "Civilization is with us to stay. I worry more about the toad's and tree frog's songs. I want that stew to be yeasty with tadpole, muskrat, and otter bones, loons' bills, lady's-slippers, skunk cabbage, jack-in-the-pulpits, and moose and bear pies, not just an ossuary of human relics. Otherwise my moss is not going to survive."

Hoagland never grows bitter. In his mid-fifties, he began losing his eyesight. After making the rounds of Manhattan eye doctors, he was told that his condition was inoperable. Then he found a young woman eye surgeon who bravely said she could try the new procedure she had just learned in med school. After all, what did he have to lose? He was already blind. The operation succeeded. As soon as he could see, his lifelong stutter faded away. Now, along with the birds he learned to identify by song alone, he can once again see.

Ted writes: "As Renaissance men of a new kind, we should feast our eyes." And that's what Hoagland does, practicing a kind of holism in which the whole—the essay—is more than the sum of its parts. And though his walkabouts often go in the direction of raw loneliness, human failing, and numbing personal loss, an immense vitality always breaks through, a passion for life. On a visit to his house I observed how bouts of typing (no computer for this Renaissance man) alternated with short walks to look at birds and snakes. Later he dandled his girlfriend's grandchild on one knee while his pet snake—

a python rescued from one of his students—slithered across the other leg. In northern Vermont he exalted the pleasure of wandering through the "back forty," but later reported getting giddy from the human density of Cairo and Calcutta. There are wild streaks in everything and everyone and Ted is the man to track them down. He loves it all. What better recommendation for an essayist, for a friend?

What sets Hoagland's essays apart is the detail: his ability to give a character great depth with an economy of words, his willingness to plunge deep into dangerous personal territory, to resist covering up his vulnerability, and to open his sense of personal failure, loneliness, and fragility for all to see.

In his essay, "The Ridge Slope Fox and the Knife Thrower," he writes: "Of course my own "snowfall" at the moment is this upsurge of loneliness, in which a failure is implied: failure, to begin with, because one must dodge off to a solitary refuge. We like to blame the need for second homes on society, saying that our cities are unliveable, but the failure is personal, first of all. Alone at last, with the trees bulging above us in shapes that have defined and preserved the world, we find that we're incapacitated for living alone also."

Ted's habit of attention, his passion for life, keeps his work fresh and true. After twenty-five years of reading and rereading my friend, I have come to understand that there is no straight line and no path that is narrow. The world he gives us is a rushing mountain stream carrying all kinds of fascinating arcana, hard facts, and wise trajectories; it is a stream that changes courses in storms, moves boulders, cuts banks so the roots of things shows. That's the kind of wild course on which his prose pushes us, and what a keen and compassionate push it is.

The "courage of turtles" is Hoagland's courage and, like the animals he so loves, there is no breast-beating, no self-congratulation, no "shining of the epaulets," as he calls it. He just lives, and one never doubts that his intentions are purely generous: to unravel the enigma of what it is to be alive.

—Gretel Ehrlich
  February 2003

Writing Wild

Among the booming items in the book business lately have been volumes on the problems and the rise of women, on black life and liberation, on radicalism, on Indians, and on what is called "ecology," often erroneously, by which is meant environmental issues, alarums and wistfulness. With all but the first of these categories, a publisher's main difficulty has not only been to find willing readers, but enough writers. The environment, for example, and in particular the wilderness, was not a splendid and traditional subject like religion, endowed with the effulgent ponderings of entire centuries. New as a concern, intellectually marginal, the product partly of an emergency situation and partly of nostalgia born from the nation's affluence, it has had no backlog of dependable interpretation, no cadre of interpreters in training. Apart from a few scientists who quickly had their say, and after the classics of Thoreau and Darwin and various explorers' journals had been reprinted, who would write the books to satisfy this appetite? So many writers who in their knockabout careers have evinced an affinity for wild places are primarily novelists. And in fact the wilderness no longer exists at all except in the terms the public allows it to. It's said there are only two places left in the contiguous states that are more than ten miles from some kind of road, and probably it's becoming impossible for any writer to depict from firsthand experience a real wilderness. From now on an act of imagination will be required, equivalent to the effort of a man who is not a war veteran writing a war novel: even if the writer be Stephen Crane, some of the richness of reality is going to be lost. The frontier will be portrayed as merely harsh and not gleeful, or else as simply gleeful and not harsh. With wet feet in the snow, he can perhaps relive a little of the harshness—but how the glee, which comes only from being at home?

Still, the call goes out for somebody to fly to Baffin Island or Baja California for the book clubs or to do a drive-around book here in the States, squeezing into any corner of the continent that may yet appear pristine. Sometimes the proposal is made to me, with a payment being offered many times what I am used to. I'm inclined to accept, believing that driving around is part of a writer's vocation. I know by now that I'm unlikely to find a wilderness, but in looking at the sandhill cranes of Jackson County, Mississippi, the yellow rails of Brazoria County, Texas, I may learn something.

I set off to these wildlife refuges and salt swamps, touring in fat-wheeled marsh buggies and pirogues with motors on them, looking for alligators, chatting with the refuge manager. We stop at a golf club and talk with an old wolf trapper, now the greenskeeper, and pull up by the fence of a Texas prison farm to watch the prisoners being disciplined (it seems to be a local joke). By myself, I do a little walking. The acreage I've come to see may be large or extra-large, but it is not a wilderness, and invariably it is empty; almost no visitors. Where are these book-club readers I'm supposed to be writing my account for? On the highways, certainly, but not out in the bush. The roads are full and the woods empty, or where they aren't, on a few established paths like Vermont's Long Trail, a repair job on the footing costs up to two or three thousand dollars per mile.

How long will these readers continue to miss walking in the woods enough to employ oddballs like me and Edward Abbey and Peter Matthiessen and John McPhee to do it for them? Not long, I suspect. We're a peculiar lot: McPhee long bent to the traces of *The New Yorker*, Matthiessen an explorer in remote regions that would hound most people into a nervous breakdown. Abbey angry, molded by what is nowadays euphemistically called "Appalachia." As a boy, I myself was mute for years, forced either to become acutely intuitive or to take to the woods. By default, we are the ones the phone rings for, old enough to have known real cowboys and real woods. McPhee and I were classmates at prep school. I used to watch him star at basketball; attendance at the games was required, and if we in the bleachers didn't cheer, the head-master's assistant wrote our names down. But cheered though he was, he too somewhere must have picked up a taste for solitude.

We are old-fashioned craftsmen all, and in our disparate ways children of the thirties, and solitude, among our subjects, should keep us in fish and chips even after the vogue for death-of-nature books has dampened. Perhaps there's rather little to be said about solitude. It amounts to what Saul Bellow once said about loneliness: a plankton upon which the whalelike ego of a novelist must feed. But since such feeding remains a necessity for each of us, reader and writer alike, we seldom lose interest in solitude. At home in Vermont, lounging on my lawn, I look up at a higher tier of land where only black bears live. I'm on the brink of embarking upon still another trip to some bleak national swamp or public forest, and I think, Good God, who needs it? Like anybody else, I'm lonely enough right in the bosom of family and friends. But excitement, the hope of visions and some further understanding—that old, old boondoggle perpetrated by the wilderness—draws me on.

(1973)

I

Animals

The Courage of Turtles

Turtles are a kind of bird with the governor turned low. With the same attitude of removal, they cock a glance at what is going on, as if they need only to fly away. Until recently they were also a case of virtue rewarded, at least in the town where I grew up, because, being humble creatures, there were plenty of them. Even when we still had a few bobcats in the woods the local snapping turtles, growing up to forty pounds, were the largest carnivores. You would see them through the amber water, as big as greeny wash basins at the bottom of the pond, until they faded into the inscrutable mud as if they hadn't existed at all.

When I was ten I went to Dr. Green's Pond, a two-acre pond across the road. When I was twelve I walked a mile or so to Taggart's Pond, which was lusher, had big water snakes and a waterfall; and shortly after that I was bicycling way up to the adventuresome vastness of Mud Pond, a lake-sized body of water in the reservoir system of a Connecticut city, possessed of cat-backed little islands and empty shacks and a forest of pines and hardwoods along the shore. Otters, foxes, and mink left their prints on the bank; there were pike and perch. As I got older, the estates and forgotten back lots in town were parceled out and sold for nice prices, yet, though the woods had shrunk, it seemed that fewer people walked in the woods. The new residents didn't know how to find them. Eventually, exploring, they did find them, and it required some ingenuity and doubling around on my part to go for eight miles without meeting someone. I was grown by now, I lived in New York, and that's what I wanted on the occasional weekends when I came out.

Since Mud Pond contained drinking water I had felt confident nothing untoward would happen there. For a long while the developers stayed away, until the drought of the mid-1960s. This event, squeezing the edges in, convinced the local water company that the pond really wasn't a necessity as a catch basin, however; so they bulldozed a hole in the earthen dam, bulldozed the banks to fill in the bottom, and landscaped the flow of water that remained to wind like an English brook and provide a domestic view for the houses which were planned. Most of the painted turtles of Mud Pond, who had been inaccessible as they sunned on their rocks, wound up in boxes in boys' closets within a matter of days. Their footsteps in the dry leaves gave them away as they wandered forlornly. The snappers and the little musk turtles, neither of whom leave the water except once a year to lay their eggs, dug into the drying mud for another siege of hot weather, which they were accustomed to doing whenever the pond got low. But this time it was low for good; the mud baked over them and slowly entombed them. As for the ducks, I couldn't stroll in the woods and not feel guilty, because they were crouched beside every stagnant pothole, or were slinking between the bushes with their heads tucked into their shoulders so that I wouldn't see them. If they decided I had, they beat their way up through the screen of trees, striking their wings dangerously, and wheeled about with that headlong magnificent velocity to locate another poor puddle.

I used to catch possums and black snakes as well as turtles, and I kept dogs and goats. Some summers I worked in a menagerie with the big personalities of the animal kingdom, like elephants and rhinoceroses. I was twenty before these enthusiasms began to wane, and it was then that I picked turtles as the particular animal I wanted to keep in touch with. I was allergic to fur, for one thing, and turtles need minimal care and not much in the way of quarters. They're personable beasts. They see the same colors we do and they seem to see just as well, as one discovers in trying to sneak up on them. In the laboratory they unravel the twists of a maze with the hot-blooded rapidity of a mammal. Though they can't run as fast as a rat, they improve on their errors just as quickly, pausing at each crossroads to look left and right. And they rock rhythmically in place, as we often do, although they are hatched from eggs, not the womb. (A common explanation psychologists give for our pleasure in rocking quietly is that it recapitulates our mother's heartbeat *in utero*.)

Snakes, by contrast, are dryly silent and priapic. They are smooth movers, legalistic, unblinking, and they afford the humor which the humorless do. But they make challenging captives; sometimes they don't eat for months on a point of order—if the light isn't right, for instance. Alligators are sticklers too. They're like war-horses, or German shepherds, and with their bar-shaped, vertical pupils adding emphasis, they have the *idée fixe* of eating, eating, even when they choose to refuse all food and stubbornly die. They delight in tossing a salamander up towards the sky and grabbing him in their long mouths as he comes down. They're so eager that they get the jitters, and they're too much of a proposition for a casual aquarium like mine. Frogs are depressingly defenseless: that moist, extensive back, with the bones almost sticking through. Hold a frog and you're holding its skeleton. Frogs' tasty legs are the staff of life to many animals— herons, raccoons, ribbon snakes—though they themselves are hard to feed. It's not an enviable role to be the staff of life, and after frogs you descend down the evolutionary ladder a big step to fish.

Turtles cough, burp, whistle, grunt and hiss, and produce social judgments. They put their heads together amicably enough, but then one drives the other back with the suddenness of two dogs who have been conversing in tones too low for an onlooker to hear. They pee in fear when they're first caught, but exercise both pluck and optimism in trying to escape, walking for hundreds of yards within the confines of their pen, carrying the weight of that cumbersome box on legs which are cruelly positioned for walking. They don't feel that the contest is unfair; they keep plugging, rolling like sailorly souls—a bobbing, infirm gait, a brave sea-legged momentum—stopping occasionally to study the lay of the land. For me, anyway, they manage to contain the rest of the animal world. They can stretch out their necks like a giraffe, or loom underwater like an apocryphal hippo. They browse on lettuce thrown on the water like a cow moose which is partly submerged. They have a penguin's alertness, combined with a build like a Brontosaurus when they rise up on tiptoe. Then they hunch and ponderously lunge like a grizzly going forward.

Baby turtles in a turtle bowl are a puzzle in geometrics. They're as decorative as pansy petals, but they are also self-directed building blocks, propping themselves on one another in different arrangements, before upending the tower. The timid individuals turn fearless, or vice versa. If one gets a bit arrogant he will push the others off the rock and afterwards climb down into the water and cling to the back of one of those he has bullied, tickling him with his hind feet until he bucks like a bronco. On the other hand, when this same milder-mannered fellow isn't exerting himself, he will stare right into the face of the sun for hours. What could be more lionlike? And he's at home in or out of the water and does lots of metaphysical tilting. He sinks and rises, with an infinity of levels to choose from; or, elongating himself, he climbs out on the land again to perambulate, sits boxed in his box, and finally slides back in the water, submerging into dreams.

I have five of these babies in a kidney-shaped bowl. The hatchling, who is a painted turtle, is not as large as the top joint of my thumb. He eats chicken gladly. Other foods he will attempt to eat but not with sufficient perseverance to succeed because he's so little. The yellow-bellied terrapin is probably a yearling, and he eats salad voraciously, but no meat, fish or fowl. The Cumberland terrapin won't touch salad or chicken but eats fish and all of the meats except for bacon. The little snapper, with a black crenelated shell, feasts on any kind of meat, but rejects greens and fish. The fifth of the turtles is African. I acquired him only recently and don't know him well. A mottled brown, he unnerves the green turtles, dragging their food off to his lairs. He doesn't seem to want to be green—he bites the algae off his shell, hanging meanwhile at daring, steep, head-first angles.

The snapper was a Ferdinand until I provided him with deeper water. Now he snaps at my pencil with his downturned and fearsome mouth, his swollen face like a napalm victim's. The Cumberland has an elliptical red mark on the side of his green-and-yellow head. He is benign by nature and ought to be as elegant as his scientific name (*Pseudemys scripta elegans*), except he has contracted a disease of the air bladder which has permanently inflated it; he floats high in the water at an undignified slant and can't go under. There may have been internal bleeding, too, because his carapace is stained along its ridge. Unfortunately, like flowers, baby turtles often die. Their mouths fill up with a white fungus and their lungs with pneumonia. Their organs clog up from the rust in the water, or diet troubles, and, like a dying man's, their eyes and heads become too prominent. Toward the end, the edge of the shell becomes flabby as felt and folds around them like a shroud.

While they live they're like puppies. Although they're vivacious, they would be a bore to be with all the time, so I also have an adult wood turtle about six inches long. Her shell is the equal of any seashell for sculpturing, even a Cellini shell; it's like an old, dusty, richly engraved medallion dug out of a hillside. Her legs are salmon-orange bordered with black and protected by canted, heroic scales. Her plastron—the bottom shell—is splotched like a margay cat's coat, with black ocelli on a yellow background. It is convex to make room for the female organs inside, whereas a male's would be concave to help him fit tightly on top of her. Altogether, she exhibits every camouflage color on her limbs and shells. She has a turtleneck neck, a tail like an elephant's, wise old pachydermous hind legs and the face of a turkey—except that when I carry her she gazes at the passing ground with a hawk's eyes and mouth. Her feet fit to the fingers of my hand, one to each one, and she rides looking down. She can walk on the floor in perfect silence, but usually she lets her shell knock portentously, like a footstep, so that she resembles some grand, concise, slow-moving id. But if an earthworm is presented, she jerks swiftly ahead, poises above it and strikes like a mongoose, consuming it with wild vigor. Yet she will climb on my lap to eat bread or boiled eggs.

If put into a creek, she swims like a cutter, nosing forward to intercept a strange turtle and smell him. She drifts with the current to go downstream, maneuvering behind a rock when she wants to take stock, or sinking to the nether levels, while bubbles float up. Getting out, choosing her path, she will proceed a distance and dig into a pile of humus, thrusting herself to the coolest layer at the bottom. The hole closes over her until it's as small as a mouse's hole. She's not as aquatic as a musk turtle, not quite as terrestrial as the box turtles in the same woods, but because of her versatility she's marvelous, she's everywhere. And though she breathes the way we breathe, with scarcely perceptible movements of her chest, sometimes instead she pumps her throat ruminatively, like a pipe smoker sucking and puffing. She waits and blinks, pumping her throat, turning her head, then sets off like a loping tiger in slow motion, hurdling the jungly lumber, the pea vine and twigs. She estimates angles so well that when she rides over the rocks, sliding down a drop-off with her rugged front legs extended, she has the grace of a rodeo mare.

But she's well off to be with me rather than at Mud Pond. The other turtles have fled—those that aren't baked into the bottom. Creeping up the brooks to sad, constricted marshes, burdened as they are with that box on their backs, they're walking into a setup where all their enemies move thirty times faster than they. It's like the nightmare most of us have whimpered through, where we are weighted down disastrously while trying to flee; fleeing our home ground, we try to run.

I've seen turtles in still worse straits. On Broadway, in New York, there is a penny arcade which used to sell baby terrapins that were scrawled with bon mots in enamel paint, such as KISS ME BABY. The manager turned out to be a wholesaler as well, and once I asked him whether he had any larger turtles to sell. He took me upstairs to a loft room devoted to the turtle business. There were desks for the paper work and a series of racks that held shallow tin bins atop one another, each with several hundred babies crawling around in it. He was a smudgy-complexioned, serious fellow and he did have a few adult terrapins, but I was going to school and wasn't actually planning to buy; I'd only wanted to see them. They were aquatic turtles, but here they went without water, presumably for weeks, lurching about in those dry bins like handicapped citizens, living on gumption. An easel where the artist worked stood in the middle of the floor. She had a palette and a clip attachment for fastening the babies in place. She wore a smock and a beret, and was homely, short and eccentric-looking, with funny black hair, like some of the ladies who show their paintings in Washington Square in May. She had a cold, she was smoking, and her hand wasn't very steady, although she worked quickly enough. The smile that she produced for me would have looked giddy if she had been happier, or drunk. Of course the turtles' doom was sealed when she painted them, because their bodies inside would continue to grow but their shells would not. Gradually, invisibly, they would be crushed. Around us their bellies—two thousand belly shells—rubbed on the bins with a mournful, momentous hiss.

Somehow there were so many of them I didn't rescue one. Years later, however, I was walking on First Avenue when I noticed a basket of living turtles in front of a fish store. They were as dry as a heap of old bones in the sun; nevertheless, they were creeping over one another gimpily, doing their best to escape. I looked and was touched to discover that they appeared to be wood turtles, my favorites, so I bought one. In my apartment I looked closer and realized that in fact this was a diamondback terrapin, which was bad news. Diamondbacks are tidewater turtles from brackish estuaries, and I had no sea water to keep him in. He spent his days thumping interminably against the baseboards, pushing for an opening through the wall. He drank thirstily but would not eat and had none of the hearty, accepting qualities of wood turtles. He was morose, paler in color, sleeker and more Oriental in the carved ridges and rings that formed his shell. Though I felt sorry for him, finally I found his unrelenting presence exasperating. I carried him, struggling in a paper bag, across town to the Morton Street Pier on the Hudson. It was August but gray and windy. He was very surprised when I tossed him in; for the first time in our association, I think, he was afraid. He looked afraid as he bobbed about on top of the water, looking up at me from ten feet below. Though we were both accustomed to his resistance and rigidity, seeing him still pitiful, I recognized that I must have done the wrong thing. At least the river was salty, but it was also bottomless; the waves were too rough for him, and the tide was coming in, bumping him against the pilings underneath the pier. Too late, I realized that he wouldn't be able to swim to a peaceful inlet in New Jersey, even if he could figure out which way to swim. But since, short of diving in after him, there was nothing I could do, I walked away.

(1968)

The War in the Woods

Even in the present day there are a few individuals scattered about the world who have a power of communicating with animals that corresponds, perhaps, to ESP. It is more easily believable, however, since we can see that animals themselves, both wild and domestic, communicate with each other across the barriers of species and of habitat. Bits of filler about these people appear occasionally in the understrata of the news: some herdsman or charcoal burner in a corner of Afghanistan, a leopard hunter, an elephant driver, a racetrack groom. The best animal trainers undoubtedly have had this special capacity along with their daring and verve, but more often it seems to be a man who does not put the gift to any especially profitable use, who lives humbly, as snake charmers and village madmen do, and whose insights bring him as much sadness as gaiety—whose allegiances are torn. I've known trainers who at least were acquainted with the Berlitz equivalent of animal talk, the phrase-book forms—how to arrest the attention of a wildebeest or comfort a whistling swan—and once I heard a firsthand description of the real article, a wandering fellow who appeared, Pied Piper-fashion, at a zoo-animal dealer's and asked for a job as a cage hand. He went into all the cages and soothed the pandas who were just off the boat, encouraged the toucans, and babbled softly to the llamas, gesturing, mumbling, making small sounds. He lived in the sheds with the animals for as long as he stayed, and was a queer, inoffensive, skinny person of no recognizable age, with a timid, energetic stoop like Danny Kaye's. Animals of every type hurried sociably to meet him at the bars when he drew near, following him as far as their cages allowed: an immediate reaction from the first day. He was invaluable as an employee. The creatures who were on hunger strikes took food, and none of them injured themselves in struggling to escape while they were being crated. And yet the prison-like routine saddened him—being warden, and then shipping them off when telegrams from around the country arrived. Soon he was on the road again, with his suitcase.

This was thirty or forty years ago. The chance for such a singular changeling to spring out of the throng has lessened as the rest of us see fewer animals, have less to do with animals—even a farm boy is becoming quite a rarity. The animals we do know something about are manufactured as commodities: our million steers like cardboard cutouts and our frenetic, force-fed hens. Most of the dogs in the pet shops come out of virtual factories now, and dogs are notable because they go three-fourths of the way in preserving a semblance of an interchange between animal and man. They go so far as to learn English, they cringe on cue and look laudatory. For reasons that are as intense as they are inexplicable, dogs really want to reach us, and when they do, our kindness or our wizardry, our amazing *imaginations,* bring them joy.

Interestingly, though, some of the wild animals make advances to us too—like porpoises and the primates and certain birds. Campers often have a camp weasel or mouse hanging about, and mountain lions on many occasions have poked their heads into a tent and sniffed the sleeper in his sleeping bag, peaceably and curious—the big tracks came and went—or bounded invitingly around while he pulled the eiderdown over his head. Both the Indian tribes and early settlers developed legends of the friendliness of mountain lions to travelers and children which, if exaggerated, must still have contained a core of truth. In the southwestern U.S., Indians even revered them—it was believed that their urine, in drying, hardened into a precious stone—and in Argentina they were known as "the Christian's friend." Wolves did not establish such a reputation for curiosity about human beings, but wolves are related to dogs, and the ferocious Russian wolf is outvoted in folklore by numerous Mowgli-prototype stories of wolves on the Indian subcontinent, in Rome and Italy, and even in Vermont. (In 1780, Ethan Allen, leading a search party, found two lost little girls, aged five and seven, who after forty-eight hours were located in the company of a timber wolf.) Of course, among the duchies of the animal kingdom there are plenty of creatures who feel no affinity for men at all, or for kinkajous either. Still, if they have backbones, they do perhaps feel an affiliation with the pulse of life itself. Reptiles eat with great relish, preferring twisting, living prey, the livelier the better; and recently a small boy, washed overboard in the Atlantic, was rescued hours later clinging to a large sea turtle which was swimming on the surface at a stately, level pace. Presumably this act of keeping him afloat was not an act of mercy on the turtle's part (though some turtles do know about "drowning"—they drown ducks, catching them from below by the feet and pulling them underwater). The turtle probably just felt comfortable in company with the boy, animal-to-animal, felt a sort of rudimentary comradeship, so that it made no objection to being utilized as a life ring.

Bears are not as chummy, however; hence our word "bearish." They are exorbitant eaters. They must sleep for six months at a stretch and they must eat enormously in order to be able to sleep, so their main connection with people is that they like most of the foods that people do. The strangely delicate or lonely accord a puma gives evidence of feeling as it touches its nose to a man's nose as he lies sleeping, having circled a deserted lake to reach his camp, or when it follows him for half a dozen miles, placing each foot exactly in his footprints and playing hopscotch-like games—this is not the style of a bluff bruiser like a bear. Bears are lugs, and they have dim eyesight but superb ears and a superlative nose, maybe the best on earth. They're brainy too, and they've distinguished between their front and hind limbs so long and diligently that the paws have acquired different shapes. They really do love food, eating ingeniously, omnivorously, such items as horse plums, wild apples, parsnips, shadberries, lupine, Solomon's seal, Epilobiums, chipmunks, beetles, rhubarb, and watercress and spawning fish and carrion meat. Zoos feed them loaves of whole-grained bread baked with molasses and supplements. Naturally they're broader-beamed in the rear than in the front, though since they don't often kill game (polar bears are an exception), their mouths are modest in dimension. They have a good set of teeth tucked inside but the mouth isn't sharklike, isn't proportioned like cleavers and axes, and they don't eat desperately, the way shrews do; their timetable is leisurely; they fatten like a woodchuck, moving from feast to feast as between cheerful surprises, scooping fruit, pruning the branches with their paws. They like our leavings too, if they can find a dump, and people who eat bears report that their meat tastes much the same as our meat used to taste to cannibals, or like the other famous omnivore, the pig. Bears may be tall and rangily built or stocky, squat, and with a pot, the short bear perhaps heavier than the large-looking fellow, just like the many varieties of man; and with their overall man shape and size, their spirited minds, their manlike wails and grunts, they have intrigued people for centuries. In societies where they didn't serve as a manhood test, they were captured alive and employed as crude gladiators in underground arenas, fighting dogs and bulls. The gypsies made them dance for coins, training them by torturing their feet with heated irons. Grizzly Adams, the mountainman, slept with his bears on cold nights (as some gypsies must have), and bear rugs were standard bedding throughout the northern hemisphere at times—they're still *de rigueur* for "dens."

Bears are fairly casual about how they pass the winter. Protected from the snow by their warm coats, they just roll in under a fallen spruce when food gets short, pulling a few boughs over themselves, as often as they take the trouble to search out a cave. They choose the north side of a mountain so that the sun won't melt them out, but don't necessarily trek back to the same area year after year. They hibernate singly; cubs are born to a mother every other winter while she lies in a doze, waking only to bite the umbilical cords. Sometimes a woodsman on snowshoes will notice a rhythmic succession of puffs of steam rising from a tiny hole in the cover of snow and know that he's passing a sleeping bear. It's as personal as an experience I once had, of finding a grizzly's tracks in mud alongside the Bowron River so fresh the water was still trickling into them.

Bears are a kind of shadow of man, a tracery or etching of him—as mutes and schizophrenics and idiots sometimes are—a view of him if he'd stayed in the woods, among the rocks, instead of becoming community-minded. The "wild-man-of-the-woods" whom northwestern Indians fear wears a bear's shape, though he is humanoid in his sexual proclivities—he catches Indian girls; his face and his coat are a mask. Even a real bear's face is quite a mask, from the standpoint of an animal trainer. The stolid, terse muzzle, the small, practically hidden eyes, the thick, short fur overgrowing the features, give the trainer no window to the bear's emotions such as he has in a lion's great eyes. A tiger's white *whiskers*, as flexile as they are, are worth a good deal toward saving the trainer from harm, and the expressive lip, the subtle, definitive index of roars are worth much more—not to mention the tail and the curl of the toes. By comparison, a bear's lips hardly move, he has no whiskers to mention, no particular tail, and blocks for toes, and though he may occasionally chop his jaws before attacking, emitting a low breathy growl, often he won't. His hasty antics when he meets you on the road and prepares to make good his escape cause you to wonder which way he actually intends to go; and a trained bear, losing the restraining element of fear, becomes even more bouncy, cryptic and clownish.

Grizzlies do roar and *waw* and make all the faces of Baal, but grizzlies have not been trained in recent times and they can pretty well be written off, relegated to the paleontologist. In a few spots they are managing to make a stand, feeding on the moose that hunters wound—inland grizzlies with bush to roam. The polar bears—"sea bears"—are in a worse predicament, being hunted with airplanes. Part of the bears' plight may be our own, although they need so much more space that they are being squeezed off the earth sooner than we. The black bears are more apropos, being gerrymandering scroungers who manage to fit into any dab of forest that presents itself; in any few square miles of tangled growth they can set up house, eating beech-nuts and leopard frogs, and render themselves almost indiscernible.

15

But in those woods, that concealed bear is like the mercury in a thermometer or the bean in a jumping bean. He moves so fast (when once he moves) when you come upon him that you know he's the forest's reason for being, or the nearest thing to a reason for being that you will ever see.

I talked to a man who had lain helplessly under a grizzly. He was living in Manson Creek, a settlement of twenty citizens in north-central British Columbia where the mail was delivered every second week. He was a clear-faced, well-built, balding man in his late thirties, and a disaffected philosopher, a man who had read mightily on his own but had no one to talk to, who had left Indiana University, estranged from his wife. He read half the night by the light of a Coleman lamp and wrote during the day, hoping to finish a book; but he liked the rough life, skiing out to look at wolf kills, and though he worried about his marriage, so far as I could tell he was holding up under the pressures of isolation, except that he needed to air his thoughts.

The encounter occurred when he was driving along a dirt road that wound for a couple of hundred miles to a mining camp. He'd stopped his car and climbed down a bank, aiming for a promontory where he hoped to see into a valley. Instead he blundered into a bowl-like depression a dozen yards wide in which a grizzly, waxing fat with the hunting season, was feeding on a moose carcass. The moose had gone there to die and the grizzly's quick nose had found it. The brush was wet, the wind blew loudly in the fellow's face, so that the bear may not have scented him, or may have scented him and waited. At nearly the same instant they saw each other, close up—the bear's head lifting, bloody and aswarm with flies. This shocking sight, really before he could take it in, was followed by the impact of the bear bashing him over. Flung as if hit by a bus, he was not immediately reactive, yet the bear seemed loath to bite him. It lurched and bunched its neck, he said, and swatted at him, raging. Lying on his back, he drew up his feet as a buffer. It was so big he saw it as a shape then, without color, but in the same factual detail as if he were a third party observing. And though its charge had knocked him sprawling, a sort of disgust or revulsion, apparently, a wish not to contact him with its mouth, kept it from grappling him more closely. Reaching around his legs, it raked and gashed him, roaring with fury but reluctant to use its mouth.

He said he'd had no nightmares to confuse his memory of the accident (he thought of it as that); nor did he expect any. And he was not a sentimental man who would falsely anthropomorphize the bear's behavior; he was living in the bush to write a philosophical study and take a breather, not in order to feed the finches. The bear started leaving, but bumped against the moose, lunged over it, then paused, unable to pull itself away, as if the outrage of being interrupted when eating was too obnoxious for it to just be able to back away from him and leave. It seemed "torn," he said—wanting to rush for cover and yet standing in the middle of their little amphitheater, boiling with insult.

When a grizzly mauls a man the real destruction it does is with its mouth: In bedside interviews, people who have been bitten have described the cumulatively catastrophic damage inflicted on them by a series of chomps. Even so, in most cases the man survives; the bear bites near his neck but doesn't quite get there, and runs off, leaving him mauled but alive. This bear, likewise, torn between its obvious abhorrence of approaching my informant and the urge to wreak havoc on him, hesitated, bawling and swaying, chopping its jaws. Finally it attacked again, lacerating his sides, pummeling his arms when they were interposed, reaching around his boots as he lay balled up on his back and kicked and, deaf to himself, probably shrieked. Outweighing him by several hundred pounds, it growled like a bass banshee, but it was so absolutely aghast at their proximity—holding its face away as if at the stench of him—that its blows were just tentative. Afterwards the doctor found dozens of scratches on him but not many substantial hurts. One claw had cut through his wallet and through the money in the wallet. And for my friend, as well, once the first terrible glimpse and charge were over, the really ghastly horror of the experience was the matter of scent. He could avoid watching the bear but he couldn't escape its smell. And, as soberly, methodically, as he was speaking to me, he couldn't describe it either, except as odious suffocation—violent, vile aversion. It was not like pyorrhea, nor like a garbage pit; it was everything fetid and scarifying and strangling rolled into one disgusting cloud which was more frightening than all the injuries and pain. Hunters call the smell cabbagy and go wild with excitement when they catch a whiff, but he was lying right underneath the mouth, which was its source.

If bears usually go to such considerable lengths to avoid our company, why do we search out theirs? It seems to be in order to count coup. Even at the taxidermist's, where the bears arrive daily in trucks, you notice that the youngster who is in charge of rugged work, like sawing off their heads, does it with a Homeric zest. "You see how we treat you?" he tells them, rolling their corpses and slapping the contorted mouths. A hunter after grizzly must spend a thousand dollars or more in transportation costs simply to get to grizzly country, and in New England bear hunters are usually bear hunters by chance, the bears are so wary and shy. Only about three percent of those killed in Vermont, for instance, have been inveigled to their deaths with bait. Ten percent have been tracked down with hounds, and the rest fall prize to hunters who "stand and stalk," in the official Fish and Wildlife phrase, which means that they're out in the woods carrying a gun, maybe after deer, when they happen to pitch upon a bear.

I've gone on several hound hunts, as well as stand-and-stalk hunts and ambushes. But hound hunts are the realistic ones; also, the hounds, being agents, interest me. Grizzlies have seldom been hunted with hounds (though some of the Indians did, adding themselves to the pack to give it extra authority), and even in running down black bears, which are neither so dangerous nor the size of a King Kong, the first problem is finding dogs gritty enough to hold the bear—make him come to bay. The smell is strong, goodness knows, and the bear, though big and vital and thick-skinned, cannot run faster than a dog, especially in the fall, when he is necessarily fattening himself (very old bears die during hibernation because they weren't able to fatten up enough). Therefore if a bear is lurking around, no worthy hunting dog will have much difficulty scenting him or catching up; the feat is to conquer him and send him scrambling up a tree. When they contact the bear, most dogs stop dead a

moment, then promptly swing around and dash for home. Some
sportsmen call a bear hunt successful if they can only catch their
hounds by the end of the day. On Monday mornings, the local radio
stations broadcast appeals for "a Walker hound lost on the Long Trail
under Hazen's Notch."

Besides the Walker breed, others that can be worked on bear are
Blueticks, Black-and-tans, Redbones and Plotts; and Airedale blood
is sometimes bred into a pack for extra grit. Basically, there are two
jobs—the strike dog's and the hold dog's. Working alone, the strike
dog finds a cold trail and works at it till he approaches the bear and
makes him feel uneasy enough to get up out of his noon bed. He
needs to have an excellent nose and an instructive voice which carries
well, and to be a dog of self-sufficient sense but not too fast, since the
rest of the pack is not released until he is full-out on a fresh track.
The hold dogs, fast as fickle lightning in a scrimmage, specialists at
"pulling fur," are the fighters who will risk their skin. The bear may
run for twenty miles altogether, fighting wherever he can set his back
against a ledge or a big tree and only running on again when the
hunters draw near. States like New York and Pennsylvania have outlawed trailing bears with hounds because they think the animals may
have a hard enough time as it is; and the contest does include a quite
peculiar proxy element. Besides the metaphorically turncoat nature
of the dog's role—who leads his master to any creature, to a woodcock
or a slew of truffles—there is a mameluke-style madness too. The
dog is kept chained the whole year to focus all his personality on his
brief spurts of work, then let loose for a few weekends in the fall to
run and run, trying to crowd in a lifetime's excitement before he's
chained up for another year. Dogs are very much like other animals
(watch a mother training her pups), except for the one central disloca-
tion that they are no longer able to collect their food. Even hunting
dogs, when lost and starving in the woods, can't, and so with this
linchpin removed, they're like a Chinese girl hobbling on bound feet
for her husband's accommodation, or like the birds which feudal
young ladies kept, which didn't require caging because the front of
their bill was broken off—they couldn't pick up their own food from
the ground and only ate from their possessor's hand.

A bear's about the biggest game. Foxes are for horsemen in open country, and coon hunting is not much of a sport; it just boils down to watching the dogs do a job. The raccoon doesn't run very far before climbing a tree once he is chased in earnest; the dogs only have to un-ravel the evidence of where he is. Bobcats are a better quarry because the chase is more complex. The cat has a poor nose but compensates for the handicap with his eyes and ears, and will slip through the boondocks for many miles, using marsh ice and deadfalls to confuse the scent—the females are said to be harder to tree, as if they valued their lives more hotly. Bears, being so large, so manlike anatomically and yet lusciously furred, wily and yet raunchy, "understandable" but possessing a beast's stamina, are way ahead of the other North Ameri-can game animals as prospective adversaries. They can kill dogs—they're brutes—but since their pleasures, their sense of play and diet, their cast of instincts, their strategy or reasoning, are within a realm which we can reach by an effort of empathy, we can pretend that we're Jack-and-the-Beanstalk and they're a personal sort of Goliath, which is both fun and very bolstering.

The Vermont season extends three months, starting September 1. During September a bear's coat is so flimsily rooted and thin that you can see right through it, so a scrupulous hunter doesn't shoot the bears he runs across but restricts himself to training and conditioning his dogs for the grueling, more businesslike pursuits of October, when the woods still belong to him. In November the deer hunters are every-where and any hound is shot on sight. This bloodless September stuff suits me fine, however. My companion is Paul Doyle, a gentlemanly, diffidently chatty insurance man in the town of Orleans, Vermont, whose engrossing hobby is chasing bears. As a hunter he is compelling and leaderly, and young men gather about him; he's in his forties and has a family of four daughters but no sons. He's a good-humored, re-sourceful talker, making it all as individualized as he can. He talks about the game as though they were a bunch of comic understudies for mankind, a shrewd and shadowy tribe whose delight is playing jokes and tricks: if the bugger outsmarts him and the dogs, that day he gets away. He's dry, doubting, but rather fond when mentioning the resi-dents of the many farms we pass as we roar around by truck on the dirt roads towards various hunting grounds. He receives frequent calls from people who think that a coon is threatening their chickens or their corn, or who claim they've seen a bobcat's track. The tracks are often illusory and the wind may have blown down the corn, but it gives him a chance to chat a while and maybe write some insurance. For eighteen years he himself farmed, and he grew up on one. Besides, he enjoys people and is a man whose hunting is primarily combative, the dogs being deputies and proxies. He's not the type of hunter who prefers the company of animals and who would just as soon sneak across somebody's woodlot on the way to a kill as first go to the house and get acquainted with the owner.

Here are three hunts. Doyle, I and his three dogs, which are a Plott-and-Bluetick cross, rode in an International Scout, a jeeplike truck, and Bob Cody and Eric Gilfallen, sidekicks of his, rode in their own vehicles behind, each with a pair of dogs. Eric, who brought along his little son, is a trainee for IBM, a sloping-nosed, blue-eyed fellow just growing out of being callow, a modernized young man whom I tended to like better each time we met. Bob Cody, a bus driver in Burlington, puts up a tent on Doyle's lawn on weekends for the sake of these hunts. He's a kidder, a staunch-looking, husky person who tilts and fusses with his square-billed cap like a coach giving signals.

On the first hunt, we went to the Duck Pond Road in the township of Glover. It's a defunct jigsaw road, scarcely navigable, that twists past abandoned farmsteads and log houses for a dozen miles, with the acres of overgrown red clover and alfalfa fields and orchards everywhere that attract bears, mile after mile of new-fledged wilderness that has not been bulldozed because a strip through the middle of it is slated to become a superhighway. Tuffy, Doyle's strike dog, trotted ahead, urinating repeatedly as he warmed to the occasion. He was butter-footed in the beginning, as stiff as if he were walking on ice, having hunted in Holland, Vt., the day before and treed a yearling, which the hosts and landowners there shot. He has grasshopper legs, a long gazelle waist and a broad face for a dog, providing plenty of space for his teeth and for his smelling-chambers. He's even blacker than a bear, and doesn't lope or pace the way a wolf does, for instance; his gait is gimpier, pointier, pumpier, dancier; his legs seem to dangle—long girlish legs—

and there's a trotting-horse quality to him—he has a thin tail and shaky, mule-jigging legs. His ears flop incongruously, like a cartoon puppy's, and yet he sniffed like a jackhammer as he started hunting more smoothly, after relieving his bowels and getting the excess of high spirits out of his system. The stark, gaunt persona of a working dog, whether a sled, hound or attack dog, emerged—the scarred face flattening like a janissary's, the eyes going gaily daft. His tail swung with the degree of interest the smells he encountered aroused. Checking the sides of the road, he knew that we were after bear, not the raccoons of August, when he had first been exercised, and so he only honored raccoon sign with a moment or two. When he found a bobcat's trail he "opened up," as the saying is, his voice falsetto when he first used it, but Doyle went into the woods and led him back.

The chokecherry bushes along our course were fully fruited, and we found clumps where a bear must have rummaged, stripping leaves off the branches and treading down the surrounding brush. But this was action of a week before, there was no scent for Tuffy, and although we generals could see the score, the soldiers who would have to fix on the bear and fight him for us had nothing to go on. We poked around an old millrace and an old house site, where a porcupine as round as a turtle was lurking down among the salty timbers. We looked into a pond, looked at the crumpled barns and farm layouts—eighteen abandoned farms, they said. It was all lovely and elegiac—the farms where nobody lived anymore and the dense second-growth wilderness which eventually would be leveled again for the highway.

A heavy dew had made scenting ideal but there was no bear scent. We drove over to Barton Mountain in the next town, and leaving the dogs in their boxes, searched for some traces of bear in another neglected orchard grown up with spruce and scrub maple, a place where once in a long while a bear is seen in the daylight sitting on its ample rump and raking apples up: maybe a farm boy will sneak close and shoot at it, pulling the gun off-target at the last instant for fear of angering it. Doyle says these current farm kids are losing their touch. He was out helping a family tap sugar trees last March, and keeping quiet about it, saw the boys drilling holes in ashes, lindens, oaks. They tapped any tree that wasn't a spruce. When he himself was young he and his brother would go looking for honeybee trees in the summer. The technique was to take a cigar box, substitute a piece of glass for the sliding wooden top, and put sugar water scented with anise oil inside. Then they would pinch a few bees off the flowers and put them in. The bees, loading up, flew home and brought back others, and quickly more. At intervals he and his brother moved the box fifty or a hundred feet closer to the hive, judging by the direction that the bees were flying. If they moved it too fast they'd lose their bees, so it was a two-day project, until finally the entire hive was shuttling back and forth from the cigar box. One time they traced a swarm for several miles to a grizzled hollow maple tree on the top of a bald hill. They left it intact until the winter, when the bees would be in hibernation, then went with a crosscut saw and cut the tree down, but they discovered that in the meantime mice had moved in and eaten all the loot—the honey and the combs, even the bees.

Doyle walked ahead of me, conversing softly, hardly audible. He talked about "pushing a snowshoe," the treks he makes in the winter. We found a deer skeleton, well picked and scattered, and loads of deer droppings, which although pellety ordinarily, soften up in September when the deer eat apples. No bear turds, however. Doyle and Bob Cody and Eric, each casing a different hillside, got on their walkie-talkies and used up some of their nervous energy. We had started out at six o'clock and it was ten by now, so there were pleasure airplanes in the air, a helicopter, and chain saws going, and truck traffic just below us. The radio itself was jammed with conversations, two or three on every channel: French Canadians, people down in Connecticut gossiping, and even some drawlers from Houston, Texas, brought in by the "skip" phenomenon. Eric told Doyle that he ought to change his rabbit's foot to a side pocket if he wanted his luck to change, Doyle prognosticated on where the bears might be hiding, and simultaneously on the radio channel two boatmen on Long Island Sound were advising one another about what sails they ought to use.

We went over to a ridge on May Mountain where Doyle had farmed until recently and which he hopes to develop as summer real estate, with lawns and artificial lakes. Bob Cody came across a smudged bear print beside a stream, too old for Tuffy to get going on, but since the stream chattered appealingly, we had lunch, let Eric's son, who had been cooped up in the jeep, climb some rocks and stretch his legs, and freed the dogs from their boxes to drink. Bob seemed to grow beefier and more phlegmatic as the heat increased and as our schemes were disappointed. Eric became less adenoidal and adolescent, more like somebody's husband, more grown-up, agreeable and witty. Old man Doyle, whose hair is gray, was wearing his farmer's chore-face—lumpy and tough, his big jaw masticating gum, his eyes narrowed and inaccessible. It was a first lieutenant's face (though he has never been in the service), and a face such as full-time big-game guides wear. His enthusiasm for hunting developed late; if it had seized him as a youngster he might have gone out West to where the wildlife was still large. He trapped bears before he hunted them—this while he was milking cows for a living—baiting them with spoiled fruit in a ravine. The first he caught was a three-legged bear which lay low when he came to check the trap—he was also patrolling his electric fence for a branch that was grounding the wire. He wouldn't have noticed he had a bear except that the trees were peeled completely white for yards around, where it had suffered. Bear traps, teethed medievally, are the cruelest of tools. Eventually Vermont outlawed them, but before that Doyle and many another farmer had stored theirs away in souvenir status, after a private discovery.

Doyle still carries a slingshot to sting bears with but used to be rougher on those that bayed than he is now. If nobody along wanted a trophy, he used to put the animal through an ordeal of three or four hours anyway, running it up a tree and forcing it down to the ground again, he and the gang of kids with him firing bullets into the trunk next to its head. It would have to fight the dogs for the movie cameras, and "tree," then scramble down and "tree" yet again, being hit with stones in its rear end all the while, and run for its life as a finale. If it injured a dog or if anything in the scenario went wrong, of course it was a dead bear. He sold a few bears that he shot to unsuccessful hunters from the city. But all that was in the savagery of his thirties. Now he lets the animal off with a warning if no one along "needs a bear," as he puts it—that is, someone who hasn't already at some point shot a bear. And sometimes he reminisces sympathetically about how the whole world must have seemed to fall in on a bear he caught last week, being chased so far and suddenly finding itself surrounded by more dogs and human beings than it had seen in a lifetime.

Almost every young man needs to bathe in blood at least once, if only his own. The problem is that nobody else can do it for him beforehand and there are many more young men than bears nowadays; automobile accidents take the place of bears. Bear is a big word; Doyle uses it as much as he can; it makes for a better hunt. By now he's such an old hand that he orchestrates the hunts, overseeing the sequence of excitements as well as the hounds and the bear. In preparation for our next trip he'd checked all week for tracks as he drove from town to town making his rounds, and the next Saturday we went out to Brownington Pond and let Tuffy loose in the labyrinthine cedar swamp which stretches behind it. Tuffy peed on fifteen trees, and so did we, and Doyle and the two younger hunters, as part of the gearing-up process, imprinted bears' feet in the mud by thrusting their bunched knuckles in to represent the toes. (In contrast to the black bears, a grizzly has claw tips marked way out in front, which you may miss at first, like a delayed explosion.)

The chokecherry bushes were stripped and trampled, the thorn apples, crab apples and cranberries had been sampled, and there were scatterings of real tracks too, scuffed and undiagrammatic. Tuffy mouthed a dried bear stool aggressively. Though he is tarpaulin-black, his two partners, Jeff and Zeke, are a pretty brindled brown, with reddish eyes, Jeff ash-faced. Weighing sixty pounds, they stand thigh-high to a man and, like Tuffy, have a fanatic, glassy, vacuous look, a hysteric look, like slaves from the world of Buck Rogers. They were rattling their tails against the panels of the truck, whimpering to go, fighting each other in their impatience. Jeff is the fastest dog—if he jumps a bear he can get half a mile ahead of the pack, although he hasn't quite as fine a voice or nose as Tuffy. Zeke ranks as the second most useful dog because his nose is best, but he is not as tough or bear-minded as Tuff; he'll tie himself up trailing a coon. Tuffy is worth maybe $400 and was bought from a famous string of dogs in Olympia, Washington, that destroys a hundred or more bears a year in some of the seed-woods of Weyerhauser.

This second hunt turned into the classic variety. As it grew plain that at last they all were going to be given something to do, the crated dogs howled pathetically to be let loose. Tuffy had struck a fresh track, voicing the news with abrupt, hornlike barks in monotone at fifteen-second intervals. Guessing that it might be a sow bear with cubs who would only circle within a mile or two when she was pursued, Doyle released Zeke to help Tuffy, thinking he'd put in the other dogs later. But the bear, a young male, streaked straight to the east instead, through the township of Brownington toward Charleston, territory which no doubt was familiar to him from his nightly meanderings. With Zeke and Tuffy ragging him, he followed a series of nearly impenetrable swamps that Doyle calls Bear Alley and that connect in a seven-mile rectangle bordered by hard-top roads and other barriers. Neil, Eric's little son, had been left in the truck with the main radio, and he saw the top of the bear's head rushing through the grass, aiming for a sag between ridges of high land, with both dogs hard after him. Since Neil couldn't manage to operate the radio, however, we tramped through tamarack, cedar and pine, jumping brooks and stumbling through the muddy sloughs, because in order to hunt bear on foot you really have to outbear the bear—go where he goes. The red shirts with buckskin vests looked like a combat uniform, and the men in them slogged about in confusion and listened painfully.

At last, hearing the dogs' mournful-sounding, hectic barks above us in the cut on the ridge, we ran for the three vehicles to try to head the creature off at one of the old logging roads which intersect Bear Alley. A bear's a beast, but once he has been treed and let go he will tree the more readily on the next hunt because of the experience. It doesn't induce him to become fiercer; like the dogs, he is being trained for the later time when you decide to kill him. The bears fare best who take a risk, such as swimming a lake or plunging through a populated area where the dogs are seduced and bewildered. Otherwise the bear had better simply stay on the ground and battle grimly, taking the gumption out of each hound individually, until they drift home one by one and he is left in silence to go his way. Of course for the bear the paradox is that such a truculent nature will get him into trouble in other situations in a settled region like New England, and

furthermore he doesn't know until late in the game that the dogs after
him aren't just an unusually pertinacious gang of farm collies and are
being followed by hunters.

The radios were more than playthings now, as Bob and Eric
checked separate hills and ridges in the jeeps, listening for the barking.
They kidded Doyle about his age, asking if he was panting from floundering in the swamp, but it was like a group of military scouts putting
together information. Finally we all raced for a notable big pine on the
crossroad that severs Bear Alley from farmland and from higher open
ground at its east end. Sure enough, just as we got there we heard Tuffy
and Zeke arrive, hectoring the bear in the tangle of brush and trees.
The bear stayed out of sight, so Doyle let loose Jeff, who was frantic,
and Bob added his two mature dogs, Belle and Duke, and Eric his two
pups. We could hear the ki-yiing when the bear clipped somebody;
with so many in the fight he didn't have time to take hold and chew.
Smelling us, he didn't come in our direction, and as soon as we moved
toward the sounds of scrapping, he started right back toward Brownington Pond again, since there were no rough mountains at hand for him to
turn into. "He won't stop to eat cherries!" Doyle shouted, laughing. He
said the dogs don't know enough to stop and listen for each other, they
only hear their own yelping, but now that they were in a tight pack
none of them was going to lose its bearings.

Paralleling the swamp, swinging into it from time to time on the
gridwork of lumbering roads, we could interpret the noises of the
chase and see tracks spattered here and there. It was a summery
weekend morning like the last one, so all around us other recreational
activities were under way: people playing badminton and gardening,
private planes cruising above us. The bear treed about quarter to
ten, after some final sparring, having run five miles on this, his second
lap. He was in a jungly patch of marsh next to a pasture filled
with Holsteins and junk autos. The cows seemed to be curious more
than upset.

We got the farmer's permission to drive as close as we could.
Doyle put some bullets in his revolver in case of an emergency; cameras and rifles were unlimbered too. The bear was seventy feet off
the ground in the crotch of a tall poplar, the only impressive tree

around. A woodpecker was pecking a rotted spar nearby, and the bear himself, perhaps because he was so high, apparently did not recognize that this was a life-and-death meeting, or else he was maintaining his dignity. He seemed as removed from our mundane glory-whoops and the dogs' inane tromboning as a bear in a zoo; or maybe every wild animal by now has come to look like an animal in a zoo. He twitched his nose, lifted his head to see if there wasn't a branch higher still, and opened his mouth a little, like a gorilla yawning, playing it close to the vest, not wanting to draw attention to himself in case we were ready to go away. He licked his paws for the moisture on them, because he must have been very thirsty. He was resting. Doyle guessed that he was three or four years old and weighed upwards of two hundred pounds, though he was a bit thin. He had large, lengthy arms, a handsome, straight substantial head, and did not appear panicky, just uncomfortable and uneasy. In the beginning he pushed his tongue out of his mouth because he was thirsty and hot, but later he did it as a signal of pugnacity, looking down at the dogs and tilting his head slightly, as if he didn't wish to show us he was looking down. Animals are alert to note where another animal is looking, and many of them—from bighorn sheep to wolves—scrape their tongues in and out between their teeth to indicate a willingness to fight.

Throughout, Bob Cody shrieked and yelled, at a pitch; Eric crowed and thumped the tree trunk with a post. They encouraged the dogs to yelp and leap as high against the tree as a man could have, and they excited them so much that Duke and Jeff began to tussle uproariously. The bear was so high up that I had to walk away a hundred feet to see him. He leaned back on his rump above us, looking at the tops of other trees and at the branches of the poplar above him, as if for an avenue higher and higher. As he became increasingly unhappy, he moved his gray muzzle in confidential ruminations like a traveler who finds that the traveling companions with whom he's penned are in fact renegades. Eventually, while the dogs were being disciplined and the cameras were clicking, while we were festively busy at the base of the tree, he began coming down. Altogether he'd had nearly an hour's rest. His long, relaxed, powerful, gorilla-type arms grasping the trunk slung him upwards or downwards or around the tree with very little effort.

Much hollering on our part; guns were grabbed again. He paused halfway down, hanging in place like a telephone lineman and watching us and looking off. His life hung in the balance, although he didn't know that. The hunters really didn't know that his life hung in the balance either; they knew they'd shoot him to save the dogs but they didn't really comprehend that he'd be dead. Which is the trouble with most hunters, and why when one of them shoots another, the shooter generally collapses, vomits, has to have his rifle taken away immediately, has to have his remaining companions sleep beside him, hold and comfort and reassure and protect him, even keep him from doing violence to himself. Suddenly the man realizes that he has been dealing with the miracle of death.

But after considering, the bear climbed back up. Doyle cut a twig for a toothpick and told the dogs, "You beat the son-of-a-gun! That's all we wanted." Between the dogs' baying, the Choctaw yells, Bob's banging a pole against the tree for the last footage in the camera, there was a terrific racket. I noticed that although I couldn't smell the bear himself, I could smell uprooted grass and bark torn off the tree. He was extremely discomposed by now, stirring up there. After ten more minutes, he came almost all the way down, making no fuss when he started, just swinging down feet first in silence, with his long forearms clutching the trunk, his vigorous body like some ancestral figure's. He seemed to be hoping that we were prepared to call it a day if he simply came down, uncontentious, nonchalant. It's hard to keep a good bear up a tree, as Doyle had said, but we didn't give in to him and he hung overhead for a long while, chopping his jaws softly and snarling—a fluffing, breathy sound. Then he climbed clear up again. The noble dimensions of the tree and the bear's moxie were making it a perfect treeing.

Since the cameras were empty and this was only supposed to be an exercise, Doyle and the others caught their dogs. Immediately, even before they'd leashed them, the bear came skidding down, hasty as a fireman. When he was six feet from the ground he leaped straight out for cover. One of the hounds got loose, unfortunately, so that they all had to be released so the single dog would not come to grief. They ran the bear for two or three more miles, back east toward Charleston and the big pine. Eric and Bob in the two jeeps, knowledgeably speeding around to an intersection, contrived to meet the bear just as he emerged in a clearing. Letting him go by, they intercepted the dogs while he was still tiredly breaking brush within their hearing.

"Tuffy seems to be lost, Paul!" they told Doyle when we reached them, because kidding the latecomer is traditional in hunting.

A week later, we attempted somewhat wistfully to recapitulate these triumphs by taking the dogs to Brownington swamp at dawn again. Lakes of fog lay between the hills; frost tufted the goldenrod, the fields of hardhack and the evergreens. We listened to a farm boy shouting at cows in the distance. Doyle once ran a herd-testing station, and as we dawdled by the truck, feeling that this repeat performance would never equal the last time, he talked about the sidelines that a farmer has, like trucking Christmas trees to New York City in the frantic weeks before Christmas, or cutting his cedar woods to sell to the fence-post factory. Then the sugar bush—a hillock of maple trees—which could take maybe four thousand taps if you wanted to kill yourself but which you tap with one thousand, feeling overworked at that—and finally have the hill logged off for cash. Lately, most farmers plan for the profits involved in real estate. Doyle says that even Bear Alley has been changing hands. He himself has acquired a real estate agent's license to complement his insurance business; yet on these hunts he's such an obvious woodsman, such a chunk-jawed, rugged deadeye, that one has the impression of a vocation lost.

The scenting conditions were ideal: no rain to wash the traces away but a dousing of dew to spice and accentuate whatever there was. We led the dogs on leashes into the brush to get a fast jump on the bear if Tuffy, who was out ahead, found one. Bloodhounds have the best noses of any dog, but they are slow and not aggressive, and they walk on their ears when their heads are down. Slogging through the mud, the streams and over deadfalls, we saw an osprey's nest and paths of coons and porcupines. Deep in the swamp there was a tin shanty where several lumberjacks had lived. There was plenty of bear sign too, though nothing recent. Tuffy was puzzling along an unproductive trail; we listened to him respectfully, wading in tangents whenever he turned. We climbed a sunny knoll and waited. He was on a beechnut ridge to the south, croaking like a chicken; then he entered a sugar orchard. Eric and Bob went off to listening posts on crowns of hills around the countryside, so there was lots of compass-reading and horsing with the radios. "The needle in the haystack," said Doyle. Once he killed a wild boar that had wandered into this part of the state from a private game preserve. "He was all shoulders when we saw him run, so we knew that if he wasn't a wild boar he must be a buffalo."

The French Canadians came on the radio again, speaking a French like leaden Spanish, and half a dozen Americans. The chain saws were starting up like motorboats. Getting tired of waiting for Tuffy to strike something, we drove around to a crossroads and caught him. We drove to the town of Westmore, checking in various orchards, finding deer beds and bushes that the bucks had stripped when rubbing velvet off their antlers. At midmorning we went to look at a cow carcass which a woman had buried a week before, using her tractor, and which she said a bear was digging up. Unlike so many tips, however, her report turned out to be true. The evidence of digging and chewing at the black remains was plain; also the tack which he had taken through a hemlock woods towards the hiding place where he lay up during the day. Spirits surged, and though the scent was dry, for his sins we tramped round and about for another hour or two with all due military drama, generating in ourselves the sensation that the war in the woods hadn't actually been won a century ago, that we were needed, that this bear exhuming the week-old carcass of a cow was a real emergency.

"Look out, now. There's a black dog loose. I don't want you jumping out of your skin thinking he's a bear, if he comes up behind you," Doyle kidded Cody.

We drove back to the notable white pine at the end of Bear Alley, where we had listened to the dogs ki-yiing in the screen of trees. It wasn't far; and here too we found tracks—giant, hand-sized imprints in the road, like Sanskrit underlying the language of the many tire and boot marks. This may have been the bear whose endeavors we had just been inspecting at the cow's grave, or even the same bear we had treed in the poplar tree the week before. He had to eat something, and bears aren't overly plentiful today. Necessarily, there will be more and more of this business of letting the bear go after treeing him; bears will be run up a tree quite regularly; it will be like a kind of bear-baiting. Bears may become one of the group of animals whose welfare will be associated with the paper industry, since they hide out in the pulp woods. I think that Doyle probably would spare all those his dogs tree except that earning the $100 guiding fee pleases him. It's not the sum of money, which doesn't seem as much to a busy insurance agent as it might to a man who was still milking cows for a living, but rather the role in which he earns it: professionally guiding hunters. A hundred dollars is little enough to pay for a bear in the 1970s, and enormous numbers of hunters in Massachusetts and New York are eager to pay it. Sight unseen, they call him up and say flatly that if he can find them a bear—if he knows where one is living—they will be up in four hours, right then and there, any time, any day. It puts him in a quandary.

I stopped at the taxidermist's next day. By coincidence, a bear had just been brought in, lying in a pickup truck. It had been shot in Franconia, New Hampshire, and was a male of seven or eight, weighing perhaps three hundred pounds. The hunter, a wiry long-haired man from Florida, was inside the shop consulting about prices. He had a sharp and knowing tipster's face, clever and gay. His wife had come along for the ride. She was pregnant and pleasant-looking, wearing white lipstick, her hair rinsed a white-blond. He was as short as she, and they appeared to have achieved the marriage-of-friends that most of us seem to be heading for. The bear lay on its back, its legs extended upwards, each one bent differently, so that its posture was like a man lying *in extremis* next to the site of a catastrophe. In height it might have compared to a fourteen-year-old boy, but it was built like a barrel. After its head had been sawn off, what remained looked like a prisoner must look after visiting the guillotine, a circle of vital red stuff jamming its neck. It looked truncated and shortened and uncompleted, like an uncolored figure in a coloring book. The paws also were cut off to be mounted and all the rest of the bear, in its ragged September coat, was thrown away. After asking whether they ought to cut off "steaks," the Floridians tooled out of town in search of a covert where they could dispose of the trunk and legs. They were flirting and celebrating because, as the fellow said, this was a big event. Thousands and thousands of guys are out in the woods and in a lifetime of hunting you may only manage to see one bear.

(1971)

Hailing the Elusory Mountain Lion

The swan song sounded by the wilderness grows fainter, ever more constricted, until only sharp ears can catch it at all. It fades to a nearly inaudible level, and yet there never is going to be any one time when we can say right *now* it is gone. Wolves meet their maker in wholesale lots, but coyotes infiltrate eastward, northward, southeastward. Woodland caribou and bighorn sheep are vanishing fast, but moose have expanded their range in some areas.

Mountain lions used to have practically the run of the Western Hemisphere, and they still do occur from Cape Horn to the Big Muddy River at the boundary of the Yukon and on the coasts of both oceans, so that they are the most versatile land mammal in the New World, probably taking in more latitudes than any other four-footed wild creature anywhere. There are perhaps only four to six thousand left in the United States, though there is no place that they didn't once go, eating deer, elk, pikas, porcupines, grasshoppers, and dead fish on the beach. They were called mountain lions in the Rockies, pumas (originally an Incan word) in the Southwestern states, cougars (a naturalist's corruption of an Amazonian Indian word) in the Northwest, panthers in the traditionalist East—"painters" in dialect-proud

35

New England—or catamounts. The Dutchmen of New Netherland called them tigers, red tigers, deer tigers, and the Spaniards *leones* or *leopardos*. They liked to eat horses—wolves preferred beef and black bears favored pork—but as adversaries of mankind they were overshadowed at first because bears appeared more formidable and wolves in their howling packs were more flamboyant and more damaging financially. Yet this panoply of names is itself quite a tribute, and somehow the legends about "panthers" have lingered longer than bear or wolf tales, helped by the animal's own limber, far-traveling stealth and as a carryover from the immense mythic force of the great cats of the Old World. Though only Florida among the Eastern states is known for certain to have any left, no wild knot of mountains or swamp is without rumors of panthers; nowadays people delight in these, keeping their eyes peeled. It's wishful, and the wandering, secretive nature of the beast ensures that even Eastern panthers will not soon be certifiably extinct. An informal census among experts in 1963 indicated that an island of twenty-five or more may have survived in the New Brunswick–Maine–Quebec region, and Louisiana may still have a handful, and perhaps eight live isolated in the Black Hills of South Dakota, and the Oklahoma panhandle may have a small colony—all outside the established range in Florida, Texas, and the Far West. As with the blue whale, who will be able to say when they have been eliminated?

"Mexican lion" is another name for mountain lions in the border states—a name that might imply a meager second-best rating there, yet ties to the majestic African beasts. Lions are at least twice as big as mountain lions, measuring by weight, though they are nearly the same in length because of the mountain lion's superb long tail. Both animals sometimes pair up affectionately with mates and hunt in tandem, but mountain lions go winding through life in ones or twos, whereas the lion is a harem-keeper, harem-dweller, the males eventually becoming stay-at-homes, heavy figureheads. Lions enjoy the grassy flatlands, forested along the streams, and they stay put, engrossed in communal events—roaring, grunting, growling with a racket like the noise of gears being stripped—unless the game moves on. They sun themselves, preside over the numerous kibbutz young, sneeze from the dust, and bask in dreams, occasionally waking up to issue reverberating, guttural pronouncements which serve notice that they are now awake.

Mountain lions spirit themselves away in saw-toothed canyons and on escarpments instead, and when conversing with their mates they coo like pigeons, sob like women, emit a flat slight shriek, a popping bubbling growl, or mew, or yowl. They growl and suddenly caterwaul into falsetto—the famous scarifying, metallic scream functioning as a kind of hunting cry close up, to terrorize and start the game. They ramble as much as twenty-five miles in a night, maintaining a large loop of territory which they cover every week or two. It's a solitary, busy life, involving a survey of several valleys, many deer herds. Like tigers and leopards, mountain lions are not sociably inclined and don't converse at length with the whole waiting world, but they are even less noisy; they seem to speak most eloquently with their feet. Where a tiger would roar, a mountain lion screams like a castrato. Where a mountain lion hisses, a leopard would snarl like a truck stuck in snow.

Leopards are the best counterpart to mountain lions in physique and in the tenor of their lives. Supple, fierce creatures, skilled at concealment but with great self-assurance and drive, leopards are bolder when facing human beings than the American cats. Basically they are hot-land beasts and not such remarkable travelers individually, though as a race they once inhabited the broad Eurasian land mass all the way from Great Britain to Malaysia, as well as Africa. As late as the 1960s, a few were said to be still holding out on the shore of the Mediterranean at Mount Mycale, Turkey. (During a forest fire twenty years ago a yearling swam the narrow straits to the Greek island Samos and holed up in a cave, where he was duly killed—perhaps the last leopard ever to set foot in Europe on his own.) Leopards are thicker and shorter than adult mountain lions and seem to lead an athlete's indolent, incurious life much of the time, testing their perfected bodies by clawing tree trunks, chewing on old skulls, executing acrobatic leaps, and then rousing themselves to the semiweekly antelope kill. Built with supreme hardness and economy, they make little allowance for man—they don't see him as different. They relish the flesh of his dogs, and they run up a tree when hunted and then sometimes spring down, as heavy as a chunk of iron wrapped in a flag. With stunning, gorgeous coats, their tight, dervish faces carved in a snarl, they head for the hereafter as if it were just one more extra-emphatic leap—as impersonal in death as the crack of the rifle was.

The American leopard, the jaguar, is a powerfully built serious fellow, who, before white men arrived, wandered as far north as the Carolinas, but his best home is the humid basin of the Amazon. Mountain lions penetrate these ultimate jungles too, but rather thinly, thriving better in the cooler, drier climate of the untenanted pampas and on the mountain slopes. They are blessed with a pleasant but undazzling coat, tan except for a white belly, mouth and throat, and some black behind the ears, on the tip of the tail and at the sides of the nose, and so they are hunted as symbols, not for their fur. The cubs are spotted, leopardlike, much as lion cubs are. If all of the big cats developed from a common ancestry, the mountain lions' specialization has been unpresumptuous—away from bulk and savagery to traveling light. Toward deer, their prey, they may be as ferocious as leopards, but not toward chance acquaintances such as man. They sometimes break their necks, their jaws, their teeth, springing against the necks of quarry they have crept close to—a fate in part resulting from the circumstance that they can't ferret out the weaker individuals in a herd by the device of a long chase, the way wolves do; they have to take the luck of the draw. None of the cats possesses enough lung capacity for gruelling runs. They depend upon shock tactics, bursts of speed, sledge-hammer leaps, strong collarbones for hitting power, and shearing dentition, whereas wolves employ all the advantages of time in killing their quarry, as well as the numbers and gaiety of the pack, biting the beast's nose and rump—the technique of a thousand cuts—lapping the bloody snow. Wolves sometimes even have a cheering section of flapping ravens accompanying them, eager to scavenge after the brawl.

It's a risky business for the mountain lion, staking the strength and impact of his neck against the strength of the prey animal's neck. Necessarily, he is concentrated and fierce; yet legends exist that mountain lions have irritably defended men and women lost in the wilderness against marauding jaguars, who are no friends of theirs, and (with a good deal more supporting evidence) that they are susceptible to an odd kind of fascination with human beings. Sometimes they will tentatively seek an association, hanging about a campground or following a hiker out of curiosity, perhaps, circling around and bounding up on a ledge above to watch him pass. This mild modesty has helped preserve them from extinction. If they have been unable to make any adjustments to the advent of man, they haven't suicidally opposed him either, as the buffalo wolves and grizzlies did. In fact, at close quarters they seem bewildered. When treed, they don't breathe a hundred-proof ferocity but puzzle over what to do. They're too light-bodied to bear down on the hunter and kill him easily, even if they should attack—a course they seem to have no inclination for. In this century in the United States only one person, a child of thirteen, has been killed by a mountain lion; that was in 1924. And they're informal animals. Lolling in an informal sprawl on a high limb, they can't seem to summon any Enobarbus-like front of resistance for long. Daring men occasionally climb up and toss lassos about a cat and haul him down, strangling him by pulling from two directions, while the lion, mortified, appalled, never does muster his fighting aplomb. Although he could fight off a pack of wolves, he hasn't worked out a posture to assume toward man and his dogs. Impotently, he stiffens, as the dinosaurs must have when the atmosphere grew cold.

Someday hunting big game may come to be regarded as a form of vandalism, and the remaining big creatures of the wilderness will skulk through restricted reserves wearing radio transmitters and numbered collars, or bearing stripes of dye, as many elephants already do, to aid the busy biologists who track them from the air. Like a vanishing race of trolls, more report and memory than a reality, they will inhabit children's books and nostalgic articles, a special glamour attaching to those, like mountain lions, that are geographically incalculable and may still be sighted away from the preserves. Already we've become enthusiasts. We want game about us—at least at a summer house; it's part of privileged living. There is a precious privacy about seeing wildlife, too. Like meeting a fantastically dressed mute on the road, the fact that no words are exchanged and that *he's* not going to give an account makes the experience light-hearted; it's wholly ours. Besides, if anything out of the ordinary happened, we know we can't expect to be believed, and since it's rather fun to be disbelieved—fishermen know this—the privacy is even more complete. Deer, otter, foxes are messengers from another condition of life, another mentality, and bring us tidings of places where we don't go.

Ten years ago at Vavenby, a sawmill town on the North Thompson River in British Columbia, a frolicsome mountain lion used to appear at dusk every ten days or so in a bluegrass field alongside the river. Deer congregated there, the river was silky and swift, cooling the summer air, and it was a festive spot for a lion to be. She was thought to be a female, and reputedly left tracks around an enormous territory to the north and west—Raft Mountain, Battle Mountain, the Trophy Range, the Murtle River, and Mahood Lake—territory on an upended, pelagic scale, much of it scarcely accessible to a man by trail, where the tiger lilies grew four feet tall. She would materialize in this field among the deer five minutes before dark, as if checking in again, a habit that may have resulted in her death eventually, though for the present the farmer who observed her visits was keeping his mouth shut about it. This was pioneer country; there were people alive who could remember the time when poisoning the carcass of a cow would net a man a pile of dead predators—a family of mountain lions to bounty, maybe half a dozen wolves, and both black bears and grizzlies. The Indians considered lion meat a delicacy, but they had clans which drew their origins at the Creation from ancestral mountain lions, or wolves or bears, so these massacres amazed them. They thought the outright bounty hunters were crazy men.

Even before Columbus, mountain lions were probably not distributed in saturation numbers anywhere, as wolves may have been. Except for the family unit—a female with her half-grown cubs—each lion seems to occupy its own spread of territory, not as a result of fights with intruders but because the young transients share the same instinct for solitude and soon sheer off to find vacant mountains and valleys. A mature lion kills only one deer every week or two, according to a study by Maurice Hornocker in Idaho, and therefore is not really a notable factor in controlling the local deer population. Rather, it keeps watch contentedly as that population grows, sometimes benefitting the herds by scaring them onto new wintering grounds that are not overbrowsed, and by its very presence warding off other lions.

This thin distribution, coupled with the mountain lion's taciturn habits, make sighting one a matter of luck, even for game officials located in likely country. One warden in Colorado I talked to had indeed seen a pair of them fraternizing during the breeding season. He was driving a jeep over an abandoned mining road, and he passed two brown animals sitting peaceably in the grass, their heads close together. For a moment he thought they were coyotes and kept driving, when all of a sudden the picture registered that they were *cougars!* He braked and backed up, but of course they were gone. He was an old-timer, a man who had crawled inside bear dens to pull out the cubs, and knew where to find clusters of buffalo skulls in the recesses of the Rockies where the last bands had hidden; yet this cryptic instant when he was turning his jeep round a curve was the only glimpse—unprovable—that he ever got of a mountain lion.

Such glimpses usually are cryptic. During a summer I spent in Wyoming in my boyhood, I managed to see two coyotes, but both occasions were so fleeting that it required an act of faith on my part afterward to feel sure I had seen them. One of the animals vanished between rolls of ground; the other, in rougher, stonier, wooded country, cast his startled gray face in my direction and simply was gone. Hunching, he swerved for cover, and the brush closed over him. I used to climb to a vantage point above a high basin at twilight and watch the mule deer steal into the meadows to feed. The grass grew higher than their stomachs, the steep forest was close at hand, and they were as small and fragile-looking as filaments at that distance, quite human in coloring, gait and form. It was possible to visualize them as a naked Indian hunting party a hundred years before—or not to believe in their existence at all, either as Indians or deer. Minute, aphid-sized, they stepped so carefully in emerging, hundreds of feet below, that, straining my eyes, I needed to tell myself constantly that they were deer; my imagination, left to its own devices with the dusk settling down, would have made of them a dozen other creatures.

41

Recently, walking at night on the woods road that passes my house in Vermont, I heard footsteps in the leaves and windfalls. I waited, listening—they sounded too heavy to be anything less than a man, a large deer or a bear. A man wouldn't have been in the woods so late; my dog stood respectfully silent and still, and they did seem to shuffle portentously. Sure enough, after pausing at the edge of the road, a fully grown bear appeared, visible only in dimmest outline, staring in my direction for four or five seconds. The darkness lent a faintly red tinge to his coat; he was well built. Then, turning, he ambled off, almost immediately lost to view, though I heard the noise of his passage, interrupted by several pauses. It was all as concise as a vision, and since I had wanted to see a bear close to my own house, being a person who likes to live in a melting pot, whether in the city or country, and since it was too dark to pick out his tracks, I was grateful when the dog inquisitively urinated along the bear's path, thereby confirming that at least I had witnessed *something*. The dog seemed unsurprised, however, as if the scent were not all that remarkable, and, sure enough, the next week in the car I encountered a yearling bear in daylight two miles downhill, and a cub a month later. My farmer neighbors were politely skeptical of my accounts, having themselves caught sight of only perhaps a couple of bears in all their lives.

So it's with sympathy as well as an awareness of the tricks that enthusiasm and nightfall may play that I have been going to nearby towns seeking out people who have claimed at one time or another to have seen a mountain lion. The experts of the state—game wardens, taxidermists, the most accomplished hunters—emphatically discount the claims, but the believers are unshaken. They include some summer people who were enjoying a drink on the back terrace when the apparition of a great-tailed cat moved out along the fringe of the woods on a deer path; a boy who was hunting with his .22 years ago near the village dump and saw the animal cross a gully and fired blindly, then ran away and brought back a search party, which found a tuft of toast-colored fur; and a state forestry employee, a sober woodsman, who caught the cat in his headlights while driving through Victory Bog in the wildest corner of the Northeast Kingdom. Gordon Hickok, who works for a furniture factory and has shot one or two mountain lions on hunting trips in the West, saw one cross U.S. 5 at a place called Auger Hole near Mount Hor. He tracked it with dogs a short distance, finding a fawn with its head gnawed off. A high-school English teacher reported seeing a mountain lion cross another road, near Runaway Pond, but the hunters who quickly went out decided that the prints were those of a big bobcat, splayed impressively in the mud and snow. Fifteen years ago a watchman in the fire tower on top of Bald Mountain had left grain scattered in the grooves of a flat rock under the tower to feed several deer. One night, looking down just as the dusk turned murky, he saw two slim long-tailed lions creep out of the scrubby border of spruce and inspect the rock, sniffing deer droppings and dried deer saliva. The next night, when he was in his cabin, the dog barked and, looking out the window, again he saw the vague shape of a lion just vanishing.

A dozen loggers and woodsmen told me such stories. In the Adirondacks I've also heard some persuasive avowals—one by an old dog-sled driver and trapper, a French Canadian; another by the owner of a tourist zoo, who was exhibiting a Western cougar. In Vermont perhaps the most eager rumor buffs are some of the farmers. After all, now that packaged semen has replaced the awesome farm bull and so many procedures have been mechanized, who wants to lose *all* the adventure of farming? Until recently the last mountain lion known to have been killed in the Northeast was recorded in 1881 in Barnard, Vermont. However, it has been learned that probably another one was shot from a tree in 1931 in Mundleville, New Brunswick, and still another trapped seven years later in Somerset County in Maine. Bruce S. Wright, director of the Northeastern Wildlife Station (which is operated at the University of New Brunswick with international funding), is convinced that though they are exceedingly rare, mountain lions are still part of the fauna of the region; in fact, he has plaster casts of tracks to prove it, as well as a compilation of hundreds of reported sightings. Some people may have mistaken a golden retriever for a lion, or may have intended to foment a hoax, but all in all the evidence does seem promising. Indeed, after almost twenty years of search and study, Wright himself finally saw one.

The way these sightings crop up in groups has often been pooh-poohed as greenhorn fare or as a sympathetic hysteria among neighbors, but it is just as easily explained by the habit mountain lions have of establishing a territory that they scout through at intervals, visiting an auspicious deer-ridden swamp or remote ledgy mountain. Even at such a site a successful hunt could not be mounted without trained dogs, and if the population of the big cats was extremely sparse, requiring of them long journeys during the mating season, and yet with plenty of deer all over, they might not stay for long. One or two hundred miles is no obstacle to a Western cougar. The cat might inhabit a mountain ridge one year, and then never again.

Fifteen years ago, Francis Perry, who is an ebullient muffin of a man, a farmer all his life in Brownington, Vermont, saw a mountain lion "larger and taller than a collie, and grayish yellow" (he had seen them in circuses). Having set a trap for a woodchuck, he was on his way to visit the spot when he came over a rise and, at a distance of fifty yards, saw the beast engaged in eating the dead woodchuck. It bounded off, but Perry set four light fox traps for it around the woodchuck. Apparently, a night or two later the cat returned and got caught in three of these, but they couldn't hold it; it pulled free, leaving the marks of a struggle. Noel Perry, his brother, remembers how scared Francis looked when he came home from the first episode. Noel himself saw the cat (which may have meant that Brownington Swamp was one of its haunts that summer), once when it crossed a cow pasture on another farm the brothers owned, and once when it fled past his rabbit dogs through underbrush while he was training them—he thought for a second that its big streaking form was one of the dogs. A neighbor, Robert Chase, also saw the animal that year. Then again last summer, for the first time in fifteen years, Noel Perry saw a track as big as a bear's but round like a mountain lion's, and Robert's brother, Larry Chase, saw the actual cat several times one summer evening, playing a chummy hide-and-seek with him in the fields.

Elmer and Elizabeth Ambler are in their forties, populists politically, and have bought a farm in Glover to live the good life, though he is a truck driver in Massachusetts on weekdays and must drive hard in order to be home when he can. He's bald, with large eyebrows, handsome teeth and a low forehead, but altogether a strong-looking, clear, humane face. He is an informational kind of man who will give you the history of various breeds of cattle or a talk about taxation in a slow and musical voice, and both he and his wife, a purpose-ful, self-sufficient redhead, are fascinated by the possibility that they live in the wilderness. Beavers inhabit the river that flows past their house. The Amblers say that on Black Mountain nearby hunters "dis-appear" from time to time, and bears frequent the berry patches in their back field—they see them, their visitors see them, people on the road see them, their German shepherds meet them and run back drooling with fright. They've stocked their farm with horned Here-fords instead of the polled variety so that the creatures can "defend themselves." Ambler is intrigued by the thought that apart from the danger of bears, someday "a cat" might prey on one of his cows. Last year, looking out the back window, his wife saw through binoculars an animal with a flowing tail and "a cat's gallop" following a line of trees where the deer go, several hundred yards uphill behind the house. Later, Ambler went up on snowshoes and found tracks as big as their shepherds'; the dogs obligingly ran alongside. He saw walking tracks, leaping tracks and deer tracks marked with blood going toward higher ground. He wonders whether the cat will ever attack him. There are plenty of bobcats around, but they both say they know the difference. The splendid, nervous *tail* is what people must have identified in order to claim they have seen a mountain lion.

I, too, cherish the notion that I may have seen a lion. Mine was crouched on an overlook above a grass-grown, steeply pitched wash in the Alberta Rockies—a much more likely setting than anywhere in New England. It was late afternoon on my last day at Maligne Lake, where I had been staying with my father at a national-park chalet. I was twenty; I could walk forever or could climb endlessly in a san-guine scramble, going out every day as far as my legs carried me, swinging around for home before the sun went down. Earlier, in the valley of the Athabasca, I had found several winter-starved or wolf-killed deer, well picked and scattered, and an area with many elk antlers strewn on the ground where the herds had wintered safely, dropping their antlers but not their bones. Here, much higher up, in the bright plenitude of the summer, I had watched two wolves and a stately bull moose in one mountain basin, and had been up on the caribou barrens on the ridge west of the lake and brought back the talons of a hawk I'd found dead on the ground. Whenever I was watching game, a sort of stopwatch in me started running. These were moments of intense importance and intimacy, of new intimations and aptitudes. Time had a jam-packed character, as it does during a mile run.

I was good at moving quietly through the woods and at spotting game, and was appropriately exuberant. The finest, longest day of my stay was the last. Going east, climbing through a luxuriant terrain of up-and-down boulders, brief brilliant glades, sudden potholes fifty feet deep—a forest of moss-hung lodgepole pines and firs and spare, gaunt spruce with the black lower branches broken off—I came upon the remains of a young bear, which had been torn up and shredded. Perhaps wolves had cornered it during some imprudent excursion in the early spring. (Bears often wake up while the snow is still deep, dig themselves out and rummage around in the neighborhood sleepily for a day or two before bedding down again under a fallen tree.) I took the skull along so that I could extract the teeth when I got hold of some tools. Discoveries like this represent a superfluity of wildlife and show how many beasts there are scouting about.

I went higher. The marmots whistled familially; the tall trees wilted to stubs of themselves. A pretty stream led down a defile from a series of openings in front of the ultimate barrier of a vast mountain wall which I had been looking at from a distance each day on my outings. It wasn't too steep to be climbed, but it was a barrier because my energies were not sufficient to scale it and bring me back the same night. Besides, it stretched so majestically, surflike above the lesser ridges, that I liked to think of it as the Continental Divide.

On my left as I went up this wash was an abrupt, grassy slope that enjoyed a southern exposure and was sunny and windblown all winter, which kept it fairly free of snow. The ranger at the lake had told me it served as a wintering ground for a few bighorn sheep and for a band of mountain goats, three of which were in sight. As I approached laboriously, these white, pointy-horned fellows drifted up over a rise, managing to combine their retreat with some nippy good grazing as they went, not to give any pursuer the impression that they had been pushed into flight. I took my time too, climbing to locate the spring in a precipitous cleft of rock where the band did most of its drinking, and finding the shallow, high-ceilinged cave where the goats had sheltered from storms, presumably for generations. The floor was layered with rubbery droppings, tramped down and sprinkled with tufts of shed fur, and the back wall was checkered with footholds where the goats liked to clamber and perch. Here and there was a horn lying loose—a memento for me to add to my collection from an old individual that had died a natural death, secure in the band's winter stronghold. A bold, thriving family of pack rats emerged to observe me. They lived mainly on the nutritives in the droppings, and were used to the goats' tolerance; they seemed astonished when I tossed a stone.

I kept scrabbling along the side of the slope to a section of outcroppings where the going was harder. After perhaps half an hour, crawling around a corner, I found myself faced with a bighorn ram who was taking his ease on several square yards of bare earth between large rocks, a little above the level of my head. Just as surprised as I, he stood up. He must have construed the sounds of my advance to be those of another sheep or goat. His horns had made a complete curl and then some; they were thick, massive and bunched together like a high Roman helmet, and he himself was muscly and military, with a grave-looking nose. A squared-off, middle-aged, trophy-type ram, full of imposing professionalism, he was at the stage of life when rams sometimes stop herding and live as rogues.

He turned and tried a couple of possible exits from the pocket where I had found him, but the ground was badly pitched and would require a reeling gait and loss of dignity. Since we were within a national park and obviously I was unarmed, he simply was not inclined to put himself to so much trouble. He stood fifteen or twenty feet above me, pushing his tongue out through his teeth, shaking his head slightly and dipping it into charging position as I moved closer by a step or two, raising my hand slowly toward him in what I proposed as a friendly greeting. The day had been a banner one since the beginning, so while I recognized immediately that this meeting would be a valued memory, I felt as natural in his company as if he were a friend of mine reincarnated in a shag suit. I saw also that he was going to knock me for a loop, head over heels down the steep slope, if I sidled nearer, because he did not by any means feel as expansive and exuberant at our encounter as I did. That was the chief difference between us. I was talking to him with easy gladness, and beaming; he was not. He was unsettled and on his mettle, waiting for me to move along, the way a bighorn sheep waits for a predator to move on in wildlife movies when each would be evenly matched in a contest of strength and position. Although his warlike nose and high bone helmet, blocky and beautiful as weaponry, kept me from giving in to my sense that we were brothers, I knew I could stand there for a long while. His coat was a down-to-earth brown, edgy with muscle, his head was that of an unsmiling veteran standing to arms, and despite my reluctance to treat him as some sort of boxed-in prize, I might have stayed on for half the afternoon if I hadn't realized that I had other sights to see. It was not a day to dawdle.

I trudged up the wash and continued until, past tree line, the terrain widened and flattened in front of a preliminary ridge that formed an obstacle before the great roaring, silent, surflike mountain wall that I liked to think of as the Continental Divide, although it wasn't. A cirque separated the preliminary ridge from the ultimate divide, which I still hoped to climb to and look over. The opening into this was roomy enough, except for being littered with enormous boulders, and I began trying to make my way across them. Each was boat-sized and rested upon under-boulders; it was like running in place. After tussling with this landscape for an hour or two, I was limp and sweating, pinching my cramped legs. The sun had gone so low that I knew I would be finding my way home by moonlight in any case, and I could see into the cirque, which was big and symmetrical and presented a view of sheer barbarism; everywhere were these cruel boat-sized boulders.

Giving up and descending to the goats' draw again, I had a drink from the stream and bathed before climbing farther downward. The grass was green, sweet-smelling, and I felt safely close to life after that sea of dead boulders. I knew I would never be physically younger or in finer country; even then the wilderness was singing its swan song. I had no other challenges in mind, and though very tired, I liked looking up at the routes where I'd climbed. The trio of goats had not returned, but I could see their wintering cave and the cleft in the rocks where the spring was. Curiously, the bighorn ram had not left; he had only withdrawn upward, shifting away from the outcroppings to an open sweep of space where every avenue of escape was available. He was lying on a carpet of grass and, lonely pirate that he was, had his head turned in my direction.

It was from this same wash that looking up, I spotted the animal I took to be a mountain lion. He was skulking among some outcroppings at a point lower on the mountainside than the ledges where the ram originally had been. A pair of hawks or eagles were swooping at him by turns, as if he were close to a nest. The slant between us was steep, but the light of evening was still more than adequate. I did not really see the wonderful tail—that special medallion—nor was he particularly big for a lion. He was gloriously catlike and slinky, however, and so indifferent to the swooping birds as to seem oblivious of them. There are plenty of creatures he wasn't; he wasn't a marmot, a goat or other grass-eater, a badger, a wolf or coyote or fisher. He *may* have been a big bobcat or a wolverine, although he looked ideally lion-colored. He had a cat's strong collarbone structure for hitting, powerful haunches for vaulting, and the almost mystically small head mountain lions possess, with the gooseberry eyes. Anyway, I believed him to be a mountain lion, and standing quietly I watched him as he inspected in leisurely fashion the ledge that he was on and the one under him savory with every trace of goat—frosty-colored with the white hairs they'd shed. The sight was so dramatic that it seemed to be happening close to me, though in fact he and the hawks or eagles, whatever they were, were miniaturized by distance.

If I'd kept motionless, eventually I could have seen whether he had the proper tail, but such scientific questions had no weight next to my need to essay some kind of communication with him. It had been exactly the same when I'd watched the two wolves playing together a couple of days before. They were above me, absorbed in their game of noses-and-paws. I had recognized that I might never witness such a scene again, yet I couldn't hold myself in. Instead of talking and raising my arm to them, as I had with the ram, I'd shuffled forward impetuously as if to say *Here I am!* Now, with the lion, I tried hard to dampen my impulse and restrained myself as long as I could. Then I stepped toward him, just barely squelching a cry in my throat but lifting my hand—as clumsy as anyone is who is trying to attract attention.

At that, of course, he swerved aside instantly and was gone. Even the two birds vanished. Foolish, triumphant and disappointed, I hiked on down into the lower forests, gargantuanly tangled, another life zone—not one which would exclude a lion but one where he would not be seen. I'd got my second wind and walked lightly and softly, letting the silvery darkness settle around me. The blow-downs were as black as whales; my feet sank in the moss. Clearly this was as crowded a day as I would ever have, and I knew my real problem would not be to make myself believed but rather to make myself understood at all, simply in reporting the story, and that I must at least keep the memory straight for myself. I was so happy that I was unerring in distinguishing the deer trails going my way. The forest's night beauty was supreme in its promise, and I didn't hurry.

(1971)

Howling Back at the Wolves

Wolves have marvelous legs. The first thing one notices about them is how high they are set on their skinny legs, and the instant, blurred gait these can switch into, bicycling away, carrying them as much as forty miles in a day. With brindled coats in smoky shades, brushy tails, light-filled eyes, intense sharp faces which are more focused than an intelligent dog's but also less various, they are electric on first sighting, bending that bushy head around to look back as they run. In captivity when they are quarreling in a cage, the snarls sound guttural and their jaws chop, but scientists watching pet wolves in the woods speak of their flowing joy, of such a delight in running that they melt into the woods like sunlight, like running water.

The modern study of American wildlife may be said to have begun with Adolph Murie, who, writing about the wolves of Mount McKinley in 1944, realized there was not much point in a scientist's shooting them; so few wolves were left that this would be killing the goose laying the golden eggs. In those days even the biologists dealing with animals which weren't considered varmints mainly just boiled the flesh off their heads to examine the knobs on their skulls, or opened their stomachs to see what they ate. The scrutiny of skulls had resulted in a listing of eighty-six species and subspecies of the grizzly bear, for example (it's now considered that there were a maximum of only two), and twenty-seven specified New World wolves (again, now revised down to two). Murie, in the field and looking at scats, could do a more thorough investigation of diet than the autopsy fellows, who, as it was, knew almost nothing else about the life of wolves.

Murie and Ian McTaggart-Cowan in Canada were the best of the bedroll scientists. They could travel with dogs all winter in the snow or camp alone on a gravel bar in a valley for the summer, go about quietly on foot and record everything that they saw. No amount of bush-plane maneuvering and electronic technology can quite replace these methods, by which the totality of a wilderness community can be observed and absorbed. Young scientists such as L. David Mech, who has been the salvation of wolves in Minnesota, which is practically the only place in the lower forty-eight states where they still occur, try to combine the current reliance on radiotelemetry with some of that old bedroll faithfulness to the five senses shared by a man with the animals he is studying.

Big game, like elk and caribou, and big glamorous predators have naturally received first attention, people being as they are, so that much more is known about wolves than about the grasshopper mouse, though the grasshopper mouse is a wolf among mice, trailing, gorging upon small mammals and insects; in fact, with nose pointed skyward, it even "howls." On lists of endangered species you occasionally find little beasts that wouldn't excite much attention on a picnic outing, but despite all the talk about saving the fruits of two billion years' worth of evolution, the funds available go to help those animals that tend to remind us of ourselves—rhinos, whales, falcons—and there aren't many lists of endangered plants.

So it is that the predator specialists are predatory. A hawk man drops out of the sky for a visit; he has radios attached to assorted raptors and albatrosses and swans, and flies around the world to track their migrations. During his chat about perfecting antennas it is obvious that he is full of what in an animal he would call "displaced aggression." The scientist Albert Erickson, who has worked on grizzlies in the north and leopard seals in Antarctica, was known as "Wild Man Erickson" when he studied black bears in Michigan. The Craighead brothers, Frank and John—territorial, secretive and competitive—have been working on a definitive study of grizzlies (which are also territorial, secretive and competitive) for umpteen years, scrapping with the National Park Service at Yellowstone and embargoing many of their own findings in the meantime. Maurice Hornocker, who is now the definitive mountain-lion man and who trained with them, is just as close-mouthed—as close-mouthed as a mountain lion, indeed. Down in Grand Chenier, Louisiana, Ted Joanen, the state's alligator expert, is equally able and reserved. One doesn't understand right away why he happens to be devoting his life to learning more about alligators than anybody else, rather than ibises or chimney swifts or pelicans, until he gets to describing how alligators can catch a swimming deer, pull it under the water, drown it and tear its leg off by spinning like a lathe, and then points to one's own twitching leg.

Wolves *would* be more of a loss to us than some exotic mouse, because they epitomize the American wilderness as no other animal does, and fill both the folklore of childhood and that of the woods—folklore that would wither away if they all were to die, and may do so in any case. We know that the folklore was exaggerated, that generally they don't attack man, which is a relief, but we treasure the stories nonetheless, wanting the woods to be woods. In the contiguous states the gray wolf's range is less than one percent of what it used to be, and that patch of Minnesota wilderness, twelve thousand square miles where they live in much the same density as in primeval times, is greatly enriched by the presence of wolves.

Wisconsin didn't get around to granting its wolves protection until they had become extinct, but Mech got the Minnesota bounty removed and almost single-handedly turned local thinking around, until there is talk of declaring the wolf a "state animal" and establishing a sanctuary for it in the Boundary Waters Canoe Area. Mech is a swift-thinking, urbane, amused man, bald, round-faced, not a bit wolflike in appearance, although he is sharp in his rivalry with other scientists. As an advocate he knows how to generate "spontaneous" nationwide latter-writing campaigns and can gather financial support from the

National Geographic Society and the New York Zoological Society, from Minneapolis industrialists and the federal government. He has a soul-stirring howl, more real than reality, that triggers the wolves into howling back when he is afoot trying to locate them, but his ears have begun to dim from a decade or more of flying all winter in flimsy planes to spot them against the snow. Sometimes he needs an assistant along to hear whether a pack at a distance is answering him.

That wolves do readily answer even bad imitations of their howl may have a good deal of significance. Observers have noticed the similarities between the intricate life of a wolf pack and the most primitive grouping of man, the family-sized band. Often there is a "peripheral wolf," for instance, which is tolerated but picked on, and as though the collective psyche of the pack required a scapegoat, if the peripheral wolf disappears another pack member may slip down the social ladder and assume the role, or a stray that otherwise might have been driven off will be adopted. The strays, or "lone wolves," not being bound by territorial considerations, range much farther and frequently eat better than pack wolves do, but are always seeking to enroll themselves.

What seems so uncanny and moving about the experience of howling to wolves, then hearing them answer, may be the enveloping sense of déjà vu, perhaps partly subliminal, that goes right to one's roots—band replying to band, each on its own ground, gazing across a few hundred yards of meadow or bog at the same screen of trees. The listener rises right up on his toes, looking about happily at his human companions.

Wolf pups make a frothy ribbon of sound like fat bubbling, a shiny, witchy, fluttery yapping, while the adults siren less excitably, without those tremulous, flexible yips, although they sometimes do break pitch into a yodel. The senior wolf permits the response, if one is made, introducing it with his own note after a pause—which is sometimes lengthy—before the others join in. Ordinarily pups left alone will not answer unless the adult closest to them does so, as he or she returns to protect them. Wolves howl for only a half-minute or so, though they may respond again and again after a cautious intermission, if no danger is indicated from their having already betrayed their position. Each wolf has a tone, or series of tones, of its own that blends into an iridescent harmony with the others, and people who howl regularly at a wolf rendezvous soon acquire vocal personalities too, as well as a kind of choral sequence in which they join together—cupping their mouths to the shape of a muzzle on cue.

I went out with a student of Mech's, Fred Harrington, who records and voice-prints wolf howls. His wife was along, doing the puppy trills, and so was the trap-line crew, who attach radio-collars to the wolves they catch. We stood at the edge of a cutover jack-pine flat, with a few tall spruces where the wolves were. The sun was setting, the moon was rising, squirrels and birds were chitting close by, and we knew that a radio-collared bear was digging its winter den just over the rise. Howling is not a hunting cry and does not frighten other animals. The wolves howled as if for their own edification, as a pleasurable thing, a popular, general occasion set off by our calls to them, replying to us but not led by our emphasis or interpretation. If they had been actively scouting us they would have kept silent, as they do in the spring when the pups are too young to travel. To us, their chorus sounded isolated, vulnerable, the more so because obviously they were having fun, and we all felt the urge to run toward them; but they didn't share that feeling. A pack needs at least ten square miles for each member, as well as a deer every eighteen days for that individual, or a deer every three days for a pack of six. The figure for moose is one every three days for a pack of fifteen, Mech has calculated. Thus, howling between packs does not serve the function of calling them to confabulate. Instead, it seems to keep them apart, defining rough boundaries for their separate ranges, providing them mutually with a roster of strength, though by howling, mates in a pack do find one another and find solidarity.

In Algonquin Provincial Park in Ontario thousands of people howl with the wolves in the early autumn. Whether or not it is a high point for the wolves, it certainly is for the people. I've gone to one of the favorite locations, where the ground is littered with cigarette butts, and tried, except the day was rainy and the wolves couldn't hear me. Nobody who has had the experience will fail to root for the beasts ever after. Glacier National Park in Montana is next to Canada, like Mech's country, and they may manage to become reestablished there; Yellowstone Park has a small vanguard. In East Texas a few hundred survive, hiding in the coastal marshes. These are red wolves— relic relations of the gray wolf that inhabited the Southeast and lower Mississippi Valley and are probably now doomed, pushed up against the sea, with no reservoir such as the wildlands of Canada provide from which to replenish their numbers.

Apparently a special relationship can exist between men and wolves which is unlike that between men and any of the bears or big cats. One might have to look to the other primates for a link that is closer. It's not just a matter of howling; owls with their hoots and loons with their laughter also interact with wolves. Nor is it limited to the mystery of why dogs, about fifteen thousand years back, which is very recent as such events go, cut themselves away from other wolves by a gradual, at first "voluntary" process to become subservient to human beings as no other domestic creature is, running with man in packs in which *he* calls the tune. Another paradox is that the wolves which remained wolves, though they are large predators that might legitimately regard a man-shaped item as prey, don't seem to look upon him as such; don't even challenge him in the woods in quite the same way that they will accost a trespassing cougar or grizzly.

In the campaign to rescue the wolf from Red Ridinghood status, some scientists, including Mech, have overdone their testimonials as to its liberal behavior, becoming so categorical that they doubt that any North American wolf not rabid has ever attacked a human being. This does violence to scientific method, as well as to the good name of countless frontiersmen who knew more about the habits of wilderness animals than it is possible to learn today. (What these scientists really mean is that none of their Ph.D. candidates doing field work has been attacked by a wolf so far.) Such propaganda also pigeonholes the wolf in a disparaging way, as if it were a knee-jerk creature without any options, like a blowfish or hog-nosed snake.

But the link with man remains. Douglas H. Pimlott, who is Canada's wolf expert, explores this matter in *The World of the Wolf*. He mentions behavioral patterns that are shared by man and wolf, and by indirection might have come to influence wolves. Both hunt cooperatively in groups and are nearly unique in that respect; both have lived in complex bands in which the adults of either sex care for the young. He mentions the likelihood that there are subconscious attributes of the human mind that may affect wolves. After all, the bonds between a man and dog penetrate far beyond the awe of the one for the other—are more compulsive, more telepathic than awe—and cannot be fully explained under the heading of love. Wolves, like dogs, says Pimlott, are excellent readers of signs because of their social makeup and their cruising system of hunting, which does not depend as much on surprise as the habits of most other predators do: "They instinctively recognize aggression, fear, and other qualities of mind which are evidenced in subtle ways by our expressions and actions. . . . In hunting we stalk deliberately, quietly . . . in winter we move through the woods and across lakes and streams deliberately, as a wolf does in traveling over his range, hunting for prey."

These movements indicate to wolves that we are superior predators—superior wolves—and not prey. It could be added that wolves, like dogs, take a remarkable delight in submissive ritual, ingratiating themselves, placating a bigger, more daring beast—this part of their adaptation through the millennia to life in a pack, in which usually only one or two members are really capable of killing the sizable game that will feed many mouths; the rest dance attendance upon them. Of course not only the fellow prowling in the woods is predatory. In the city, when much more driving and successful men emerge on the street for a business lunch, their straight-line strides and manner, "bright-eyed and bushy-tailed," would bowl over any wolf.

(1972)

Bears, Bears, Bears

Bears, which stopped being primarily predatory some time ago, though they still have a predator's sharp wits and mouth, appeal to a side of us that is lumbering, churlish and individual. We are touched by their anatomy because it resembles ours, by their piggishness and sleepiness and unsociability with each other, by their very aversion to having anything to do with us except for eating our garbage. Where big tracts of forest remain, black bears can still do fairly well. The grizzly's prickly ego is absent in them; they are unostentatious woodland animals that stay under cover and do not expect to have everything go their way.

Grizzlies never did inhabit the forested East. They lived on the Great Plains and in the Rockies and Sierras, much of it open or arid country; apparently they are more tolerant than black bears of hot, direct sun. In such surroundings no trees were at hand for the cubs to flee to and the adults developed their propensity for charging an intruder. For their own safety too, the best defense was an assault, and until we brought our rifles into play they didn't trouble to make much distinction between us and other predators. They still are guyed in by instinct to an "attack distance," as the biologists call it, within which their likely first reaction is to charge, whereas if they perceive a man approaching from farther off, they will melt away if they can.

Bears have a direct, simple vegetarian diet supplemented by insects and carrion or fish, so they need less operating space than a wolf, which weighs only about one-fourth what a black bear weighs but must obtain for itself a classy meat meal. Nevertheless, according to several studies, black bears require from one to five square miles apiece just to gather their food, and units of at least fifty square miles of wilderness for their wanderings and social relations. In this day and age such a chunk has other uses too. Loggers will be cutting on parts of it, and boy scouts holding encampments, canoeists paddling the rivers, and hikers and hunters traipsing across. Black bears were originally found in every state but Hawaii, and still manage to survive in about thirty, if only in remnant numbers, so that they seem able to co-exist. They are coated for living up on the windy ridges or down in the swamps and hollows, where even the snowmobilers can't get to them during the winter because they are under the snow, and they give promise of being with us for a long while.

Probably the most ardent investigator of black bears right now is Lynn Rogers, a graduate student at the University of Minnesota. He's thirty-four, red-bearded, crew-cut with a wife who used to teach English and two children, and he is another one of David Mech's protégés. He works in Isabella (once called Hurry Up, until a leading citizen renamed it after his daughter), which is a logging village, a tiny crossroads with more bars than grocery stores, settled by "Finlanders," as they are called, in the Arrowhead region of northern Minnesota, now the Superior National Forest. The logging is fading as aspen grows up in place of the old stands of big pine, but the Forest Service plants red or white pine where it can (there is more jack pine, however), and the swamps are forested with black spruce. The lakeshores are pretty, with birch, cedar, red maple, fir and white spruce, and the whole place is bursting with bears. On a seven-mile stretch of highway near Rogers's headquarters thirty were shot in one year. This was before the townspeople became interested in his work; now they let the bears live.

Bears, Bears, Bears

Rogers is a two-hundred-pounder with a rangy build and a small-looking head, no more bearish than Mech's is wolfish. Though there are scientists who come to resemble the animals they study, more often they look like athletic coaches, animals being in some sense our behind-hand brothers and these the fellows who watch out for them. Rogers could well be a coach, except for the streak in him that makes him extraordinary. In the woods he moves at a silent trot, as only the rarest woodsmen do. His thoughts, insofar as they could be elicited in the week I lived with him, seemed almost exclusively concerned with bears—catching them, amassing more data on them. He seldom reads a newspaper or watches television, and likes to kid his wife about the "fairy tales" of literature which she taught in school. When he takes a day off, it's to snap pictures of beaver or to wait half the day in a tree for an osprey to return to its nest. He's lived only in Minnesota and Michigan—grew up in Grand Rapids—but once he did stop off in Chicago, when driving between the two states, to go to the natural history museum. If you ask what he'd like to do when his achievements are properly recognized, he says he'd want to stay in Isabella and study lynx or else fisher.

As he sits in a brooding posture at the kitchen table, his body doesn't move for long periods and he thinks aloud, not so much in actual words as with a slow series of ums and ahs that seem to convey the pacing of his thoughts. But he lectures nicely, full of his subject, and in the woods whatever is lummoxy drops away in that quickness, the dozen errands he's running at once—searching for a plant whose leaves will match the unknown leaves he has been finding in a given bear's scats, examining a local bear-rubbing tree for hairs left on the bark since his last check. If he's lost in his jeep in the tangle of old logging roads, he gets a fix on the closest radio-collared bear and from that figures out where he is. If he's near one of them and wants a glimpse, he lifts a handful of duff from the ground and lets it stream lightly down to test the wind before beginning his stalk. When he's radio-tracking from the plane that he rents, he watches his bears hunt frogs, or sees one surprise a wolf and pounce at it. If a bear in a thicket hasn't moved since his previous fix and is close to a road or a house, he may ask the pilot to land, if they can, to see whether it has been shot. Then, on the ground again, suddenly he'll climb an oak tree to taste the acorns on top, spurting up the branchless trunk without any spikes, his hands on one side pulling against his feet on the other. Lost in the yellow fall colors, munching bear food, he shouts happily from the tree, "What a job this is, huh?"

Wildlife biology as a profession interests me. Like the law, my father's vocation, it's one I follow. It's a stepchild among the sciences, however—badly paid, not quite respected, still rather scattered in its thrust and mediocre in its standards, and still accessible to the layman, as the most fundamental, fascinating breakthroughs alternate with confirmation of what has always been common knowledge—akin to that stage of medical research that told us that cigarettes were, yes, "coffin nails," and that frying foods in fat was bad for you. Partly because of its romantic bias, as a science wildlife biology has a tragic twist, since the beasts that have attracted the most attention so far are not the possums and armadillos that are thriving but the same ones whose heads hunters like to post on the wall: gaudy giraffes and gorillas, or mermaid-manatees, or "same-size predators," in the phrase ethologists use to explain why a grizzly bear regards a man thornily. It's not that the researchers have hurried to study the animals which are disappearing in order to glean what they can, but that the passion that activates the research in the first place is the passion which has helped hound these creatures off the face of the earth. Such men are hunters *manqué*.

Game wardens are also that way, but have the fun of stalking, ambushing and capturing poachers, while so often the biologist sees his snow leopards, his orangutans, his wild swans and cranes, vanishing through change of habitat right while his study progresses—wondering whether his findings, like other last findings, invulnerable to correction though they soon will be, are all that accurate. Anthropology can be as sad a science when limited to living evidence and a primitive tribe, but the difference is that woodcraft itself is guttering out as a gift, and apart from the rarity now of observers who can get close to a wilderness animal which has not already been hemmed into a reserve, there is the painful mismatch of skills involved in first actually obtaining the data and then communicating it. Scientific writing need only be telegraphic to reach a professional audience, but again and again one runs into experts who have terrible difficulties in setting down even a small proportion of what they know. Eagerly, yet with chagrin and suspicion of anybody with the power to do the one thing they wish they could do (suspicion of city folk is also a factor), they welcome television and magazine reporters and interrogators like me, sometimes in order to see their own stories told, but sometimes to try to help save the animals dear to them—as if our weak words might really succeed.

But we observers have a piece missing too; maybe we put on our hiking boots looking for it. Like some of the wildlife experts—or like Lady Chatterley's gamekeeper, who was in retreat when he went into the woods—we don't entirely know why we are there. Not that an infatuation with wild beasts and wild places does us any harm or excludes the more conventional passions like religion or love, but if I were to drive by a thicket of palmettos and chicken trees way down South and you told me that a drove of wild razorback hogs lived back in there, I'd want to stop, get out, walk about, and whether or not the place was scenic, I'd carry the memory with me all day. It's said of a wilderness or an animal buff that he "likes animals better than people," but this is seldom true. Like certain pet owners, some do press their beasties to themselves as compresses to stanch a wound, but others are rosy, sturdy individuals. More bothersome to me is the canard that *when I was a man I put away childish things*, and I can be thrown into a tizzy if a friend begins teasing me along these lines. (A sportswriter I know has gone so far as to consult a psychiatrist to find out why a grown man like him is still so consumed by baseball.) Rooting around on riverbanks and mountain slopes, we may be looking for that missing piece, or love, religion and the rest of it—whatever is missing in us—just as we so often are doing in the digging and rooting of sex. Anyway, failure as a subject seems more germane than success at the moment, when failure is piled atop failure nearly everywhere, and the study of wildlife is saturated with failure, both our own and that of the creatures themselves.

Rogers is a man surpassingly suited to what he is doing. Like me—it linked us immediately—he stuttered and suffered from asthma when he was a child, and he's still so thin-skinned that he will talk about suing a TV station because it has edited his comments before airing them. But with these thick-skinned bears—pigs-of-the-woods—he is in his element. Just as it was for me while I stayed with him, each day's busy glimpses and face-offs fulfilled his dream as a boy twenty or twenty-five years ago: to track and sneak close to, capture and fondle a noisy, goofy, gassy, hairy, dirty, monstrous, hot, stout, incontrovertible bear.

For their part, the bears have been *engineered* to survive. Whereas wolves have their fabulous legs to carry them many miles between kills, and a pack organization so resilient that a trapped wolf released with an injured paw will be looked after by the others until it is able to hunt again, a bear's central solution to the riddle of how to endure is to den. Denning does away with the harsh months of the year and concentrates the period when a bear needs to eat a lot in the harvest months when food is at hand. Although its breathing and heart rate slow by one half, and its metabolism subsides so that it loses only about 5 percent of its weight a month (half the rate at which it would shed weight during ordinary sleep), its temperature doesn't fall much while it is in the den. This distinguishes bears from bona-fide hibernators like bats and woodchucks, and means that they can give birth in the security of the den and can defend themselves if attacked. The bear's sense of danger is reduced, so that the carefully surreptitious visits Rogers makes in midwinter go off with a minimum of fuss, but in its easily defended hole it can deal even with a pack of wolves.

Males sleep alone, but a sow has the company of her cubs—generally two or three. They are born around the end of January and den with her again the following winter; then in June, when they are a year and a half old, she permits a brawly big male, often several in sequence, to disrupt the close-knit life that she and the cubs have enjoyed since they were born. He or she drive them off and roam a bit together for a week or two, but by the device of delayed implantation of the ova her new cubs are not born till the middle of winter, which gives her a respite. The cubs are exceedingly little when they do arrive, weighing just over half a pound apiece—half what an infant porcupine weighs. The porcupine possesses quills, open eyes and other faculties to meet the world, whereas a bear cub has a great deal of developing to do in the dark den. Its eyes won't open for forty days, and small as it is, it isn't a drain on its fasting mother when suckling. Like a baby ape, it has a long interlude ahead of intimate association with her, an intimacy that will help make it far more intelligent than most animals.

Bears scrape out a depression for themselves under a pile of logs, a ledge or fallen tree, usually pulling in a layer of dead grass and leaves for insulation (paying a high price in heat and weight loss if they don't—one of the facets of denning that Rogers is studying). Some woodsmen claim that bears will position the entrance to face north in order to postpone the moment in the spring when meltwater chills them and forces them outside before the snow is gone and much food has become available. Emerging in mid-April, the adults look in fine shape; with their winter fur they even appear fat, though they shrivel rapidly during those first weeks as they tramp about trying to find something to eat—as if the fat cells are already empty and simply collapse. In Minnesota they break a path to the nearest aspen stand and climb or ride down the young trees to bite off the catkins at the tips of the limbs. They sniff out rotten logs under the snow and bash them apart, licking up the insects that have been hibernating there. A mother will take her cubs to a tall tree, such as a pine, and install them on the warm mound of earth at its base in a resting spot which she scrapes on the south side, nursing them and sending them scurrying up the trunk whenever she goes off in search of a meal. Then when the horsetails and spring grass sprout, the family begins to thrive.

The coating of fat that bears wear most of the year—and which was the frontiersman's favorite shortening—is of indirect use to them if they are shot, blocking the flow of blood, making them difficult to trail. Their flat feet, too, leave less of a track than the sharp feet of other game. Altogether they are excellently equipped, and if they don't insulate their dens or choose a sensible location for themselves, they'll probably come through the winter all right anyhow; the snow, melting to ice from the heat of their bodies, freezes into an igloo around them, complete with a breathing hole. If the complicated physiology by which they are supposed to fatten at an accelerated rate in the fall doesn't take hold (sometimes a mother gives so much milk that she stays thin), they muddle through even so, just as orphaned cubs do if they must winter alone without any denning instruction. The only dead bear Rogers has ever found in a den was a nineteen-year-old female, which despite this exceptionally advanced age, had given birth to two cubs. They had milk in their stomachs but apparently had been killed during her death throes.

In the past four years* Rogers has visited a hundred and six dens, first observing the bears' autumn rituals and later crawling inside. He has an advantage over his friend Mech simply because bears do den; he can head right for any bear wearing a functioning radio—in 1972 there were twenty-seven of them—and, after tranquilizing it, attach new batteries, which with luck are good till the following winter. He can outfit the yearlings with radios before they leave their mothers, and the habit of denning makes bears of any age easier to trap. His traps consist of two 55-gallon barrels welded together and baited with meat; far from finding the contraptions claustrophobic, the bears crawl comfortably in. Occasionally, when an animal is too bulky for the trap—as happened last summer when Rogers was trying to re-capture a 455-pound bear whose collar had been torn off in a mating-season imbroglio—he sets foot snares at its favorite dump. This involves choreographing where the bear should place its feet by putting tin cans and other junk and branches close about the trap along its path. The snares are an unerring type developed in Washington State, where for some unfathomed reason (they seldom do it elsewhere) bears tear apart young trees to eat the cambium lining the inner bark, and the timber companies have declared war on them.

By comparison, Mech's wolves are will-o'-the-wisps. From an airplane a frustrated Mech may see one of them wearing a collar whose radio went dead years ago. Even Maurice Hornocker, the mountain-lion man, who works in Idaho, has a simpler time of it because his subjects, while they would be just as hard as a wolf to catch with an

---

*I.e., as of 1972. I have not tried to incorporate his more recent findings, partly not to steal any thunder from his own presentation of them. My account here is deliberately anecdotal, incomplete and imprecise, so as to be scientifically useless whenever it does not cover fairly familiar ground.

ordinary steel trap, obligingly leap into a tree in the winter, when snowed into a valley and pursued by hounds, where he shoots them with a tranquilizing dart and, climbing up, lowers them gently on the end of a rope as the drug takes effect. The best that can be said for wolves in this respect is that at least they do howl morning and evening in certain seasons, and are sociable souls, so that to keep tabs on one is to know the activities of five or ten others.

A heat scientist who is collaborating with Rogers in studying the biology of denning hopes to insert a scale underneath a wild bear so that a continuous record can be obtained of the rate at which it loses weight, to be collated with the winter's weather—weight loss being heat loss in this case, since the bear neither eats nor excretes. Another scientist in Minneapolis, a blood chemist, is creating from the unprecedentedly wide sampling of bears' blood that Rogers has sent him a profile of its composition, by season and in relation to sex, age, body temperature, sickness or behavioral peculiarities. In concert, they are studying particularly the breakneck conversion of food to fat during the late summer, and a nutritionist will analyze the many foods the bears eat. Rogers has charted their diet through the year, drawing on the evidence of scats, his walks and sightings from the air and their radioed locations. The scats he sifts in a pan of water. Leaves, wasp heads and carrion hair float to the top; seeds, tin foil and twigs sink to the bottom. He's also investigating the fine points of telling an animal's age by counting the rings in a cross section cut from a tooth. Like the rings in a tree, a dark annulus is deposited in the cementum every winter while the bear sleeps and a light one during the bright part of the year. The live-bear biologists pull out a lower premolar and the dead-bear biologists take a canine, but there are also false annuli to confuse the count.

Wildlife biology used to be rather hit-or-miss. Rogers's predecessors would hogtie a trapped bear once in a while and clap an ether cone on it, then proceed to take weights and measurements. From dead bears they catalogued parasites, and looked for placental scars on the uterus. Sometimes a bear was caught and tagged to see where it would travel before a hunter shot it, or it might be color-marked so that it could be recognized at a distance, and transported and released somewhere else to see whether it "homed." To maintain sovereignty, every state's game department insisted on going over much the same ground with these prankish experiments; more seriously, a study of bear depredations on livestock, if any, would be made, because the stereotype of bears as menacing varmints had to be discredited before the legislature could be persuaded to remove the bounty on them, forbid killing them in their dens and give them the spring and summer protection that animals regarded as game receive. In state after state it would be pointed out that back in 1943 California had declared the grizzly its "state animal," but by then twenty years had already elapsed since the last grizzly had vanished from the state. Arkansas and Louisiana set out to right the violence of the past by importing several hundred Minnesota black bears at a cost of up to six hundred dollars apiece. A few have sneaked into neighboring states to delight the outdoorsmen and give the pig farmers the willies (for it's no legend that bears relish pigs), and so Mississippians have had cause to wonder and whoop at the sight of bear prints in the mud, for the first time since back in the era when Faulkner wrote his masterpiece *The Bear.*

In the late 1950s tranquilizers began to be employed, then radio collars. A woodchuck in Maryland bore the first such device; now even turtles and fish are saddled with transmitting equipment, and there is talk of substituting a microphone for the beep signal in the case of certain outspoken creatures like wolves, to record their life histories vocally. Some experts distrust such tools, suspecting that the hallucinogen in the tranquilizer, the obtrusive handling of the animal while it is immobilized, and having to wear an awkward collar may alter its personality and fate. But Rogers is a believer. In Minnesota he has captured a hundred and eighty-three different bears, some many times—one a day during the peak of the summer. Earlier, in Michigan, he had assisted in catching about a hundred and twenty-five. Flying four hundred hours in 1972, as much as his budget allowed, he totted up more than three thousand fixes on his bears. Of the thirty-seven he had put radios on during the previous winter, he could still monitor eighteen in late September and locate nine others whenever he wished to pay his pilot extra for a longer search. One of the travelers, a three-year-old male he had first tagged in its mother's den, went clear to Wisconsin, nearly a hundred and fifty miles, before it was shot.

To place all this in perspective, the State of New Hampshire, for instance, until recently had only one bear trap, a converted highway culvert that was trundled out three or four times a year. The game wardens got so excited when it was used that two of them would sleep overnight in a station wagon parked close by so as to be there when the door clanged. Before Rogers's program began, the most sophisticated telemetric figures on black-bear territoriality had been drawn from the State of Washington, where seventeen bears had been radio-located four hundred and eighteen times from the ground.*

At Rogers's cottage the phone rings with reports of sightings, friends recognizing his ear tags and collars; everybody keeps an eye out the window in the evening for bears crossing the fields around Isabella. He likes these neighbors and talks endlessly—bears, bears, bears—and his wife Sue loyally wears shirts with big bear tracks painted on them. She's witty, slightly conspiratorial, and a great help to him, pushing him as she might urge on a student of hers who was talented, but disorganized. The data keeps pouring in because he has such a network of methods set up to collect it, and he's out gathering more every day besides. One has the feeling that without her the study might strangle in congestion. He mentions an expert he knew in Michigan who in the course of a decade had collected more information on bears than any other man there, but who, as the years went on, could never write down what he'd learned and get credit for it. Finally, to cushion his disappointment, his chief transferred him to the task of collecting a whole new raft of raw data on deer.

Rogers has received a modicum of funding from the state's Department of Natural Resources, the federal Forest Service, the National Rifle Association and other disparate groups. Mostly, though, it is some Minneapolis magnates who call themselves the Big Game

*The Craighead brothers, however, who began their grizzly studies in Yellowstone Park in 1959, have captured altogether more than five hundred and fifty grizzlies.

Club who have backed him, and particularly a poker-faced depart-
ment-store owner named Wally Dayton, who will drive up, go along
on a tour with the enthusiastic Rogers, see a few bears, and head back
toward the Twin Cities without a hint of his own reactions, except
that shortly thereafter the university will get a contribution ear-
marked for his work. At first, in my time with him, it had seemed
sadly chancy to me that he had been afforded so little official support
for a project I knew to be first-rate. But soon such a sense evaporated;
rather, how lucky it was that this late-blooming man, who creeps
through the brush so consummately that he can eavesdrop on the
grunting of bears as they breed, had discovered at last, after seven
long years as a letter carrier in his hometown, what it was that he
wanted to do! In his blue wool cap, with Santa Claus wrinkles around
his eyes because of the polar weather he's known, shambling, blundering, abstracted at times, he is an affecting figure, a big Viking first
mate proud of the fact that he can heft a 240-pound bear alone. He
kisses his wife as he starts out, one pocket full of his luncheon sandwiches, the other with hay-scented packets of scats he forgot to remove after yesterday's trip (they smell pleasant enough, and he likes
carrying them as boys like carrying snakes).

In grammar school, with his breathing problems, he couldn't rough-
house and was kept indoors—the teacher would give him a chance to
tell the rest of the class what birds he had spotted out the window
while they had been playing. As his asthma improved, he and a friend
named Butch used to jump from tree to tree or swing on long ropes like
Tarzan, until Rogers took a bad fall and was hospitalized. They swam
in the summer, plunging into deep ponds and kicking their way underwater along the turtle runways on the bottom to go after snappers,
whose meat they sold in Grand Rapids for a dollar a pound. They
would never leave off exploring any pond where the fishermen told
them there was an oversized fish until they'd determined whether or
not it was a great six-foot pike. He still laughs remembering the times
when it turned out to be nothing more than a carp.

In adolescence his stutter was the difficulty and he took extended
solitary fishing trips. Boyish, he once went through an entire winter in
Michigan without wearing an overcoat to see whether he could tough

it out, having read of a man who went into the woods stark naked one fall to find out if he could clothe himself with skins and prevail. He was a colorful postman not only because of stunts like this but because hordes of dogs congregated about him on his rounds, following him for hours; in the afternoon sometimes he carried the little ones home in his pouch. He did some judo and boxing in gyms and got into street fisticuffs; he still likes to step into a fight where the odds are three or four against one and knock all the bullies out. Even after he had returned to college and met his wife and started studying bears, Rogers almost lost a finger when some bear feces got into a cut and he refused to go to a doctor at first. Only recently he inflicted what he is afraid may have been a permanent strain on his heart by racing through a swamp after an athletic bear scientist who makes it a point to always keep up with his hounds.

One might speculate that, like Jack on the Beanstalk, he *has* to be boyish to be so indefatigable at sneaking up next to these furry ogres. He speaks proudly of his two plane crashes while out spotting bears; his one mishap when a bear chewed him occurred when he was working in front of a high school class with an underdosed bear that climbed to its feet and staggered off, and he was so embarrassed that he tried to wrestle it down. Like a denizen of the woods, he seems full of anomalies to an outsider. He was a Vietnam hawk and hippie-hater during the war, but was glad not to serve in the army himself when his asthma offered him a chance to stay out. He's a member of Zero Population Growth and is thinking of getting a vasectomy, yet kept asking me what it was like to live in New York; didn't the girls smoke an awful lot and wear too much makeup? Though he is working on his doctoral thesis, only lately has he entered what he calls a transitional stage away from his parents' fundamentalist beliefs. He went to a Baptist parochial school and junior college, and not till he went to Michigan State, after the mail-carrying years, did he encounter a serious argument against the theory of life propounded in Genesis. Taught Darwinism for the first time, he had to learn to stop raising his arm in astonishment in biology class and quoting the Bible. The teacher was nonplussed and would suggest "See me afterwards," but then would avoid the meeting, and the students naturally thought he was funny.

Offended, Lynn also postponed matching up his parents' ideas with the rest of the world's. He was superb at bear-catching, after all, and felt he was working at real biology, not bookish stuff, and because he was keeping his thoughts to himself, when he did argue about evolution it was usually just as a doubting Thomas with a more convinced fundamentalist, not with a scientist who might have had it out with him. He still seems to be waiting for the rejoinders which never came when they should have, to explain things for him.

"Darwin is full of holes too, you know," he said to me in the jeep, looking to see whether I'd answer, but I smiled and shrugged. For years he and his friend Butch, swimming, leaping from tree to tree, had lived with the dream of Tarzan in their minds, but it was just Butch who had been allowed to go to the movies. He would come back after the show and tell Lynn about Tarzan's feats.

On one of our mornings together, a caller notified Lynn that a bunch of grouse hunters had pumped enough birdshot into a bear caught in one of his foot snares to kill it, so he went out to do an autopsy. It was a mother with milk in her udders and two surviving cubs which had run away. She was brownish compared to an Eastern black bear but blacker than many Western bears. Her feet were cut from stepping on broken glass while garbage-picking, and years before her right ear had been torn off. While he worked, the hunters who had shot her showed up, hoping to claim the skin. They were rough, heavyset customers, one a battered-looking Indian, and the witnesses to the killing, who were also grouse hunters and were standing around in hopes that *they* might get the skin, were too scared to speak up until after the culprits had left—which they did just as soon as they heard Rogers talking about getting the law after them. Then when the witnesses, two St. Paul men, after he'd helped tie the gutted bear onto their car, felt safe enough to enlighten him, Rogers could scarcely believe his ears, that people were so chicken-hearted. He hollered at them, threatening to take the bear back, went to a phone and called all the game wardens around.

We drove to several other dumps—perhaps a desolate sight to most people, but not to him. Gazing up at the white gulls and black ravens wheeling above, he imitated how his bears weave their heads, looking up at the birds. He told cheery stories, wretched stories. Somebody in Isabella had gutshot a bear with a .22, and the beast took five months to die, at last going from den to den in the middle of winter, in too much pain to be able to sleep. It died in the open snow, its belly bloated with partly digested blood, having shrunk down to ninety pounds.

That afternoon David Mech's crew from Ely delivered one of his radioed bears, #433, which had been caught in one of their wolf traps. They'd already tranquilized it, and he treated its banged paw; "Poor 433, poor 433." He marked down the latest data on it and drove it back to its home territory. Sometimes he howls to a pack of Mech's wolves for the fun of it until they answer him, and has caught about twenty wolves in bear snares, enjoying his own mystic moments with them. He uses a choker on the end of a stick while he tapes their jaws and wraps a weighing rope around their feet, careful not to let them feel actually in danger of strangling, however, or they go mad. Crouched over them, he achieves an effect similar to that of a dominant wolf; the thrashing animal gives up and lies quietly. Sometimes a possumlike catatonia slips over it and it loses consciousness for a while.

The next day, because one of the newly orphaned cubs had been caught in a snare, he had a chance to tag it in order to keep track of its fortunes. Thanks to the marvelous alimentary system bears have, young orphans tend to stay fat, and they hang together through their first winter, but with no mother to defend a territory for them, many questions remain about how they eventually fit into the pecking order of the area. All summer he had been in radio contact with two cubs a poacher had orphaned in June, when they were not long out of their mother's den. They'd been keeping body and soul together, traveling cross-country in a haphazard fashion, presumably scuttling up a tree if a wolf or another bear materialized, until a Duluth, Missabe and Iron Range Railway train killed them. They had begun by eating their mother; maybe could not have survived otherwise, since they were unweaned. One can imagine them at first simply scratching at her udder in order to reach the milk curdling inside.

In a barrel trap Rogers had caught a three-year-old male, blowing like an elephant because of the resonance of the barrels. Bears really can huff and puff enough to blow the house down. While it chuffed at him through one vent he injected the drugs Sernylan and Sparine into its shoulder through another, then lifted the door and rubbed the bear's head as it went under, boyishly showing me that he could. This was unfortunate because the bear's last waking image was of that dreaded hand. Licking its nose and blinking and nodding while the shot took effect, it kept its head up, straining, sniffing as though it were drowning, or like a torture victim struggling for air. Once Rogers live-trapped seven bears in a single day, and once in the winter he handled five bears in one den—four yearlings and their mama. He says that in his experience all really large bears are males, though a hunter sometimes thinks he has shot a "big sow" because the males' testicles retreat into their bodies after the breeding season.

Later he shot a grouse for his supper, and showed me a few empty dens, of the ninety-four he has located so far. We drove to a bleak little hamlet called Finland to check on bear #320, a sow he had already pinpointed more than two hundred times in his studies of territoriality. She goes there every fall to eat acorns, staying till the snow is thick before hurrying twenty-odd miles back to her home stamping ground to dig her den. "What a job!" he said again, exuberantly showing me balm of Gilead, climbing an oak tree or two, pointing out a dozen different kinds of birds, and halting by the road to jump up on the roof of the jeep and do a sweep with his antenna to see whether another bear was near.

In a typical day for as much as six hours he will jounce along abandoned logging trails, then go up with his pilot for another four hours, the plane standing on one wing most of the time in tight circles over a succession of bears. Cautious pilots cost the project money, but he has found a young man who is paying for his plane with bear-study money and is daring enough. Wearing a head-set, homing in according to the strength of the beeps entering each ear, Rogers directs him by hand signals. Sometimes the beeps sound like radar chirps, sometimes like the *pop-pop-pop* of a fish-tank aerator. On the ground they are still more accurate, to the point where he can distinguish not only a bear's movements across humpy terrain but its restlessness during a thunderstorm, its activity pawing for ants, or digging its den.

These bears produce more cubs than the mothers of Michigan, which ought to signify that they eat better; yet the cubs seem to grow slower. Rogers tabulates the temperatures for each week of the summer, believing that the weather may be as important a factor as the availability of food. At the end of a hot summer with plenty of blueberries, the first-year cubs he was in touch with weighed only an average of thirty-two pounds, but another year, when there were practically no blueberries but the temperature was cooler, another group had managed to fatten to an average of forty-seven pounds. An older bear once expanded from eighty-nine to two hundred and fifty-five pounds in a year, and another gained ninety-five pounds in forty-two days, ending up at three hundred and eighty, and nevertheless crawled into a barrel trap, getting so stuck that Rogers had to stand the barrels on end and lift them off to free the poor fatty.

Despite these gourmand triumphs and the fact that his bears face little hunting, Rogers finds that the average age of the population is only about four and a half—just about the same as biologists calculate for much more severely hunted places like Vermont, where almost a quarter of the bears are shot every fall. Even without the attrition from hunting, the mortality among cubs, and more especially among yearlings and two-year-olds, is high. Nobody has quite figured out what happens to them. G. A. Kemp, a researcher at Cold Lake, Alberta, has theorized that the population is regulated mainly by the adult boars, which kill the subadults if there is a surplus. The Craigheads, working with the grizzlies of Yellowstone, have suggested that dominant bears—grizzlies that occupy themselves principally with being king of the hill around a dump or other gathering point, rather than with eating—seem to lose the will to live when defeat comes, and fade from the scene.

Bears don't mature sexually until they are four, which, combined with the circumstance that the sows only breed every other year, and plenty of eligible sows not even then, gives them one of the lowest reproductive capabilities of any animal. Now that his research has extended through several years, however, bears that Rogers handled as infants, then watched play on their mothers' backs, are themselves giving birth. Occasionally he tracks them for a full twenty-four hours, using student assistants, discovering when they travel and how far and fast. In this wild region, they do most of their sleeping in the dark of the night, from midnight to five.

From his plane in the fall he photographs the terrain in color so as to delineate the zones of vegetation, mapping these to compare with his radio-marked bear ranges for the same area. Keying the bears to the vegetation indicates the feed and habitat they prefer, and also which logging practices of the past have benefited them. Logging, like a forest fire or a tornado, brings in new growth, and even in the primitive section of the national forest, where cutting is not allowed, bears haunt the openings where vetch and pea vine have had an opportunity to sprout and where the windfallen trees are dry from the sun and teem with bugs. On the other hand, clear-cutting does them no good because, like other game animals, they are uncomfortable without hideouts nearby. Sometimes the Forest Service, adding insult to injury, sprays on a herbicide to kill the young aspens and birch—the trees here which are most palatable to wildlife; Rogers is on the watch for any birth defects in his new cubs that may result.

In the spring and early summer the bears' diet is salady—early greens in shady places, and clover, grass, plantains, pea vine and vetch. They dig out grubs, chipmunks and burrowing hornets, clean up wolf kills, eat dandelions, strawberries (the first of the berries), juneberries, bilberries, thimbleberries, chokeberries, chokecherries, rose hips, haw apples, wild plums, hazelnuts and osier dogwood. Raspberries, although abundant, are not eaten in the quantities one might imagine, perhaps because they grow singly on the cane, but bears do feast on blueberries in midsummer, pausing only for a week or two to give closer attention to the berries of the wild sarsaparilla plant. In Michigan and New England they stay above ground into November, munching nuts in the hardwood forests and apples in derelict orchards, but in Rogers' wilderness the last crop eaten is the fruit of the mountain ash—red, berrylike clusters. By October most of the bears have chosen their dens and are puttering around—they excavate less than grizzlies—sleeping more and more, gradually letting their bodies wind down, except for a few savvy males which journey to Lake Superior to visit the dumps at the resorts there, eating until the snow covers their food before making tracks back. The Craigheads, indeed, think that grizzlies may possess an instinct to enter their pre-dug dens during a storm, when the snow will cover their tracks. When a bear stops eating and its intestines are empty, a seal of licked fur, pine needles and congealed digestive juices forms across the anus, putting a period to the year.

Usually they are tucked in their dens before the first harsh cold snap. The cold itself doesn't affect them except to put hair on their chests, but once the food supply is blanketed over, their interests are best served by going to sleep. During the winter their tapeworms starve to death and their cubs have maximum protection, and, for the rest of the year, they generally give every evidence of invulnerability to natural disaster because of the array of foods that suit them. In 1972, for example, when a June frost had ruined both the blueberry and mountain-ash crops, the Isabella bears needed to improvise an unsugary diet of salads right into the fall, then ran out of fodder entirely a month earlier than usual; yet when they denned they wore the same good belting of fat.

Disease, too, like malnutrition, is uncommon among bears; their preference for solitude helps ensure that. One of the mysteries that have intrigued biologists, therefore, is how predators or quasi-predators, especially such redoubtable beasts as bears and wolves, regulate their own numbers. Most prey animals are kept within bounds by being hunted—if not, they pop like popcorn until an epidemic combs through them—but what natural force rides herd on the hunters? Among bears, the burly males unquestionably pluck out and kill a proportion of the wandering young if an area becomes thick with them—as will a sow with cubs of her own kill other cubs—and the device of delayed implantation of the ova probably offers a kind of hormonal "fail-safe," by which some of the bred mothers simply do not wind up pregnant by autumn, if conditions are bad during the summer. The complexities of fertility and sterility operate as a balance wheel for wolves and mountain lions also. Several studies on these other animals are coming to fruition now, and more and more evidence points to sterility in conjunction with territoriality as the answer. To compare the findings is fascinating.

Mountain lions are geared for a life alone, and each inclines so sedulously to solitude that they rarely fight one another. The toms, in particular, according to Maurice Hornocker, don't overlap in their ranges. The females are slightly more tolerant; besides accepting some overlap among neighbors, they make adjustments of range from year to year so that those with big yearling cubs to provide for and train occupy more space than does a mother with newly born kittens. In the snowy country of central Idaho the females each have a winter range of from five to twenty square miles, and a male will encompass the home territories of two or three females, like smaller geometric figures within his own bailiwick, though he steers clear of actual contact with them except to consort briefly to breed. Mountain lions neither cooperate nor directly compete in hunting, and their scent-marking, which seems to be done mostly by the toms and which takes the form of periodically scratching with the hind feet a shovel-shaped scrape in the soil or in needles and leaves under a tree, compares with the punctilious, gossipy sort of urination male wolves indulge in and the regular round of rubbing-trees boar bears maintain. The lion is different, though, in that he doesn't pursue a rival to punish him if he is trespassing. Instead, his territoriality has been likened by Hornocker to a system of "railway signals," which, merely by notifying one cat of the presence of another, effectively "closes" that track to him. Since male mountain lions will sometimes kill kittens they come across, as boar bears kill cubs, it makes ethological sense for the species to insist upon a territoriality that is exclusive—only one dangerous male is regularly in the vicinity. On the other hand, the females, upon whom falls the responsibility of feeding the young, benefit by being willing to allow some overlap in their ranges; they can follow the game as it drifts about.

A newly grown lion setting out in its third summer from its mother's abode rambles along in an easy fashion with, in effect, a safe conduct through the territories of older lions but no desire to settle in and try to rub shoulders with them, until eventually it locates a vacant corner of the world to call its own. This impulse to clear off, which is present in young wolves and young boar bears as well, discourages inbreeding and helps to ensure that a lion lost from the population anywhere is likely to be replaced, that no plausible lion habitat goes undiscovered for long. The reclusive temperament of mountain lions befits their solitary techniques in hunting—based on the ambush, the stalk—and the way that they hunt, in turn, dovetails naturally with the abrupt, broken country they are partial to—terrain not so suited to the convivial, gang-up manner of pursuit which wolves, living usually at a lower, flatter elevation, prefer. But as is true of wolves, lions feel the urge to breed only after they have managed to establish a territory; or to put it the other way around, they do not take up permanent residence, even if they find an empty niche, until they locate scent signs and symbols around indicating that here they will be able to breed.

Despite Mech's discovery that lone wolves, dispensing with territoriality, roam more widely and often eat better than wolves in a pack, those in the prime of life do pair up and live in packs within a territorial discipline if they can. They put up an outright fighting defense once they have plumped upon ground of their own. Perhaps the fact that they fraternize so freely contributes to their readiness to fight; being sociable, they want company, but place a strict limit on how much they want. Hornocker speculates that such gregarious predators can afford the luxury of an occasional test of strength (though their howling and scent posts allay much of the need), whereas a solitary cat cannot. A mountain lion, depending wholly upon itself, must keep fit, and so as an economy measure the race has evolved a gentlefolk's way of spacing its populace about.

Individually too, bears have no other creature to lean on except themselves, but grazing the forest meadows as they do, they can nurse an injury along when necessary, and aggressiveness toward their own kind has a biological function for them. The bullying of the weak by the strong first puts good virile genes in the cubs, then weeds out the dullards among the yearlings and two-year-olds. The ladder of dominance in a wolf pack is a matter of still greater importance, because in the relatively level country wolves frequent, where game is easier to find than in a lion's convoluted topography and where there is more of it to go around, they must have no last-minute doubts as to who is boss; they must all streak after the same beast, swarm upon it, dodge its front hooves and bring it down. The bickering and the spurting of pee on each other's piss that they like to do is not just boundary-marking, but reaffirms which one—to judge by that tangy thermostat deep inside the body (and even a dog can distinguish one unit of urine in sixty million parts of water)—will lead the charge.

Wolves and bears are fastidious in their sexual clocking, breeding only so that the bear cubs will be delivered during the denning period and the wolf puppies into the lap of the spring. If a female lion loses her kittens, however, she may come into estrus again almost immediately. She has the onerous task of killing food for the litter, as sow bears do not and a bitch wolf need not, and is more likely to lose some of them, and so is equipped for another try. But like the bear, once her young are developing, she does not breed again for two years because no pack structure surrounds them to nurture them in the meantime. (The bitch wolf can go right at it the next February.)

Both bear and wolf scientists remark on how many of the females they study are barren in years when, to judge by the calendar, they ought to give birth. When an animal requires several square miles to stretch its legs and its psyche and to forage for food, inhibition assumes an importance. The creature must not simply be physiologically ready for offspring; it must have a great spread of land at its disposal, a competence, a self-confidence, and a wolf pack is wonderfully elastic in regulating this sort of thing. The strongest youngsters, with the wherewithal of nerve, fan out at the age of two to colonize new territory, but the old pack—parents, pups of the spring and yearlings of the year before, and sometimes older shrinking violets who haven't yet made the transition to independence, or an adopted senior widowed wolf—continues to hold the fort.

If the hunting is good in winter it's very good, with deer floundering in deep bogs of snow, but if it's bad, there are no summer beaver moseying about to be ripped up and no baby animals for hors d'oeuvres. When faced with starvation, a pack will evaporate rapidly from eight or ten or twelve to the single primary pair, as the others, barred from eating the sparse kills, head away in desperation to try their luck elsewhere. Then, from the odds and ends of packs that have disintegrated, a new apportioning of the countryside occurs. Sometimes a big pack will coalesce for a season if two former littermates, each leader of a family on ranges that adjoin, meet affectionately again, maybe after weeks of howling to each other, and throw in their lot together. In a pack, although several females may be nubile, only one of them conceives, as a rule. The lid is on unless the dominant animals are put out of commission, whereupon all sorts of pairings become possible.

Like other recent studies (Jonkel and Cowan's in Montana, for instance), Lynn Rogers' investigations suggest an almost equally ingenious instinctual realpolitik for bears. No pack exists—though grizzlies occasionally are prone to live in a loose sort of pack arrangement—but the boar black bears of Minnesota each roam over a chunk of geography averaging more than sixty square miles during the June–July breeding season. This is about the same freehold that a small wolf pack would use, but since the bear does not need even remotely as much land for food, he merely bestirs himself to be certain that no other male is around where he is at the same time. Males overlap, in other words, and Rogers thinks that two miles is about the buffer they insist upon, scratching, rubbing against so-called bear trees for the purpose of warning lesser males to beware. In his experience, sows seldom make use of these signposts, but do, by contrast, appear to enforce a severe territoriality upon each other, driving other sows, including large ones, beyond distinct boundaries that they lay out. Although Rogers hasn't figured out the method of marking that they employ, because the area involved is usually less than ten square miles,* it is easier for them to exclude a trespasser than it would be for a boar to try to do the same. The boar is excellently situated, since six or eight or more sows live within his stamping grounds. Though each will be receptive to him for only a few weeks every couple of years, he doesn't have to depend on the mood and good health of any one of them in order to breed. They don't wait upon his welfare either, because each lives within the roaming range of several boars— the smaller specimens giving way before the fearsome bruisers, but skulking back. Boar bears are more likely to come to grief than sows because of their wandering disposition, yet whenever one is killed,

---

*A. M. Pearson of the Canadian Wildlife Service gives a grizzly density of one bear per 10 square miles in a study area in the Yukon Territory, with the average sow's range being 27 square miles and the average boar's range 114 square miles, figures influenced by the local food supply as well as by the nature of the beasts involved.

others are on the scene—the whole uncanny setup being just the reverse of how mountain lions live.

June is an ideal month for bears to breed. They have had about three months to flesh out and recover their aplomb after the winter's sleep and plenty of opportunity remains for serious fattening before they slip below ground again. Wolves court and breed in the most grueling month instead—February, just when they should need to save their energy—but their love life goes on year-round and culminates extravagantly on the midwinter hunt. It's a time when all prudent bears are hoarding up their fat and their newborn young under the ice and snow; the cubs grow from half a pound to five pounds before they even see the sun.

Bears hoard, wolves spend. Under the circumstances it's no wonder that scarcely half of the bitch wolves conceive, that though a wolf gives birth to at least twice as many pups as the sow does cubs, half of them probably won't survive for a year. Even the five or ten square miles the sow defends against other females would be more land than she needs for herself, if she weren't also defending nourishment for her cubs and for those of previous years. The winter of their first birthday, they den with her, then in the following summer are driven off as she keeps company with her paramours, but they are not driven outside her territory; they are still welcome there. They split up and den separately from her that fall, weighing maybe eighty pounds. In their third summer the mother appears with a new brace of cubs, and now they must keep severely clear of her. The males, not yet sexually capable, are full of urges and strike off on free-lance jaunts, as wolves and mountain lions of the same age do, each trying to light upon an empty space among the crazy quilt of bear bailiwicks that intersect throughout the forest. One young bear may travel thirty miles and set up shop, only to have a close shave with a resident bear, after which he will dash straight back to his mother's domain to recuperate for a little while before sallying forth on a different tack. Because he's slower to mature than a wolf or mountain lion, when he does find a neighborhood that suits him he has a couple of years to explore the district before committing himself. By scent he makes the acquaintance of the various sows he will pursue and the boars he must rival, eventually reaching at sexual maturity a weight of perhaps two hundred and seventy-five pounds when fat in the fall or a hundred and seventy-five pounds in the hungry spring.

Young males are the pioneers when bears resettle an area such as grown-over farmland. But they must cool their heels until a food shortage or some more arcane pressure pushes the sows toward them. Their sister cubs tend to linger in the mother's realm, living in isolation but protected from molestation by other sows because of the territorial right which they retain. One obvious effect of this procedure is that whenever a new sow does breed, her partner will probably have originated in another region, but as long as her mother remains sexually active, it appears that she will not do so. She lives there in reserve—in limbo, as it were, like an unhatched egg—in a section of her mother's territory as small as a single square mile, against the day when the elder sow meets with a disaster, whereupon the range will pass to her. Then her turf may shrink a bit, as the sows on the borders challenge her boundaries, but sooner or later she blossoms to the task of defending it.

When Rogers was starting his study, he almost ran out of funds in August when the bears he was tracking left their haunts after the agitations of the mating season, and went for trips he hadn't expected—vacations, the impulse might be called. The males sometimes travel substantial distances and mingle festively without much quarreling, and he was paying his pilot to chase them. The sows don't wander so far, but may go ten or twenty miles, as if to eat new plums and cherries, or merely ramble into an unfamiliar loop of land adjacent to their regular duchy, which for the time being they stop patrolling. This custom is another means by which bears discover gaps left by mishaps and exploit them so as to keep the countryside producing bears at full capacity. It is also a kind of relaxation which wolves could not afford because the territoriality of a wolf pack is based on the exigencies of hunting.

These are exciting discoveries, and of the several authorities engaged in zeroing in on the details, I didn't doubt that Rogers was the best. I liked his rushing way of driving and hiking and his enormous hunger for data. I liked his enthusiasm for the unfashionable black bear (there are many more scientists studying the wolf), and as we toured, enjoyed being in the shadow of a man larger and more vivid than myself—though with his bigness, as with the bigness of big women, went an affecting vulnerability. His ums and ahs annoyed me, yet I was saying um and ah myself by now. We kept remarking how we had each spent hours after school alone, daydreaming of seeing wild animals in the woods and searching out their hideouts and handling them—not imagining that such good fortune might ever really be ours. Here we were, he said, in woods that many people drive a thousand miles to camp in, people who felt that if they could happen upon a bear it might make their whole summer excursion—and we could see one at any time.

Rogers has actually put radios on seventy-two over the years, and when he's trying to enlist somebody's support or testing a student who wants to help him, he generally goes to a den. The kids (or I, or Wally Dayton) crouch down on their hands and knees, peering into the troll-like crevice where mushrooms grow. Whether or not the smell of the bear actually persists inside, it *seems* to, and one is reminded of humble caves that a boy might run away to, and of digging to China, and of bottomless cracks in the earth. In the fall, after the bear has gone to sleep in its new hole, Rogers will tie a thread across the mouth so that on his next visit he will know whether it has woken up and scrambled outside for an interlude.

Whenever he gets near a bear in the flesh, as in mixing with them in their dens, he comes into his own—decisive, direct. Where other biologists explode the tranquilizer into an animal with a dart gun, leaving a wound, perhaps knocking the bear out of a tree so that it is killed, he does almost all his injecting by hand. The sows stand chuffing at him, slamming their paws on the ground to scare him, but he runs at them, stamping *his* feet, and stampedes both sow and cubs into separate trees. Then he climbs up and sticks the needle into their round rear ends, before lowering them one by one on a rope as the drug takes effect. Approaching a bear denned under the snow, he slips off his parka so it won't squeak as he crawls. Wriggling forward underground, he carries a flashlight in one hand and the syringe in the other, fastened to the end of a stick. If the bear is awake and panics and begins to come out, he rolls quietly to one side of the entrance and hunches there, poking it with the drug as it lumbers past; it can't get far. Sometimes bears make a blowing sound, like a man loudly cooling soup, which he listens to, not taking the warning to heart unless it is accompanied by a lifted upper lip—this being a true giveaway of belligerence. "It's like driving in town. You've got a traffic light to tell you when to stop." Usually, though, the bears stay becalmed, resting in their nests, merely sniffing the syringe when it is presented to them, making no more objection to the prick than they would to an insect's bite. He takes his time; the air inside the den is dead and hardly carries his scent.

Weather causes worse problems. Some days Rogers has to break trail on snowshoes for his snowmobile for miles, and must put the needles and vials of drugs in his mouth to warm them; the tubes of blood that he collects go in his shirt. For his blood-tapping and temperature-taking he must haul the bear outside, and if there are cubs he deals with them, squeezing into the furthest recesses, but finding them unresisting once the mother has been subdued. Newborns have blue eyes and pink noses, and the smell left by his hands does not make the mother abandon them. He listens to their hearts, measures the length of their fur and wraps them in his parka until he is finished examining the mother. Even knocked out, the bears are all right in the cold, although in the summer they sometimes need to be bathed in cool water after panting in a metal trap; he washes off the matted mud if they've been struggling in a snare. After he's through, he replaces the family just as it was—wriggling inside the den, dragging the cubs and mother in after him, adjusting her posture and limbs so that she'll wake up feeling natural.

On September 22 we spent a red-letter day together, starting at a dump where gulls and ravens whirled above us and Rogers scanned the line of trees for any fat rear end that might be beating a retreat. He flew for long hours, locating all the bears whose radios were functioning; then back on the ground, as a check on his methods he went to three of the fixes to confirm that the bears were where he'd marked them. He inspected seven denning places, showing me how he discovers the hole itself by the raking that bears do as they collect insulation. This is while the ground is clear of snow, so he memorizes how to find it later on by lining up the nearby trees. Number 414's chamber last winter was under a clump of boulders, fifteen feet back through a passage. Number 320's was under a bulldozed pile of birch that the loggers had left. A few miles away we watched a female preparing a small basket-shaped sanctum under the upturned roots of a white pine, from which she sneaked, like a hurrying, portly child, circling downwind to identify us before clearing out. Another bear, a hundred-pound male, was hollowing a den under a crosshatch of windfalls just above a patch of swamp. He too scrambled silently away downwind ahead of us like a gentleman disturbed in a spot where he's afraid perhaps he shouldn't be.

In a pea-vine clearing Rogers photographed three bears eating and obtained some scats. He tasted bear delicacies as he walked, spitting out prickly or bitter leaves. In one of his traps was a young male, chopping its teeth, clicking its tongue, with a strong ursine smell of urine. Rogers answered with the same sounds, and when he let the bear loose it bounded toward the woods like the beast of a children's fairy tale—a big rolling derrière, a big tongue for eating, and pounding feet, its body bending like a boomerang.

We ate rock tripe off the rocks, saw moose tracks, wolf scats, two red-tailed hawks, three deer and a painted turtle. The dogwood was turning purple now, the aspens golden, the plum bushes red, the pin cherries brown, and the birches and hazel and thimbleberries yellow. There was pearly everlasting, and blue large-leafed aster still blooming in the woods, and sweet fern that we crushed in our hands to smell. Alders had grown up higher than the jeep on some of the roads we followed. "Doesn't have too much traffic," said Rogers.

There is sometimes a sadness to David Mech's work, when he knows in advance from the blood tests he does which of his wolf pups is going to die. But Rogers's cubs are hardier, the winter hold no terrors for them, and when they do disappear it is not due to the sort of anemia which an investigator can foresee. I thought very highly of him—this admirable animal-catcher, this student of wild foods and smells, this scholar of garbage dumps. Because his bears like dumps, so does he.

(1973)

Lament the Red Wolf

1

Gas rationing is in order, the Environmental Protection Agency suggests. What will young people do? Ordinarily a fuel shortage accompanies a war, when they have various surrogates. It's not really that driving equals living dangerously, however. People drive more dangerously in the Alpes-Maritimes than in America, and in Italy a car itself perhaps can represent more precisely a man's own personality—at least, to hear the honking, it seems so. When I was living in a village in Sicily, the padrone of the lemon groves lying all around would wake up the populace after midnight with the peremptory note of his Ferrari's horn as he sped home. He was signaling to have his front gate opened, and to hasten the job, began a tattoo of toots right as he entered town. But distances, not speed, characterize American driving: trailers, campers and the like. Or a retired couple, as their first project, will set out to tour from coast to coast, reserving a motel room each morning four hundred miles ahead. Youngsters, above all, start off, having the breadth and complexity of the continent to familiarize themselves with.

Geography has glamour in America. The whole excitement of driving here implies some opposite new place to reach, and other nationalities like us for this. The English, arriving in Boston, promptly want to head for Arizona to meet the Navajos. Thomas Wolfe celebrated the cross-country railroad, the auto's smoky, rumbling precursor; and how Walt Whitman would have loved to drive, finally to run plunk up against the shining Pacific. Although there used to seem to be no need to go beyond the sea—whichever sea—because almost everybody's ancestors had crossed over from the other side, those two grand bulky oceans, separated by such a spread of miles, did much to mute for us the sadness of the end of the frontier.

What is ominous is that we know that once they have been instituted, alterations and restrictions in the scope of life are never quite relaxed. Actual rationing may not come to pass, but in the meantime the spontaneity of travel has become a privilege, not a right; a freedom that was traditional has been pinched off. It would be easier to assent to the call for a return to the simple life—long walks, and so on—if we hadn't already made so many localities uninhabitable, on the theory that everybody who lived in them could pop onto the freeway and drive someplace else for a day off. Nixon, jumping into his jet or speeding along the thruways near San Clemente to let off steam, was only a souped-up version of the rest of us.

I have driven clear from east to west and west to east half a dozen times, and yet this closing of the open road strikes me as an immediate personal loss. When my native iconoclasm builds up in me until I want to knock people's hats off, I pile into my car and drive away with the window open, and soon find myself singing "God is good, God is great!" at the top of my lungs into the roaring wind, looking out at the tire recaps along the highway in Pennsylvania—then, two days later, at alligators, which are the spitting image of tire recaps, in the watery Louisiana woods.

This trip I was wolfing, though. I had a hand-cranked siren in the trunk that wolves will answer to, and a wolfish, lunging husky along,whose beastly nostrils at my ear and boisterous snuffles from the back seat kept the car from becoming completely a car. I'd been to Minnesota to see how the black bears manage, because there is some hope for them, and now I wanted to have a look at an officially endangered species, and while I was at it, perhaps at the animal which in America is the worst off, Texas's red wolf. Even with the crush in the world, some creatures do thrive—the scavengers and compleat omnivores like possums and coons, and beasts that move into a disrupted habitat by preference, like cottontails and ground squirrels. Others, more conspicuous—the arrowy, showy predators and hearty herd creatures like buffaloes and prairie dogs—or animals that are too single-minded or delicately attuned, haven't much chance. One's interest swings back and forth between the two groups.

Conservationists assume that a day will come when we will all want to pick up the pieces—that if only they can hold onto such living entities as the green turtle and the right whale for a little while longer, the consensus of civilized opinion will swing behind them. It is a questionable assumption, and so the gloomier, more visceral individuals go instead on the hunch that something may happen whereby finally the saved animals will inherit the earth. This isn't sensible, is misanthropic, and is a view they keep to themselves, but the most vivid observation to be made about animal enthusiasts—both the professionals who work in the field and, in particular, the amateurs—is that they are split between the rosiest, well-adjusted sort of souls and the wounded and lame. (More professionals are rosy, more amateurs are lame.) Animals used to provide a lowlife way to kill and get away with it, as they do still, but, more intriguingly, for some people they are an aperture through which wounds drain. The scapegoat of olden times, driven off for the bystanders' sins, has become a tender thing, a running injury. There, running away—save it, save it—is me: hurt it and you are hurting me.

Wolves are well suited to cupping any wounds that we wish drained. Big and concise enough to command the notice of any dullard, they are aggressive, as the wounded themselves wish to be aggressive. Once passionately persecuted, in just the kind of turnabout which people relish, a wolf can now be taken to represent the very Eden we miss, and being a wolf is thought to be the best at what it does in a world which demands that any creature to receive attention must be the "best." Although in fact red wolves are inferior to other wolves at wolfish deeds, their name "red" adds a cachet, concealing their ineptitude from everybody except their friends.

Luckily for me, the scientist working with these little wolves, Glynn Riley, was not under contract to *The National Geographic*, or otherwise operating under the notion that he should hoard his findings. On the other hand, he wasn't a certified scientist either, but a trapper who simply had interested himself and learned more than the degree-bearing scientists had been able to. This meant, in the first place, that he was suspicious of any writer from the big city because of the campaign of the urban humane societies against the leg-hold steel trap—a threat to his livelihood, as he conceived it, which loomed importantly to him, if not to me. Also he felt none of the curiosity in chatting with me that the full-fledged *National Geographic* biologists are likely to reveal, even as they hold back the yarns and lore they plan to jot down for their own profit at some future date. One can wheedle considerable information from them sideways, so to speak, and it is not as lonely with the *National Geographic* biologists because the rapport goes both ways, whereas after a week or two with a trapper, one begins wishing that maybe he'll ask a question about New York City.

Instead of growing less susceptible to the debilitations of solitude, as I get older I am more so. It's a peculiar life: Tuesday, hurrying along Sixth Avenue in New York, Wednesday, after a flight, exploring Dog Canyon in the Big Bend country near the Rio Grande, startling the vultures off a lion-killed deer in a dry stream bed overhung with black persimmon trees. To drive the distances involved helps cushion the switch, but then one runs out of gumption that much sooner at the site one has come so far to inspect. More than once I've had to dash away from scenery that was unimaginably lovely because I knew my time was up, that if I lingered, my mind, like Cinderella's, would soon be crawling with transmogrified mice. I've had crying jags and such, once in the room which serves as office for water pollution control for the Louisiana Department of Wildlife and Fisheries, headquartered in Baton Rouge. It was an appropriately empty, watery spot for crying, and funny because to actually deal with water pollution in Louisiana would require an office suite the size of the Pentagon. I'd spent a clutch of weeks with four French-speaking fur trappers in the Cajun salt marshes that front the Gulf in the southwestern part of the state, and now after my contact man here in officialdom got through arguing his budget request for the ensuing year, we were to set off on a night trip by skiff so that I could stay awhile with several fresh-water trappers in the cypress-tupelo gum tree swamps between the Mississippi River and Lake Maurepas. I couldn't stem the tears.

Air travel and the telephone, too, make for hysteria. A few spins of the dial and we can talk to almost anybody in the world, and in towns like Hackberry or Buras, Louisiana, or Alpine, Texas, at the first strong pinch of loneliness I've known that I could jump into my Hertz Ford and hop a plane for home. The trouble is, at home I've often wanted to catch a plane for Alpine—to be back in Dog Canyon again listening to the javelinas yap and fuss; then, uneasy there, might want to streak for Philadelphia. A friend of mine does let this panic take possession of him. His acquaintances in Hawaii, Los Angeles and London hear from him, the times being rough and events going badly. Since he is an endearing chap, they say yes, he can come, and await his next move. He's reassured by all the invitations and calls or writes his other friends to tell them he is going to Hawaii, London, Los Angeles, or Mexico City. He calls the airport for fare and timetable information, but in the end, more frequently than not, re-laxed at last by the show of affection, he goes nowhere at all.

In Minnesota, Lynn Rogers, the bear expert, had been rather guarded with me, as though he were feeling vulnerable himself and did not welcome the possibility that somebody else might get a handle on him which properly ought to be his. By contrast, Glynn Riley had no suspicions of me as a lay psychologist, didn't care what I thought of him and wasn't concerned with the riddles of motivation. Instead, he was alert to the good name of his profession, and while he told me freely about his boyhood, his screw-ups in school, and courting Pat, his wound-up, stringbean wife—she has a certain flash and dazzle to her eyes and hair, and used to fold herself into the trunk of his car to get into the drive-in movies when they were kids—with the equanimity of a man at peace with himself, he would do this only on his own front porch. Never would he let me bounce about the country with him on his regular rounds, as Rogers had, checking traps and palavering with the ranchers, lest I see a trapped creature and write of its struggles. I couldn't convince him that an exposé of trapping was very low on my list of priorities; I'd seen plenty of trapping and knew that if the fellow wasn't one of a kind, like Riley, he was probably by now a grandfather who wouldn't be around by the time the controversy resolved itself. Similarly, the trapper employed by the wolf scientists in Minnesota, an old-timer who catches the wolves that they can't, won't let anybody else watch how he works. If he is in his pickup with one of the Ph.D. candidates, he will drive past a likely trap-site, giving no sign that he has noticed it, and stop a hundred yards beyond, leaving the young man in the truck and walking back to set the device with his back turned, lest at this late date these doctoral scholars, discovering his secrets, might desert their latter-day vocation for the sake of becoming a master trapper and compete with him.

In spite of being thin-skinned, Rogers had liked lecturing on bears and appearing on television and in the papers, but Glynn Riley had let me drive down to see him solely in the hope that I might pry loose from the Bureau of Sport Fisheries and Wildlife in Washington his appropriated funding, and more too, so that he could put radios on the wolves and hire a spotting plane and someone to help him. As I had seen, they were being as slow as a taffy-pull up there, but he was also sick of blathering to newspapermen—sick of their errors, ignorance, perfunctoriness, misemphasis—and though I explained that letters might accomplish what he wanted,* that I had hopes of doing more with the wolves than merely publicize them, he remained correct with me, not to be cozened.

The dog-wolf family is thought to have originated in North America, migrated to Eurasia, where the gray wolf defined itself as a prodigy of the Northern Hemisphere, and then returned. Some biologists think that red wolves may be descended from a primitive wolf that stayed in North America during this diaspora and were hounded into the southeast lip of the continent by the returning grays. Others speculate that they are an offshoot of a worldwide race of primitive wolves of the early Pleistocene which have disappeared elsewhere; or, on the contrary, that they are a product of the devious ice-age ge-

---

*Sure enough, writing to Washington, I did elicit the funding he had wanted, but along with the funding came a supervisory bureaucracy, which pleased him less.

ography blocked out by the glaciers which did so much differentiat-
ing among animal species. Another theory is that the red wolf
sprouted from a common ancestor with the coyote in the Pliocene,
and is not directly from the gray wolf's line. Coyotes, like Old World
jackals, are "brush wolves" that became miniaturized for pursuing
smaller prey in broken country where a hefty predator might not operate as well. They can put up with hotter temperatures—ranging
into Central America—but not with the deep snows and freezes that
arctic gray wolves know.

Red wolves are short-coated and long-eared, with stilty, spindly
legs for coursing through the southern marshes or under tall forests.
They have the neck ruff, almond eyes and wide nose pad of other
wolves, but not the massive head and chest, and so their angular ears
and legs seem to stick out plaintively. Anatomically their brains are
primitive, almost foxlike among the canids, and they have impressed
naturalists as being as rather rudimentary animals, fragile in their social linkups, not very clever, unenterprising and almost easy to trap.
Besides the pacing gait that they share with larger wolves and a flat
dash, they bound along like modest rocking horses, standing up on
their hind legs to peer over a patch of tall weeds. They are an unem-
phatic, intermediate sort of animal, behaviorally like wolves, ecologi-
cally more like coyotes. They howl like wolves, not like coyotes, and
snarl when threatened instead of silently gaping the mouth, as coyotes do. They scout in little packs, unlike coyotes, which have
stripped away a good deal of the pack instinct for better secrecy in
crowded country and better efficiency at gleaning small game. A
grown male weighs about sixty pounds, midway between a coyote's
thirty or forty and a gray wolf's average of eighty pounds; but skinny
as he is, the red wolf can live on a coyote's diet of cotton rats and
marsh rabbits, and whereas a gray wolf needs about ten temperate
square miles to feed himself—coyotes can get along as densely distributed as one every square mile—the red wolf again is in between.
Five square miles supplies his food, and ten to forty is enough to
stretch his legs and psyche with other members of the pack, about
half what a pack of Minnesota timber wolves requires.

The earliest observers—William Bartram in 1791, and Audubon
and Bachman in 1851—were definite on the subject of a smallish,

darkish, long-legged wolf inhabiting the region from Florida to what is now central Texas, and north to the Ohio River. It was primarily a forest beast, piney in its affinities. The first government biologists of this century, men like Vernon Bailey and Edward Goldman, backed up the idea of a specifically southern wolf still more strongly, although the animals on the eastern seaboard had been exterminated already, and were gone everywhere east of the Mississippi by the 1920s. They did range the Ozarks and the river bottoms of Louisiana and the East Texas prairies, but because some of these latter had started hybridizing with an invading legion of coyotes, a body of opinion claimed that red wolves might never have existed at all except as hybrids of a coyote-gray wolf cross, or maybe as local grays, colored to suit the climate, in much the way that "white" wolves developed in the north. Since gray wolves possess such a fastidious sense of self that a cross of the sort would be a rarity, the rival proposition was offered that though red wolves might have existed as a true species at some point, they'd crossed themselves into extinction even before white men arrived.

Wolves are special beasts, so variable genetically that they partly live on disguised as dogs. Dogs, too, dance attendance on a breadwinner, cheerfully accepting the ups and downs of life with a master just as wolves stick with the pack, and bark and rush at an intruder close to the "den," otherwise marking their passage through life semantically with squirts of pee. If dogs were to inherit the earth they would quickly turn into wolves again; and coyotes carry the flag for wolves most directly, becoming bushy-necked and wolfish in appropriately remote surroundings, or little more than wild dogs when they live close to a city. Indeed, gray wolves would need only a nod from the voters to get a foothold in corners of their old range—Maine, for instance. Brought in, they would soon be at home, parceling up the timberland wherever the human populace is thin, until the deer found themselves in a density of two or three hundred per wolf.

But red wolves are so far gone by now—none has been photographed in the wild since 1934, and they are considered present in pure form in only two of Texas's two hundred and fifty-four counties—that the main effort to protect them involves not only shielding them from human intervention but from encroachment and dilution by coyotes. This situation is unusual. The rarest breeds of ferret, parrot, and so on, even manatees and prairie chickens, depleted in numbers though they are, seldom require protection from other animals, and it is this peculiar rattle-headedness—that these last wolves will so amenably let a coyote mount them—which has called into question their right to be regarded as a species. Mostly the museum scientists, such as Barbara Lawrence of Harvard, rather than the outdoor workers, have been occupied with challenging them, but recently a formidable young taxonomist at the University of Kansas, Ronald Nowak, with a friend named John Paradiso from the National Museum in Washington, has computerized a much larger body of evidence than Lawrence's and has taken up the cudgels for them. The current majority view is to return to the belief that *Canis rufus* (called *Canis niger* for a while, but scientific names sometimes change more frivolously than common ones) is indeed a discrete creature, only lately decimated.

Nearer the East Coast, there were no other predators to replace the wolves when they had been killed off, but west of the Mississippi, coyotes from the plains slid in as soon as the shattered packs stopped defending an area. Coyotes could withstand the poisoning and trapping campaigns better, and the hard logging that the settlers did among the old-growth trees actually benefited them by breaking down the forest canopy. According to the evidence of skulls in the National Museum, the red wolves of Missouri, northern Arkansas and eastern Oklahoma met their end in good order as a species, not mating with the coyotes as they were superseded. (It is a textbook theory that a true species is supposed to preserve its racial purity even more stubbornly in a border area under pressure.) But around the turn of the century, on the Edwards Plateau of central Texas where the same blitzkrieg of white settlers from the East was followed by an invasion of coyotes from every other direction, the demoralized red wolves for some reason began to accept coyotes as their sexual partners, and in the delirium of catastrophe created with them a "Hybrid Swarm." This "Swarm" thereupon moved eastward slowly, as ordinary coyotes were doing anyway at every latitude clear into Canada—and naturally was irresistible. Bigger, "redder" than coyotes, with such a piquancy of wolf blood already, these hybrids absorbed the wolves of Texas's Hill Country and Big Thicket all the more readily. They bred with true wolves and true coyotes and wild-running domestic dogs (even a few escaped pet dingos)—anything they met and couldn't kill—becoming ever more adaptable, a shoal of skilled survivors in a kind of canine Injun-territory situation.

The beaver trappers in the West had hiked out of the mountains and switched to hunting buffalo when the beaver were gone. The buffalo hunters were soon wolfers as well, and bounty-hunted them for a living after they had run through the buffalo. They sold the skins and paved the mudholes in their roads with heaped wolf bones, so many thousands were killed. Throughout the 1800s strychnine was the poison used. Then a drastic potion, sodium fluoroacetate, known as "1080," was introduced, and by the 1940s, a device called the "getter gun," which when implanted in the ground fires cyanide gas into the animal's open mouth when it pulls on a trigger knob baited with scent. From 1915 on, most of the wolfers were employed by the U.S. Biological Survey, which under the umbrella of the Interior Department eventually metamorphosed into the Bureau of Sport Fisheries and Wildlife. Thus by a piece of bureaucratic irony the same corps responsible for reducing the Midwestern red wolf to its final extremity is now the agency in charge of trying to preserve it. Even some of the personnel have been the same, which gives credence to the frequent complaints of calculated foot-dragging that conservationists have made.

To a taxonomist who looks at skulls of the period the record now seems plain as to how succinctly coyotes supplanted wolves in the hardwoods bottomlands along the Mississippi and in the Ozark Mountains. But the salaried wolfers naturally preferred to continue to see themselves, like the old-timers, as dealing with wolves, and so they kept on totting up an annual kill of thousands of "red wolves" in the official tabulation. As late as 1963, 2,771 were reported to have been done away with in the federal program of control. The year before, however, an obscure dissenter, Dr. Howard McCarley of Austin College, Texas, had published his contention that many of these were either coyotes or hybrids, and that the red wolf was nearly gone. Once his discovery was confirmed, the received opinion among biologists, who had taken so cavalier a view of *Canis rufus* until then, reversed abruptly to the notion that the creature may well have existed, but no longer. Since there was nothing to be done about it, the poisoning was allowed to continue even in the Texas coastal counties where in fact a few survived, till 1966. Fortunately two Ontario scientists, taking the matter more seriously than most of the Americans, journeyed about one summer in the meantime playing recorded wolf howls in wild places and listening to the answers that they got—sundry barking mutts, coyotes and coydogs. They were privately financed and soon ran out of funds, but they did learn that while McCarley had been right about the broad belt of territory he had studied, down on the muggy coast between the Vermilion River in western Louisiana and the Brazos in Texas a tiny remnant of voices was answering their Canadian wolves in kind. What with the lengthy delay in publishing these findings in a recondite journal (like McCarley's, earlier), and of bringing them to the attention of the federal specialists, not until 1968 was an organized recovery effort initiated, and not until 1973 was enough money provided to really begin. The scientific method depends upon a scoffing skepticism on the part of rival investigators to puncture a weak argument, but one reason why the biologists did not do more for the red wolf is that so many of them dillydallied while they scoffed.

Part of the appeal of Southeast Texas is that some of its residents tend to deprecate the charms of the place. They'll say that the landscape is mosquito-bitten and unlovely, the colors washed out, that a tourist who wants scenery ought to move on. For a hundred years an army of Texans have believed themselves to be a Chosen People on the grounds of their good fortune—rather like the Victorian British, and in contradistinction to the Jews, for example, who historically have interpreted *mis*fortune to be the insignia of blessedness. Many people have believed that they were Chosen, but none more badly than the Texans. Standing one evening in the Chisos Basin, an old Apache stronghold which is probably the pearl of the western section of the state, I must have looked affected by the colors because I heard a Dallas fellow drawl behind me, "Well, you think you'll buy it?"

Minnesota had seemed fairly familiar—bleaker and flatter than northern New England, wilder than around my home in Vermont, but not more so than northern Maine, which has a moose herd three times the size of Minnesota's and a wilderness region three times as large. Lakes were interspersed through a balsam fir and white pine forest, and the natives had that clamped-down modesty cold weather brings, because you can't cultivate too grandiose an opinion of yourself when a three-foot snowfall at any time for half the year may shut you in. In Isabella, Minnesota, there was an individual called The Pig Farmer because of his supposed smell, who when the spring floods came would slosh around in two feet of water in his swamp cabin, eat cold food, and sleep in a wet bed instead of bothering to move to higher ground. Maybe nobody else can be as glum as a Great Lakes Finlander, but near my house in Vermont is a barn with a whole cavern smashed in it which the farmer himself fashioned one night by driving his bulldozer against the wall when he heard that his youngest son, too, was going to leave the farm.

People who are bundled up much of the time, with stacks of firewood half the size of the house, and the sense that things will most likely go wrong if they haven't already: this is the America which stretches next to the Canadian boundary from the Atlantic Ocean to the Great Plains. The warm-weather rain forest of the Pacific might alter even a woodsman's outlook substantially, and, otherwise, the Rockies will give him big ideas, but what happens where the plains begin is that all of a sudden there are no trees. *No trees!* People started wearing big hats not simply because the brims were shady and wouldn't catch in the branches, but to help break up the landscape. It was a vast change, and in a huge country without forests to enforce a different perspective, many of them got to feeling big in the britches as well as in the head. Indeed, the big got bigger. Whereas in the woods that fellow with the swamp shanty and two cabbagey acres owns everything the eye can see, on the prairie it takes a rich man to feel so proprietary.

Down in Texas, the hats, the vistas and the britches, the distances to be ridden, were more expansive still. To be thirsty in Texas was a powerful thirst. The rich grew filthy rich, but before that the Indians, whom the Texans dispatched with an implacable efficiency that was the envy of Indian-haters everywhere, had included some of the continent's stiffest tribes. Not only Apaches, but Comanches, and not only Comanches, but the Attacapas and Karankawas of the Gulf Coast, who in the early years were rumored to enjoy a man-bake as much as a clam-bake, eating a castaway's buttocks and arms right in front of him as he died.

The "Kronks," as the white men were wont to call the Karankawas (or, in an earlier, more authentic spelling, "Carancahueses"), were a robust people described as standing almost seven feet tall, with slender hands and feet, sensitive faces, and hair to their shoulders, with snake rattles tied in it and bangs in front, who swam superbly and cruised between the islands and sandbars of Galveston Bay in little fleets of dugout pirogues. They communicated with smoke signals—Y's and V's, diverging, curling, spiraling columns or twin zigzags—and employed a six-foot cedar bow with a three-foot goose-feathered arrow. Two families might travel together in a pirogue with a small deck at either end and the baggage heaped in the middle, erecting at night a single shelter of skins thrown over poles on the beach. They worshiped the sun, and on ceremonial occasions blew the smoke of a fire in seven sacred directions. They had a personalized god named "Pichini" and a dread god "Mel," in whose grim celebrations they played a dismal-sounding stringed instrument five feet long, which bellowed like an alligator. For gayer festivities they had a tambourine made from a tortoise shell and a reed whistle. They talked in whistles and sign language as well as words, and counted on their fingers, going from the pinkie to the thumb, which was the "father." They were a voluptuous people, the women grabbing for the penis of an enemy's corpse. It was said that they masturbated a good deal, and their name Karankawa was generally translated as "dog-lovers," because of the horde of voiceless dogs they kept, though their detractors claimed that the love went to even further extremes. The Lipan Apaches called them "those-who-walk-in-water" because they shot fish while wading, rather than from a boat. The Tonkawas called them "the wrestlers" because they liked to wrestle and were good at it. They wore a breechclout of Spanish moss, with a wreath of palm leaves as a hat and perhaps a cock partridge's feather behind one ear. They slept wrapped in deerskins and kept their firesticks in a skin bundle, used wooden spoons and fishbone needles, and red and black pots with conical bottoms that would stand upright in the sand. They ate seafood and every kind of meat, from buffaloes to skunks and reptiles—nursing their children for years to shelter them from this rough diet. The children, their foreheads sometimes flattened as a form of decoration, played with wooden dolls, and the adults tattooed blue circles on their own cheeks, and lines from eye to ear or parallel lines descending from the mouth. With vermilion they accentuated their eyes and striped themselves red and black and white, unmarried girls with the simplest, thinnest line, but married individuals decorating themselves with flowers, birds and animals, and hanging colored stones and conch shells from their ears and the wings of the nose.

The Karankawas smelled of alligator grease, which was their chief protection from the bugs. After the whites had outgunned them, they hid in the thorn-brush thickets and behind the endless screen of man-high roseau cane. Since they had fought against the Comanches and Jean Lafitte's pirates, as well as against more orthodox settlers, and since they had numbered probably only about four hundred warriors when La Salle first landed on the Texas shore to establish a fort in 1685, they were all gone before the Civil War, when settlement really started. The last canoeful of able-bodied men deliberately paddled for the open sea during a storm, the legend goes, and the few women and children left begged their way on foot along the coast to Mexico.

Wolves, too, were a force that molded early Texas, and the optimists would claim that if we can just hold onto a smattering of them, when the time comes that people want to pick up the pieces we will have them around as a force to be observed once again. The difficulty is that though there are as many buffaloes alive as the buffalo reserves can hold, buffaloes are not a force anymore; indeed, buffaloes not in the millions may not *be* buffaloes. Neither are Big Brown Bears a force, nor Mounted Indians. That former midcontinental prairie community of mounted Indians, gaudily iconic big brown bears, and buffaloes and rattlesnakes and eagles and gray wolves that once existed centering around what is now Nebraska and Wyoming represents our idea of the pre-white New World better than the coastal or woodland aboriginal cultures do, and we all turn a bit sorrowful, reading of the buffaloes shot by the millions for their tongues, of whole dramatic nations of plains Indians starved or served up smallpox or ridden under the ground. Yet we wouldn't then and wouldn't now have had it any other way. What could we have possibly done with all those goofy buffaloes besides shoot them right off? Land of opportunity, land for the huddled masses—where would the opportunity have been without the genocide of those Old-Guard, bristling Indian tribes?

A pause is necessary when speaking in defense of wolves for some mention of their fearful destructiveness. The settlers had good reason to be afraid of wolves, the same reason that the Indians had for howling to each other when they surrounded an isolated cabin: wolves digging under a dead man's cairn to wolf down his spoiling remains, wolves disemboweling the family cow, feeding on her thighs and abdominal fat, burying their heads inside her, although her entrails lay unbroken and she was still alive and watching them. When wild game was no longer available, wolves killed the new livestock prodigiously—such stupid, lavish, feasty beasts presented to them on a tray. They soon cast off their wilderness inhibition against killing too much to eat; there was no sating them, and for a cattleman no living with them—at least the big buffalo lobos. It was either them or him. No honest-minded naturalist can peer at a caged wolf without recognizing in the old sense its wicked air. That sharp and fabled nose hooding the teeth, the bright eyes all the more dangerous for being downcast, the uncannily tall legs and twitching ears—these, with its lugubrious howl, were what the pioneers feared.

The first settler straggled into the wilderness with a single-shot rifle, leading a couple of mules, with a crate of brood hens on the back of one and two piglets in a sack to balance the load, some seed corn, potatoes and soldier beans, and dragging a long-suffering cow with a half-grown bull at her heels which the fellow hoped might manage to freshen her again before he butchered it. In the north, he settled in a beaver meadow where a little wild hay grew, and planted his potato peelings, living off boiled cowslips, sour dock, dandelion greens, Indian turnips and goldthread roots in the meantime. In red-wolf country, he lived in a hot hut with a scrap of cloth hanging across the door hole to fend the mosquitoes off, and saw his cattle, too, turn gray with malaria or bog down dead. He was afraid of wolves. The prairie was theirs, not his, and if they swept through in cavalry style, mocking his gun, and killed his mules, he was in a bad way. If they killed his cow, his children would have no milk; if they drove the deer out of the neighborhood and killed his chickens and hogs, the whole family might starve. A bachelor mountain man, wrapped in hides, here today and gone tomorrow with a pack of curs, could afford to be more nonchalant; he had no kids wandering alone along the streambank poking at the muskrats with a stick, and if he stretched his lungs at night he could holler from his bedroll louder than the hooting packs. When he shot a deer he tied his neckerchief to it to keep the wolves away until he lugged the last of it to camp. Still, sometimes these self-sustaining hobos were the ones who reported the attacks; the wolves were hunting something else and in their speed and happiness (they have been seen to jump up on the rump of a running moose and briefly ride there) happened to blunder on the man and turn toward him. In Kipling's *Jungle Book*, wolves were "the Free People."

A real wolfer lived for his wolves, trailed them for days, smelling their pee and fingering their toeprints to distinguish the bitch from her mate, slept out in order to waylay them on the trail, and when he'd shot them both, walked from his hiding place to scalp them and strip off their skins in an act quick as sex, leaving the white frames grinning in the grass. That yodeling, streaking wolf—he strung up snares that yanked it into the air and kept it hanging there, upright as an effigy, choking, kicking, till he came in the morning and hugged and punched it and cut its throat, or bound its jaws with barbed wire and carried it home across his horse to tie to a tree in the dooryard to tease for a week.

Here in littoral Texas the pioneers found an old-growth forest of large sweet gums, elms, loblolly and longleaf pines, hackberry trees and beech and oak. Wild violets and blackberries grew where the trees gave out, and then the prairie extended toward the sea: bluestem bunch grasses, Indian grass, gama grass and switch grass, with bluebells and milkweed spreading blue and white during the spring and buttercups and Indian pinks under these, the terrain broken by occasional sand knolls covered with yaupon and myrtle brush where the wolves denned and hid out. Next came a marsh of spunkweed, cattails, cutgrass and the same spartina that the colonists on the Atlantic shore had fed to their livestock. A bayshore ridge fronted the Gulf, beyond which the wolves and pioneers and Indians crabbed and beachcombed, collecting stunned redfish by the wagonload after a storm. Wagonloads of oysters, too; and in the bayous mullet seethed among gar, catfish and bullheads. Out in the tides were weakfish, black drum, channel bass, gafftopsail cats, sand trout. Summer was the fishing season; in the winter everybody lived on wildfowl and game. Prairie chickens could be caught by hand when they got drunk on fermented chinaberries; so could the geese when their wings froze together when the rain blew cold.

There was yellow fever, and hurricanes that washed away entire hamlets, and influenza in the winds and hock-deep water that the cattle still stand in. The wolves fed on sick waterfowl from everywhere north to above Hudson's Bay. They still eat sick birds, mainly cripples from the hunting months, which is when the ranchers make their tax money, charging ten dollars a day per hunter. Red-winged blackbirds and robins continue to flock in million-bird masses, and blue and snow geese arrive from Canada by the tens of thousands, along with teal, gadwalls, canvasbacks, pintails, shovelers and widgeons. The federal government has a bird refuge at Anahuac in Chambers County and two near Angleton in Brazoria County and one in Cameron Parish, Louisiana. The managers of these burn over the brush to plant millet and other goose food, and bring in cattle to keep the grass cropped green and short and to chop puddles in the ground with their hard hooves.

It seemed unbelievable that these last uncompromised wolves should have been discovered here in the salt marshes—next to Houston, Galveston and Beaumont, Texas's most industrial and populated section—instead of in the piney woods and hillbilly thickets always listed as their home. Metro Houston grew by six hundred thousand during the 1960s to a total of two million people, America's third largest port by tonnage; yet the wolves had ranged within Harris County itself and beside Galveston Bay and over in Jefferson County, within sight of some of the new subdivisions, through intensively productive rice fields, next to several of the state's earliest oil strikes, such as Spindletop.

Oil wells pump like nodding grasshoppers, bird watchers creep about on the lookout for avocets and phalaropes, and now that the deer are mostly gone, the wolves chew on stillborn calves and the carcasses of bloated steers that died of anaplasmosis. It was the last place the authorities had thought to look (for the debunkers, still a debating point), but the industrial buzz, the waterways and highways may have served to delay the coyotes for a little while. The older wolfers I dropped in on mentioned animals weighing ninety pounds or more which they hunted half a century ago with their July and Goodman hounds—roping them or clubbing them in the water when they took to a bayou to escape the dogs. Nowadays the wolves altogether add up to only one or two hundred sorry smaller specimens, because these final marshes are so mosquito-ridden that a calf, for example, may smother from the balls of insects that fasten inside its nose. Heartworms kill or invalid the grown-up wolves, plugging up the heart valves so that they suffer seizures if they run, and hookworms starve the pups. Tapeworms, spiny-headed worms and sarcoptic mange plague them indiscriminately, the spring floods drown their dens, the summer heat renders them somnambulistic and the saw grass rips their fur until their tails are naked as a rat's. In Chambers County alone there are ten cattle ranches of better than ten thousand acres, but the only cattle that can survive the bugs and watery winter footing are an indigenous mongrel Brahma breed.

Still, the ranchers have built many windmill-driven wells that bring fresh water to the wolves and other wildlife as well as to the cattle. The U.S. Soil Conservation Service has constructed raised cow walks above the standing water, and the oil companies have laid oystershell-based roads running upon embankments which provide the wolves with direct access nearly everywhere. Where the sand knolls that used to be their safe haven have been bulldozed away, windbreaks of salt cedar, huisache and Cherokee rose have been planted that fulfill the same purpose. Better still are the innumerable miles of canal banks channeling water to the rice fields, in which a pair of wolves will excavate their various emergency holes to foil a flood or hunter, a practice which also cuts down on puppy parasites.

Rice farming has introduced a "horn of plenty," as Glynn Riley calls it, in the way of rodents. The fields stand fallow every third year, and when they are plowed and reflooded the rice and barn and cotton rats and gobbly mice and big and baby rabbits must scrabble out across the levees to another field in a frenzied exodus which the wolves attend delightedly—just as up north in dairy country, coyotes will follow a farmer's mower at haying time to bolt the running mice, or follow his manure spreader to eat the afterbirths which are included in the mess. But the wolves' best staple lately is another creature tendered up to them by man, the nutria. Nutria are furry water rodents five times the size of a muskrat, and locally more catholic in habitat and diet. Introduced from Argentina to Avery Island, Louisiana, in the 1930s by a Tabasco Sauce mogul who dabbled in natural history, they escaped during a hurricane, and being tolerant of brackish water, made their way successfully along the edge of the Gulf and the Intracoastal Waterway, reaching the Rio Grande around 1967. They are a resource in Louisiana—the pelts are worth four or five dollars apiece—but in Texas they are shot as pests because they burrow through the levees and breed exuberantly and eat a lot of rice. They leave fingery tracks—have delicate fingers which can pluck up a single grain of rice—though, when abroad, they are so clumsy that they have been a blessing to the beleaguered alligators as well as the red wolves. The gators grab them in the water and the wolves snatch them in the fields at night when they venture out to feed, and for the wolves there is a nice balance to it because whenever the water gets so high that the nutria achieve a degree of maneuverability, the dry-ground rats are in a panic.

In spite of this abundant provender, coyotes have now seized all but two of the last seven counties under study; there is talk of a "Dunkirk Operation" to salvage a few wolves and whisk them to some sanctuary island such as Matagorda (already teeming with coyotes)—or, as it soon seemed to me, there may be no hope. It may not matter much if we bear in mind the continentwide accomplishments of coyotes in resettling wild areas; these wolves have been grist for the mill, making them bigger and "redder." But such considerations did not temper my irritation at the officials I met who should have cared about what was happening and didn't. The arrangements of the national Wild Animal Propagation Trust to distribute red wolves for a breeding program among cooperating zoo directors had collapsed without getting started. A noted biochemist in Minneapolis who had been interested in doing blood protein studies of the species had been forced to quit for lack of funding. The state of Texas had made no move to resurrect the wolves from unprotected varmint status, or even to make legally permissible the little gestures of help that Riley was receiving from a couple of local enthusiasts. It was both sad and comic; he was entirely on his own—other federal agencies in the neighborhood, and even other chains of command within the Fish and Wildlife Service, seemed indifferent to the matter—yet, as a trapper, he had faith that here in Chambers and Jefferson counties his lone trapline could halt the tide.

Riley lives in the small town of Liberty, and grew up in Wortham in the East Texas brush not far away. His father did some trading in scrub horses and thin cows, and if there wasn't any money in the house it still was a good life for a boy. Now he's thirty-eight, calls his father Pappy and has that cowpoke look of not putting much weight on the ground when he walks. His face is trim and small, his body slim, his hair curly and neat and his voice mild. Like many wildlife men, he prefers being inconspicuous, and nature has given him the wherewithal. After a good supper he'll say that he's "full as a tick." He hasn't finished college yet, having dropped out several times, and is country-religious, so that although he is subject to more than his share of professional frustrations, if he is speaking bitterly and doing a slow burn, suddenly in midsentence he'll undergo a change and say of the other individual in an altered tone, "But bless his heart." "The good Lord gave the wolf forty-two teeth to eat with," he says in the same folksy way; and broadcasts wolf howls from his tape recorder on the telephone to callers. "Sounds like a pack of Indians." He says a mountain with a wolf on it stands a little taller, and that a wolf represents everything a man wants to be. "He's free, he's a traveler, he's always on the move, he kills his food. He's *worth* three hundred deer."

With none of the pained air of a late bloomer, Riley instead seems simply different in this age of Ph.D.'s, and himself suggests that some-day his own head ought to be nailed on the wall at the Smithsonian In-stitution alongside the red wolf's. He is a first-rate trapper, has killed "a jillion" coyotes for the government, and therefore is as skilled at politicking with the old ranchers and trappers as any government agent is going to be. Since he is not a cosmopolitan man, his worst dif-ficulty has probably been in dealing with what ought to be his natural constituency, the conservationists "up East," that redoubtable big-city crew of letter writers whom other scientists have rallied to the cause of the whooping crane, brown pelican, and what not.

From the start trapping has been his passion—on the first day of his honeymoon he insisted upon running his trapline—and he used to measure the tracks of the coyotes in Wortham against the sizable wolf tracks in Stanley Young and Edward Goldman's standard book, *The Wolves of North America*, discovering right as a teenager that these were no longer any variety of wolf, though everybody around still bragged them up as such. He knew of one old beech tree down next to the Trinity River which still carried the claw marks of a black bear that decades ago had climbed it, and knew an old hunter who as a boy had crawled into the briar jungle there after two hounds, thinking they had treed a squirrel, when, lo and behold, one dog jumped over his head to get away and he saw the bear sitting with its back against the tree, swatting the remaining pooch. Of course no bears are left in Texas now within six hundred miles for Riley to see, and his bitterest experience as a boy was when he had to sell his rifle and borrow a friend's one fall, in order to pay the landowner's fee, when he wanted to go hunting.

He loved the howling, the matching of wits, and went to work for the Bureau, eventually being put in charge of these last wolves be-cause he'd grown so good at nabbing coyotes. He's in the position of knowing more about them than anybody else, yet watching a succes-sion of schooled young men arrive to make their academic names studying the animal before it vanishes. They must turn to him for help, as do the cameramen and journalists who show up in Liberty, and he's evolved a quietly noncompetitive attitude, putting the fun of his work ahead of the rivalries of a career. He traps a few wolves to attach radio collars to, and traps calf-killing wolves when the ranchers complain, before they get caught in one of the mangling four-trap clusters that the ranchers set. (The old method was to drag a dead cow roundabout, strewing chunks of tallow laced with strychnine behind it.) Mostly, though, he traps coyotes, especially prophylactically along the edge of the Big Thicket where the middling tracks of the hybrid swarm already have met and mingled with the wolves' large pads.

WOLF AT WORK, says a sign in Riley's office. He claims he "probably would have amounted to something" if he hadn't become fascinated with wolves, but that the country "wouldn't be complete" without them. With people already wall-to-wall, he frankly couldn't comprehend why anyone who was enough like him to show up at his door in the first place would want to live in New York City for much of the year. He was uncomfortably amazed, and every morning talked to me at first as if he were seated in a dentist's chair—I being the dentist—so that his role in whatever I had in mind achieving for him professionally could be over and done with. My lunging husky did serve as a recommendation. Riley laughed at how very furry he was, although in Minnesota, where the dog had also served to break the ice with the predator men (everywhere he tended to offend the ranchers and the farmers), they would immediately begin to talk about a wolf pup they knew back in the bush that was about his size and shade of gray.

Another favorable factor for me was that I'd read some of the literature of this infant science of predator ethology. A poorly, skimpy showing it makes, on the whole—perhaps a good month's read—but few of the journalists who seek out these field men have bothered to look into it at all, and since the field men themselves are not readers outside the particular pocket of their specialty, they are impressed when somebody has taken the trouble. Besides, as boyish as I was (like Riley, I had the sense that these adventurous predators, just as they *eat* all other animals, somehow *contain* all other animals)—still trying morning and night to catch sight of a wolf, peering into the spoil-bank thickets in the rice fields just as I had done thirty years before, speeding across the greasewood West as a youngster en route to Los Angeles on the Super Chief: by midmorning he would have managed to relax with me.

As kids both of us had climbed to many "caves," which usually proved just to be stains on the face of the rock when we reached them, but hoping to find some magic beast, a cougar or a wolverine, whatever the continent's legends might contain. So now in the evening he took me out to a coyote family's rendezvous, where with the siren we got them howling. Out wolfing again at dawn, we tried to provoke the soundless wolves, but instead it was the snow geese from white-wolf country, wheeling in platters by the thousands, that answered us. We saw coots in the ditches and an alligator so long it looked like two, half in, half out of the water, and more serrate and flat-looking than I'd anticipated. We saw fish popping in Oyster Bayou, and crabs and fat brown water snakes, and an armadillo with a tiny pointed head and papery ears; saw pelicans flying, and wavy lines of white ibises and cormorants, and roseate spoonbills like scoops of strawberry ice cream high in the air, and plenty of mink and otter tracks. Otters lope in a way that even in the form of prints communicates their speedy eagerness.

Riley himself walked rapidly, hunkering down to feel the depressions left by a wolf's toes. He bent right to the ground to smell its scenting station—a wolf's squirt smells milder, not as musky as a coyote's—to distinguish how much time had passed. The far-flung spatters were a diagram for him. He loves toes, hopping with his hands, his fingers in the toes, and never now encounters a wolf or coyote that he can't catch if he wishes to. Often he chooses not to, unless he wants to shift them around, but in any part of Texas he can envision the land much in the way that coyotes do, knowing where to find their prints and how to catch those toes. He's like a managerial cowboy, with wolves and coyotes for his cows.

His traps have toothless offset jaws, with a long swiveled drag to minimize the damage done. He attaches a bit of cloth steeped in tranquilizer for the wolf to mouth so that it will sleep. Sometimes, too, he removes a spring to weaken the bite, and adjusts the pan until the jaws close at a touch, so not the slender leg but the resilient paw is pinched. He boils the traps in a black dye, then coats them with beeswax, and has a shed full of dark-glass bottles of wolf, coyote and bobcat urine, with bits of anal gland chopped in, or powdered beaver castor and beaver oil—two universal lures from his old haunts along the Trinity—to sprinkle on a mudbank above the trap, although in fact the wolves are gullible enough to step into a trap lying open on the ground if it is placed well, and coyotes, though cleverer, are nearly as curious as they are clever, so that anything that stinks may draw some of them in.

Wolves scratch at a scent post after wetting it, whereas bobcats scratch beforehand, and neither is especially intrigued by the other's sign, but to trap either animal he employs the scent of an interloper of the same species. Wolves love to cross into the territory of another pack and leave their mark to razz the residents, like kids painting their colors on a rival school. Some of the feral dogs he traps run snapping at him, but wolves and coyotes are dumbstruck as he approaches, and after a bark or two will do anything to avoid offending him. Generally they hunch down, "sulling," facing away. I saw him bring a hybrid back and maneuver it into the netting of a holding cage, supplying a pan of water before he went to lunch. The coyote dipped its chin into the water to verify that it really was going to be permitted to drink, then held its head away from the pan until we left. He shoots these, saving the skull and skin and looking for any telltale vestiges, such as the placement of a certain vein on the rear ankle that red wolves bequeathed to the hybrids which neither gray wolves nor coyotes quite duplicate, or perhaps some feathers on the forelegs inherited from a stray bird dog. Or he may discover a coyote's little teeth set into a wolf's lanky jaw. The wear on the incisors will show its approximate age. Wolves have more forehead in their skulls than a coyote, and grays have more than reds, but dogs, which are dish-faced, have more forehead than wolves. Wolves boast big wide cheeks, big teeth and a proportionately lengthier, narrower braincase than coyotes or dogs, and the sagittal crest along the ridge of the skull where their powerful jaw muscles attach is more pronounced, but a dog's crest is higher than a coyote's. Coyotes, though, like wolves, have more space provided within the margins of the skull for their hearing organs than dogs do.

Wolves' hind legs usually swing in the same line as their forelegs—they single-foot, as foxes do—whereas dogs put their hind feet between the prints of their front feet and show a shorter stride.

With his tape measure for checking tracks and a siren for censusing, Riley goes about looking at the feet of wolf-chewed calves to see if they had ever really walked or were born dead. If something did kill them, he sees whether they were pulled down by the ears, dog-style, or by the belly and the hams, as a proper wolf would. Everywhere he stops his truck to look at tracks—at the short feet of feral mongrels dumped sick originally from hurrying cars along the Interstate, at the wide feet of "duck dogs" lost during hunting season, and at the big heelpad and long foot of a true wolf. For the record, too, he collects skulls and skins "off the fence," wherever the ranchers are still poisoning. When he catches notable beasts that please him—two black coyotes that I saw, for instance—he "transplants" them.

"You transplanted them to heaven?" I asked.

"No, no, somewhere that they're going to be real happy."

2

Texas encompasses considerably less state-owned park and recreation land than New Jersey, and for its size, remarkably little federal acreage too, because one of the terms of its annexation to the United States was that the federal government acquired no public domain. Its history has been all private enterprise, and whereas Florida and Southern California have fetishized their sunshine, Texas has promoted the notion of space. Conservation legislation of any kind has had a difficult time making much headway, and many a landowner profits more from selling his deer to the hunters, at two hundred and fifty dollars per season per man, than from his cattle. Minnesota's wolves range mainly on government land, but Texas's live on private property, which means that their fate is tied to the inheritance tax and the local tax rate on land. If the ranching oligarchies fare badly, if their oil runs out or the assessors decide to put the squeeze on them in favor of new industry or summer development, or if a younger generation, coming into possession of the key spreads of property, wants to be rich in money instead of open spaces and maybe live elsewhere, it will spell the end of the red wolves.

In 1803 the U.S. purchase of Louisiana brought Anglo-American settlers to the eastern border of what is Texas. In 1821 Mexico gained her independence from Spain and the first Anglo colonists received permission to cross the boundary and settle southward on the Brazos under a Spanish-type "emprasario" system, whereby one energetic, commanding man was given a land grant on which he undertook to establish upwards of two hundred families, exercising quasi-judicial authority over them. This was a different conception of how to do things from the homesteaders' democratic methods in the American Midwest farther north, but within fifteen years the population of Texas quintupled. By 1830 the government in Mexico City was trying to forbid new Anglo settlements, to restrict immigration to Catholics, and otherwise pinch off the fast-developing trade relations between these Protestant citizens and their former homeland in the States. The Texans' War of Independence followed in 1836, but the emprasario method of settlement continued, and by the time that Texas joined the Union in 1845, the population had again quintupled, to nearly a hundred and fifty thousand.

Thus Texas was annexed, but on its own say so—take us as we are—its land its booty, and fashioned in its infancy by Spanish-Mexican autocracy and in its adolescence by successful revolt and outlawry. In all the pulling and hauling there had been no eastern-seaboard counseling, no older-brother leavening by Virginia and Massachusetts army generals who supervised the birth of other states, or by a moderating President and Congress in Washington. In quick order the Civil War began, in which Texas, a slave state, went with the South, deposing its elected governor, Sam Houston, who was a Unionist, in the process. More revolt, hard riding and bitterness through Reconstruction, until by the onset of the new century Texas's population had increased to three million, but the crest of settlement had included an embittered surge of Southern veterans—burnt-out families grappling for land to assuage their loss. The Mexicans had been bundled off or reduced to a serf class, the Indians done away with, the wildlife mostly extirpated, and in a pride-heavy, insular setting soon to be thoroughly lubricated with oil there was little influence to dampen the frontier swagger.

Booted boys and behatted giants fish from the boardwalk at Port Aransas, knifing the croakers that they catch with enthusiasm. Even Cokes look bigger in Texas; and eating habits remain Brobdingnagian, with funny consequences for the midriff. But in Odessa I went to a "rattlesnake roundup" advertised for the municipal coliseum, and found the entrance thronged with ticket holders. This seemed what I was after—the old Texas rite for ridding the calving range of snakes—except that the crowd turned out to be fans attending a rock concert. The "rattlesnake roundup" was way around in back inside an adjunct shed, with three cars parked at the door.

Texas is still a good place to be rich in. Money is the stamp of excellence, yet in the southeast sections a more rooted conservatism, involving the illusion of an old-family tradition, has been carried over from the states nearby. Since it is a conservatism essentially unburdened by the weight of tragic circumstance of the Old South, one needn't become a contortionist to imagine that this is indeed the good life. Part of a wolf-seeker's regimen is to visit these grand mansion houses, and everywhere he encounters gracious living in the form of magnolias and spacious acreage patrolled by black cowhands—peacocks, guinea hens and fancy breeds of goose strolling the grounds, ten-foot alligators in private pools, pet deer in live-oak groves festooned with trailing moss. Quail and mourning doves, mimosas, pecans, orange trees, big-kneed cypresses, four cars in the garage, cool patios with iron grillwork, long lawns, little lakes, and girls and their daddies—girls so pretty Daddy doesn't quite know what to do with them.

These men of good fortune—men like Joe Lagow of Anahuac, and R. E. Odom, who lives across the Sabine River from Texas in Louisiana—glanced at my Vermont license plates, New York face, and gray husky, and talked to me with caution. Lagow is a short jay-bird of a man who serves as county commissioner and on a number of committees, and with his in-laws owns twenty-six thousand acres of snow-goose, red-wolf country. When I called to him across his aviary to ask if he was Joe Lagow, he swung around agreeably and said, "Yes, I'm what's left of him." Odom is younger and more reticent, even a little feline and courtly, in the Louisiana manner. We had tea in his jewel box of a house, served by his white foreman. With his mother he owns a matchless spread of land in what is called Gum Cove, a luscious loop of grazing ground a few feet above sea level, enclaved within the badlands of Cameron Parish and reachable only by ferry across the Intracoastal Waterway.

The time is past when Southern ranchers can be bamboozled into a reflexive show of hospitality, and various of these men gave me to understand, with conscious irony, that they were conservationists because they were conservatives and it would only be when new views took command that the ecology of their grasslands would be disrupted—smiling as they said this because of course a visiting Northern journalist was likely to represent those views. Nevertheless, the parade of exotic scribblers and photographers whom the environmental vogue is bringing to the door has started them thinking that the wolves that den on their mesquite knolls may be among the perquisites of wealth here on the Gulf; they've told their cowhands to quit killing them. It's the little operator, leasing pasturage for forty cattle that he has his hopes pinned on, who is still likely to put out traps, and if his few hundred acres happen to lie athwart a wolf run, it won't much matter how many thousands more stretch trap-free all around.

I went to Wolf Corner in Thompson, Texas, just beyond the Houston city line, where a trapper named Charlie Grisbee has nailed up as many as thirty wolves or hybrids at a time. Grisbee wasn't home, but on his starchy lawn a wooden wolf was chasing a wooden family of ducks. It was a suburban sort of house interfaced with stone, all spruce and neat, with blue Pullman curtains in the windows of the garage. I'd asked whether Charlie was married and people had said very much so; they didn't think his wife especially liked his trapping, but that it "went with Charlie." A single twenty-pound coyote was hanging on the rack at the corner of a field next to the highway—attenuated-looking, rotting, twitching in the strong wind off the Gulf, with its head and tail hacked off, its rain-stained, rabbity fur and rabbity legs no longer distinguishable as those of a predator. In the grass for yards around were tibias, scapulas and backbone scraps, along with dewberries and Indian paintbrush, but some developers had now got hold of the field. I picnicked on the porch of a preempted farmhouse with a veteran fig tree for shade and honeysuckle all about.

In Danbury, in Brazoria County, I talked to Andrew Moller, among other old wolfers. Though Brazoria didn't bounty scalps, some of the fellows would deep-freeze what they caught and cash them in elsewhere. Moller is ninety-one. His grandfather jumped ship from a German whaler and bought land on Chocolate Bayou for five cents an acre, unfortunately sold off later. Once Moller was safely born, his father and his uncle had taken off for an adventure of their own, riding down the coast to Mexico for a couple of months, wading their horses across the many rivers they encountered at the mouth. And "in nineteen and eleven" he, a chip off the same block, had treated himself to a thousand-mile wagon ride around Texas, before paying thirty-five dollars for sixty cows, which over the next forty years he husbanded into a herd of fifteen hundred cattle. A traveling man, he mostly rented pasture for them. He trucked them to the Davis Mountains in West Texas, and to two decommissioned army camps in Arkansas and Oklahoma—unexpected long-grass pasturages on easy terms which he had hit upon during his hunting trips—always "keeping at least a nigger hired." Once he bought a thousand mares at four dollars a head, all of them running wild—he had to catch them—but sold them for ten dollars a head to a bootlegger who pirated them across the Sabine to Louisiana undipped and uninspected. Two of his old hands visited him recently in Danbury. He fed them catfish "and never heard two niggers laugh so much."

Using Walker hounds and Trumbulls, Moller caught little wolves in the nineteenth century when he was little and big ones when he grew up, till the barbed-wire fences were strung. A coyote, like a fox, will dodge into thick brush, he says, but a wolf "leaves the country." To catch him you first have to convince him that you are going to by running him ten miles through the sage and salt grass without letup. "Run a V on him" with other riders until his hind end wobbles and he hasn't gained a yard and begins to despair; then it may take another five or ten miles. Or if they could drive one into the Gulf of Mexico, they would keep roping him while he bit the ropes in two, until at last they drowned him. To run the wolves, even without a kill, kept the packs busted into isolated pairs which were less troublesome to the cattle, and generally Moller would catch the pups at the family rendezvous each fall. Sometimes, though, a varmint hunter would shoot a calf by mistake as it rose up suddenly in the grass. He'd had a couple of hog dogs as a boy that would chase any pup they came across, and with these he began wolfing on Chocolate Bayou, where the Amoco oil refinery now stands. In "nineteen and two" he was helping a trapper friend trail the wolves that hobbled off dragging the trap behind them, except it got to be such fun that they quit trapping and simply ran the creatures—ran them into swimming water where Moller would strip and grab a club and manhandle the wolf out to where the dogs could throttle it. Or he might rope it, haul it home to the hog pen and feed it cracklings and offal until his wife complained about the stink.

Moller is a well-set-up individual with pink coloring, a long face, a big pair of ears and nose, and a mellow voice. In 1895 eighteen inches of snow fell and half his father's cattle died. They skinned two hundred hides that week that fetched a dollar a hide in Galveston, both working as dollar-a-day cowboys afterwards, his father eating alligator tails and getting a dollar apiece for their hides too. Or they would paddle down Chocolate Bayou with four deer carcasses, put them on the city boat and trade them for a sack of green coffee in Galveston. In 1900 a hurricane blew down the house and washed away half the people who lived in the area, he says; one husband and wife held hands, grabbed hold of some driftwood and floated for thirteen miles.

The game was so plentiful—from cranes to doves—that on their hunts sometimes they couldn't hear the hounds for all the birds hollering. Sometimes, too, there were so many wolves about that when they went out after geese they couldn't creep close to a pond where a flight had just landed before some wolf would bound into the water to see whether any cripples were in the bunch, putting them all to flight. Moller captured the spring pups by riding up on a sand knoll where a lot of wolf tracks converged and prancing his pony around until its hooves broke through into the den. Then, on the following day, he'd jump the gyp-wolf (mama) there, and the day after that the pop. Once at the South Texas Wolf Hunters Association meet at the

King Ranch, the Mexican hands had butchered a beef and hung it up for everybody to help himself, and brought out horses—the members had only had to bring along their own saddles. They all painted numbers on their dogs to score them in the chase, and Moller and a buddy stayed out late hounding a wolf until at last the creature "set his bucket down." He was exhausted, so they roped him, whipped the dogs away, and tied his mouth and carried him back across a horse, and at the big bonfire slipped off the ropes and heaved him into the crowd of wolfers to start the hunt all over again.

The cowhands close to Houston are mostly black, not Mexican, as they are toward the Rio Grande, or white, as in the bulk of Texas. Slingshots, in the old journals, are known as "nigger-shooters," but since at least the work was manly in the old days, for some of them it may have been a tolerable sort of place to be a slave—alone on horseback hassling the cattle much of the day. It still would seem to add up to a better life than growing peanuts in Mississippi, although the shacks along the road look just as rickety as Mississippi's, and though many of the people one encounters have a peculiarly screwed-tight intensity to their faces—extraordinary faces that a traveler sees nowhere else in the United States—as if they had been scorched in a crucible, like black faces in Mississippi. Can it simply be the sun?

One morning I was chatting with a rancher who said he wanted to kill all the turkey buzzards in the sky as well as the red wolves. There are plenty of buzzards. We could count about fifteen standing about in the treetops and roosting on fence posts. Overnight the rain ditches had filled, the sky still smelled of rain, but as we visited, the sun broke through, lying at a cannon's angle, the kind of morning sun that made you answer to it, irradiating dead as well as living things. Greens bled into blues and reds, white was black and black was white: too much color and too bright. The wind, which had been chilly, began to heat. Then, in this incredible intensity of light, what the buzzards did, following some lead from an elder, was all at once to spread their wings, not in order to rise and fly, but holding them outflung to dry.

What we were witnessing was not unfamiliar. Everybody has seen pictures of a totem pole topped by a raven carved with its wings outstretched, the Earth's creator, according to the maker of the totem pole. Ravens are the buzzards of the North. What we were privy to— fifteen buzzards spread-eagled, metal-colored in a violent sun— would have transfixed an Indian of the Northwest, would have provided a whole life's ozone to a woodcarver, a vision any warrior would have died for, if in fact his excitement didn't render him invincible. Fifteen images of the Creator in a rising sun would have propelled a great chief into his manhood after walking naked for a month; except we have no divine signs now.

I had settled in Anahuac at a café-motel where the lady displayed her late husband's Yale diploma in the office as a talking point. She missed Arkansas, claimed it had been an awful mistake for them to have left Little Rock nineteen years before, and looked that Southern mixture of left-over hopefulness and untidy despondency—hard shoulders and forearms but vulnerable breasts and soft hands. She served a rueful menu of chicken-fried steaks and heavy catfish to lonely oil workers and roaming fishermen. I was discouraged, angry at the way the wolf project was on the back burner for everybody but Glynn Riley. In Washington there was a mixture of flutter and indifference—even to get information had required a personal visit—and over the years Texas's Parks and Wildlife Department has taken what might politely be described as a minimum of interest. (Their black bears were allowed to fall practically to the vanishing point before receiving partial protection.) The wolves' blood characteristics had been studied not at a Texas medical center but in Minneapolis, and in Houston itself the concern, if possible, was fainter yet. The director of the Museum of Natural History, Dr. Thomas Pulley, an influential man, was not so much uninformed about the wolves as agin 'em. He hadn't exhibited the handsome skins that Riley had sent him, and liked to take the long view, speaking of man's impact on the world as related to evolution like the glaciers, belittling the notion of interfering as "causey, like preserving mustangs." He seemed bankerly in manner, a small-city, big-fish iconoclast with the mocking cast of mind that often develops in isolation, rubbing up against mostly laymen. He said that when he and his friends hunt deer they see plenty of coyotes.

118

The Houston zoo director, a civil servant, was not as self-assured. He had no wolves and agreed with me that though the zoos in San Antonio and Oklahoma City did keep one or two, it was incongruous that the only propagation program in the nation was way off in Tacoma, Washington. He said that to construct a "wolf woods" would cost only about seven thousand dollars, but that to raise such a piddling sum among the multimillionaires of Houston would be difficult because controversial, and so his efforts on behalf of disappearing species were devoted to the St. Vincent's parrot and Galápagos tortoise.

Riley carries hurt wolves to a veterinarian friend, Dr. Buddy Long, in the town of Winnie. Long pins together any broken bones (wolves will tear off a splint), administers penicillin and distemper shots and worms them. He is a man who "likes old things," and is the angel of Riley's program, having sunk thousands of dollars of his own modest funds into the work. He has a scrunched-together, matter-of-fact face, the mouth creased for smiling, and propagandizes as he makes his rounds among the cattlemen, several of whom still trap but who will telephone him when they catch something, if they don't like the idea of inviting a government man to poke about their property. The animal is a sad sight, clinched into a clutch of traps, with its feet mauled. Whatever toes are left he tends, or if the wolf is dead, he leaves it soaking in a tub for whenever the scientific community gets around to wanting to know what a red wolf looked like under the skin. At the time of my visit he had no legal authority to keep wild animals, and when the wolves he treated were ambulatory not a zoo in the country was prepared to take them, and so one night he'd leave the door of the pen open.

Long is a bit older than Glynn Riley, well settled in one of those delicious marriages that are a pleasure to catch sight of, and, as luck would have it, has been bolstering to Glynn. Through studying blood parasites he had become interested in the wolves, and now kept captives of his own in a big breeding arena. White on the lips and chin, with broad cheeks, narrow noses, a pointed attention and that skittery bicycling gait—whirling, almost fluttering, away from me along the fence—they were still jazzed up from the courting season, when they had chased each other all over Chambers County. Unfortunately this

119

same month or two coincides with the calving season in the region, so that the ranchers see more of the wolves when they least want to.

Long took me wolfing along Elm Bayou, East Bayou, Onion Bayou. A blue heron was eating baby alligators, though in a few weeks it might be summering in one of the suburbs of Chicago. The geese in their yapping thousands flew up from the fields around us; they would soon be on the tundra. Long said that skunks are thick, and that though a grown wolf would have enough sense to steer clear of a rabid skunk, a blundering pup might get bitten and carry the disease into the packs.

"Around here you can look farther and see less than anywhere in the world," he said. But we inspected the "swimming holes" where the stockmen swim their cattle across the Intracoastal Waterway every fall, then in the spring again, bringing them back to higher ground. We saw the burros that they use to halter-break the yearling colts, tying colt and burro neck to neck. He spoke about the problems of a cow vet. "Sometimes they won't get well and sometimes they won't die." At the fence gates we found wolf tracks. Now that the fields were drying off for spring the baby rabbits were hopping from the nest, and the wolves had scattered off the levees to catch them. Long said that sometimes the wolves will run a ranch dog right through a screen door, and twenty cattle through a fence, and pass the house again that night, barking so as to rib the dog. When hunted, they will circle into a herd if no other cover is close, and hamper the men from getting a shot at them by sticking beside the cattle.

Among the many lice-chewed cattle we saw one fine high-horned bull with a long dewlap, ears that hung down at a steep angle, a hump big as a camel's and a penis like a rhino's. He was a pretty mouse color, all the prettier for being so dangerous-looking underneath that comely pelt. "That one would try to get in your back pocket with you," said Long as we negotiated the gate.

The only other strong ally of Riley's I was able to find in Texas was Hank Robison, who sells cigarette lighters and ballpoint pens in Houston. A lobbyist and crusader, he has worked to get the local bounties removed. He lives in a workingman's district, has gold in the front of his mouth, is self-educated and self-conscious about it, and financially must live by his wits, he says. But posters of lions and tigers stare off the walls of his small house; his blinds are dog-chewed. He talks like a dogged cross between a crank and social worker and is a fervid letter writer, keeping a file so that no officeholder can get away with not replying to him. He has a flatly single-minded fighter's face, taking you for where you stand, and when knocked down, obviously will not stay down, because his delight is just precisely to get up again. He camps in the Big Thicket on weekends and lives for his family as well as for wild animals, and yet in him I thought I saw what I notice in other enthusiasts and in myself: the injured man who recognizes in the running wolf his wounds.

Riley could comprehend a person preferring to live in the city if he liked going to the movies or had the money to eat in restaurants, but what he couldn't understand about the Eastern cities was the matter of muggers. Working with wolves, he wasn't afraid of muggers. "Why don't they clean them out of there?" Like Lynn Rogers in Minnesota, apparently he had a picture of himself walking down the avenues and, if he saw a mugger, punching him in the mouth. Of course, being familiar with firearms, he could adjust his image when I said that the mugger was likely to be armed, but he continued to presume that the solution lay in individual acts of heroism. What neither man could grasp was how *many* muggers there are.

Glynn has poisoned pocket gophers in East Texas and prairie dogs in West Texas, and out in Muleshoe in the Panhandle did rabbit counts for the Bureau, where he saw some odd spectacles: a badger and a coyote turning over cow chops in a partnership to eat the beetles underneath; an eagle snatching a duck from a windmill spillway. The eagles perched on the boxcars where feed was stored to spear the pack rats living underneath, and early one morning he watched a coyote filch a rabbit from an eagle, the coyote's chest fur shining nobly in the sun. Once in a while he'd drive a hundred miles or so to chat with an old wolfer who had shot the last gray Western lobos at their watering holes. One time the fellow had ridden here to the Gulf to dispose of a hog-killing red wolf: lay waiting for it behind the pen the night that he arrived, and when he heard the hog scream, shot the wolf, and the next day left—too many people here, not that big

Western country. "We thought there'd always be another wolf. We didn't know they would ever play out," he told Glynn.

Riley's best thrill, when he has visited the study crew in Minnesota, has been to feel with his hands the outsized tracks the wolves make there in the fluffy snow. Gray wolves are real wolves in a way that red wolves aren't, and the black taiga wolves of the Yukon and the white arctic wolves are larger still. Some day he hopes to have a hand in studies of them all: jaguars too. He's a predator man and he wants size—dire wolf, cave bear! Then, because he was a novice on snowshoes, he began to make strange tracks himself, falling down and flinging out his arms. For days it was the joke in camp: *that's* where Glynn Riley from Texas fell down, and *there's* where he fell down again.

Like old-time trapping, Riley's is a lonely business. His best friend lives six hundred miles away in the Trans-Pecos town of Marathon, Texas. He's a mountain-lion hunter whom I'll call Mike Marfa, and the two of them became acquainted at what Marfa likes to call "rat meetings," where the varmint-control technicians of the Fish and Wildlife Service get together to talk shop, mostly about killing rodents and rabbits. But these two were men who had a penchant for pulling down a bigger creature and, beyond that, were outdoorsmen with a vocation for it (Marfa likes to say that he's already caught enough coyotes to fill ten diesel trucks). When the two of them do manage a visit they can hardly contain their pleasure. They open the pungent brown bottles that Riley sets such store by, bobbing their heads like connoisseurs above the beaver oil and bobcat urine, two years in the brewing though Marfa likes to tease Riley that it is where you put the trap, not so much what you sprinkle on it, that does the job.

Marfa is another man who knows more than many of the professors do who hold Chairs on the strength of their investigations into ethology, and sometimes comes back snorting from the symposia he goes to, saying he'd like to hear from the guy who *catches* their lions for them. For years he was the state's principal lion hunter, when the Bureau had a hundred and fifty trappers giving the coyotes a going-over. He was paid a little more and got up earlier too, he likes to claim, kidding Riley, and went out on muleback the whole day long, chasing after his hounds, instead of tooling about in a pickup truck like Riley and the rest, to prune the lions back to the edges of Big Bend National Park from a line which corresponded more or less to U.S. Highway 90. When I first met him he was on his way home from an excursion to Florida where he had demonstrated for the World Wildlife Fund that the Florida panther was rarer than Florida's wildlife officials had believed. His pack of mottled Walker hounds—a home brew he has bred and culled and whittled on over the years, and doesn't sell or swap or loan, he says, any more than a carpenter would his tools—were sleeping in a fresh pile of hay in the back of his truck, so placid after traveling so far that they spoke well for him. He and Riley took them for a run after bobcat along a bayou bank, but then, although Riley was eager to have him stay overnight and go to the Houston Fat Stock Show, which happened to be on that week, and although he himself was wistful about the possibility too, he said he had another twelve hours of driving ahead and didn't want to keep the dogs cooped up any longer than that. He's the type who scoops up every hitchhiker on the road, otherwise stopping nowhere, but compared to Riley, his mannerisms are gruff and harsh, and he is proud of going all day in the Big Bend desert without either water or food. Like so many other wildlife men, he was not in the Marines when he was a youngster and probably should have been. Where the bear man, Lynn Rogers, had made the burler's leap to city living in Minneapolis in the winter, Riley and Marfa had not. Riley had relinquished much of his hunter's spark, however, to a reflective attitude that suited his present work, but Marfa, whom Riley rather looks up to, was just as hot as ever; he had quit the Bureau and when he wasn't working on an experimental program to transplant mountain lions from the Big Bend country to South Texas, supported himself as a private lion hunter in the Big Bend region, and by trapping the last few lobo wolves down in the Mexican states of Durango and Chihuahua.

Marfa let me delve about with him a bit in his own territory, first wanting and then deciding that he didn't want a full-dress magazine article written about himself, but through both men I caught a sense of the cycle of wolf and coyote hunting.

The coyote is of course the "barking wolf," the Trickster of so many Indian tribes—a deity to the Chinooks and the Navajos, a subtle animal with a taste for the suckled milk in a lamb's stomach, for instance, which the simpler-minded bobcat does not share—the New World version of the jackal, and yet a creature so highly thought of that the pregnant women of certain Indian tribes would wear its testicles next to their stomachs to ward off difficulties. The fall is nonetheless the season when the guileless pups are dashing around; it is a chance to wipe out the year's crop while they are wet behind the ears, and was the season for the getter-gun until the getter-gun as a device was disallowed. Any witches' brew could be used to bait the knob—possum juice, rotted gopher, dead rattlesnake or frog—and since the pup took eight or ten leaps to die, more of the hunter's time was consumed in locating its little corpse in the brush than in any other part of the job.

In the winter the getters weren't as effective and the sort of guy without any particular skill who had coasted along in the fall by putting out a lot of them took a back seat to the serious trapper. Winter is the mating season, and the emphasis is on catching the adults as they hustle about, pissing at scenting stations and trailing one another. Sex is what interests them, not picking up the quaint and curious scents that getter-guns are baited with. The trapper, milking the bladders, cutting the musky anal glands out of the specimens he bags, creates some scent posts of his own or activates others—a turkey wing lying next to a sheep path—that the smarter coyotes will step up to. In a bog in Anahuac, the fellow might set his trap at the end of a footlog, with a wad of moss under the pan so that a raccoon's weight won't depress it.

In the spring and summer the animals lose interest in everything except their pups, and travel in a beeline between the den and hunting grounds. Trotting back full-bellied from a long drink at a spring, they may stop for a moment and piddle at the turkey wing or even investigate the *outré* smells on the bait knob of a "getter," but generally this is when the professionals hunt for dens. Den-hunting is a specialty, intuitive, distinct. The steel-trap men are condescending about the cyanide go-getter—a kind of scatter-shot method, a glib, perfunctory tool—and yet compared with trapping, den-hunting is downright purist and arcane. It's catching the animals alive, by hand, in their hidden home, and some predator hunters hardly bother to trap at all, killing a presentable quota of coyotes just by finding and digging up the year's new dens. Usually they ride, because a coyote fears a man on horseback somewhat less, and what the hunter looks for is a bustling hodge-podge of tracks that, as he studies them, begin to offer evidence of radiating from a given point which the coyotes have tried to conceal. Often the den faces southeast from a slight elevation, and he may try to call one of the parents toward him with a "squeaker" made from a piece of a cow's horn which emits a rabbit's squeal. If, having dismounted, he sees the coyote first and holds his fire until it scents him, he will have the benefit of its last quick anxious glance in the direction of the den to guide him on, before it takes evasive action. If the grownups attempt to decoy him he shoots them, then looks sharp for the first pup, which will streak for the hole as soon as it sights him. He tumbles about in the brush, grabbing the pups and clubbing them, or if they are very young he must dig, hooking them out from underground with a wire prong twisted on the end. If either parent has escaped him, he will bury a dead whelp with one foot exposed and set traps alongside it and by the den.

In sheep territory the javelinas root holes under the woven fences that coyotes also make use of, and this is where the ancient craft of snaring can be practiced. Then, by contrast, there are hunters who are primarily marksmen and shoot the creatures from a helicopter. But none of these systems will suffice after the less vigilant 70 percent of the population has been eliminated. There are always a few coyotes which flatten down instead of bolting when the helicopter makes its pass over the chaparral, and which keep their pups clear of the getter-guns. For these holdouts some studying is necessary; the animal becomes individualized, and a Riley or a Marfa becomes interested. Or they may meet an animal like Adolph Murie's blithe classic coyote in the valley of the Yellowstone which trotted toward him carrying a sprig of sagebrush in its jaws that it tossed up and caught and tossed and caught.*

---

*Murie, *Ecology of the Coyote in the Yellowstone* (Washington, D.C.: National Park Service, Fauna Series Number 4, 1940), p. 38.

When the Fish and Wildlife Service supervisors in San Antonio decided that the Big Bend mountain lions had had enough pruning, they set Marfa on a series of eccentric research labors, such as catching sixty coyote puppies "by Friday" for a sex-ratio study, collecting adults for a test of poisons, or gathering coyote urine and red-wolf skulls. (The number of red wolves killed in order to verify their existence as a species and then to train successive research cadres must surpass the number so far "saved.") Finally Marfa went into business for himself, charging the sheep ranchers two hundred and fifty dollars per lion, and more for the Sierra Madre lobos he has been capturing in Durango lately, working for the stockmen's association there. In some respects a wolf is more vulnerable than a coyote, because of the complexity of its social life and because it is bolder and therefore more accessible, but since it travels farther, in another way it is less so. These are "named" wolves, the last of their kind in an enormous spread of territory, in their way almost as endangered as Riley's wolves are, and correspond to the famous "outlaw" wolves of the American Great Plains a half a century ago. Like them, they're quirky, lonely, queer, atypical beasts, final survivors because they have allowed themselves only the sparsest pleasures. Marfa carries a handful of traps as he rides his mule around for a period of days or weeks to spy out some small chink in the precautionary tactics of the wolf he is after—some stray indulgence by which it still tries to amuse itself that has escaped the notice of all the other trappers who have had a go at it. These Mexican lobos have short pretty heads, and you must know the length of the neck and stride in situating the trap.

One such wolf, "Las Margaritas," took him eleven months to catch, humbling him, he says, and in the meantime, it was claimed, slaughtering ninety-six cattle on a single large ranch nearby. The only entertainment left "Margaret" after so many narrow escapes in a lengthy career was killing steers, once she was safely inside a pasture. She was poison-proof because she fed at her own kills and nowhere else, and never a second time at one of them. Already missing two front toes, she would follow a different route coming and going. If she arrived on a logging road, she exited by way of a cattle track; if through a canyon, by a high pass. She avoided other wolves, although from loneliness she sometimes would howl behind the ranchers' barns. She would not go close to the message stations of other wolves, but instead would squat wistfully to make her mark at a safe distance, so that he could not catch her by the ordinary technique of setting a trap at a scent post or manufacturing a bogus station with the urine of a foreign wolf. Some outlaws, he says, entirely give up trying to communicate with other wolves and use only their own scenting stations. Once, indeed, she did step in one of his traps, but the hole carved into her foot by the two toes that she was missing happened to fit across the pan and saved her. She jumped for her life.

She traveled continually, having been hunted with hounds often after a meal, and there was no predicting where she would go. Over the years, hundreds of traps had simply been left blind for her in paths across the mountainsides she ranged, which gradually had lost their human smell and any surface scars to show the ground had been worked on. But some of them had become boneyards for other animals that had been caught instead, and the rest she avoided by her spartan custom of stepping mostly on the rocks and stones, or else on ground too hard to dig in without leaving a permanent sign. On the road, if there was any indication that a rider had dismounted or that a man had left his truck, even the day before, she immediately veered off, not waiting to discover what he might have been up to. Without the fellowship of a pack, with nowhere safe enough for her to go to relax except among the actual cattle herds, killing was her life and her relations with her pursuers her only intimacy, so when at last Marfa did catch her—when he had almost given up—it was in a trap that he had left blind some weeks before next to a corral she liked to hang about. She pulled the stake out of the ground and painfully dragged the trap as far as she could, but all the ranch hands turned out to chase her down. Only then was it revealed that notorious "Margaret," so security-ridden that she squatted meekly to piss like a bitch, all along had been a male.

When this methodical search had palled, Marfa dashed off behind his light little slipping lion hounds—skinny so their feet hold up and so they can twist through the canyon cracks and into any boulder pile (for which he has a "climbing dog")—to run down one of the infrequent lions left. He sight-trailed for the pack over the alkali ground, where the scent, as dry as smoke, had blown away. Where there were grass and sticks again they'd pick it up. Salt blocks, windmills and fencing are what makes ranching here. Durango is also the starving country where wetbacks come from, and any deer whose prints show up is tracked relentlessly. There are human outlaws in the Sierra Madre as well, and Marfa, lean from his regimen of two meals shoveled in twelve hours apart, living very nearly on a level with a lion, with the two expressions that his face falls into—boyish and bleak— went about with his rifle handy and his bedroll and mule and dogs.

Another noteworthy wolf he caught because his dogs showed him its single small inabstinence. It liked to go up on top of a mesa to a water tank with an earthen dam and wallow in that one soft place on a long-dead skunk lying in sweet-smelling grass. He captured a wolf called Wide Gait using a month-old turd which he had saved from its former ladylove, whose Spanish name meant Nearly Black and whom he had trapped previously with an old turtle shell. "Dead as a hammer," he says.

Turds represent survival in the desert or the woods and are beloved by animals for that: a meal put to use, the gift of life. Of a woodsman, too, you'll hear it said, "He was the best deer-hunter that ever took a shit in the woods." Marfa showed me how to distinguish a ringtail's scats (small-bore, on top of a rock, containing scorpion pincers and tails) from a raccoon's; a kit fox's fuzzy-toed, dainty prints from a gray fox's; and trundled me about, pointing out abundant lion scrapes in the sandy canyons we explored next to the Rio Grande. Lions scratch with their forefeet for their feces and their hind feet for urine, partly hiding the first but ballyhooing the latter. Their front feet make a bigger, rounder print, so people sometimes think one track is two.

This is country where one finds the arrows wetbacks put together in the dry streambeds with stones—where once in the Christmas Mountains Marfa found the skeleton of a "wet" who had gotten himself lost. He pointed out a mountain in Coahuila, a twelve-hour walk up a canyon tributary to the Rio Grande, which has a cave so big a plane could fly into its mouth, and cool high pine forests where a few black bears are still holding out. He spoke about another sanctuary, in Chihuahua, where until recently all the American cats could be found—jaguarundis, ocelots, bobcats, lions and jaguars—though now every such Shangri-la in Mexico is shrinking faster than a puddle on hot city pavement. The last of the grizzly bears, he says, was blown up with nitroglycerin wired to a honey-smeared log.

An ocelot leaves more scent than a bobcat and doesn't fight the dogs as hard; a jaguarundi is lithest in the thickets and the toughest to trail, he said. Lions and lobos are a force, a *frequency*, if you will: once maybe the trombone, now the oboe in the orchestra. They are the Headless Horseman who, once he is gone, exists only in fairy tales, and although most of us can get along without hearing the oboe's note or seeing the Headless Horseman ride, in Riley and Marfa I had come close to locating the people who can't. Marfa, in particular, who has hunted jaguars in the jungle in Campeche too, talks about retiring to British Honduras, where in the wet woods he envisions the cats forever plentiful, leaving a trail for his dogs "as strong as a garbage truck." In the desert in the early morning he lets the vultures be his guide and trucks his dogs to where they are. Then, with the water *tinajas* fifteen or twenty miles apart, he gets his lion.

Red wolves howl in a higher, less emotive pitch than gray wolves and don't blend with each other quite as stylishly, though they do employ more nuances and personality than a coyote family's gabble. A coyote's howl sounds hysterical, amateurish by comparison, chopped and frantic, almost like barnyard cackling, or, in an early description, "like a prolonged howl the animal lets out and then runs after and bites into small pieces." The only likely-looking wolves I actually saw during my several visits were two smashed dead on the highway, which I passed at high speed as I was leaving Texas. They were red, sizable and somber, at least from the perspective I had by then accumulated. They were probably mates, the second having lingered alongside the first, and now were angled affectionately rump to rump—the copulative position—in death.

Once, too, alone one night along Elm Bayou, I howled up a wolf a quarter of a mile away that sounded querulous and yowly, variable and female. We were beginning to converse, but I left it to answer another wolf howling a mile beyond. This wolf and I talked back and forth, until I started to wonder. The sound jerked and creaked too unsteadily for a wolf and yet was pitched too low to be a coyote, and wasn't barky enough for a feral dog—almost like a windmill. In fact, that's what it was; I'd left a real wolf for a windmill.

In these inquiries I had begun to glimpse the noble stretch of science when it grabs hold of a sea of data and persuades it to jell. In a still-primitive, ambiguously motivated backwater area of scholarship there was nevertheless a majesty to the picture as it emerged. Predators are smarter than herbivores, usually need to sleep more, and possess the invaluable ability to vomit, and when the findings on these biggest beasts are combined, one understands better the grizzly with its "attack distance" developed for a life on the plains, the black bear thriving by gourmand eating and a love of holes, the mountain lion avoiding competition and starvation by avoiding wolf country and its own kind, the wolf avoiding competition and starvation by a hierarchal social existence. Unluckily, the very means of population control that had enabled each of them to prosper while ruling the roost—the graphic social life, in some cases, and the slow, problematical birth rate of more solitary creatures such as bears or eagles—is now depleting them. These discoveries were being made, on the one hand, by scholars many of whom might have been laughed out of the lab if they had been working in another branch of science, and on the other, by observers in the field whose woodsmanship was only a faint shadow of that of the centuries when the wilderness (and these animals) were real. But I'd met men who wouldn't have done badly in any era of woodsmanship.

(1974)

Nature's Seesaw

I live at the top of Vermont, next to Canada, and moose leave their tracks in my garden occasionally, investigating the vegetables out of curiosity without eating them, in the same way that they may emerge from the trees onto the lawn to stare at my crowing rooster to see what he is. With no wolves around, they are increasing by 15 percent a year, though the pioneers had wiped them out, along with the wolves. But caribou, which originally shared that old-growth forest, have not come back because the caribou's mossy, lichenous diet was destroyed along with those virginal woods. Instead, deer (called "Virginia" deer at first) moved north, thriving on the cutover vegetation. So I have deer, too, around my place, which are periodically thinned back by a severe winter, when the snow gets taller than their legs. Moose, being bigger, don't mind the snow, but will die from a brainworm that deer carry (and seem immune to) if the deer get too thick. The two animals are in balance here, in other words. The moose can't move too far south because of the deer and the deer can't go much further north on account of the snow.

Opossums also migrated up, finding the new habitat to their liking—in old books they too boast the sobriquet "Virginia." But they

131

stopped short of my latitude simply because their naked tails froze in Vermont north of approximately the White River. Raccoons and skunks are similarly opportunistic creatures but have no such problem with frost, so I do see them. My rabbits are snowshoe rabbits, however. The cottontails' northward swarm stopped at about the White River because of the depth of our snow and our mean winters.

Canada lynx, like the caribou, had disappeared when our primeval forests were felled for charcoal. But bobcats, more versatile, moved up from cottontail country to fill the lynxes' ecological slot, toughing out the cold weather by ambushing a deer in a snowdrift, perhaps, and strangling it, then camping for a month by the carcass. In the summer they eat rodents, birds, everything, and I hear them scream from the mountain ledges above my house. Or my dog may tree one, growling from a spruce limb above my head in the dark of the night.

The balance between predators and prey—bobcats and rabbits, fisher and porcupine—is different from the relationship between parallel species, such as moose and deer, fisher (a large form of weasel) and fox, fox and coyote, or coyote and bobcat. Red foxes had thickened to fill the void in predators as nineteenth-century sheep farming and twentieth-century dairying replaced the charcoal industry, and hedgerows, underbrush and woodlots grew back. Foxes eat what cats eat, plus impromptu berries, nightcrawlers, slugs, grasshoppers, woodchucks and cows' afterbirths, while combing a meadow for voles. I've had them so bold that, chasing the rooster of mine, they've slammed right into my knees. Even southern gray foxes, a slinkier, nocturnal, tree-climbing species, have recently materialized in the north country.

And turkey vultures have begun to follow the interstate north every summer to compete for carrion with our wilderness ravens and farm-field crows, which are resident all year. Ravens nest on my cliffs, driving off the crows, though they are very much shyer toward people than crows. Nor do they mob hawks and owls as boisterously as crows do. Red-tailed hawks and barred owls patrol the notch where my house is, but if I walk downhill for an hour or so to the swamps along Willoughby Lake, I will see red-shouldered hawks instead, or hear the five-hoot tattoo of a great horned owl at dusk.

Though the trout-fishing will probably never equal the prodigality of pioneer times, the crash in fur prices has brought beaver and even otter back, while bears—an estimated two thousand inhabit Vermont's nine thousand square miles—are making out fine, fattening in derelict orchards on defunct farms and upon old-field budding aspens in early spring. One bear tried to hibernate in my hayloft, after climbing an apple tree next to the garage and biting apart a birdhouse that a mother deermouse was nesting in, after the swallows had gone south. After I repaired the box, a flying squirrel settled in.

When mice colonize my house, I can't bring in a bear to stop their scuttling, but what I'll do is catch a three-foot garter snake and insert him through a hole in the ceiling to eat the babies. During the summer, this stratagem works. In the winter an ermine moves in and does the trick. Less tractable was the problem of the porcupines that for years kept chewing on the floor of my garage in their hunger for salt. Fishers had preyed on porcupines on the frontier, as martens had preyed on red squirrels, but the fishers and martens had been trapped out. The martens' demise was a boon to goshawks, Cooper's hawks, horned owls, bobcats and other enterprising hunters that can grab a quick squirrel. But the porcupines, equipped with quills, had no such effective secondary enemies, at least after country people stopped eating them (and squirrels), around the 1950s. In 1957, the state of Vermont, responding to complaints, started to release the nucleus of a new population of fishers, one hundred and twenty-four, acquired from Maine. One site happened to be close to my house, and quite soon I began finding porcupine skins inside-up on the ground and picked clean, until their numbers were in reasonable balance again.

Fishers, like bears and beavers, in taking to civilization, have spread through New England, prompting the recent reintroduction of sixty martens, too, in central Vermont. Vermont alone has perhaps one hundred thousand deer; and wild turkeys, reintroduced to the state in 1969, are nearly all over—so that, altogether, the New England region is richer in wildlife than when Henry Thoreau was writing *Walden* one hundred fifty years ago. There are exceptions, of course. Loons (which require an undisturbed lake to nest on), wood turtles (which frequently try to cross roads), warblers and other songbirds that winter in Latin American rain forests, are stymied and gradually vanishing, even as more protean actors elbow in. The busy coyote, which has migrated east through Ontario from the prairie Midwest in the past forty years, eating house cats, road kills, wild grapes, leopard frogs, coon pups and whatnot, may be the most notable of these. Though the settlers killed off the wolves and "catamounts" (mountain lions), they didn't shut off the future need for a middle-sized predator, and the "brush wolf" or "trickster" of nineteenth-century lore turns out to fill the bill.

Flux itself is balance of a kind, and along my stream, which feeds eventually into Lake Memphremagog and the St. Lawrence River, the local pack of coyotes has thrown the foxes and bobcats into a tizzy: Coyotes will kill and eat grown foxes (as they did the cocker spaniel next door), so the foxes simply withdraw from our mountain notch in years when I hear the coyotes' flamboyant howls. The coyotes also answer my harmonica, and may sneak into the garage and drag a twenty-five-pound sack of dog food into the woods. They search the stream bank for fishermen's discards, flush and leap high for a woodcock, then eat its eggs, or discover a fawn. They can't kill a bobcat, but will sweep through in January and devour the bobcat's hoarded winter larder, creating a very grim situation for the bobcat. Being as versatile as African jackals, coyotes prosper in the tracks of humans in the way that jackals follow lions—and we're doing better than lions.

In the years when coyotes den on the mountains above, my fields aren't scoured for meadow mice as thoroughly as they would be if the foxes were at work. Coyotes range farther out, so there is a surplus of rabbits and mice close in. Marsh hawks and red-tails then take over some of the foxes' micromanagement role, as well as owls, fluttering like gigantic butterflies in the moonlight, as I sit outside watching them and the bats. Coons, too, help take up the slack, afraid of the coyotes but at least able to scramble up a tree if they have to.

One banner noontime in August a flock of real butterflies descended upon my goldenrod—hundreds of Monarchs fattening for their autumn flight toward Mexico. Half a dozen snakes, safe from any hawk because they were next to the house, and my special garden toad who has swelled so big that no snake can swallow him, were basking in the sun. A few years before I had paid one hundred and ten dollars to have a pond bulldozed; and already a great blue heron was frogging in it; bear, moose and deer tracks marked the margins; and the sky's mysteries were reflected on the surface.

I could see all these things because I had just paid fifteen thousand dollars to have my vision restored—a cheap price for new eyes that, with plastic implants, saw as I did fifty years ago. Plastic eyes—and more wildlife running around in New England than when Thoreau was alive? Nature is complicated.

(1994)

Wild Things

In the current happy excitement about whether we may soon discover signs of primitive life on Mars, there is a weird and tragic incongruity—because at the same time we are losing dozens of more complex but unexamined species every day right here on earth, and doing little about it. And these aren't all just the proverbial varieties of beetle with which our planet is profusely endowed. Creatures such as tigers and rhinos are also disappearing, which from childhood have been part of the furniture of our minds. Indeed, they may have helped to create our minds. When you see a lion or a tiger at the zoo, you know innately that your ancestors did, too. And even if classic children's authors like Dr. Seuss and Maurice Sendak now tend to create "wild things" that are alloy animals instead of simply using the realities of a jungle, as Kipling did—Shere Khan, the tiger; Hathi, the elephant; Baloo, the bear; Kaa, the python; Bagheera, the panther—these alloy animals are surely blended from the same old veldt or jungle citizenry that shaped our imaginations to begin with and make us respond emotionally to amalgams.

I was lucky as a child because I not only had books in the house that allowed me to conceive of myself as Mowgli, Dr. Dolittle, Little

Black Sambo, and other people whose lives were intertwined with those of imaginary creatures—I knew a whole spectrum of creatures myself. Living in the country, I could read *The Wind in the Willows* and encounter real toads, moles, woodchucks, muskrats, or weasels outdoors. And in 1951, at the age of eighteen, I got a job working with real tigers, elephants, monkeys, and panthers in the menagerie of the Ringling Bros. and Barnum & Bailey Circus, crossing America for fourteen dollars a week, all I wanted to eat at the cookhouse, and half of a triple-decker bunk on the first of the three trains (seventy cars) that carried the show to the next town on its nightly hops. We didn't realize then the rarity of what we were doing: that the big circus would temporarily close in 1956 and never again perform outside under canvas, and that tigers, for instance, would become desperately endangered—their ground-up vitality used as a potion for human fertility (which the world hardly needs).

We'd arrive in each town about 4:30 A.M.; the elephants and the big top on the second train two or three hours later; and then the performers around eleven. So we were on duty in a casual fashion for sixteen hours a day, interspersed with naps, or swims if the circus lot lay alongside a river, or playing with the animals. There were twenty-four Indian elephants, led by Ruth, Babe, Jewel, Modoc, and other matriarchs, plus some ninety horses. Being allergic to hay, I didn't take care of them, but delighted in trusting my life to the beneficence of those elephants, lying near their feet in the sun or walking closely between them on errands. Instead, I was assigned to care for an old chimp and a baby orangutan, a black rhinoceros, a pygmy hippo, and a gnu, a mandrill, several mangabey monkeys, the two giraffes, and a tapir. But I yearned more especially to commune with the big cats, and eventually was apprenticed to "Chief," a Mohawk Indian, who had charge of *them*. The next summer, when I came back, I found that Chief had been clawed during the Madison Square Garden engagement, had married his nurse from the hospital and stayed there in New York. Thus I had them to myself till I went back to school.

Lions are straightforward, sociable folk, easy breeders, and blessed with a humdrum, sand-colored coat that people have not wanted to strip from them and wear on their backs. Also they're lucky enough not to share a continent with the crazy Chinese, inventing mystic applications for their pulverized bones. I had a pair of lions, a maned male and a splendid female, who patiently managed to share the cramped cage, five feet by five, that Ringling Bros. provided for them. That companionship, with their bodies overlapping, seemed to calm them so much you hardly felt sorry for them, compared to our solitary, pacing tigers. I used to sleep under the lions' cage at night, if we stayed over in a large city for other performances, both because of the protection that their paws, hanging out between the bars, afforded me from wandering muggers and for the midnight music of their roars—glorious-sounding, staccato strings of roars that they exchanged as communiqués with the circus's troupe of lions who performed in the center ring under the whip of Oscar Konyet. (He was such a high-strung man, he sometimes had to stand and whip one of the side poles for a while after his act, in order to decompress.)

Tigers are more moody and unpredictable. Unlike lions, they don't form gangs or "prides," and can't be herded in the ring by somebody who knows their group dynamics and can turn the leaders and stampede them. They're more willowy and individually explosive, and must be dealt with singly, or persuaded subtly, in a sort of time-fuse confrontation. You can apply affection, but it's more a matter of slow seduction, one-on-one in the training sequence, than just becoming pals with a bunch of fractious, energetic, snarling lions. Our resident tiger trainer was a gentlemanly Englishman, Trevor Bale—not a chair-wielder in the familiar American "fighting" style of Clyde Beatty, who tried to overpower the animals instead of drawing them out, and who Konyot was imitating. The suppler, more courteous European tradition of animal training—epitomized by Alfred Court when I was a child, and by Gunther Gebel-Williams when I was middle-aged—also had had a great American practitioner, the tiger trainer Mabel Stark, who, when I saw her in California in 1953, was a quarter century past her prime and crippled by strokes but, tottering and without the use of one of her arms, still could inveigle cooperation from a cat. I was only a cage boy, not a trainer—a dreamer, not a player—but I regarded my tigers as God's cymbals when they roared and God's paintbrush when they didn't, and though of course I thought their captivity was a kind of travesty, the idea that wild tigers might not even outlive my own life span wouldn't have occurred to me.

There was a store in downtown Manhattan I used to visit, near where the banana boats came in, that sold pythons, pangolins, parrots, ocelots, tiger cubs, leopards—what couldn't you buy? And a couple of cigar stores in Times Square displayed as a sideline shrunken human heads at a hundred bucks apiece. These were the long-haired heads of Indians killed in battle, then carefully skinned off the skull and gradually steamed down to about the size of an eating-orange and stuffed to assume the proper physiognomy by Jivaro tribesmen in Ecuador, which sailors brought in from Guayaquil (though you wondered whether the middlemen weren't putting in an occasional order for more killings for the gringo market).

For all the looting of the earth's wild places, there seemed to be no end to them. The *National Geographic*, and "Bring 'em back alive" Frank Buck, and my own aspirations to be an explorer said so. My first elephant ride had been at Frank Buck's compound at the New York World's Fair in 1939, indeed. And I remember how little fuss was made one May, in 1953 or 1954, when I went backstage at the circus during its performances in Boston and two little baby tigers had just died, caged with their mother. The bosses were sorry about it (as about the cagehand who was lying in a pile of straw on the cement floor with high-fever pneumonia), but there was no sense of a significant financial or gene-pool loss. On the books—I notice from the circus's archives from the early 1950s—adult tigers were carried at a valuation of only about eleven hundred dollars apiece; a polar bear, twelve hundred; a sun bear, two hundred. Chimpanzees were about six hundred dollars; orangutans about two thousand; and "Toto," the star-attraction gorilla, ninety-eight hundred. Giraffes were worth twenty-two hundred; cheetahs, a thousand.

Most of our cages were old army ammunition wagons from World War II, eleven feet long and partitioned so that, for instance, the two lions were housed with an enormous yolk-yellow, black-striped male Bengal tiger who must have weighed a quarter of a ton. In the tiny space allotted to him, he ignored the two lions on the other side of the dividing screen and seemed the very picture of dignified placidity, with regard to caretakers like me. Though the lions didn't ask for trouble, sprawling over each other's legs in their claustrophobic cage, they were plainly prepared to shred anybody who reached inside. They bristled and snarled like furniture scraping a floor, their handsome lips contorting into gigantic peach pits, if you had to disturb them while cleaning their cage with the long iron rod that pulled the dung out. But the tiger just lay on exhibit, stuffed unjustly into his narrow box, with an extraordinary tranquillity that was much more seductive than the bluff normalcy of the other two. In his peacefulness, he was cryptic, like a hostage king. You felt sorry for him, yet respectful: including the new workhands who had just joined the circus because they were hungry (gulping that first meal down) and wanted to sneak out of their town. And one of these neophytes, showing off for the townie girls after the afternoon show, perhaps after prodding old Joe, the ruddy-maned lion, to roar, might move the few feet on to silent, watchful Rajah, Joe's still bigger counterpart in the adjacent cage, and instead of tormenting him, might tentatively begin to pet that beautiful black-and-yellow coat through the bars, which were spaced wide enough to get even your elbow through. And—about once a year—when that young man, half-soused, did so, while the girls oohed and aahed, Rajah would wait till the hand moved up past his ribs to his magnificent shoulder, then whirl in a flash and grab and crunch it, pull the arm all the way in, rip it out of its socket and claw it entirely off.

This is not the place to itemize all the other mishaps that might befall a fourteen-dollar-a-week man, crushed by a wagon that rolled over him on the lot or tumbling off the circus train en route to somewhere at night, never to reappear. But his stump would be sewn up and he'd get a free night in the hospital, then be put on a Greyhound bus for wherever his home was, still howling in agony at every jounce.

We used to scratch the rhino's itchy cheeks, and the jaguar's risky flank, the cheetah's reluctant scalp, the hippo's willing tongue, and the four leopards' luxurious coats. It was complicated fun. Bobby, the rhino, for example, wouldn't have deliberately hurt somebody, but he didn't know his own strength when playful—or particularly care— and might inadvertently have crushed an arm against the bars in lurching about. For him, as for Chester, the large hippo (Betty Lou,

141

the pygmy hippo, was rather unfriendly), who gaped his huge maw so that you could stick your hand in and scratch his tongue and the walls of his mouth, it was a natural procedure, akin to how the tickbirds along the Nile would have searched both their bodies for parasites. The cheetah, by contrast, growled softly, if touched—didn't like it, but probably wouldn't bite—whereas the jaguar objected with a mild rumble, and undoubtedly would have if he could have done so without bestirring himself. He was a frank, solitary animal, like the tigers but less complex than them, and a night roarer like the lions, but less bold and various in how he emitted his messages, maybe because he had no other jaguars to answer him. He was penned in a cage three and a half feet in width, alongside the cheetah's pathetically similar space (the fastest animal on earth!), with a Siberian tiger confined in the third compartment of the wagon who appeared to have gone quite mad, he was such a coiled spring of rage. Whereas the two giraffes, Edith and Boston, leaned down and licked the salt on my sweaty cheeks every hot day, the Siberian would have minced me, as he tirelessly made plain.

I believed at this point in my life that no man was complete without a parrot on his shoulder, or at least a boa constrictor looped partly over him like a friend's arm. I wasn't one of these people who think it necessary to choose between cats and dogs. I liked them both; and when I say that tigers were my first love, I mean simply sexually. I was a bad stutterer, still a virgin, could scarcely talk to other people, and felt at home in the circus partly because aberrancies were no big deal there. And we had two great big orange females compartmented in the two halves of an eleven-foot ordnance wagon who regularly, when they were in heat, presented their vulvas to me to be rubbed. So, standing at chest level with the floor of the cage, I used to reach in and gingerly do it; Chief had showed me how. And there was an ex-con who, like so many other hoboes, had materialized one day in Ohio, worked a little while, and then vanished in Indiana. The idea that caged creatures need some solace came naturally to him. He even rubbed the old chimp's penis. What's now called "homophobia" was not a problem for him. I was bothered by that, but also by the fact that the chimpanzee was infinitely stronger than me and very disgruntled—being, after all, an individual who had been raised closely with people to perform as a cute baby in the center ring, and then abandoned to solitary confinement when he outgrew his childhood. Though he was lucky, in fact, not to have been sold for experimentation like the rest, he didn't know that, and I thought I fathomed his resentment clearly enough to steer clear of his hands and teeth, which you would be at the mercy of while masturbating him. But this fiftyish guy just out of jail went to the cage and talked to him sympathetically, when he happened to be working nearby, and reached in and massaged him a bit, like you might ease the nerves of a murderer and be in no danger, nor even ask for a cigarette in exchange afterward.

The white-ruffed, orange-and-black lady tigers, however, needed to come to the bars and swing around, squat down, and present their hind ends to be rubbed, which meant that, unlike the chimp, they weren't in a position to grab me—their mouths faced away. Then the one I was doing would stand (the other tiger in the meantime observing edgily), pace off and turn and come back and try to kill me, swiping downward with one tremendous paw extended through the bars and a roar like the crack of a landslide, bringing tears to my eyes. Knowing what was coming, I liked to step back just far enough that her paw missed me but the wind of it made my hair hop on my head, and her open mouth three feet away ended up in a deliciously subliminal snarl that she could ratchet up to motorcycle volume if she wished to. The other tiger might share her agitation briefly and chime in, and Rajah wheeled and sprayed pee around, scent-marking the ground outside of *his* cage.

Yet this was not much more furor than when tigers mate naturally. Soon she would return and squat for me to put my fingers into her vagina again; then maybe roar, swipe at me, and come to the water pan peaceably, when I slid it under the bars for her to drink from at her leisure, while I watched without giving offense, close by. I'd talk to her in her own language by making a soft chuffing sound, blowing air past my lower lip, and she answered, as zoo tigers also would, in New York or wherever I went, as long as I kept in practice. Because the secret lies in relaxing the lips, it's the opposite of a trumpeter's embouchure.

Intimacy; and I believed that I had a sixth sense. Another year, at Mabel Stark's little zoo in southern California, I climbed into a mountain lion's cage. She was another female in heat whom I had been petting through the bars. She bounded at me immediately, thrusting her paw straight into my face like a muff, but keeping her claws withdrawn.

Our four leopards—during my circus years—were utter beauties, hand-raised by the veterinarian's wife. She was an aerialist, bold, supple and strong, with white skin and black wavy hair that hung to her hips. All four loved caresses, especially Sweetheart, who was the handsomest leopard I have ever seen, with a splendid, white, breastly undercarriage and a rich, dazzling top coat, like camouflage for an empress—the mother of the rest. With her, you didn't have to be gingerly. You could simply donate your arms to her and push your face against the bars while she crouched over them, licking them like long hunks of meat with her thrillingly abrasive tongue, or else twitched her tail and purred like steady thunder as her stiff-napped, Oriental-carpet back was being scratched. Her two grown daughters milled and whirled over and about my arms and next to my face, as swift and electric as four-foot fish—the tails an extra length, lolloping up and down like puppets. The daughters purred also; and the yearling male, who was unrulier because he was beginning to shed the docility his kittenhood had trained him to, would vault around and sometimes seize my hand in his teeth and pull it as far into the cage as it would reach, without breaking my skin, but pressing down threateningly if I resisted him. Then when he had my arm under control, he flipped over on his back underneath it and in mock fashion "disemboweled" it, as if it were a gazelle that he had caught by the throat, with all four paws bicycling upward against the flesh. But instead of destroying my arm, just like that mountain lion in California, he kept his claws in.

In East Africa, as a tourist, you watch lions from the safety of a well-roofed Land Rover, comprehending, nevertheless, as soon as a lioness stalks toward you, why early people invented spears. And you grieve for the thoughtful-looking, suffering elephants existing in shattered little herds, who have obviously witnessed so many other elephants being butchered for their ivory. Safaris are a well-oiled industry, tooled for an ever-shrinking theater of operations, but you need to reach into your mind's eye for the kind of intimations of our origins that came much more easily in Africa even twenty years ago.

When I went to southern India—flying from Nairobi to Bombay, and taking an overnight sleeper from there to Madras, in 1993—I found that wildlife viewing, like everything else, was very different in this vast disorganized democracy. As in Africa, the remnant wilderness preserves were shrinking, were strangling really, and the larger beleaguered animals knew it. But the crush and kaleidoscope of people was unlike anything I was used to. Yet it did not involve mass anarchy and the collapse of tribal certainties, or cruel politics and looming starvation, like Africa's. Democracy is invigorating.

Forty years had passed since I had been a mute young man who could speak freely only to animals and had played with Ringling Bros.' elephants and tigers. Yet though I had become more interested in people, I was still typecast as a nature writer from that early handicap and sent off to wild places to pursue old loves. In Bombay, Madras, and the newly industrial city of Coimbatore, I was lingering and lagging to walk the raucous, prismatic, mysterious streets, thereby disrupting the schedule of my local handlers, who wanted me out of town and up in the mountain scenery as soon as possible, where they hoped to make money from my visit. They were travel agents—Air India had given me a free plane ticket on the assumption that I would go up into the Nilgiri Hills and write about sambars and sloth bears, tigers and tahrs. If I publicized the ecotours they were projecting, they figured that lots of rich Americans might follow me and they could accomplish what they each aspired to do, which, because they were young men, was either to pay for a marriage to a Brahman or else fly to California and go hang-gliding in the Sierras.

I was a laggard because I loved Madras, for example, and walked or rickshawed in the streets all day, then explored the huge iridescent crescent beach in the moonlight (though was startled to find the unmarked graves of a few of the city's destitute underfoot at the duneline). Like Bombay, Madras was a far less berserk, vertiginous city than the African ones that I was familiar with. Religion, and democracy, too, were the glue. People believed in their gods and their souls, and had the hope of the ballot. They weren't going to crack me on the head just for a chance at my wallet. Indeed, in New York, a dead pauper fares much worse than an anonymous burial on that immortal great beach, with ridley sea turtles climbing out of the waves to lay their eggs next to you. I found a new hatchling scrimshawing the sand, and helped it into the sea.

The train out of Madras I'd been supposed to be on derailed into a ravine. We went by its wreckage and stopped for three passengers with broken arms. (In Kenya, a train two days *after* the one I was on had crashed off a bridge into a river, with numerous deaths.) And from Coimbatore we drove to the towns of Pollachi and Anaimalai and up into the Anaimalai Hills to a high old British logging camp called Top Slip because the teakwood and rosewood had been slid downhill from there, but which is now the Indira Gandhi Wildlife Sanctuary, though with the aid of elephants it's still being partially logged. The hushed, handsome, rising and plunging forest had a panoply of birds—golden orioles, scarlet minivets, racquet-tailed drongos, pretty "dollar birds," and crow pheasants, green barbets, blue-winged parakeets, blossom-headed woodpeckers, and mynah birds. We saw these, and tahrs (an endangered wild goat) and sambars (a large dark form of deer), big bison, and wild boars, a black-and-white porcupine, mongooses and civets, green parrots, magpies, hoopoes, hornbills, plentiful chital deer, red with white spots, and flamboyantly plumaged jungle fowl, langur monkeys, macaques, mouse-deer holes, and a nine-colored pitta bird.

I was traveling at this stage with Salim, a young university-educated Shiite Muslim from Madras. His father was a travel agent posted to Abu Dhabi, his mother a Hindu, his early schooling Catholic. His first language had been English because his father otherwise spoke Urdu. Our local guide, Sabrimathu, was about seventy years old and what is called in India a "tribal," meaning from one of the fragile indigenous tribes, the Kadar. Despite a few protections the government gives them (analogous to the position of American Indians), they tend to miss the British when you talk to them, because the British praised and encouraged their tracking skills. In the present money or bureaucratic economy, with a seething agglomeration of

subcontinental humanity everywhere, they are at best an after-
thought, like an eccentric, illiterate great-uncle in a ragged dhoti marooned in the attic. Sabrimathu carried a little sack of tobacco leaves
to chew, and a bush knife; and like the British, I was delighted to listen to him communicate with another Kadar man on the opposite
hillside by means of langur barks, regarding the whereabouts of a
dozen elephants we were following. We broke off hastily when the
other man let us know they had a baby with them.

Originally, Sabrimathu said, two peoples had inhabited these high
woods. The Kadar carried spears and lived by gathering small creatures and forest plants, or scavenging from red-dog (dhole) kills, if
they could surround the pack and drive them off. With brands from a
campfire as weapons and windfall shelters, they could coexist with
the forest's tigers and also the bison, which are like the African buffalo. But there was no way to stand up to the elephants. They'd had
to hide, run and hide, abandon any permanent settlement that the
elephants approached. The other tribe, the Kurumbas, used bows
and arrows to hunt with, shooting birds out of the trees for food and
skirmishing with Sabrimathu's group, whose language they didn't
speak. They, too, fled the elephants when a playful herd or a rogue
bull in "musth" rampaged through, but feared the teak loggers and
the British more, and so vanished north.

Sabrimathu's group numbers only a few hundred now, in ten or
fifteen tiny communities of thatch huts, on this rugged borderland
between the Cochin district of the state of Kerala and Tamil Nadu,
where I'd come from. He had a confiding face, unkempt gray hair, a
woodsman's elastic sense of time, and a blurry sort of shuffling manner by which he tried to elide and conceal his feelings when supervisors and clerks condescended to him. Of course, on the contrary, I was
all ears, like the British naturalists and tiger hunters who had formerly
employed his skills, or the World Wildlife Fund researcher he said
he'd caught a long python for and put it in a burlap sack. He pointed
up a forest stream to where the pythons bred; and later pointed at a
knot of crags under a cliff of the Perunkundru Hills, where a leopard
mother retreated each year to bear her kits; and to a distant thicket of
sidehill evergreens where a tiger generally did the same. Up on a bare

saddle of scree, a bit of footpath was visible where he had met a tiger coming toward him—that situation where, he said, you "just stand still and see whether your time has come." It hadn't, though once a tiger jumped at him in the underbrush when he was helping a forestry official track a man-eater. It missed. He was injured another time, when he surprised a bison on a narrow trail and it charged and knocked him out and horned his arm; he showed me the scars, healed by forest medicines.

The British had naturally encouraged the Kadar people to become the mahouts here, capturing and training the local wild elephants—which they tentatively did, overcoming their age-old fears. I remember hearing, in northern Canada and Alaska, how the New World Indians at first had been unsatisfactory guides on grizzly-hunting expeditions because even though they might be wizards at tracking grizzlies, having practiced for thousands of years equipped with "stone-age" weapons, their purpose in doing so was mainly to avoid the beasts. They were so fearful that newcomers—white bullyboys with fat-caliber rifles—still made fun of them. But here, in this other kind of devouring, homogenizing democracy, it was not the raj or later visiting whites but other Indians who made difficulties. And about twenty years after independence, Sabrimathu's remnant tribe, so fragile anyway in the new India, had been ousted from their livelihood as elephant handlers by a new people: cattle herders, more adaptable and sophisticated, the Pulasaris, who came up from the plains—at first two families, then more. After apprenticing with the Kadar, the Pulasaris had finagled or genuinely convinced the authorities that they would be better at doing it.

We stopped at their camp, located beside a boisterous small river, the Varagalear, in a cut between hills in the deep lovely woods, where they earn about sixty dollars a month, three times a laborer's wage, for working a dozen elephants. We arrived in the evening as the usurpers were finishing washing the beasts, and they jeered at poor Sabrimathu's chagrin as they showed us a five-year-old they were training to blow on a harmonica, lift one of her feet with her trunk, and cover one eye with her ear. She lay down in the swirling warm stream with only her trunk raised above the current to breathe, while the foreman washed her tusks, lips, and eyelids. The others were not as tame, and after being watered, washed, and fed, were chained for the night, though the wild herd kept close tabs on them from nearby and sometimes came down in the night and mingled with them.

The several families of interlopers had small children, and it was idyllic, with the foaming creek and the rushing wind in the trees, miles from another human sound, yet protected from any wandering tiger by the throng of elephants, swaying on their rhythmic feet and swinging their idiosyncratic trunks to private tempos. I remembered feeling this safe in the circus, sleeping under the big cats' cages, knowing that any mugger who crept up on me would provoke a roar that would stop his heart, or if he swung a little wide in the dark, he'd encounter the row of elephants, who would step on him.

Naturally I wanted to see a tiger, though there wasn't much chance of that. We drove to a few overlooks where they occasionally were sighted on a beach of the stream below, but didn't walk anywhere after dark. An old Kadar man with prostate problems had been seized in Sabrimathu's little hamlet the year before, when he needed to pee in the middle of the night and left his hut. But the same villagers went out in the woods every day, gathering teak seeds from the forest floor to sell, or honey and beeswax from clefts in cliffs and hollow trees, or sago, cardamom, ginger. Or they collected soap nuts for making shampoo, or guided the Forestry Service men on inspection tours, in order to obtain the rice that had become their new staff of life and didn't grow here. They also used to catch civets for the perfume industry, and had guided tiger-rug hunters, but these latter ventures were now illegal and what poaching went on was done by gangs of in-and-out thugs with connections to outside smugglers, not by naive tribal people. Sabrimathu reminded me of various aged Eskimos, American Indians, and African subsistence hunters I've met too briefly over the years, who, like him, knew a thousand specifics no one will know at all when they are gone, though nobody they had any contact with seemed to care much now about what they knew. They too lived wind-scented, sunlit, star-soaked, spirit-shot lives. Humble on one level, proud on another, Sabrimathu was vulnerable to exploitation and insult partly just because he was so tactile and open to

everything else. Like those millions of American Indians who disappeared way before their time, he was rooted in place. He could be
chopped like a tree or shot like a songbird.

Early on our last day at Top Slip, I woke Salim—my young travel-
agent, biology-major, Muslim-Hindu-Christian escort—and told him
I'd like to go on a bird walk. Amenable though sleepy, he drove me
ten miles downhill through the woods to Thunnakadu Reservoir,
which is a pretty lake that was created in 1967 and looks perhaps four
miles long. The valley it drowned is also lovely, set between protected bands of forest highlands of the Cardomon Hills and flowing
toward the Malabar coastline on the Arabian Sea. The road we traveled gets only one bus a day, and at the lake there was no settlement
at all except half a dozen wooden cabins for the road crew. They were
still asleep, so we simply walked across the top of the dam to the wild
side of the lake, as the fragrant, misty blues of dawn were broken by
the strong-slanting yellow sun. Cormorants and kingfishers were
diving, and pond herons prowling the bank, and we saw a fishing
eagle. There was a bamboo raft tied ashore, of the sort the Kadar use
to go angling for arm-length larder fish that they can dry. Salim's
knowledge of the birds we heard and saw was that of a practical-
minded young man of many interests. He was impatient with India's
religious sectarianism, and rather favorable toward the social changes
that the brave women's movement in big cities such as Madras were
aiming for. He'd traveled some, and wanted to travel more, and so the
antiquarian curiosity that foreign tourists like me displayed was not of
much interest to him. He said, for instance, when I asked, that, yes,
Gandhi's example was still remembered in India, not ignored, but not
followed either. A modern capitalist, commonsense democracy was
what he wanted, with money, decency, mobility.

We walked and chatted on a footpath along the lake, while red-
wattled lapwings, the "policemen of the forest," kept noisy watch
over our progress, along with several "babblers," the "seven sisters"
birds, so called because they always move in a group. A big Brahminy
kite, white-headed but otherwise a beautiful orangey brown, was
being hassled by a bunch of crows above the trees, much as birds of
prey are in the United States. We saw a leopard's precise tracks, and

then a largish tiger's sprawling pugs, and four bear feces, berry-filled, in different stages of drying out, as if this path was a thoroughfare. Though Salim had never seen a leopard or a tiger, he was in favor of turning back, yet not insistently so. There was no disputing what we were looking at—the tiger and the bear could have been nothing else—yet, after all, we could have expected that these animals would come down to drink and forage a bit at night, before climbing the bluff behind the lake again.

Overhead, a troop of langur monkeys swinging in the branches had begun to whoop the alarm. It had been quiet except for the bird calls at dawn and sunrise and a few magpie and lapwing minatory cries. But entering this neck of the woods provoked a monkey cacophony, a real hollering that seemed part fearful bark or howl and part self-important fun—a rather gay razzing once they were accustomed to us and had done their primary job. We continued our stroll for another quarter mile, occasioning lots of hubbub because each marginal youngster had to prove that he knew his duty too, not just the sentinels and the leaders. But then there was an added note, deeper in pitch, exasperated and abrupt. The langurs' hullabaloo at first had masked it, or the fact that with our presence so much advertised, we had now felt free to gab in normal tones, and therefore heard the gravelly, landslide-sounding rumble a little ahead of us as just perhaps some sort of patriarchal intervention from within the monkey clan—not superimposed.

We kept walking. It was repeated. Not only bigger lungs and a lower pitch: The temper of the roar was totally different, like a combat colonel interrupting the chatter of a bunch of hyperexcited privates. Rajah had roared horrendously at me a few times when I had been hosing his cage or cleaning it with the long iron rod and had bumped him inadvertently. And from a distance of forty years, those capsizing blasts reverberated for me.

"That's not a monkey!" Salim and I said simultaneously. Then, in about the time that a double-take takes, "Isn't that a tiger?" We each nodded and smiled—then after three or four steps, stopped in our tracks. The lake was on our left and the woods extended to the bluff, a few hundred feet high to the right, which was one reason why a nettled tiger, too, might feel he had been hemmed in. That he had roared at us, instead of waiting silently in the undergrowth beside the trail to simply kill us, was a good sign. On the other hand, he could have withdrawn up the valley, or a hundred yards to the side, without our ever knowing about him. He or she was obviously not doing that. Was he lying on a kill? Or was she a lady with some half-grown cubs? The roars, instead of ceasing when we turned around and started walking back toward the area of the dam, now redoubled in exasperation, as if the tiger, like the two caged females I'd masturbated in the circus, had flown into a sudden, unreasonable rage. Furthermore (from the volume and tone, I guessed he was male), he was now paralleling us, maybe forty or fifty yards in—not visible, but roaring repeatedly, not letting us depart without a terrific chastening. He could have cut us off and mauled us, or driven us into the lake, but didn't; and eventually we met four Kadar men in dhotis who were collecting teak seeds and told them about him. Like us, they turned around immediately and fled at an inconspicuously quick scuttle.

The crew chief, when we got back to the road, said in Tamil to Salim, "Oh, you shouldn't have gone there. That side of the lake is where the tiger lives." The estimate of the wildlife warden at headquarters was a census of thirty-five in these seven hundred square miles.

Being a fan of adages such as "a stitch in time," "an apple a day," "turnabout is fair play" or "what goes around comes around," I was pleased by the symmetry of an old tiger cageboy like me who had tried to be superkind being spared in India forty years later. As in grizzly country, I was glad, too, that it was still possible to experience a fright from a wilderness creature. In this Tamil Nadu region in 1993, one didn't hear talk yet of tigers being poached for the Chinese aphrodisiac market—only elephants for their tusks and sandalwood for its scented properties. But there are close to a billion people in India, and scarcely two thousand tigers. And since Indira Gandhi had decided that tigers ought to be protected, a number of generations have grown up that are less afraid of people, at the same time as the territory available for them to roam in is being constricted from every side. Like grizzlies, the point about tigers is that from our standpoint they are unpredictable. They fly off the handle when pressured, and need more than just a specified number of square miles to provide a food source or enough prey animals. Like the Kadar, they are elastic in their sense of time. They need space for their whims and passions and shifts of emotions. They weave more as they walk.

An Australian orthopedist had turned up at Top Slip after lecturing at a conference in Coimbatore, instructing the local doctors in how to handle broken backs—a commonplace where people climb coconut trees. But the hospitals were full of people with lung ailments from the dust that was everywhere, he said, or who'd gotten busted in road crashes.

We drove back down from these rosewood, teak, and tamarind forests to Anaimalai and Pollachi, and then to Mettuppalaiyam, in several hours of the wildest riding I've ever experienced. It's a nation where huge painted diesel lorries and long blue buses careen at dizzying speed past countless oxcarts, hundreds of bicyclists, and thousands of pedestrians on jerry-built highways through continuous strings of makeshift villages. Not, however, merely like Africa, because of this quintupled congestion of people walking and crossing against the tenfold vehicular and animal traffic: cattle, goats, donkeys, and camels, jalopies, pickups, taxi-vans, swarming scooters, mopeds, occasional tractors, and hosts of schoolchildren, urchins, waifs, toddlers, and folks struggling on canes and crutches. And it's not so much that you fear dying (that the bullock with red-painted horns, struck broadside, will do you in) as that some of these confident, innocent citizens going about their business—hour by hour, more individual humanity in puce and aquamarine saris at instant risk than you have seen anywhere else in the world—are going to get smashed up into the air or crushed under the tires. Little unattended kids, grumpy old men strutting along because of their back and leg ailments, mammas shopping purposefully for beans and sunflower seeds from vociferous peddlers, customers at stand-up tea shops half-forced out in the traffic, or wedding parties at colorful, compact temples of stone and plaster likewise spilling outside. The many schoolyards debouched into the street, plus dozens of markets constructed of stucco and low-slung canvas. And many people, to save rupees, were walking for miles with only a rudimentary familiarity with the dangers that motor vehicles can pose. Nor were the drivers' skills uniform. Obtaining a license was not so much taking a test as paying a bribe, and the road often whittled down to a single lane.

We whizzed along at velocities approaching airplane speed, with corkscrew, brake-slamming maneuvers, for several hours, stopping one time for rice, fried fish, and tea; then slept overnight in Mettuppalaiyam at a hotel with fleas, before boarding a narrow-gauge railway train in the dark of the morning to go thirty miles up to the resort town of Udagamandalam, or "Ooty," as it's called, where British colonials are said to have invented snooker at the Ooty Club. Mettuppalaiyam, though, is a paper-company city where a siren awoke everybody at 6 A.M. for the shift change—eucalyptus plantations all around provide the pulp.

Nevertheless, the clip-clop of steel-shod oxen on the pavement was constant; and the all-night, dimly lurid-looking orange neon lighting was reminiscent of the 1930s in America. So was the hunger. Whereas in Africa I had seen people who were literally starving to skin and bones (and other people knocked dead on the highway in much sparser traffic because they were even less used to cars), the hunger that I saw in India, whether in Bombay, Madras, Coimbatore, or Mettuppalaiyam, was like missed-meals nutrition during the Depression in America. As I waited for this train, for instance, I was eating a banana on the platform. I'd half-finished it when a group of schoolgirls came along, perhaps twelve years old, neatly dressed in their uniforms. They looked presentable, conventional, not "untouchable," and one, a bit more confident, reached out tentatively toward my banana. "May I?" When of course I handed it to her, she immediately wolfed it down, as two other girls tried to grab it away. It may have been her only breakfast, but in Africa I had seen girls and boys of the same age in rags in a war zone who hadn't eaten in a couple of weeks. And in America in the 1990s, by contrast, if you offered a half-eaten banana to a beggar on the street, you might be wiping spittle off your face.

The vegetarian politeness and busy energies of so many of India's famous personalities make the place seem more channeled than it actually is. One forgot that both Indira Gandhi, and then her son Rajiv Gandhi, when he took over the prime ministership, had been assassinated—the latter near Madras in 1991; I visited the spot—not to mention *the* Gandhi, before that. And when I'd arrived at Bombay's airport, I didn't realize that an estimated four thousand people, primarily Muslims, had recently been killed in sectarian rioting in that city alone. I was apprehensive enough to be landing alone with no reservations in a strange country at 3 A.M., but noticed my Sikh taxi driver was semihysterical. It turned out that he'd been waiting at the airport for nineteen hours for a fare, and this because it was the safest place to hide. All of the Sikh or Muslim cabbies, he said, had fled there. Yet I soon went around to visit the hanging gardens, a Jain temple, Mahatma Gandhi's house, the Prince of Wales Museum, the aquarium with triggerfish and eagle rays, the island of the Elephant Caves, the monumental arched Gateway of India that the British built in 1927 at the port, and other stuff, like any charmed-life tourist.

Ooty is up at 7,500 feet, twice as high as Top Slip, and by paying a couple of dollars in baksheesh I got to ride in the little blue-and-red, coal-fired engine with a gazelle painted on the side that was pushing the ramshackle five-car train. We rode through sugarcane and rice fields and mango-fruit and betel-nut plantations; saw mushroom farms and truck gardens for carrots, beans, and potatoes, plus coffee and cinchona (quinine) production. The engine gripped the grades, belching white steam and black smoke (*I-think-I-can, I-think-I-can*). Roses bloomed in the cuts, between dark tunnels and white cataracts. We had trekkers from Europe doing their walkabouts, and a bunch of army recruits whom we dropped at a training base at Wellington halfway up, and two elderly Canadians. The man, a civil engineer in far-off spots like this, had never married till his sixties, but had once adopted four orphans as foster children here, and was now revisiting them all to see if they belonged in his will, as he told me later at the Southern Star Hotel.

I-thought-I-could, I-thought-I-could, the little cog train began to say. The fireman dropped off lumps of coal for poor women (I assumed, unless they were his relatives) who gathered at hidden nooks along our route. The coffee fields had been lower down. At cooler altitudes were green-tea plantations, for which the Nilgiris, or Blue Hills, are famous. But there were also long green ravines and thickly forested tangents extending down the mountainside that contained fragments of the holy forest of original wild vegetation, as complex as Creation, that are called *sholas* and preserve God's own infinitely harmonious unruliness. At least in southern India, when you visit a temple you may find parrots nesting in the walls, monkeys perched on the turrets, and a cobra coiled in the quietest of the recesses. Similarly, an uncut forest is regarded as having some magic, perhaps a reservoir of the godhead. It is going to get cut, but it is also loved.

Ooty, "Queen of the Hill Stations," is a spacious, vaguely rakish, prosperous little city with film and fertilizer factories, assorted tasty eateries, and shops and hotels. Too quickly, we left in a 1977 Willys Jeep named Theena on a drive of several bumpy hours to an isolated trekkers' cabin at Mukkurthi Reservoir, because my mission, courtesy of the Indian government, was still to see some wild places. Salim, my dark-browed, acned, saturnine, big-featured, practical-minded, Shiite-Hindu-Christian, biology-major guide from the metropolis of Madras had handed me over to a new guy. Habib was a sunnier Ooty man from a tea-growing family, with a business degree. He was a Sunni Muslim who loved to hike and hang-glide, as well as the good life otherwise, and hoped that whatever I wrote would draw enough Californians to Ooty that he could use his money from "inbound tourism" to enable him to travel to California himself, where he wanted to hang out in the Bay Area just as much as an American might wish to come here. Habib was a handsome outdoorsman with an eye for the majesty of nature, a curiosity about history, and sympathy for the aboriginal peoples still left around. Like Salim—who was linked a bit with university life in Madras, and had put me in touch with a few of its activist idealists, without wishing to be one—Habib was quite an interesting man. In fact, he'd deserted his middle-class background and gone off to live in a three-family village of Toda herdsmen in a place called Parson's Valley, after falling in love with a Toda girl, for half a year. On one of his hikes last month, he had crouched in a hollow and watched two mating tigers climb past him toward these high grass hills where we were now—the epitome of harassed, focused wildness, he said, though splendidly colored—red, white, black, orange, and yellow.

And the national Electricity Board had caused half a dozen finger lakes to be created for hydroelectric purposes, supplying power plants downriver at Paikara. Overlogging and a drought had then scoured and eroded the slopes brown. But small ragged crews of men, camped in lean-tos, were replanting, putting in fast-growing acacia seedlings that could be cut for firewood or wattles for hut-building to truck to the city in a few years. (You *must* believe that human beings are a good idea to like India. Everything is people, people, people, but without the vaunting religious assumptions of human superiority of the West.)

I walked several miles at sunrise, encountering fifteen gray-black bison coming off the mountain for a morning drink, before I turned back. We rightly feared each other; I'm sure my heart beat just as fast as theirs. At intervals, a winding creekbed a hundred yards wide had been permitted to keep its tall, tangled *shola* trees and undergrowth, and this is where the whooping black monkeys that I now heard and other wildlife hid—the deer, the elephants, the "white panthers," and "black panthers" that the caretaker at our cabin, Gopal, and his wife, Agniesh, described. They were old folk from Mysore who had gone north and worked at a hotel at the Taj Mahal for a while, being used to Europeans, but had returned here, where thirty years ago Gopal had guided British hunters on horseback after tigers, elephants, tahr, bison, sambar, and chital, with a pack of thirty-six hounds specially trained for the pursuit of different quarry. He was paid a hundred rupees whenever they killed a tiger, at a time when a laborer's monthly wage was fifteen rupees. Now he just watches through the window when a tiger strides by on the jeep track outside and, if it's rutting, stops and paces and sprays pee and chuffs at him. His young son, Aiyappan (named for a god who can take human form), walks back and forth to Ooty every week to school. This is, incidentally, the territory where the children's story *Little Black Sambo* was written.

We gave Aiyappan a lift. The rolling landscape, even largely stripped of trees, retained an exhilarating sweep way off to the far horizon, where the biggest mountaintop still represented the Todas' afterlife, Habib said, a site where the living tribespeople make an effort to visit the spirits of their ancestors at certain intervals—though like all their less convenient customs, this one was under siege. Not many Todas were still observant enough to undertake a hundred-mile walk for such an ancient purpose. But just the lunging terrain can seem to speak exultantly at a distance, as it goes sailing over lakes, blue gulfs, and mystery forests, up toward the drifting clouds.

It was Sunday. Back in Ooty, the cart horses had been turned loose for the day. The week's washing was spread in Brobdingnagian proportions across a whole vacant field near the public faucets, and the roadside tea houses were cheerfully crowded. A Communist hammer and sickle had been chalked on one of the buildings. A little beyond that, a dozen green quarter-moon flags were flying from a tin hovel, alongside a loudspeaker horn for praising Allah. Further on, nestled in a lusher garden, stood a Hindu temple decorated with a sculpture of Ganesha, the elephant-headed, pot-bellied god, riding on a rat, and other emblems and effigies. We drove to the top of Dodabetta, at 8,700 feet the highest mountain in the Nilgiris. It's cold and bouldery and wild up there in spite of the excursion road that has been built, and formidable creatures like leopards and tigers come out at night—though one might repeat that in this part of India, nature shares at least symbolic full citizenship with humanity. Each may be mistreated, but people are part of nature, not a biblically sanctioned master race.

Habib said his Toda girlfriend had married another man after he broke up with her. Although she continued to live in her home village, she commuted by bus to a job as a lab technician in Coonoor, making rabies vaccine. The Todas, when they adapt to contemporary conditions, tend to do pretty well, he said, though only about seven hundred and fifty are left in the world. Because of their reputation for integrity they may be hired to manage a tea plantation, for instance. The ones who stay in the traditional settlements of four or five stone-and-mud, wattle-and-grass-roofed huts in a cluster on a hilltop are rather demoralized, however. For one thing, they'd always fermented their own home brew, but now alcohol comes too strong, too available, from the store; and the people who surround them in numbing majorities, like the Badagas, or the various outlanders and flatlanders who have migrated in, are swamping the Todas.

After a night's sleep in Ooty, we drove out to Bigupathimund Camp, which is high up in the mountains, near the head of two lively streams, with forests all around, but also a far-flung view—one of Habib's favorite spots. The four Toda families who lived in a small mud-walled compound there knew his friendly interest to be sincere and so welcomed us. The government gives each Toda man five acres to farm when he marries, so they had a fine moist little saddle of the mountaintop under cultivation, thick with carrots and onions, though wild boars and bears occasionally marauded through. I heard shouts all night, and a large animal rushing by our shelter once in the dark. Next morning they asked if I had a gun, because of one particular wild pig that sticks and stones and hollering couldn't deter. A leopard, too, had been around, but no tigers for a year or so.

We were staying in a rest house that the British had built. The Todas are tall, rather light-skinned or coffee-colored, and have Aryanish, delicate features. But because they are vegetarians and stay-at-homes, they were not used much as hunting guides by the British officers who vacationed here. Indeed, the Badaga watchman at our house offered to procure us a bunch of prostitutes from his village three miles downhill at about a dollar apiece for the night—as he said he often did for Forestry officials and other guests. The Todas complained of the noise and atmosphere of debauchery inflicted on them by these revels. Such a tiny remnant, really, on a small reserve, they had a much more serious problem, too. They'd just suffered the loss of their sacred buffalo, which had been stolen from the precincts of the temple nearby in the woods that they had maintained, they told me, for at least two hundred years. And she could not simply be replaced by buying a water buffalo in the marketplace, because a temple buffalo must be descended from another temple buffalo. Definitively, she must also be able to roam free in the *shola*, going and coming whenever she wishes, not penned up, and therefore would now be at risk, in this jammed and polyglot, impious age, of being grabbed and butchered for food by people of other allegiances, or simply captured and led on a rope to some faraway market for sale. Their ordinary buffaloes also roamed free, but the calves were kept at the settlement so that the mothers would return at night, whereas this one temple buffalo is always supposed to be totally free, keep her calf where she wishes, and live in the forest, not in camp.

So, they were in anguish over the unknown fate of this sacred, very personable, particular buffalo. They are a *buffalo people*, and by chance we had arrived at a point, February 15, when they were planning to go and rededicate their temple—one of only two active temples that all of the Todas had (a third having fallen into disuse). They wished to try to reverse a long sequence of bad luck, and pray for the buffalo's welfare, and ask that she be taken care of, wherever she was. Their other domestic animals, mainly cattle but a few buffalo, numbered less than twenty, anyway, and this band was so vulnerably small that when they held a dance for us the next evening by firelight in the little mud compound of four houses, only two men and five women performed—singing and shuffling in a swaying, rotating circle, with four kids watching. An old man blew the two-foot bamboo flute. This was blackened and sounded a bit like a piccolo; then when he hung a tin cup on the end to alter its tone, like an oboe.

Our host, as Habib spelled his name, was M'Thekalmudi, a thin-mustached man whose face looked like Joe DiMaggio's and who gave his age as forty-nine and his wife's age as twenty-seven. Three of the kids were theirs and the other his younger brother's. The women could have nothing at all to do with the rituals of the temple, but otherwise seemed rather equal and free, though they did perform a periodic ritual of obeisance to a husband or elder man, kneeling and placing his foot on their heads. But some Hindu women do that as well. Everybody gradually got happier, in dancing. Yet M'Thekalmudi confessed in his language with some foreboding that even the flute "didn't sound right."

M'Thekalmudi's wife brought me a ceremonious cup of buffalo milk, had me remove my shoes, and let me squeeze into her house, which was loaf-shaped, with a low, rounded roof. Half the horizontal space was taken up by a sleeping platform made of boards and dried dung. The small door was also wooden and could be locked—small doors discourage animals, wild or tame, from coming inside. There were no windows, but several oil lamps set on niches or shelves, and a mud fireplace with a rack for firewood and a smoke hole going out. Wood and bamboo had been used to frame the mud walls, and there were mattocks hanging from the rafters, and buffalo-horn-shaped tree branches, religious in nature, plus a few framed family pictures tacked up. At the back wall were shelves for clothes and food in storage vessels, and on the floor, several stainless steel pots that contained water. It was smoky but cozy—my hostess gracefully communicating in sign language—and the next day I saw her sister and her lugging pails of cows' milk down the hill toward the Badaga village to sell for cash, a six-mile round-trip. The buffaloes' milk was always kept separate. The Kota tribe were also neighbors of the Todas, and furnished them with pottery and bush knives in exchange for milk, or perhaps for meat when a cow died, or when a male buffalo was sacrificed after a man had died—because the Todas did not eat meat, just left it in the forest for the Kotas or hyenas or whomever.

In the morning the men prayed in a short, low, windowless, grass-roofed, barrel-curved minor temple, built of wood and fitted slabs of stone, that was located right in the village, as they did every day—not a place that even Habib could venture inside—after the rituals of milking their buffaloes and smearing some buffalo cream in their hair. An upright stone slab stood in front, and also two large round stones in the village's council area. A boy must be able to lift one of these, stand up, and hurl it over his shoulder before he married and became a man.

Habib said he'd left his girlfriend's Toda family after six months or so because the routine of lazing on a hillside watching their seven cows graze all day long finally became boring, though he'd liked the purity of it. Now he watched his own family's ten acres of tea shrubs grow. I teased him when he said he was religious, asking him if he wouldn't rather make a pilgrimage to Mecca than go hang-glide in California after the tourists began paying him to bring them here. He said Mecca, yes, but not as much as California.

Then we accompanied the men on their poignant trip to the central temple, a humble walk through field and forest of a couple of miles. Eight Toda men and two boys were involved, which—for such a powerful occasion—was all the more affecting; and when we got close we took our footwear off. Through Habib, M'Thekalmudi said, "We all used to be healthy. Could run up any mountain and not have to stop. But now we don't exert ourselves." Everyone had abstained from sex last night after the dance and had fasted this morning. They wore no western clothes; instead they had on white cotton dhotis and the knitted buffalo-wool shawls that their wives make for them, which take four months apiece.

Traditionally, the men would have spent January alone at this temple, living only on rice and milk from the temple buffalo, neither smoking, drinking, nor visiting women. But they hadn't this year because of the stolen buffalo. We stopped first at a whetstone pool of clean spring water (it was lined with whetstones you could sharpen your bush knife on). Here everybody bathed once again, though they had done so in the village too, and put sandalwood powder in dots on their foreheads.

We approached the temple in attentive anticipation, and my unspoken worry that it might seem anticlimactic proved needless. It stood in a riveting cup-shaped grotto, noisy with bird and monkey calls, in a sumptuous, unspoiled forest. It was conical, very lofty and exceptional-looking, grass-roofed, with a siding of bamboo withes bound together and overlaid with more grass, except for the bottom five feet, which was constructed of upright stone slabs that the grass overhung. I would guess it was thirty-five feet high, altogether. Inside, I was told, five twelve-foot stone pillars lent additional support, and some much taller teepee-style treeposts. Inset in the front was a gnomish round stone door, with a buffalo skull fastened over it, and other wood and metal emblems. In a half circle outside were several concentric stone walls and, between them, a slender stone slab. Behind the temple was a comely huge "temple tree." But they let nature choose the species that it would be. And another large tree stood in front, though this one had been vandalized by intruders with graffiti. Nearby was a three-foot stone upon which, until about a hundred years ago, a naked man, chosen from a different village each year, used to sit fasting for fifteen days, except for the buffalo butter poured over him every third of those days—"shortening his own life for the glory of God."

Of course the soul of the whole place should have been the temple buffalo, free-roaming, divinely descended, ultimately from the original Buffalo given to mankind at the Buffalo Tree. M'Thekalmudi sent a runner several miles to that very tree of life to bring me a peeled foot-length sprig, which in itself formed horns like a buffalo's. He said they come here, however, for both deaths and festivals; "any good or bad."

They knelt and prayed in unison for a time, led by an older man. And we saw, on our leisurely walk back to the hamlet of Bigu-pathimund, a large gray stone which was a woman who (even though it wasn't her fault) had passed too close to the temple. She'd been sick, and her brothers, in carrying her home on a litter, had taken the shortest route, and she was turned to stone in an utter instant.

"If you do wrong," M'Thekalmudi added, speaking of the present, "God will lead the tiger straight to you in the woods."

We also saw "the leap of joy," an incredible jump marked by two black stones that was once made by a man of legend, returning from a journey, when he was told that both his previously barren wife and his buffalo had given birth to babies. He had a sack of grain on his shoulders at the time, so if you try to duplicate his jump, you should, too.

And, crossing a ford of the stream, we saw where the sun once entered the earth for a brief spell and the world went dark, after two Toda villages had been quarreling about who "owned" the stream. "The temple brought the sun down," M'Thekalmudi said. And now the figure of a praying god is gradually rising from a rock in the middle of the water—hands together, and with a helmet head like an astronaut's—a little more every year.

One of the men, walking down to the valley for cigarettes after the ceremony, saw a leopard and then a bear along the stream. He told me they have a special calming sound that they utter from the belly, when they encounter an elephant deep in the woods, so the elephant thinks, *Oh, that's just a Toda.*

We left the Todas, and drove for several hours out of the high country, through tea and cinchona plantations, to Kotagiri, and down to the Moyar River Valley, then wound up that into another sizable forest preserve, and finally traveled another twenty unpopulated miles to a town called Thengumarahda, reachable from the end of the dirt road only by boarding a coracle, a circular little buffalo-hide skin-boat, and then walking across a mile of rice and peanut fields. A mountain called Kodanad loomed overhead, with many cliffs and draws and stringy waterfalls and other visible complexities. To climb down to Thengumarahda from the road on top of Kodanad took five hours, if you didn't lose your way, Habib said.

The rice had just been cut with scythes. Wheeling lines of oxen, five abreast, were trampling it to separate the grains from the grass, which would later be fed to the animals as hay, and the grain then tossed in screens by groups of women to separate the chaff. The peanuts were planted in alternation, as nitrogen-rich legumes. All told, three or four crops a year were fitted in. Though sugar cane might have been more profitable, the wild elephants found sugar juice irresistible and would come stomping into the fields after it at night. They sometimes broke down banana trees, too, to get the fruit, and the watchmen would throw firecrackers or firebrands at them. But the banana orchards they'd damage were not so extensive. Coconuts were an elephant-proof crop, as well as limes, and there were little plots of mulberries, chili peppers, betel nuts, and whatnot.

Thengumarahda had been established as a Gandhian agricultural cooperative of a hundred and fifty families on five hundred acres at the time of independence in 1947, Habib said, and was the only one of maybe forty of these idealistic projects in India that had survived. Factionalism, greed, debauchery, and "free enterprise" had brought the others down.

I wasn't functioning as a journalist checking facts on this brief tour, however. Rather, I was listening to the ancient music I was hearing: like how they bang two pans together if a tiger comes. We were situated again in a former British rest house used by the Forestry Service. A bare tiled-floor, whitewashed structure at the edge of the village, it had a splendid view of the ramparts of Mount Kodanad going up two or three thousand feet, with a lot of forest in between and half a dozen wooded pocket sanctuaries to gaze at higher up, ideal denning places for a hyena family or a mamma bear or big cat or an old elephant that just wanted to be off by himself. In India the ivory poaching has decimated only the males, because female Indian elephants (unlike their African counterparts) do not have tusks. So what you have are herds of angry females who have witnessed a number of cruel, treacherous, lingering deaths of bulls that they've known well—shot from ambush—whose tusks were then hacked off. The smugglers' ("bandits") trail was pointed out to me, in fact.

If chased by an elephant, you run in a zigzag, hide, and dash away when discovered, hide again and dash if rediscovered, then turn suddenly, and turn again, because an elephant, though fast in a straight line, is less maneuverable than you are. It will stop and listen for you, raising its trunk to sniff the air, sometimes pawing one foot, and spread its ears "like a cobra's hood." It can push down the sort of tree you might be able to climb, so you want to get up into the rocks or squeeze into a culvert under the road, if you can run that far. But when Habib once did, a mile from here on a little jeep track, the elephant found where he was and knelt and reached as deeply as she could into the culvert to grab him with her trunk. Then, when that failed, she got up and stood over it and stamped her feet, trying to squash it in on top of him.

We saw a wedding procession, led by a man with a sambar-skin drum and a man with an oboe-length flute. The new couple, returning to town after the ceremony, stopped their approach at the first tea house and were offered free cups of milk by way of welcome. *We* had tea so hot you had to pour it back and forth from cup to saucer (which of course is what you want in a spot where boiling is essential).

That night, a leopard came into somebody's house through an unshuttered window and killed a goat, but was unable to pull it loose from its rope and get it back out the window—so simply crouched, licking its blood at the throat. The owner of the goat, in trying to save it, had been so flustered when the leopard looked at him as if she might pounce that he tripped and broke his arm. But his neighbors, rushing over, frightened the leopard out. This same troublesome female, with kittens to feed, had grabbed a small boy one evening a few weeks before and started to haul him away by his head. But he was quite heavy, slow to drag, and his father bravely gave chase, caught up, and rescued his son, who was all right now, though we saw the tooth marks.

The Irulas had been the indigenous tribe here along the Moyar River—hunters and trackers, snake catchers and soothsayers—and still had a few cohesive villages in the forest. My impression was that they were holding together marginally better than the Todas or Kadars: this partly because they still had a recognized function. Few people in modern India cared whether the surviving Kadars, such as Sabrimathu, could still track tigers, or whether the few Todas who were left, like M'Thekalmudi, still sang poems to their Temple Buffalo, if they could find her. But the Irulas until very recently had caught cobras for snake charmers all over India—they were the ur-snake charmers—and also as guard figures for traditionalist temples in places where the native cobras had been wiped out. They also caught crocodiles for the World Wildlife Fund's "Crocodile Bank," near Madras, from which Moyar River breeding stock may be re-seeded to other zoos or wildlife preserves anywhere crocodiles will be wanted, down the road. Nor are the Irulas' clairvoyant powers to be sneezed at in a country where spiritual telepathy is not confined to mosque, church, or temple. Nonetheless, they, too, were hunkered down in hard-scrabble poverty.

We met Murukan, a young Irula man named for an ancient Tamil and Hindu god always seen with a trident. His other name was Bear because, five years earlier, he had been gripped and bitten by a bear—he too has scars—which his father drove off by ripping a handful of thatch from their roof and setting it afire. He said his grandmother was so tough that she once killed a bear with her bare hands that had attacked her when she was coming home from the market on the footpath. His grandfather, a famous hunter who had simply ignored the skein of new wildlife laws that were instituted during his lifetime, called the forestry officer of the Moyar district to his house when he knew he was dying and turned over a whole stack of three hundred skins of animals he had killed with his muzzle-loader over the years—deer and bear for meat, and prowling leopards, or whatever. He had done what was only natural, and not then sold them to smugglers, but wished to be sure his family would not get in trouble. His other gesture, in preparing for death, was to go to their private temple in the woods and remove the statues that mattered to him, such as, Murukan said, a five-foot brass cobra, a silver tiger and a silver bear, a gallon-sized god's head and a sacred ax, and bury them secretly in a pit where not even his descendants would ever discover them, so that they wouldn't suffer the neglect he foresaw for all precious objects and the beliefs undergirding them.

Of course he was right; they would have been stolen. Even the live cobras Murukan still catches to guard the little temple now get killed by passersby who don't realize or accept their significance, and the wider market for temple cobras has dried up. Another Irula family began catching pythons, instead, for a shoe-leather dealer. They got paid the equivalent of five to twenty-five dollars—for a python "large enough to eat a small child"—but started experiencing strange mishaps and very bad luck, and soon stopped.

Murukan's father collects tamarind seeds in the forest for about a dollar per thirty kilos, though it can be dangerous because the elephants collect them also. Other Irulas spend the night on platforms in the paddy fields for a dollar a night, throwing firecrackers or lighting piles of hay to fend off the wild pigs and elephants. (Three years ago, two of them had been stomped on and killed.) Murukan himself—wiry and untidy like a man of the woods—collects honey for a living every March, and had spotted nine beehives on the cliffs so far by a careful reconnaissance. The bees place them as inaccessibly as they can, but he slips on a bedsheet with eyeholes cut in it and works at night, rappelling down the cliff from above, with a burning stick tied to his belt for extra protection and a big tin jar to fill. Each of these hives may provide him with about ten dollars' worth of honey and wax. And there were eleven Irulas, he said, working the ramparts of the cliffs stretching above us, who find two or three hundred hives altogether, though the bears and the leopards diligently compete with them, sometimes almost alongside.

As many as forty British officers used to come to the Moyar River every year to hunt on horseback with tiger hounds; and four Irulas, including Murukan's grandfather, served as trackers, while their wives did the cooking. "The bad tigers but not the good tigers" were killed, and because Irula girls were famously beautiful, some of the bachelor Englishmen would pay a bride price for one of them and carry her off as a mistress to Mysore, Bangalore, or the Malabar Coast. It was not considered too bad a fate, compared to that of the girls who were simply stolen, or seemed to be—eloped or were kidnapped and disappeared. The magical part was that a certain large-ruffed, three-tined sambar deer would come for them and stand on the riverbank, and the next time they went down for water they were never seen again. But when the parents went to the temple to pray, the message conveyed was that their daughter was alive and safe. And what was exasperating was that the Irulas suspected another tribe's magic, the Kurumbas', was operating and surpassing theirs. A Kurumba scout in human form, walking down from his village way up in the Nilgiris for many hours, would have been seen around the Irulas' settlement for a few days, chatting with people, observing everybody. Then he'd leave (and this happened until the 1980s), and the next thing they knew, the sambar materialized on the riverbank again—an apparition they dared not shoot.

The Todas had told me that the first Toda man had found the Buffalo Tree—where buffaloes were given to mankind—when he happened to be resting underneath it and discovered a horn half-buried in the ground, and became curious as to what the horn was. So I asked Murukan how the Irulas had discovered their own special woods temple, from long before his grandfather's time. It is separate from the several Hindu temples in the valley and the other temples— tiny, prehistoric stone lean-tos that Habib was showing me—whose origins and provenance nobody knew. *Theirs,* the Irulas', was built of mud and grass, over a black stone that, he said, a cow had kept going to, secretly, voluntarily, and dripping her milk upon. When the people who owned her figured out that she was always coming back from the forest with an empty udder, they were angry and followed her, intending to kill whoever was stealing their milk. Instead, they discovered that she was honoring and feeding the black stone. So they built the little mud temple, and, by legend, the stone will crack if any impieties are committed around it. This is where they still bring the skins of chital deer and other creatures that they shoot for food, not selling them but building a hutment with them, praying over them, and later laying others on.

I asked whether Murukan ever encountered a tiger. He said, through Habib's translation, that, yes, four months ago, when he was doing one of his preliminary searches for beehives up a tributary valley—he pointed it out—he had seen a tiger with kittens that "could leap sixty feet" and had just killed a cow. She was crouching over it, sucking blood from its throat and, like a nervy cat, tapping the top of her head with the tuft on the end of her tail. No tiger had killed anybody recently, but five people had been killed by elephants in the past eight years (one man tusked to death in front of our rest house). Yet the elephant is "the king of the jungle," he said, and shouldn't be shot, no matter what he does. During the latest frenzy of poaching, an elephant had been found in the forest here, disabled and kneeling but still alive, with his trunk nailed to the ground with a sharpened crowbar, and L-shaped cuts under his cheeks where his tusks had been cut out. That kind of thing "may be why they're mad."

The Irulas live in an older, though now subsidiary, hamlet called Hallimoyar, three miles by trail from Thengumarahda. Hallimoyar is named for Queen Halli (plus Moyar), called Hallirani, whose ruined fortress overlooks Thengumarahda from an isolated, heroic-looking spur where she and possibly a thousand men won renown by holding out against the army of Tippu Sultan, the so-called Tiger of Mysore, on one of his predatory raids of the late eighteenth century. The actual village, though, is down in a lovely, well-watered glen in the palm of the valley, under the generous shade of banyan and mango trees, with banana orchards and paddy fields, and even a couple of vacation cottages owned by rich tea planters from the highlands. Thengumarahda is much busier during the daylight hours than Hallimoyar, having many more people—perhaps five hundred. But both shut down at dark, except for the glow of a few oil lamps and a couple of generators, and of course firelight.

The daily routine in Thengumarahda begins at dawn or a little later, when the women get up, bathe, walk several times around a ceremonial minty plant that grows in the houseyard, and do "puja," praying at the family altar. They bring coffee to their husbands and, in old-fashioned households, kneel ritually to him, as according to the adage, "Whether he is grass or a stone, he is still my husband." After sunrise the cattle, which had been closely penned in the middle of the village overnight, have been milked and are moving out of town in one direction. Then when the streets are clear of them, the buffaloes are herded out in another. And flocks of goats follow last—all to graze on the slopes and bottomlands three or four miles out of town.

Men do the herding. The women get the children off to school, and process the surplus milk into ghee, collect and dry the night's dung for fertilizer, carry water to refill their storage containers, gather thorn fencing, or work in small sisterly parties in the fields, alongside a little brigade of men. It is not a money economy (though we met a woman who said she would buy thirty-two kilos of raw rice for the equivalent of seven dollars and convert it to fifty kilos of white rice to sell in her store). But there was abundant food, and to a visitor it seemed sufficiently idyllic that I had to remind myself it was no fun to fear this mother leopard every time she had cubs. Last year she had succeeded in carrying away two babies, and now the men were setting a homemade box trap for her again, with a goat inside. Also, I stopped by the medical clinic on a day that the young student who doctored people was in. With his undergraduate degree, he was studying for his exams to enter medical school, and meanwhile was paid by the government to commute by bus from Satyamangalam to Thengumarahda once a week to give out pills, put on splints, and tell people when they ought to go to a hospital. He said the diseases here were respiratory funguses from the animal dung and TB and asthma; intestinal troubles from the sewage gutters and the stream water; scabies and other skin ailments; and venereal disease from what he called loose morals resulting from the people "having no entertainment," plus the forestry officials bringing germs in and inflicting them on the local girls whom they hired when they were in town.

I was now accompanied by two more travel agents, besides Habib. Mahesh and Danesh were from Madras. Mahesh, the older, more sleek and posh of the two brothers, had just married a Brahman stockbroker's daughter and had plans for the Moyar River valley. He spoke of it as a "product" to "market," and had contracted for half a dozen new skinboats to be built so that his father's big agency could bring in tourists and have them float to or from Thengumarahda. I wasn't enthusiastic about the idea (in fact, have postponed describing this trip for several years in order not to assist the project) and told Danesh, the younger, less socially ambitious, still slightly rebellious brother, that I hoped he'd protect the town as best he could from what might happen if it became a "profit center." He had once saved a village girl from drowning in a well, which was regarded as quite extraordinary: a rich university student from the city risking his life for a peasant girl. And Danesh had another village girl's name tattooed on his shoulder, and said his present girlfriend was not from Madras either, but another region, a lesser social class, and spoke a language he didn't know: so they used English. In the old India, before you could make money writing airline tickets, he said his caste would have been that of a metalworker.

With Danesh and Habib, I went to visit the town blacksmith, a modest, cheery man pounding iron implements over a bellows stove. Then to the brickworks, and the yard where all of Thengumarahda's red roof tiles were made. There was a basket maker, too, and a sizable house filled with silkworm cocoons, a cottage industry that the village had recently started and made a go of. And the town raftsman received a living for poling people and freight across the river in his buffalo-hide skinboat, which, being round and framed with bamboo, could spin in the currents like a carnival ride. The town fisherman, whose name was Kaliappen, netted catfish, carp, and eels to sell and, on the side, guided hydroelectric and forestry surveyors or foreigners such as me.

The town potter was also a sculptor, creating the temple statuary. Like an artist, he acted a bit offish and prickly when Kaliappen took me to see him. Asleep on his veranda at an hour when others weren't, and naked except for a G-string, he was mildly drunk. Humorous, well-knit, fiftyish, and disgruntled when he was told that I might write about him for an American magazine, he departed from type by wanting anonymity. Instead of being pleased and beginning to preen, like your average artistic hustler, he didn't wish for any publicity. He "worked for the gods," he said, through Habib's translation. "What I do is between me and the gods!" Then, as Kaliappen rebuked him for being huffy to a visitor, he softened his manner, told me he hoped that I "lived like a king of kings," and asked politely if I had "walked all the way from America." But he repeated that his name should not be linked with his sculpture, which was an offering to God.

Kaliappen said that we Americans got on an airplane just as if it were a bus. But though a waterman himself—he had a snug skin-boat—he'd never seen the ocean. (Nor had Murukan; so the two of them eventually went to Madras on the same train as me, courtesy of Mahesh—who was not too bad a guy—for a first awesome look.) Kaliappen, being a neighbor of the sculptor, then offered us the hospitality of his own verandah, where we sipped coconut water and ate onion and chili rice patties, as the parakeets came screaming back to roost in the coconut palms over us and the sun set.

With Kaliappen as our guide, we drove ten miles upriver the next day in Theena, our 1977 Willys Jeep. Though the riverbank was adorned with a gallery of tropical trees of the most majestic, convoluted proportions, the floor of the valley, unirrigated and under dry ridges, was a veldtlike landscape of scrubby thorn trees, a few foxes and chitals, and no place for a walker to hide if attacked. He showed us where some forestry officials had shot a wild buffalo for a barbecue, and where two years ago an engineer, foolishly on foot while crossing between loops of the river, had been mashed by a mother elephant, who let nobody retrieve his body for the next two days.

We saw five sambars—glorious big deer—and two lithe black bucks—antelopes with spirally horns—all running away; and several quail. The elephants had scoured a red salt lick with their tusks and trunks into the shape of a huge fry pan. It made us glad to spend the night at a cement-block camp by the river that the hydrologists had built, empty now but uncrushable if a herd came through, as tracks showed that they often did. The purling river was seductive, however, with its deep sand beach and noble trees. We tiptoed back and forth repeatedly from the impregnable house to the luscious riverbank, despite hearing that Kaliappen, Mahesh, and Mahesh's father—"the M.D.," they called him, meaning managing director of the travel agency—had been surrounded by elephants and marooned on the riverbank for six hours on the last trip. I was angered when somebody found a harmless trinket snake, an inoffensive species like a garter snake in the U.S., and disabled and dissected it while its heart was still beating. But during the night the stars formed a diamond pattern in the center of the sky and hyenas came sobbing to the fringes of our camp. We slept outside in order to feast upon the sky's beauty, but the price of doing that, of course, was that I dreamt that a hyena was creeping up to devour my foot.

In the morning we got into Kaliappen's coracle, the prototype of what the tourists would ride, and pushed off. The flow was brisk, the current a clean earthy brown. Skimming along as probably the first rafters in months, we saw a plenitude of creatures that had come to the Moyar to drink, or lived anyway under the drapery of trees. Brown catlike monkeys and midsized swinging langurs, peacocks and jungle fowl, black bucks and chital deer, and several sambars that spooked when they saw us. Eight wild buffaloes that had been wading in the water also ran. An eagle watched us from a limb, and several vultures were circling a kill that was up on the bank, out of view. A blackish crocodile slid off the beach and others, swimming, slowly dived. There were Malabar squirrels, one lying dead, apparently of a snakebite, and parrots, bulbuls, hoopoes, bee-catchers, hornbills, and a fish owl moaning *boom-oh-boom*.

"Don't you want other Americans to see this?" Habib asked me.

"But they won't," I suggested. "Everything will drink at night."

Kaliappen said that the monkeys had already fled from us so precipitously because their blood is sometimes drunk as a tonic for asthma—just as bear meat is chewed small and fed to infants to make them grow strong, and tiger dung is rubbed on skin ailments, and ground-up bits of elephants' teeth are swallowed for internal aches.

Drifting swiftly on, paddling to avoid an occasional patch of rocks, we found that buffalo hide was a wonderfully resilient covering for a boat if you hit, and roundness an ideal shape for collisions because you just spun around and rolled off. I told them that much of America had been explored by fur trappers in skinboats.

We passed a tree house where hydroelectric technicians sometimes lived while measuring the river's volume and pace. With their ladder, they were safe from the elephants, but otherwise the trees were really too big for them to have climbed.

Floating around a few more bends, we noticed an unusual-looking rock in the shallows by the left shore. It was longer, wider, and higher than most. Kaliappen suddenly muttered, "That's a dead elephant!"

This was a find—sad, mysterious, curious, lucky. But as we approached, dipping our paddles to slow our progress and steer close but not too close, our voices rose and the rock moved. It scrambled to get its feet under it and upright, while we paddled like mad to the opposite bank, jumped out of the skinboat as quick as we could, and clambered up out of sight of the now very lively elephant, which had merely been bathing. We found ourselves in a fallow field with no cover to hide in from the behemoth if it followed us; then scattered at a crouch so it would have to pick only one in particular to chase. Kaliappen yelled at me to take off my white shirt so I wouldn't stick out. But my skin was still pale. Scrunching down, I tried to become earth-color.

After we had waited awhile and determined that the elephant had left without even smashing our skinboat (as had happened to Kaliappen's last), we discovered that we had landed under Hallirani's lofty fortress on its remarkable crag. The field was strewn with random ruins, such as a five-foot temple built of three stone slabs, with another slab laid on top, very ancient, though some contemporary coins had been inserted in the back wall as an offering. The figures of a woman and a lion were discernibly carved in it; and two-foot-high stone hovels of a similar construction stood nearby, that you could have crawled into. Other carved stones lay about in the grass; also an urn for grinding rice, blackened with age and too heavy to lift. I hadn't enough energy to climb to Hallirani's unconquered high-up redoubt, but Habib said that the huge rainwater cistern that had enabled her to withstand Tippu Sultan's siege was still intact—you could take a dip in it—and several links of the thick iron chain that had held the gate, and much of the brick wall that had plugged the gaps between the natural ramparts of rock. And he'd even found a goodly portion of her wooden palanquin, he said. He was trying to interest a university or the government in investigating or salvaging what was left.

When we got back to Thengumarahda, we heard that two cobras had been tussling in a breeding ritual across the little stream from our rest house. An elephant cow and calf had eaten two banana trees when the watchmen fell asleep; and that mother leopard had slipped into town yet again, slid inside somebody's house, grabbed another goat, and gotten away with it.

We talked to a seventy-year-old man who was cultivating a mulberry field. He'd bought a goat for five hundred rupees, nearly a month's pay, he said, and had tethered her next to him as he worked, so she could browse and still be safe. But within a month this same leopard had crept up in the heat of the day, pounced over his stooping back, and seized her, thrown her over *her* back, and carried her up to the spiry knoll where she had her two kittens—kind of a miniature of Hallirani's refuge, I suggested. He laughed, pointing out just where to climb if I wanted to try bearding her at the mouth of her cave. The queen had lived "at the time when the gods lived here," he told me in Tamil, through Habib's translation.

He showed me a thicket where a bear and her cub had slept last night. Monkeys were whooping in the trees, and he said he'd rather "dig bulbs in the forest" than kill animals for food. His settlement of a dozen families was called Pudha Kadu, "New Place," and had its own little whitewashed mud, dung, and stone temple, a single room with a head-high thatched roof. One of my sculptor friends' terracotta elephants stood at the entrance, facing a black rock that had been chosen from the Moyar's riverbed after much deliberation by a young boy "who had god in him," the old man said. Inside were five other river stones that had been similarly identified by this inspired boy. Each was painted with eyes and a turmeric forehead dot. Six brass plates leaning on a shelf depicted a female deity named Masiniyathi, and there were several holy elephants, and a vessel holding coconut water that people sprinkled on themselves, and two china plates containing a sacred ash to dab on one's forehead. Three paintings showed the god Murukan with his trident, riding a peacock; and jolly Ganesha with his sidekick, the rat; and their joined male-and-female parent, Siva and Parvati. Women couldn't enter the temple. Men had to bring the ash and coconut water out to them.

Our Murukan was less used to Europeans, less sophisticated than Kaliappen, and conscientiously poured out my jug of boiled drinking water in order to refill it from the tap because the tapwater looked clearer to him. Though Kaliappen loved wild things and was an enthusiastic observer—instinctively a conservationist—he wasn't twinned with them like Murukan. Agile, stocky Kaliappen had once "ridden" a wild buffalo to distract it from trampling a friend who'd been knocked to the ground—had also "ridden" a black buck that he'd caught sleeping, for fun. But Murukan, like Sabrimathu, had a willowy, weavier quality, as spontaneous as the boughs that bounce in the wind, versus a "civilized" superstructure of iron.

We went to see the headman of Murukan's Irula village of Hallimoyar. His name was Siddan and he lived in a one-room concrete house decorated with plastic mango leaves and yellow flowers hanging over the open doorway. A Rotary Club had just paid four hundred rupees to have his cataracts removed at the regional hospital, so he had perhaps more reason than usual to be cheerful. However, the dispiritedness of old age and shattered traditions still seemed to underlie his mood. The government did provide the children of registered tribal people with free schooling, uniforms, and so forth, but he missed the British. He had worked on a coffee plantation six miles uphill, and "We lived like kings," he said in English. "Nobody was hungry." At least not tribal hunters in this Shangri-la, with forest skills. He told me that a cow giving ten liters of milk a day would cost him five thousand rupees, and a buffalo giving half that much, three thousand (or about one hundred dollars). You could borrow up to two thousand rupees from the government, but you'd have to give half back to the authorizing officials as a bribe, plus interest on the whole. Wages were a dollar a day.

A forest fire was burning in a hanging valley; we watched the smoke. But at our rest house I was surprised to see the forestry officers lounging on the porch, watching it so casually. They said they'd "book" somebody for starting it, some hapless shepherd who might have had a campfire, though it was out of the question that they would actually climb up to the fire to try to put it out. A sandalwood smuggler might have been the culprit, Siddan said, or merely the prism of a broken bottle left there years ago, and not the nearest shepherd at all.

Next day, a holy man, a sadhu, hiked into Thengumarahda. Tall, thirty-something, with uncut hair and wearing an orange turban and orange shorts, he was sitting on a stone wall along the wagon path, nodding to people he knew. His air of exuberance also made him stand out. As it happened, this was his hometown. He had a wife and four children here, he told me with Habib's help, but a year or so ago he had had a vision from God. He had talked with God, and with his wife's acquiescence "because it was from God," he had left home to wander the world. His face looked buoyant, and besides his scanty orange clothing, he wore multiple strings of brown beads and had painted red and white tridents on his forehead and bare chest and arms. He carried only a plastic bag such as animal feed is sold in, into which the villagers on his travels could pour donations of rice, to keep him going, or where he put the cannabis plants that Habib said he probably picked wild. Inside the plastic bag was a pretty pouch made from a chital deer's red-and-white spotted skin. Inside this special pouch—as he showed me when I asked—he had a plate-sized brass gong that he struck, and a conch shell that he blew, before he said his prayers.

According to Habib, freelance sadhus like him sometimes fulfilled a role similar to that of psychotherapists in the West. They talked and listened to families whose temple priest might seem consumed with performing the daily rituals, or otherwise oblique, opaque, and obtuse. Many hamlets had no priest, and sadhus, by their lectures and by stimulating acts of charity beyond their own needs, offered visible testimony to consecrated traditions that otherwise could have lapsed. They also revisited abandoned shrines, forgotten temples, and other precious sites in their impromptu roamings, under the ancient rubric that improvisation can engender inspiration. And by trusting themselves not just to humanity but to the wilderness, they were generally able to pass by elephants and tigers without being molested.

Seeing my interest was sincere, this sadhu told me I could go with him tomorrow to a temple in a valley an eight-hour walk away that "belonged to the animals." That is, the valley did; but as a consequence the temple still had its silver statues. Once, a man from Thengumarahda had walked all that way to steal them, but fell so sick a week later he had to walk all the way back and return them.

Kaliappen ended up taking Habib, Danesh, and me on a stroll that was nearly as challenging. We went on a picnic to catch some fish and look at crocodile drag-marks in the sand on a plump beach three miles below Hallimoyar. The river rustled by in corded currents under grandly proportioned trees. We built a driftwood fire for cooking, and napped when we weren't doing anything else. An elephant path crossed the Moyar at this point, and we found hyena prints and dung with sambar hair in it. You could wade out in the silky water and sit on a knobby rock, or cradle yourself on the lowest limbs of two or three of the biggest trees that arced over the river.

Though it ran hip-deep near the bank, and though a cow was reported to have been bitten on the nose upstream the day before, we trusted Kaliappen's assurance that he knew the nature of crocodiles and enjoyed the afternoon till sunset: whereupon we started walking back to Hallimoyar on the ox-wagon track. A brown-and-white Brahminy kite was being buzzed by a swift gray hawk. We'd seen a black buck, fleeing us in a hurry, on our trip in, and expected to stumble upon other animals as dusk approached. A river temple stood along the trail with a cobra living in a termite mound alongside that Murukan had said he'd put there. A rich tea planter from the heights had paid to have the site spruced up. It was an open-sided platform with pillars supporting the roof and lions on top of that, as well as other stone or terra-cotta statuary brought from afar, not merely the sort of mud figures that people made for themselves to save money and then painted white, as often is the case. But the situation was genuinely antique, rediscovered in historic times (Murukan had told me) by a shepherd who used to lie under a certain shady tree here, as his cattle nibbled through the woods—but felt uncannily itchy when he did. His curiosity had been so aroused that he dug with his knife and finally unearthed a clay figurine which, when he cut into it, bled.

Though I'd hoped to see the cobra—and there was also a trench for fire walking—we weren't inclined to linger because we'd already waited too long, while dawdling at the beach. It was growing dark. The twelve hours of night would belong to the animals; and as Kaliappen reminded us, five years ago a husband and wife from Thengumarahda who were praying at this temple had been knelt on by an elephant. Furthermore, we smelled carrion. In a comfy Land Rover in East Africa a tourist will follow vultures, but on foot in India at nightfall, we didn't want to know what animal had killed the carcass whose odor was pungently wafting to us.

Clouds hid the moon. We distanced ourselves from whatever might be guarding the meat. Fortunately the path was composed of a whitish soil that we could fix our eyes on. But then I happened to glance up, from telepathy perhaps, and dimly noticed that we were all about to collide with a baby elephant. How nice, I thought for just a second, a baby elephant. *A Baby Elephant!* Then, sure enough, the mother's shape loomed indistinctly in the gloom, five yards away. Her shadowy trunk hardly moved, not yet swinging forward and up; her tree-trunk legs looked the very pattern of patience. But as we alerted one another agitatedly in whispers, her great ears did spread out above us like a cobra's hood. We could also make out other females at her shoulders—two, three waiting, maybe four.

"We're totally trapped. Our luck has gone all bad," whispered Kaliappen.

The elephants were preparing to enter the road, so we didn't run backward. Instead we ran upward, up the side of a rocky ridge that fortuitously stood to our right. They could have charged uphill, but rocks are not to a pachyderm's liking. The steeper and more bouldery it was, the better for us. We scattered, but angled slantwise along the slope to a dropoff that seemed high enough that their trunks couldn't reach us if they followed and stood on their hind legs. Collecting there, we agreed it was the best we could do. Looking down two hundred feet at the trail in a slice of moonlight, we saw more elephants in the dusk. Another group was arriving. We tried to count; thirty or forty were slowly shuffling toward the river. It was amazing, almost surreal in the dark. Fearfully, we lit a fire on a flat part of the rock—and heard a groan from some of the matriarchs below, as though they were murmuring, *What are these crazies gonna do, set the valley, too, on fire?*

After the assemblage apparently had vanished toward the river, we yelled for a couple of hours before a gust of wind caught our voices properly and carried them to the night watchmen in Hallimoyar's paddy fields. Bravely, they set out to rescue us, though in fact they didn't know who we were, and thought we might be bandits, smugglers, poachers, or whatever, seeing our fire. They said later that they had been as scared of us as of the possibility that elephants might be blocking the road. The fire would have protected us for the rest of the night from cats, bears, bison, dholes, or hyenas, but we were impatient and glad of their cooperative spirit.

Back at Thengumarahda, a troupe of actors of the Koothu Theater in Madras was performing the great Hindu seventh-century epic cycle of the Mahabharata for the villagers. The show, in bravura style, lasted for eight hours through the night, and though not puppetry, reminded me of the classic Sicilian puppet shows that dramatize in marvelous fashion the epics of Charlemagne.

Swiftly, the next day, we left by oxcart, skinboat, and soon our Willys Jeep again. Back to the mad, pool-table traffic of India, with me hallucinating accidents from the death seat that never quite occurred. The rickety horse wagon piled with sugarcane and the lorry overloaded with gravel converging just ahead of us on the skinny, skinny road—surely we couldn't squeeze through? But maybe precisely because we were traveling at sixty and shimmying, we would do so. To have slowed, or steered less reflexively, might have meant a smashup.

In Coimbatore, the "Pest Man," the "Auto Consultancy," the "Polio Clinic," the "Bone-Setting Hospital," "Guru Travels," and cracker shops, tool shops, pickle shops, flower shops, diamond shops, peddlers selling watermelons, mustard seed, tomatoes, people plaiting palm leaves for roof thatch, spinning coconut fiber into ropes. A red-headed devil's effigy hung from a beam in a building being constructed, to forestall accidents. On several doors three stripes were drawn with ashes, top and bottom, mourning a death. And in the morning in many neighborhoods, women in saris stooped to draw complex, improvised, geometrical but wavy designs with rice powder on the sidewalk in front of their doors, which mutely but sometimes quite powerfully broadcast the state of harmony or else dissonance in their households—the daily mood engendered by the kind of spouse and children they had. (It's supposed to be rice powder so that the ants may eat, too.)

In Madras, "Eve-teasers"—bumptious men who torment women in public places—shared the clattering streets with beige and yellow sacred cows, which roamed free, willfully, impulsively, though always glad to find a banana skin or an orange rind, and were milked and fed grass by the very poor. Bullocks, on the other hand, labored with a rope strung through their septums. We have won the earth from other vertebrates by our exceptional lubricity; and foreplay remains the basis of most commercial advertising, as billboards everywhere make plain. But people in India rock their heads agreeably, as they talk to each other, to show sociability, which to a Westerner is confusing because the motion looks instead like a minute form of head shaking, as if they're disagreeing.

My plane's departure from Madras was delayed because in New Delhi there were bomb scares at the airport. Businessmen were leaving the capital with their families before the religious riots that were scheduled for tomorrow. So, feeling in suspension, I persuaded a guy at the terminal to drive me up a nearby hill where Doubting Thomas (according to some reports) was crucified. It seems natural that, in his regret or sense of guilt for having at first doubted Christ's resurrection, Saint Thomas would have been the apostle who proselytized the farthest afterwards—clear to the Bay of Bengal, perhaps, here to recapitulate Christ's fate. I've felt a link to Thomas because my parents used to call me "Doubting Thomas" when I was young and rebellious and "doubted" their Episcopalian liturgy. Maybe among his minor complaints at the last was a bellyache just like mine from eating curried rice and vegetable patties on a banana leaf.

Yet on this cathedral hill, schoolchildren were planting trees, while a gang of jackdaws disputed possession of the sky with some vultures and kites, and the smell of uric acid and rotting carbohydrates drifted up from Madras's five million people below. But I also saw an egret sitting on a cow's back, and a blackbird on a buffalo. Cashew trees, brisk kilns, papaya trees, droves of white ducks on the way to market, and even a drove of pigs. The Cooum River divides the city.

Brahma, Vishnu, and Siva—Creator, Preserver, and Destroyer—riding, respectively, on a Swan, an Eagle, and a Bull, had topped Saint

Thomas's appeal in India. More din, more heterogeneity, plus the androgynous exuberance of so many sculpted figures from the animal kingdom scrambling like totems up the compact temple towers. Metaphors, of course, but with a bit of glee or mischief thrown in, and the undergirding of real elephants, cobras, lions (yes, lions lived in India), and tigers maybe only a day's walk away.

One does not leave wild places hopefully now. Alloys indeed are what we'll have. Virtual wildernesses and realities; metafictions. "Albino king snakes" are already in the pet stores, and "ligers" and "tiglons" in the dealers' catalogs that hobbyists use. (Apparently, selling a cross evades the endangered species laws.) But I exaggerate. Winnie the Pooh was an alloy of a kind, and the rear-guard actions for preservation many people are fighting will stave off curtain time for a while.

When I remember that Siberian tiger caged in eighteen square feet in the circus, or the black-maned but supernumerary movie lion I cared for in California in 1953—who had been relegated to a reinforced piano box—I can't romanticize how such things were fifty years ago. The cruelty was abominable, but was still encysted in a world that seemed closer to being whole. Ultimate wild things are incidentally dangerous—white sharks, gorgeous tigers, harpy eagles, polar bears—as well as unpredictable. Tigers are less athletic, more complicated, than a leopard, which may sometimes seem like a single, lengthy muscle. A tiger's spirit, when ferocious, feline, and imperial, can parallel ours, though without the monkeying primate qualities that have given us our berserk streak that invents the end of the world. Tigers are less heartbreaking than the beleaguered elephant because they are not social creatures and are reactive, not innovative. But they are an apex, a kind of hook the web of nature hangs on. To know them, and elephants, marked my life.

(1997)

Behold Now Behemoth

A bristly, lovely, although hot and fearsome recklessness invigorates God in the Old Testament when he loses patience. *Behold now behemoth, which I made with thee,* he says to Job, who has been complaining of his unjust sufferings. But justice is not what the majesty of Creation is all about. Consider, for instance, the hippopotamus. *He moveth his tail like a cedar . . . his bones are like bars of iron . . .*

For me, too, religion needs to wear a mask of jubilation. Yet unmixed glee is beyond my capacities. I begin to flag if I am required to be upbeat for many hours at a stretch—though I have in fact had just the sort of biblical experience that warrants a lifelong commitment to the happy tangents of faith. It happened during my late fifties, when two eye operations restored my sight after three years of legal blindness. My vision had shrunk to the point where I couldn't see faces, birds, or trees. Through my telescope I studied the rising moon or the way that branches interlaced, but even the lenses of such an instrument could barely recapitulate what my eyes with ordinary eyeglasses had formerly seen.

Quite suddenly, however, within a period of half a dozen weeks, the miracle of the streaming clouds, the blowing grass, the leaping birds, the upspread trees, and the variety of expressions on my friends' faces was given back to me. For possibly an entire year, in the exalting aftermath of regaining my eyesight, I was incapable of being depressed. I simply needed to glance out the window and couldn't believe how golden the sunshine was, how softly green each leaf, or how radiant the city night could be, with its great arclike sparkling bridges and hooded mobs of apartment houses, each of the thousands of lives packed inside signified by a small yellow light. If I was in the city, the slant of lion-skinned building stone on a skyscraper's face was breathtaking. In the country, I was lifted to rapture by the prismatic pointillism of the wildflowers, or a sea of seed heads shimmering underneath the black outcrops on a mountainside, the puce and pink of a slow dawn, the white slats of birch bark under a purple rainstorm medallioned by a rainbow or slashed by a crimson shaft of half-set sun, a sky big enough to fall right into forever and ever if I lay on my back and didn't grip the grass.

And, of course, I didn't neglect to look up Christ's miracle-working episodes, impromptu as they were. Set against the scale of eternal redemption, the temporary plight of the blind and sick whom he had encountered accidentally was not his preoccupation. But pity for their anguish mixed with his practicality when he asked whether they "believed." Presumably, since God had created heaven and earth, God could cure blindness, leprosy, or whatnot with or without "belief," but Christ's own powers, swift and serene though they seem, may have needed that extra catalyst. Indeed, in Mark 8, the act requires two applications of Christ's hands: the first restores the blind man of Bethsaida's sight only to the extent that people look to him *like trees . . . walking about*. So *Jesus laid his hands on his eyes again*. Rather like my surgeon.

I was truly, sadly startled, though, in the midst of my exuberance, to notice how many of my friends' faces had changed during my blind years. They looked battered, bruised, disheartened, bereft of illusion, apprehensive, or knocked a bit awry by the very campaigns and thickets of life that I was giddy with delight to have regained. I was seeing the forest, I decided, while they were engrossed by the trees. Like a prisoner sprung from a dungeon, I didn't care about minor harassments, frictions, frettings, inconveniences. The sky, the clouds, the colors and movement, and my sudden freedom were plenty for me. I could be irascible, impatient, and hard to get on with, but never unhappy; that's not what life was for. Instead I was charged up, alight, Lazarus-like, and I realized that such a marked alteration in my friends' faces and the cast of strangers' expressions could not be the result of my having just been "away" for a while, but that everything was clearer. The fox-red coat of a deer in June; the glow of a checkered, fat garter snake, its white skin shining between its black scales; a goldfinch's trampoline bounce on the wing; the fire-engine pace of a chimney swift tearing around; leaf shadows running on a tree trunk like a crowd of squirrels as the wind blew. Such a lovely, vivid, vibrant world—what does it matter if your marriage is going rancid? "Cheer up, for heaven's sake!" I wanted to say when the shaft of a stranger's glance on the street told me a tale of misery. Funky neon at midnight in the city, or raindrops zigging down a windowpane, a sky of feather-blue, a sky of sleety pewter, a lady's dachshund walking like a leashed salamander down the sidewalk (and the piercing pleasure of a toddler seeing it), old bricks on a town house or a church front.

In Manhattan I went to services at the church where I'd been christened more than fifty years before, and both before and after my crucial operations I seemed so other-worldly or beamish to the vicars and the vergers that they assumed I was one of the homeless, fiftyish men who were mingling with the well-heeled parishioners for the sake of the sandwiches served afterward. There was no end to how glad I was at any hour to wake up, step outside, or simply pour and stir a cup of coffee and stretch my feet into the spill of zebra-patterned sunlight that the venetian slats threw on the rug so marvelously.

Behold now behemoth, God says. . . . *He lieth under the shady trees, in the covert of the reed . . . the willows of the brook compass him about. Behold, he drinketh up a river, and hasteth not: he trusteth that he can draw up Jordan into his mouth.* Or, God continues angrily to Job, *Canst thou draw out leviathan with an hook. . . . Canst thou put an hook into his nose? . . . Will he make many supplications unto thee? . . . Wilt thou play with him as with a bird?*

I use the King James translation, and Leviathan may be either a whale or a crocodile, though this spiky, vivid description goes on to resemble in its particulars a scaly, toothy crocodile, who, like the often dangerous hippo, could make the Jordan River terrifying. The biblical Hebrews were an inland people, not seafarers like the Phoenicians; but on the other hand, the author of the Book of Job is considered to have been a later, more traveled and worldly individual than some of the other writers. The Revised English Bible of 1989 splits this chapter, 41, into two entries divided by Chapter 40, so that Leviathan can represent both of these wondrous and unconquerable creatures. And the whole glorious dithyramb to the animal kingdom—peacocks, lions, wild gleeful goats, formidable wild oxen, wild nifty asses, dashing ostriches, soaring cliff eagles—recited by God pridefully to the much abused Job out of a "whirlwind," is in marked contrast to that earlier, more famous God, whose injunction to Adam and Eve at the beginning of Genesis is that they and humankind should *subdue . . . and have dominion over the fish of the sea, and over the fowl of the air, and over every living thing that moveth upon the earth.*

The Hebrew God is whimsical, jealous, inconsistent: mad, of course, very soon after that first chapter of Genesis, at Eve and Adam, with somewhat the same tone of thunderous petulance he later directs at poor Job for rather less reason. (Job's long sufferings have been the result of a sort of a sporting bet between God and a manipulative, teasing Satan, not punishment for an impulsive act of disobedience at the behest of some newly fledged Serpent.) Even in the single book of Deuteronomy, where Moses transmits, at God's instruction in Chapter 5, the Ten Commandments (plus at different points a considerable amount of merciful detail as to how bond servants, widows, orphans, and destitute wayfarers shall be treated), God also decrees, in Chapters 2 and 3, the genocide of the tribes of Heshbon—*the men, and the women, and the little ones*—and also of Og—*utterly destroying the men, women, and children, of every city.* And again, in Chapter 20, God ordains a further holocaust: *Thou shalt save alive nothing that breatheth. But thou shalt utterly destroy them; namely, the Hittites, and the Amorites, the Canaanites, and the Perizzites, the Hivites, and the Jebusites; as the Lord thy God hath commanded thee.* Deuteronomy does contain the brief, winsomely generous admonition in Chapter 25 that *thou shalt not muzzle the ox when he treadeth out the corn* (in other words, not let him feel hunger), but it also includes, in Chapter 28, the dire warning that if God's established "holy people," the Jews, don't follow his commandments, they will become cannibals from famine, conquest, siege, and plague, eating their own children. And in Exodus 20 and 34 the vindictive threat is floated that a father's sins will be visited upon his children even to the fourth generation—although, in fairness, Deuteronomy 24, Jeremiah 30, and Ezekiel 18 contradict this. *I wound, and I heal*, he says in Deuteronomy 32.

He seems a berserk and hideous deity in some of the more perfervid remarks that Moses and others record or attribute to him. He is an angry caliph who might better suit the Serbs or Hutus of the 1990s or the Hitlerian Catholics of World War II, and he did not have much appeal for me as a boy, though the Old Testament stories we heard in church and Sunday school were riveting—the drama of baby Isaac almost being sacrificed by his father, Abraham; of Judith cutting off the head of Holofernes; of Joseph sold into slavery by his brothers; of little Moses in the bulrushes; of Job's faith and loss of faith; of David fighting Goliath with a slingshot; of Samson rendered powerless when the treacherous Delilah cut off his hair (Judith a heroine but Delilah a villainess). The sheer, gala accretion of these tales, extending over a good number of centuries, had more narrative weight than did the thirty-year story of Jesus, from Bethlehem to Calvary.

But Jesus spoke for a God whose teachings I could better swallow. His, too, in its abbreviated way, is a matchless tale. Born in a manger, although he was the Son of God, because there was no room at the inn, yet visited in his infancy by wise men and shepherds drawn by a radiant star; healing blind men and lepers, raising the dead, and throwing the money changers out of the Temple, accompanied by a small band of "fishers of men"; betrayed by Judas for thirty pieces of silver and crucified between two criminals, dying in agony and thirst after several hours but forgiving his captors, "for they know not what they do," and on the third day rising from the dead to sit at the right hand of God himself. A most direct parable—just lengthy enough, yet coherent and confirmed by four testimonials. You can't beat it for what it is, and the interpretations within our own language and time have ranged from "Onward, Christian Soldiers" to Martin Luther King. You see on TV the pomp of the Pope, versus Mother Teresa. And whatever these elaborations have become, the central addenda of Christianity seem as essential to me as the Bill of Rights added onto a basic Constitution. Judaism without the Sermon on the Mount seems a religion incomplete, *lex talionis*—an eye for an eye—without the Golden Rule: *Whatsoever ye would that men should do to you, do ye even so to them* (Matthew 7).

Jesus added to the undercarriage of Judaism not to destroy *but to fulfill,* he says. And like Moses before him, he went into the wilderness on a walkabout, up to a mountaintop for revelation—which I take to be more evidence of biblical ambivalence about the idea in Genesis that the wilderness ought to be bridled and ruled, that the snake and crocodile, the elephant and hippo, the whale and lion should have no untrammeled territory left in which to strut their stuff and play their fateful, antique roles. Still, as against the legend of Christ, shimmering and imperishable as it is (and, indeed, priests and ministers wear desert dress), you have Judaism beginning not with a baby's birth but with the very universe. You have the theater of Eve and her Serpent; then Noah's brave Ark; wise Solomon; the visions of Isaiah; Jeremiah and Zechariah; Daniel in the Lions' Den; Jonah in the Whale; the Song of Songs; and zestfully on. No wonder so many Jews have regarded themselves as a people chosen by God.

My own bias is against a monotheism so people-centered, and thus the Old Testament God who most appeals to me is least "Hebrew." ("There is no certainty that the author was an Israelite," says Marvin Pope, a leading scholar of the Book of Job.) God's magnificently hair-raising answer to Job from out of the whirlwind outguns anything of the sort in the New Testament, which after all is more fit for the advent of Saint Francis, lover of tiny birds, or the pacifism of Martin Luther King than for the preservation of old values. *Where wast thou when I laid the foundations of the earth?* God declares (a lover of carnivorous tigers as well as small birds).

> *. . . When the morning stars sang together? . . . Hast thou commanded the morning since thy days? . . . Hast thou entered into the springs of the sea? . . . Have*

the gates of death been opened unto thee? . . . Hast thou perceived the breadth of the earth? . . . Where is the way where light dwelleth? and as for darkness, where is the place thereof? . . . Hath the rain a father? or who hath begotten the drops of dew? Out of whose womb came the ice? and the hoary frost of heaven? . . . Knowest thou the ordinances of heaven? . . . Canst thou lift up thy voice to the clouds? . . . Canst thou send lightnings? . . . Wilt thou hunt the prey for the lion? or . . . provideth for the raven his food?

For me, that's plenty good enough as an underlying Constitution, an underpinning for my American Transcendentalism, as well as a basic link to other world religions and beyond them to the grandfather, or "pagan," spiritual impulses that occasionally well up in so many of us at the ocean, in the woods, or during slam-crash thunderstorms or to the extraordinary hallucinations that afflict us when someone we love dies. Genesis's intolerance of wilderness was tailormade for the Industrial Revolution. It covered the clergy on every lame excuse they gave for ducking their heads as the skies and fields and rivers turned sooty-black and breathing space and sunny light and a whole panoply of flashing creatures disappeared. Just as on other issues, such as slavery, child labor, racial prejudice, and colonial genocide, the church was rarely in the vanguard to intervene but, rather, brought up the rear of the mainstream, snubbing the earnest mavericks while the situation rapidly grew worse. In my lifetime alone, perhaps half the species that were alive on earth when I was born will have been snuffed out.

Christianity displays these contradictions in Saint George slaying the dragon while Saint Francis plays with birds, in Androcles plucking a thorn from the lion's paw while Saint Patrick drives the snakes out of Ireland. And Judaism has faced its own immiscibility in the task of peace-making in Israel, where rabbis and religious folk have not seemed to play an adequate part in whatever reconciliation has been accomplished with the Palestinians. Instead, it's been mostly the work of military men and secular idealists, as if the Jewish religion itself is incomplete, a religion of resistance, of "silence, exile, and cunning" (in James Joyce's analogous definition of how art should be engendered), but not yet a religion brought to closure, not yet a savior's religion here on earth.

189

No stretch of grief or the imagination, no precedent in science or logic can get a handle on this catastrophe—half of Creation extinguished in a single life span. Noah did not materialize again to save God's handiwork, or even a Mother Teresa. Flying beings, swimming things, creeping, crawling, running existences, long-legged or short-winged, brought to life over many, many millennia, had no escape and simply blinked out. People, says a friend of mine who is a Congregational minister, "are born in solidarity with Creation but live in brokenness with Creation," or, as he adds, "in sin."

The author of the Song of Songs, another extravaganza, might testify to that. You may recall some of his imagery: *Your eyes are doves behind your veil, your hair like a flock of goats streaming down Mount Gilead. Your teeth are like a flock of ewes newly shorn . . . your parted lips . . . like a pomegranate cut open. . . . Your two breasts like two fawns, twin fawns of a gazelle grazing among the lilies.* (This from the Revised English Bible, which is more lyric here.) *Come with me,* the speaker adds to his new bride, *from the summit of Amana, from the top of Senir and Hermon, from the lions' lairs, and the leopard-haunted hills,* to civilization. The duality of nature in the Bible is like that in other ancient epics, such as *Gilgamesh,* the *Odyssey,* or *Beowulf,* and our own literary figures, Melville, Hardy, and Conrad. Psalm 104 boasts affectionate references to wild goats and rock badgers, storks, whales that sport in the sea, wild donkeys, and young lions *seeking their food from God.* But in Psalm 102, *I am stricken, withered like grass. . . . I am like a desert owl in the wilderness, like an owl that lives among ruins,* the writer says. Though the King James Version uses the intriguing alternative translation, "pelican of the wilderness," wild places are not habitats where you'd want to be.

And in Isaiah, Chapter 34, after the Lord has sated his bloody wrath upon the residents of Edom, *horned owl and bustard will make it their home; it will be the haunt of screech-owl and raven. . . . It will be the lair of wolves. . . . Marmots will live alongside jackals. . . . There too the nightjar will return to rest and . . . there the sand-partridge will make her nest, lay her eggs and hatch them, and gather her brood under her wings; there will the kites gather, each with its mate . . . they will occupy it for all time, and each succeeding generation will dwell there.* (The King James substitutes unicorns and cormorants, bitterns, dragons, satyrs, and vultures for some of these; and the American Revised Standard Version, porcupines, ostriches, and hyenas.) Likewise, when Babylon is overthrown in Isaiah 13, *marmots will have their lairs in her, and porcupines will overrun her houses; desert-owls will dwell there, and there he-goats will gambol; jackals will occupy her mansions, and wolves her luxurious palaces.* Sounds like the epitome of desolation but also like a bit of fun. The desert fathers lived closer to nature than we do.

Here, as in Job, the wilderness is presented as an antithesis to cities and to agriculture, certainly not one that man wishes for, yet one that, for God's superbly diverse purposes, continues to celebrate the glory of life on earth. Though God had been mean to that Snake, back in Genesis, for tempting Eve (*Upon thy belly shalt thou go, and dust shalt thou eat all the days of thy life: And I will put enmity between thee and the woman, and between thy seed and her seed . . .*), wild animals are generally God's children, too. What he envisions for them at the end of time is summed up in Isaiah 11. *Then the wolf will live with the lamb, and the leopard lie down with the kid; the calf and the young lion will feed together; with a little child to tend them. The cow and the bear will be friends . . . and the lion will eat straw like cattle. The infant will play over the cobra's hole, and the young child dance over the viper's nest. There will be neither hurt nor harm in all my holy mountain; for the land will be filled with the knowledge of the Lord as the waters cover the sea.*

No permission is given to Isaiah, Job, or Genesis for the holocaust mankind has visited upon the natural world, whereby the rhinoceros may soon be as scarce as the unicorn. Behemoths, crocodiles, and the soaring eagles and fearsome lions that enriched, mythologized, and demonized the banks of the Jordan as manifestations of God's majesty are long gone, with their like being pursued to the edge of the planet. The blackened woods, the sooty skies, Leviathan more than decimated: God is not just. He is cryptic, elliptical, even countenancing your death, *my* death. Like sand in a wasp-waisted egg timer, we tumble through the slot before we're quite ready to, and the tumbling process does not ensure fairness even in priority. You and I, born the same year, may die thirty years apart. Justice is not God's department; justice is a man-made concept, except in the somewhat different sense that character is often fate as, in fact, Job's is, finally wining him back God's favor or, to be exact, *fourteen thousand sheep, and six thousand camels, a thousand yoke of oxen, and as many she-asses,* so that he's exactly twice as rich as before God allowed Satan to toy so cruelly with him. In life we don't necessarily see people receiving their just desserts, but over a couple of decades we do notice their muddied faces and bitten nails if, although as rich as Croesus, they have lived nastily. Time wounds all heels.

The Old Testament God seemed as primitive as a tribal sheik, being too much constructed in the splintered, banal image of man. Thus the New Testament, although less dramatically embellished with centuries' worth of narrative, convinced me more as a boy. I was a Tolstoyan then, and from that teenage base of idealism I discovered jubilee "shout" singing in the black Pentecostal church I used to go to in San Francisco in the late 1950s. I later discovered Saint Francis's hymn of adoration called "The Canticle of the Creatures":

> Most high and most holy, most powerful Lord....
>   To Thee and Thy creatures we proffer our praise:
> To our brother the sun in the heavens ashine,
> Who brings us the beauty and joy of our days,
> Thine emblem and sign.
> We praise thee, O Lord, for our sister the moon,...
> For our brother the wind, for the bright of the noon,
> For all of Thy weather.
> For our sister the water, so humble and chaste,
> For beautiful fire, with his perilous powers,
> For our mother the earth, who holds us embraced,
> Who delights us with flowers...

Transcendentalism naturally followed, and I stopped describing myself as a Christian. Nevertheless, Psalm 148 does say it all: *Praise the Lord from the earth, you sea monsters and ocean depths; fire and hail, snow and ice, gales of wind that obey his voice; all mountains and hills; all fruit trees and cedars; wild animals and all cattle, creeping creatures and winged birds... Praise the Lord.* And Psalm 150, the famous one: *Praise the Lord. Praise God in his holy place, praise him in the mighty vault of heaven.... Praise him with fanfares on the trumpet, praise him on harp and lyre; praise him with tambourines and dancing, praise him with flute and strings; praise him with the clash of cymbals; with triumphant cymbals praise him . . .*

Behold now behemoth, which I made with thee! An electrifying injunction, and for practicality a lifetime I've been doing just that—observing zebras, and genuine behemoths like elephants, hippos, giraffes, whales, jaguars, and grizzlies. I have believed that they were indeed "made with me," and by the age of eighteen I was already thrusting my hand down a circus hippo's mouth to scratch the back of her tongue and the inside of her cheeks, much in the way that tickbirds, or "oxpeckers," do in Africa, searching out leeches. I also communed with Siberian and Sumatran tigers, both now almost extinct, and black-maned lions and Indian elephants, and I rubbed a rhino's itchy lips on sweltering afternoons, not in a trivializing manner but single-mindedly, with a passion that had begun with turtles when I was five or six—like that of city kids for dinosaurs nowadays. Leopard seals and eponymous leopards, killer whales in the Arctic and Antarctic, and Nile River crocodiles: I've traveled far and wide since then to glimpse these stirring beings. *Canst thou draw out leviathan with an hook? . . . Will he make many supplications unto thee?* Can you *make a banquet of him* or *part him among the merchants?* God asks Job jeeringly, and, alas, it's come to pass that we can, with religion frequently a handmaiden to the merchants.

On the street, with my rejuvenated sight—fifteen-thousand-dollar plastic implants—I seemed to see right back into the exhaustion and poignant anxiety in the recesses of other people's eyes, the thwarted potential for love and fun and dedication, the foiled altruism, now in abeyance, and the exasperation. And yet I could also see the imp that lived in them, the child that hadn't died. So often the variables that exist in somebody's face, from mirth to aggravation, add up to the wish to still believe in virtue, hope, and God.

"I have seen the Elephant," the gold rushers and other frontiersmen used to say after they returned to town. For me, with a lifelong belief that heaven is on earth, not nebulously up in the sky, I see it every dawn and sunset, and in the head-high joe-pye weed, smelling like vanilla in July (and used by the Indians in treating typhus, colds, chills, "sore womb after childbirth," diarrhea, liver and kidney ailments, "painful urination," gout, and rheumatism). I see it in the firmament at night and in a stand of spruce or a patch of moss beside a brook. And during the time when I was blind I could smell it in the scent of a blossoming basswood tree, or hear it in a toad's trill, or lay my head flat on the ground and gaze at the forest of fervent moss, inches away, a beetle or a caterpillar crawling. *Behold now behemoth.*

(1995)

II
Places

Of Cows and Cambodia

During the invasion of Cambodia, an event which may rate little space when recent American initiatives are summarized but which for many of us seemed the last straw at the time, I made an escape to the woods. The old saw we've tried to live by for an egalitarian half-century that "nothing human is alien" has become so pervasive a truth that I was worn to a frazzle. I was the massacre victim, the massacring soldier, and all the gaudy queens and freaked-out hipsters on the street. Nothing human *was* alien; I'd lost the essential anti-egalitarian ability to tune out on occasion, and everything was ringing in my ears. Of course, even my flight itself was part of a stampede of people who were doing the same; and since my wife and I happened to be involved in a kind of low-grade marital crisis, too, for all my dovish politics, during my last few days in the city I had been going to mean and bloody movies and reading dirty books, as I usually do when in a trough of depression.

I have a hundred acres, mostly woodland, which I'm informed is probably generating enough oxygen for eighteen hundred people to breathe. I don't institute many improvements, both because of my ignorance and because, for instance, instead of chopping deadwood for the stove, for twelve dollars I can buy sufficient stove-sized scrap from the bobbin-and-dowel mill down the road to cook and heat the house four months. A ten-mile stretch of Vermont state forest adjoins my land, and there is more forest beyond, so what I really do is walk. An old overgrown stagecoach road which has been kept open by hunters' jeeps and loggers' wagons winds with appropriate slow grandeur up through a pass and down into a wild valley, where there are several ponds and much birdlife and an abandoned log shack or two. A long brook rattles through the undergrowth and evergreens for miles, and the ridges roll up to haystack humps and aggregate themselves into the broad miniature mass of Mount Hor, which on its other side looks off a giddy cliff into a spring-fed lake several miles long. There is a smugglers' cave beside the lake where silks and whisky used to be stored; the Canadian border is only fifteen miles away, and for a whole summer a revenuer slept in a hammock in the woods along the shore, posing as a poet but listening for sounds. Another nearly lost, forgotten smugglers' camp—this dating from the Civil War, complete with cemetery and cellar holes—lies up behind an opposing mountain across the lake. Around on my side of Mount Hor a deep, traditional sort of cave corkscrews into the mountain a hundred feet or more, a place where hunters lived, and once an eccentric called Leatherman, who wore skins and lived off whatever he could catch or kill. Hor is a fastness for bears. I've heard descriptions of how six of them have died of gunshot wounds in the valley below. The surviving bears, like shy, fleet Indians still holding out, sometimes hoot to their mates at dusk in June—a single quiet hoot with a growl at the end, which distinguishes the sound from an owl's call. Plenty of deer skirt through, and on the mountainside you can find boggy glades where single deer have made their beds in the fine grassy patches, leaving the imprint of themselves after they run. There are frogs on the paths—occasionally a charged, invigorated snake with a frog in its mouth. I've seen mink holes along the brook, and glimpsed a pair of tiny shrews playing at the entrance to their burrow. The porcupines, after huddling in congregations through the winter, spread out and fight for territory during the spring, with piercing, nasty screams, though in the evening you can hear them chewing bark high in the spruce, their teeth sounding gravelly-voiced.

My collie, Bimbo, who accompanies me, tangles with mystery creatures like mother raccoons fifty yards back in the brush. He has enough finesse not to get torn by them or squirted by skunks, and kills woodchucks with a chop of his jaws and a snap of his head, mouthing them hungrily to break the bones, lingering over the body and salivating. But then he lets them fall and, trotting home, finishes off last night's helping of dry dog chow instead. Before I adopted him, he wolfed down crusts of bread on his visits to the house, running four miles for the privilege. Though he is uncompromising with strangers, he's almost overly loyal to me, having had so many other masters that he keeps a weather eye peeled for the day when he may find himself alone, starving again. He sticks beside me in the woods rather than ranging out, but chases any deer we see with businesslike directness wholly wolfish for the moment, testing the air before finally happily lying down in a stream, and by his manner telegraphs the different creatures whose tracks he smells. He avoids gun-carrying people, having seen some shooting, and is afraid of thunder, indicating its approach before I hear it come. He is most cheerful in the morning, as if the day as it advances saddens him—he points up a somber nose. But he's a great ground-scratcher after urinating and a dramatic posturer with other dogs, his sense of self perhaps enhanced because he lives in isolation in the country and meets few other dogs. He fights sharply and seems to take a rich and realistic view of the citizenship of all the animals in the world, making no unnatural distinctions between those wild and tame. Cows, cats, and fishers intrigue him equally. Meadow mice are a pleasure to hunt, but in bear country he doesn't wag his tail as much and walks with gingerly circumspection through the smashed berry thickets, the rank and muddy wallows. When we set out, he springs with all four feet off the ground and catches my hand in his mouth, and when we get back to the house he pulls off the burrs that have stuck to me, breathing lovingly. There are two things difficult about him. He personalizes cars, and chases them with an inimical bold heroism, since he's been hit three times. And in an apparent attempt to aggrandize himself, he loves to roll on the moldering bones of redoubtable strange animals. Worse than just using a dead deer, he singles out a picnicker's ordure to roll in if he can, smearing his fluffy fur with excrement, wearing it like epaulets, as the most mythic material of all. Afterward he romps and struts; it gives him a tremendous lift to smell so thickly like a man.

Besides believing nothing human should be alien, we used to aspire to another condition: as D. H. Lawrence said, we must *live more intensely.* We thought that, vague and dreamy, we were letting life slide by. But I was joining a mass swing of people looking for country acreage who had begun to feel so hard-pressed that their main effort was just to disengage themselves. They were of different politics and different vocations, yet some of them felt that if they lived any more intensely, they might have to be hospitalized.

Although we're swamped in populace and intensity, a few ridges over from me was a commune—twelve or fifteen persons in their twenties whose response to these dilemmas was more hair of the dog. Instead of barricading themselves behind thousands of acres of forestland, as I was trying to do, they intended to chum and combine with some of these overnumerous souls. And with the aspens trembling, field flowers blooming, the blue sky and the lavish landscape, their admirable experiment seemed to be working out. The children were sunburned and muscular, doing without diapers and caring for each other. They lived in a Children's Tent, and while there was some uncertainty and ear-pulling, mostly they roamed between adventures, catching toads, feeding the hens. The grownups slept in pairs tucked into plastic lean-tos or hunters' tents under the spruces—there was one lofty-looking tepee. They had a geodesic dome which wowed their visitors and was intended to be transformed into a candle factory eventually, as well as a roomlike area covered with sheets of plastic draped over poles where the cooking was done, and a large produce garden that didn't succeed, owing to the acid soil.

Consistent with their life style, they tried to welcome strangers, even explaining their beliefs to sightseers if asked to, or letting a hitchhiker camp with them for a week or so on a probationary basis. Since several were veterans of an ill-fated commune farther south in the state which had turned into a kind of motel for traveling hippies, this time they'd bought enough land for an agricultural existence, but without buildings, so that in these first months nobody could stay over unless he bestirred himself at least to pitch a tent. They built an outhouse, chicken house and cow shed, repaired their road, attempted to incorporate as a private elementary school so they could educate their own children, avoided obtrusive drug use, helped their neighbors hay in exchange for the loan of farm equipment, and wisely went to meetings of the local Grange so that the local people could see firsthand that they were not dragons. The men were fit-looking—the long hair didn't appear to be a mark of bereavement—and the girls eloquent, graceful, appealing; they had big eyes, and as in many communes, they got the job of dealing with outsiders. I felt wistful when I dropped in. Obviously, no notable amount of work was being done. Everyone went off on jaunts into the countryside or swam or gathered firewood or sat talking all day in the cook tent, fixing salads of sorrel, lamb's-quarters and wild mustard leaves with little berries and raw eggs stirred in. They made butter and ice cream and pots of sugared oatmeal, and boiled milkweed and fried cornbread. It was a summer idyll. Lying underneath the trees, they never did get the log house built that they had planned.

By October, like grasshoppers who'd danced the harvest time away, they were looking for winter quarters to rent, stung by the frosts, worried for their children's health. It developed that the townspeople were not so friendly after all; nothing was available. They were college folk, so they weren't really going to have to stay and freeze, but it was interesting to note that the most favorably disposed faction in town were older persons who could remember living off the land and looking rather ragged themselves during the Great Depression. Also, the oldsters connected the rootless appearance of these hip types with the itinerant loggers from French Canada in earlier days—long-haired, linguistically a puzzle, with underfed dependents—and therefore weren't afraid of them.

This corner of Vermont is without industry, and when a summer resident shows up again the following spring, the winter news of friends and neighbors is likely to be bad—bad luck, bad health—

because so many younger people clear out, and there is hardly any way for a man who has stayed around to have advanced himself. Seventy-five years ago the town had factories manufacturing cheese, knickers, shoes and butter tubs, and what was then the longest power line east of the Rockies. Seventeen miles long, it carried 800 kilowatts and was the hobbyhorse of the inventive-minded middle class, although at that time farm boys still went into the woods after spruce chewing gum, which they cut off the trees with sharpened poles and steamed and sold downtown for a dollar a pound. Later they saved their gum money to buy battery radios and "windchargers," noisy windmills that turned and turned on the roof of the house and kept the batteries charged.

Since then whole settlements have disappeared in the outlying sections of town, and the country has grown so wild that one of the postal clerks has killed twenty-three bears so far. The saying is that you need only soak your feet in a bucket and set the salty water out by the back door for deer to drift right up to drink. A deer is just a joker like oneself; he's not much better at hearing a man move toward him in the woods than the man may be at hearing him.

Like most of the other abandoned farms, mine has its residue of projects that failed: a stunted orchard, an attempt at raising Christmas trees. The soil was marginal, and the family tried to keep goats at one time, and they had cows but the barn burned. Failure makes some men rough on their wives. There are stories of how the man who lived here during the thirties wouldn't bother to cut the stovewood short enough to fit the kitchen stove, wouldn't even cut down more than a week's supply, in case, as he said, he died; his wife could cut down her own trees after that. By and by he did die, and she moved off the place, saying that she was sick and tired of "staring at that damn mountain." Another, more sensible enterprise of theirs had been raising hunting dogs.

Woodcock fly up; a little fox runs down the road. In the springtime, when I arrive, being in my own fields is plenty for me—airing the house and stepping in and out, discovering again that the night sky exhibits stars by the thousand if they aren't blotted out by lights. No matter how brutal the winter has been (last Christmas fifty inches of snow fell in a single week), the grass is coming up like kettle-drums; birches and pines, which grow as much as three feet in a year, are mustering themselves and shooting up. Goldfinches pick apart the dandelions; sapsuckers chisel for bugs underneath the maple bark. I roast potatoes to eat in their jackets like rolls and take walks on the drizzly evenings, listening to my brook, admiring the treetops against the sky, comparing spruce with fir, red spruce, white spruce, red pine, white pine. I watch the bats over Little Fish Pond, hearing trout jump that sometimes sound so big I step back under the trees, afraid somebody is heaving stones.

The young men hunt hard in season, turning their attention to the sport, but the old men think about it all the time; it is an elixir to them. They seem to feel they'll live longer if they are still able to shoot, as though in dealing death they are immortal for the moment. Far from shying from the ghastly antics of the dying deer, they recount these covetously, like a formula that may stave off the same collapse in themselves—the creature jerking its legs up as it fell, twitching and groaning on the ground. These tales can extend through half an afternoon, each man has killed so many deer, often outwitting the game warden, too. Porcupines and groundhogs can be hunted much of the year, and some people do so when times are grim, either for the relish of the kill and as a means of staving death off, or else for food. When neighbors quarrel, they hear each other next morning out in the woods shooting small game; and in the fall, when the hayfields are mown and visibility is good, they both lay up a store of gutted groundhogs, later grinding the meat with onions, apples and sunflower seeds into a matchless burger steak. Years ago people put up barrels of salted smelt caught in the spawning season, bins of root vegetables, canned green tomatoes, and grated horseradish cut with turnip. Then in midwinter, after letting a barrel of hard cider freeze, they'd drill a hole in the middle and tap the nearly pure alcohol, which made a man's heart feel as if it were wrapped in soft cotton.

In farming country old people are not sequestered away, and when somebody dies nearly everyone knew him. Only last week in the drugstore he may have crossed his fingers and said with a mild smile that he was hoping for a clean bill of health from the doctor.

The butchering, the weighing of each cow's fate every few months, also makes death a familiar companion. Not every cow that doesn't freshen promptly is sent to slaughter, but she goes "down the road," to bob in terror under the auctioneer's prodding. It's personal—rather like a slave auction, perhaps. "What a pretty lady this is! Look at the teats on her! Keep her in the pasture this summer, and then if you don't like her, cut her throat in the fall!" Milk farmers are involved in all the intricacies and ambiguities of life-and-death power, and generally are glad to be. Since they work mostly around the barn, they're paler than the farmers who grow crops. Not until the 1960 census did Vermonters come to outnumber their cows, and several say the reason they were in no hurry was that they simply *liked* cows. In the isolated gores and valleys cows were a kind of harem. They could withhold or volunteer part of their milk, and if well soothed and happy they gave more. Even with machine-milking, the udders need a good old-fashioned warm-fingered stroking beforehand, and when a cow is bred artificially, the technician massages her cervix as well as squirting in the semen. After he leaves, a skillful farmer will squat down for a while and in a friendly fashion rub and squeeze her teats.

Against the sense of exuberant release I felt on long walks in the woods was the knowledge that this in fact was just a hermetic patch of wilderness with highways on all sides, scarcely larger than a park: it was a ship in a bottle, and I was only hiding out. The commune idealists, who read *The Whole Earth Catalog* as a life's chart, seemed doctrinaire, not easy company, so on days when I wasn't out with the dog hunting for smugglers' camps, I started accompanying an artificial inseminator from Newport Center named Donald Nault on his regular rounds. I had the frivolous notion that I might be watching the way human procreation would eventually be carried on, each liberated woman choosing semen that suited her from a listing of donor traits. Instead, the cows, pinned in their stanchions, looked around at us like immobilized moose turning to watch the wolves approach to eat. But as Nault kneaded them the experience became less unpleasant or fearsome, obscurely peaceful. They visibly relaxed, as though an ill wind had blown through the barn but had left them unharmed.

Nault has five kids and lives in a frail-looking frame house, shingled gray and set on a hilltop that overlooks most of his working territory, which is twenty-five miles square. His wife is a stocky, pretty woman, an ironist, a pertinacious mother, who stuffs bitterns and flying squirrels to decorate the living room. He is a good explainer and seems to smile more than most people do, although he's perfectly prepared to yell. He's gangly and has short gray hair and the open-faced look of a high-school science teacher, with thin-rimmed glasses, a spacious physiognomy but narrow bones. His voice is flat-timbred and dispassionate-sounding; he breaks his vowels in half, twanging the halves in different tones. He keeps bees and hunts with bow and arrow for hobbies, and works in the 4-H program, a much more free-wheeling proposition than scouting, being geared to what farm youngsters can do off in the boondocks by themselves. Like the bulk-milk pickup drivers, the feed dealers and John Deere men, he's one of the county's peripatetics. According to tax figures, his corner of it has seventy-six hundred cattle, of which he services about half (the rest still rassle with his competitor, the bull). Even allowing for the heifers that are too young to breed, this means he services at least ten cows a day because he does free repeat breedings when the first doesn't take. He's off three days a month, including Sundays, but gets no other vacation, and is paid at the rate of $2.80 per cow. The fee the farmer pays is $7.

I learned about the business, along with a good deal of outright gynecology, riding around with Nault from farm to farm, seeing the lightning rods atop red barns and white houses (summer people reverse the colors—red houses and white barns). The farmers took no more notice of us than of meter readers, and though the days turned out to be rawer than I'd expected, with sometimes afterbirths and once a dead calf on the floor, there was the pleasure of the pasturage and roller-coaster woods and the big-siloed, spruced-up farms lying in front of the dramatic silhouette of the Green Mountains, Jay Peak jutting up immediately in front.

Besides enjoying the guided tour, I was glad for the friendship between Nault and myself. We were contemporaries and whatever we didn't have in common tended not to come up. But the hard monotony of breadwinning communicated itself too, just as it does whenever one absorbs the routines that another person must live by. We'd pull up by a milkhouse, built of cement for easy cleaning, with cold spring water tumbling into black slate sinks and a torpedo-like five-hundred-gallon milk cooler gleaming, milk stools hanging up beside breeding charts and bacteria counts sent by the creamery. The milkhouse is for people, but the dark barn, drafty and partitionless, smells of fermenting silage and wet, fleshly herd politics. The cows have topknots where they've been dehorned and side-set eyes, trusting noses and flappy ears.

Nault steps into his rubber boots and syringes semen into a catheter, which he holds crosswise in his mouth while working with his hands. He is medical in manner, not chieftainish like the farmers, and though I admired the delicacy with which he handled the task, I pitied him the tedium of pounding round and round between a hundred farms year after year, none his. Some of the fellows envy him his free-lance life, however. Leaping land values, the overall slide toward change, cause a hollering across the countryside. Farmers think of retiring on the money their acreage would bring; yet dairying really has never been more profitable, they say. A hundred pounds of milk will buy two hundred pounds of grain, but a cow only needs to eat about a pound of grain for every three or four pounds of milk she produces during the winter months, or one to nine or ten pounds when she is pasturing. This is the ratio that matters. Also, about one acre of grazing ground and one of hay are necessary to support a cow in New England, and so if she brings in a yearly profit of perhaps two hundred dollars after all expenses, then each acre is worth a hundred dollars a year to the farmer and he will only continue keeping cows as long as that hundred dollars does not seem too paltry a sum when measured against the prices the land speculators offer him.

Whereas in the old days a man might dabble in winter logging or the Christmas-tree business or maple sugaring and take the chance that a few cows would catch pneumonia while he was gone, now it's best to be a specialist, with all the thorny breeding questions and mastitis and Bang's disease and vibriosis to watch for. Little farms must have the same expensive milk-handling equipment as big ones, so that the little operators are being bought out. Efficiency demands that they get rid of the mediocre milkers, then feed the good producers all the protein they will eat, whether in the form of short early-cut hay and high-value alfalfa and clover, or store-bought nutrients like beet pulp, citrus rinds, and chopped-up corn, wheat, barley, oats and molasses ground together. Most of the cattle Nault breeds are black-and-white Holsteins, which yield an average of 14,900 pounds of milk a year, far outperforming the brown-and-white Guernseys or Jerseys. Genetically Holsteins are also more trustworthy than Guernseys and, being big, are worth two hundred dollars as beef just as they stand. Jerseys do keep a hold on some farmer's affections because they're quite emotional and heated, yet small, easy to manage, and their milk tests high in butterfat, which means a premium is paid.

The landscape grew more familiar as we tooled around Nault's territory. Sometimes, during the afternoon, we went right back to the same farms, driving through gray rain squalls, past fields of timothy, rye grass and vetch, and stands of lusciously foliaged trees in the townships of Troy and Coventry. We saw Canadian Frenchmen with De Gaulle's nose at the age-old New England occupation of gathering stones. We passed the house of the district's healer, a seventh son of a seventh son, who can cure everything from dropsy to the twist in the postman's hip, which got out of its socket as the poor guy leaned from his driver's seat to reach the mailboxes. This healer is a rough type and doesn't pray beside his customers; he simply puts his hand on the ailing area and holds it there for ten or fifteen minutes, telling raunchy jokes meanwhile.

Once we passed a mink farm, consisting of cage-filled sheds and several horses waiting in a vacant lot to be killed, cut up and fed to the mink, then drove up the first grade of the mountains to a brown slumping home isolated in deep woods, with a toolshed in back where a brown cow was tied. No grownups were around. A girl of twelve, who had been left in charge, came out of the house, handed Nault seven one-dollar bills and watched him work. Afterwards we coasted back to moneyed, rolling pasturelands, with immense barns equipped with stanchions by the hundred, all electrically hooked to the fire alarm so that the cows would be freed automatically in case of a disaster. Indeed, the latest innovation is to dispense with stanchions entirely, letting the creatures mill as they wish about the barn, only walking them through a "milking parlor" twice a day, because the more benign they feel, the more milk they will brew.

These new procedures naturally discourage the *machismo* bent of many farmers, which is why lots of them still keep bulls. The snorting beast costs hundreds of dollars to feed, more than the farmer saves in breeding fees, and it inhabits a stall where otherwise he could stable a milker. Yet some people will alternately utilize Nault's super variety of semen and their own yokel bull, and then, to his consternation, instead of raising the fine new calves which have the perfected genes for future stock and selling off the quirky local progeny, as often as not a man will keep his own bull's calves and send Nault's scientific infants straight to the butcher's block.

I am describing what I did in the aftermath of the Cambodia invasion, not a story with an end but of interest to me because it is what I would do again in the event of other invasions, or practically any other kind of trouble; it is the only thing that I can think of. I liked being poised near the Canadian border the way I was, and found that ducking quickly into the woods and living by myself had helped: up early, aware of other creatures besides man, with the sky-clock of sun and stars.

After hiking awhile around Mount Hor, I began going across the road to explore a large steep formless upland known as Robbins Hill, after a rifle-toting family of Raggedy Anns who have disappeared. I'd been learning to recognize the common trees, and a riotous arboretum of these were crowded together on Robbins Hill in what was an orgy for me. Young trees, particularly, send me into a hustle of needle-squeezing, bark-tapping and branch-waggling. I can't believe how straight and true to type they are, how springy to the touch and brown and green. To discover so many examples together in deep grass—lacy cedars next to hemlocks next to wavy larch and beech and yellow birch—was grounds for glee. Laughing to myself, I rushed from one to another, touching the leaves—perfect little maples, perfect little balsam firs. There was a flowering shrub called moose missy by the old people and a flower that they called frog's mouth.

Now this was all escapism—a word that's going to lose its sting. I was escaping to recuperate, my ears grateful for the quiet of the woods. My wife flew up to join me as soon as she could, and except for her company, I found the old people best to be with, rather than those my own age, saddled with mortgages and emphatic politics. My neighbors told me about fermenting beer forty or fifty years ago that had a head so thick they could write their names in it or spoon it off for sandwich filling. They'd make next Christmas's plum pudding on Christmas Eve, to marinate in brandy for twelve months, and serve last year's. The husband remembers skidding logs down off Robbins Hill with oxen one winter after a forest fire. The fire leapt across the road on some loose birch bark that caught the wind, and he remembers how pathetically the porcupines squealed as it caught up with them. There was only one farrier in the county, a man named Duckless, who shoed oxen for icy winter work; he did it as a kind of stunt. Oxen are stiff-legged and can't lift their legs as a horse can, so he employed a block and tackle and canvas sling to hoist them up. Since they are cloven-hoofed, each foot needed two shoes. The dogs would collect from the farms nearby as if a bitch had come in heat. Dogs love a blacksmith's visits because they chew on the hoof parings—the parings are taffy to them.

My friend Paul Sumner went foxing with his dog as a youngster, following the fox for many winding miles and hours. He'd get $25 for the skin at a time when the daily wage at the sawmills was less than $1.50. A fisher skin was worth still more. He had a Long Tom rifle which had a kick that knocked him down and a bolt action so loud that if he missed when he was deer shooting, the animal would stop running and listen, mystified by the strange sound. There were ten Sumner children, and necessarily the boys hunted for meat. They'd get one rabbit started, and in dodging about, it would scamper through every other good rabbit hiding place, scaring up a throng. After each snowstorm the father would tramp around the swamp, leaving a great circle of snowshoe tracks beyond which the younger kids were not supposed to go. Though they were very poor, the saying was that no woman could be admitted into heaven who cut more than four pieces from a pie. Paul still makes his own bullets, weighing out the grains of powder as some men roll their cigarettes. He used to make shot for his shotgun by mincing up a flattened pipe, and would hike off for days with a bait pail and traps into the Big Woods over in Essex County, carrying a few bottle caps with wax and string in them to heat the kindling for his fire on a wet night, later pouring his supper grease on the next morning's firewood. He remembers Halley's Comet in 1910, having climbed Mount Hor especially to see it, sleeping on the crest and watching a duckhawk fly up at dawn out of a tree and kill a fast-flying duck with such impact that both of them fell from the sky. He remembers fishing in Canada and catching northern pike four feet long. If the line broke, by jinks, he says, the fisherman jumped in the lake and wrestled with the fish, almost like another man. The blueberries were as big as thumbs and turned the hillsides blue.

He tells the legend of how oak trees acquired scalloped leaves. There was a man who signed a pact with the Devil according to which, after enjoying his handsome looks and riches, he would have to give himself up "when the oak lost its leaves." But oaks never do lose all their leaves; some cling stubbornly to the trees all through the winter until fresh foliage sprouts in the spring. And so the Devil, who was a bad loser, ran around and round the archetypal oak, chewing on its leaves, marking the edges with his teeth.

In the cavalry down in Brownsville, Texas, after World War I, Paul used to feed his horses sugar cane for a treat. His barracks mates kept an ocelot for a mascot; and there was a pet terrier in a bar they patronized which was so tough the customers would throw a tennis ball at it as hard as they could, down the aisle between the tables and the bar, and the dog, bounding in the air, would catch it on the fly. Back in Vermont, Paul, who was always a fisherman, located an old quarry hole with bass swimming at the bottom of it. A man lived nearby in a tar-paper shack, ten feet by six and all grown over with blackberries— "The house was only standing up because the termites inside were holding hands." It stood under a fine white pine that the fellow called his "sunflower tree" because the needles seemed so radiant when the light was right. He raised tomatoes on the remains of a defunct outhouse and baked his bread in loaves so big around, a slice was the size of a pane of glass. He spent his days bucking firewood for money, though flourishing his rifle when people came to pick it up (he'd grab a broomstick and aim with that if they were kids). He was so fussy that he wouldn't let anybody touch his cartridges, afraid they'd leave some sweat on them and tarnish the parts of his gun, and yet his house was stuffed with junk, scarcely allowing room for the bed and stove. He never washed his dinner plate, just dumped more food on it, but every few weeks he would scrape off the detritus and fry that too, calling it "stodge."

Another character on that road was the Turkey Buyer, who ranged about the state in a truck carrying gobblers. When he passed a farm that raised the birds he would screech to a stop, jump out, run up to the door and tell the farmer that one of the turkeys from his truck had got out of its crate and scurried in among the farmer's turkeys; would he please help catch it? Together they would catch one of the farmer's turkeys, and then the Turkey Buyer, with many thanks, would drive away.

Dan Tanner was a neighbor of Paul's too. Dan was a seven-footer who had once killed a bear which went after a string of fish he'd caught by stabbing it with a sharp stick of heartwood just underneath the arm. He was exceedingly tough; his wife, Abbey, used to wash the blood off all the men he licked. A good trout brook made up in their back field, most of it underground for the first mile. Nevertheless, there were some holes you could fish through and catch short little trout, discolored from not having seen the sun. Tanner ran a still that cooked his booze so hot, the pots and tubing jounced. He set aside a jug for Saturday and one for Sunday, but usually he'd finish Saturday's before sunset, vomit it up and finish Sunday's too. He didn't trouble very much about the law and feuded with the game warden. One time in the winter when the warden was trailing him, Dan carefully tossed the doe he'd killed behind a rock and turned downhill, taking small steps, down to a brook, then walked backwards in his own tracks, stepping exactly in each step, and hopped behind a dead spruce on the ground, where he lay still. Pursuing him, the warden passed by and looked in vain for Tanner's tracks across on the other side of the brook. Thirsty, he stooped to drink, and Tanner fired a shot into the water just underneath his nose.

Paul, who is a father, a widower, is a less violent man. He suffers from angina but cuts pulpwood for a living at nineteen dollars a cord. One corner of his farm is about to be razed for an interstate highway, and parallel with that will be a power line, so his years of retirement will probably be spent between these fierce belts of activity. For much of his working life he was a lineman himself for a power company. The photos on the wall show him in climbing boots high on a leaning pole with a tree fallen on the line. He's got blue eyes and a jug-handle pair of ears, a puckery, sharp-witted face, a twisty smile. He jokes a lot, collapsing in laughter, swinging his arms, although he has a sense of misery as well. In wintertime he needs to shovel the snow from in front of his windows in order to see out; it gets so deep that he can walk right onto the roof when the ice must be scraped off. He grows winter apples, which are not picked until after the first snowfall. The frosts seem to condition them; that's when the deer prefer them too.

He who fights and runs away lives on, and that's what I had been up to. As the summer closed I went again to the roots of the brook under Mount Hor, finding the split-pear prints of deer and listening to the ravens honk. There is a "boiling spring" that Robert Frost used to visit, according to reports. The spring no longer boils, having become choked with leaves—it never did boil in the Westerner's meaning of the word; they don't have hot springs here—but it still tastes pristine and heads a cold and lively stream. Talking with the various old men, each one with a heart condition, I sometimes felt the need for haste in gathering information: even a sense that if the fellow should suffer a stroke before my eyes, I would bend over him, urgently asking, *Where was that cave? Who was it that you said lived there?*

Each of them, after his own manner of doing things, was in the process of selling off his land—at least the relics on it, like wagon wheels—pretending that he was just trying to "get rid of the stuff," impatient that the buyer hadn't come for them, and watching as his pastures, laboriously maintained since the nineteenth century, grew back to tangled wilderness. In September I accompanied a man I am fond of into the jungle that had formerly been his lower pasture and now was on the point of being sold to me. He was in his middle eighties and walked very slowly, like a frail Galápagos turtle, looking incongruously weightless but leaning heavily while I helped him to edge through the willow-alder thickets. We looked for the old fence line, where bits of barbed wire lingered on the trees, and the stump of a black cherry tree that he thought the bears had killed, and a round rock called Whippoorwill Rock, and a big butternut, and for the place beside the stream where his brothers and he had once successfully rigged a power saw operated by a water wheel. The alders were a jungle, yet he struggled much farther into the center of the property than I'd expected, calm and slow about it, swaying a little when the wind blew. Many landmarks had been obliterated, but he found a few. The growth was swamp grass now, smothering in spiraea brush. Remembering as he went along, he persevered so far that I was afraid that even with my help he wouldn't be able to extricate himself again.

(1971)

Walking the Dead Diamond River

For many years the New Hampshire Fish and Game Department has made a census of ruffed grouse along nine habitat routes, each about forty miles long, representing when taken together every variety of cover within the state. Lately new highways and real-estate schemes in the southern counties have forced the biologists to shift some of these, and some of the paths have been preempted by motorcyclists or Sunday walkers, so that even if the grouse population in the area hasn't declined, the annual count can't be tallied as scientifically as the censuses of the past; understandably, this is discouraging to the men who do the counting.

Recently I had the fun of walking the wildest, northernmost Grouse Survey Line, which crosses the headwaters of the Connecticut and Androscoggin rivers, country as remote and untarnished as any in New Hampshire—owned by several lumber companies and by Dartmouth College. It's country emptier than the much better-known Presidential Range and the other mountains and valleys of the White Mountain National Forest, lying to the south. My companion was Karl Strong, who is the department's senior biologist north of Concord.

This walk used to be made in midwinter on snowshoes, as well as during the summer when the broods of new chicks can be counted, but now that life is softer for everyone, it's done twice in the summer instead. There are three cabins in the course of the forty-two miles where Strong and his partner used to pack their supplies and sleep over, but first they dispensed with their packs, trucking their gear in ahead of time, and now they arrange to drive home each night. In fact, it was lucky for Strong that we did it this way because on one of the nights of our walk, August 24th, a freak killing frost developed that would have wiped out his vegetable garden if he hadn't been at home to hose down everything early in the morning. He raises about fifteen different vegetables, freezing or canning them so that his family can eat them all winter. Gardening is his passion, though one day in June when I talked to him he was on a schedule of waking up every three hours at night to feed an orphaned puppy. He's a reserved, lean, soft-spoken man, pale in complexion like a Scandinavian, not in any sense a softie in appearance but a cold-weather man, and the depth of his affection for living things does not show immediately. In talking to paper-company officials I found he is called "the missionary." When I mentioned this to him he laughed and said that his grandfather was a minister and that, like a minister, he puts in lots of work and accomplishes little.

He's a deer specialist; the grouse census is a job that he does for New Hampshire's bird biologist, who works with ducks and pheasants as well. He's uncannily attuned to deer and astonishes the paper-company foresters because he can actually smell a deer two hundred feet off. A gland in the deer's heel cords gives off a sex scent which Strong describes as resembling the smell of a certain fungus that is found in rotting birch stumps. He can smell porcupines too, but no bears, except for "dump" bears. This Grouse Survey Line is Strong's particular darling. He's walked it himself for fifteen years, watching his body gradually age when measured against its miles and seeing the trail and rivers change as logging and even sport fishing become modern industries. Logging may soon be done with laser beams or thin pressurized jets of water. Already the more technologically advanced companies cut pulpwood with monster-sized timber harvesters that can sheer a tract of forest right down to its roots, and then, right on the scene, the logs can be fed into chippers which dice them into paper-making fiber, chip-sized, to be trucked to the mill like freight. This is not done in New Hampshire yet, but there have been plenty of changes.

Though Strong's grouse path is mentioned in the Appalachian Mountain Club's *White Mountain Guide,* he hadn't been eager to have me accompany him because it is never hiked on, is purposely marked only very obscurely, and could be destroyed for useful game observation if the outdoor fraternity ever really discovered it. A path through splendid country that is traversed twice a year, not worn into ruts by a river of feet, is nowadays a great rarity and a precious one. He said I could come along if I could keep up with him, didn't get blisters, and if I recognized to begin with that any account of the New England wilds must be more of an elegy to pleasures now past than a current guide.

We started at Second Connecticut Lake to go to Cornpopper Spring, which is under Magalloway Mountain. The sky drizzled intermittently, the temperature stayed around 45 degrees with the first of the gusty cold front that killed several gardens that night, and we walked with clenched fists and "dishpan hands," as Strong put it. It was miserable enough, but the raindrops stippled the beech leaves beautifully and the firs in the rain looked as gray as steel. My hat was red, which looks black to a deer or a bear but which birds, with their sharp color sense, are alert to, so Strong planned to be extra alert himself.

Once out in the woods, he seemed younger immediately, lighter and gayer than back in town, remarking on the balsam smell in a soft voice that would be well suited to love-making—his wife packs notes into his lunch with the sandwiches—and reminiscing about a day in 1959 when he caught his limit of big fish in a beaver pond that we saw on Smith Brook, using only the naked hook itself, which he had twitched like a fly. We saw a kingfisher plopping from high up to catch a chub there, and a merganser diving. The forests around the Connecticut lakes are a baronial showpiece owned by the power companies that maintain the lakes as reservoirs, but we soon got into bushwhacking country where the tourists don't come. Strong says that by nature he should be a Democrat, believing the Democrats are closer to the Biblical injunction that we must be our brother's keeper, not dog-eat-dog as the Republicans are, but that the tourists are making him more conservative. He walks with quick quiet strides because the grouse try to steal away on the ground if they hear a man at a distance. When he thinks he has heard one of them call, creaky and peeping, he tramps noisily into the brush and claps his hands to scare up the covey so he can count it.

The low country was lush, with raspberry bushes in hoops and flowers head-high. We saw a broad-winged hawk, and saw beaver-work in the sandy-bottomed brook that we crossed and recrossed— Strong said he thought the man who had laid out the trail must have been on snowshoes, unable to see the water. Strong himself made the mistake of blazing it recently with a paint called International Orange, which in some way sets the bears off; nearly every blaze was chewed. Up in the woods, the trail was cool and shadowy till we got into a logging area, where I learned from smelling the birch stumps that white birch is odorless (which is why it is used for Popsicle sticks), that black birch smells like wintergreen (and is a flavor for chewing gum), and that yellow birch has a delicate, mellow, somewhat minty smell. The stumps of the latter were a wonderful yellow-orange inside. We saw one a hundred years old, just downed.

In the rain the skidders, which are a kind of modified, big-wheeled tractor most effective at hauling logs, had churned several hundred yards of poor Strong's trail into a comically gucky concrete-colored soup. The ruts, four feet deep, were running with rain. Slipping like a monkey on roller skates and balancing wildly with his arms, he insisted on walking the route anyway, laughing because laugh was all he could do.

We descended to Smith Brook again, finding a clearing where five bunkhouses and a horse hovel had once stood, near the remains of a log-driving dam and a tote road, trestled and corduroyed. We saw a doe and a fawn, purple trillium ("stinkin' Benjamin") with its wine-colored berries, Canadian dogwood with bright red bunchberries, and a grouse's scrape-hole in a dusty spot where the bird had bathed itself. We saw a brood of three (our count was eight for the thirteen miles that day). Up on Hedgehog Nubble we found the abundant turds of a moose that had wintered there. Moose winter high and deer winter low. New Hampshire has very few moose but if they were anywhere, they would be here. At the turn of the century the last three caribou in the state were sighted and shot close by.

The clouds swelled gray and silver, settling on us. Sometimes the sun poked through, which hurt the eyes in a sky so dark. Strong smoked when we took a break, to let his liver "release its sugar," telling me that's why a smoker stays thin. We saw a waterfall, and moose and bear tracks, and more than one tucked-away valley with ferns, mosses and snapdragons, usually the site of an old hunting cabin with the owner's Army dog tags tacked on the door and some claw marks where a bear, hungry in the spring, had tried to break in. The resident hummingbirds flitted close to my red hat, sometimes half a dozen in the space of an hour, to investigate why it was the same color as their own throats. Up on Diamond Ridge at three thousand feet was a cold fir forest, very remote. Strong hunts from a cabin on Magalloway Mountain, using a muzzleloader to make it a bit harder for himself. Last year he and his friends sighted in on a mama bear with her hackles up and three cubs, and there was lots of black smoke but no kill. He told me how tough it is to pull a three-hundred-pound bear out of the woods, or even one weighing two hundred pounds; they stretch when you pull but they don't move. Boy, he said, they seem smaller, though, when skinned out.

He has no laws to assist him when he advises the timber operators on behalf of the wildlife as to what they should do (nor do they seek his advice—he just goes around offering it). He's always polite, the foresters say, and will come into the offices of the Brown Paper Company and simply tell them, "Well, we blew it," when a key stand of evergreens has been cut and some deer are going to die as a result. The whole forest is wildlife habitat, of course, but he restricts his marking activities to the 10 percent of the woods where the deer winter, or he wouldn't get anywhere. Even so, and being prudent, he cannot expect that more than about three-fourths of the trees he marks will be spared. Deer must shelter under mature softwood growth like fir or spruce in a snowy climate. The boughs block some of the wind

219

and catch part of the snow, holding it up where it evaporates. Deer don't browse on trees of this sort unless they are starving; instead they look for young hardwood saplings like maple, poplar and birch to gnaw on and peel, not trees of a size yet worth harvesting commercially. But before any other consideration they must have shelter. Rather than freeze in a zero wind or flounder about in deep snow where a dog could kill them, they will stay in a softwood grove and slowly starve.

In the north woods if there were no logging going on there would be few deer, the pickings would be so slim—just a frontier of big trees better suited to the life style of caribou, which eat moss and lichen. But Strong's job is to intercede with the foresters so that a mix of clearings, glades, openings and sizable timber for shelter is left. Although the personnel are getting brisker, more impersonal, the companies, feeling the pressure of the times, make a big stir about "multiple use"—land with game on it, land lovely for hiking—and he can appeal to that. The traditional cutting cycle used to be seventy or eighty years and the best foresters cut only about a seventh of the timber at hand in a decade, so that timber of every age was growing. Now in the rush for "fiber," younger and younger trees are cut, the cycle is down to forty years, and it's increasingly complicated to manage a forest so that the different requirements of dozens of creatures can be fitted in. Rabbits, for instance, thrive in an area five to fifteen years after the woods have been cut, and grouse fifteen to thirty-five years afterwards, but some of the furbearers and birds need much older timber.

The next day we were back at Cornpopper Spring, starting from there by 7 A.M., with the weather even a little colder but the sun a bit brighter, the wind having blown the rain away. We had ten and a half miles to go to Hell Gate on the Dead Diamond River, where the Fish and Game Department has a camp. Strong said he felt like putting his snowshoes on; the only way to get good and warm was to put on a pair of heavy snowshoes. His father came from the lumbering country of Patten, Maine, and he remembers pouring kerosene on a crosscut saw as a boy to make it go through a gummy pine. They hunted together.

Then in 1944, while he was a Navy medic, his father was shot in the woods for a deer (an average of five hunters a year are killed in New Hampshire).

The first mile of this section was a logging road now, and for a while farther on, alongside a glacial esker, a farmer had taken his tractor and plowed a track of his own so that his friends in their vehicles could reach a vacation cabin he'd leased. We met some loggers, who seemed like direct but limited men, a notch below the state-employed people I was meeting. We stood at the edge of a clearing watching three of them work without being detected by them. Strong's lip curled in amusement; what kind of woodsmen were they? He waited for them to notice us until he got tired and, like an Indian feeling benevolent today, simply walked peacefully away through the trees.

Since grouse usually run before they fly, a windy, disruptive day like this one was bad for hearing or spotting them. They were plentiful because June, when the chicks were new and likely to die of pneumonia if chilled, had been very droughty—a June without storm is not good for the trees but is good for the grouse. Once grown, they are rugged birds and winter right on the scene, eating birch buds and diving deep into the snow to sleep, leaving no tracks on the crust for a fox to follow. Strong said that the foxes were beginning to build up again after a rabies epidemic in 1969. In the previous siege, in 1963, he'd had to take twenty rabies injections in the stomach as a precaution. It's best not to check for rabies in wildlife too often, the biologists say, because you'll find it so regularly that the fewer checks you make the fewer epidemics you discover. We saw both fox and bobcat scats. Fox dung is surprisingly dainty and small-bore, even considering the animal's whippet-thin body. Bobcats, and especially Canada lynx, look leggy, pathetic and light as air, too, when their coats are skinned off. They are dumber than foxes if judged anthropomorphically by their IQ, but are so superbly cautious and stealthy, so hard to see and so wild, that by their own lights they are smart enough. In a lifetime Strong has sighted just three.

Raw deer-season weather. Strong blew his nose with his fingers, and pointed out where his nephew at seventeen had hit a bear with six shots, the bear dashing on till it finally dropped, nipping off strips of its own intestines as they fell out and trailed. (The nephew has never come hunting since.) We watched two hummingbirds feeding on jewelweed in a glade where Strong once saw twenty. We noticed a woodpecker hole high in a stub where two swifts were nesting. In the depths of the woods we came on a deer lick, with well-defined trails homing in like the spokes on a wheel; I heard one deer flee. The mud was white with minerals, and the roots of the trees had been exposed by the hooves. Strong used to lie here in a blind on moonlit nights to observe the goings-on—three or four deer at once pissing and shitting and drinking in the shallow pools, contributing nearly as many minerals back to the lick as they removed.

We picked hatfuls of hazelnuts for Strong's teenage daughters, and saw lots more neon-red bunchberry and bear-chewed blaze trees, but the trampled-looking grass that I would have assumed was another sign of game turned out to be just a casualty of the hard rains. We talked about how most naturalist writers rate poorly with full-time workers in the field, Thoreau, Fenimore Cooper and Ernest Thompson Seton included. But I was wearing Strong's spare pair of rubber boots, and their good fit seemed to represent the friendship budding between us. Doctors, as another group which cultivates the outdoor life, also run into a lot of kidding from the professionals. Strong told me about two who had crashed in the Pemigewasset drainage while flying over the White Mountains one February and, with a surgical saw, tried to cut some green poplars next to their plane to make a fire. They died, which wasn't so funny, but if they had gone to a softwood grove a couple of hundred yards farther off, they could have broken off plenty of dry wood from the dead bottom branches just with their hands.

We were on the grassy banks of the East Branch of the Dead Diamond River, whose headwaters spring ten miles away we had seen the previous day. The day before it had taken me until the late evening to get the bones of my hands feeling warm again, yet now we were sweating already. The temperature was 58 degrees (whenever Strong saw a grouse he took wind and temperature readings). We lunched partly on hazelnuts—a squash-seed taste—overlooking a thunderous sixteen-foot falls and its twisty catch-pool, a stretch where once in the 1950s

Strong caught and threw back two hundred fish in a couple of hours. People had hiked in from what was then the closest road, in Maine, to catch four-pound brook trout, but now these holes were empty of fish.

We watched a bulldozer cracking down trees for a winter haul road, which would need no gravel, only the natural mud architectured into shape on the night of the first freeze, whereupon for the next five months the log trucks would roar back and forth on the ice. However, this was a forest whose patterns Strong had helped to create, and even his management plans for the streams—that the skidders not silt up the spawning beds by operating along the banks—had been followed, so what we saw was not agitating to him. We followed the old tote road on the riverbank, used in log-driving days. We'd crossed from the large township of Pittsburgh (312 square miles) to the Atkinson and Gilmanton Academy Grant (fourteen square miles of woods, once sold by the aforesaid academy for four hundred dollars). Dartmouth, which owns the adjoining College Grant (forty-seven square miles) near Hell Gate, leases the recreational rights to this land at a dollar an acre annually so that its alumni and guests may feel free to spread out. Like most other state people, Strong resents the exclusion of the general public by these rich guys, but like me he had to admit to being glad that these woods would resemble a wilderness a little bit longer than unprotected forests. On the other hand, in the fall Dartmouth men kill only about seven deer for every ten square miles of land they have, whereas the public on ordinary timberland kills twice that many. This is not favorable news to a man like Strong who on his snowmobile tours finds twenty deer starved to death per square mile in the cramped wintering yards on even the public lands.

We argued about hunting—not that I could sensibly oppose hunting deer, but there are other beasts. I teased him as to whether this predatory "naturalness" he touted so highly wasn't downright dog-eat-dog Republicanism, but he wasn't to be hobbled by consistency, and pointed out again that too many tourists with city ideas were turning him in that direction anyway. Of course, the yearly symbolic deer he killed was like his assiduous gardening or the cabin he'd built for himself on Magalloway, as I understood. He said, though, that wildlife was public property, for all the people, and that therefore he resented anybody who posted his land against the free access of hunters. My answer was that, first of all, wild animals were perhaps the property of no one but themselves, a question I was willing to leave moot if he wished, and secondly that I resented any man's going on any land, public or private, and shooting some creature, dwindling in numbers, whose like I might have trouble ever seeing in a natural state, and then tacking its hide on his livingroom wall—*that* concept of private property was offensive to me.

Strong said, Well, if his hunting something really means that you may never see its like again, I agree with you, he ought not to be hunting it, it should be a protected species; that's what biologists like myself are for. What I'd left out of the equation, however, he added, was the fact that many people who post their lands do not do so out of any beliefs corresponding to mine. Rather, they seem to think that in buying a piece of land they're buying the wildlife that lives on it too, along with the pines and the apple trees.

Okay, that infuriated me too; we were agreed. He'd started defining us as conservationist versus "preservationist," but I laughed and said, Look, if *you and I* name-call and can't get along, then what hope is there that the wilderness forces can ever combine? He smiled. I said, Bear in mind too that some of the people who object to hunting are not as ignorant about the woods as you think. What arouses them is not that a deer is shot which otherwise would eventually starve to death, but that the hunter gets such a kick out of killing it.

Do you see hunters butchering cows for kicks during the off-season? Strong asked. It's not the pain, it's the death, and it's not the death but the stalk and the woodsmanship and the gamey wild meat the fellow is after; the completeness of each of these complemented by the others. I understood what he meant, but to be one up I asked why, if the woodsmanship is the heart of the matter, there are so very few archers in the woods—archery requiring woodsmanship of such a high order that it does overshadow the kill. Strong said bow-hunting is just too hard to do for all but that handful of hunters. Success comes too hard, and most hunters are firearms buffs as much as they are woodsmen and enjoy the big bang and the bird-in-the-hand. Besides, he saw no reason why the kill ought to be overshadowed. The naturalness of the kill was akin to all of the other pleasures one felt in the woods, and in no sense skulky or inferior. It was his business to see that no animal was hunted into oblivion if he could help it, but to have a deer herd protected like the animals in a zoo, just to be looked at, never shaken up by a hunting season as by the whirlwind of natural predation—this was not woods or wilderness, he said angrily; this kind of situation would arrive soon enough as it was, as I should know.

We waded the East Branch just above where the Middle and West Branches join, a black-looking shapely knoll in front of us and a high hardwood ridge beyond, all forest land everywhere, with bluish tall firs in the foreground that Strong had managed to save. The day before, I couldn't have believed today would bring prettier country, but it was like parkland in Colorado—forest and wild grasses interspersed. Though I was getting a charley horse, the marvelous ungrudging succession of Valhalla views, of black knolls, green grass and green trees, the forest unrolling, the sandy-banked river bending alongside—and long-legged Strong—put energy into my strides. As he talked, it became evident that this wasn't just Dartmouth country; it was also a private playground for a good many Fish and Game officers. They could get through the gates and camp and fish where no one else could.

Strong talked about his difficulties in the National Forest. There, too, the deer yards received last consideration, and the federal foresters fibbed to him, outmaneuvered him, or tried to treat him as some kind of hick in order to escape interference with their timber sales. In Canada, where he's gone as a consultant, the Crown Lands are sometimes overcut just as badly. A cord of softwood on the stump is worth $6, and if there are fifteen cords to the acre, on these vast tracts it begins to add up.

We saw a red-shouldered hawk, a meadow mouse, and bobcat droppings with a whole little mouse skull intact in one. There were the tracks of a raccoon that had been hunting tadpoles, two garter snakes, a goshawk's nest in a dead beech, and lots of deer prints. Two big red deer bounded off, showing each other the way with their fleecy tails. We were in the principal deer yard along the Dead Diamond now, country that Strong tours during the winter. He said the deer often die with their stomachs full of non-nutritive wood, having run off their fat during the hunting season and the season of rut, but if there are loggers working nearby they can survive off the sprouty tops of the fallen trees.

On a suspension footbridge we crossed to Hell Gate Camp, four grizzled huts in a breezey hayfield. We watched a party of Fish and Game recruits being taught how to disarm a hunter. They had been issued bird books and were learning how to identify ducks. As a biologist, Strong has no police duties. Most of the time he wears no uniform, and unlike the wardens who were instructing them, can drop in on a hunting or fishing camp in the guise of a hiker; even noticing a violation, he can move on if whatever is wrong strikes him as really not very important.

These hearties do not let you go without having coffee with them. The next morning we were delayed again while pleasantries were exchanged. I met no woodsmen among them but I did meet outdoorsmen who, feet up on the table, relished being here in this kingdom, with the white water hissing outside, instead of down at the office in Concord.

We waded the Little Dead Diamond, still steaming after the frosts of the dawn. It's a noisy, energetic tributary stream, chiseling potholes and digging rock sculptures in rhythmic curves out of the limestone strata above Hell Gate. We followed it uphill. Six or seven years ago Strong used to catch his limit of ten trout here in an hour while he ate lunch, or feed crumbs to as many as twenty that were visible in the clear water. Now he's lucky if he catches three little ones. The spring freshet, loaded with rocks and ice, wipes them out of the fishing holes, and the stream is too precipitous to be repopulated from the main river below. Until recently a new population would always wash down from the gentler stretches—the stream heads at Mount Pisgah—but now these nursery pools too are being heavily fished by people who reach them in rough-terrain vehicles. No surplus exists.

My left leg was swollen tight with charley horses, yet this walk of eight miles through dense, choppy, unpretentious country which had never been settled or farmed seemed like the best scenery of the trip and a kind of climax. It was ambush country; you couldn't see far, but hidden away there were several quite glorious wilderness elms that Dutch elm disease hadn't found. We saw a splatter of tracks left by a sprinting bobcat alongside the stream. The stream popped and sparkled in the sun, pincering past obstructions, cutting a hundred corkscrew twists.

Leaving the Little Dead Diamond, we took its South Branch, ascending toward Crystal Mountain. Usnea moss ("old-man's-beard") hung from the dead limbs in the stands of young fir, a delicacy for the deer. The masses of moss covering the ground which Strong remembered from some of his early visits had disappeared since the last logging, replaced by raspberry thickets. We ate as we walked, and saw traces of every other creature that had been feasting also, every animal one might expect except for skunks, which stay nearer farmland. There was a new beaver dam, the drowning marsh trees turning red. There were firs and alder—maybe good woodcock country—as well as thick overgrowth scrub where the maple trees had been logged. We saw two broods of grouse, the first mother leading two chicks and the second five. It was a lovely high-ceilinged day, platter-blue, good weather for grouse to be out and about. (Our average count for the whole grouse survey was one bird for each mile and a half walked.)

We crossed into Dix's Grant from the Atkinson and Gilmanton Academy Grant, both owned by the Brown Paper Company. Parts of the bed of the South Branch had been preempted by their logging trucks, so it was badly messed up. Where it forked, we turned from the South Branch to Lost Valley Brook, climbing south through a concealed niche in the ridge, a little lost valley indeed, very isolated in spirit, where a decade ago Strong was marking thirty-inch birch, and hemlock and pine forty inches through. Now even the six- and eight-inch pulpwood is being removed. We found a dead shrew with fine-grained gray fur, and lots of deer sign. The skidders had cut ruts waist-deep, partly overgrown, no joke to fall into.

We talked about naturalness again. The Indians, Strong said, thought that one could no more own land than own the stars; that's why they "sold" to the whites so cheaply. We were drinking from the brook and I happened to remember how, in the Book of Judges, God told Gideon to choose an army to defeat the Midianites by taking his men to a stream and picking the ones who drank directly from the running water on their hands and knees, animal-like, not the more civilized ones who lifted the water to their lips. Strong liked that, but I said that maybe it just meant that the beastly fought better. He told me the latest promotional scheme involving his department was to transplant some ptarmigan from Colorado to Mount Washington's tundra and see if they lived. Unfortunately the question concerned not just the ptarmigan but New Hampshire's twelve fragile square miles of alpine ecology. Would the birds choose the rarest buds to eat, and what would the tramping feet of the hunters do?

At the source of Lost Valley Brook we entered a thick, dark, gloomy wilderness forest of pole-sized fir and paper birch that is one of the watersheds of the Dead Diamond and Swift Diamond rivers. The Swift joins the Dead fifteen miles or so below Hell Gate, and the waters of both go into the Magalloway River (where they meet the paved road), then into the Androscoggin, then the Kennebec, and finally into the ocean at Bath, Maine. Even up top here it was swampy, though, with many toad pollywogs enjoying the bogs; frogs, which start bigger, would be out of the tadpole stage by now, said Strong. We spotted some hawks, garter snakes, hummingbirds, bumblebees, high phloxlike flowers, red mushrooms, and false Solomon's-seal with red berries. Often the ground was cut every which way by beaver channels, like an obstacle course. Moss, muck and sucking mud, bank-beaver holes, wild grasses and sedges, poplars, cattails. The temperature, 60 degrees, up 15 from when we had started, had me wet with sweat. Fourmile Brook, a portion of which was our destination, heads at a pond so remote that it is stocked with trout thrown out of an airplane.

This brook drops away down the ridge at such a steep pitch that the water sounds like a pistoning motor. We found an antique ax head, broad, rusty as ochre. The last go-through by the loggers had been recent, and so the growth was jungly and low, with plenty of the bugs and berries and wetness grouse like, but for some reason the hauling had been done with a bulldozer, not a skidder, and the ground had not been damaged too much. There was a heady honey smell everywhere from the flowers—purple, blue, yellow—and millions of bugs. Big-toothed poplar, willows and birch, moosewood and silver maples, alders, jewelweed and shadbush. More deer sign, more pollywogs; a grouse brood of four, cheeping like chicks, trilling like mice.

Fourmile Brook is a good deal longer than the name indicates, with bad footing, and we spent much time on it before reaching Fourmile Camp. This is a tin-roofed government shack seventeen miles by woods road from the highway, in a clearing surrounded by hills. The wind from the south carried the smell of the pulp mill in Berlin, New Hampshire, a smell more fecal than what one encounters in the actual lavatories at the paper company. If I stepped off into the brush for a minute Strong said, "Is that you or Berlin?" It's a nagging, boiled-cabbage, boiled-egg smell at best, carried also on an opposite wind from the Canadian mills sixty miles north, or on an east wind from those of Oxford County in Maine. A wet light snowfall in the winter seems to sharpen it even more, which for a man with Strong's educated nose must be disturbing. We found a bear's droppings, and I remarked how queer it was that a man's would have affected us as more disgusting. He said the reason might be that compared with wild animals people overeat so enormously that they don't digest as much of the fermentable material. Not being a scientist, I suggested instead that maybe we're so egocentric we prefer to believe even the badness of some of our smells exceeds that of other creatures'.

A truck had been left for us at the camp. As we drove back toward town alongside the Swift Diamond River, we saw it had turned the color of mud from fresh logging that day. So had a stream called Clear Stream. Under New Hampshire's Clean Waters Act a fine of a thousand dollars a day can be levied for offenses like this, but it hasn't as yet been invoked.

Samuel Taylor Coleridge is said to have walked as far as forty miles in a day, and Carlyle once logged fifty-four in twenty-four hours on a walking tour. Wordsworth, the champion in this league, was calculated (by De Quincey) to have totted up 175,000 or 180,000 miles in a lifetime of peregrinations afoot. "I have two doctors," said Sir George Trevelyan of English-style walking, "my left leg and my right."

The American brand of walking of course has a different mystique, almost forgotten lately, which dates back to the frontier and has little to do with the daily "constitutional" and therefore should be exercised in a setting so brawny and raw that the mileage can't even be guessed at. Since my own sports as a boy were running and walking, my image of athletic prowess has been a related one, but I was glad to get home to the soft bed and fortifying dinners of the Colebrook House Hotel each of these evenings. I'm lucky I wasn't born a few centuries ago. For the sake of the exultancy I feel in wild places I probably would have tried to get in on some of the exploration, and as I'm not that strong physically, I would have been one of the substantial number in almost every party who died. Even in balmy weather, when I've been alone on a true frontier, a hundred miles from the nearest dirt road, I've had crazy, incongruous sexual fantasies assault me, like a blanket pulled over my head, as if by them I sought to hide from more powerful fears—of grizzlies, illogical avalanches, of twisting my ankle or getting lost. Yet between these bouts with the fantastical, during which my eyes actually shut at times, I was all eyes, all elation and incredulousness, living three days in one.

Strong stretched his legs the next day on the last lap of eight miles. We both hoped we hadn't been chatting so much that we'd spooked any grouse, so he stayed in front of me, letting me see if I could keep up. We went from Fourmile Camp up a steep hardwood ridge which is part of Crystal Mountain, and down the other side. Many squirrel tracks at the rain pools, a red squirrel and chipmunk confronting each other on a short log (the chipmunk the one with the food in its paws), and a rapid goshawk. Goshawks will plunge right into a pile of brush after a grouse, like an osprey hitting the water chasing a fish. Strong said he saw his last peregrine falcon in 1954. In those days he would see up to fifty horses going home at night on their own along these trails from the logging sites.

The ground where we climbed was heaped with slash sometimes five feet high, wet from the night's rains, and the skidders had cut tank traps everywhere, making walking a sweaty struggle. The grouse we disturbed called to each other. The cocks live alone, each in his own territory, to which he tries to drum mates in the spring. The females nest on the bare ground, usually in some slight depression that they find at an elevated place near the base of a tree. They eat catkins, clover, foliage, and fruits, but the chicks are not vegetarian; they eat beetles, ants, spiders, snails, flies, and larvae, which are richer in protein and vitamins.

In a clearing we found the remnants of a loggers' supply wagon. Spruce had been the climax forest and now that the big old second-growth hardwoods had been removed also, mostly fir was appearing, a short-lived, fast-growing species that buds early in the spring, risking the frosts but shooting up, its root system shallow and its limbs flimsy. Yet a fir woods, too, requires at least forty years to reach a commercially plausible size, and in modern business enterprise who's going to sit around for the next forty years with real estate like this, watching the dragonflies? Every management shakeup brings a change in plans, and Strong in his advocacy position with respect to the land is naturally on the firing line.

Understand that a bear, for example, needs a minimum of about five square miles to forage in for his food supply. This is not counting the extra land he will roam through in the course of a year, which might comprise seventy-five square miles, or more than two hundred if he is hunted hard. The five square miles is an irreducible wilderness area that will grow his food, and although other bears may overlap with him, he will include their territory in his wanderings. A single deer's primary range for feeding is forty or fifty acres. A mink's, in a fertile marsh, may be only twenty, and a raccoon's ten, though, like the deer, they will each ramble a mile or more on occasion, utilizing the food-stuffs and crannies of a much larger acreage, and could not live in a wild state for long if really restricted to such a space. Yet if an acre is now to become worth $1,000 as recreational property, is that raccoon worth $10,000? Is a bear worth $3,200,000? As in the suburbs, a raccoon can parcel together a home out of snips and pieces of people's backyards, but otter, bears, bobcats and so on cannot. I had teased Strong about hunting, but I hoped he knew that the teasing had been a result of my admiration, that I understood that hunting by men like himself was never the villain in wildlife management. Rather, it was the summer people like me, who come crowding in, buying up, chopping up the land after the loggers have skinned off the trees.

A brook going downhill gave us a steady grade to the Swift Diamond. The temperature rose to 80 in the afternoon, from 45. Squirrel and deer country, with lots of witch hobble—deer food. We met mosquitoes and saw a rabbit, an owl's feather in the leaf muck, and a woodchuck's tracks (a type darker than the reddish farm chuck inhabits these forests). Seeing a red squirrel chitting at us, bold in the certainty that we couldn't touch him, I had a sudden memory of the chattering exhilaration which as a boy I had felt just after a close brush with death in a car. So must this squirrel feel at dusk when an owl swoops at him and he swerves round a tree trunk and escapes, feeling the wind of its wings.

The Swift, like the Dead, was employed originally for freighting out the virgin softwoods, so that there was no need to build roads into this country at all until, scarcely ten years ago in the case of the Swift, the loggers came back again for the hardwood trees, which don't float as well. We followed the road alongside the Swift for half a mile, then waded it and struck up Nathan Pond Brook, through a narrow wild brushy defile under Cave Mountain, with yellow birch and soft and hard maples and cone-bearing alders ten feet high. The hummingbirds swarmed to my red hat again, and there were goldfinches, purple finches, and blueberry thickets where we stopped to feast, and shoulder-high joe-pye weed, fireweed, goldenrod, and beaver activity and engineered ponds.

Legally as well as perhaps geographically, it is no longer possible just to throw a pack on your back in the Northeast and hike cross-country for weeks, because casual camping has been prohibited. But here in this obscure little bypassed valley bursting with undergrowth the illusion of the old hiking freedoms persisted. Even the vivid fish in their pools didn't give me the feeling of claustrophobia and pity that I often get, looking at trout cramped into a brook. They had space and a churning current and complexity enough in their habitat to baffle a hunting mink.

(1972)

Mountain Notch

The little mountain in the Northeast Highlands of Vermont where I live is a knoll of low-grade granite and occasional schist more than three hundred million years old. One can date its origins, therefore, to about the time amphibians emerged on earth, and to the age of ferns. It stretches from west to east in the shape of a whale, with stunted spruces clinging in clefts of bare rock on the very top, and chatter marks gouged on the surface by the sole of the last glacier that worked it over, about twenty thousand years ago. At the whale's forehead are free-fall cliffs four hundred feet tall, so that, from a certain angle at a certain hour, at a distance of three miles, the mountain looks like a wave of breaking surf facing the rising sun. But on foggy mornings the clouds hide these dimensions and contours, making the mountain bulk bigger (if I want it to be bigger) than it really is.

A pair of bobcats generally dens in the jumbled boulders around the bottom of the cliffs. I encounter them by the evidence of their tracks, or when my dog trees one of them in the dead of night. An exasperated, rasping, extraordinarily fierce growl from a low branch overhead announces that this is not another of the local forest animals—no silent coon, or hissing fisher, or muttering bear. In high

summer and in the mating season, in February, the bobcats will sometimes exchange a few loud, declaratory screams.

Fishers are large relatives of the weasel. Like raccoons, they den in
hollow trees, and leave their five-toed tracks when they lope through
our small valley, which is notched into the south slope of the mountainside. In the winter they are especially on the prowl for porcupines,
which they strip so cleanly of flesh and bone that only the flat skin remains, inside up, on the ground. Coons try to hole up in snowy weather,
but porcupines remain more active. Fishers breed in March, right after
the female's previous litter has been born. Porcupines breed in December, the male performing a clumsy, poignant, three-legged dance while
clutching his testicles with one front paw. The colony of porcupines
then winter quite sociably among boulders underneath spruce and
birch. The mountain's band of deer, in the meantime, have crossed a
hardwood ridge opposite the cliffs and gone down into a cedar woods
alongside Big Valley Brook, a thousand feet lower, where they can
chew the cedar bark and other favored foods, and where part of the
snow, caught overhead in the thick screen of boughs, evaporates.

The coyotes who raise their pups across the notch from my house
howl in the fall and winter months, but carefully keep mum during
their denning season so as not to betray the location of their pups. In
the spring, only the pups themselves are likely to break the silence
of the den—and then only to yap wistfully for a moment in the middle of the night in answer to the yapping of our dog pup, when we
have one.

June is the best time to see bears. Every other year, males from
far and near come calling upon the sow who seems to make her headquarters in this notch. They are great romancing bachelors, and they
roam the road in broad daylight, too impatient to wait till dusk. Her
yearling cubs, whom she has already ceased to mother at the start of
the courtship, must cast about incautiously for new quarters; you see
them grazing in the field well past dawn and drinking at midday at
the brook. The old bears welt some favorite birch-tree trunk, standing up and scratching competitively. Walking, one will notice the
dead logs they have beaten apart in search of grubs; and if I have gotten just muzzy-headed enough after a hike of eight or a dozen miles

and lean over a bashed log, I find myself experiencing some of the same hungry, busy, humdrum interest in what is there that the bear must have felt.

Behind the rock crest of the mountain is a pocket bog with pitcher plants. Also a spring which tumbles in upon itself in the form of a whirlpool, so that any leaf that you drop in promptly disappears. The deer summer in this high mixed woods of fir and spruce and birch and beech and maple, descending maybe half a mile at night to browse the patches of moosewood, hobblebush, fire cherry, mountain ash, shadblow, vetch, and wild apple saplings at the edge of the fields. A pair of red-tailed hawks nests each year somewhere along the whale's back, in trees that I have never located. There are broad-wingeds, too, and once in a while a goshawk. Barred owls bark at night, and ravens inhabit the cliffs, croaking eloquently at midmorning and in the afternoon—but not the marvelous peregrine falcons, or "ledge hawks," as the farmers used to call them. Forty years ago they would stunt during the spring courtship season with flirtatious giddy dives down from where the ravens flap.

Woodcock do a more modest but still spectacular swooping mating flight over a strip of alder thicket, where they later hunt earthworms. And below the alders is a beaver pond, which a pair of otters visits. Swimming playfully in sequence, they sometimes look to me like a sea monster. The patriarch among the beavers swims out toward them bravely and thwacks his tail on the water to warn his clan.

There are snowshoe rabbits, each intricately snug and custombound within the space of a handful of acres, bathing on a pleasant day in the same patch of dust that a ruffed grouse has used. And chipmunks—that courageous warning trill an individual, though hidden, gives, that may endanger it but save the race. There are congeries of songbirds, from indigo to scarlet-colored; three species of snakes in my woodpile; and trembling poplars, white-leaved in the wind, and all the manifestations of the moon.

(1981)

Up the Black to Chalkyitsik

Wilderness has a good many meanings. Bitter cold or uncommon danger can make of any patch of the outdoors a "wilderness," but nothing precludes balmy weather from the equation; nor are snakebite and quicksand essential ingredients. My happiest experiences in wilderness landscapes happen to have been in Alaska, and my favorite town there is Fort Yukon, a dot of a place thrown down near the junction of the Yukon and Porcupine rivers, one mile north of the Arctic Circle, eight hundred seventy-five river miles from the Yukon's Canadian headwaters, and a thousand winding miles from its debouchment into the Bering Sea. Canadian traders of the Hudson's Bay Company established the fort in 1847, not so much to protect themselves from the Gwich'in Indians of the region as to fly the flag and fend off the Russian traders operating from a station five hundred miles downstream. (Russians had discovered the mouth of the Yukon in 1834.)

This was the first English-language community in Alaska, but after Alaska was sold by Russia to the United States in 1867 for a price of $7.2 million, the Hudson's Bay Company was forced to move its operations eastward to British territory. Fort Yukon continued to be a fur-buying center under American auspices, however, and then it became a gold-rush way point for the riverboats headed for the Klondike frenzy near Dawson City at the turn of the century, and finally the site of a small radar base after World War II, as well as an administrative sub-hub for six or eight Indian villages in the surrounding fifty or sixty thousand square miles, a huge terrain, abutting the Brooks Range from the south, that is equivalent in size to two Irelands and includes the so-called Yukon Flats, which is an area of forty thousand lakes and one of the richest breeding grounds for waterfowl in the world.

Though the radar base has closed, Fort Yukon (pop. 650) is still fairly busy, a jumping-off point for winter trapping trips and summer jaunts up the Coleen, Chandalar, Christian, Porcupine, Sheenjek, and other pristine rivers that feed this portion of the Yukon. Thirty-year-old flying boxcars roar off the airstrip to bomb forest fires in the out-back in July and August, till it sounds like a war zone. Surveyors for the Bureau of Land Management, or the Fish and Wildlife Service, federal and state social workers, construction crews, oil geologists, and health and sanitation experts bunk at the Sourdough Inn while they attempt to carry out various Sisyphean projects. Alaska is the land of the dubious contract, as one gradually discovers, and, besides the more drawn-out scams, is full of white people who are angry about whatever they were doing down in the Lower Forty-Eight before they came up here, how long they kept doing it, and who they were doing it with. They lend a frenetic or malcontent air to a mainly Indian village like Fort Yuk (as they sometimes call Fort Yukon when they're in Fairbanks). Other whites, with better intentions, may feel they are being defeated as they struggle against intractable problems like fetal alcohol syndrome and a rising suicide rate and, like the first group, ask the perpetual questions, "*Shall* we stay in this crazy state?" and "Where are we going on vacation?"

Baja, Belize, Bangkok, or London over the Pole may be where they go, on the high salaries paid. Paris, New York, and Tokyo are about equidistant from Fairbanks by airplane, so one has the feeling one can go anywhere in a matter of hours—to the edge of the earth on the coastal plain of the Arctic Ocean, over the Brooks Range, where polar bears cross scent lines with grizzlies and wolverines, as maybe two hundred thousand caribou sift through; or to the Champs Élysées and Trafalgar Square.

This can be exhilarating but, if you've gone off the deep end over the long lightless winter, demoralizing too; freedom becomes vertigo. Of course, the complicated skies above Fort Yukon aren't really light-less even then. The sun flirts with the horizon, the moon rises, stars spangle the firmament, and the northern lights flicker, shoot up, and glow. You see what you look for—a collapsing conclave of "neo-Indi-ans, salt-and-pepper Indians," as they were described to me by a flipped-out social worker, whose wretched and dangerous job was to take abused children away from violent mothers and drunken fathers; or a lively, self-reliant, age-old, resilient subsistence society still hold-ing its own with at least some degree of élan beneath the drumfire of soap-opera television and do-gooding welfare programs, beer-hall bravura and bathos, and satellite-powered telephones. At the Sour-dough Inn, one tilts back in a barber's chair at the pay phone to talk to New York. There's a daily mail plane and other amenities: the Alaska Commercial Company general store; the community hall, with shower baths and washing machines. The University of Alaska has put up a million-dollar log building for extension classes. The town has three churches; a Lions Club for bingo and Budweiser and a two-dollar cup of moose stew, if you're hungry; a new little historical mu-seum established in the hope that tourists will come; a Wycliffe Society Bible translator, putting psalms into Gwich'in (though Eng-lish has swamped Gwich'in by now); and Fort Yukon's federally funded psychologist, who estimates that a fourth of the citizenry shows up every year in her office, which is situated between the town-owned, tin-walled liquor store and the bootlegger's green ply-wood house, which opens for business when the liquor store closes.

The river itself, spraddled out with its islands to a width of three miles at this point, imparts importance to every settlement alongside, and its armies of salmon—kings, silvers, and chum—churn by invisi-bly from July through September, heading for Canada to spawn but at hand for the netting meanwhile. In the winter, frozen, it's a causeway for sled dogs, and during the summer, if you camp on its banks, you can lie at midnight watching a thousand swallows whirl in the wind, and the giddy sun loop like a rolling lasso along the rim of the forest, while the town's chained packs of dogs bay jubilantly at each other from several backyards. Although the Bureau of Indian Affairs has

239

built rows of pastel prefab housing in a newer quarter, many residents prefer to live in the old log cabins close to the river and venture out in snowtime to run snare lines and trap lines. Six to ten thousand mink and two or three thousand marten skins are marketed through Fort Yukon's "A.C." store in the winter.

I fell in love in Alaska, with the person in charge of tracking tuberculosis all over the state, and therefore have visited Eskimo villages like Point Hope and Kotzebue and Crooked Creek, Indian villages like Angoon and Tanana and Sleetmute, Anglo towns like Dillingham and Tenakee Springs, while she tested and chatted with patients. I've seen the Copper River, the Susitna River, the Koyukuk River, and the Killik River, hundreds of miles apart, going from south to north. I've barged on the Yukon, summered in Fairbanks, wintered in Anchorage, and twice, when I've been in the north on other business, have dropped in by mail plane with a pack and a tent to walk Fort Yukon's dirt streets—streets refurbished with gravel after an ice jam during spring breakup in May 1982 floated six-foot bergs into town.

If I walk half a mile from the airstrip, I reach Fred Thomas's cabin, and he greets me with emphasis. (Everything he says is with emphasis.) And if it's lunchtime, Charlotte, his wife, will take out some beaver meat to feed us, knowing that, coming straight from the city, I will enjoy that. She is fifty-six, comely, husky, reddish-skinned, smooth-complexioned, aging gracefully, and, in the manner of Indian wives in these villages, does not talk to white strays such as me unless her husband is present, but has many visitors of her own sex and race, with whom she is warmly responsive.

Fred is sixty-four, compact and wiry, built smaller than Charlotte, with a beardless, keen, concentrated, round, predator's face, bristly short hair that is turning white, and a relaxed but peripatetic look. As a family man, he did maintenance work for seventeen years at the radar base in order to raise his six children well, and only trapped and hunted in his spare time, though still managing to average about fifty foxes and two or three wolves a year. But now he has resumed the calling of woodsmanship that he loves.

Fred's mother was a Gwich'in from a band that lived on the upper Porcupine (the Dagoo Gwich'in), and his father, Jacob Thomas, born around 1880 in Wisconsin, had worked on a Mississippi riverboat for a little while before joining the 1898 gold rush. He'd arrived late and mostly trapped mink and moose-hunted in the Klondike for meat to sell to the miners at a dollar a pound to keep things going while his partners dug holes. Nothing panned out for them, but as "Tommy the Mate," Fred's father worked on the Yukon boats for fifteen or twenty years, before settling down to have Fred and six more children and to carve out a life for himself far from other white men.

It was July 1919 in Fort Yukon when Fred's parents put him and most of their belongings in a boat and paddled twenty-five miles up the Porcupine River to the mouth of the Big Black River, and paddled, poled, and lined their laborious way up the midsummer shallows of the Black for two hundred more miles in the course of a month to its Grayling Fork, where they built a trapping camp, which has remained the heart of Fred's own family's activities ever since. They would stay out from August—when they already needed to begin laying in wild foods for the winter—till the following June, when the muskrats, last of the fur animals to lose the lush nap on their coats, finally did so, and the river was high and yet safe enough to travel upon with boats stuffed with furs, dogs, and youngsters.

Fred has a vaguely "Irish" look, which is darkened and blurred with the admixture of Athapascan Indian, so that he reminds me of several of the Cajun trappers I have traveled and camped with in southwestern Louisiana, and like them, he speaks the elided English of someone not so much bilingual as caught between two languages and master of neither. His two sons, however, live within yards of his house and trap and collaborate with him in the old-fashioned way (seen also in Cajun country, or any tribal region I've known) by which an older man becomes simply as strong as the number of his grown sons. And two of his brothers go out from Fort Yukon every fall to trap from cabins of their own on the upper Black. Flying in with the winter's supplies, they don't have to start as early as in the old days.

Fred spent so much time on the Black when he was a boy that he had only three years of schooling, but he is a sophisticated man, nevertheless, partly from watching hundreds of servicemen from all over the United States matriculate through a tour of duty at the little base at the edge of town, and partly because he contracted tuberculosis as a young man. After trying the local boneyard of a hospital and realizing he would die like the other Indians and métis there, he lived for three years alone in a tent to clear his lungs, never spending a night indoors. That, too, frighteningly, was of no avail, and so his father at last, pulling strings as only a white man—even a "squaw man"—could do, persuaded the government to send Fred to a sanatorium in Tucson, Arizona, to recover. So he's seen orange trees, though never an apple tree, he says.

His mother's father, Ab Shaefer, was also a white man, a whaler from Nova Scotia who had jumped ship in the Arctic with three other sailors about two decades prior to the gold rush by pretending to go on a caribou hunt. The ship's officers pursued them and shot one man, but the rest escaped and, it being summertime, passed safely through the Eskimo country of the Arctic Slope and crossed up over the British Mountains, which in the Yukon Territory correspond to the Brooks Range, and then were saved from the terrors of winter in the interior by the Indians at Crow Flats, the Vunta Gwich'in. Anyhow, on his way home from Tucson in 1945, Fred stopped off in Chicago to get acquainted with a few of his Shaefer relatives and saw a big city.

Ab Shaefer and one of his companions had married two sisters at Crow Flats village, near the head of the Porcupine. (The third of these surviving whalers floated down the Porcupine to Gwicha Gwich'in country at the village of Beaver on the Yukon River, thirty miles below Fort Yukon, and married a woman there.) And Shaefer, living at Crow Flats and Old Crow and trapping with his in-laws along the upper Porcupine's tributaries, like the Bell River and the Eagle River, sizable in their own right, which run to the Northwest Territories, went so happily native that he simply ignored the gold rush when it occurred, almost next door; did not participate. Fred has not many memories of Shaefer—except that he said, "Well, I'll be damned!" a lot—but remembers his own surprise, as a small boy visiting with his mother and father at his grandfather's winter camp on the Bell, where some of the vegetation was new to him, when he was sent out of the cabin to get dry firewood and chopped at a leafless tamarack, thinking it was a dead spruce, but found that because tamaracks drop their needles in the fall, it looked dead yet was alive. The other whaler who lived in Old Crow drowned in the currents of the Porcupine around that same year, and Fred last saw Shaefer in 1943, during his own scary siege with TB, when the old man came down the Porcupine on a riverboat to Fort Yukon to change boats and go up the Yukon to Dawson City (in this age before ubiquitous planes) to live in an old-age home.

Now it was Charlotte's father, a Tranji Gwich'in named Henry William, from Chalkyitsik, the one village that exists on the Big Black River, who, Fred told me, was sick. He suggested as we had lunch that we might make a trip of it and bring Henry William some fresh salmon. The Indian Health Service doctors at the hospital in Fairbanks had discharged him after an operation for what they'd described as "an intestinal infection." Presumably, he had been sent home to die in familiar surroundings of bowel cancer. In Fairbanks, Henry had got sick of store meat—what he called "meat with no blood in it"—and the doctors and everyone felt that it was a shame he wasn't enjoying his meals these last weeks.

I said sure. A New Yorker born, I come to Alaska's high wilds like Alice diving down her rabbit's hole, and that great city, as I gaze back at it from the Northwest Orient Airlines Boeing, smokes like heartburn personified or a multiple smashup of racing cars. But in a dozen hours I can be smelling wood smoke, tending a supper fire in front of my tent, camped in Fred's yard, or with my friends Beri and Mary Morris (who manage the Alaska Commercial Company store), whose spare cabin lies close by, or else in the Anglican churchyard. Its veteran minister was on sabbatical on the occasion of this visit but had told me before to camp there, to cut down my chances of being robbed. Wilderness buffs sometimes raft or canoe for five or six hundred miles down the Yukon, surviving mazes of rapids and sloughs, though still less than halfway to the river's mouth, and then beach their craft on a sand spit within hooting distance of the Sourdough Inn, make camp on the beach with exultant relief, and rush to tuck in to a huge, candlelit, tablecloth meal and chat long-distance on the telephone, only to return to the spit and find everything gone.

Fort Yukon is full of violence—one of the worst posts to be a state trooper in the whole state—and stories abound of white people who commute to marriages elsewhere, grinning meanwhile, come dusk, when an Indian mother on welfare shows up at the kitchen door wanting grocery money, beer money—a town of gunfire by night but considerable sweetness by day. I was camped, in fact, on the riverbank inside the fenced yard of another couple, the wife a retired schoolteacher here, the husband the man who installed satellite dishes and suchlike necessities. They may raise the northernmost tomatoes in the United States, and probably the northernmost honeybees. They were out, when I heard a knocking at their door and the voice of an English lady calling them. My tent was up, but my sleeping-bag zipper was stuck, so I went to introduce myself, tell her they were out, and try to persuade her to unstick it for me.

She did, although she exclaimed, "Oh, what an impossible nuisance you are! You're like my son when he goes on a trip with the Scouts. You've come all the way from New York, and you don't know how to zip your own sleeping bag? I suppose you're a world traveler too—we get those. How do you function?"

"There's always somebody to do it," I said.

In her forties, blond, younger than I, she turned out to be Fred's sister-in-law, Mrs. Johnnie Thomas.

For a novel that I was writing, I had become curious to learn more about Bigfoot, or "Brush Man," as the Gwich'in call the phenomenon, translating from their own word, *Naa-inn,* for Bigfoot. Sure, Bigfoot had lived in these river valleys, a number of people told me. Some had seen him or knew of circumstantial evidence of his existence. All had heard the stories, as well as others, about an odder, perhaps still more intriguing humanoid wild being: the Little People. These tiny, aggressive, quite talky inhabitants of the taiga and tundra had prodigious strength and cryptic personalities, living mostly underneath the earth and snow but contacting human beings more confidently than Bigfoot. They were self-sufficient, for one thing. They didn't need to steal food from a campsite, as Bigfoot would, and didn't hunger for the companionship of women either, like Bigfoot occasionally. They played quirky and raffish—or sinister and heartless—pranks, yet also were capable, when the spirit moved, of doing a good turn: saving a lone traveler's life or extricating him from great danger, if he pleaded with them. Whenever they proved troublesome, the only way to quiet them was to build bonfires over their burrows, boil pots of water, and threaten to pour that down their holes.

Bigfoot was a kind of howling fugitive, by comparison, an outcast figure apparently in need of fellowship with man at the same time as—glimpsed at the end of a trail or across a frozen lake—he fled from him. So I asked my new English friend, who had already heard about me from Fred, who I should seek out to talk about Bigfoot.

"And *Vanity Fair* magazine in New York City sent you to Fort Yukon to find this stuff out?" She laughed.

"No, *Vanity Fair* is sending me to Anchorage to find out about 'Alaska's Millionaires.' But that gets me to the state, and I come here. Or *House & Garden*, or another one, sends me."

Having fixed my zipper, she felt it improper to chat much longer, saying Fort Yukon wasn't Britain and she hardly ever missed Britain, much less went back. "I'm certain you'll manage. Ask on Front Street and ask Fred and Johnnie."

Front Street, a dirt track alongside the river, is where the row of old-timers' log cabins is—white prospectors', traders', and trappers' cabins at the turn of the century that now belong to their descendants, of mixed race but in solid-looking housing unmessed with by the Bureau of Indian Affairs. In no time, asking along, I met a middle-aged Indian woman, married here but originally from the village of Beaver, whose sister had been abducted by a Bigfoot, she said. All one summer her brother had tracked the two of them through the mountains, hearing the girl's cries receding in front of him wherever he followed, and had never caught up. A very sad thing. On the other hand, as kids they used to go out and shout down a Little People's hole that they knew about—not really afraid, as their parents would have been—for the fun of hearing words come back, she said.

"What words?"

"I forget. But you knew what they meant. Grouchy."

Getting interested, she led me into her house, which was a jumble of river and trapping equipment and furniture and cartons of food, with several kids, and two other women, who had dropped in. Her husband was heavy, paleish, drunk, sixtyish, reclining in the slatted sunlight in a broken easy chair, and unfriendly, assuming I worked for the government or a social agency.

"Why don't *you go?*" he told me, rousing slightly.

"He just wants to know about Brush Man," the lady explained.

"Brush Man!" he said, with a dim smile. "You're talking about olden days—my father's days, my days. My friend fed a Brush Man one time. Is that what you want to hear about?"

"Yes," I said.

"A whole family of them, three babies and the two big ones, came to his fire hungry, in the winter. He was a hundred miles from nowhere, camped in the snow. And he had half a moose left that he had shot, so he let them eat that. Just watched them eat, and they didn't say nuthin to him. Only he said you could tell what they thought without speaking. Why don't you go now?" he repeated.

Back at Fred Thomas's, I asked what *he* thought.

"Sometimes they're a downed airman," he said.

"A Bigfoot is?"

"I don't know. You see what you're looking for. It could be a pilot that's scared shitless, running around in the woods, gone off his rocker, after a crash."

"And how about before there were planes?"

"Well, then it might be an Eskimo," he said. "Or a family of Eskimos."

"Yes? How?"

Fred explained that before the whites arrived and instituted jails and asylums and so forth for crazy people and murderers, they were likely to be expelled from their settlements, or they ran away before they got killed. "And where would they go?" He pointed north toward the handful of Eskimo villages spotted along the Arctic Ocean and Arctic Slope north of the Brooks Range, six hundred miles or more above where we were. "They'd come down here, if they survived. All crazy and shaggy, mumbling Eskimo."

"There was a war on, anyway, with the Eskimos," Charlotte added.

"So he'd stay in the woods and be crazy there? Steal fish, steal food, look at the women from a hiding place?" I asked. This was an explanation, if not an answer.

Charlotte said when she was a girl she knew people who used to leave sugar, tea and salt for a Bigfoot at a certain rock on the river-bank, where he'd come down and pick the stuff up. And he learned to leave a few furs there, in return, for them to sell.

We went to check Fred's fishnet, which was set on a fifty-foot line, buoyed by empty ammonia bottles, out at the point of a mid-channel sandbar two miles south of town and a mile from shore. The net seemed ludicrously short and small, in the scale of the vast yellow river, but three king salmon were tangled individually in its monofila-ment—a red forty-five-pound male, a reddish twenty-five-pound fe-male, and a paler twenty-pound male. As Fred very carefully landed each of these, I sat holding the previous one under my feet in the lit-tle skiff to keep it from leaping back into the water. They filled the boat with their anxious and strangled despair, and if we had tipped over they could have lived, while we would have drowned very quickly, not just because of the water's hand-numbing temperature, but because its immense freighting of silt soon fills your clothes like a crushing weight and drags you down.

Yet such an easy catch of flesh exhilarated Fred and me, rather like a windfall of money. It suddenly made life seem more secure and, day after sun-swept midsummer day, is a commonplace coup on the Yukon. Besides providing for his father-in-law, Henry William, in Chalkyitsik (frontier Indians often chose two first names for their "white" name, because they would name themselves after several new friends, though sometimes an unscrupulous white man might "charge" them for his), Fred wanted to send a salmon or two on the mail plane to the Natsit Gwich'in of Arctic Village, on the Chandalar River, in the Brooks Range, the most remote and self-sufficient of these Gwich'in communities. In exchange, his friends there would mail him a caribou next winter. Even out in his bush camp, he seldom has a chance to eat caribou. Small bands of the Porcupine Herd strag-gle as far south as his Black River country only about once in every five years.

At home, Charlotte filleted the three fish, dropping the organs and roe into a jug to rot for trap bait and cutting the backbones into sections, which Fred would stick into punctured tin cans and hang close to his traps and snares. His practice is to set out literally hundreds of these in November and just leave them be until March. In his smokehouse, he also has strings of goose wings stored, which, when dipped in beaver castor, he will tie in low spruce branches to attract lynx. He laughed and told me he'd once caught thirteen two-hundred-fifty-dollar lynx in a single night, when they were moving through his trapping territory in one of their strange, periodic migrations, and how he had remembered then that his father, in hard Depression times, had wished he could catch even two thousand dollars' worth of fur in a season to feed his family of nine.

Charlotte showed me their photograph album, which, like other Fort Yukon photo albums, consisted, apart from its wedding and graduation memorabilia, of numerous pictures of dead bears and moose, *in toto*, then the same moose and bears being skinned; and of trap-line cabins and stilted caches on chutelike rivers, or trap-line catches pinned in a row on a clothesline rope in front of one of the cabins for the camera. The meat represented a winter's food and the line of wolf, fox, otter, mink, beaver, marten, and fisher skins a year's worth of money; so what else ought to be in an album of memories?

Jimmy Ward, the son of another old-time white settler, turned up for supper. We ate a snow goose, which Fred had shot last spring, and some pickled strips of dried salmon and left-over beaver, with store-bought spinach and rice. Jimmy Ward is a white-haired, black-bearded mischief-maker of whom it is no exaggeration to say that he is frequently drunk. He had been besieged in his cabin by gunfire one night a few months before and been carted away for a night in jail after the shoot-out, and while he was gone, his cabin had somehow caught fire and burned to a shell. Now the government had placed him and his Gwich'in wife in a ninety-cents-a-day government prefab for the rest of his life and, he announced cockily, he was sitting pretty.

"It was an active winter in Dodge City," he said. U.S. Representative Don Young's cabin—summer home to Alaska's perennial congressman—had also been set afire; and so had the Fish and Wildlife

Service's cabin, from which the eight-and-a-half-million-acre Yukon Flats National Wildlife Refuge (itself as large as Massachusetts and Connecticut combined) is managed. So he didn't know whether to be insulted or flattered to be in such company. Tomorrow he and his wife were going out to camp in a favorite slough up the Yukon a couple of dozen miles and put out their fishnets and rabbit snares and lean back and enjoy themselves. After you'd split, smoked, and sun-dried a few hundred salmon, with those smells on the wind, you'd soon have a young black bear to cure too.

This is his summer camp, of course. In the winter Jimmy's trapping camp—like Fred's, it was his father's before him—is not on the Yukon but one hundred sixty miles up the Porcupine, between two of the Porcupine's principal tributaries, the Coleen and Sheenjek rivers, a less traveled territory, although as fall gets in the air in Fort Yukon, one hears people telling each other, "I'll see you on the Sheenjek," "I'll see you on the Coleen."

Jimmy said he wanted to die on his trap line, not shrink to skin and bones in a hospital bed, as several friends had. "I'd rather fall down in a rat tunnel and die."

Fred said that one spring he and his brothers had caught thirteen hundred muskrats on the Black. Last winter he and his sons had trapped about eighty lynx, forty marten, forty mink, fifteen red foxes, two wolverines, and seventy-five beavers. No wolves, but his brother Albert, who is based seven miles upstream from them, had got six.

Jimmy argued with him about how high a lynx snare should be set. But they agreed that the most fearsome creature in the bush is a "winter grizzly," a bear that is too hungry to hibernate and has woken up desperate and on the hunt for a quick meal. Jimmy mentioned, however, that he had once shot at a Brush Man. It had been standing on the ice of a lake, and he'd fired at it twice, but it wouldn't fall and didn't drop down on all fours to run from him either, as a bear would have done; instead it ran into the trees on its hind legs. So *he* ran, and was too scared to come back the next day to check on the tracks; instead had cleared out of that valley entirely.

I said Fred had said that Brush Man could be a downed airman instead of a Bigfoot, or else an Eskimo exiled from the North Slope villages, or maybe (I wondered) a Koyukon Indian, from the next tribal group, down toward Galena on the Yukon, where I'd also been visiting and where I'd seen snares set around a homestead cabin for Bigfoot—or Woods Man, as the Koyukon Indians called him, because their slightly milder climate on the Koyukuk River grows more woods, less brush.

"I don't see why you have to limit your options," Jimmy answered. "If you see a Brush Man, he could be a pilot that's crashed, or he could be an Eskimo that's lost his marbles, or he could be a Bigfoot. Couldn't he? When I first saw *you*, I thought you were James Watt, because you wore glasses and you asked too many questions and you smiled too much."

We laughed. It was not impossible that the horrendous secretary of the interior would turn up. Worse folks did. Later on that first trip, Jimmy had decided I was really a fur buyer who was scouting around from cabin to cabin to see everybody's catch by pretending to be a writer asking questions. At the end of my stay, he had swung around to believing my story about what I was, but then, just on my last day in town, I'd walked over to Fred's house and paid him two hundred fifty dollars for two little wolfskins. So Jimmy didn't know what to think. Gleefully, now, he informed me that I looked older. And he asked if I owned one of those tube-shaped tents and mummy-style sleeping bags that all of the river floaters and mountain climbers and trail hikers who passed through town had.

Because one of my annual pleasures is to be put down by Jimmy Ward, I said yes.

"You zip yourself inside that, and it's like a grocery sack for the old grizzly bear. You're all wrapped up for him. He can just drag you anywhere, and you'll never get to see who he even is. You'll be zipped inside, where he can hold you nice and still."

Fred said Jimmy shouldn't have shot at that figure on the lake if he didn't know what it was. When he was fourteen, he, Fred, had almost shot his own father. It wasn't a simple case of buck fever, because he had killed his first moose three years earlier, but he was hunting moose and saw something brown through the brush across an opening, and because his father was supposed to be out overnight on the trap line, he took aim. But what had happened was that his father's lead dog had broken loose from the sled and gotten snagged in one of the traps. So his father was returning early to mend the dog's foot. Fred didn't fire, and within a few years he had his own nine-day trap line, with six overnight cabins on it.

Darkless summers are a jubilant time. I've been spoiled for some of my usual Vermont haunts by summering in Alaska, where, for instance, the daylight is continuous in Fort Yukon from May 13 through August 4. The sun's manic ball never dips below the edge of the sky. Instead it revolves incessantly, looping to different levels like the motorcyclist who rides around and around inside a giant barrel at a carnival, while the swallows dive after bugs and packs of sled dogs halloo to each other back and forth across town. Like the dogs, I found depression impossible. People, birds, bugs, dogs, didn't sleep much, and the sun, as if bleary from overwork, turned orange and red within the halo of its yellows.

That evening, before our departure for Chalkyitsik, I sat at the Sourdough Inn with some smoke jumpers from Montana, a fisheries expert from Anchorage, two mining men from Fairbanks, and a helicopter pilot from California, originally, by way of Vietnam. One of the "millionaires" I had interviewed in Anchorage for the magazine in New York in exchange for my air fare had made his money developing a shopping mall but had arrived in the state as a bulldozer driver. Had got off the plane drunk, he said, because of the breakup of his marriage; had rented a car and weaved toward the friend's house where he would be staying and immediately was impressed with Alaskan hospitality because the trooper who stopped him didn't arrest him, merely led him to his destination and wished him good luck. In the same spirit, he offered to introduce me to a woman friend of his and to take me sport fishing. But what was most special, he said, was that people here, whatever they did, were the best. Pipe fitter, electrician, dozer operator, geologist, bush pilot—they could work at thirty below or go round-the-clock in the summer and maintain quality. That trooper who had stopped him stood six foot five and "could have stopped the gunfight at the O.K. Corral."

I'd found the same thing. The pilot from New Jersey with whom you flew to lost little villages through snowstorms, fog, mountain ranges, either could cut it or pretty soon quit and went home—or died. The riverboat captain who ferried you to Yukon River settlements either could pick out the braiding of hundreds of channels that led him past hidden sandbars to his destination in the course of a week or grounded at a cost of ten thousand dollars. Mostly, I'd traveled with my tuberculosis supervisor, who flew to Eskimo and Indian villages, doing skin tests to discover latent cases of this antique disease, examining active or former patients, talking to the district nurse or a local health aide, and occasionally speaking to the populace in the school gymnasium. We slept on the floor of the health clinic or a first-grade classroom or maybe the gym, staying a couple of days in a town of a hundred and twenty souls before moving on.

The district nurse, living in a center such as Bethel or Nome and flying out to a half-dozen individual villages, seventy or a hundred-seventy miles away, which were under her own supervision, had life-and-death power. Not just in the sense that she quickly developed emergency-room skills; but there was no doctor on these scarce visits—a few days per village every six or eight weeks. She determined who got plastic surgery after a fire, or special prenatal care, or a timely cancer exam, or plentiful painkillers. With a limited budget, she authorized a mercy flight or a seat on the mail plane for somebody who wanted to see a doctor—or else she said no. I—whose eyelids froze shut in about five minutes in Arctic villages at forty below—had been much impressed by the stamina and panache of these women, sheltering humbly under their wings.

I napped on a cot in Fred's smokehouse for a few hours, till breakfast time, when we ate bacon and eggs. Fred's neighbor, a wide-cheeked, husky man who lives in a blue house across the road and takes phone calls for him, came over to help truck our gear to the riverbank. Fred had me store my valuables behind his daughter's picture on the mantel, which was the safest place there was, he said: his daughter who's working to be a lawyer in Massachusetts.

"There's no give-up in this guy. Good man for a trip," the neighbor told me. He drank a cup of Yukon-yellow river water. "Well, there's my coffee this morning."

Fred was zipped into a black windsuit, with a snazzy white life belt buckled to his hips. It was August 1, and as we got out on the water he remarked that it must be the first day of fall, because the thousands of bank swallows that nest in catacomb colonies in the river's cutbanks had begun vanishing, to get a good start on their flight to South America. So had the smaller flocks of white Arctic terns, which go nearly to Antarctica for another darkless summer at our antipode: true light-loving birds. Because Fort Yukon lies within the wide bowl of the Brooks Range and the more southerly White Mountains and Crazy Mountains, summer temperatures can go to one hundred degrees, but the first killing frost occurs around the third week of August. Our boat, flat-bottomed, square-bowed, thirty-two feet long, four feet wide, and powered by a forty-horse Evinrude, had been built for Fred by the local fur buyer to fit the chop of the Yukon's currents and the Porcupine's surge, plus for shallow-draft marsh running—a salmon boat, a muskrat boat.

In such a boat I'd crossed the Mississippi's mouth after muskrats and garfish, armored prehistoric-looking creatures as big as king salmon. On the Mississippi, dodging the high wakes of supertankers and containerships, our skiff had seemed like an anachronism. But on the Yukon, whose silent roar is bridged only once between Dawson City and salt water—a stretch equivalent to the Mississippi between Minneapolis and New Orleans—I felt natural.

After three breezy, down-slipping miles, we turned up into the Porcupine, which at its mouth looked to be about a third of a mile wide. The Porcupine is itself a major river, more than five hundred fifty miles long. Its waters are a rich shade of gray in the sunshine, not Yukon yellow, but just as cold and fast when you dip your hand into it. Less thickly silt-laden than the Yukon, it wouldn't cram sand into every interstice of your clothing if you found yourself unexpectedly swimming in it, but like any Arctic river, it has *gravitas*.

With the Porcupine's constant turns, and the sun's vagrant positioning over us, the water constantly changed color. It turned black and mirrored the sky, or shifted into a spectrum of handsome grays. Loons were flying determinedly every which way with breathless speed, propelling themselves in a goose's posture except that they held their heads lower. Snags in the current porpoised rhythmically, with their roots or stumps stuck down in the tangle of driftwood along the bottom, but their free ends poked out so much like whiskery heads that it remained a surprise to pass them and look back and notice that they really were stationary, and to watch gulls land on them even as they bobbed. Seals, farther toward the Yukon's great debouchment, do swim upriver for two hundred miles to feast on its salmon.

We slid by the mouth of the Sucker River, and then that of Eight Mile Slough, which looked just like the Sucker's mouth, though the Sucker in fact is a fairly intriguing river. Sloughlike in its sluggish currents, it is named for the bottom-feeding species of fish that thrives here, and it is a fine territory for beaver. A man used to live right here and make a good living from them (though he had to pay a price, with the nickname "Sucker"). Fred himself trapped along the Sucker River a good deal during the years when he was a wage slave for the air force because he could reach it easily from town—from foxes, he made a gold mine of the radar-base dump—and he had his two scariest experiences with grizzly bears here. Thousands of animals must have watched him from hiding places over the years, he says, but only twice has he realized it telepathically, and each time it was a grizzly, flattened down close to the ground, "with its nose going like crazy," along the Sucker, in springtime. He thinks an animal that large and formidable may be required to "register" on him; that the brain waves of slighter wildlife slip past. On each occasion, he made cautious haste to clear out, and then the grizzly cleared out. He is live-and-let-live with grizzlies, and he has prevented his sons, too, from shooting them when it was not necessary for self-protection and when the carcasses were too far out from home to be dragged back to feed to the dogs.

At Seventeen Mile (a location measured from Fort Yukon), the Porcupine looks about a hundred fifty yards wide, and there is one cabin left from what was once a small Indian settlement. Then we glided by the modest-looking outlet of the Grass River, where, as in the Sucker, whitefish can be netted in great numbers and the pike that congregate to devour them can be jigged for. The Grass River is a couple of hundred miles long, counting its tributary, the Little Black River, which curves in a parallel course through the same country that is drained by Fred's Big Black River. Only one trapper works the Little Black River nowadays, and as with all of the other rivers around, this relative emptiness of what is very familiar country to Fred, full of a hubbub of memories of dozens of families who worked the vast drainage of the Porcupine for furs, depresses him. It's not like the changes afflicting woodsmen in the Lower Forty-Eight, where development is consuming everybody's old haunts. In much of Alaska, though perhaps temporarily, the land is emptier. Old-timers who went everywhere as a matter of course die off, and young people stay in their villages in the winter, drinking their government checks.

At Twenty-five Mile, chunks of ebony water appeared in the swift gray roil of the Porcupine. Then blocks of obsidian water. A sand spit split the river from the entrance of its tributary, the Big Black, on the right-hand side. We entered it. Two hundred miles up was where Fred's home was, but we were going only seventy-five, to Chalkyitsik, where Charlotte had come from. The Black, at first about sixty yards wide, narrowed to fifty, spread to seventy-five, shrank again, and swelled, mirroring meanwhile the tiers of white clouds. The current was slower than the Porcupine's, with cherry-colored gravel visible on the shallow bottom and frequent grassy banks that were vividly green. Chattering kingfishers scolded us from both banks, darting between their roosting trees. Plentiful loons of three different species flew by in speedball haste, with giggles, and raffish large flappy ravens, croaking, and little mew gulls that nest on the tundra, and sizable herring seagulls. We saw five pintails and a family of goldeneyes, several mallards and a number of mergansers, or "sawbills," which dive and catch fish and therefore, like a fish-eating grizzly, are considered too "fishy" to be good eating.

At Steamboat Slough there used to be a cabin shaped like a steamboat—five-sided, and pointed at the bow end—which had been built by some cheechako prospectors after the gold rush for fun. "And then it fell down. And then it burnt up," Fred said.

Abundant dark-green spruce trees grew twenty to fifty feet high for miles. But a few lightning burns are interspersed through this forest, with dead black spars remaining that have refused to fall over, and alder thickets and willow woods that are gradually growing up in place of the burned spruce. Since these burns are of different ages, the new vegetation is accordingly lower or higher, but other patches have burned in one wholesale sweep, except where the wind's whimsy has spared odd vibrant clumps of waving spruce trees.

Besides fire, permafrost is the other tyrant here—Fort Yukon in winter is one of the coldest inhabited places on earth—and creates what is called "the drunken forest." Where lightning spares a stand of trees long enough for them to begin to grow big, their roots meet the barrier of the permafrost and are stymied until, top-heavy, they reel, they slant like cartoon sailors, surviving for years at desperate angles.

Mostly, though, the spruces and willow-poplar woods alternated with a rhythmic pleasantry, often facing one another across the river, and on the mud flats in front of the willows, moose, in feeding, had left their tracks. By the banks where poplars grew, we saw beaver workings; and on the grassy swales above the gravel beaches, bear paths. Black bears were the best meat legally available now, so Fred kept his .30-.06 at the ready. Moose weren't supposed to be hunted for a few more weeks, but he was mentally noting each location where he saw tracks to tell his two sons and five brothers about in Fort Yukon, as well as some of his in-laws in Chalkyitsik. He pointed out the signs of beaver to me with a more detached, merely professional interest, because they were in someone else's trapping territory.

"Goddamn, it's falltime! They're getting their food piles ready already."

The Yukon Flats stretch for nearly three hundred miles and host perhaps two million ducks during the summer. The Wildlife Refuge proper, which we were within (and within which trapping and hunting are permitted), is four times as large as Yellowstone National Park, and it serves as a sort of duck factory from the standpoint of the Fish and Wildlife Service, producing, as the birds fan south over the continent from California to Maryland, an estimated four hundred thousand "hunter days" of recreation. Rounding the many bends, maneuvering between the frequent sandbars, we saw wigeons and scaup and canvasbacks and startled up a golden eagle, which had been eating a dead duck on a beach. As it flapped in a circle to gain altitude, the trees almost forced it to graze our heads. Both white-fronted and Canada geese appeared, and later a bald eagle; then an osprey's nest. And we saw a number of sandhill cranes, tall gawky birds who seem to shift and balance themselves as edgily on their legs as on their wings. And a great number of hectic loons, intent upon getting rapidly from one place to another and then back again, as if they knew they were already rare in the Lower Forty-Eight.

The copses of willows and spruces changed sides too, from left bank to right bank, or right bank to left bank. The water was seldom deeper than three feet, and so clear that the salmon that run up the Big Black cannot be netted in any quantity because they can easily see the strands even during the summer's night. The cherry-colored pebbles on the bottom, and the clarity of the clouds reflected upside down ahead of us, and the black and silver riffles just ahead of them, were very beautiful, with the constant bending of the river's course revealing new vistas of trees, new beaches of sand or stones that we were coming to, or a little oxbow that had filled up with earth in the spring floods and grown up with grass, where animals came.

When I could hear him above the water's rush, Fred was telling me of trips like this up the river in falltime, with as many as thirty people transporting themselves to trapping camps above Chalkyitsik—camps at Red Bluff, Doghouse Slough, Salmon Fork, Grayling Fork, and the topmost tributaries of the Big Black—and how they'd sometimes get stranded in inadequate water and have to live on just the fish that they angled for and the ducks that they shot. The worst year, it was a month before a rain at last released them and they got off the river's "high bottom" in their slow, old, deep-draft inboard motorboats. And when they did, they poled around just three bends and saw two moose on the bank and shot them and camped right there and—between the thirty of them—ate all eight legs in a couple of days.

After four hours and maybe forty miles, we stopped at Englishoe Bend for lunch. It's a campsite where Fred regularly stops, next to a muddy slough where nets for whitefish can be set, in grassy waters that are aswarm with pike, and opposite a long gravel bar where he said the women used to collect hundreds of tern eggs in June and then go back a week or two later to gather a hundred more, that the robbed parents had relaid. Board tables and butchering racks had been nailed between the poplar trees. We saw the fresh tracks of a three-year-old-size bear, which had wandered around in search of relict scraps, and heard the *chirp-chuk* of a ground squirrel, a delicious animal that Fred kept a watch for thereafter, to shoot for Henry William if he could, while we boiled salmon and potatoes for lunch and laid the salmon skins on a stump for the magpies to pick. *"Chuk, chuk, chuk."* With cupped hands, he tried to call the ground squirrel out of its den.

Only seven government staffers are assigned to care for these eight and a half million government acres, and they live and work in Fairbanks, more than an hour away by plane. So the original Gwich'in caretakers pretty much still have it, insofar as they go out, plus the fly-in white hunters and fishermen, who are not numerous enough to put undue pressure on the animals but can unnerve and infuriate an on-the-ground trapper by landing at his muskrat lake and making waves that throw both rats and sets out of kilter for a week, or by landing and shooting a particular moose that was slated for his winter larder. Only an average of six and a half inches of precipitation falls in a year—a desert's quota—but the fact that so much stays as snow for so long and is underlain by permafrost makes it a duck factory anyway.

Fred said the Indian families had acquired their "white" names when passing whites would bestow a first name such as William or John on a man and eventually his sons and daughters got another first name tacked on ahead of that one. Fred himself, being three-fourths Caucasian, is another story, but he always chose the Athapascan life— and indeed, with the provisions of the 1971 Alaska Native Claims Settlement Act, passed under the gun of lawsuits by native groups that were holding up construction of the Alaskan oil pipeline, it be- came financially desirable to be classified as a "Native." In hindsight, he realizes that his own and other families probably could have, and certainly should have, founded their own statutory village on the upper Big Black River at its Salmon Fork, where there is an aban- doned ancestral Gwich'in village site, at which his brother Harry still traps, fifty miles below Fred's cabin. If the proposal had worked, the government would have built them a school, brought in a generator, mail service, and other courtesies, and they could have set up a store, passed a restrictive liquor ordinance, and otherwise established a quiet place to live for themselves, with opportunities for going into business, if they wanted to. Chalkyitsik has survived into the post-World War II era because it's at the head of navigation on the Big Black. The little tug *Brainstorm*, pushing a barge with barrels of fuel oil, stacks of lumber, and heavy items of replacement machinery, still makes it that far up the Black once every year at high-water time in June. But some other villages are supplied solely by air.

With my friend Linda, I'd been to several of these, on the Kuskokwim River or the Chukchi Sea. It had become unusual for me to travel alone. I was spoiled, in fact; never in a tent without being in her arms; never in an isolated settlement without sleeping in the warmth of the health clinic, surrounded by the appurtenances of first-aid gear and medicines supplied to these places, or else in the womb of the school, in which all these communities focus their assets: the one sure oil furnace and hot-water heater; showers and laundry machines; and a communal kitchen stacked with cases of government-surplus peanut butter, canned peaches and peas, macaroni, and jack cheese. When I had insomnia, I'd wake in the middle of the night on a wrestling mat on the gym floor and shoot baskets—an ace at sinking three-point baskets at 3 A.M., being so utterly relaxed at that hour, my wrists loose as flippers, my fingers a pianist's, my eyes a dead-eye's. I don't believe a man should travel far without a woman's company; it's unnatural; and even when the war between the sexes comes to the fore, man is born of woman, spends nine months inside her, and depends upon her for long sustenance. Nor can I imagine dying with any degree of resignation, even of old age, anywhere but in a woman's arms. That women are taking over the Western world is no surprise; I've expected they would. They're awesome. The only protection from the power of women is a woman, and the best are the feminists, because they have all the virtues of men.

Fred tried to call the ground squirrel out of its burrow for Henry William's supper before we started again. *"Chuk, chuk, chuk."* But it wasn't fooled. The afternoon sky already looked cold, but autumn holds no terrors for a ground squirrel: as from Fred's rifle, it just goes underground. There were still plenty of dragonflies and many mosquitoes. "Where do they get all *their* food?" I asked. "There aren't that many of us around." Goldeneyes were running on the water, leaving patterns of footsteps like skipping stones as they took off, and we saw a mother merganser with twenty flightless though fast-swimming babies in tow. Four fledgling red-tailed hawks were awkwardly testing their wings between spar trees, and periodically we slid past a watchful, affronted owl.

The so-called mew gull, which mews, is a seacoast gull that nests along interior lakes and rivers and is so versatile that it feeds on swarms of flying insects like a swallow, but also upon bugs in a field, and on fish, crustaceans, and mollusks. It likes the gravel bars of the Black River to lay its three olive-colored eggs on. The babies, by now a month old and almost full-grown, still couldn't fly, but wore as camouflage a mottled brown, like the bars where they stood, ungainly, uneasy, as we went by.

More kingfishers agitatedly flew up and down between bankside sweepers—uprooted trees leaning over the current—and spar trees. At Agnes Bar (named for a local woman named Agnes Druck), Fred told of sneaking back here one time on a gaggle of honkers who thought they had seen the last of him and bagging nine of them with three shotgun shells. "This is my supermarket, this nice river."

On another occasion along through this stretch, during a spring flood just after breakup, he had lost control of his canoe and was swept violently under a sweeper and nearly flattened and swamped. "Whoa!" he'd yelled, forgetting he wasn't still behind his dog team—which had been part of his problem: he'd been sledding for so many months.

Then we spotted a moose in the water, which had been drinking. It wheeled and ran up out of the river and onto a high bank, where it stopped and stood surveying us, like a wild horse with horns, just the way that a hunter would want it to do.

"Lots of hamburger!" Fred laughed and said that it had "a three-year-old's palm." Shortly before freeze-up, he said, when he's hunting hard, he sometimes likes to sleep in his canoe, to be well placed at dusk and at dawn. But the warmest part of the day is also a good time to hunt, when moose and bears may wake from their noon naps and

want a drink. Nowadays, when he hasn't strong arms for hard paddling, he hunts from this noisy skiff, but once he missed a shot at a
moose when he'd just cut his motor and his own wake caught up with
him and rocked his boat as he was firing.

We watched the riffles, watched for smooth but quick currents,
following the cutbanks but avoiding disturbed water. Past bend after
bend after bend, we watched the taiga and willow scenery unfold—
the "drunken forest" of leaning spruces narrating where the permafrost rose momentarily underground; then placid tree lines
again—until, three hours from Englishoe Bend, we rounded yet another bend in the river and suddenly sighted a bluff in front of us with
several log buildings on top, a dozen beached skiffs at the base, and a
sandy path leading up. Some kids were playing on the beach, and a
couple of fishermen were flapping and tossing their short nets about
to dry them in the wind. The Black River fishhooks around the bluff,
past the mouth of a good fishing creek that faces the town, and so for
both reasons Chalkyitsik is named Chalkyitsik, "Fishhook Town."

Walking up the path, we met John William, Fred's brother-in-law,
a shambling but big-built, handsome, Indian-looking, young-looking
forty-nine-year-old and born-again Christian, who promptly began
lavishing elaborately scatological invective upon Fred, pausing only
to introduce me as an honored visitor to the Reverend David Salmon,
the Gwich'in minister of St. Timothy's Episcopal Church in town. It's
said of the Yukon Athapascans that they're born into and die in the
Episcopal Church but "shop around a lot in between." Just so, an
evangelical family of fundamentalist preachers with Tennessee accents had dropped into town, and John enthusiastically let us know
that he had fallen under their spell. Also, the state trooper whom I
knew from Fort Yukon was here to deal with three teenage kids who
had smashed up the town's pickup truck. Chalkyitsik, with only a little off-again, on-again general store, has a mere handful of teenagers
and a single truck and perhaps one mile of road, which runs from the
school to the dump. But they had snatched the keys and driven that
far and come to grief on the way home.

"Sure feels like falltime. A few leaves turning yellow," John
William said. He borrowed enough money from Fred to buy some

sugar for our tea at the store, and he knocked on a friend's door and borrowed a small slab of moose meat to give us a good supper that evening.

"Going to make an Indian out of him yet. I already gave him some beaver meat and some snow goose and salmon, and he's only been here two days," Fred said.

John's house was as old as he was, John told me. The leaky sod roof was covered with plastic sheeting, and the walls were lined with flattened cardboard cartons for insulation. It stood next to the store and was hooked into the store's generator for electricity. He had a deep couch for me to sink into, two *Newsweeks* and a *Real West Yearbook* on the table, a wood stove fashioned from a steel barrel, and a Coleman white-gas burner for cooking. John took out his old violin and horsehair bow and played "Be Nobody's Darlin' but Mine," as Fred told me later he had been doing for visitors for thirty years. He'd been the storekeeper for a while and now was village council president. He had had eleven years of schooling, including stints at Bureau of Indian Affairs boarding schools in Sitka on Baranof Island, in southeast Alaska, and in Phoenix, Arizona, because he had impressed his teachers as being promising.

"But still it was just a glimpse," as he told me, of the immensity and complexity of the outside world and the wealth of cultivation beyond the watershed of the Yukon. Unlike a lot of the Indians and Eskimos I had been talking to around Alaska, who felt that they'd been unfitted for life in both worlds by the experience of being partially immersed in each, he wasn't sorry to have gone Outside. Liquor had been his weakness, he suggested, and *Newsweek*, he said, remained his link. In Alaska opinions tend to be strong and unambiguous, and many Eskimos and Indians are consumed by a rankling bitterness toward white rule, white society—and even a death threat whispered or yelled at a strolling white man who is transient in the community isn't uncommon, especially in Eskimo towns such as Barrow. But John wasn't angry. He had come back to Chalkyitsik to settle, not with the sort of ringing and emphatic choice of how he wanted to live that Fred had made. He was divided. He knew that there were other ways of living—with music, books, and bustle—that appealed to him. For

Fred, the deeply drastic changes in Fort Yukon—like the "wine scramble" on the Fourth of July, when grown men scrabble in the middle of School Street to grab a bottle of wine; the crime wave, including a double fratricide last year; the rising rate of drownings and outright suicides all along the Yukon—were not cause for personal alarm but simply confirmed that the old life in the bush, with his brother Harry fifty miles below him and his brother Albert trapping seven miles above him on the Black River, was best.

There are many young men with a mocking bitterness toward everything they can identify as "white." They drink bottled beer, drive snowmobiles and "big-horse" outboards, and envy their fellows who fly off to be educated elsewhere, yet with a full dose of self-flagellation as well as a rancid, vituperative resentment of an outlander walking by. Then maybe, alas, you hear they've shot themselves while cleaning a rifle or have taken their boat out and rolled it over within sight of shore—a favorite sister possibly witnessing this in horror as the river effortlessly seized them and pulled them down. But it's not the fiftyish people who do this, or even share the fury, as a rule. Several times I met men or women of late middle age who said wistfully that the happiest years they'd ever known were when they'd left their native villages and gone and lived with a white friend in Seattle or Salt Lake City, removing themselves from Indian life altogether. It wasn't politically popular to say so, but sitting in an ancestral cabin isolated on a reach of riverbank no longer inhabited by others, they might confide.

Old people, however, had no such memories of a romance with a lonely Anglo schoolteacher, perhaps; no williwaw of doubts assailing them as they remembered a sojourn ten years before in Santa Cruz, where a summer lover had spirited them after a tryst on the Yukon and where they had worked on the amusement-park boardwalk, running a kiddie ride, until the lady in question—an anthropology professor on sabbatical, a social worker on furlough, a federal accountant, or whatever she was—after one drunken binge too many, bought them an Alaska Airlines ticket home. In these villages you may meet an Indian woman who at one point was carried off too—by a white barge worker, a store manager, a bush pilot, a fire fighter, a hydrologist—and then gently sent home because, in Juneau or Los Angeles or Tulsa, she no longer looked so good. It was not that her hair was less black and lush or that the measurements of her bust had shrunk, but that she didn't know what to do; she had to be led by the hand everywhere. She became meek and confused, too easily bossed around and too tempted by liquor, or frightened of it, and couldn't pull down a healthy paycheck, and sat by the TV all day if left alone.

But the women somehow survive this kind of experience better. More flexible or philosophical, they go to work in the village post office and grocery store, or the village or tribal office, with enhanced skill. There seems to be a marked difference in how "Native" women bear up under the stress of demoralizing social change. They can remember the big-legged oil-field guy carrying them off to Houston when his contract expired and his wife, by letter, had informed him that he shouldn't expect to move back in the house. So instead he brings his Fort Yukon girlfriend to roost in a condo by the Ship Canal or Chocolate Bayou, and they lie in bed in a luscious *X* late every morning and drink shooters late into the night, living off his Prudhoe Bay earnings, while he phones divorce lawyers or tries to get through to his kids on the phone—him climbing her body half the night, in between bouts of snoring like a walrus—until one day he begins shaking his head and says, "Oh, no, no, it's no good. I'll drive you to the airport."

No, she protests, and he "kindly" gives her another chance. But he begins joking about "firewater" when they drink, and the fun goes out of so much of it. She feels foreign, inadequate, a dumbhead. She sneaks off to try to make it on her own in Houston, but finally her family sends her a little money, and a barmaid takes pity and deposits her on a plane for Minneapolis, where the stewardesses can steer her to the gate for Fairbanks—where the ancestral, rapacious cold itself is as steadying as a hand on her elbow.

"The hawk almost got you?" they say in the Arctic when you've just survived a close call.

But we didn't talk of these things in John William's log cabin in Chalkyitsik. Nor did I ask about his personal history. Instead John and Fred agreed that it was too bad the Englishoe Bend ground squirrel hadn't come out of its burrow, because John's rabbit snares were turning up empty and it was animals like these, cooked in their skins, that the old man found most palatable in his last illness. He was tired of eating pike, which were the easiest fish to catch in midsummer. Salmon swam by the town all the time but would not bite a hook, because when spawning they don't like to eat and the Black is as clear as glass in August anyway.

We went to look at John's new cabin, of which only the deck had been laid in quite some while.

"You better finish it," Fred said. "Your rafters look like deadfalls from lying there on the ground."

"I'm going to build a Log Cabin Syrup-type cabin," he said.

They talked more about wild foods. Fred said his mother used to bake hoot owls and that if you first boil and then bake a loon, it's pretty good too, though most people don't know that. We walked for a mile or two around John's snare line to see if Fred had any suggestions for improving it. Fred has been snaring rabbits in a serious way for half a century, in town and out of town, for a garnish for a meal or living off them when he had to, and never gets on a plane without a roll of picture wire in his pocket, in case the plane goes down and he has to set snares to survive—gave me some wire, for safety's sake, when I left him—and he said it was harder in the summer, without tracks in the snow to read like a newspaper.

John observed that a shot rabbit tastes better than a snared rabbit, because it hasn't strangled slowly in the snare, while its juices soured. He pulled an imaginary bowstring back close to his eye and sighted along his outstretched arm. But we weren't seeing rabbits that you could shoot at, either.

We went up on Marten Hill, where the old man was going to be buried and where Fred said he himself hoped to lie. Cranes were calling from the sky, and we also heard a ground squirrel's *chuk*, which made us all grin but was frustrating to the two men trying to tempt Henry William to eat. The view was low-lying but splendid—to the northeast, Frozen Calf Mountain; to the southwest, Bear Nose Mountain. Immediately beneath us lay Marten Lake, a modest dab of water that the "black ducks" (as they call white-winged scoters here) arrive at in legions on Memorial Day, even more concentrated than the mallards, which need less open water and arrive two weeks earlier. The Chalkyitsik hunters lie on this sunny cemetery hill and blast away as the exuberant, amorous scoters, which have wintered down the Pacific coast, swoop up again off the level of the water in wavering lines, sometimes without having landed, and skim up the slant of Marten Hill past them to have a look-see at the other lakes all around.

Fred talked bolt-action versus lever-action versus pump-action guns and showed me where they lay and how they fired. Probably more hunting fun is had here in this week or two, he said, than anywhere else around the village, so he'd like to have his grave dug where he can hear the guns and laughter and remember how it was. In their gleeful, flirtatious courtship activities on his own hunting ponds, farther up the Black, the ducks are so very unwary that, alone and paddling quietly after them, he can get close enough to shoot several, and then go home when they fly off, but come back and do the same thing again before dusk.

Before we returned to the village, he and John showed me two sites where arrowheads have recently been found that indicate raids that were staged upon these Chalkyitsik Gwich'in more than a hundred years ago by Indians of the Koyukon group, living hundreds of miles to the west, and by Gwich'in Athapascans from northeast on the Porcupine, who almost within living memory had attacked an outlying encampment by surprise one night, thinking it was the main one, with such force that they might have wiped out everybody if they'd got their target right. All these Athapascans, living south of the Brooks Range, also warred intermittently with the Eskimos, whose territory lay only two hundred fifty miles north of Fort Yukon. The animosity lingers in muted form at Native American rights conferences and the like, and in Fairbanks bars. But Fred told me the story of the last Gwich'in who had died at Eskimo hands. He had come home very sick after a long hunting trip in the northern mountains and simply took to his bed, saying nothing about what might be the matter with him. He asked that he be buried with the regular ritual (which in those days meant being placed in a tree), except for one special stipulation: that nobody examine his body closely for three years, but then to do so. And when the period was finally up and his sons carried out these filial instructions, they discovered an Eskimo lance head—serrated like a harpoon head that holds sea animals—at the center of his bones. And they realized that by remaining silent, he had succeeded in bringing the long cycle of vengeance, counter-vengeance, and counter-countervengeance at last to an end.

Not just the local Indians and Eskimos tend to take a leery view of each other, but the whites who work with Native American Alaskans often choose sides. Alaskan Eskimos, if one can generalize, were more innocent until recently of whites' duplicity and brutality than the various Indian and Aleut bands. Because of the climate and remote locations in which they lived, they had been "discovered" later, and perhaps protected a bit better by the missionaries who interceded with the whalers, adventurers, and officials who visited their villages during the summer. The "Red Power" political movement and the rage accompanying it were slower to reach the Inupiat Eskimos of the North Slope than the Indians of southeast and central Alaska. Consequently, a traveler is more likely to be threatened with a beating or with getting shot in an Eskimo village nowadays—Indian activism having reached a more political, sophisticated stage. Thus traveling much there takes a bit more intrepidness (not counting the fact that my eyelids freeze shut). And I am a stutterer, and Eskimos will make fun of a handicap more readily. Their culture, pummeled by the exigencies of the Arctic, makes less allowance for handicaps; their religion itself seems simpler.

But with my nursing friend, I had an entrée and a protected status. Sometimes people even took me for a doctor at first, because I was accompanying a nurse. I would go with her as she visited patients: not just kids, but old men and women dying of liver cancer—to which Eskimos are particularly susceptible because they are subject to hepatitis B, a precursor disease. The bed would be by the window of the back room of the small, slapped-together, government-built house. The man lying there looking out would glance up, politics and Red rage being far from his mind, if indeed he didn't disagree with its premises from the different perspective of his own generation. Linda

would feel his pulse, take his blood pressure, and do the mildly painful business of drawing blood, unless perhaps he was so close to terminal that she had the option of not doing so. She would ask if he was
where he wanted to be—would he rather be in town at the hospital?
No, no, he said, with his eyes fastened on the landscape again. Did he
know that he could have a sedative or an anesthetic shot anytime he
needed one—had the village health aide made that clear to him, and
did he trust her to do it? Yes, he said. Linda explained with tender-
ness that she herself was from Anchorage and would not be back, but
she would talk to the district nurse and that if he told her of any way
she could help him from now on, she would. Resigned, his gaze outdoors, he smiled no.

At John's cabin, John showed me the moose shoulder blade he
hunts with during rutting season in the early fall. The Gwich'in will
gently brush a moose scapula across the bushes and branches as they
walk through the woods or canoe a small creek, imitating the sound of
a bull's antlers in order to provoke the approach of other bulls. At this
time of year, a hunter doesn't necessarily try to walk softly. He may
deliberately break a few sticks underfoot to mimic the noise of a bold
bull that is looking for trouble. People who have hacking coughs, people chopping firewood—even drunks vomiting their breakfast at the
edge of the village—have unwittingly attracted a rutting moose. Because moose don't eat much during their rut but drink lots of water,
you hear the water slosh in their bellies as they come. A 1964 vocabu-
lary listing gives eleven different Gwich'in words for "moose."

Fred and John talked about hunting in the old days, when if you
met a cow and a bull, you shot the cow once, and then the bull once,
and then the cow, and then the bull, swinging your rifle back and
forth so that neither escaped, but husbanding your shots because
each bullet ruined at least a couple of pounds of decent meat. Fred's
father apologized if he needed more than two shots to immobilize a
moose, but then would patiently let it die in its own time. With
moose, you try for a heart shot—under the shoulder and from the
side—but in hitting a bear, you place your shots not so much for a
quick kill as to break the bear down so that it can't charge, with shots
into its shoulder bones and chest, or the face and eyes. After a moose

died, the Gwich'in immediately cut off its ears, for reasons of piety which Fred has forgotten, just as they would cut the muzzle off a wolf and tack it to a tree, or put a piece of moose meat into the campfire at night if wolves howled to share their kill in this manner with them. Bears, as they died and afterward, were treated with special respect and gentle solemnity, befitting a manlike creature whose spirit would go back into the pool of bear spirits and help to determine how much luck the hunter would have at hunting bears again. But except for putting meat on the fire when wolves howled, Fred's riverboatman father didn't allow "superstitious" practices in his household.

Fred and I ate moose for supper, while John preferred to boil the heads of the two salmon we had brought. Henry William, John's and Charlotte's father, came over to share a bite and to meet me. Gaunt-chinned, pale, and crumpled over, leaning on his cane even after he was sitting down, Henry William wanted to tell me his story but was too tired to say more than a very little.

With John's and Fred's assistance, he said that the first time he had ever seen a white man was early in this century, when his own father had taken their family cross-country from the Big Black River to the Little Black River, and down the Little Black to where it meets Big Creek to form what is thereafter called the Grass River. But instead of continuing down the Grass to the Porcupine and to Fort Yukon, they went up Big Creek to its headwaters, at a rise that on its other side overlooks the Yukon River opposite Circle City, which is now the village of Circle, pop. 81. At the turn of the century Circle City was a small trading metropolis, two hundred ninety-two river miles below the larger hubbub of Dawson City, and by sled, about a hundred sixty miles northeast of Fairbanks. In fact, in 1896, just before the Klondike strike, Circle City had boasted twelve hundred citizens, a million dollars in gold extraction a year, two theaters, an opera house, twenty-eight saloons, eight dance halls, and the sobriquet, "The Paris of Alaska." The Klondike rush, much richer, had partly depopulated it, but even in 1906, fourteen years after the first Circle City strike, a quarter of a million dollars' worth of gold was taken out of there.

Although the William family was a bit late to see Circle City in its glory, the buildings did remain, and everything was new to them, he said—even flour. They bought some flour and stirred it into water with some newly acquired white sugar and poured this white whiteman's gravy on their moose meat, not knowing any other use for it. After the meal, he, Henry, had carefully felt his face and looked at his hands to see whether he might not be turning white, too.

"Right down here in America we get a square deal," said Henry. "But in Canada, no. Shoot him! Shoot him! In 1919, natives scared of police. Grab a guy and smell his breath and maybe shoot him. Take a girl to the station and all screw her before they let her go."

After their initiation in Circle, the family had gone to Canada, but ended that unpleasant sojourn after World War I and came back to the Big Black River to set up a homesite at Doghouse Slough, upriver about twenty miles from Chalkyitsik. John, who consequently has some land rights at Doghouse, said he wants to open a "Doghouse Restaurant" when the tourists come, and that although he doesn't know how it used to be with those Canadian Gwich'in up the Porcupine and Yukon, now (on the grass-is-greener theory) "The girls are friendlier up there in Old Crow. They're more relaxed."

"But I'm sure that goddamn Seward bought this country from Russia," Henry told me—as if I, as a white American, could somehow share in the credit.

"Beautiful mornings, with the mallards and the laughing geese talking. On the Salmon Fork it's like Marlboro Country. Fast river. White mountains." John laughed, teasing Fred because it was Fred's brother Harry who actually trapped the Salmon Fork, whereas Fred's Grayling Fork, named for its grayling, a troutlike fish, was fifty miles farther up the Black, and "dark like a dungeon," and too shallow and slow-moving for salmon to choose to spawn. With no salmon holes, it had no salmon—"except for a few strays that missed the turn," as Fred himself admitted with a grin. Even the otters that wandered into his Grayling Fork got starved out by winter or else would put their feet into his mink traps simply "to get a scrap to eat."

Henry William let them kid each other without comment. Now that Belle Herbert had died—supposedly the oldest person in the United States, at 129—he was Chalkyitsik's senior citizen. Belle had lived so long that she outlived her family and dwelled alone, though comfortably, with a string that ran from her house to a bell in the next house, which she could ring if she had to.

Fred and I went back to the riverbank and put up separate tents, I with my air mattress to sleep on and Fred with a bearskin. We stood watching the river's ripples and fish surfacing and muskrats making *V*'s as they swam about. Fred called the muskrats closer to us with squeaking sounds—saying his father "couldn't call a muskrat to save his life"—just as he does from his canoe when he is hunting them with a .22 after the ice goes off the lakes in the spring and they have so much freedom to swim anywhere that you can't trap them, but the fur's still good. Then the days have lengthened like mad, and the males think he's a male and the females also think he's a squeaking male, and both come for him. Between pursuing the muskrats and the gleeful ducks, it's such a happy time of year that he once tried to tape-record the sounds of May, to play back for himself in midwinter, but wound up mostly with his own voice cussing the recorder.

We built a smudge fire to fend off the mosquitoes, and John and Fred talked ducks, fish, and mosquitoes. But John said he was tired of fooling around alone in the woods. He wanted to get married now, "either to a white woman or to a red woman." Fred, being an old married man, said it wasn't so bad being alone. He regularly had only two lonely moments on the trap line, both in the early fall. The first was when his kids went back to go to school, and the other, right afterward, was when the geese went headlong overhead, which they did just as soon as their young ones had grown wings that could fly. Sometimes the geese's heading south seemed a little lonelier, maybe because his kids, but not the geese, were sorry to go.

A cousin of John's stopped by and, when I brought up the subject of Brush Man, said he thought he'd spotted one once but now doesn't believe it, because he was a kid. His father had told him they'd traveled overland from the Lower Forty-Eight, just as the miners did, but, unlike the Klondikers, they couldn't go home again.

John said, "A guy here shot one a few years ago, but they paid him back—he blew his head off a little later." And expressing his impatience with white-style "proof," he added that "if they aren't still on the Yukon, they used to be, that's for sure. *Used* to be. Now you might have to go up north, up where the big bears are. They don't like the helicopters and all the stuff around Fort Yukon. Everybody's got a finger in the pie."

"But you mean they're in the mountains?" I asked him.

"And farther away than that. Way up north; what's that place called where it's so wild?"

"The Arctic National Wildlife Refuge?" I said.

"Empty place. Yes, that's it. You don't know what you'd find."

In broad daylight, we slept awhile, grateful that our tents were dark. Then we breakfasted at John's with the state trooper, Dan Hickman, whom I knew from Fort Yukon and whom John seemed quite interested in courting, both in the manner of a local politico and as someone who was fascinated by people who had found their niche in life. The trooper, in his turn, was curious to get to know Fred, because Fred had been the foreman on a local jury that recently acquitted a Fort Yukon Indian of the charge of threatening a policeman with his chain saw. A certain electricity flowed between them, therefore. Alaska has two varieties of trooper—the giant macho guys who look prepared for rifle duels, icy shoot-outs, treks by snowmobile, and bush-plane chases; and these more limber and amenable officers, who can tactfully adjudicate racial or domestic disputes. The tough troopers used to be sent to Native villages, but now that the Natives have organized and acquired collective wealth and clout, one meets the tougher troopers in the white cities and towns, whereas the skillful negotiators go out to Eskimo and Indian communities—men like Hickman, who say "Caucasian " instead of "white" and "Athapascan" for "Indian," even though the locals themselves happily use the informal terms. Our man, besides being less massively built than your stock-in-trade Alaska trooper, was the son of a trooper and probably from birth had been free of the compulsion to vaunt his manhood.

We talked about a pending case where two trappers on the Black were said to have shot fourteen moose last winter to feed their sled dogs, instead of feeding them fish and rabbits the way everybody else does now that fly-in hunters from Fairbanks compete for moose. John kidded Hickman about the Mad Trapper of Rat River, a famous mystery figure who fifty year ago in Gwich'in country among the tributaries of the upper Porcupine River in the Yukon Territory led the Royal Canadian Mounted Police on a forty-eight-day midwinter steeplechase and shooting match. The Mad Trapper was a canny Swede named Albert Johnson, not a Gwich'in, and his stamina was superhuman, but even so, Alaskan troopers, as well as the Mounties, have to take some kidding in these Native villages about him, the trooper's job, meanwhile, being to cultivate contacts for solving a crime later on.

In the two weeks, altogether, that I spent around Fred, I never heard him speak of the bush as menacing or unmanageable. But from childhood on he has heard stories about berserk white men coming to grief in the drainage of the Yukon and the Porcupine: "Old Man Rice," for instance, a Southerner who did not like Indians because their skins were dark. He and a German immigrant, known on the Black River as Smitty, had had adjoining trapping territories along a rich beaver slough near the headwaters of the Salmon Fork. When Fred was young, they'd quarreled over who the slough belonged to, and shot each other one April. At least this was the theory. April is the season when trappers shoot beavers on the thawing ice, as their trap sets become less effective and the hungry animals emerge to forage through newly melted holes. Because the German's three dogs were discovered dead on their chain in front of his cabin later, the police, the Thomas family, and other neighbors drew the conclusion that Smitty had expected to come back. Apparently Old Man Rice was whipsawing lumber out on the ice for a boat he was building, when Smitty bushwhacked him. But presumably he played dead, when shot, to get his revenge. Then, at breakup, both bodies, as well as the boat, floated away. Neither individual had any friends—the one because of the language problem, the other because of his prejudices about Indians—so nobody cared very much, but it was the kind of insolubly enigmatic murder in the wilds-beyond that can provoke rumors of crazy-bad Injuns, or maybe a Bigfoot.

There is still a yearly toll of migrants into the Alaskan bush who come to a bad end. On a lovely, pristine river like the Coleen, a famished body will be found, twisted inside its muddy sleeping bag in a little tent that the rains have pounded askew, with its plaintive diary,

the entries growing incredulous, frantic, pinched, sliding toward inco-
herence. The man may have made his way into the wilderness on his
own, or been dropped off by a bush pilot who forgot about him, or
else when the pilot did return, as scheduled, the wanderer was dead.
No licensing procedures, no training requirements exist for people
who wish to immerse themselves in frontier conditions. The plane,
needless to say, just drops them off, and in an hour—as I've heard
tell—the person may find himself wet to the waist in the spring thaw,
with his pack soaked through, and no dry ground to stand on. The
temperature is 33 degrees, and although he may not know the word
for hypothermia, he is suffering from it. He has dry matches, he
thinks, but where to build a fire? The expensive pilot has been told
not to come back for three months.

Calamitous adventures are commonplace in Alaska. You can
struggle for your very life for days in the muck and muskeg across
Cook Inlet from Anchorage, within sight of its silvery skyscrapers.
The same sort of dithery idealism that sends young people off to become hippies in Vermont and Oregon, or to demonstrate in front of a
government building, propels them to risk their good health in a
quick study of wilderness skills—a oneness with nature you can't
back out of. The plane flies off and leaves you, and you build a hut,
shoot meat and throw it up on the roof, and maybe learn enough
about trapping to feed yourself that way too. You learn the intricacies
of meats in balancing a diet; your woodpile is an object of high labor
and devotion. But your candles run out; the night extends for eighteen, twenty, twenty-two hours. Will the pilot ever remember? One
meets people in Alaska who have literally frozen their buttocks off,
wading for many miles through deep snow, though it may be that this
ordeal began as a lark.

Pilots are heroes in the state, and one soon grows keenly fond of
them—an unrequited fondness, as a rule, because once they have delivered you deep into the tortuous chaos of the Brooks Range, for example, they will drop you off and fly away to risk their lives alongside
somebody else, dropping onto a dot-sized landing strip along another
river, and then by day's end maybe five other parties as well. In the
summer, pilots make lots of money and the sky doesn't darken to

crimp their fun. Geologists, prospectors, surveyors, kayakers, hikers, mountain climbers, Native people visiting around (or pregnant, undergoing contractions, or schoolchildren going to a basketball game with a rival town), government experts of a dozen stripes with doctoral degrees or axes to grind or a sudden furlough—the complete cosmology of contemporary humankind in Alaska hops in and out of their aircraft. In many villages they are the sole reminder of the stopwatch tempo of the outside world, roaring in and out with insulin and bread and beer, housing specialists and sanitary engineers, wolf hunters, glaciologists, archaeologists, and behavioral scientists who intend to study bighorn sheep. The roar, the preliminary passage overhead to scout the runway, is followed by the abrupt, whooshing landing, a quick palaver, exchange of passengers and heaving of baggage onto the ground, possibly a cup of coffee, a ham sandwich, and up again, with that frenetic sangfroid.

A pilot is the one white man an angry Indian can't make fun of, because he covers ground, sees game, does good, carries the mail, and earns money putting his life in jeopardy. But the roar punctuates the static life of his sinking culture with news of its cruel eclipse. One of my social worker friends spoke of these Indian villages as becoming like "fox farms," which, during the boom of the twenties, when furs were in vogue, sprang up all over. People would pick a small island isolated enough so that foxes would drown if they tried to swim off, and breed and feed them till they overran the place, killing a crop when prices were right. But when the stock market fell and prices crashed, the people stopped bothering to catch and deliver fish to their fox-farm islands, just abandoned the places. The foxes turned into living skeletons, cannibalized one another or tried to survive for a little while on sea wrack and injured birds. And this, he thought, was about what would happen to these settlements, nurtured with hothouse oil-fed welfare programs, when the Prudhoe Bay fields run out.

The pilots, who teethed in Teterboro, New Jersey, or Huntsville, Arkansas, and who may go on to fly airliners someday pretty soon, are not overly interested in the deterioration of Indian culture and the morale of these villages, or in the private survival dramas of young hippies on a tiny quilt patch of ground sliding under the plane. Life was passing those guys by, too. You dropped them off and picked them up five months later, and they'd eaten some ducks and porcupines, masturbated to beat the band, fished a little, scratched in the riffles of their creekbed for signs of gold (of which they knew next to nothing anyhow), taken a fuzzy picture of a wolf that had surprised them by visiting, and gut-shot a moose that then got away. This is not really what life is all about. Of course, the white hippie may have originated in Teterboro himself and have his own perspective on things, but the pilot is a vivid reproach to younger Indians, who have no way of remembering how their society is supposed to work and see only its present decay, into which the plane plunges with groceries, hospital services, and so on; then darts off to cover ten other villages, carries native leaders to their lobbying meetings and kids to the dentist—living refutation of some Red Power arguments about the self-sufficiency of Native culture now. Old people, accustomed to living by the fishnet and snare and a few well-placed bullets a year, hardly care except when they look at their daughters and sons.

White sufferers, on the other hand, have come *from* home, are not *at* home, and are an entirely different breed. They can leave, if they want to, and go back where they came from, but in unusual cases, when they don't, they get into still steeper trouble, not just pulling a trigger on themselves or suddenly drowning, but a kinkier, lengthier unhappy ending. We have in America "The Big Two-Hearted River" tradition: taking your wounds to the wilderness for a cure, a conversion, a rest, or whatever. And as in the Hemingway story, if your wounds aren't too bad, it works. But this isn't Michigan (or Faulkner's Big Woods in Mississippi, for that matter). This is Alaska. You get into trouble here and it's not a cold spell, it's eight months of cold; whereupon if finally the ice goes out on the river and you're on the wrong side, how are you going to get back?—for days, floes splitting around you. And Fred, though he recognized that people from my world often went into the bush to get away from the ailments of what they called civilization (so did he, partly, from Fort Yukon's tensions), had no idea what a crazy constellation of distresses these migrants sometimes brought with them. Nor, in the serenity of his duck lakes and stick forests, did he quite realize there were ills that might never be healed.

Alaskans take for granted, but then tend to conveniently forget, the round of psychodramas of a good many migrants and newcomers, who may arrive with the fervor of born-agains, with furniture piled on the car, with infants in tow and maybe a master's degree, riding their last dollar and gallon of gasoline into Fairbanks to throw themselves on the mercy of the first working-class family that smiles at them and has a lawn to mow—a meal for a mow—but may not last half the year. It's a tradition that you grubstake newcomers and hope they work out. That's how the state grows. Nor should anyone arrive too auspiciously. People who have managed their lives well elsewhere wouldn't be here.

In the towns of McCarthy and Manley Hot Springs, however, while I was living in the state, mad gunmen shot multiple sets of victims dead in fathomless rampages—the McCarthy murderer a short-term resident in this white community reachable only by air, the individual in Manley Hot Springs, a man who had driven as far west of Fairbanks as you can go. And so drifters on the Yukon receive less of a welcome than they used to, even from whites, and in the towns at the end of the last road you can't be sure of a grubstake now. Reversing the fundamentalists' old view of the wilderness as satanic, people thought it was Eden for just a while, and satanic souls may head straight for Eden if they can, to see if their madness abates.

After the thick, frantic dramas of the gold rush, from 1885 through 1906—a hundred million dollars in gold; the Northern Navigation Co. ran thirty-two stern-wheel river steamers at once on the Yukon alone—veterans of World War I arrived, not simply for healing purposes but with the zest of the twenties too. What better place to roar? And in the Great Depression, hungry men came on a shoestring, needing grubstakes.

(These, mostly, were the pool of men whom I knew during my wanderings in the Stikine and Skeena and Cassiar and Omineca districts of British Columbia during the 1960s, men in their fifties and sixties by then but still able to get about pretty well if they needed to, though I met a few who had preceded them by twenty or thirty years, now going blind and lantern-jawed. When you walked to their cabins, usually by a river that they could fish in, a creek that they could pan

277

in, if you wanted to stay over, the general etiquette was that you split wood for your helping of moose meat and a night's lodging, like in the thirties. Not just the supper's kindling and a summer night's firelight, but wood for the *pile*—"to remember you by when I'm all by my lonesome," as one guy said. He panned enough to buy his boat gas and groceries. Gold was hourly wages to him—so many hours put in: so many rice-sized grains or hangnail-sized flakes wound up in the bottle he kept. "There never comes a time when there's no gold in a place that has gold." That and his woodpile was all he needed. My book *Notes from the Century Before* was about such as him.)

Then World War II vets migrated to Alaska; then sixties hippies; then Vietnam vets: each group with its quota of nuts and hard cases. You read any old-timer's memoir of Alaska and you'll find some paranoid soul marching from the village of Dillingham, on the Bering Sea, over stupendous country to the village of Sleetmute, on the Kuskokwim River, in rags and burned black by the sun and the frosts. Or from the Kuskokwim, over another hump of the Alaska Range, to the Yukon River. Or from the Yukon over the Brooks Range to the Arctic Ocean, raving and muttering, mad as a hatter. These are the iron men, who survive. But others just go out and camp, get cold, wet, and hungry, shiver, and die.

In 1981, shortly before my first visit to Fort Yukon, a Texan starved to death near the Coleen River, only about thirty miles off the thoroughfare of the Porcupine River, and because his death needn't have happened and he kept a poignantly detailed, frightened diary, discovered by a newspaper reporter, it made headlines. But another such death, in 1975, affected Fred more personally, because it was on his own Big Black River. He and his son Jimmy may have been the last people to see this man alive.

Fred was working at the Fort Yukon radar base during those years and so on September 24 was on his way back "downtown" with Jimmy after a vacation at his trapping camp on Grayling Fork. The first night he stopped at his brother Harry's cabin, fifty miles down the Black, at its Salmon Fork. He could easily have made Chalkyitsik, seventy miles farther down, by the next night but became curious, seeing a new cabin going up on the bank at a bend halfway there, and stopped to say hello. The fellow, who looked to be in his late twenties, told Fred he had served in the Vietnam War and "wanted to get away from people." Yet he was pleasant, and although they were hurrying to get their skiff downriver before freeze-up, Fred and Jimmy stopped to camp and get acquainted with their new neighbor.

He'd made good workmanlike progress with his carpentry, but Fred remembers being surprised at how little exploring he'd done roundabout. He had paid a Chalkyitsik Indian named Paul Ben to ferry him out there with six five-gallon cans of gasoline (half of which had been burned on the trip), five gallons of kerosene for his lamp, and a rubber raft, which of course would be useless within a couple of days, when the river froze up.

"He had no calendar or radio or watch, because he was trying to get away from everything, and he had three or four sacks of oatmeal—that was his long suit for food—but I didn't see no rice or macaroni or stuff like that," Fred said. Fred's brother Harry, on a visit, had given him a hunk of moose meat to help him get started, and it was hanging in a tree where the bears couldn't get at it. But the "camp robbers" (gray jays) were pecking away at this at a great rate. He claimed he didn't begrudge them what they could eat, but didn't seem to realize that they would eat lots, just peck and peck and peck and fly away to store what they got for a rainy day. "They can do an awful job on your store of meat."

He had brought a fishnet, but it was lying on the beach, not in the water, where it should have been right now during the fall whitefish run, and he said he didn't know how to set it under the ice, a skill he would need in less than a week. Fred tried to tell him that freeze-up is the time to be working like hell laying in food for the winter while you still can. First whitefish and then the suckers are running past on their way back from their summer hangouts in ponds and creeks to deep holes in the river bottom, where they can get below where the ice will reach. Setting his nets in these few weeks, Fred fills a couple of washtubs with fish each day to throw up on top of his cache to freeze. And this is also the time when young rabbits born during the summer are foraging hungrily as the green things die off and the first snows begin hemming them in, before predators have caught large numbers of them. Before the fur bearers get prime, a trapper will devote days to stringing a regular maze of rabbit snares, laying up meat for himself and his dogs. Fred and his brothers caught sixteen hundred rabbits one very fine fall and threw them up onto the cache along with the whitefish. Their twenty dogs ate twelve pounds of cornmeal boiled with twelve pounds of these (or of moose fat) a day. By October it's a matter of grabbing all the flesh you possibly can, so, in the bitter weather, you can devote your energy to trapping.

Also, now that the willows alongside the river had lost their leaves, the moose would be leaving the valley for higher ground and wouldn't be back till the snows drove them down. So, quite apart from the legalities of the hunting season, it was crucial to bag one first. Yet it was easy for me to imagine this newcomer's sense of peace and relief. In the late summer he had built a sound cabin, and he felt that after surviving combat in Vietnam he could survive anything. He had a .30-06 for big game, but no .22 for rabbits and grouse. Rabbits, indeed, were all about, feeding on the tops of the trees he had cut for his house, but he said he'd seen enough killing; he was enjoying watching them.

"You talk about a man digging his own grave! He wouldn't let Jimmy shoot a few of them for him," Fred said. The ducks were already gone—Fred ordinarily goes into winter with forty ducks hanging in his cabin—but he'd had no shotgun to shoot them when they'd been around, and said he didn't know how to set snares for additional meat at the beaver house that Fred had seen half a bend upstream; nor was he interested in learning. He seemed reluctant to kill anything. Two days before, he had watched a bull moose across the river but hadn't shot it, wanting, he said, to wait till it crossed to his side— he didn't realize the dark, hungry time was almost upon him and he should paddle like hell to get meat when he could. His few gallons of kerosene would quickly burn up. Fred uses nine-hour candles, thinly wicked, fat with wax—three of them set on spikes inside his cabin, so he can see while he skins, and one outside, sheltered in a punctured tin can hung by a wire under his snow roof to welcome him home from the trap line.

Paul Ben had gotten this poor fellow started, and undoubtedly Paul Ben would have looked in on him again to check on his progress after a while, or at least have come back to invite him down to the village for Christmastime. But what neither Paul Ben nor the man had anticipated was that Paul Ben would go to Fairbanks and get shot in a barroom brawl and not be in a position to take care of him again. Perhaps Fred is nagged by guilty regret that he himself, down in Fort Yukon, hadn't made inquiries. Paul Ben's Chalkyitsik friends may be too. Apparently the stranger, as Fred speculates, having watched the late-summer traffic of skiffs (such as Fred's) going by, was fooled into thinking there would always be people passing and had not been told that the winter trail the dog teams and snowmobiles used did not follow the Big Black River's endless windings, but cut cross-country considerably back in the bush from where he was. If he'd explored at all, he would have found it, and certainly would have discovered, too, that a Fort Yukon trapper named Harry Carroll, who winters in Chalkyitsik, had a trap-line cabin only two bends, or three river miles, down the Black from him. Harry Carroll didn't actually stop in more than once a week, but when the poor guy was starving in January he could have got his mitts on a whole stack of mink, marten, and lynx carcasses there to subsist on till the next time Harry came by. In fact, if he hadn't waited until his strength gave out, he could have hiked down the river to town in two hard days. Tracks showed that, late in the game, suffering hunger pangs, he had left his cabin in desperation and struck through the woods for a mile or two, but had missed both Harry Carroll's cabin and the winter trail.

The sad story, which in its particulars was like the dithering behavior of the man who had starved to death near the Coleen, except that this man was so close to help, puzzled Fred—unless you took it to be simply a story of suicide. He didn't think his having been in a war might have had much to do with it. The idea of people retreating here to lick their wounds, wool-gather, and recruit themselves seems odd to someone at home in the place, with a year-round raft of bread-winning skills, amid brutal extremes—Fort Yukon's recorded temperature range is −78 to + 105. You can craft a snowhouse around willow boughs, or sleep on the boughs where coals have warmed the ground, with maybe a moose-skin propped up to cut the wind and a leeward fire—and on and on, if you know these things—but it's not the best site in the world for eremitic experiments or peace-love theatrics.

In Alaska you meet people who are still boiling mad at what they were doing before they got here, and it sticks in their craw that they have children growing up five thousand miles off, under another man's auspices, and their money from whatever project they failed at is gone. Children, money, time, love—what isn't lost? Such a honcho stands next to another in a bar (or next to an Eskimo who under different circumstances would be ranging behind a dogsled after caribou), and you may see the fur fly. The younger ones build nomad-type houses out of scrap wood, with cupolas and whatnot, and provisional marriages—one couple I knew "married" each other on a heart-shaped bed of purple fireweed—and hybrid careers. A bit of oil-rig wrestling at Prudhoe Bay, a bit of gold smuggling to Mexico City, or buying emeralds in Bangkok and hustling them back. "Gone to Goa," said a hand-lettered sign on the door of the jerry-built house of my fireweed friends, when I stopped in. Next time, Lethe-land; same people zonked out. Another man, a loner, has constructed bottle-shaped refuges dug into the ground in the deep bush that he can parachute to if he feels the need to, each with supplies and a plug.

Lassitude or pugnacity: if these are two of the stock reactions outsiders have to their awe or distress engendered in Alaska, I'm subject to lassitude. Fred was, I think, politely astonished, if not irritated, by how little advantage I took of my overnight stay in Chalkyitsik. He'd brought me so far in his boat, introduced me around, charged me a sum, and I had disappointed him by not venturing on my own into the cabins of older Indians who spoke English as a second language, at best, and might tell me Bigfoot or battle stories or lore even he didn't know. And of course he was right. He had watched me barge into old-timers' houses in Fort Yukon often enough, but here I sat engulfed in John William's broken-springed sofa, reading an out-of-date *Newsweek*, unless he led me out to meet people. Perhaps he wasn't reminded of the young veteran who'd got himself all the way to the upper Black River and then starved to death because he had ceased to exert himself, but I made the connection. My gush of energy in just getting to Chalkyitsik had exhausted me, which naturally puzzled Fred, for whom it was a boat trip between his and his wife's hometowns.

I'd first had to leave New York, entailing a fight with my wife—our marriage then being in its waning-fireball stage, her boyfriend calling her every day and spinning the dial on his phone to produce a Bronx cheer of clicks if I was the one who picked it up at our end. The flight to Seattle was an ordinary red-eye, with sleepy yuppies loosening their ties, the tempo of business breakfasts ahead. But the Alaska-bound passengers in the Seattle terminal are a breed apart. Headlong young men with grandfather beards and bristly mustaches; hectic but more ill-assorted souls, middling in age, who had fouled their nests and were banking on better luck in the "Last Frontier," hoping its rigors could swallow their bile. The profile airport clerks use to distinguish potential hijackers is presumably not applied to Alaska flights, or a third of the passengers would be pulled out of line to be questioned discreetly.

Then, on the Boeing, "Man Mountain," as he introduces himself, is your seatmate, an acidulous presence, obese as a bear, with a part interest in "the third creekbed down" in a nameless wing of the east Wrangell Range: that is to say, a Pleistocene creekbed, under another prehistoric creekbed, under one of the myriad present creekbeds in this almost roadless region of rock, ice, and snow. "The western end of this country has been ruined by the eastern end of this country," he says, with which I cannot entirely disagree.

Or the man next to you, in a "halibut jacket," with big hands, may be a Cessna pilot who earns up to twelve thousand dollars per long frenzied day during the brief herring season, spotting schools of fish for the boat he is contracted to, in highly hairy dogfight maneuvers over the ocean, competing with other spotter planes.

Or he owns a chain of California gas stations and has just opened a new one on the Glenn Highway for a tax loss and for fun and games, where he can let his hair down, hunt moose with an Uzi, hang out with mechanics who look like the Confederate general staff, and talk about "necktie parties" with them.

Alaska is also a place where people like big shaggy dogs. At the Anchorage end of the flight, with a bizarrely frozen musk-ox, mountain goat, and polar bear, all glass-encased, looking on, one sees them rassling a crate with a husky in it off the conveyor belt—"Going to count salmon!"—while kindred burly spirits with U-shaped beards yank at huge backpacks, at hundred-pound cardboard cartons wrapped in masking tape, and at reinforced trunks, as if aiming for a winter "assault" on Mount McKinley, as perhaps they are.

In Anchorage, there'd been my reunion, delicious but tense, with the friend who had taken me on TB investigations all over and who I had hoped would go to Fort Yukon too. She couldn't and so resented my going, and inevitably the division of allegiance and memories between New York and Anchorage caused stomach ache, heartache, split-screen images of what was going on in one place at the same time that I was busy elsewhere. Infidelities are chickens to eggs, until it's hard to remember who started what; and my dark-haired Anchorage friend had turned me down when I wanted to transfer my home here, so the wrongs at issue had become a cat's cradle, indeed.

Some Alaskans like to call Anchorage "Los Anchorage" because of its temperate climate and nondescript sprawl, but the glass skyscrapers reflect a most muscular, lovely cloud action, as well as the big Chugach Range of grassy white mountains very closely crowding the city. You can hear wood frogs croak, see a pet caribou penned in a family's front yard directly across the street from the Atlantic Richfield oil company's headquarters, eat splendid king crab and other seafood that's fit for a king, and admire a couple of volcanoes across Cook Inlet, a glistening wide arm of the sea.

Fairbanks, more bleak and extreme in winter and summer, has a giddy, ad-libbed quality, being a long way from succor if the roof falls in. When I'm not exhilarated, I get lonely in Fairbanks; I get like a dog hearing thunder, after a while, and rush about seeking company, which in Fairbanks means people with breaking-up marriages as often as not. More hair of the dog.

I'd spent a couple of days there, visiting trailers, walking the tunnely corridors of the state university, huddled in an igloo of a hotel at a downtown crossroads where people have hunkered through a lot of tough winters. There's a great government store for buying maps in

Fairbanks, and one or two riverfront restaurants overlooking the muddy Tanana River, and a bare-bones airport which is freight train, ambulance, and grocery store to that world.

Fort Yukon, where I had come next, is a more precarious place than Fairbanks by common standards: e.g., more gunfire, farther from a newspaper, a boiled shrimp, a CAT scan. In Fort Yukon the river is still primeval, and the stars, like the permafrost, hump close. The sky, where the weather god lives, is one story up. But as a consequence, if you don't panic, there's a dignity, even a gravity, to the spot; you could find worse spots to die.

Anyway, here I was in Chalkyitsik, on the roof of the world, irritating Fred Thomas by sitting on my ass on the morning of our departure reading month-old news of Manhattan in *Newsweek*. I should have gone to the camp meeting the night before. I'd liked Jerry Falwell in Anchorage, and this would have been better. The village was emotionally hung over, but as we undertook a final tour of his in-laws' cabins, something stronger seemed to be laced in their tea. Though Chalkyitsik had voted itself dry recently, the state trooper told me that, with a telescope at the end of Fort Yukon's runway, he had watched bootleg liquor being loaded for the flight here. I was finally feeling peppier, coming out of my shell and getting in shape for talking with people with dark skins, "Native"-looking faces, and heavy accents—which, alas, takes extra energy for me because, like most of us, I am a prisoner of my upbringing—but our time was up. John, who wanted to keep us around for another night, said the highbush cranberries were ripe and that the three of us should go pick a bunch. Or go fishing, maybe—wouldn't we like to stay? My middle name is Ambivalence, so much of my life, it seems, has been accidental, and I was willing to, but Fred got us into the boat about 4 P.M.

The bluff, with its tall view of swift water, is a congregating point for the villagers, who have rolled several logs there to sit on. Just watching the river makes you feel you are accomplishing something, and a clever eye can read news upstream and down from the wrack and the roil, the shadows of salmon, the impetus of quick birds, fat fish, inches of current. Two kids were poking a stick in a muskrat's hole, and we had half a dozen other people to wave us off.

A muskrat, too, would have been a treat for old Henry William. Fred's one regret was that we hadn't procured him any wild meat. Even I knew how good muskrat or squirrel can be. But it wasn't more than two or three bends down the river that I felt the boat rock silently, as Fred was wont to do to alert me. Looking a hundred yards in front of us, I saw two swimming heads close to the left bank.

"Bears," he snapped in a low voice, while reaching for his gun, because with only the tops of the heads showing, I didn't know. They turned, watching us, not sure what we were or what they ought to do. Fred revved the outboard motor so that they wouldn't reach shore soon enough to get away. Then he cut it and drifted down because of their reluctance to leave the shelter of the water. He didn't want to shoot one of them there and have to haul its carcass onto the beach. They were yearlings, he muttered, born the winter before last—he could tell from seeing only their heads, while their bodies were still underwater, as we waited for them to scramble up onto the mud. The mother had probably kept them with her until about a month before, when she would have driven them away in order to mate again, in accordance with her bearish two-year cycle. If we had not intercepted them, they would presumably have stuck together through another winter, hibernating as a pair and bolstering each other in the meantime.

At last we were so fearfully close, they did swim into the shallows, crouch for a hesitant moment, then dash out of the water in that adolescent spirit of *Oh, we've done it now! We better run!* As wilderness bears, they may never have seen a person before and did not really try to tear away until Fred's first bullet hit the smaller, plumper, blacker cub. Each weighed perhaps a hundred pounds, but one was larger, rangier, and browner.

Obviously they had never seen an animal shot. The black one stumbled, glanced at us, flopped down, got up. Fred fired four more times in slow succession, as our skiff drifted past, although he deliberately did not turn his gun on the brown cub as well, as it fled.

Shocked, seeming to sorrow like a human figure at what was happening, the black cub kept looking our way as it fell again and struggled up, swaying, gazing at its wounds and sniffing them, trying to absorb the separate calamity and mystery of each shot. Finally it fell and rolled up on one shoulder but could go no farther and began to kick reflexively, bled at the throat, began a wholesale jactitation, and died.

"Meat for the old man," Fred said.

We pulled ashore, checked that the little bear was dead, and recapitulated its story as told in the prints. Fred said that the two of them had just started out from this beach for a cooling swim, probably not intending to cross—had been eating highbush cranberries back in the brush but came to the river because the day was hot. Two sets of footprints entered the water, and two emerged. The larger bear had then paused at the first explosion of Fred's gun and its impact on his stumbling sister before bounding into the willows, where the mud became sand. The other set of prints meanwhile milled and bumbled about, were sometimes blotted by having been sat or fallen on, staggered slackly, and ended with the limp body of the bear herself. Fred, who is not afraid to make fun of himself, said he had aimed at the shoulder the first time, the way he does with bears—"to stop 'em, break 'em down"—but had hit her in the loin. He had then aimed at the shoulder again and had hit her there—he showed me—but too high. Next, he had aimed at the side of her head but had hit her jugular vein. Like tracks, the bullet holes were tactile evidence.

When I asked if he had spared the other yearling because of me, he shook his head. But the people back in Chalkyitsik (and later his wife, Charlotte) were so surprised at his restraint that I didn't quite believe him. He is known as a man who never shoots animals he can't eat, however, and as a conservative trapper who always leaves his trap lines with a breeding stock to repopulate them, even letting a creek valley "lie fallow" for a year, his fur buyer in Fort Yukon told me afterward.

After buzzing back to Chalkyitsik to tell John William about the meat, we returned to the mud bar, where Fred cut off the little bear's right shoulder and arm for his own family's use. The browner, humpier twin was poised on his hind legs, wraithlike, back in the willows, trying to figure out why his sister wasn't getting up. If John William really wanted him, all John had to do was hide on the far bank come evening, Fred said.

Sliding downriver, we saw horned owls and sparrow hawks crying *killy-killy-killy*. A couple of bald eagles swerved away from us in the air, sailing up a tributary. We saw many loons; many, many ducks. On flat stretches, the river meandered practically in 6's and 8's, marvelously slow going on a brightly cool day with the world afresh. A whole loop would bring you just about back where you'd started, and climbing the bank, you could see that the next loop would do almost the same. The geese feeding there would simply move over again.

We stopped at a Fort Yukon family's new cabin, chinked with sphagnum moss and overlaid with a sod roof; also boasting a seven-dog log doghouse. Tracks showed that both a mink and a fox had been foraging in the yard. "First sign of fur I've seen," Fred remarked happily.

Arriving at Englishoe Bend, we moored the boat and horsed two two-pound pike out of the slough by leaning over the stern and wiggling a trolling spoon past them on a broken fishing pole. They struck in five seconds. One spring, Fred caught fifty pike in two hours in the slough grass here. Another day, he shot a hundred thirty-nine muskrats on the ponds nearby. The point in a wilderness is that when you do this sort of thing, the slough or pond fills up quickly again with pike or muskrats from the virgin sloughs and ponds all around.

Pike are ferocious predators—eat baby waterfowl and muskrats as well as fish–and so their livers taste extremely rich, like the top of the food chain in these waters, which is what they are. We also fried a bear steak with bacon. Our bear had fed on salmon, leaves, and roots as well as berries, so she tasted complicated, munificent, protean, like the mistress of a larger realm, and Fred claimed that sometimes when you're eating a blueberry-fed bear you would swear she's had sugar sprinkled on her. One June, going upriver, he and four brothers lived on a bear cub the entire way, roasting it whole all during the first night, then boiling parts of it each successive night.

"Damn, sounds like springtime!" he said when the sandhill cranes started calling on the two river bars in front of our camp. *Garrrooo. Garrrooo.* Wide-winged, five feet tall, and yet small-headed, they seemed exuberant that their summer's householder duties were done. A wedge of what he called "laughing geese" (white-fronted geese) skimmed overhead, crying *Kla-ha! Kow lyow! Ka-la-ha! Glee-glee!* And the various loons that we had heard before were howling up a storm, a regular hootenanny. The geese tootled. The cranes said *tuk-tuk*. The loons yodeled and wailed in falsetto.

Fred slung a mosquito net over four posts that were set in the ground and cut spruce boughs to serve as his mattress and laid them inside, with his bearskin on top, and his three-hundred-dollar Arctic sleeping bag and his .30-.06 rifle. He'd fed the magpies our scraps and put the remaining wrapped food on a bench twenty yards off, with some tin cans piled on top to give warning if a bear scrounged by. It was bait, so he made sure my tent was out of his field of fire.

In the lambent dusk we fed sticks to our supper fire, building it bigger than was proper for cooking, and watched the endless unfathomable tales the flames told. Fred talked about trap lines, which might be ten to thirty or forty miles long. Your main line followed a river, and "side lines" five to fifteen miles long would weave up each sizable creek. He talked strategy for catching marten, lynx, beaver, and mink, and about how he puts out hundreds of steel leg-hold traps and wire neck snares in November, leaving them in place into March, because "no matter how many animals come through the country, you can't catch them if you've got no traps out." Around now, he said, the ducks on the lakes are all moulting—when the young can swim well but can't yet fly. This is when the whole village of Chalkyitsik used to turn out and paddle slowly in a fleet of canoes down Ohtig Lake, which lies only about five miles behind town, driving the total year's crop of young and grownups into the narrow end, where nets were strung for them, and other people waited on shore with clubs, if they tried to climb out. That one lake could fill Chalkyitsik's needs, give up all its babies before they flew, yet be as good as new the next year, replenished by ducks from the dozens of undisturbed lakes round about.

He told me about the most recent gold rush in this area, during the 1940s, when small nuggets were found on the axle of a fish wheel twenty-four miles above Fort Yukon, on the Yukon, and a couple of thousand people poured in and put up a tent city. But it amounted to nothing more than that. If it wasn't somebody's hoax to bring in business, they figured that an old-time prospector coming downriver on a stern-wheeler must have lost his pokeful of gold overboard, or a Klondike barge had turned over.

He also told me about one fluke winter when a wing of the Porcupine Herd of caribou had migrated right through his Grayling Fork country and he'd shot ten of them. Fed a lot of people. Another year, however—this was before World War II—at around this same point during the summer, thirty people, including his dad's whole family, had started from Fort Yukon for their trapping camp at Grayling Fork, but the water in the Black was so low that they got stranded at about where we were now. For that month they couldn't budge, waiting for rain. They just jigged for pike and stalked ducks and shot small game in order to survive. Finally enough rain fell that they reached Salmon Village, at Harry's Salmon Fork, in about two more weeks of struggling. There at last somebody shot a moose.

"Everywhere you went, people had a pot on the fire and were offering you a piece." But then the skies rained so hard that the river went half over its banks and choked up with new driftwood that they had to dodge as they went on, hugging the banks.

He told me about a "magic" war between two shamans of rival villages, in which good old-fashioned poison, supplied by a miner, won the day.

And Fred said that in the Eskimo-Indian wars, which were fought across the valleys of the Brooks Range before the white men interfered, the Indians would try to wipe out the Eskimos, whereas the Eskimos would try to adopt any Indian children they captured—"because maybe Indians are smarter." He laughed.

He said the Eskimos hold more of a grudge against the Indians for the old feuds than vice versa; and that on the Kobuk and Noatak rivers, the inland Eskimos will still camp on islands overnight, instead of going up on the heights to sleep—which would be a better place for a hunter—because of the defensive habits they formed when they were scared of Indian attacks. (Of course, in Eskimo towns, you hear accounts of these campaigns that are quite the reverse.)

He said a moss-chinked house is the healthiest place to raise a baby, because the moss "breathes." And again he talked of hunting muskrats in his canoe with his .22 in May, his favorite time of year, quietly calling them to him one by one but paddling clear of the grizzly bears, down from their winter dens on the mountainside and hungrily digging out roots and muskrats from the edge of the pond.

On this short, bright night, the cranes and loons whooped, trumpeted, and hollered, above the river's continuous rustle: a party babble—hilarious voices—and young ones being schooled. I'm not accustomed to wildlife sounding loud when humans are around—short of Africa anyhow; and that, too, is being silenced. I told Fred that at home I was a person who would take in animals that were unwanted or had been "outgrown," such as South American parrots and African pythons, so that I ran a refugee center at times, sort of end-of-the-world or end-of-the-line. Hobbyists who went in for exotic animals in larger ways were willing to pay three times as much for a "liger" as for a lion. A "liger" is a cross between a tiger and lion. "And then what do they do with them? It's crazy," I said. "I took care of some circus elephants when I was younger, and now I take care of parrots, and I see that parrots use their beaks for the same purposes—reaching, pulling, prying, tasting—as elephants use their trunks. But they're both disappearing. It's like archaeology to know these things."

Fred smiled to show he understood, and we went to bed.

"Goddamn high bottom, I'll tell you!" he shouted next morning, as we traversed the river's numerous shallows. The river had fallen a few inches overnight and brought the bed closer. In the strong wind Fred steered for high waves instead of avoiding them, because where the waves were, the water would be deeper. At second sight, the river's course already seemed homey to me with its landmarks of gravel bars, winter-skinned knolls, and leaning trees. Bird heaven, just for the moment. Kingfishers, owls, diving ducks—the ducks gabblers and busybodies, the kingfishers florid, aggressive personalities, the owls buffaloed by the sunlight, though velvet-glove killers. Actually, we'd heard several owls whooping it up during the night, but the gleeful-sounding loons had been so vociferous or argumentative as to overshadow them. Owls put out a lot of noise when on their own turf and not maintaining hunting silence, but not like a loon. Loons have a fish-eating gaiety, like a barking seal's, versus the meat-eating reserve of an owl or a wolf. All of them howl and all of them bark, but the fish eaters seem to enjoy doing it more, as if with freer spirits—like the yelling that gulls often do versus the subdued mewing of hawks. Maybe it's because the earth is three-fourths covered by water and their ancestral experience of food hunting has been so bountiful. The confidence of loons, seals, porpoises, and gulls reflects the amplitude and ubiquity of the sea. Our gulls of course were tracking the spawning salmon, skimming above their shapes underwater, certain that such a riot of fish would provide a feast.

Eventually the Porcupine's sea-green, sea-gray waves, triple-sized, swallowed the Black River's dark ropes of water, and in the wind there we had a deep-water chop, a new lilt and velocity. Then after twenty-five brisk, breezy miles of tangled low forest that seemed like a narrative I'd just come in on—it had started more than five hundred miles earlier, in the Mackenzie Mountains—the Porcupine's gray-green currents met the great yellow Yukon. This was no contest at all. Like motes among the forested islands, two other skiffs were busy on tiny errands, checking fishnets or carrying vegetables to families in fishing cabins downstream. We were scooped into the massive, monumental flow like a motorized wood chip wiggling upstream, and duly arrived in the sunny and slightly truculent town of Fort Yukon, where most of the kids were swimming in Joe Ward Slough, named for old Jimmy Ward's father, who was more of a public figure than Fred's father, Jacob Thomas, though Jacob was maybe a better father than Joe Ward had been.

I went to the Sourdough Inn and sat in the swiveling barber chair next to the pay phone and placed some long-distance calls. A party of floaters who had rafted down the Porcupine from Old Crow were celebrating their safe arrival with a kitchen-cooked dinner in the dining room and joking about "catching the subway home." On the windowsill sat an ant the size of a cat, constructed of wires, facing a poster on the opposite wall, which showed a rat that seemed to be tunneling through, with the legend: *I gotta get outa this hotel!*

I ate mashed potatoes, beet-and-cottage-cheese salad, and chicken-fried steak with the floaters and joined them for a look at the town's new stockaded museum. We saw a Gwich'in awl made from a loon's bill; a moose's stomach displayed as a cooking utensil into which hot stones would be put; a three-pronged fishing spear; and a whistling swan's leg bone, such as Gwich'in girls had to drink through during their first menstrual spell. In the "white" graveyard next to the museum is a plaque:

In Memory of the People
Of the Hudson's Bay Company
Who Died Near Fort Yukon
Between the Years 1840 and 1870
Many of Them Being
Pioneers and Discoverers and
Explorers of Various Portions
Of the Yukon and Alaska.

I went back to Fred's in the bright dusk. He was still up and took me to see the log cache on stilts where he and his brother Albert store furs. By now everything was sold except miscellany, but he looked for a silver fox I wanted to see. Found a cross fox, instead, whose yellow, black, and red shadings were probably even prettier. In another gunnysack was a "bum lynx" Charlotte was going to sew a hat from, and a small wolf she wanted for parka ruffs.

"You never know what you'll find when you tip a sack upside down," he said. We discovered, indeed, six wolves in another bag, two of them black wolves seven feet tall.

I sat on a case of shotgun shells as we talked some more. Flying boxcars were taking off to bomb a forest fire, and Fred remembered he'd wanted to give me a bottle of matches and a roll of No. 3 picture wire for rabbit snares for my flight south, in case the plane went down and I needed to live off the land. He showed me how to tie and set the loops, having just made two hundred forty beaver snares for the winter, and the same number for lynx. Dry and chatty, he said he goes to Fairbanks every couple of years for a medical checkup and doesn't mind the flight as long as he's prepared.

I put up my tent by the river and the next day heard of a grizzly bear that learned to mimic the bawl of a cow moose calling her calf, while lying in wait on the trail. And, again, of the man who had once fed a family of starving Brush Men who sat with him beside his camp-fire talking to him only by mental telepathy. Of how to set snares around one's cabin for a murderous Brush Man. And of the Little People, the trickster gnomes who live underground and are as strong as a dozen men—of the stealing but also the good turns they do. Probably the only way you can scare Little People into returning what they have stolen from you is by boiling pots of water and standing over their underground holes and threatening to pour. Brush Man you cannot speak to, but Little People will talk to you.

(1984)

In Okefenokee

Okefenokee Swamp in southeastern Georgia comprises about six hundred square miles. It's home to perhaps twelve thousand alligators, a hundred fifty black bears, six hundred otters, eighteen thousand white ibises at the peak of the summer, nine hundred great blue herons, a hundred fifty sandhill cranes, twenty-five ospreys, forty-five hundred egrets of three species, four thousand wood ducks, and assorted populations of pileated woodpeckers, wood storks, barred owls, red-shouldered hawks, parula and prothonotary warblers, and numerous more commonplace songbirds. All told, there are forty kinds of mammals and forty of fish, thirty-five species of snakes, fourteen of turtles, eleven of lizards, twenty-two of frogs or toads, within the national wildlife refuge, which is by far the largest in the eastern U.S. And yet it's not really such a swatch of swamp—thirty-five by twenty-seven miles at its longest and widest—considering the ecological and even mythological freight that it must carry for all of the uncountable wild wetlands that have been drained, plowed, and subdivided.

Okefenokee is much smaller than Florida's Everglades (which is a national park), but because of its isolated location it has been less injured by the pressure of development at its boundaries. The soil at surrounding drier elevations is the color of a supermarket shopping bag, and indeed the principal industry roundabout is raising and cutting twenty-year-old slash pines for pulpwood that goes to manufacture paper bags. The swamp lies in the shallow dish of an old seabed, forty-five miles west of Georgia's present lush coastline and about the same distance east of the rich pecan-, peanut-, tobacco-, and cotton-growing country that begins near the prosperous city of Valdosta. It forms the headwaters of the Suwanee and Saint Marys rivers, and for the local Indian tribes, too, it was a region of mystery and legend, a hunting ground more than a home, until the Seminoles, the last of the tribes in the area, hid there as white settlers spread across the South after the War of 1812, raided the whites who were encircling them, then finally were driven out by army troops in 1838, escaping toward the deeper fastnesses of the Everglades.

Okefenokee was the last haunt of the panther and wolf in Georgia. They and its mosquitoes and reptiles—as well as the raffish reputation of its "swampers," the families who lived on its islands and hunted and trapped its hammocks and watery "prairies" by poling themselves in dugouts or trudging knee-deep through the peat bogs—kept most other people out. Some swampers were said to be descended from Civil War draft dodgers. At dawn and dusk they would let out ululating two-mile "hollers" that went on for a minute or two from their feeling of pride and primacy, and they were serious moonshiners, distilling corn whiskey from the sugar cane and white corn that they grew in locations no federal agent was likely to reach on his own or alive. In towns like Fargo, at the southwest corner of the swamp, a bootlegger could park his high-springed truck loaded with jugs in front of the post office and chat for an hour and nobody thought twice about it.

However, the whole swamp was logged for its cypresses and crisscrossed by a network of tramways in the first quarter of this century. Earlier, during the 1890s, a brief but concerted attempt had been made to drain it to create agricultural land with a canal, which remains to this day the principal pathway inside. Because wildlife refuges differ from national parks in that their first purpose is supposed to be the preservation of habitat, off this canal one travels into Okefenokee only by canoe and only by precut water trails through the sea of floating lilies and other vegetation to wooden camping platforms set out on the prairies five or ten miles apart, each trail and platform being reserved for a single party of canoers by arrangements made with the refuge manager beforehand.

In my capacity as a chronicler of other people's vacations, I paddled about forty miles on a four-day trip last spring that wound through the more familiar passages of the swamp from refuge headquarters near the town of Folkston, on the east side, to the Suwanee River at Fargo on the western edge, as part of a group of eighteen people, including two guides provided by an outfitting company called Wilderness Southeast. Except for our guides, who were women of thirty-four and twenty-two, and two teenagers on spring vacation, we were mostly in our fifties—a marine engineer from California, a career IBM man, an army defoliant chemist, a closemouthed, wise-looking country lawyer from Kentucky, a folksy, rawboned radiologist from Valdosta, a hospital head-of-pharmacy, a Cincinnati school-teacher, and the wives of the IBM man, the defoliant chemist, the lawyer, and the radiologist. Although, except for the teacher, these women were housewives, our guides were enthusiastically liberated women who immediately asked us men whether we were wondering where the real, *male* guides were. To distinguish us and help us remember each other, they had us attach animal names to ourselves, such as Art Aardvark, Beetle Bob, Betty Bee, Bear Bill, Betsy Beaver, Bobcat Bob, Evelyn Eagle, Polly Parrot, Jackass Jason, Ouzel Ottway, Possum Pollard, Ted Turtle, Lynn Lynx, Mary Mouse, and so on. I thought it a vaguely humiliating procedure, but it did furnish us food for thought about each other. Jason, the radiologist, was anything but a jackass, for instance, and his wife, "Polly Parrot," besides being a regent of the Daughters of the American Revolution, whose grandfather had been toted about in his infancy on the back of a male slave, had recently gone through an Outward Bound program, rappeling down cliffsides, and had soloed in an airplane. "Mary Mouse," the teacher, wore a sweatshirt saying "It's sporty to be forty" and said she made a habit of spending summer vacations in places like New

Guinea or Newfoundland, when she wasn't picking up pocket money delivering vans nationwide from a factory in South Bend. "Bobcat Bob," on the other hand, did look like a likely hunter, and "Evelyn Eagle" gave the impression of being an outdoorswoman who probably did truly aspire to wings. "Possum Pollard" looked as if he could play dead in court and then wake up and surprise the opposition, and "Ouzel Ottway," a bachelor pharmacist, was a passionate Sierra Club devotee and was signaling as much, because John Muir, the founder of the Sierra Club a century ago, often wrote of the water ouzel as his favorite bird.

We had compulsory campfire gatherings for group-think purposes in the evening, our leader Viva!—she spelled it with an exclamation point—having worked previously as a counselor in juvenile-delinquent prerelease programs. She encouraged us to explore our behavior patterns and do things differently from what we were used to (indeed, on the application forms, the fee for the trip had been labeled "Tuition"), but this was a rather unnecessary suggestion, because although the self-employed people—lawyer, doctor, marine engineer—didn't much change their personalities, which at home and on the job were approximately the same, the men who worked as cogs in large organizations had turned zany by the second day. The IBM man became bombastic and mock lecherous and the army chemist "fuzzy," eccentric, bewildered, "unstrung." Viva—who paddled with me for most of the trip—spoke of her "listening skills" and "confrontation skills" in Reality therapy and Gestalt therapy, but I got quite fond of her even as she tried to tinker with my motivations, because she was so sympathetic, affectionate, vulnerable, and earnest, and her own personality seemed so contradictory. She had a skinny straight nose, a string-bean frame, and a frenetic metabolism that grew desperately hungry at frequent intervals, so that she would stop paddling in the midst of a downpour to gobble nuts and dried fruits almost in sight of our tent frames. She confessed that she had been disillusioned by the "fail rate" among her contingents of delinquents but that she believed everyone had control of his own destiny; and for all the intensity with which she tried to mold us into a unique, "bonded" group, permanently enriched by the experience of crossing this swamp, she said she herself "burned out" quickly in groups. Ours was the only one she had scheduled herself to guide that spring. She usually preferred to stay in the office or else went out for extended sojourns alone in a cabin in the woods.

It's a phenomenon nowadays that youngish retired people, or prosperous couples on the verge of retirement, venture in increasing numbers into outdoor group adventures led by young ideologues from what is left of the counterculture, who pay themselves almost nothing (Wilderness Southeast's partners got $8,500 a year) but who believe in a special agenda of education, activism, and behavior modification, often incongruously at odds with the beliefs and careers of their customers. What they all do have in common is the modern conviction that life is lived in modest niches—whether one occupies a slot at a huge corporation or mildly does one's own thing, protectively colored by a graduate degree—that our aspirations are complexly and dauntingly circumscribed, and that life must be selective and specialized.

We had spent the first night in a small piney graveyard in Folkston and next morning left solid land at the entrance to the Suwanee Canal near Chesser Island, paddling ten miles on this twenty-yard-wide relic of Harry Jackson's 1889–95 attempt to drain Okefenokee, while listening to cricket frogs gick-gicking, carpenter frogs calling with a sound like a hammer tapping, pig frogs grunting like impatient hogs. These species are not musically the prettiest of amphibians—not like toads or spring peepers—but here in their confident legions they reminded us that their race probably fathered all of the vertebrate music on earth. We stopped to watch two warblers weaving a nest of Spanish moss and several fishing spiders poised to grab insect larvae on the rims of the lily pads. Viva said she was "heavily into snakes and spiders. It's like a secret, looking for spiders, because nobody else is."

Fish crows flew about uttering *uh-uh*, and *uh-uh* again, for which reason they are known as virgin birds, our younger guide, Nancy, told us, while paddling in her black bathing suit in the stern of the *National Geographic* photographer's canoe. He, "Bear Bill," was a former quarterback and "monster back" for Arizona State, and she was a sharp, smart naturalist, just out of the University of Vermont, who, with her chipmunk cheeks and sorority hairdo, looked collegiate when paired with him, though neither in fact was unduly so. Viva and I raced ineffectually with them, when we had a chance, though mostly our job was to harry poor Pollard, the Kentucky lawyer, who was casting for bass at the rear of our procession of nine canoes, quite competent with his rod and possessed of an eye that loved currents. But he was supposed to keep up.

Under the warm sun, the alligators lying on both banks seemed more assured in the presence of humans than they would have been in chilly weather, when they have to make allowances for the sluggishness of their own bodies by sliding into hiding underwater much sooner. Their heads were flat-looking and grimacey because of the long mask of their mouths—a grin that is two hundred million years old. Swimming alligators have horsey heads, however; the eyes and high nostrils are emphasized, instead of their fixed somber smiles. They look more like a sea horse than a sea horse does (though the inches between their nostrils and eyes denote their total length as measured in feet).

When they bellowed, the gators sounded like motors starting up, not like horses whinnying, and, besides answering each other, felt obligated to answer the airplanes that crossed the swamp. Such an outlandish challenge from high above may sometimes conceal from them the triumph of their position at the top of the food chain here (since people in a wildlife refuge don't kill them for their skins or to eat their tasty tails). A baby alligator's first meal is likely to be a crayfish, but the adults eat an occasional bear cub whose mother was forced to cross deep water between islands; and they will camp under the nursery trees where colonies of ibises, herons, and egrets nest, to devour not only the nestlings that have the misfortune to fall but also the raccoons that otherwise would decimate the baby birds ensconced in the branches above. Alligators create new water trails through the matted plant life during their nocturnal wanderings and dig essential water holes used by many other creatures during a drought.

One twelve-footer we met, after we had left Suwanee Canal and entered the narrow passageways of Chase Prairie, hissed and blew itself up formidably when it felt surrounded, but then let us slide by in a gingerly file, without flailing its muscular tail. The tail is both a chief weapon and the alligator's main means of travel; but they have a variety of sounds, including the primeval roar of conquest that a great one will utter when it charges and seizes a deer mired in mud and lifts it bodily out and swaggers back to its pool with the deer gripped crosswise in its jaws—a roar that sounds more Triassic than contemporary, more like a titanic burp than a lion's intellectual roar, and therefore more nightmarish and terrifying, which surely helps to stun and immobilize deer. On the other hand, a male in courtship hums *umphs* underwater in such a way that the water vibrates deliciously around the female, until she closes her eyes, puts her chin on his head, and twists her body around his. And this is the sound the alligator hunters of Okefenokee used to imitate, groaning softly while mouthing the end of a punting pole thrust into the water near where they knew a gator was lurking.

On Chase Prairie we heard an osprey mewing as it hovered above a fishing stretch, and two hawks crying to each other connubially, two owls barking back and forth informatively, two cranes garrooing as they beat by in uxorious, coordinated majesty, a woodpecker cukcukking loudly from a line of cypress trees, and a bellowing alligator in full rut—all at once. Chase Prairie is named for the chases the swampers used to conduct, one man driving game animals off the hammocks and islands, another poling fast after them in his dugout or jonboat as they waded and swam to escape.

We were in the midst of pond lilies and bonnet lilies, bladderworts and pipeworts, neverwet and maiden cane, pitcher plants and pickerelweed, wampee and hardhead grass—all that mob of plant life that defines the swamp. The leaves and stalks, dying off in the winter, settle on the decomposing layers of peat on the bottom, ten or fifteen feet thick from the centuries of vegetation that have rioted on the surface in the sultry sun and died and rained down on the impermeable clay understrata. Their constant decomposition produces gases that now and again push up whole mats of this peat, called "blow-ups," which, if they float for long, catch seeds of sedges and grasses and, as they get larger and larger, twenty yards across and more, are called "batteries," so solidly bound together that they can support a person, though often swaying under his feet because they may be floating on six feet of water. ("Okefenokee" comes from an Indian name meaning "land of the trembling earth.") Then cypresses, buttonbush, titi and gallberry shrubs and bay tree seedlings grow and send down roots that eventually stabilize the battery, until, when enough of a patch of dry soil has formed that finally the old swampers could have camped there on their alligator hunts, the battery is called a "house." "Hammocks" are large "houses" where hardwood trees like water oaks, laurel oaks, swamp maples, black gum and sweet gum trees have gotten a foothold. Also, there are as many as seventy regular islands in Okefenokee Swamp, most of them former sandbars left from half a million years ago, when, probably, this area was part of the sea. On the islands are forests of loblolly and slash pine, as well as large cypresses, magnolias, and other glories. But the swamp is gradually, over the millennia, filling in; the actual open prairies that are most "swampy" constitute only 15 percent of it today.

At lunch we'd talked of trips down the Snake River and the Grand Canyon, into the Smokies, the Sierras, and the Wind River Range, all taken under the tutelage of America's drifting populace of "wilderness guides"; and as we paddled along in wildlife-refuge-type silence, I doubt that many of us failed to think intermittently of retirement strategies and financial stratagems, of midlife crises, romantic tangles, children-at-a-standstill, or whatever middle-age hex happened to be enlivening our existence at the time, while my austere, frenetic friend Viva—who would certainly have risked her own life in a flash to rescue a stranger—sat ready to help us or save us.

Nancy was as enthusiastic a naturalist as Viva was an educator. At her urging we stopped to look at larval dragonflies preying on other larvae under the lily pads. After a year or two of doing that, the nymphs metamorphose and crawl onto a stalk, to dry in the sun and pump blood into their wings for some still more dramatic hunting activities performed in the air. We stopped to watch this occurring too. And there were predatory diving beetles, known as "water tigers" in their larval stage, and hunting-diving grasshoppers, as well as the fishing spiders waiting on the water lilies. Cormorants flew over, black, agile diving birds, which old fishermen across the South still like to call "nigger geese" because they're dark and fly like geese, although they live on fish, not plants, as geese mostly do. The many turkey vultures soared with a dihedral cock to their wings; and the few ospreys with a flat, boomerang-type crook to theirs. In this cost-effective era, no spectacular bird such as an osprey can expect to be allotted enough space to nest and feed its brood unless it pays for its acreage by being ogled by hundreds of human beings. The pair nesting along our route were magnificently wild-looking, nevertheless, with their brown capes and backs, white heads and underbodies, their handsome straight postures when they clasped a branch, and utter mastery of the air, oddly combined with a repertoire of chirps, cheeps, kiweeks, and kyews.

We used yellow fiberglass Mohawk canoes and green Eureka tents, and when we reached our camping platform, which measured twenty by twenty-eight feet in the midst of a mile-square parcel of water, Viva had us stand in a circle and massage one another's shoulders. The sunset was only a rip in the clouds, but ruby, carmine, and puce all the same, and ibises, egrets, herons, and storks flew home in discrete flocks to their several roosts and rookeries after the long day's frogging and fishing. Being bird buffs, we didn't mind feeling caged in their garden spot, but, after a supper of salami and cheese, went out again in our canoes to see more alligators by shining our flashlights into their eyes, which reflect like coal embers. Nighttime is when alligators come alive and hunt, so we located a number of them, their eyes that prodigally passionate color. The raccoons' shone bright white, by contrast, as they foraged the house and hammock margins; and the spiders on the lily pads had eyes that glittered emerald green. Frogs had white eyes, and besides the cricket, carpenter, and pig frogs, bullfrogs were croaking, and pickerel frogs that sounded like two balloons being rubbed together. Bear Bill, Violet Viva, and I (Ted Turtle) slid close to a raccoon that was feeling for frogs in the shallows under the silhouettes of tall trees. He was silvery and ghostly in our flashlight beams, displaying a stand-up, tiptoe curiosity elaborately tempered with fear. Up on his hind legs and down he went, ears pricked, fluid with tremulous life, until, still undecided about us, he finally fled.

The white-eyed frogs would gobble the emerald-eyed spiders, and the white-eyed raccoons ate the frogs when they could, but the coal-eyed alligators would devour the raccoons eventually. For each, it was a case of waiting and traveling, waiting and traveling, and by quiet paddling toward a coal-colored pair of eyes we got close enough to a middling gator to have killed it as the old gator hunters would have done, with a .22 bullet shot into one of the red coals, for twenty cents a foot for its belly skin.

Sunrise next morning was another blaze of reds glimpsed through the clouds. A ten-foot alligator cruised close to our platform, belatedly waiting for the couple of coons who had swum over during the night to climb the posts and scavenge our leftovers. So much of nature's picturesqueness is really a series of relentless tests of stamina. This Jurassic beast, like hundreds of its toothy fellows in the Okefenokee that are just as big, floated unobtrusively or lounged on the bank night and day, waiting for hunger to operate irresistibly on the possums, coons, rabbits, deer, and bobcats living on various dabs of land surrounding this wet prairie so that they'd enter the water to swim from one to another to feed. (Overpopulation alone would force most of the year's crop of young to do this, but wise veteran animals wait for autumn, when temperatures fall, to relocate or range about much.) And the herons, watchfully statuesque in shallow water, waited by the minute or hour for some frantic frog, hidden in the mud but smothering for air, to make a desperate dash for breath.

Large birds, with the freedom of the skies, swept toward their hunting grounds to the west—the egrets flapping and sailing, the herons with a rocking slow down-beating flight—while we sat and gazed at their grandeur over our Sierra Club cups of scrambled eggs. The Sierra Club, like any other significant institution, combines bits of the sublime with the ridiculous. What's ridiculous are these smallish metal cups from which its wilderness votaries are supposed to eat all manner of meals, from steaks to soup, with a single spoon, which our particular outfitter provided on a red cord to be worn around the neck betweentimes, along with a hand lens for looking at plants and a whistle for emergencies. All good fun, perhaps—like our leaders' "teachable moments" and "solo time" or "private space"—except that my tentmate, Bill, from *National Geographic,* and I were out of temper because, in order to discipline us for what they claimed was his snoring, they had made us take our tent down that morning, although after canoeing a circuit we would be coming back to the same platform in the afternoon. And sure enough, three miles out, the clouds burst with the first of what would add up to five inches of rain. The wind ribbed the water; everybody was drenched and chilled, though the tree swallows swooped down festively to grab disoriented insects, and wading birds rushed in hasty uncharacteristic glee to grab subsurface creatures that the wild water forced out. Viva and I in the last canoe watched the black paddles of the eight craft ahead of us rising and falling, like fish crows descending to feed and rising swiftly to descend again. She teased me, but then assuaged Bill's and my chagrin by installing him with Nancy and her in her own tent and me in Mary Mouse's, to shiver, be comforted, and sleep.

It was a rough storm, testing everybody's cheeriness. Our IBM man performed a comedy routine that had worked well, he said, during bad thunderstorms on dude-ranch rides in the Rockies. He seemed to be the most Thoreauvian of us all and most objected to the regimented parts of the trip, but everyone who signs up for wilderness trips has a soft spot somewhere, a feeling for wild things—which is to say for the underdog, nowadays—underneath a frequently quirky, abrasive, or camouflaged exterior. We all had in common a respect for privacy, individualism, and self-sufficiency, a love of birds, plants, and animals, and because we were, in the manner of the eighties, a "single-issue constituency," we had no political arguments, being content to ignore everything else. Gone with the 1970s was the unanimity of the old alliance on civil rights, a dovish foreign policy, and the "ecology movement." When one of our number said she believed in shooting any robber you caught in your gunsights, somehow none of the rest of us objected, because she'd also said that she believed in "protecting God's creatures."

Next day the sun smiled, and the flocks of ibises arrived again, with their splendid red bills. We paddled to Floyd's Island, past blooming iris, pipewort flowers like upright hatpins, and the flowers that the bladderworts send up like innocuous buttercups while the voracious bulk of the plant beneath the surface consumes minute crustaceans and water larvae. Everywhere there was neverwet, its spadix shaped like a thick pencil, white with a golden tip. And when the bottom lifted under us and scraped our canoes, we entered into effusions of greenbrier, wild grape, pepperbush ("poor man's soap"), yaupon, holly, titi and gallberry (both favorites of the honeybees), and, especially, thickets of the "hurrah bush" (a relative of fetterbush and staggerbush), as the swampers called it because it is so dense that anyone struggling through might wish to yell "Hurrah!" at the end.

We saw and heard an otter chirping to its mate; saw the personable kind of lizard known as a skink on a loblolly bay tree; heard yellow-throated and prothonotary warblers—the latter golden orange—and mockingbirds, catbirds, red-winged blackbirds, and one painted bunting, which was blue, green, red, and brown. On the island were some magnificent live oak trees that the loggers had spared, one with resurrection ferns spreading high from a crotch and another with a beehive inside. Floyd's Island was the site of the Seminoles' last encampment in Okefenokee. Under their resident chief, Bolek, called "Billy Bowlegs" by the whites, they raided a settler family on Cowhouse Island, on the northeastern edge of the swamp, killed seven people, and then retreated most of its width and much of its length to Billy's Island, pursued by troops under General Floyd, who chased them on here, whence they escaped unscathed.

On Billy's Island, a little later, we encountered a diamondback rattlesnake and saw where the "Good Black" and "Bad Black" cypress loggers had been quartered (the latter were prisoners who'd been bailed out of jail), as well as the site of the "juke" where Good Blacks danced, or "juked," on Saturday nights.

The sun seethed on the currents in myriad popping points of light or lay like a platter of gold where the water was still. Because of the peat's tannic acid, Okefenokee's water itself is the color of dark tea and a perfect reflecting medium, so that on the narrower waterways, lined with gum and bay trees and cypresses festooned with Spanish moss, a photograph not only is arrestingly beautiful but may look the same upside down. When a wind blows, however, the re-splendent image of the trees on the water is broken into zebra zigzags.

We finished crossing the swamp at Stephen Foster State Park, on the Fargo side, where the Suwanee River starts flowing in earnest, and paddled six miles downstream past many Ogeechee lime trees, whose fruit makes good pies and preserves, and water tupelo and black tupelo gum trees, whose blossoms are a nearly peerless honey-making source for the bees, and then camped at the fishing camp of a famous old-time bootlegger and guide named Lem Griffis, now an apiary and campground run by Arden, his gentler, law-abiding son. The river was at its highest level in ten years—the people on Wilderness Southeast's previous trip had eaten a canebrake rattlesnake that had been flooded out of its usual holes—and we built big bonfires for our final two evening confabs, with mosquitoes whining near us of a size that swampers say "will dress out at a pound."

We had white stubble beards and white-and-black beards, and the women were as sturdy as those with the beards. Our lawyer said that when the bull alligators in rut were bellowing, it was just what he'd heard the hippos in Kenya say: *"I want some!"* Our doctor repeated to us several times that he'd "promised my wife's daddy thirty-seven years ago that I was going to take care of her, and he would kill me now if he saw her in this swamp." But she was the one who had rappeled down cliffs and soloed in an airplane. Our Thoreauvian IBM man—whom my heart went out to because he kept trying to pretend that there weren't eighteen people on this trip—grew quickly impatient when the sociable moments veered at Viva's urging toward a conventional group-grope session. He would grab his wife's hand and say this was their wedding anniversary, for God's sake, and they had to get to their tent—which really did have the desired effect the first night.

By the time we quit paddling, my shoulders were getting stronger and my back felt delightfully limber, as though I could push on to California if only some of the populace between Fargo and there would clear out of the way. Both Viva and I were heading for solitary spells in isolated portions of the Appalachians. Bill, the photographer, on the other hand, was returning to Miami, the base from which he often goes to crisis assignments in Central America. Nancy, equally a modernist—her mother a socialite, her father an airline pilot, and she a Miamian who had chosen to go to the University of Vermont—was on her way to a career in wildlife management. More and more women are entering the environmental fields and gradually transforming the predatory bent of those vocations. The wardens used to be hunters who preyed on lesser hunters—who poached the poachers—but now the swing will be to a more protective, even "maternal" approach, which will be necessary if wildlife is to survive at all. And this is going to be how the wilderness will be experienced in the next century: in groups of twenty people, by prearrangement, led by specialists in group dynamics to preselected birding or bear-viewing sites, and efficiently out. Otherwise there won't be any wilderness.

I poked around Fargo a little and looked up Barney Cone, aged sixty-six, who has retired after many years as the refuge's patrol officer and has the likably boiled look of W. C. Fields. As we talked, riding around in his pickup truck, he would raise two fingers from the wheel every time that we met another vehicle. Before his day, he said with a lawman's aplomb, plume hunters had combed the swamp after egrets, and when plume sales had been outlawed, the swampers went after gators. When the refuge was established, in 1937, that had to be stopped. He'd paddled its water trails with a partner by night for thirty-five dollars a week, watching for the gas lamps that the poachers mesmerized the animals with. "At first, if you made a case against a poacher, the judge would just about run you out of court. But gradually it got to where they were sending them off for a year and a day," he said.

The local sheriffs wouldn't help him, but the state game wardens sometimes did, and the sheriffs at least didn't interfere with him the way they warned the moonshiners about the revenuers' raids. Not until "nineteen and thirty-eight" had a paved road reached Fargo, so before then the moonshiners had pretty much run everything during the rainy season, when the roads were mud, and the dry season, when the sand was a trap. "Shine" sold for $4.50 for a five-gallon jug. A hundred-pound sack of sugar cost that (if you didn't raise your own), but you made two jugs of shine with that hundred pounds, soaking it for three days with a mash consisting of fifty pounds of cornmeal and fifty pounds of whole-grained rye that had already soaked together for three days to get good and sour, then "running it off" (distilling it).

"How else did people make money?" I asked him.

"Oh, dipping turpentine, or at the sawmills," he said. "They cut cypress for crossties for the railroad, they cut black gum trees and water oaks for plywood and boxes. Sold peat moss. Raised those backwoods cows that you didn't have to feed, or the hogs too. Ate wild meat and huckleberries," he added with a laugh, though he'd stopped eating bear meat after a plague of screwworms reached Georgia in the 1930s and bored into the bears—burrowed into the cattle too, till the cattle got so sick the bears started catching up with them, and of course that sent the swampers out after the bears with their dogs. "That hurt the bears a whole hell of a lot. The beekeepers were already after them."

The price for alligator skins had risen from twenty cents a foot at the turn of the century to fifteen dollars a foot in the 1960s, but in 1955, during a drought, the swamp suffered four major fires, the gators each time going into their holes underwater to try to survive. Even so, he found many of them whose tails had been scorched because they hadn't been able to get all of themselves inside. Without law enforcement the population would have plunged. The hunters used a "pig pole" with a barbed spear or hook on the end for fishing up the animals that sank after they had "shined" them with the lamp and shot them from real close. "They'd fill the boat and pile them out, kill some more and pile them out, four or five at once, and go on ahead and next day come back to all of the piles and skin them out. Or in a dry spell, they walked the swamp looking for holes in the mat where a gator was and haul him out and ax him in the head.

"You know what a redneck was?" Barney continued with a chuckle. "A redneck didn't just mean somebody who got himself sunburned out in the fields. It meant a man who only buttoned his shirt collar to go to church, so his neck looked chafed on Monday morning."

I went back to Folkston, on the east side of Okefenokee, and talked with Ralph Davis, who's seventy-three and mostly Irish but one-eighth Cherokee. He says he helped survey the refuge's boundaries. Claims jokingly that, after that, the government men chased him for forty years in airboats and motorboats because of his poaching, until finally they had sense enough to save themselves some money by hiring him. He says by then he knew the swamp so well at night he could hardly find his way around in it during the day. He'd killed maybe a thousand gators, though tried to limit his kill to bulls by leaving the pools alone where he saw babies. He got a dollar a foot for skins in the Depression, and since he could kill twenty-five or thirty in a four-or five-day excursion, it was very good money.

Mr. Davis seems quite "Cherokee" in his sentiments, bad-mouthing the Seminoles, saying that the seven-footers of an unknown tribe buried in mounds before history began were probably "a better class of Indian" and joking about "hundred-and-fifty-pound coons" coming as tourists to the swamp "to look at the coons." In a kinder tone, he speaks of how he loves the smell of "spirits of turpentine," which is best from a green young tree—you can put either crude pine gum or its spirits directly onto a cut or pour the liquid on the dressing after bandaging it. And a few drops on a lump of sugar will defeat a cold. From March to October was the gathering season. The pine trees were precisely scarred, about chest-high, and a two-quart can was hung on a nail underneath to catch the drippings, emptied once a month. They got paid from thirty to fifty dollars for a fifty-gallon barrel, and the resin left after the spirits were boiled off was used to caulk their boats with. (More famously, by pitchers in baseball.)

Davis, a chair-loving fellow but vociferously folksy, claims his father named Bugaboo Island—the wildest island left in the swamp—once when the wind caused two trees to rub together all night, moaning above his campsite. Honey Island had bee trees, and Blackjack Island blackjack oaks. John's Negro Island was where a slave stolen from a man named John was secreted. The Chesser family arrived in "eighteen and fifty-eight," and their homestead on Chesser Island, now watched over by him, has been restored by the refuge management, with its cane-boiling syrup equipment, its "hog gallows" and toothed otter traps, its gourds hanging up for purple martins to nest in and clear the air of mosquitoes and flies, the whole yard scraped bare so wandering snakes or scorpions would have no place to hide. While he was growing up, the Chessers cultivated melons, corn, peas, beans, and sweet potatoes, and ran loose livestock in the swamp, and grew about thirty acres of sugar cane, which made a clear, sweet syrup of renown. A bobcat skin was worth only fifty cents and a fox three dollars, but in the winter he and his friends would go out after fur for a week or so in a twelve-foot dugout, carrying their traps, their bacon and sweet potatoes, pushing themselves with an eight-foot pole with a Civil War bayonet strapped to the top end to fight off alligators, planning to meet other kids who were trapping at a certain "house" in the middle of the swamp and camp there, drink and swap stories, butchering a deer or a "piney-woods rooter"—one of the bristly, gray, big-headed, big-tusked, wild-running hogs. At dawn they'd let out a couple of old-time Okefenokee two-mile, one-minute hollers to wake up the sun and wake up the swamp.

Okefenokee is sometimes called the Yellowstone among wildlife refuges, it's so important. Yet as I drove around its perimeter it seemed awfully small and fragile, like a drop in a dynamo, when I knew what encircled it. In the town of Waycross I met Johnny Hickox, a round-faced, mellow-looking gentleman of fifty-nine in gold-rimmed glasses, with a straight short smile, a farmer's sloping shoulders, and bib overalls. Though neither a retired lawman nor a re-formed outlaw, he grew up on Cowhouse Island, "dipping turpen-tine" from the collection pails for sixty-five cents a day in his first job, then hunting alligator belly skins, until, after World War II, you could make fifty cents an hour at the sawmill. The steers his father raised in the swamp grass sold for only ten dollars, and bearskins had no better use than being cut into wads to stuff in the holes the pigs dug under the fences, to scare them back inside. ("Most pitiful thing, to hear them holler for mercy if a bear caught them!") His grandfather at the turn of the century had earned only ten cents a day, logging cypresses, including the services of his horse. But in that era you could buy swampland for eleven cents an acre.

A guy and he would spend two weeks "pushing a pole," wander-ing a whimsical course from Waycross to Fargo with a load of traps, and sell whatever furs they'd caught, then enjoy another two weeks poling back, with many stops. No swamper ever starved in the swamp. There were so many fish to catch that "you had to hide from them to put your bait on," Johnny says. Four-pound pickerel, two-pound "mudcats," and the smaller "buttercats," which are catfish with yellow on their bellies. Twelve-pound bass, swarms of perch, and delicious soft-shell turtles. His great-great-grandfather had fathered twenty-one children, by only one wife—which is one reason nearly everybody around this patch of swamp seems to be related to him—but nobody went hungry.

There is no lawman-outlaw edge to Johnny Hickox; and from the tourist park where he works, he took me out along the "Wagon Road," a water trail that logs used to be floated over, to "Sapling Prairie" for a picnic in a jonboat with a light motor on it—though he paused to demonstrate his push-poling for fun, telling me it was a skill that, like riding a bike, you never lose the hang of. He said these old water trails "tuckered out" if not cleared by a government cutter boat or a big alligator swimming through occasionally, and he pointed out a few other trails leading off through the wet maze of sedges, lilies, swamp grass, and bushes to former haunts where he had camped and earned a living with his ax and fish lines and traps. A gator was eating bonnet lily roots, while a "Florida cooter" turtle steered well clear of it. He pointed out swamp iris, and wampee, with an arrow-shaped leaf and hot roots that the Indians seasoned meat with, and Virginia chain fern, and "soap bush," whose leaves make suds when scrubbed, and "hen-and-biddies" pitcher plants, named for the lineup of their bloom and leaves, and pipeworts, also called "ladies' hatpins."

"I was married to this swamp," he said happily, though he has four grandchildren already and his wife still pampers him. He showed me what bears like to eat—black gum berries, greenbrier berries, highbush blueberries, live oak acorns, wild-hive honey, and palmetto fruit—as if to indicate how much abundance they also found here.

We ate our sandwiches on a "house" on Dinner Pond, ten miles out, facing one of only two virgin stands of cypress trees left in Okefenokee, and listened to a Carolina wren sing *tea-kettle, tea-kettle, TEA-kettle.* Two paired cranes flew overhead as if they were married. The trees' strange "knees" sticking out of the water and the hanging Spanish moss (which old-timers burned in smudge fires to keep the mosquitoes off) gave us the pleasure of their company, not to be encountered widely in the South anymore because cypress fetches so much as a log and air pollution kills the moss. Eight or nine days' traveling in the jonboat would bring us to the Gulf of Mexico, a happy trip, he said.

Southerners, like New Englanders, whom I know better, are survivors by temperament. But they use talk instead of taciturnity, zaniness instead of stoicism, as their method of getting by, and that's more fun. We agreed, over our tea at Dinner Pond, that neither of us would ever see a wilderness that was as pristine as what we had loved before. But wildernesses have a special value, apart from sheltering so many primeval creatures that elsewhere are nearly gone. The South is becoming homogenized into the rest of America because so many Northerners are moving there. And it may be that regionalism will survive best in wild places such as Okefenokee, where the South is not the "Sunbelt" but remains the South to eye and ear. Cypresses and ibises, wood storks, snowy egrets, timeless turtles, hordes of frogs, hurrah bushes, and Ogeechee lime trees can preserve alive our sense of human as well as natural history.

(1984)

O Wyoming

Saturday, September 3. My nineteen-year-old daughter, Molly, and I have driven from Vermont to Dubois, Wyoming, to enjoy an eight-day pack trip along the southern edge of Yellowstone National Park. But smoke palls the town. Most of the customers at the Branding Iron Motel (which has a corral for people to park their horses in overnight) are Apache women from the San Carlos reserve in Arizona, who are here to earn $6.38 an hour on the fire lines—with yellow coats made of survival cloth, red backpacks, hard hats, kit bags, canteens, and other gear piled on the lawn. At the laundromat across the highway, the scent of smoke is everywhere—drawling, burly men in town for a couple of days are calling the Dakotas on the pay telephone and washing heaps of redolent clothes (redolent with memories for me, because I fought forest fires in California in 1953), between pit stops at the Outlaw Saloon or the Rustic Pine Bar, "The World's Most Unique." However, the conflagration burning what will wind up being a third of the park this very dry summer has crossed what was to have been our route, so we've changed our plans, with the idea of exploring part of the Absaroka range, a spur of the Rockies just outside Yellowstone's southeast boundary. (*Absaroka* was the Crow Indian word for "Crow," and the range was a contested territory for the Crows and Shoshones.)

We've been riding for several days in Jakey's Fork and Torrey Canyon, two valleys of the Wind River Range, another core spur of the Rockies, which is also touched by the Continental Divide, for the extraordinary beauty there and to get our sea legs under us, in a manner of speaking, or to warp our legs into the weird-feeling shape horseback riders have. Riding on a "lower" animal may fit very well with the human ego, but not with the human physique. All that personable meat and muscle moving under me—a whole butcher shop's worth, by the standards of the city—is terribly touching and comradely. I don't ride very well, but twenty or thirty years ago I did some riding and have happy memories and a feel for negotiating with horses. Besides, even though in this day and age he will be sold for forty cents a pound to make dog food when he slows down (yes, even here in the cowboys' "wild" West: specifically, he will be shipped to a vast abattoir in North Platte, Nebraska, to be knocked on the head), a horse is a quirkily sentient creature, like us, sometimes cheerful or conscientious, sometimes gloomy or rebellious or conniving.

Because it's the end of the dude ranching season and the horses are about to be driven some miles away to their winter range on the Shoshone Indians' reservation, where they'll go "barefoot" till spring, we had been put on a miscellany of horses who hadn't yet lost their shoes. But now, on our pack trip, led by Press Stephens, vice-president of the Wyoming Outfitters Association and a resident of Shell, Wyoming, a village of fifty people in the Big Horn Mountains northeasterly of where we are, I am on Buffalo. Buffalo is a strawberry roan with frost on his rump, only seven years old but until recently an actual wild horse, a young stallion roaming Nevada's Ruby Mountains until he was captured, castrated, branded, and shod. Though he carries people on his back just for about three months a year, he has adjusted quickly to domestication and has managed to take my measure in almost no time. In his case this revolves around the question of whether I will slacken my reins enough for him to snatch mouthfuls of food by the wayside as we travel along. I know that, on principle, a rider shouldn't, or his ride will become purely an occasion for the horse's eating, irregular in direction, all fits and starts. But on the other hand, in my middle age, I've turned more benign than I used to be, no stickler for rules, and more hopeful that people and animals will enjoy their lives.

Lars, a contemporary of mine, a patent lawyer from New York City, a large athletic man who eats, walks, and sometimes even talks prodigiously, and like me is a dude on this trip, seems to be the same way. He sits on his horse in the manner of Sancho Panza, with the reins in a nobly insouciant droop, and lets his beast eat so often on the narrow trails that I end up impatiently barging ahead and not letting Buffalo eat on the trail at all.

Lars, because of his size and crew-cut and half-hidden but overall competence, looks like an army colonel, but we have a real colonel along, Lars's friend Pat, an artillery officer from Arkansas and West Point—chairman of the English Department there, in fact—a smallish, red-faced, appealing man whose tales of Korea and Vietnam contrast with a present enthusiasm for teaching Virginia Woolf.

We packed out of a trailhead at Brooks Lake, above Dubois, and, after a few miles of climbing Brooks Lake Creek, went over the Continental Divide at Bear Cub Pass, from the Wind River (which is to say, the Missouri and Mississippi River) drainage to the Snake River (which is to say, the Columbia River) drainage. Wyoming is the classic state for basin-and-range, sagebrush-and-bunchgrass, parkland-and-forest scenery. It's the New England of the West in the sense that it's the founding fathers' West, haunt of the mountainmen and site of the early trappers' rendezvous on the Green River, not far from where we are, and then of quintessential cowboying.

Over the Divide, on the Pacific side, the stands of spruces get a little more serious about being spruces, and lovely sloping meadows alternate with them, and serious, speaking cliffs loom above the sidehills. After descending to Cub Creek, we went up it and camped by and by on a white sandy flat at eight thousand feet among lodgepole pines and knee-high willows, where a modest trickly brook comes in. The sky has stayed turquoise blue most of the time, except when the wind shifts Yellowstone way and carries smoke from the fires over us, acrid and propelling charred clouds, though, even so, we are somewhat sheltered from it. Molly and I unsaddled the horses and helped with the ten packhorses, while Lars and the literary colonel helped Press put up the tents, and their wives, Marit and Ann, helped his wife—my old friend Gretel—set up the part of the camp devoted to nourishment. Press and Jack Swenson, his horse wrangler, were talking about what they call "horse wrecks," which is just as it sounds: pack trains derailed on a mountainside.

This high country was too snowy for Indians to live in regularly, but they hunted elk, moose, and bighorn sheep here, as whites do now. Press, our leader, is mid-thirties, a converted Easterner or self-created cowboy from Atlanta (his father a Coca-Cola executive), by way of South Kent School in Connecticut (where at sixteen he started chewing tobacco, he says), Bowdoin College in Maine, and a year playing rugby and studying art history at the University of Madrid. He has been doing this sort of thing for the past eighteen summers, though he also rodeoed off and on for about the first ten years after he got here. He compares that sport to fast downhill skiing in the rhythmic techniques and physical prowess required, having quit both (and chewing tobacco, "another stupid thing") at about the same time. He is strong, tall, and—as this is his last tourist trip of a strenuous season—thin, with a twisty grin, a fin of a nose, and a gusty voice, slurring his words in a tenor monotone that sounds like the wind. He's a gentle man—Gretel met him at a John Wayne movie festival in midwinter, where they'd each gone to alleviate bouts of cabin fever, and she noticed him because he had tears in his eyes—who loves these mountains and reels off the names of dozens of creeks, trails, routes and passes, aspects of mountains, and private hideouts for camping whenever he can possibly bring them into the conversation. He wears red suspenders, which he likes to pluck when introducing himself and launching into a little peroration, almost as if he were a tall-tale spinner, but otherwise is modest about everything except his dislikes. As is the case with so many people who make their living outdoors, serving as hosts in the wilderness, he has by now had a bellyful of guiding sport hunters, is sick of the butchery of the hunting season (this week beginning again); is sick of gun blasts, elk "murdered," black bears, antelope, and moose knocked over, not for food anymore but for stranger motives.

Because of our inexperience and despite Press's deft assistance, it takes us about four hours to set up or strike camp, which in this era of backpacking seems like a turn-of-the-century way to go about traveling, but on the other hand, somebody in my kind of shape couldn't go far anymore in this tall terrain except on the back of a horse. We eat well too—no freeze-dried food—and the conversation has more spaciousness, I suspect, more elevation, more of a frame of reference, animal, vegetable, mineral, than if we were walking. Press used to teach history-of-civilization night courses at Central Wyoming College (or "Country-and-Western College," as they called it), while wintering on an Indian reservation, watching an outfitter's herd of horses, and intriguing juxtapositions come naturally to him. And Gretel Ehrlich, with *The Solace of Open Spaces*, has emerged lately as a star writer of this region. She has just won a Guggenheim Fellowship, whose first check she spent on a new refrigerator and on bailing a friend out of jail. Over the ten years I've known her, she has added gravity to her beauty and other substantial virtues and sits her horse at the rear of our caravan with the look of a matriarchal squaw (or Georgia O'Keeffe)—solid and still, observant and straight. Her small dog, Rusty, a Kelpie–Blue Heeler cross, trots inseparably a few paces behind her.

Though we're both animal lovers, we irritate each other by "spoiling," respectively, Rusty and Buffalo. I don't think she should encourage Rusty to eat off her plate; she doesn't approve of my feeding Buffalo my orange peels while taming him down. Besides, as a wild horse, won't he get a bellyache? Press and she ask. Where could he ever have digested such tastes before? I laugh, being a native New Yorker talking to Wyoming ranchers: "Don't think you know all the tastes of the wilderness just because you live here! Any spirited horse that lives wild will have tasted dead fish in a stream and carrion killed by a snowslide for the sake of the salts they have." Gretel laughs in return and tells me that Rusty is her psychiatrist and deserves to eat off her plate. He does indeed listen whenever she speaks, cocking his head like the RCA Victrola dog.

Jack, the wrangler, who sings Jimmy Buffett songs to the little horse herd as he rounds them up near dawn, is five years younger than Press, ten years younger than Gretel, and twenty-five years younger than me. He's a likably knockabout ornithological field assistant, wildlife photographer, and adventure guide, who has recently studied shearwaters in Hawaii and has counted the catch on Russian trawlers for the U.S. government. He plans, not long after our trip is over, to go to the Himalayas in search of a yeti to take pictures of. Says he will look for one at between eight and twelve thousand feet, just the sort of altitude conducive to such a creature's good health but where climbers from Europe and America, ambitious for K2 or Everest, don't bother to stop.

Sunday, September 4. Today we rode to the head of Cub Creek, at a level of ten thousand feet. Saw a sharp-shinned hawk, a Swainson's hawk, a raven family stunting, magpies, several sets of elk tracks, some bear-bashed logs, some dashingly black-and-white Clark's nut-crackers flying overhead, heard gray jays whistling, and saw a golden-eye duck on a pond. It has rained in these mountains only twice all summer, and every form of plant life has retrenched to its survival mode, but high up here, the melting snowfields have kept the creeks flowing and the water table close under the soil.

I should mention that the lenses inside my eyes are clouding over with cataracts—this seemed like a good way to spend the time waiting for an eye operation, taking my daughter for her first trip out West. So when I say that we've seen a sharp-shinned hawk, I mean that my friend Jack did. I, too, am interested in hawks and yetis, but I see most inaccurately at this point. The big old silvery blowdowns in the forest look like silver horsemen to me. The packhorses standing together look like mounted Indians. Masses of trees spread over a sidehill look like Paul Bunyan and Babe, his legendary blue ox. But I do see the smoke crimson the sun or block the passes on both sides of us periodically, like a wind-borne narrative of the conflagration in Yellowstone, which is two or three dozen miles from us at its leading edge. But the fire doesn't preoccupy me, as it does Press and Gretel, because this isn't my home and I long ago removed my heart's strings from Wyoming (I, too, was here in my teens, when a first visit counts) to Alaska, where there is more space and time. I wrote Yellowstone off. What I really care about are the evolving tragedies of bureaucratic mismanagement in Alaska's wildlands.

Cub Creek heads at a flat pretty pass, and we rode over that to the head of the south branch of the South Fork of the Buffalo River, one of the Snake's largest tributaries, eating our luncheon sandwiches next to a collection of tiny black springs that popped from the raw tundra soil, where we were squeaked at by voles while Press described the vicissitudes of doing an oral history of your hometown, each family complaining about the "play" it received, or absence thereof.

Sticker, our strongest, most independent-minded packhorse, who Buffalo pals with, was "Indian-broke," as they say, and also was a bucking horse for a while, till one day he simply stopped bucking: realized it wasn't necessary. He is head shy and won't tolerate being examined or stared at, but will stand still to be loaded or unloaded as long as nobody looks at him. All of these horses are leased from a man who owns nine hundred and fifty, picking them up wholesale roundabout by the semi-rig load and looking them over when he gets home, walking through his corrals, figuring out which can be used to carry dudes, which for cowboys, which for packing, which for rodeos, and which should go straight to North Platte for Fido to eat. Buffalo, being a "government horse," from federal land, with whitish numbers that were freeze-dried into his neck when he was caught, cost the man only a $125 adoption fee.

These high-altitude trees "feed" by straightening up, not spreading out to catch the sun, probably in order to offer the heavy snows a slimmer target, but just below timberline they're grouped talkily enough, in clusters. We saw a moose with its dinglebell swinging and a hatrack perched on its head, augering fast up into the timber from a willow swale. The avalanches here architecture the timber into ribs along the side ridges, cutting chutes that determine where anything lives; because we're in steep country now. We've followed new forks off of forks, the trail dipping down, then scrabbling up through scree and brush, to a "nameless drainage," as Press puts it, at the head of the north branch of the South Fork of the Buffalo River, a little ways from the shoulder of Wall Mountain (11,600 feet), and near one head of the Yellowstone River too. Yellowstone water, however, eventually reaches the Gulf of Mexico through the Mississippi, but Buffalo water reaches the coast of Oregon, so we are camping on a slant of ground by a frigid swift mini-watercourse among stubby chest-high spruces a few hundred feet below the Continental Divide.

Press says he loves these wild camps: "The wild specter to it. There's a magic about timberline, a mystery to why the trees grow just exactly to here and not ten yards further." This is the highest and roughest place he's ever stayed with a party, and for the latrine he has dug a "four-day hole," choosing a noble outlook for the throne. Besides canvas and food, his essential kit is an ax, a shovel, a bow saw, and a pistol. At this altitude the snows of the fall could begin falling anytime now. That's what Press, Jack, and Gretel joke about, whereas we tourists joke about bears, specifically a "timberline bear," a grizzly you can't climb a tree from. Jack had seen the tracks of a grizzly making its way along this creek as we rode up, and for a while, with field glasses, thought he might have spotted a bighorn or a bear among boulders or clumps of vegetation on the far ridge, thrown into relief against the backdrop of the blue sky, but after two hours it still hasn't moved.

Labor Day, September 5. Molly is a pretty good rider and is of course delighted to have nineteen horses to watch and get her hands on. But her deeper pleasure in what we are doing has transformed her face: more glee than sophistication, and as "boyish" as "girlish." Presumably it has transformed mine too. Lars, only thirty-six hours out of Newark Airport, is an astonishing athlete, climbing our ridge, up and over, leading the "assault" on Wall Mountain. And Jack, still more light-legged and in training for his pursuit of the yeti of myth, did the same climb in only a T-shirt and shorts. As the group's senior member, I was glad to stop partway up, once we had crossed the Divide, and laze on the bank of a lovely green tarn with a single duck floating on it and the tracks of an itinerant coyote and a couple of elk discernible in the moss at the outlet, where Bliss Creek starts.

Bliss Creek (or "Crick," as they say) is named not for ecstatic emotions but for a horse rustler who made his home in its meadows, two thousand feet lower than we are, and used to steal horses in the vicinity of Cody, Wyoming, east of the Divide, and bring them up here and over to the settlement of Jackson, on the Pacific side, then steal a few Jackson horses and drive them up and over through here and sell them in Cody. It worked for a time, till in 1896 he was hanged at the creek's mouth.

Bliss, which goes into the Shoshone River, then the Bighorn River, the Yellowstone, the Missouri, the Mississippi, and the Gulf of Mexico, finally—like the nameless mini-creek that rushes past our camp, a mile away, and that flows instead to the Buffalo River, the Snake River, the Columbia, and the Pacific—starts just as upwellings of black water from thimble-sized springs seeping underground from the white remnants of the winter's snowfields. But Bliss immediately slices into a series of corkscrew clefts, sharply dropping, which I enjoy staring down into through my binocs, when I'm not following Lars's hiking feats above me on Wall Mountain. He's such an enthusiast that, discovering a hundred-dollar bill in one of his pockets this morning, he wanted to fling it away. "What use is money!" He's asking Press about buying a ranch somewhere around here, "to preserve this way of life," and is thinking about digging a latrine as admirable as Press's in his own hundred acres of woods on the Hudson when he gets home. Speaking of permanences, we're finding chunks of petrified wood amid about ten thousand years' worth of volcanic ash. But along most every ridgeline, summits or spurs of rock poke up like turtle or camel or bobcat heads, or ancestral otters, bears, vultures, and other totems. Our horses—which are brought in to lick salt and remember their provenance every morning, even when we don't plan to use them—were found this morning under a giant statue of Lenin at timberline on another creek.

I had a friendly dream last night: a friendly woman, encountered by chance, who wanted to make love with me. Breakfast was Cream of the West cereal and Western Family creamer in our coffee. Small throngs of rosy finches are larking about, and we've seen water ouzels, water pipits, and three red-tailed hawks chasing a Swainson's hawk. Fireweed fluff is blowing, and there are harebells and asters. The ground is honeycombed with voles' holes, and pikas live here, storing small hay piles. Yesterday's "timberline bear" is still stationary, but our hay-colored gulch leads up to the rim of the world with only a backing of sky. That's where the tarn is, and the black wall of Wall Mountain, and the plunge down toward life-giving forests again, a place where people can live. At the inlet of the black-and-green tarn, thirty acres of water surrounded by spongy tundra and a litter of lichen-decorated (green and red) rocks, we saw three migrating Baird's sandpipers—Arctic nesters that winter high up in the Andes—picking up tiny crustaceans or nymphs. I drank Mississippi-destined water, thinking of Pilottown, the ultimate village that stands by a boardwalk on stilts at the very mouth of that river, where I've visited, a hundred-plus miles below New Orleans, and all the turbid life these snow waters are going to pass between here and there. Then I followed the record of horse shit back to camp, till I heard the neck bells.

Ordinarily one looks from a cold aerie like this toward the forest as a refuge where one could build a campfire in an emergency, or climb a tree. (I remember an Eskimo telling me that that was the difference between his race and mine: Mine couldn't bear living long without trees.) And except for the human face and form, no sight is more precious and tender to a person undergoing the sensations of dimming eyesight than the incredible shapes of trees. Yet nevertheless, with the sky turning charred, the air smelling barbecued whenever the wind blows news of the fires our way, we get chatty and gay for a moment, realizing the one zone that's safe is where we are. No fire can trap and incinerate us above timberline.

Tuesday, September 6. The wind buffeted our tent all night with boisterous, mean gusts, though fortunately from the south, blowing sand and not snow. Molly talked to her mother in her sleep, saying, "I'm all right. I'm not hungry. I'm not cold." Reassuring words, but I wake up abruptly with anxiety if she coughs or talks. Her posture when riding is sort of great, and she looks golden-faced when the sun hits the frames of her glasses, but at least since the age of eight she has been worrying me by choosing in macho fashion (origins unknown: certainly not me) to underdress when possible against chilly winds.

Another personage I've worried about subliminally is Buffalo, whose gait has become a bit humpety or wobbly. I should have called for a consultation (to be truthful, I'm such a tyro at riding that I've never saddled a horse unassisted). But finally Press noticed and found that a nail from his left hind shoe was scratching the frog of his foot, and—calling him "Son" to soothe him—has reshod that hoof.

The stream is bruisingly cold when we wash (to the eye, like seething pewter), and lighting the little steel stove becomes life's focus, while we hear the wind hiss, and wait for the sunshine on the rimrock of the west ridge to slide slowly down nearer us, and for the dwarf willows to collect yellows, and for the short spruces on the east slope to invent individual long shadows. It's another uncannily cloudless day with no hint of the fire, if the wind stays southeasterly. We leave our camp where it is for another night and ride up on the whaleback ridges west of Wall Mountain, seeing a prairie falcon sailing over the bare alpine heath, and a ferruginous hawk, and rosy finches tumultuously flocking, perhaps after snow fleas, and a migrating goshawk crossing the Continental Divide and then diving down toward the squirrely spruce woods again, where it belongs. We come to the head of Wallace Creek and then to the head of Turner's Fork, which is named for Press's old boss, so he jumps down to have a taste of its water; and we go up onto an ultimate knob of rock at 11,300 feet—Jack Swenson all the time afoot, bare-armed and in shorts, though the temperature is in the forties, in training for his pursuit in a couple of months of the Abominable Snowman in Nepal.

From this knob of the Divide, above the Buffalo Plateau of the Teton National Forest, we look down at Simpson Meadow, and at Jack Davis Peak, which is named for the "last old-time cowboy in the Jackson region," says Press, who knew him, and at the south fork of the Marston Fork of the Shoshone River. Also across at Yount's Peak, farther off, at the headwaters of the North and South forks of the Yellowstone River (and named for Yellowstone's first game warden), and at Thorofare Mountain, which separates Yellowstone water from the Thorofare River. Beyond them we cannot see because of the vast gulf of smoke being churned up by the so-called Mink Fire, a little way down the Yellowstone. The scope of this fire (like the halving of

Yellowstone Park's grizzly population recently) seems to be a result of bureaucratic meddling, however well-intentioned, in a wilderness of terribly limited area, an area insufficient to absorb misguided planning. So as I see what's going on, I'm glad that after loving Wyoming in my teens, I tied my heart's strings to Alaska, with wildlands a hundred times larger, postponing being utterly heartsick over something like this.

Riding about, we see springs that are the very sources of the Snake and Shoshone rivers. See ridges like animals' heads, and ridges like rows of molars, and the wonderful amplitude of the saddles swinging in between, with, a bit lower, convivial-looking trees placed talkatively, where the grim avalanche chutes haven't imposed an implacable order. Through glasses we pick out the minute and tentative figures of three sheep on a stratified hump above Simpson Meadow and Lost Creek, our only "game" for these days at timberline; and in the opposite direction see Smokehouse Mountain, Coffin Butte, Crescent Mountain, and Ramshorn Peak, above Frozen Lake Creek. Then the hysterical smoke swallows everything, glowing red from the sun as if from ubiquitous fires that foreshadow the end of the world.

The terrain is like tussocky or mossy moor, interspersed with spindles of shallow soil that supports sedge grass and bluestem hay, or else barrens covered with blackish slag broken into scree. Except on the latter stretches, Buffalo likes loping uphill to overtake any horse that may have gotten ahead of him (particularly if I click my tongue), but then he may suddenly try to rush to one side of our progress, where good grass grows—playfully, as if to convince me that he and I are just on a grazing expedition. Lars, the lawyer, meanwhile is exclaiming to his very dear wife, Marit, a weaver and helpmeet type, how full of possibilities life is. But Pat, our literary artillery colonel (his wife, a fourth-grade schoolteacher, is a fellow Arkansan), is the opposite in the sense that he stays in character even more than he wants to. In these V-cut, ramparted valleys that mount toward the edge of the world, he finds himself irrelevantly figuring where he would place 105- and 155-millimeter howitzers to defend our position, as if this were Korea or Vietnam—both campaigns, he says, having scarred him.

O Wyoming

Wednesday, September 7. One is tired of a tent site by the fourth day, having slept at the same head-to-heels slant, on top of the same stones, voles, and willow stubs, for three nights running. This is a harsh, scrabbly environment anyway, with only a veneer of dirt on the basic rocks, and thin stingy air with the imminence of winter on it, up where mammalian life gets difficult. But at the same time all these conditions are exhilarating on a summer day, even if you just walk off somewhere by yourself and lie down spread-eagled, gazing at the convex sky. The closer you are, the bigger it swells.

Jack left to catch the horses at 7 A.M. but didn't bring them all in till half-past eleven. Buffalo hangs out with Grump, Arlene, and Sticker, the tough, brown, "Indian-broke" former bucking-bronc packhorse, and they move lots at night; but when faced with a mare named Irene, he lays back his ears. Every horse has nip scars. By talking, feeding him cookies and orange peels, and lingering with him, I've gotten Buffalo willing to hang around camp sometimes when let loose in the evening, until the others are well under way. The cusps of his teeth still mark him as young at age seven. A horse isn't "smooth" in the mouth until ten, Press says.

We have F-15 interceptors accelerating overhead, inflicting sonic booms on this pocket of wilderness because it is marked on the pilots' maps as "uninhabited." Gretel and Molly mutter ironic comments about "men" as they wash the camp dishes (though maybe more at my loafing than at the airplanes).

We rode down a couple of thousand feet in altitude and a distance of three or four miles to camp in a gentler terrain of fine meadowland by a slow piece of stream under big old spruce copses in ground-squirrel and red-squirrel country, choosing a spot where the sunrise will hit us and warm us by eight in the morning, if the smoke keeps blowing toward Oregon instead of toward us. Today was splendid, though we saw no game. What's also remarkable is the absence of wildlife such as elk, sheep, and moose when you glass far-distant slopes out of rifle range.

I've been astonished at the scarcity of animal tracks, because if they should be anywhere, they ought to be here in Wyoming's grass mountains, designated as a national showplace, with prime summer feed, and the drought and fires elsewhere should have funneled them in all the more. It seems to confirm what I'd heard in Dubois about how badly overgrazed and overhunted Wyoming is. This beautiful alpine fodder—sedge grass that's 14 percent protein—goes untouched because the fall and winter and spring ranges that the animals must depend on during the year's hard seasons are overused. In the Big Horn Mountains, where Press himself lives, he says there is no place that you can go on a wilderness trip without meeting cattle and sheep. It's one reason why he brings his summertime customers here. Wyoming's Fish and Game Department is funded by hunting and fishing license sales, not general state revenues, so there is a maximum emphasis upon kill or "harvest" figures, on game earning cash by being killed, not the attention to conservation matters that occupy fish and game departments whose funding attunes them to other concerns. And much of the old winter range has been carved up for summer homes (called "ranchettes") or grows sugar beets and beer barley, besides the miles devoted to cattle. It's important that the cowboy heritage be maintained in this setting of its heyday, but in this age of cheap instant travel, when these last roadless paradises like Yellowstone *do* really belong to everybody, the question is even more urgent whether beef should be the emphasis here, in competition with rare, dwindling collections of wildlife, instead of in states like Georgia, which are already more efficient producers of beef than any part of the Old West. Georgia can't preserve for the rest of us herds of elk, abundant moose, healthy scatterings of bighorn sheep and grizzly bears, wilderness meadows, creeks, and forests, and a sense of what the Wild was.

Thursday, September 8. Before sunrise the valley was misty, though the billowy-looking mountains and frog-headed ridges at the far end rose out of the pretty white haze (not, I think, smoke)—raw land that is "holding the world together," as a farmer I know back in Vermont says of his own patch of undeveloped acreage. I walked with the light-legged Jack up to a trail on the slope opposite our camp to look at some bear tracks. I'd thought I'd seen grizzly tracks yesterday along a creek bank but foolishly hadn't jumped off my horse to check for sure, presuming somebody coming along behind me, with better eyesight, would confirm them. We see bear tracks because grizzlies

are protected here, unlike other game. These new ones were fresh
and clear, and from the precision of the claw marks we assumed they
were a small grizzly's. Anyway, they went in both directions, as if he
or she had made a round trip, so I followed them—"Follow the toes,"
I kept saying to myself—toward the bear's first destination, to find
out what he'd been after. They led me a couple of miles through a
lovely wide saddle between Crescent Mountain and Coffin Butte, a
spacious high pass, which itself crossed the Continental Divide, with
two patchy glaciers above me on my right. At the head of Du Noir
Creek, which flows sixty miles southeastward to the town of Dubois,
then into the Wind River, the Bighorn River, and eventually the Mississippi, I found a cluster of white-barked pine trees, whose nuts are a
principal food for bears fattening for hibernation at these altitudes.
The creek cuts a humpy but precipitous slot in the crumbly conglom-
erate rock, and I sat looking down into that and across up at the
streaks of silver meltwater running down the pitch of Coffin Butte
from remnant snow and the shrinking little glaciers. "Hold out a
week or two more, and there'll be new snow!" I told them loudly. It
was an impeccably balmy day, as happy for me as when I'd sat by the
green glacial tarn at the head of Bliss Creek, gazing down at the
corkscrew slit of that water's course toward the Shoshone River, except that today, in effect, I had the bear's company.

Starting back, I followed his or her returning tracks to a shallow
turquoise lake immediately east of the Divide, where a sheep had in-
cised half a dozen footprints in the bank when it had come down to
drink. I lay there in the veldt-tan grass of the watershed saddle a long
while, picturing myself as bear bait, both hoping and fearing that
Toes would return, and so still that a hawk stooped over me and
buzzed me repeatedly to see what my condition was. My condition
under that turquoise sky by that turquoise lake was happy! And at
suppertime I headed home. In up-and-down country, the country is
everywhere, and the wind was all wrong for stealth now, alerting any
wild animals that might be ahead of me, but I got glad about that.

Friday, September 9. Press and Jack like to joke that their outfit
runs "on diamond hitches and duct tape," everything is so thoroughly
taped up. I'm the same. Yesterday I lost my binoculars from not being

able to see where I had put them, and today a crown on my back tooth fell out. I was nauseous at first, expecting pain, but when the pain didn't come I stopped feeling nauseous. I remind myself that sometimes a dude is doing his share just by keeping up, filling his belly.

"A horse that farts will never tire./A man who farts is the man to hire," says Press. He is "on a See-Food diet. If I see food I eat it." He's reading the fine writer Jim Harrison and slinging the "bear box" up and down from a tall tree limb night and morning. He speaks of the people in Wyoming who don't live by tourism—and for whom the satellite dish isn't "the state flower"—living "like coyotes," by scavenging elk horns that have been shed in the winter, for China's horn-as-an-aphrodisiac market, by gold panning, trapping, cutting firewood. Maybe the best sheep rancher he knows is working as a jailer in Riverton because of the effects of this summer's drought. Press's previous trip was with a psychiatrist from the East and seven of the man's patients. That was fine, but some of the hunters he takes out bug him. One almost shot him, aiming through a scope sight that shut off the hunter's side vision. He talks about rodeoing: A Nez Percé Indian named Jackson Sundown, who is in a class by himself in rodeo history because he rode every horse he ever got on to a standstill, was never observed being bucked off. Nowadays the cowboy has to stay on for only eight seconds. The heart of rodeoing is in Henrietta, Oklahoma, he says, but he likes the big Canadian broncs best. More northerly horses are bigger.

I should mention that he came within possibly a day of dying on the trip a couple of weeks ago. He'd developed an abscess on his butt, which he thought was a boil and ignored; developed blood poisoning; a raging fever; couldn't ride; walked alone ten miles out to a road; got himself to a hospital and located a competent doctor and underwent surgery just in time. He got out of bed for this special outing and has been riding by means of a child's round air-filled life preserver, which he fastens to his saddle each day to keep his weight off the wound. Gretel, too, in bronc mishaps and two lightning strikes, has nearly died.

Last night I dreamed of traveling on a passenger ship, and a shoot-'em-up there. We're camped by a purling stretch of what might be described as the south fork of the South Fork of the Buffalo River, which flows to the Snake by and by. But our tents, underneath very nobly old-looking, hardy, sizable spruces that, with this short growing season, probably predate the white man here, are pitched between two steep creeks, which, plunging down six or eight hundred feet from the stubborn snowfields above, are doing the work of the world and producing a wonderful, perpetual ruckus, a noise to induce dreams of the sea. In the outdoors, water is where the action is. It contains all sounds when it runs and, in the sunlight, wrinkling like an elephant's skin, all colors too. It speaks in tongues.

A flock of geese labors south with a beat like heat shimmering, Molly says. Blundering blindly around in my sunglasses, I remind her of Ray Charles, she says. It's odd to think about, but we communicate with our horses by tucking our fingers into their lips. Regardless, Buffalo spooks at light-and-shadow configurations sometimes and needs more than the reins, needs talk then. This complex valley with rimrock and headlands and red and green meadows, up and away from the population centers, is "holding the world together," says Press, like my farmer friend. And we agree it shouldn't have to be "used," can just be looked at occasionally, or *not* be looked at, just exist by itself.

There's a bitter quarrel between the Indians on the Wind River reservation—the only Indian reserve in the state, but almost as large as Yellowstone Park—and the many whites with inholdings or on nearby ranches about water rights, always a cruel issue in the West. The Indians have won a substantial water allotment, based on their treaties, in a recent court fight but are driving their white neighbors into a fury by not *using* it all, letting some of the water stay in the river and flow right by, just listening to it and looking at it as it goes.

We rode up on the high flanks of Crescent Mountain (11,375 feet) today. It's one of the mountains where hunters shoot sheep, like Whiskey Mountain of the Wind River Range, under which, in Torrey Canyon, I saw a good number of petroglyphs last week. Torrey has a valley with three or four lakes and an exploding brawny creek that twists in its rocky bed with the force of an omen, in otherwise very dry country. With monoliths and burial sites, a fertile floor and nesting ospreys and eloquent cliffs, it's a place full of the ancient presence of man. We saw representations of owls, eagles, and what looked like "airplanes," and what looked like sprites. Also thick-bodied, sinister figures, and armless hands and legless feet stuck onto trident shapes. Bow-and-arrow men; mountain sheep. Skulls; death's-heads; thunderbirds; crowned, toothed "masks" complete with illustrated "brains." A horned dancer with one arm up and one arm down; and various skeletal frames, some of which looked to be inspired not so much by a human or animal array of bones as by the fossils that occur side by side with these cryptic scratchings in the sedimentary beds.

But we're too high here for such evidence of habitation. The snow may get twenty feet deep, and the cold intolerable. And Crescent Mountain is volcanic in origin, scattered at the top with blackish slag or tuff that is speckled with bilious-colored lichens and tinkles like broken slate when dropped, though some of the mountain's shoulders are undulantly grassy or comfortably dark with timber. We rode close to the summit and climbed a bit, then descended over a shelving ledge of compacted snow to a miniature crater lake that was chocolate at first, later purple, as the sun's angle shifted. There are elegant ramparts and turrets to gaze at, and abrupt, intimate cliffs to peer down, reminding me of some of the dioramas at the Museum of Natural History in New York that engraved themselves upon my enthusiasms when I was a child. You can see why this has become a final hideout for sheep, but on the other hand, two were shot here a week ago. We met their heads strapped to the back of a packhorse going down to Dubois on our second day out and, probably as a result, saw none today.

Borrowing my colonel friend's field glasses, I went off alone and studied the several levels of the view. In such a spot I like to scare myself by imagining I'm in some giddy fix, on some ultimate knoll, where nothing is higher, and must climb off. Except for the line of smoke, the sky was cerulean blue and soundless, spreading over the world. In this crazy-hot summer, ice in the Du Noir Glacier on Coffin Butte must be melting that fell as snow hundreds of years ago. It was a sailing view, a vulture's view. And Lars was catching California golden trout that the Fisheries biologists (with their zany ideas for the "wilderness") had helicoptered in. Californian indeed, with their spotted tails, fluorescent red bellies, and longitudinal red stripes on olive sides, and with spawn in them.

Climbing out of the crater (perhaps a volcanic vent?) that the lake is in, I frightened myself while slipping on the steep scree by suddenly visualizing the pitch as becoming nearly perpendicular. You can do that: have your eyes play tricks, turn a sixty-degree slope to eighty-five degrees, and nothing for you to hold on to but pebbles and gravel. Scrambling and sliding, I gave myself a cardiologists' stress test. It told me I should have a normal life span.

Saturday, September 10. Last day. In the wee hours I heard taps on the tent and thought it was rain. Went outside. There, thought it was only the spruces shedding their needles. The roar of water from the two tumbling creeks was so pervasive it seemed to be floating the tent, and I thought the taps might be an illusion produced by that. Still, the smell of the sky did have rain in it. And sure enough, rain came in earnest by breakfast time. Hallelujah. Third rain of the summer. Not yet snow. The temperature stayed in the forties, as we whirligigged slowly down toward home through tall rain-forest-looking woods of Douglas fir, Engelmann spruce, lodgepole pine, with dank-looking ponds and swamps alongside, past finger meadows and willow breaks now springing rib-high. The aspens have yellowed too. At lunch my chapped lips burst blood into my sandwich once again. ("Put horse shit on them. That'll keep you from licking them," Jack joked.) The switchbacks got like a merry-go-round as we went lower in the cold rain—the wind "strong enough to blow Christ off the Cross," as a wrangler said when we met him.

It's not that one does anything so very different in these alpine valleys with a vista of runneled headlands and mauled ridgelines, lens-shaped glaciers and snowslide chutes, and the Continental Divide, at the top of the world. One sits (or *I* do) picking at loose flakes of skin, biting one's nails, thinking of the politics of one's marriage, friendships, or career, replaying in one's tediously repetitive mind old conversations or correspondence from weeks or months before and two or three thousand miles away (or that never took place at all). In other words, one remains human; one doesn't calcify into rock. But fitfully there's a feeling of peace, which comes not just from the beauty spread out everywhere, but from a far-flung frame of reference.

We got back to the world of pickup trucks with collie-huskies bounding around in the back—where Gretel heard that a skunk had killed one of Rusty's new puppies at their ranch and that alfalfa was heading for one hundred dollars a ton. At the laundromat across the highway from the Branding Iron Motel, a poignantly lonely fire-fighter from Chicago, not black from the fire but black, was at the pay phone, calling home.

(1989)

Wowlas and Coral

In Belize you will meet determined birders, working on their "life lists," trying to sight a jabiru stork. You'll meet a roofer from Milwaukee taking the winter off; a junk bond salesman who has lost his job for "liquoring the Indians" (selling to bankrupt savings and loans' execs); a cashiered chef from Santa Monica; an advertising person jettisoned in an agency shake-up. I, too, had lost my job, as a college professor, for political incorrectness, and was looking for a rain forest respite, coral sand beaches, Mayan ruins, preferring a mainland landfall to an island destination because of the resonance of continents—jaguars and mountain lions, whole Indian nations, and the knowledge that I could walk from these mangrove swamps and limestone plains clear to Alaska or Argentina, should I so choose.

What I did was get myself to Miami and on board a TAN SAHSA jet for Belize City. TAN SAHSA is Honduras's airline, and en route to Tegucigalpa, after crossing the aquamarine Caribbean to Quintana Roo and paralleling the heel of the Yucatán—and after the stewardesses had served rock cornish hen (you could do worse than TAN SAHSA)—it dropped me off in Belize, an English-speaking democracy formerly known as British Honduras. The country achieved independence from Great Britain in 1981 but, being coveted by Guatemala, still keeps two thousand of Her Majesty's troops on its soil to thwart these designs. About the same size as El Salvador, which has six million people, and Vermont, which has six hundred thousand, Belize is only a third as populous as Vermont. It boasts seven hundred species of trees, as many as in the entire continental United States, and fifty-four kinds of snakes, six opossums, ninety bats, twenty-three fly-catchers (ocher-bellied, sulfur-rumped), and five kinds of wildcats. Though regarded as a political anomaly by Honduras and Mexico too, it won admission to the Organization of American States in 1991, partly by denying U.S. forces landing rights during the invasion of Panama. The British are said to have coached the Belizeans on this.

As an oasis of tranquillity, far less populous than when a million Mayans lived here a thousand years ago, Belize has lately received some spurts of anxious refugees from civil wars in El Salvador, Honduras, Guatemala, and Mexico. And from the seventeenth century it was a hideout for the so-called Baymen, Scottish and English priva-teers who hid in the river mouths that indent the mangrove swamps and robbed Spanish shipping. The world's second-largest barrier reef further sheltered them from retaliation, and one buccaneer in particu-lar, Peter Wallace, who is said to have arrived with eighty companions at the mouth of the area's most navigable river in 1638, may have given that river and the country his name (Wallace; Willis; Belis). On the other hand, a Mayan word for "muddy" is *beliz*.

Jamaica's governor, the nearest British authority, intermittently put the kibosh on such freebooting, whereupon the Baymen would buy slaves and cut logwood, a small, locally abundant tree whose heartwood provided red and purple dyes for Europe's woolen indus-try. When new technology eclipsed this livelihood, they shipped ma-hogany, Spanish cedar, pine, oaklike Santa Maria trees, and splendid sacred Mayan ceiba or "silk-cotton" trees (for their fluff), at the lofty top of which godlings once dwelt. Slavery among off-duty pirates in the woods became more of a meritocracy, a looser, more rascally, rum-punch, miscegenatic operation than regimented plantation slavery, and white supremacy was hard to maintain. Kidnapped Mayans and escaped slaves from elsewhere were added to the Creole brew; and

Carib Indians began arriving about 1802, after surviving tribal annihilation on some of the Lesser Antilles islands, which they in turn had conquered from the Arawaks. (*Carib* meant "cannibal" in Arawak, and thus the Caribbean vacationlands have an ambiguous semantic ring.) Later additions included Sepoy mutineers deported from India, Chinese coolie wanderers, Mosquito Indians from Nicaragua, Mexican mestizos fleeing the Caste War in the Yucatán, and disgruntled U.S. Confederates deserting the ruined South after the War Between the States.

In 1798 the Baymen had secured their hold on the territory by beating off a fourteen-vessel Spanish fleet at Saint George's Cay, near Belize City; and by 1871 the uncharacteristically reluctant Crown was persuaded to formalize its relationship with the colony. Bananas, citrus fruits, cacao beans, sugar, molasses, coconuts, and tortoise shell in dribs and drabs were not exports to make a merchant banker's mouth water, and the market for mahogany petered out: thirteen million board feet exported in 1846, three million in 1900. Chicle tapped from sapodilla trees as a base for chewing gum then replaced mahogany, just as mahogany had replaced logwood as a forestry and economic base early in the nineteenth century, but after a boom of thirty years or so, synthetics were invented, which by World War II had rendered chicle superfluous too. Sugar and citrus are the main crops now, and—in the forests—ecotourism and marijuana. Ecotourism, indeed, may have supplanted marijuana. You meet rapscallions aiming to run ecotours who seem not altogether unlike eighteenth-century logwood buccaneers.

Hard-drug courier planes drop off enough white powder when refueling for the flight north that Belize City has a cocaine problem, however. It has become Footpad City, which is a shame because otherwise it has a flavor like Mombasa's a couple of decades ago, a peaceable, planetary hum that can transport you out of the Americas for a very cheap air fare. Stay awhile, but seek security.

From the airport go to the Fort Street Guesthouse, if you are midscale. (To Mom's, on Handyside Street, if you are traveling light.) In a wicker chair on the Fort Street veranda, with a margarita and a glass of iced rain water and a lovely bouillabaisse in front of me, I found my cover pierced immediately. A British naval officer seconded to Belize's navy paused in flirting with my traveling companion to say, "You look like a college professor who's just been sacked. That special seediness."

"You're right. You should work for the CIA," I told him.

"Don't think they haven't tried to bribe me," he remarked, amused that an American diplomat was approaching, with his mother, to have supper.

There on the veranda I also met a local beer brewer, and an elderly butterfly hunter who was rumored to have been fired from his job in London only four months short of when his pension should have kicked in; and then Sharon Matola, who is the soul of conservation in Belize. She is a thirtyish woman who ran away from Baltimore with a Romanian lion trainer and toured with a circus in Mexico, before coming to Belize as a jaguar trainer in a movie company. She cajoles party ministers to set aside swaths of rain forest in reserves, and British soldiers to help her build the Belize zoo. And there was a Yorkshireman who flies Puma helicopters for the Royal Air Force. He told me about the fun of lowering a snake scientist into the jungle to capture boas, imitating the man's herculean rassle with a thirteen-footer, until the shy herpetologist himself showed up for supper. A diminutive person, he confided that he had recorded thirty-three species, including a frog new to knowledge.

Belize City has sixty thousand people. Hurricanes flattened much of it in 1931 and again in 1961, so the seat of government has been moved to a village called Belmopan, fifty miles inland, though no one who had a choice moved. At the Swing Bridge over Haulover Creek you are in the center of town. Putt-putts and pitpans (river craft), lobster boats, sailing sloops, and little lighters tie up here, or you can get on a dive boat and rent scuba gear. Banks, the post office, police station, Lebanese stores, Hong Kong restaurants, the green Catholic church, the president's green frame house, and the People's United Party's blue headquarters are close at hand. You can buy papayas and Bombay cloth, see Ibo and Ashanti faces speaking the Jamaican patois which is street English, overhear lots of Spanish, and visit the Mennonite furniture mart nearby. Pale, burly, blond, in straw hats and bib overalls, Belize's six thousand Mennonites came from Manitoba by way of Chihuahua in Mexico in search of clean living. They raise Belize's chickens, breakfast eggs, and green vegetables, converse in a sixteenth-century Swiss Anabaptist Low German, and look at you aware that you are going to hell. Some are such fine mechanics that they are called Mechanites. Others use a horse and buggy and have been departing for Bolivia or Paraguay to start the gargantuan drama of pioneering primeval jungle all over again.

Colorado surfers, Gurkha artillerymen, Boston remittance men pass slowly by, as the muggers with shoeshine kits circle them. I'd heard of Belize on the Yukon River, where some of the young placer miners operating in solo couples spoke of winters in Placentia like a luscious secret, ducking down when the creeks froze up and paying in nuggets. ("What do you make in a year?" I'd ask, and they laughed, aghast at my gullibility. "No placer miner makes anything; they break even.") It was twice as expensive as the rest of Central America yet half as expensive as North America, and no need to feel sorry for anyone: just sun, swim out to wrecks, eat fish, smoke dope. Red parrots, blue grottoes, Indian pyramids. Buy in dollars, not quetzals, cordobas, lempiras, balboas.

Haulover Creek is lined with slapped-together shacks of misfitted boards in cheap landsmen's pastels or deeper, sea-savaged mariners' colors, some built of salvagers' booty off the teeth of the reef, some out of junkyard crating and hurricane damage. Nothing to make you weep unduly if it blew down again, but handy and homey, set up on stilts; people run for the concrete schools in a flattening storm. The gardens are hedged with conch shells, sharks' heads, turtle skeletons, crocodiles' skulls. Then on Albert Street and Regent Street you've got more substantial white clapboard two-story houses, in the modestly porticoed, gingerbread-and-iron-railing style of superseded British colonial ports worldwide, as you walk south of the Swing Bridge to the handsome brick Anglican cathedral, the first in Central America, constructed in 1812–26 from a Christopher Wren parish-church design—three Mosquito Coast kings were crowned here by the British—and Government House, a ramblingly graceful white wooden mansion of the same era.

On Orange Street live the Zabone family of woodcarvers. And the Swing Bridge is worth half an hour any time. But after a day or two you may want to head for the bus station, or go to a gray house on stilts at the corner of Euphrates Avenue and Orange Street and talk to George Young, an ambulance driver who also runs a couple of ramshackle station wagons and may be pleased to drop everything and take you on a chartered tour of the country. My travel mate, Trudy, a college psychologist, and I spent four good days with him. George is fiftyish, a black Creole, the son of a sailor who would sometimes come home from the seven seas and ship out the same night when George was small, and who had an "outside family" to keep up with too. But George has paid school fees for six kids, maintains close-knit relations with them, and got to know his father fondly and his half-brothers also, before the old man's death from pneumonia at fifty-five. His mother and three brothers live in the United States, but George chose what he calls "the slow lane," staying here as a family man and taxiing occasional tourists around. He's visited them, but gets enough taste of the United States when he catches a bus to Houston for an auto dealer and chauffeurs vehicles down. After the blistering racial climate in Texas, his adventure continues through Mexico with cold mountain deserts and fogs, and the gauntlet of officials asking for bribes, wanting to ticket him if he stops to eat and gives them a chance. But the worst risk is bandits, if he doesn't stop, but drives through the night. At gunpoint a new car was hijacked from him. He wasn't shot, and begged his way back, persuading the local taxi association to take up a collection for him. In Guatemala you can have bandits and guerrillas, and the police don't just arrest you for money, like in Mexico. "They are savage. They want to hurt you. Throw you in jail and watch you suffer." Being black in Belize is never as dicey, though the two parliamentary parties, the People's United Party and the United Democratic Party, do tend to divide along racial lines, with Hispanics in the latter.

George drove us north to Crooked Tree, Guinea Grass, Orange Walk, Sarteneja, and the ruins at Altun Ha, two excavated ceremonial plazas with pyramids, temples, ball courts, and palaces, covered with irrepressible greenery and imbued with a marvelous seabed smell. In the ball-game plaza would-be kings competed in life-and-death matches.

Crooked Tree, a placid agricultural village bordering a waterfowl sanctuary on a lagoon, grows cashews and mangoes. Guinea Grass is Wild Westville, by contrast, druggy and closed-mouthed; and you can see a fortified, floodlit villa gleaming white behind razor wire. You can also rent a skiff for the twelve-mile trip up the New River, braided through mazy lambent sloughs, to the ridge and ruins at Lamanai, or "Submerged Crocodile," some of which are twenty-five hundred years old. As recently as 1867 Mayans fought the British here (five million people in Mesoamerica still speak Mayan dialects), but with the huge, vine-hung, moss-strewn, orchid-stippled trees, the vivid river, the lakelike lagoon, and the sun on the marshlands beyond, a quietude prevails. The two-square-mile center of Lamanai seems scarcely excavated, though more than seven hundred building sites have been identified and there are three temple-pyramids, one a hundred feet high, that you can climb, decorated with jaguar and crocodile and sun-god masks. It was here in the sixties that archaeologists found the largest piece of carved jade in Central America: a nine-pound head of the sun god, Kinich Ahau. Palms, ferns, and philodendrons swarm nearly everywhere, fountaining vegetation at each cleared spot, and spider monkeys gab and amble in the canopy overhead. In the limey, lichen-covered rubble you can find sea fossils, inches from the honey smell of brilliant flowers. Lichens, limestone, fossils, and flowers blend the scents of soil and sea, and nature here is veined with history. We tasted custard apples, like warm ice cream, and soursop fruit, admiring the clouds reflected on the water, and the sailing trees. Mayan civilization is thought to have collapsed a thousand years ago in the general region of Belize with a revolution of the peasantry against the nobles.

On the pearly, black and blue river, kids in pirogues were collecting firewood and catching fish for supper, and we saw several Mennonite farmers, who widely populate the banks of the New River, as we skimmed out.

Sarteneja, east of the mouth of the New River, is an isolated fishing village a couple of hours' drive from Guinea Grass through large sugar-cane plantations, the marl road strewn with cane leaves where the big trucks have passed. Wages are ten or twenty dollars (U.S.) a day, though illegals from El Salvador may work for only three, which is about the price of a pack of Independence cigarettes and a bottle of Belikin beer. George talked about how many cane cutters get bitten by "tommygoffs," or fer-de-lances. "Wowlas" are boas. The king vulture is called "King John Crow"; the screech owl, the "monkey bird"; the osprey, the "billy hawk"; the toucan, the "bill bird"; the blue heron, the "full pot," because it's so big its meat fills a pot. The otter is the "water dog." The kinkajou is "nightwalker." The tapir is the "mountain cow." Howler monkeys are "baboons." Pumas are "red tigers." Tayras (weasels) are "bush dogs." We saw cornfields and beehives, and little *milpas* growing yams and plantains. "Lots of sweets in this soil," George said.

This is Spanish country, the heartland of the United Democratic Party, whose colors are red and white, and party officials' houses were sometimes painted that. George's Creole party, the People's United Party, uses blue and white. "But your feet be lifted off the ground here if you make much noise about that," George said. "You might wind up in a well. They's a lot of wells around. You can't ax them about politics. Very distressful if you did."

Sarteneja is a beach town of sixteen hundred souls on Chetumal Bay. It's got blue water; a row of coconut palms and almond trees; a new mooring dock; some fishing sloops from which people go out in dories to dive for lobsters (called "crawfish") and conch or to angle for red snapper, bluefish, shark, and mullet; and two dirt streets of tin-roofed, cement-block houses, some hungry dogs, a nondescript one-story hotel, and several vacation huts going up. Egrets, ibises, anhingas, roseate spoonbills, and wood storks fly about, because of the lagoons and swamps, and there are frigate birds and cormorants, pelicans and agile terns stunting over the salt water, and Mayan ruins to investigate ashore. The gringos who've discovered this place—schoolteachers, diner owners—are mostly from upstate New York, though I met a stone-broke Quebecois whose single asset seemed to be a sailboat he had built; he was awaiting a buyer. In countries like Belize, no particular relationship exists between a gringo's income and how imaginatively he travels.

Wowlas and Coral

I'd come to meet Jan and Tineke Meerman, a stringbean fortyish couple from Holland who manage the twenty-two-thousand-acre Sarteneja Reserve surrounding the Shipstern Lagoon. It's owned by a group of Swiss butterfly fanciers, and Jan raises and mails out the pupae of perhaps thirty of the reserve's two hundred species to commercial butterfly farms in Europe (Britain alone has forty of these), where visitors enjoy the relaxing ambience of greenhouses full of tropical plants, waterfalls, and exotic birds. He can also, of course, cater to the bottomless market for dead butterflies, which are collected like stamps worldwide. But what has happened to Jan and Tineke—very tall, he wears a U-shaped beard; very precise, she clips her hair short; and they live by kerosene lamp in a former oil-drilling camp—corresponds to Sharon Matola's transformation from jaguar trainer to conservationist. Sharon dreamed of taming lions, back in Baltimore, and now is a front-line ecologist. Jan, a carpenter's son from Zeeland, the Netherlands, arrived in Belize as an amateur lepidopterist with some brief experience of wildlife work in Yemen and Tanzania. But in the process of going into the forest and marsh after butterflies (catching thirty quick species in any morning), and then to identify and dig up for his screened pens the food plants the larvae of each species eat, he, too, became a committed ecologist. He speaks of reintroducing howler monkeys to the eight thousand acres of gallery forest within the reserve, and of the necessary education program, which would involve the villages around. His recreation used to be collecting lucrative butterflies for the carriage trade—with a graceful tweaking motion he catches them by the wings between his fore- and middle fingers. Now it's sleeping on jaguar and puma trails in the rainy season, when the tracks show up well, listening to the cats roar or scream, and studying the habits of several individuals he knows.

Married nine years, Tineke and Jan are a good team and have a "night" dog and a "day" dog to perform different duties outdoors (bite and wag). They have a pet wowla, a small croc, some turtles, and a collared peccary. A Royal Air Force jeep stopped by with a Kew Gardens biochemist, who was studying how toxic butterflies build up their protective toxicity and how the plant that the Mayans ate to fight diabetes achieved its effect. We had a shrimp-and-grouper

343

dinner, and his military driver let me peruse a British Forces map. Then he solemnly took it back. "You have just read this map. Now I must kill you."

We talked about Belize's three coral snakes and four tommygoffs, and why hot countries have a slow pace, and how Mennonite apostates, as George put it, "try to get bad," going to bars, flirting clumsily.

We slept in the bunkhouse and in the morning walked the nature trail that Jan maintains, labeled with dozens of trees. Trumpet tree, bullet tree, mimosa, waterwood, poisonwood, strangler fig, chicle tree, cotton tree, gumbolimbo, mother-of-cocoa, royal palm, finger palm. Tiger heron, Tri-colored heron, Amazon kingfisher, pygmy kingfisher, curassow . . . the toll of birds we saw went on. Then we wound down the old Northern Highway, through a pleasant backwater of cane fields, little cattle ranches, shallow wetlands, and second-growth woods, back to Belize City, where a cabdriver excitedly hailed George to tell him that another driver, using George's other station wagon, had been arrested for running drugs. "He want you to bail him," he said. It seems that George's own good reputation had prevented the car from being impounded, however, and George was disinclined to extract the man from jail right away. The trouble was, George suggested, that jail was too soft. Imprisoned British soldiers are still forced to dig graves for a coffin full of stones and dig it up again, or to build a mountain of sand and run up and down with their packs on. *That* is jail, he said.

At the airport, Mennonites in severe frocks and blocky shoes were meeting new pilgrims from Canada, who looked as raptly distracted by God as they—while Trudy and I rendezvoused with our new guide, Neil Rogers. Neil, a rolling stone and Englishman with years of tourist herding in India under his narrow belt, seemed as symmetrical a type to my own as were the resident and visiting Mennonites. Sex in Belize City was "a melee, a free-for-all, bad for relationships," but he'd fallen in love with the co-owner of the Fort Street Guesthouse, he said. Life here was lived "on the knife edge," going either beautifully or awfully, which was how he preferred it. And I, too, am a professional traveler and only hope to die respectably of old age in my bed, not a suicide or the victim of a scary virus or a plane crash. Just as I like to eavesdrop to get an inkling of what is in store, Neil was eavesdropping upon us slinkily from behind a door as we approached, before introducing himself. He, too, had arrived "at loose ends" in this spot where reef divers "bubble around" and the sky seems so big and the world so small.

The ceiling fans, slotted blinds, the Doberman pinscher on guard against thieves, the tattooed Cockney paratroopers with pink rum punches on Fort Street, all are organized by Rita and Rachel from Colorado, who are known informally as "R. and R." Neil was lovesick (I, too, fall in love in foreign climes to anchor myself), so I went to see Alexander Featherstone at the U.S. Embassy, who told me the U.S.A. spends six and a half million dollars a year on Belize.

Travelers aim for salient sights and memorable days that slice through a cross-section of a new country. In the Pyrenees they want to spend a sunny hour with a goatherd who has been hiking these same meadows for a half a century; or they will barge in on a glass-blower on the island of Murano who's been doing that since before they were born. Spanish laceworkers who have gone blind making tablecloths in the service of m'lady; fisherfolk in the Bay of Fundy whose ancestors were riding the tides when King George squabbled with George Washington. Old wines, tapestries, porcelains, and cathedrals: Continuity and devotion are what tourists are after, because they're gone at home. Ah, the peasants in the fields, *they* still believe!

Of course, the rain forest is so old it's where snakes chose to lose their legs. They were originally lizards who found that wriggling on their bellies through the tumbled vegetation was faster to begin with. Animism, pythonic religion, a faith older than Christ or Moses, is what we look for in the jungle. Otherwise we want to chop it down.

Neil, in his Land Rover, sped us west from Belize City toward the Guatemalan border, an eighty-mile trip that till the 1930s could take two weeks of poling up the Belize River, with landings at Double Head Cabbage and More Tomorrow, at Burrel Boom, Dancing School Eddy, and Never Delay, at Black Man Eddy and Bullet Tree Falls. In the Valley of Peace, Salvadoran refugees grow peanuts. Neil spoke of the virginal spelunking in the mountains to the south, and maybe ten days' wilderness walking either north or south. His boss, Mick Fleming, at the Chaa Creek Lodge, where we were headed, had recently been on an expedition to a precipitous twist of the Raspaculo Branch of the Macal River, where no human beings may have set foot for a millennium.

Short of the Hawkesworth suspension bridge over the Macal River at San Ignacio, the British have their Holdfast Camp, with a few tanks and Harrier jump jets to foil a Guatemalan invasion. San Ignacio is a friendly Hispanic town surrounded by scenery, including Xunantunich, a Mayan ruin on the international border, and Mountain Pine Ridge, a large reach of high ground. Chaa (for Chocolate) Creek is an African-style lodge with round whitewashed thatched-roofed cottages, a raised patio for having drinks on, breadnut trees spreading overhead, with parrots and keel-billed toucans feeding in them, and the river flowing by in front. (Needs only a couple of hippos.) Mick left Uganda a few steps ahead of Idi Amin. He's English, and Lucy, his wife, is from New Jersey, and at supper, two of the guests, from Great Neck, Long Island, discussed whether their son should be sent to Yale or Princeton, while a retired British Signals light colonel with white mustaches told tales of India and Malaysia. "At my age I've got one foot on the bus stop and one foot in the grave," he said.

Next day, a retired British tank sergeant named Dick Strand, from Bath, took a group of us bumping by Land Rover to admire the thousand-foot Hidden Valley Falls on the Rio On, and then a sumptuous, arched-mouthed cave that the Rio Frío slips through, sandy-bottomed and radiant, tranquil in February, with leafy green backlighting at both ends, while the silent high ceiling seethed with black-and-white reflections of sun shafts glancing off the moving water. Strand took us up on the pine ridge to watch British cannon fire and see where survival teams live off iguanas, armadillos, and coatimundis. He has done this, and has five tours of duty in Northern Ireland to reflect on, plus better stints in Germany and Cyprus. But he came back, married a Belizean, fathered two daughters, and bought a comfortable house on which his property tax is twenty-seven dollars a year.

Next door to Chaa Creek Lodge, a herbalist from Chicago named Rosita Arvigo will give you a massage and an infusion of tonics learned from a genuine Mayan shaman near Xunantunich named Eligio Panti, who has been assisting the National Cancer Institute of the U.S. in collecting wild drugs. She has cleared out a "nature trail" in the bush, where you can examine rubber and allspice trees, mahogany and bay cedar, fiddlewood and custard apple, and the give-and-take tree, a handsome palm whose spines can deliver painful wounds that its own bark will cure. She's a tously, somewhat offish woman who lived for years with a tribe of Indians in Guerrero, Mexico, before moving here.

Neil then piled Trudy and me into a car and took us upriver till the track petered out on a fertile plain, by the Macal (which is named for the edible *macal,* or taro, plant), probably the site of the Mayan capital of Tipu, which was not decisively overrun by a Spanish expeditionary force until 1707. Previous campaigns had penetrated to Tipu in 1544, 1567, and 1608, but the Mayans succeeded in revolting in the 1630s. The classic-period sites of Tikal and Caracol, as well as Xunantunich, are not far off.

A young man, William Morales, met our jeep with his mule at a modest melon-and-squash farm, strapped our bags on the beast, and led us up a limestone gorge. The river sashayed, smiling, through tawny pools, past amber, white, and gray rock facings and forest patches, great sacred cotton "world trees," bullhoof trees (named for the shape of the leaves), tall palms, rosewood, fig, and Santa Maria trees, which were my favorites because the trunks are like oaks. Palmettos and ferns were underfoot, and vines draped everywhere, over tapir, deer, tayra, and agouti tracks. The river ran like puppies, leaping down rock ledges, with tarpon and snook in the quiet parts. "Gibnut" (agouti, a big rodent) is the national meat for Sunday "boil-ups," when everything goes in the pot—cassava, kidney beans, chilies, geese, rice, hog plums—and old-timers drink cashew wine, William said.

Most days, he rides seven miles at dawn to chain-saw a piece of the jungle for a hydroelectric project, hearing howler monkeys holler as he goes and comes; but his lungs were bothering him. We climbed a bluff to his parents' pretty farm at the lip of a waterfall on top. Antonio and Leah Morales had tried to raise cattle, but the jaguars kept killing their stock; now they were trying coffee. By candlelight we dined on homegrown corn, beans, peppers, chicken, pineapple, and coffee, and Antonio told how, when he and his brothers built watch fires to protect their cows, the biggest jaguar just sat down by one of them and warmed his back—then splashed vigorously through the stream when he saw a gun, his colors gorgeous in the firelight, and loped away. Even hunting opossums and white-lipped peccaries ("warree") for the pot is an adventure, because the men go barefoot at night on paths where tommygoffs are also hunting and will suddenly rise up—the proverbial "two-hour snake." Tommygoffs can give birth to as many as seventy young, and Antonio has seen one strike a gibnut just as he himself had drawn a bead.

Antonio is Belizean, born of Mexican and Guatemalan parents. Leah is Salvadoran, and she and her parents had to flee Honduras, too, during the so-called Soccer War in 1969, when twenty thousand Salvadorans and Hondurans died after a series of disputed games. The starlight and the silence, except for gouts of water going off the waterfall, set her story of being a refugee in relief.

In the morning's green-pink sunrise, with a hundred birds sounding like tin whistles and all the world a stage for them, Antonio led us through the woods—monkey bushes, ink plants, medicine trees, negrito trees—to a cave he'd found while gathering roof thatching and tie-tie vines. Head high once we'd crawled inside, it wound down for maybe two hundred yards, with stone shelving providing niches for occasional polychrome pots painted with monkeylike or humanoid figures, and even a few grains of corn remaining in them. There were a couple of low-ceilinged side chambers that you could scramble up into, marked by ceremonial fire rings (these caves were underworld religious sites, never places where Mayans slept), and behind an impressive stalactite an offshoot passage sloped into an ultimate cul-de-sac, which had an altar in it.

I'm crepuscular by nature and feel at peace in caves, and Antonio likes the night. He told about how as a child he'd led mule trains through the dark forest to the *chicleros'* camps, with just a bell mare to help him, the big cats never attacking. Starlight can belong to people too.

Soon we walked down the footpath to the canyon floor, with palm fronds clacking gently overhead, the pell-mell river swooshing by. A "Jesus Christ lizard" poised beside an eddy. (They run on their hind legs across a strip of water.) Neil was sitting hidden by the trail to eavesdrop upon us and, finding we were happy, put us in a Land Rover with a driver named Ricky Monzameros, who had grown up in Bullet Tree Falls, for the four-hour, fifty-mile drive to Tikal the next morning.

Ricky spoke English fluently, like a policeman, which he had been for five years. "Five years in the police and never arrested anybody. So nobody's mad," he said. He'd been stationed at Benque Viejo del Carmen, where Guatemala starts, so our entry was smooth.

Immediately the colorful poverty—the begging children in prismatic cottons—of Mesoamerica began. In Guatemala, wages can be a dollar or two a day, money is color coded because of illiteracy, and high-school graduates teach other children through the sixth grade. Teenage soldiers, green-clad, manned a roadblock, and a college student whom we picked up said that "if you stick your head up above the crowd, you'll just be another grave." Her father had been beaten to death by the police and then stuffed in the wreck of his car, which mysteriously went off the road.

A girl carried a string of fish in her hand; another, a cluster of bananas on her head; others balanced plastic water jugs. There were bicyclists, horsemen, donkeys toting sacks of corn. Very little vehicular traffic, though we saw a Ferris wheel set up alongside a general store, and brightly pink and chartreuse fundamentalist *iglesias*, for the ride to heaven, in between a long series of hand-to-mouth farms. Red shirts, red skirts. Insects sang. We jolted over the bulldozed road, and the Mopan River (which becomes the Belize) snaked slowly across swampland alongside, with waterbirds and waders all over, dashing ducks and solemn storks. Red-vented woodpeckers and white-collared seedeaters perched in the trees. We saw chestnut-bellied herons, green and red trogons, masked red tityras, yellow-lored parrots, and colonies of oropendola birds' stocking-looking nests, and an iguana in an *agate* tree. A truck full of cheese chips and pork rinds had tipped over in the soft dirt, and we saw a hunter with an old gun on his shoulder and a mongrel on a string.

Ricky's father was a hunter and a *chiclero* and taught him to find warree, gibnut, and "mountain cows" for the pot, and reptiles for their skins. At thirteen, Ricky was taught to climb and bleed a chicle tree by the traditional method—his father lit a fire under him, so he had to keep climbing. After the market for it died, they made their own gum by boiling chicle sap and pouring in a purple dye and Colgate toothpaste, for taste.

Of a philosophical turn of mind, he asked me, "In the world, Ted, are there more eyes or are there more leaves?"

"That's a good question, if you're counting insects' eyes," I said.

His tourists run to people who may be vacationing on Easter Island next Christmas, or Christmas Island next Easter, and talk to him of Machu Picchu and Botswana and Hyderabad, of real estate consortiums being reorganized, of rock stars dumping their managers. It being Sunday, we watched a mass baptism of adults on a scenic beach at Lake Petén. The young minister possessed a deeply cut, charismatic face, and the enthusiastic singing of his parishioners was gleeful, as baptisms ought to be.

Tikal was a major capital for a thousand years. In six square miles, three thousand remnant structures have been mapped. A million potsherds, a hundred thousand tools and other objects, have been unearthed. I climbed Temple IV and Temple I (a gray fox came out immediately to smell where I'd sat), saw the bronzy ocellated turkeys, the brachiating monkeys, the scarlet macaws, the floral extravaganza all about. "Undiscovered" until 1848, it seems as arbitrary a choice of site as, say, Manhattan. To try to think about the politics and commerce, astronomy and superstition, art, gardening, bombast, and war that had been concentrated in these blackened, seashell-smelling ruins would be fruit for years, and I was on a jaunt. I roamed the jungle, mused, and met a rare, white-and-black anteater, a magical sort of pandalike creature, gazed at the plazas, acropolises, and temples—a jaguar had recently borne a litter of young in one of them—and enjoyed the huge trees.

Back at Chaa Creek two days later, the supple Neil Rogers put Trudy and me into the hands of a driver named Elmo Richards, thirty-one, a friend of Ricky Monzameros's, who had grown up in a hamlet called Las Vegas, near Bullet Tree Falls. His father, too, had been a hunter, selling crocodile hides at three-fifty per foot, fer-de-lances for twelve dollars, boas for five dollars, puma skins for fifty dollars, and one-hole jaguars for seventy-five dollars. (Now a good woodsman is more likely to grow "Belize Breeze" in an off-road patch.) Whereas Ricky had escaped from his twig-fire village by joining the police, Elmo's way was more free-lance. He worked at first with his father in a slaughterhouse in San Ignacio (a hundred lambs a week for the British military), until, restless, he went to Los Angeles to visit a cousin. Like George Young—like so many Belizeans—he found the U.S. alarming, although watched relatives make a go of it. When he went outdoors, young toughs would home in on him, reaching for his beer money, his pizza money, asking, with death in their voices, whether he was a Crip or a Blood. Life was so cheap, and there seemed so little space for him to squeeze into, that he was relieved when his cousin simply gave him a secondhand truck to take back to San Ignacio. At the slaughterhouse, he would load it with meat and drive southeast to the coastal town of Dangriga, selling wholesale at every crossroads shop. In Dangriga he'd pick up a load of fish and start the return, a twelve-hour round trip. Because his sister had married a Dangriga politician, he was well rooted at either end.

Elmo, like Ricky, sympathetized with the U.D.P. party, opposing George Young's P.U.P. Party, which had recently won reelection after two years out of office. But as with George, politics made both of them uneasy. They didn't speak of possible violence, the way he did, but rather of bureaucratic retaliation in matters like a building permit, a tax reassessment. "They watch to see if you vote, because they know how you'll vote," Elmo said. When I asked him about the British, he told me they were O.K. when sober, but that in 1982 some of them had danced naked on a bar with some San Ignacio girls and had set off an all-night brawl in which four thousand people fought.

From the nondescript capital, Belmopan, a barracks village, we turned onto the so-called Hummingbird Highway, which is so rich in hummingbirds, orioles, laughing falcons, blue-crowned motmots, and swallow-tailed kites, the name seems not a hype. The gravel road swings past a dozen quick amber creeks, pocket valleys, mini-jungles, past grapefruit and lime groves and sweet-potato *milpas*. Good Living Camp. The Sibun River. Over-the-Top Camp. Alta Vista. We saw a drug czar's *finca*, a Hershey chocolate farm, a Nestlé orange-juice factory. The Maya Mountains to the west lent the scenery a panache, and finally we turned toward them and drove into the Cockscomb Basin Wildlife Sanctuary, 103,000 acres, named for the country's highest mountain (3,700 feet), whose profile is like a rooster's comb. Elmo, pleased with us, invited us to his family's next boil-up—his father dumped in pigs' tails, peppers, palm oil, chocolate, possums, bananas.

There were three cabins at the reserve, one for the wardens, one for us, and one for the three soldiers guarding us from bandits. Walking out, we swam idyllically in South Stann Creek under a spreading bri-bri tree and smelled the droves of warrees that had been eating palm nuts underneath the cohune trees. Elmo showed us tree rat, gibnut, gopher, bush dog, and ring-tailed cat tracks, plus a bullhoof root, such as he chews for a toothache, and "jackass bitters," a plant whose leaves when brewed relieve fevers. Soapseed, pimento trees, bay-leaf palm, laurel tree, Boy Job tree, My Lady tree.

The soldiers (Belize remains a democracy partly because it has only a six-hundred-man army) included a Creole corporal, tall, black, and street-smart, from Belize City; a slim, straight-shooting mestizo from Orange Walk, or "Rambo Town," as George Young had called it because of its drugs; and a Mayan from the Punta Gorda district. Kekchi and Mopan Mayans live here in the south. The four wardens were small-framed, muscular, round-faced Mopan Mayans, with the bark of woodsmanship on them, an air of watchful stillness, a less obtrusive body language, a different tempo of ears-eyes-nose observation. These canebrakes and "tumble" forests (called so because the hurricanes bowl them down) were their home, and like good wardens, they had hunted jaguars before the preserve was established, using a large gourd with buckskin drawn across its mouth, which grunted like a rutting *tigre* when you scratched your nails across the top. The Creole corporal, to my untutored eye, could have been Tanzanian; the mestizo could have been from Tijuana; and the Mayan serviceman had been assimilated to the point where he looked generically Amerindian—could have been in Arizona or South Dakota—but not these guys. Ignacio Pop, the head warden, was hide hunting a two days' walk from his village when a tommygoff bit him. Luckily, he says, he was not alone. His two friends packed him out to a logging road in the course of eleven hours and got him to a snake doctor, who cured him in about a week.

After a balmy night of insect songs and bat activity under the panoply of stars, and some more walking in the morning, Elmo drove us to Dangriga (a Garifuna word meaning "Standing Water"), whose population is climbing toward nine thousand. Sun-soaked in February, the reddish streets were a promenade for ladies carrying black umbrellas to block the heat. (The men we saw were mostly drunk.) We ate lunch in the Starlight Café, a Chinese restaurant with Christmas lights around the bar, next to the Local Motion disco and the Tropical Hotel. At night, Elmo said, some drugs or sex may be peddled, but in a more good-humored spirit than in Belize City. We heard that a local *obeah* man rises from the image of a coiled snake if you go to consult him in his cabin, that the boas grow venomous fangs at nightfall, and that a Welshwoman has been living alone in the mangrove swamps for two decades. Also an American lawyer. The Chinese fled here from the Japanese in World War II, and now a second wave is leaving Hong Kong in fear of the Communist takeover. Lebanese own many of the citrus farms. They arrived as storekeepers but have lately sold their businesses to "Hindoos" (East Indians), to become landowners. You see them less often, Elmo said, but everybody eats Chinese.

The Garifuna, or "Black Caribs," as the English called them, arrived on this coast in the early nineteenth century. They were seafarers, dugout paddlers, island raiders, cannibal warriors, whose name in the language of the Arawaks, the "Caribbean" tribe they preyed on, is where our word "cannibal" came from. Interestingly enough, only the men spoke Carib; the women, many of whom were captured Arawaks, spoke Arawak, until the languages blended. At the time of the European conquest, the Caribs, paddling from South America, had swept the Arawaks from the Lesser Antilles and were perhaps prepared to move on Haiti and Cuba. Instead they were decimated and temporarily given Saint Vincent's Island as a designated "Indian Territory," though scalawag French and English, and blacks from a slave ship that wrecked just off the island in 1675, joined the brew. The "Yellow Caribs," those with white blood, were permitted to stay, after the British reassumed control, but the Black Caribs were deported in 1797 to Roatán, an island off Honduras, and some wandered here to the mouth of Stann Creek, a former trading post set up by English Puritans from Nassau, whom the Spanish had evicted. The Mayans still seem metaphorically stunned at their self-inflicted decline as a civilization, which began five hundred years before Columbus, but the Garifuna, whose "Carib" conquest of the Caribbean was arrested at full tilt by the English, French, and Spanish, have energy to spare. They go to sea, or colonize Brooklyn (which has more Garifuna than Belize), or become schoolteachers, merchants, government clerks.

In Belize we are thrust into the climate in which we were born—body temperature, like the womb, like Olduvai Gorge. And the pyramids have such basic forces inscribed on them as the Sun, Maize, the Tiger, the Croc. Friends whom I met in Belize City like to swim nude every morning near the mouth of the brawny Belize River, five fathoms deep, where it enters the sea and dolphins and sharks and whatnot show up, fast mountain currents joining the punch of the tide.

Stann Creek and Dangriga are gentler. We hired a boat from Ringo Usher, the son of the local dentist, and headed twelve miles out to Tobacco Cay, a seven-acre island where those seventeenth-century Puritans grew tobacco and where Garifuna turtlers later settled, with a church and a school. Ringo and his father are building tourist cottages in Dangriga, and Ringo has found a dozen mangrove trees growing on a patch of reef unclaimed by anybody and, by placing drift logs in such a way as to trap coral sand washed into these shoals, is constructing a beach for more cabins. He showed us, en route. All up and down this coast, old sea-snake and saltwater-crocodile islets are being converted to money, though we did see one that has been preserved for the boobies and frigate birds to nest on. Hundreds wheeled over it; landed to roost; flew up. At one end was a special tree, where, Ringo said, the birds went to sit when they were sick and preparing to die.

The frigate birds steal fish from the boobies by "beating on them till they spit it up," as Ringo said, and we saw other avian or piscine dramas. Ospreys diving. Herons. Water birds, from limpkins to soras, from loons to grebes to whistling swans, have celebrative cries, saluting the dawn or the rising moon as if God were alive in the world. But we—lizards that we are—tend to hoard the sun, gaze out with a basilisk's impassive stare from our beach towel, when we are by the water, bathing in a kind of fugue of memories while feeding heat to our cold bones. And the breaking surf eases our hearts. *Thump. Thump.* Its failure to accomplish anything except in a cosmic time frame is comforting, yet the energy soothes and reassures us.

Tobacco Cay sits right atop Columbus Reef, so swimming from the beach, you can dive a few fathoms down the splendidly awesome wall of that, or else paddle about in the extensive shallows on top. Or you can do what I did, which was to step from Ringo's skiff straight into the hammock that Winnie and Nolan Jackson, his grandparents, have rigged on their dock and stay there awhile. The surf thundered hard, the wind blew boisterously, the sun skidded off the tossing waves. With a bit of thatch shading me, I was in heaven, though Nolan grumped that if the wind always blew like this, "we would go crazy."

It was suppertime, and going off to collect two lobsters from one of his traps for Trudy and me to eat, Nolan remarked over his shoulder, "It's a shame these poor lobsters have to die for you," a sentiment I've often shared, watching diners stuff themselves in restaurants on Cape Cod. Because Nolan didn't know us from Adam, his grouchiness seemed refreshing. People come to his hammock and little hotel for their honeymoons or divorces or a cancer recuperation or to celebrate a cash bonus, dressing in beachcombers' "sweats" as if they were pleasantly indigent. Winnie said she'd moved out here for her asthma, but demurred when we complimented the view. "It's just pretty; it's not beautiful," she said.

She baked johnnycake, fried plantains, and boiled rice and beans to go with the lobsters, while the wind blew pelagically, the thatch over us rattled, and the Atlantic crashed against the rim of the reef a short distance away. You could see why these Belizeans didn't need to be pirates at heart to find plenty of wrecks to pick over and drowned bodies to strip and dump back for the sharks. The Black Caribs who had fought subjugation on Saint Vincent's Island, the rebel Mayans who had revolted and fled to Belize from defeats in Quintana Roo, and the Jolly Roger crew of Englishmen raiding Spanish shipping from the mouths of Belize's rivers must have blended in the mind's eye of their contemporaries remarkably.

Nolan grew up on an island on Glover's Reef, which is eighteen miles farther out, an island he says his brother has now "thrown away to an American for seventy-five thousand dollars." Nolan himself shipped out on Liberty ships in 1945 with Panamanian papers to see the world. Making friends, he soon acquired a dead American's papers, too, and worked on American ships as "Josnik Kowalski," pretending his accent and darkish skin were Polish in origin, at twice the money. For seven years he traveled to Europe and the Far East, a deckhand in the summer, a fireman in the warm engine room when the weather turned cold, and stayed at the Seamen's Church Institute in New York, taking astronomy courses and studying for a mate's license between jobs. It was a fine spell, but so many regular navy men were demobilized that ships became hard to find. He remembers the brutal glitter of New York with a certain startled pleasure—the "rum shops" selling beer "for a shilling" (twenty-five cents) and "people getting drinks off you," the museums, the social possibilities, the excitement of the uptown streets, the breakneck competition—but marginal folk like him felt crowded out.

He came back to Glover's Reef and fished for red snapper, grouper, and tuna, till he lost his boat off the beach one night in 1978 when a north wind blew and he couldn't afford to buy another. Tobacco Cay, where he and Winnie started over, had been Winnie's grandparents' home, though "if you lived here you were nothing," she says. "If you lived in town you were something." Back when tortoise shell was worth ten dollars a pound, the village sent two big schooners down the Mosquito Coast to Nicaragua, after hawksbill turtles, and it still harbors a few fishing smacks. Though small and closely inhabited, built up with holiday houses, Tobacco Cay has a nesting pair of ospreys, sixty feet up in a coconut palm, and catbirds, tanagers, grackles, turnstones, pelicans, herons—and almond trees, papayas, sea grapes, under the sloping palms. The houses have solar panels for electricity, and tubing to carry rain water from the roofs to cisterns for storage. In these overfished waters, "sometimes nothing is left but your tan," Nolan says, but he remembers the bums sleeping in Central Park in December, their legs cased in newspapers that turned hard like plaster by morning because of the body's frozen moisture; they had to "break out."

I roamed the island, ringed with bleached conch shells, admiring the palm trees' idiosyncratic, windblown slant, and imagined drifting ashore here as a castaway, famished with thirst, and trying to crack open a coconut for water to survive, then hoping that another would fall before I collapsed. I swam, lazed in the hammock, and met Elwood and Sandra Fairweather, Belizeans who, like Nolan Jackson, made me a bit homesick. Elwood, in a foundered leather easy chair next to his beach shack, said in a gravelly, impenitent voice: "Twenty-eight years in New York." He and Sandra, a pretty woman with a red ribbon in her hair, had been married fifteen years and had just had a baby daughter. Sandra laughed at how long they'd delayed, and showed me some charcoal drawings she'd made, and a jaguar cub skin. Elwood has three grown kids from his first marriage, to an Italian woman in Brooklyn; he'd worked in a bookstore for eight years and then as a typographer, until computers made him redundant.

I sat in a broken wooden chair seat next to him and met his chums who wandered by: a dugout lobster fisherman, a diving guide, a buffaloed Texan, who had sailed down here from Galveston and had just lost the motor off his boat. It had dropped off the stern into three fathoms, and he had a charter arriving, a woman from Minneapolis— what would she think? Would she advance him money? Elwood dispensed a fatalistic calm. In New York he'd haunted Greenwich Village, he said, "and generally was a beatnik." Bleecker Street, the New School, Saint Mark's Place, Washington Square—we found we'd shared some city sites and obsessions of the sixties; and like Nolan, he didn't seem to have returned to Dangriga by fervent choice.

Raw rubber, Scotch, and lumber used to be scavenged from wartime wrecks on the reef when he was a child, and now drug boats are sometimes scuttled there for insurance money; people scavenge furnishings from them. Elwood's ancestors fought the Spanish at Saint George's Cay in 1798. Later another, as treasurer, signed British

Honduras's paper money. His father is a distinguished Anglican minister, who worked in New York for many years and whom I visited at the cathedral in Belize City. But with that lineage also goes the proud tradition of "going for a stick"—a cotton tree—for a dugout canoe, precursor of the Garifunas' seamanship, as well as the *obeah* stories. Even in New York, Elwood told me, an *obeah* woman can retain her powers—walk down the street with a gold chain on, and no snatcher will grab it lest it turn into a poisonous serpent in his hands. (He'll drop it in horror, and she'll stoop down and pick it up and it will be gold once again.) One *obeah* man, however, got his comeuppance, despite his supernatural powers. He liked to sleep with married women, after first slipping out of his skin so they didn't know who he really was. But he ran afoul of a clever husband who discovered where the *obeah* man had hidden his skin, and sprinkled salt on it, so that it shrank. The poor lover snuck back from his dalliance and couldn't put it on. It didn't fit! *Skinnee, Skinnee, Skinnee, don't you know me?* he cried—a song still sung by schoolkids.

Sandra, who is a dancer and a Belize City Creole, not a Garifuna, draws some wicked-looking nudes, and there are Garifuna stories of young girls propitiatorily fed to crocodiles. These perhaps balance the apparent likelihood that Garifuna men who captured Arawak women for wives in pre-Columbian times first ate the Arawak husbands, thus adding a certain vividness to life and making the victory memorable. Though not much more than do the gastronomical rituals of success and failure in New York.

We tourists wear bifocals. Pious about the survival of the sixty species of coral in the Caribbean, we nonetheless want a strobe-light vacation, both light and dark. "Ecotourism," and yet malice aforethought for when we get back and begin scrambling for money and status again. Eat well, dress well, and strip the earth to pay for it—and not just for lucre, but for the endless OJ and burgers grown in the tropics on bulldozed rain forest, the gas guzzling, shrimp guzzling, resort rambling. Tourists come from consuming countries, and once they pass Passport Control and get home again, they are Central America's problem, not yet its solution.

(1992)

I Have Seen the Elephant

Towns exist north of the Arctic Circle, and not just prefabricated white-men's towns; the Arctic has been inhabited for many thousands of years. But Antarctica is different. Individual people couldn't set foot and begin to survive there until the early nineteenth century, when they had sophisticated means to sail away immediately again. Besides, Antarctica is a mountainous continent that is believed to have sheared off of Australia as much as eighty-five million years ago, instead of a gigantic cap of ice that sits atop an ocean, as the core of the Arctic is; and therefore Antarctica manufactures its own gelid, horrendous weather, insulated by hundreds of miles of pitching ocean on all sides, instead of borrowing the climate patterns of neighboring continents and blending and chilling them, as the Arctic does. And Antarctica has no land mammals, no caribou, moose, musk oxen, polar bears, grizzlies, white wolves, hares, lemmings, foxes, as large regions above the Arctic Circle do. Only sea creatures make fitful visits to its margins (how *would* an Eskimo have lived there?), which makes its sometimes tumultuous landscape seem even starker in the mind's eye than the Arctic's pale terrain.

359

To get to Antarctica, you fly south from Miami for eight hours over the length of South America to the international city of Buenos Aires. Then you fly on again for four or five more hours, over the pampas and over Patagonia, and the strait discovered by Ferdinand Magellan in 1520, to Tierra del Fuego, and finally land in the windy frontier settlement of Ushuaia ("Ooshway-a"), Argentina's southernmost, which fronts Charles Darwin's fabled Beagle Channel. The little cruise ships that briefly flirt with the Antarctic Peninsula (the "banana belt" of Antarctica), whose northern tip still lies seven hundred miles away, beyond Cape Horn and across stormy Drake Passage, between the Atlantic and Pacific—which Sir Francis Drake blundered upon fifty-eight years after Magellan's tamer discovery—tie up here.

Mine was a stubby, two-thousand-ton, thirty-eight-passenger, ice-hardened Russian research vessel, the *Professor Molchanov*. The professor had been a distinguished Soviet atmospheric scientist who was murdered by Stalin's NKVD during the Nazi siege of Leningrad but whose reputation was later "rehabilitated"; and it is characteristic that the Russian government, now desperate for dollars, is converting even their arctic-weather ships to carry bevies of American trippers to the Antarctic, and that the few other passengers on the *Professor Molchanov* were Germans: like the Russians, a recently defeated people whose principal task dictated by the victors was that they learn English. The *Professor Molchanov* had been leased by two entrepreneurs in Connecticut and then re-leased by them to a retailing outfit, Mountain Travel, with offices near Berkeley, California, which had provisioned it in Hamburg, Germany. It was half empty, however, because of competition from the *Vavolov*, a bigger sister ship, and the *Kapitan Khlebuikov*, equipped with survey helicopters, as well as the four-hundred-passenger *Marco Polo* (formerly the *Alexander Pushkin*), the two-hundred-and-fifty-passenger *Bremen*, the St. Louis–owned *Discoverer*, the New York–owned *Explorer*, the New Zealand–owned *Asiatic*, and so on. A new destination creates a scramble.

Ushuaia, surrounded by snowy, stunted mountains, and a low timberline, resembles an Alaskan coastal town, with its hasty housing, higgledy-piggledy storefronts, and thrown-up hoardings, the off-road three-wheelers sharing the sparse streets with regular autos, the malamute prints hardened into a stretch of sidewalk paving, and the varied, occasionally Indian-looking faces. Two huge Japanese drift-net trawlers, the *Kongo* and the *Yamato*, were tied up along the single wharf, opposite the *Bremen* and my *Professor Molchanov*. This had been a convict town, and Tierra del Fuego was Argentina's Siberia, after the Yahgans, the indigenous people who hollered so vigorously at Darwin and at Robert Fitzroy, the captain of the *Beagle* in that winter of 1832–33, succumbed to European diseases, rifles, liquor, and whatnot. (Their signal fires gave Tierra del Fuego its name.) Then Ushuaia somewhat resumed its role as a prison colony during the terrible years of the junta in the 1970s, when political prisoners, if they were lucky, were exiled here. But mainly the population is descended from nearly two centuries' worth of sailors, stowaways, and other human flotsam who jumped ship or were jettisoned by their skippers in rounding Cape Horn, such as you will see washed up in other end-of-the-world ports. The "Roaring Forties" and "Screaming Fifties" these extreme latitudes were called—though you don't reach the Antarctic Circle itself until you're at sixty-six and one-half degrees south—and surviving them at all in a sailing ship was surely enough of a pedigree to hoist a beer here.

Wind shear, in this nervous, penultimate climate, made the short, gusty airstrip a bit hairy. In town, I went to Tante Elvira's, a restaurant in a gray shack on the main street that I'd heard about from a friend who lives in Topeka, Kansas, and enjoyed crab bisque, sourdough bread, and three-cheese "butter," sitting next to two local nuns, who couldn't persuade the proprietor to take their money. I got on the ship with the pilot, who was saturnine, wiry, grizzled-haired, his English resembling the sort of a seafaring Spaniard who is posted next to Gibraltar. Chile and Argentina had recently been squabbling over these scant, cold archipelagos to such a breaking point that the Pope in Rome needed to be brought in to mediate a compromise. Looking across the Beagle Channel at Navarino Island, which belongs to Chile, and at a Chilean gunboat prowling by, the pilot ventured a joke about the military mind—his own nation's as well as theirs.

Our skipper, Gennadiy Nikitin, was a young thirty-nine, both agile and stooped in his posture, rather gentle-faced, wearing jeans and a sweater, and shyly friendly to the passengers. At first the mates and helmsman had seemed more officious. "I'm Gennadiy," he said, and told me he'd served as a bridge officer on an auxiliary frigate in the Soviet fleet before transferring to civilian ships like the *Professor Molchanov*. "On the little boats in the navy they didn't notice me as much, so it was easier to leave."

The whipsaw winds, the piebald sky deepening to a red sunset, the choppy mountains separated by blunt dogleg valleys, all had a provisional quality, as though a bouncing gale or a summer snowstorm or blind-man's fog could blow in from any direction while you weren't looking. Navarino Island, which is even more sparsely populated than Tierra del Fuego, conveyed the same brink-of-the-world severity, rolling from its shingle beaches up toward an interior that you knew was quite shallow, before the melodramas of the Southern Ocean began.

The Yahgans had built dozens of bonfires along Beagle Channel, so I peopled the narrow beaches and brushy cliffs and darkish coves that we were passing, once we'd cast off, with these. The Yahgans had been a naked, canoeing people, estimated at six thousand, and are reckoned to have been among the most primitive people on earth when Darwin, then twenty-three, saw them—far inferior to Eskimos, for example, in their level of craftsmanship. They fought by throwing stones, never having invented spears or bows; didn't know how to thatch a hut for shelter from the year-round storms, living instead in flimsy grass "wigwams"; and had no priests, chiefs, or artisans: in fact, no word for the concept of "God," though a missionary did record a Yahgan language totaling over thirty thousand words. They were preyed upon by a local forest tribe, called the Onas, who were larger in stature, used better weapons, built better housing, painted themselves, and—though the Onas never ventured out onto the water—at least by wearing guanaco skins on their bodies and as hats and shoes, had invented clothes.

Standing next to me on Gennadiy's bridge was a housewife in her late fifties, married to a chemical engineer for Clorox, who said that she was making this trip partly in memory of her father, a naval architect who had designed engine rooms and had always wanted to see the White Continent himself. Another woman, late forties, was a bank vice president, single, with a doctorate in American history. She wanted to experience Antarctica as the exemplar of solitude, "the best substitute for voyaging in space." And there was a widower, a power-company president from Iowa who was wetting his feet in the new world of recreational adventure for the first time, as we steamed eastward down Darwin's channel. He was an exception to the rule that Antarctica visitors are sophisticates who have not only already been to Paris and Venice, but have rafted and trekked in Papua New Guinea and Bhutan. (The banker had toured Vietnam on her own last year.) When I asked, "Why Antarctica?" he said his friends at the Rotary Club had asked him the same. "I'll tell you later, when I've seen it," he said rather tentatively, because his wife of forty years was dead and he wasn't convinced yet about any of the choices he was trying to make.

Our ironic pilot's job was negotiating dryly with the various Chilean and Argentinean gunboats we passed, and with the Chilean navy base at Puerto William, as much as calibrating our route. We saw very few lights, so I could fantasize that the Yahgans, southernmost humans in the world, still lurked along shore. Perforce a littoral people, they lived in fear of the woodsy, valley-dwelling Onas on the Tierra del Fuego side, but when a European castaway floated off a shipwreck, they toyed with and tortured him; might burn and eat him. Aiming for the eyes, they were terrific stone throwers, if landing parties tried to rescue him, but ordinarily lived on mussels, birds, turtles, birds' eggs, turtles' eggs. They hunted seals with clubs or ate dead creatures that washed up on the beach, and fished with lines that the women plaited from their own hair. I scanned the steeply darkening, grass-topped mountains, imagining signal fires and hollers that would be exasperating and barbaric, if you had reason to be afraid of them.

We saw the tiny lights of several sheep stations and dropped the pilot near Picton Island—"Five people and a quarter million sheep," he said. I then slept a few hours, till at around two-thirty the dawn began to finger a low band of the sky with apricot and peach colors, when we were some miles off the Gibraltar-like bulk of Cape Horn—which is itself an island, longish and high-ended.

The seas now flexed in a whimsical, hard-slamming rumpus like Goliath on a binge, unimpeded by any mass of land separating the two oceans that ran east and west around the globe. The horizon tilted precipitously, and we experienced double gravity in alternation with weightlessness every twelve or thirteen seconds. The floor kept rising under my feet and tipping me back into my bunk, or altering the position of my pant legs as I tried to get dressed. The purple sea turned glinty gray, pitching us about like a double-jointed seesaw, an unhinged carousel.

"Rock and roll," Chuck Cross, our expedition leader, called it. And Greg Myer, our birding guide, who was from California, said that the rough handling we would get from this Drake Passage across the fabled Southern Ocean was how we'd "earn Antarctica." Sometimes tourists complain that they can't just fly from Tierra del Fuego and skip the nausea of the Screaming Fifties, but another of our "lecturers"—as these young chip-on-the-shoulder escorts who accompany trippers to far-flung spots are called—was a spirited Brazilian, Suzana d'Oliveira, and she said she had watched as twenty-two of "her" tourists died in a crash at Puerto William, the short Chilean airstrip, like Ushuaia's, on the Beagle Channel. Their charter plane couldn't stop on the tarmac and slid into the water like a rocking horse. At the front, the food cart blocked one exit and an emergency chute at the rear inflated too soon and blocked the other. She'd flown in on the first trip, "with the baggage and the Germans," and, being a vigorous, resourceful woman, she ran, swam, and climbed up onto the wing and pounded at the chute even as the passengers were drowning inside.

(The father of a friend of mine, as I learned later, happened to be on that plane, and survived by quickly making for the rear when he saw the fatal food cart, and dragged his wife and several others out before the chute inflated. Once outside, while they were babbling in relief, he discovered that he had already saved the life of one of these strangers before. They'd been shipmates on a subchaser that had sunk in a typhoon off Ulithi Isle in the Yap Island chain before the invasion of Iwo Jima in 1945.)

The seas swung like five pendulums at cross-purposes; and, fighting the floor, which lifted and fell away right when I'd calculated that it might plan to stay where it was, I conceived a particular love for my bed. It was a day to lose a pound. Seasickness knocked the jet lag out of me like pneumonia supplanting a common cold. From the poop deck I watched giant petrels kiting in the wind and a wandering albatross sailing tirelessly with locked wings. An hourglass dolphin porpoised through the water and two rockhopper penguins were doing the same. I remembered my first intercontinental sea voyage from Manhattan to Lisbon and Palermo, on my honeymoon in 1960.

The ship creaked. The Russian crew, ice hardened, was from Murmansk, though Sergey, the sallow-skinned radioman, was Belarussian in ethnicity, and Dalî, the bartender, was Georgian—a very angry Georgian because she'd been at home visiting her family during the bitter fighting four months before in Sukhumi. Shells had hit her house, her brother was killed in the battle, and Dalî ran through forests and brambles to save her life, collecting bruises that she could show me still. Their wages were microscopic, ranging from six dollars a day for an able-bodied seaman to sixteen dollars for our excellent captain, and so by the end of the voyage we travelers were giving away everything we thought that we could—in my case, my boots, raincoat, hat, shirts, and socks. I teased Gennadiy that the *Professor Molchanov* was togged out like a spy ship because of the electronics with which it did research when not ferrying rich Americans. He'd hung off Cuba and Cape Canaveral on real spy ships, but had never landed on American soil. His complexity pleased me—a democrat whose father had spent twenty-three years in Siberia for political incorrectness but who, when talk turned to rebuilding the new Russia, quoted Genghis Khan. Like the rest of the crew, he despised both Mikhail Gorbachev and Boris Yeltsin. War was inevitable; there would always be war; Gorbachev hadn't forestalled the threat of war, Gennadiy said.

We travel partly to define ourselves and flesh out who we are, or else perhaps to try to fulfill an authentic passion (icebergs, flamenco, Alfred Sisley, whatever it is)—or to heal a central puzzlement, a grief, or a defeat, bursting a chrysalis that has held us back so we can begin anew. This is ambitious, exhausting travel, after a divorce or death, but other people travel to try to shore up their sense of domesticity, seeking a frisson of physical danger to reassure themselves that they're still spry, while amassing a secret store of shimmering memories to draw upon when immersed back home. Still others simply want to sound more interesting when asked where they've been.

The Drake Passage was stern medicine, hard too on the crew and the ship, which, under their present charter arrangements, shuttled continually back and forth across it every two weeks every year from November to April. We shuddered as if the ship were an old saddle bronco, as used to the jarring, stiff-legged hullabaloo of a rodeo as any wrangler. The hours progressively seemed to lower my braincase down onto the back of my eyeballs and the roof of my mouth and herniated my stomach into a sore, sour knot. The waves were like an out-of-sync trampoline, but then amidst coruscating sunshine, two finback whales emerged like sudden embolisms, utter masters of that same rhythm, as they rolled, breached, and blew. Much in the way we don't swallow at the same time as we take a breath, the whales effortlessly factored every unsynchronous heave into the tempo of their spouts. The spray thrown up by our bow created falling rainbows.

I was glad to sleep in bouts of a couple of hours so as to miss less, going up on deck in between. My dreams, however, were scary ones, as if to acknowledge that we were on our way to the White Continent. Yet they weren't about the tides or ice—no foundering ship and sleety, sloshing lifeboats under the lee of a titanic iceberg. Instead they went back to my late adolescence and the circus tigers I had cared for as part of a summer job. Hip-high and pungent, they stalked the floor so close to me that their bristling whiskers brushed my arm; the hair in the small of my back was electrified. Then, abruptly, in the way dreams have, a surreal telescoping of forty years occurred, to the corrosive, poignant, heart-palpitating death of my quarter-century marriage and, later, my wife's losing struggle with cancer, whose final stages I nevertheless witnessed from beside her bed. Not *all* of this, of course, but a swift unnerving silhouette of her in anger, ill health, and distress that packed a wallop and sent me up to walk the deck. I'd had a recent siege of semi-blindness myself, and my surgeon had told me after operating that I should see whatever I wanted to of the world before my difficulties recurred. So here I was, gorging my eyes on the slanting, kiting birds, the flux of black geometric waves in endless mad triangles, and the first drifting icebergs—absurdist cubes, sliced with a cake knife and white as snow—cruising the Southern Ocean (benign-sounding name!), where the Indian, Atlantic, and Pacific oceans converge, shrapneling storms with a clockwise spin: but not really concerned about a maritime disaster or any considered action of my own, just my inner baggage.

When on the open deck, I treated the rail in the rather affectionate, gingerly manner I'd perfected for tigers, staying a little bit out of reach, admiring the glistering sea without leaning right over the maw of the rushing waves. Ever since I was fifteen and went on a voyage with my father from Bayonne, New Jersey, to Galveston, Texas, on an Esso oil tanker, I've had a kind of "secret sharer" who wants to slide inconspicuously over the side of a ship, or the edge of a cliff. Unlike in Joseph Conrad's novel, he never does, so I've never been rid of him. An overriding impulse sustained for just a moment might do it, and in Antarctic waters, the act would be irreversible. You couldn't bob up to wave an arm and shout, "Throw me a line"—though I *would* change my mind. Thus I moved along toward the enclosed bridge lightly like a spectator, not hypnotized like the proverbial bird drawn to a snake. I was bored by my handicap and had survived and enjoyed two weeks on the Bering Sea not many years before, where the absurd narcissism and blind solipsism of a frivolous act of suicide would also have been thrown into relief: self-destruction in the midst of prehistoric, vaulting grandeur. But I was on this trip for keeps. If my mind skidded out of kilter in the next fortnight, there wasn't any sanatorium to check into, only the vertigo of the bucking wind, the slamming sea, the cryptic sky, the haunting grisly icebergs jostling one another in a slot between colliding banks of fog. And my mouth tasted of vomit, not majesty.

But I loved the pretty, flickering, brown-and-white, almost-speckled birds known as pintado petrels that materialized alongside us in numbers by the second day, swooping at the krill our ship turned up. Also blue and Wilson's storm petrels, and prions, fulmars, and black-browed albatrosses, lofting me with a jiggling gaiety, a certainty that I was in the right place. So often, indeed, there's a disjunction between the sights one sees and the taste in one's mouth: unutterable beauty to gorge upon, and yet seasickness; or, at the other extreme, a delicious meal in a scrumptious restaurant, when you're sitting across the table from people who are both miserable and dislikable. In the shaving mirror in my cabin, I was startled to discover that I had turned white-haired since my last ocean voyage, which had been on the *Discoverer* out of Nome. Exhaustion, nausea, dysentery, an unshakable cough, or a lady-or-the-tiger sense of imminent possibilities have gone with more than a few of my richer experiences, so it seemed natural to tiptoe alongside the shuddering rail, while en route to the one polar continent.

Wham-bam waves splashed over the bow, spraying the bridge windows dramatically. We had a two-hundred-degree, glassed-in view, and a cherrywood table with drawers full of Soviet and British Admiralty charts to pore over, plus the round radar scope that when peered into looked like a planetarium ceiling on which new icebergs began showing up like spatterings of stars. We heard occasional "growlers"— chunks of floating pack ice—scrape noisily along our hull, and saw "bergy bits," the next size up, which might stand a dozen feet out of the water, not heroic statuary like the genuine "tabular" icebergs. Flat walled, flat topped, and about a hundred feet high, these monumental constructions, sometimes castellated or jaggedly eroded or gigantically cubic, had calved off the Larsen Ice Shelf, hundreds of miles away in the Weddell Sea. We encountered them as we got within fifty miles of the first of the South Shetland Islands.

For ten or fifteen hours we sailed past spellbinding flotillas— dozens, and then more dozens. Big as a building, or a city block, or an entire neighborhood, each specimen was cut slightly differently, unevenly white with granular seams of blue or platinum, and a few had flipped over during a storm and been scrubbed at, top and bottom, by the waves. They were rounded, creased, shelved, and their patina of immaculate white had been stained with ancient interior dirt that had melted out. Their surfaces were marred by protuberances, tincolored, lead-colored, which lent them an aura of mortality. Though hard as concrete, they weren't frozen cubes, unearthly and uncompromising. They were now *aging* and could start to sing to our intuitions.

The Arctic, too, proffers this lavish plethora of white, but the Arctic has been inhabited for milllennia and is a country of myth and mysticism, anthropomorphic gods and mammalian dangers, whereas Antarctica boasts a tumultuous landscape where even moss and lichens are barely present, and seabirds and sea creatures make only fitful visits. The lore is instead top-heavy with the feats of breast-beating European explorers. So you have something different—on the order of another planet—where penguins arrive as from a space-ship every November to land on certain ice-bare beaches for egg-lay-ing. Yet twenty-six nations have established fifty research stations for human occupancy, laying claim to zones of influence, should the con-tinent's mineral resources be opened to exploitation.

We were now well inside the winter rim of the pack ice, which waxes and wanes hundreds of miles every year, and thus sailing on borrowed time. Perhaps because I'm a professor myself, my thoughts kept straying to our namesake professor, Molchanov, who had been shot in the head by one of his police guards as he lay in shackles in the snow on frozen Lake Ladoga, outside Leningrad. I couldn't re-construct how weakened by hunger and beatings he may have been, or whether he had been arrested in a general roundup of intellectuals or targeted because he was a scientist of repute who had attended in-ternational conferences, amassed a file of correspondence with col-leagues in other countries, and participated with them in some of the pioneering weather flights of the German dirigible *Graf Zeppelin*.

"He was shotten. He got died," Gennadiy said, remembering his own father's tale of a forced march from the Ural Mountains, where their family had been rich landowners, to northwestern Siberia as a boy of eleven, accompanied by his grandmother. In his years in Arctic Siberia, he had become a construction supervisor of such acumen that he won permission to move to Murmansk and build shipyards there, where he married. Gennadiy, born after World War II, enrolled in the Naval Academy at age seventeen and after eight years of service off Africa and America transferred to nonmilitary duty. He was a quick study at learning English—as he must have been at maritime science to become a captain so soon—and later he asked if I would help him translate a family memoir he was writing. His mother lived in a three-room cabin on a dab of their old property in the Urals, where, unmar-ried, he spent his leaves. Unassuming, although his bashfulness was a form of civility with these American guests, he told me that a psychological "sickness" had overwhelmed the Russian people. Even the educated ones were reading trash to distract themselves from the collapse of their country and "bury their heads in the sand." He himself was happier at the ends of the earth, meeting Americans, seeing the terrain, and reading the Russian classics in his cabin, though he didn't yet know Nabokov and said that he thought writers like Pasternak and Solzhenitsyn were "too angry." His gently gloved comments reminded me of a favorite teacher I had had, but then he'd startle me with a conquistador quotation from Alexander the Great, or a remark about women, when I asked if he was married: "Women are like a ship," he said. "They may look different, but they all work the same."

Two mornings south of Cape Horn, using the inflatable rubber, outboard-driven minicraft known as Zodiacs, we landed on a little shingly ironstone beach on a steep slope of Joinville Island, a tip of the submerged Andes just off the Antarctic Peninsula. Bouldery gravel from higher up lay on the remnant ice just above us, with cleaner swatches of bright white snow left by the miniature slides that had occurred in the summer thaw. A small colony of gentoo penguins was nesting here, several hundred creating a steady racket of cries, which were mostly unrelated to us. They were jockeying with and encouraging one another, yet the space that they had, bare of snow, was so very limited they seemed terribly vulnerable. Gentoos are the "mellowest" species of penguins, Greg Myer said, and though obviously uneasy they were not panicked by the arrival of twenty human beings on their tiny beach. Penguins' predators are leopard seals and killer whales, which hunt them in the deep, and ravenlike birds called skuas that cruise overhead to steal their eggs or seize their chicks when they are ashore. So they have no instinctive fear of an apparition approaching on foot during this relatively short period of the year when they are beached.

I sat down in the cheek-by-jowl congestion on this sparse scoop of stones and sand. In fact, I disapproved of our being on Joinville Island at all, now that I was here. It was too small for the penguins to be subjected to a crowd of people—we had all the rest of the world. Yet I was excited to be thrust among my first penguins in Antarctica, as if thousands of preceding millennia hadn't yet happened. The island rattled with subsurface meltwater and diverse rocky trickles and a spindly waterfall. Where moisture sheltered minute growths of moss, it was faintly green, but mostly the slopes were dirty white, cut by rust-colored outcroppings or scree. By the penguins' roosts you could see lightish red stains in the snow from the krill in the birds' guano. Krill are the inch-long crustaceans that during the sun-shot January summer grow in extraordinary masses underwater, weighing as much as thirty pounds per cubic yard.

My pity for the penguins was not based on there being a great shortage of them. The massacre of most of the world's krill-eating whales has been a boon to penguins because of the new abundance of food. Nor does Antarctica present a shortage of beaches in this brief window of weeks when they can hatch their eggs and nurture their chicks. The beaches are few but Antarctica is big, so there are extra beaches. The chicks were pretty large by now, January 17—astir and standing up, although still fuzzy and an infantile brownish silvery gray. The parents, besides the vociferous gabbly quarreling they did over nest pebbles with neighboring pairs—pebbles are the only nesting material and serve as anchors or markers too—and their clamorous high yodeling with red bills pointed skyward (known to scientists as "ecstatic display"), were also engaged in the long grind of waddling down to the water and uphill again, fetching food in their crops. Penguins can't fly and aren't made for walking, so it's touching to watch them struggle along in their pelagic camouflage. The dynamics are unforgiving because a colony must achieve a sort of critical mass to succeed. It must be densely populated for the chicks to survive the skuas' sneaky hawk-like dives from different angles out of the sky. The outer ring of nests suffers plenty of losses anyway. Yet if the colony is large and crowded enough to mostly foil the gathering skuas, the adult penguins must swim farther and farther out from shore to capture their share of food, then climb the slope laboriously again when they return. And because leopard seals wait for them in the waves, some never do come back. The second parent, waiting at the nest for its turn to eat, eventually must leave if it is not to starve, and the skuas swoop and tear at the single chick left behind, while other parents merely mind their own offspring.

High is certainly tougher, as you watch the penguins climb from the beach by an endless progression of clumsy hops to reach the lofty site of their special niche. Because of the work of the trip, it might be assumed that the youngest, least experienced parents have been pecked and shouldered out from below and forced to settle for space high up. But, on the contrary, the huskier, wiser-looking old birds— some of the strongest—pitch their nests on a particular ledge to catch more of the early-warming and earlier-in-the-season sun. Toiling up and down all day and swimming out to chance the leopard seals, they do their utmost until, like all the other parent penguins, they finally get played out and swim way off for an extended respite in the ocean to regain their strength. The abandoned young, meanwhile, waiting to finish growing thermal feathers and sufficient musculature to face the sea, cluster and lean into each other in what ornithologists, in an inspired bit of nomenclature, call "creches," for safety in numbers against the piratical skuas. Together, eventually they take the per-ilous plunge, and the leopard seals, lurking in the wings for these tyro swimmers, enjoy their biggest feast of the year.

I knew some book biology, but as I sat on the rocks trying to ig-nore the fact that twenty other tourists around me were in search of a vaguely similar epiphany, I was reaching for a concordance with pen-guin time, ocean time, and weather time, which is not digitalized like ours but instead goes in surges. Subsistence cultures live in surges too—sleep, eat, and exert themselves in what we might define as whims and binges—not pacing themselves with a metronome as we do. In seeking what the biologist E. O. Wilson has called "deep his-tory," we fugue back however far we can, one hundred or one thou-sand years, from clockwork timing to something a little like surge time. Hard to do. I can accomplish it for ten or twenty minutes if I try.

One of my fellow passengers had endeared himself to me on the first day—on the airport bus in Buenos Aires—by taking off his tramping hat to show me how his dog drank out of it on their hiking trips in Colorado. He was a retired officer type and track coach who ran marathons, climbed mountains, and ran up Pike's Peak annually;

indeed he had won an Olympic bronze medal as a young man, I learned later, and not from him. Geeky and scoutmasterly in a way that my writing had mostly saved me from, he therefore seemed an alter ego.

There was also a retired political science professor from Michigan: matter-of-fact, quizzical, decent, and a string bean, well up on his reading. And a fiftyish woman in the video business, with what she said were marital problems, and a somewhat anxious, haunting face, whose passion for beauty and adventure warred with her vulnerability to seasickness and other frailties. Also a likable young securities lawyer from Toronto, not yet formed or crystallized by marriage, as you had the sense he'd soon be. And a couple of travel agents from San Diego, husband and wife. The husband's tangled head of hair and fiercely bushy, jutting beard looked more like a sea captain's than any real sea captain's I've ever known. And a corrections psychotherapist from the Rockies with an extraordinarily sensitive face who read airport novels on the bridge as we passed much of the best Antarctic scenery. He reminded me a bit of the travel agent who looked more like a sea dog than the captain did, because of his misleadingly sensitive face, which turned out to be an expression of the travails childhood polio had inflicted on him. And a German engineer who worked for the Bayer Company in Cologne and told me he had visited sixty countries in eleven years of off-time rambling. Also a sales clerk from Chicago who had just lost her job and consequently had money worries, but talked most often of the great love of her life, who had flown over the Hump in the Himalayas during World War II (it turned out that our retired professor had been a landing officer at an airfield there), and was in frank search of a revelation on this journey, such as the organizers of this cruise had already facilitated for her in rafting trips down the Bíobío in Chile and the Tatshenshini in southeast Alaska. She was soon my favorite chum, along with the Toronto lawyer, the video woman, the professor, and a youngish Tasmanian environmentalist who was studying our "impact."

Mountain Travel, which began business in the San Francisco area twenty-five years ago by taking paying clients to the heights of Nepal, regards itself as the granddaddy of adventure companies, though I liked to tease them by saying that they were really just New Age White Hunters because of the spiritual spin that they attempt to instill on their trips. They were Ernest Hemingway and we were Francis Macomber. But Lynn Cross, director of their polar operations and our official escort, whose husband, Chuck, was our expedition leader, wasn't convinced. A professor's daughter from Illinois, she had gone to bartending school after graduating from college and spent the next seven years in the bar business before getting thoroughly tired of talking with people "who could never remember the next day what they'd said" and gravitating into travel as a livelihood. Now forty, she still had a wiry, waiflike look, like so many of the women who labor over the books in the back rooms of bars, emerging now and then into the Antarctica of drunks and misanthropes and ne'er-do-wells with a shyly maternal or authoritative smile, and she had retained that patient, slightly pedantic manner in handling tourists that works so well with saloon buffoons and barflies and was also vaguely reminiscent of her college major, early childhood studies—staring persuasively at people who didn't at first cooperate.

Chuck was fifty-two, his marriage to Lynn recent, and it appeared to be a complementary one. Chuck was chunky, his beard and hair a mix of black and gray, and rather bleak of face except where his thick eyeglasses managed to magnify his eyes enough to show their inner vulnerability. A mountaineer with what he summed up as "twenty years of climbing and then twenty years of skiing" behind him, he lurched when he walked as if the level ground were not his native milieu and he were attempting to push off from it. Chuck's reserve was such that I couldn't inquire whether, like many climbers I have known, he had been markedly singed at some point and climbed to get *up, up and away*. But he did tell me, rocking on his feet, that lately he was growing more content to gaze at a height of land without immediately beginning to scheme how he could get himself on top of it. He seethed with a scrambler's energy. His proudest possession was a racing sailboat in San Francisco Bay, and as a youngster he had climbed Mount Rainier twenty-five times by twelve different routes, under the influence of a charismatic English teacher at Oregon State who later died on an icefall on Mount Everest. Chuck was enthusiastic about the ocean but his stomach wasn't. He was a landsman and there was a sort of reverse-pole electricity to his movements, which seamen, even the restless ones, seldom show. Engaged in a commercial enterprise, they make their living by accommodating themselves to the tides of nature—not by conquest, like a mountain climber, who probably earns his living elsewhere.

Mountain Travel Company has a "Grand Slam" program for escorting Francis Macombers up the highest summits on every continent in the world. They count seven: Kilimanjaro (19,321 feet) in Africa; Aconcagua (22,834 feet) in South America; Djaja (16,500 feet) in New Guinea, which is classed as Oceania; Vinson (16,850 feet) in Antarctica; and of course Mounts McKinley (20,323 feet) and Everest (29,028 feet). Mad, spiky, frenetic millionaires could add Kosciusko, in Australia, and Kinabalu, in Borneo. Chuck himself had climbed two of these, and wore an orange-and-yellow expeditionary parka whose triangles a helicopter rescue pilot could spot from miles away, if he should become stranded on a snowfield or an ice face. But I trusted his integrity and flexibility, and teased him that in one's fifties or sixties we didn't need to seek an abyss. We already *had* an abyss; we were poised. I knew a man who had climbed Kilimanjaro and never bothered to learn what tribe his bearers were from.

As for the Russians, they seemed to be groping for a national persona from which they could derive some decent pride, while winning a livelihood by transporting Americans—a people so supremely confident that they must seek artificial challenges—in civilized comfort into the utmost wilds. The captain was a subtle man, a thinker on such matters, and the second and third mates, Alexandr Savchenko and Evgeniy Levakov, in nice American sweaters, with European facial features, looked like they were from Minneapolis. Evgeniy said he'd seen duty as a paratrooper in Kazakhstan during his military tour and was a father, routing his pay of ten dollars or so per day directly home. Limbo, out here on the gelid deep, was better, he said, than the spiral of disorientation, corruption, and demoralization in Russia.

The first mate, named Slava Trukhanov, was a different sort, squat and bulky, a phlegmatically forceful Siberian with a lowish brow, a sloppy sweatshirt, and the look of one of Genghis Khan's troop commanders. He was a competent seaman, had served on a minesweeper, and had quickly picked up tourist English in this new posting, but he had little curiosity to use it, preferring to gaze flatly at the quiltwork of the sea or at his panels of instruments. Because of my love for Alaska and my nine visits there, I've sometimes flattered myself that, had I been a Muscovite writer exiled to Siberia, I might have survived better than some of the Russian intellectuals did. So I took our Slava to be the mayor of the Siberian village whose boundaries I was restricted to for purposes of this fantasy. And by watching him, I found him not too bad: certainly not a bad mate to the sailors, and we had one American he took a liking to. This was an Arizonan who ran rafts professionally down American, Siberian, and African rivers, a kind, burly man, thirtyish, now beginning to worry about what kind of conventional career he might switch to. (He told me that, true to my notion of "adventure companies" just being retreads of the old White Hunter days, they were now shooting crocodiles in the Zambezi River so that they could advertise raft trips that would be trouble-free.) Slava took him down to watch Russian movies in the mess room and would impulsively walk over to him like an older brother to rub his wiry mop of hair and ask when he was going to get married and start a family like a good guy.

Across from Joinville Island is Petrel Cove on Dundee Island, which is strewn with leaky fuel barrels, rusty machinery, and collapsing tin and plywood shacks from the recent Chilean-Argentinean rivalry, and has a mile-long abandoned Argentinean naval airstrip on the stony beach, where we stretched our legs, in the absence of the fur and elephant and crabeater seals and nesting birds that must have made good use of it until not long ago. I missed the heavy, yeasty, barnyard smell of penguin dung on Joinville Island, however; the effervescent gabble.

En route to Paulet Island, just east of Joinville, we saw white icebergs that turned shark-blue underneath, like a double message, and flat little snow-covered floes that were peppered with resting black penguins, perhaps in the company of an eight-foot leopard seal, pale as a spotted ghost and sleeping off its last meal of another penguin that it had caught in a long, desperate chase underwater. Or the penguins' fellow passengers might be several silvery, greenish-gray crabeater seals, small-mouthed, sociable, and mild mannered. We also saw a sea-gray mamma Weddell's seal, a fish- and squid-eater midway between the leopard seal and the crabeater seals in size—a largish beast, lolling on a cake of ice, who Greg Myer speculated had probably weaned her single pup on an isolated beach only a couple of weeks before and now might be molting. She rolled over further on her itchy back in response to the apparition of our ship, in order to eye us better.

Paulet is a rookery for about six hundred thousand Adélie penguins, named for the wife of French explorer Admiral Jules Sebastian César Dumet d'Urville. Spiry yet already almost snowless, Paulet boasted a broad beach of slippery rocks and was marvelously raucous and smelly, seething with thousands of marching birds, or hollering paired-off sentinels, and trickly with melting runoff stained by red and green guano. The waves soughed mildly by comparison with the noise of this metropolis, once you got fifty yards up from the strand. Also, there were the remains of an emergency stone hut constructed in one quick week in March 1903 by twenty men led by the Norwegian whaler-explorer Carl Anton Larsen, more than sixty years after d'Urville's two voyages, when Larsen's ship had been caught and crushed in the ice. They'd roofed it with canvas, chinked it with guano, insulated it with sealskins, and killed and stacked eleven hundred Adélies to last them as food until spring. (Only one man didn't survive.)

Though a few raffish, piratical skuas swooped overhead, this was a place of yeasty prosperity—the penguins bravely stinky, bravely braying; and elegant, svelte blue-eyed shags (a kind of cormorant) nested in shoals among them. It's undoubtedly sentimental to ascribe "raffish" or "brave" behavior to birds, but sentiment in such a stark spot is endangered too. Those vanished whales by their absence had helped to feed this penguin city, and because the three common species of the Antarctic Peninsula have staggered nesting schedules—Adélies, chinstraps, and gentoos, in that order but often on different islands, two or three weeks apart—and dive to somewhat different depths as they search for fish and krill (gentoos as much as five hundred feet down), they dovetail more than they compete for food. The sumptuous, keening, terrifying funnel of life and death is layered like an underwater skyscraper for them. With ballasted wings, they peel off in sharply tangented Immelmann turns and barrel rolls, sideslipping, fishtailing, volplaning, whereas out under the canopy of the sky they have to either rest or nest.

Penguins surrendered their ability to fly in order to "fly" through the water better, propelled by their stubby wings, ruddering with their feet—rather in the same way that snakes gave up the capacity to walk in favor of crawling. In a hot antique jungle climate about one hundred and fifty million years ago, the lizards that eventually reinvented themselves as snakes found legs a hindrance in wriggling through the tangles, much as penguins, forty million years ago, experienced an icy climate change that capped the protein that they needed underwater. But whereas the vanishing jungle has left snakes in the unfortunate position of having made a Faustian bargain whose chits are falling due, the maritime penguin, in this particularly solipsistic weather system, is doing fine. Furthermore, the blubbery, bowling pin-shaped body and finlike wings it grew—the wings held stiffly out like arms for balance—and its big eyes and portly waddle, together with its black-and-white evening-dress costume, have won it potent friends, who may come in awfully handy if a penguin population crisis occurs over the harvesting of krill for human consumption someday. It's kind of unfair because snakes' leglessness is an esthetic curse, a death knell signaled in the Bible: *On your belly you will crawl.* But I like snakes and find that handling them soothes me like handling a string of worry beads or fingering a rosary might do. Their ancientness gives me pause, which is what nature does for us anyhow. And penguins, diving two hundred feet down or zestfully porpoising along the sea's surface at a speed that neatly matches the rhythm of their breathing, are offshoots of lizards too.

Our odd, alien party of penniless Murmansk seamen and moneyed Americans paying through the nose for two weeks of adventure steamed gently south through the night to Seymour Island, where the Argentineans have a big base of one hundred and fifty people supplied by air. From a discreet distance Seymour is a lengthy ridge of mudstone, sandstone, and limestone, which in midsummer looks to be the color of a lion's skin and is known for its remarkable petrified wood, and its fossils of an extinct marsupial, a five-foot penguin, and a marine dinosaur. The wind was up; we couldn't land, which disappointed our staff geologist, Wayne, who also leads tours of the Grand Canyon and up the Amazon with his friend Suzana. I hardly minded because we saw so many bachelor or bachelorette penguins swimming around, and occasional gray-green seals, and a minke whale afloat on the Weddell Sea, which we had now entered, plus the many stately bergs and darting birds. (Petrels derive their name from "Peter's birds," because in skimming they seem to walk on the water, like Saint Peter in the Gospel of Matthew.) Islands may appear more impressive when you lie just off them, imagining them, than if you actually land, with all the motley regimentation and boating rigmarole of going ashore.

"A piece of cake," the captain kept saying as we passed Snow Hill Island, which is larger but uninhabited by Argentineans or anyone else (though a Swedish geologist did spend two winters there ninety years ago). The Weddell Sea is named for James Weddell, the British sealer who penetrated it in 1823, and has a weighty feel. I'd supposed earlier that one might go to polar regions to recapitulate what, for example, Giovanni da Verrazano and Henry Hudson laid eyes on. But the sparse porpoising penguins vaulting like Frisbees out of the water and a few seals as noodgy as manatees couldn't lend Antarctica the plenitude of the Hudson River, circa 1524 or 1609. Instead we were in the midst of a Royal Navy of icebergs—pods and prides of them, next to which a whale looked mouse-sized—aircraft carriers one hundred feet high and therefore extending six hundred feet below the waterline, if you figured the physics of it. The biggest berg that has ever been sighted measured two hundred and eight miles by sixty miles, across its top. The Antarctic ice sheet itself contains 90 percent of the world's ice and is one and a half times the size of the United States, but nothing in nature looks more alien. One can't rightly compare icebergs to "castles," ice sculptures, vanilla frosting, or Soviet architecture, although, being human, we try to. Hard as concrete yet steadily melting, not water-colored or able to reflect the spectrum of sky colors that water does, not immutable like a cliff face, or green-clad and stream-chiseled like a mountainside, they're paradoxical. They lack what we think of as personality and in our mind's eye can throw a line to. Stately but disintegrating, cerulean perhaps in little streaks but as broad as a city block and impenetrably white, they represent the *Titanic* and death.

The waves whispered crisply against these numerous edifices. Close up, we'd see ancient grainy brownish veins in the ice, pitting it like smallpox and embodying snow crystals that may have fallen before Weddell or d'Urville or Larsen or Nathaniel Palmer—the sealer from Stonington, Connecticut, whom Americans credit with discovering the continent in 1820—had yet arrived. Thus it may be ice that's like the starlight which reaches us long after being launched, huge telegrams from prehistory yet geometrically squared off like goofy architecture, floating on the blue-black sea in gigantic blocks that are mostly an eerie, sanitary white. Originating from the Larsen, Ronne, and Filchner Ice Shelves, the bergs were positively everywhere, leaving less and less maneuvering room; and twenty-five miles short of the fog bank that marked the wall of pack ice, we turned back—though they continued to parallel us massively, like antiseptic, scarfaced monuments, till past nightfall, with periodic trios of tiny penguins as black as gnats the only speck of life, and a low pearly sky.

The map of Antarctica is tagged clear around with an extravagant foliage of names. Every cape or inlet, plateau or nunatak memorializes some ship's master, naturalist, whaler, sealer, naval officer, or adventurer lucky enough to have first clapped his weather eye upon it. Patrons, sweethearts, and home counties are also remembered, on glaciers, promontories, and islets, like a cacophony of testosterone—names hanging off the outline of the continent as thick as tassels, of people who had wanted to outlive death by flirting with it. There must have been other explorers who wished to leave only their footprints, but naturally we just know the hollerers. And so the map you study back home is very different from reality, where you hear no egos, only glaciers cracking, roaring, calving, splashing—or rumbling, thudding avalanches—and the cryptic hiss of the waves on the gravel.

I made the point to Gennadiy, and he repeated a quote from Genghis Khan: "The warrior who nails the sable skin on the wall after a battle is not the warrior who won the battle." I kept kidding him and Slava, Evgeniy, and Alexandr because the *Professor Molchanov*, its superstructure strung with electronic gizmos like a Christmas tree with baubles, *must* be a spy ship; and Gennadiy had hung off Cape Canaveral only a decade before, recording space-shot telemetry, then putting into Havana or Guinea-Bissau. Surely, too, our charts were so precise about depths because the Soviets had been hiding nuclear subs in these exotic waters?

"In the Arctic, yes," said Alexandr. "Not here. Too far."

"Then hunting subs," I insisted.

"Let me show you how you hunt subs," Alexandr said. He pulled out another chart, showing Siberia's Sea of Okhotsk, where lots of naval stuff was. His finger became an American submarine trying to sneak close, while his other hand was a Russian submarine cruising silently in a defensive position with big ears. "Subs hunt subs."

From the Weddell Sea we went through Erebus and Terror Gulf (named for the British warships James Ross employed on his terrific voyage of exploration in 1839–43) and through Antarctic Sound to the west side of the Peninsula, while I dreamt in swift jittery succession of crossing the Atlantic on a flimsy barge, and then of an imaginary lover who all of a sudden turned sadistic to me, and then of being captured crazily by Yahgan Indians in the Beagle Channel, until insomnia got me up to see the dawn.

We landed on Astrolabe Island, a toothy dot named for d'Urville's ship (and a former instrument of navigation), whose short beaches under modest, cuspy heights are a chinstrap penguin rookery. Tuxedoed, with the addition of a black line like a soldier's chinstrap, they were slightly more assertive than the Adélies, higher-headed, more attentive to us, and less dithery when we approached, waving their stubby, theatrical wings and gabbling in protest. They also were doing their "communal ecstatic display," as science calls it, which is neither communal nor entirely ecstatic, being in part a threat posture, but which also helps bind each penguin to its mate because the pitch of each bird's voice is unique. Chinstraps, too, are pebble lovers, and pebble stealers to improve their nests, and imprinted with the drive to return to the same beach every spring. But they are thought to be more monogamous than the Adélies, which are adapted for the even tougher climates south of here, and therefore must be prepared to lose last year's mate.

Like Joinville Island, Astrolabe had the feel of a secret place, but was so small we saw no skuas. (According to David Campbell's excellent book on Antarctica, *The Crystal Desert*, a pair of skuas will patrol about ten thousand nesting penguins.) Eight Weddell seals, however, were resting in a row on a cushiony bed of snow while they shed their winter coats. Lying prone, they scarcely raised up to look at us, though they did groan a bit. There were also three shouldery fur seals established on separate flat patches of rock, apart from them—bachelor bulls who emphatically objected to our presence for territorial reasons by rearing up on their flexible flippers to offer us a maximum profile of strength. Unlike Weddell or crabeater or elephant seals, fur seals have land-worthy flippers and hind legs that fold forward under them and thus can propel them in an aggressive charge faster than a running man. Like sea lions, they have external ears and doglike heads, and bulk and height constitute a territorial display for them, even encompassing the rubber-necking posture of tall, two-legged tourists like us. They could be formidable on land, but since defending a special patch of rocks in beachmaster fashion is their purpose, they don't charge far. Indeed, some of the smartest sealers used bull fur seals as wardens of a kind, to pen the females on the beach, not letting them escape into the sea, while the sealers methodically killed and skinned them (a sealer might blind the bulls on their seaward side), until just the bulls were left, presiding over a harem of hideless carcasses, whereupon they themselves would be killed.

Terns and petrols also nest precariously on Astrolabe. The snow on the tide-washed beach was algae stained, and a blue berg was marooned in a tiny cove, among black seal-sized rocks that greatly outnumbered the seals.

Cruising across Bransfield Strait from Astrolabe to Deception Island, we admired the lovely dappled brown-and-white petrels skimming for krill, and the somnolent fur seals "jugging," as it's called—sleeping on their backs in the calm waves with their flippers folded over their chests, round as jugs, like sea otters in the north Pacific do. Indeed, Antarctic fur seal skins used to be shipped to China, where their coarse guard hairs were painstakingly plucked out so they could be passed off as much more valuable sea otter skins.

At intervals we encountered five separate pods of humpback whales, blowing in a leisurely fashion, then lifting their backs in loose unison, and their broad flukes with a seamlessly synchronized rolling motion, to dive. Side by side they did this, arching underwater and serenely reappearing at an unexpected angle, to exhale their misty sighs again. The mothers had calved off the coast of Colombia, Greg said, and swum down to gorge on the dense acres of krill nourished by the round-the-clock summertime daylight here. The babies' breathing (big creatures now) was impetuous, nervous, uneven, but the mothers' slow worldly sighs, forceful and vaguely wise, got to me, straight to the heart.

I live in a place—New England—where the volume and diversity of bird calls declines a bit more every spring. Fewer birds, fewer species, a weaker chorus—altogether, I would suspect, a third sparser than twenty-five years ago, which, in real time, is the blink of an eye. And that's part of why people shell out good sawbucks and frogskins to fly to Thailand, Tanzania, the Amazon, or Antarctica to see what's left. At home, for wilderness, I hike into terrain so high that no real-estate developer has been interested yet, so the idea that the whole White Continent is still not owned seems quite incredible. But twenty-six nations have set up "scientific" stations here to fly their flags and pre-position themselves for a land grab if policies change.

Frogskins and sawbucks were terms for money in my younger days, when people sometimes ate bullfrogs and still sawed firewood: there were so many trees and frogs around. Greenbacks reminded them of a frog's skin, and the X on a ten-dollar bill of a sawhorse's legs. People might have a dried rabbit's foot attached to their key ring for good luck, and liked it when a good rat snake took up residence under the house, or if there were bats in the belfry of the church up the street to keep the summer's crop of flying bugs in control. Nature was a natural condition—not a churchless religion for its devotees, twinned with jogging, meditation, Walkmans, Prozac, or whatnot, but best accessible to those with plush incomes. We on the *Professor Molchanov* were members of the green groups, the Audubon Society, Nature Conservancy, Greenpeace, Sierra Club, Wilderness Society, World Wildlife Fund—though my early years of struggle as a writer were bankrolled by a small inheritance from my mother's mother, whose money came from logging operations among the primeval Douglas firs of Grays Harbor in Washington. What would now seem to be museum-piece trees thus founded my beginnings. And with our stomachs full of flounder, sole, shrimp, our oil-based synthetic clothes, oxblood shoes, Honda gas tanks, freeways, swimming pools and ranch houses, all wrung from the earth—the million miles of swamp and forest drained, stripped, or paved over—we *still* wear billions of frogskins on our backs and pay for our accoutrements in sawhorses.

We travelers were all pondering not this, but the quandaries of grief or a job change, how it felt to get old and retire, our marriages or sexual chevaux-de-frise, our guilt and pain. The power-company president from Iowa and I were thinking of our newly dead wives, and a friend of mine was dying of Lou Gehrig's disease, and four or five others had died of hemorrhaging or carcinogenic catastrophes before having had their proper say in the world: with more books to write, more friendship to give, and kids who still needed a great deal more of their time. Life is so very precious while you have it, yet comes with a kind of biblical itch, a scabies patch on the back that never quite quits, but keeps you going. Antarctica is mostly entropic, on the other hand, lifeless, the edge of the void, where the sweet rain that elsewhere wets our lips and keeps us alive is cruelly crystalline, yet a feast for the eyes. That we could so profoundly enjoy the lifeless sight of ice is part of the mysterious double dimension that makes us puzzlingly human. Life had chafed us—whether with polio or widowerhood or sexual abuse (as one person hinted) or sieges of stuttering and semiblindness, in my case—and it was a tonic to stray so far.

Deception Island is a volcano's caldera, an aficionado's ultimate destination, if you start from Cape Horn in a steel-hulled ketch and get across six hundred miles of the world's roughest water, then zero in on the correct beachless dot of cinder-colored rock, tall and forbidding, till you sail round it and—presto!—spy an opening in the walls like a hidden slot that is ten fathoms deep and wide enough for even a cruise ship to slide inside. A splendid anchorage, a lake of seawater five miles long and three miles wide, awaits you there, with reddish-brown ashy beaches—and chinstraps nesting on them—rising all the way to the crater's rim, where a few pocket glaciers strewn with recently exploded ash linger year-round, set off by yellowish patches of lichen. At the far end of this peaceful oval is a handsome bowl where the water is hundreds of fathoms deep, but emerging from a slit in the lip of the shore is a little hot spring where tourists take a dip that qualifies them to say when they get home that they swam in the waters of Antarctica.

Nathaniel Palmer, the Connecticut sealer twenty-one years old who went on to run guns to Simón Bolívar in what is now the nation of Colombia, and later helped to invent the clipper ship and grew wealthy trading with China, discovered Deception Island in November 1820. It became a safe harbor for other sealers and soon a major whaling station, the rusting detritus of which remains in Whalers' Bay—barracks, ash heaps, hangars, huts, hulks of machinery. But the austere symmetry of the crater is mesmerizing, a sanctuary where you might freeze and starve, but take a while to realize it. Walking about, we met a couple of Spanish military men and some Argentinean sailors and scientists and the daring crew of a sailboat that had lost its mainsail under way from Buenos Aires. British and Chilean scientists sometimes camp here, too. During the last eruption a quarter of a century ago, they'd fled with burning shirts, rescuing one another.

We cruised through the night to the Antarctic mainland, south of Trinity Island, to a thirteen-person Argentinean research station called Primavera, perched like a couple of close, colorful dots in a hook-shaped bay of purple water surmounted by shelving glaciers and other perpendicularities that looked a bedazzling white. It was stirringly sumptuous, steeply mountainous, in a smothering surplice of maybe a dozen or twenty different shades of ice or snow—crystal and diamond and custardy egg-white—in long schlossing drifts and billowy dunes, illuminated by bright effervescent sunshine. The visible peaks hinted that others must lie back beyond, while the rustling, inky water at our prow bobbed with dozens of floes that had just cracked off the sheer walls. Though lush in the way that green can be lush, it was also eye-popping because it was so white. On deck, a sort of prolonged quiet ecstasy possessed Gloomy Guses like Chuck and me, who had passed the half-century mark with many prior adventures and perhaps too many memories to process new stuff properly. We were smiling like babies.

White can indeed be luxuriant, a color for weddings and royalty and special people, of ermine and satin and lilies, but also of tusks and hypothermia, a celebrity color, or the ghastly pallor of death. These little glaciers with brown nunataks sticking out of them, calving blue and creamy bergs into the bay, had left one pitch of ground that thawed to bare scree every spring. The Argentinean scientists— two women were in charge—lived in red board buildings set on stilts above the permafrost, amidst a gentoo colony and two hundred pairs of nesting skuas that ranged out elsewhere, and sheathbills, which are another scavenger, and some Cape petrels and Wilson's storm petrels and Antarctic terns. Altogether since the camp's establishment in 1953, eleven species of birds, three types of seals, twenty-five mosses, forty varieties of algae, and a hundred lichen have been totted up here, plus two inconspicuous inch-high kinds of grasses and two sorts of insects: namely, feather lice and seal mites.

Three months is not an intolerable stretch to be stranded here, said the middle-aged cook, who volunteers every year, and the radioman and Buenos Aires scientist-intellectuals agreed, referring jokingly to a doctor posted at another base who had made himself mildly famous by setting fire to the place in order to be airlifted out before his enlistment was up. The cook offered us a hospitality gourd of maté, a herbal tea, and cookies to pass around, and Chuck gave them their mail from Ushuaia and a box of fresh vegetables. Our engine-room crew ferried some of them across the bay in a Zodiac to check experimental equipment that they had placed there but couldn't visit because their government hadn't provided them with a boat. We passengers went putt-putting in two other Zodiacs, scouting the bluish crisp floes dusted with sparkling corn snow. Half a dozen crabeater seals were snoozing on these, their green-tea or sea-turtle coats marred by two-foot scars that dated to when they were pups and a leopard seal had grabbed and tried to devour them. The two leopard seals we drifted upon were more alert, and one opened and chopped his big jaws at our approach, as a bear will do when circled. His camouflage was different, olive or charcoal-gray on top and pale ashy gray on the underside, with the eponymous spots. Twice the length of a man, he had a mouth three or four times as wide as a crabeater's, though his incisors were shorter than a bear's or a leopard's, and he had very large shoulders and flippers for purposes of pursuit. His face was grimly primitive looking, not so much like a mammal's as like a python's or an ancient sea reptile's.

Antarctica is a relic formed three or four hundred million years ago when the upper Paleozoic supercontinent Gondwanaland began breaking up into Africa, the subcontinent of India, South America, and then Australia, as Antarctica drifted south. The climate had been so temperate that marsupials may have walked to Australia from their North American origins by means of the land mass that now constitutes Antarctica. But the land bridges vanished eighty-five million years ago, and four million years ago the present ice sheets started to coalesce. Afterward there could be no grasslands or forests for castaways to colonize, no Eskimos or Indians to glower now at tour ships coming to this appendage of the Andes.

From Primavera we sailed south through Gerlache Strait to Charlotte Bay, opposite Brabant Island. Our stalwart helmsman, Vasiliy, sported a T-shirt with BOSS stenciled on it, and the supple-faced boatswain, Vladimir, and the comely, skinny seaman who had been nicknamed "Mr. Blue-Eyes" by some of our livelier passengers both wore other American giveaways. The sea had its disciplines and manifold moods that thankfully overrode the daily shortwave squawk of Moscow news. Glistering and platinum white or navy blue, it heaved and slammed, causing our ornithologist, Greg, to miss his newborn son and reflect caustically on "breeding males and nonbreeding males" vis-à-vis penguins and people (he himself had been gladly changing since his marriage); and our Boston bank loan officer to plan a trip to Slovenia, where she had ancestors, and Chuck to speak of his mentor, the English teacher killed on Mount Everest ("a little death on a big mountain") and his return here next month with a boatload of macho glacier climbers. On this trip we figured more than half of us had snapped more than a thousand photos apiece. It was like a disease, the bending, limping, stooping, gesticulating, view-finding, lens-twiddling Saint Vitus' dance that people engaged in, as though their cameras were their children and the effort was to give them an emotional experience. Lens settings, like frequent-flier mileage— some said they even bought their groceries by credit card to pile up extra mileage, one for every dollar billed if you had the right card, and then if you got divorced they'd let you split your miles—was a topic of irrepressible appeal, after the attentive pieties of the panorama had been disposed of: like coming home.

In our exhilaration at these quick takes, these brushes with exotica for which we'd come so far, we felt closer to one another as well, though so random a collection of people—the go-go San Diego couple with impeccable tans; the gentle Iowan who had risen on the ladder at his power company not as an engineer but in personnel; the Clorox chemist whose wife kept apologizing affectionately because she didn't "like chemicals"; the bearded, boyish, muscular river runner from the Arizona desert; the polio sufferer who had become a sex therapist; and Chuck, in a cowpuncher's hat, charging about like a bison. The Argentineans had posted a road sign at Primavera saying they were still 2,870 kilometers from the South Pole, and only 1,109 from Ushuaia, but I was reading Apsley Cherry-Garrard's *Worst Journey in the World*, probably the best of the Antarctica journals, about a ski trip across the winter ice in 1911 in search of emperor penguin eggs. (Emperors lay their eggs in the winter.) Also Ernest Shackleton's and Robert Falcon Scott's books about their heroic treks. Scott may possibly be said to have died because he didn't appreciate dogs. That is, he tried using Siberian ponies and motor sledges to pull his loads and they broke down, whereas his rival in the race to the Pole, Roald Amundsen, relied on fifty-two sled dogs.

And I'd brought along the diary of a distant cousin I'd recently gotten my hands on. He was an aspiring foreign correspondent who was murdered at twenty-nine in Inner Mongolia in 1905, and his voice on the page sounds a bit like mine. He'd left college to enlist in the Spanish-American War in 1898. Afterward, he moved from serving in Cuba to the Philippines to work as an administrator in the mountains of Luzon with Igorot tribesmen. But then reports of the Russo-Japanese War in 1904 juiced him up, and off he set via Ceylon, where he picked up a French adventurer as a traveling companion, a bogus or cashiered army lieutenant.

My cousin John was handicapped and doubtless partly driven by fluctuating but daily attacks of asthma, much as I'd been as a young writer-traveler by a bad stutter, except when his exuberant absorption in his surroundings distracted him from fretting about it, and therefore it let up on him. And as with me later, life may have seemed such an emergency anyway, such a leap of faith even while staying at home, that he was prepared to trust all manner of people when launching himself on a trip. The Frenchman unfortunately was a mistake. After they'd left Ceylon for China—and then headed up to Peking to cross Inner Mongolia and Manchuria on horseback to reach the battle areas by land—John's diary gradually becomes uneasy, jittery, scared, though his tone also sounds throttled by the knowledge that his companion may be reading it. His money and passport have been stolen. He suspects, first, some villagers, but later his wording is elliptical and panicky, and the journal breaks off. His body was never discovered, but his baggage was left in the last hamlet they'd stopped in. The Frenchman thereupon disappeared, after cashing John's letters of credit by forging his signature, back in Ceylon.

We marveled at the blowing, fluking whales in trios, pairs, quartets, blue-black, bundled in the gray winter. The youngest animals stood practically on their tails, "spy-hopping" as it's called, to get a gander at us, the mother maybe prompting them for educational purposes. Then, since they can't climb out on the ice floes like a seal, they'd nap in the water till our thrum woke them again. The Weddell seals, fish eaters that stay here all winter—chewing breathing holes in the ice instead of migrating to open water as the other mammals do—are little fellows next to the whales, but have more heft and rather a lovely sea-and-ice coloring and a rounder, comelier mouth than the moss-yellow, krill-grubbing crabeaters, which are thought to outnumber them by about twenty-five to one.

Growlers and discolored bergy bits slid by, and one splendiferous berg, big as a stadium, though quite stately, with bitty penguins tossing themselves about its ledgy flanks. Two minke whales escorted our bow; and all around, once we had reached the larger perspective of Charlotte Bay, we confronted a gargantuan semicircle of glacier mountains, bulging buxom and highly tiered, with numerous fresh bergs that had just chunked off and now clustered about us, church-sized, gymnasium-sized, and thus far so innocent of the ocean that they were sharp-edged, sugar-white, vanilla-new. Charlotte Bay is one of the most beautiful sights on earth, equivalent to Mount McKinley or Lake Como, though crunchy with provisionality because you could so easily die here and the very profile of the ice is changing continually. White as virginity, white as a funeral, yet so crisp I nearly wanted to embrace the icescape and be set on shore to take my chances and entrust the snowfield with my infinitesimal life. Individually we fugued, whether with binoculars or cameras, in the midst of this summer scene so starched, succinct, and crystalline, although punctuated by cannon booms from the glaciers' snouts and bursts of katabatic wind. Wellman Glacier, Bayly Glacier, Mount Johnston, and the Foster Plateau going up seven thousand feet, stood close. Despite the cold breeze on deck, I grinned until my mouth ached.

We sailed on and stopped at a place called Portal Point to look at a peak-roofed, two-room abandoned hut provisioned with 1950s tabloids and tinned foods for the British exploring teams that had holed up here. Built of wood and tar paper, with bunks, shelves, cozy glass windows, and cement blocks outside to anchor it against the wind, it seemed homey in this summer interlude. Three crabeater seals lay on their backs in the side yard wriggling to rub off their molting fur. Some gentoos were also about, placid, convivial birds with pretty white eyebrows, salmon legs, and orange bills. That they are unafraid of us is of course part of their quaint appeal, in a larger world where all other wild creatures flee. The water temperature at Ushuaia had been twelve degrees centigrade, and had fallen to three degrees as we reached the islands of Antarctica, but the pods of orca whales that will pop penguins into their mouths in about the same way we eat shrimp, and the fleets of bergy bits upon which the birds can float and hide, and the surge of storms under the theater of the sky were not digitalized. (Even for reptiles there is immense leeway, if they know their habitat intimately, not just in how much they manage to eat and how long they survive their predators, but how well they take advantage of or cushion themselves against temperature change.)

From Charlotte we sailed to Cuverville Island, another glacier and fjord spectacle, where we anchored and napped through the wee hours. Four Britishers were tenting on the beach between two penguin rookeries. By occupation they were a moss botanist, a penguin ornithologist, a geographer, and a lawyer-administrator. The geographer's task was to map people-movements as precisely as possible, because two thousand tourists a year debarked from cruise ships here and one rookery was kept off-limits to them as a "control" area, while the other was left open for free-lance meandering. Then at the end of the season the penguin and moss biologists would total up the damage that had been done. Though I approved of the idea, I immediately skewed their statistics a trifle by reboarding our ship when I found out that I was being mapped, it was such a comedown from the era of Shackleton, Amundsen, and Scott.

Ronge Island, across a gap, was not being mapped. A fur seal bull acted as beachmaster, swelling up and posturing to nearly a man's height on a rock that he'd picked, while two cows dozed on the gravel nearby. Both gentoos and chinstraps were nesting higher up, their colonies contributing a farty assertion of life's pungency to the added scent of seal urine and the seaweed's piquant smell. Penguin tracks ran uphill through the snow to where their chicks were waiting to be fed, though the doughty parents had to concentrate their ungainly steps into trenchlike paths between outcrops of rock that would have been impassable otherwise. And it was on these "highways" that tourists could cause the deaths of penguins unintentionally by punching cylinders in the snow with their boots, into which the descending chicks would fall and never be able to scramble out, and within which the adults too—waddlers almost as helpless as chicks ashore—might get trapped.

Out in the channel, a mamma humpback whale breached, blowing like a hippo, a robust personable sound, as confident as a matriarchal elephant, only more so. She was about fifty feet long, rather skinny, with the big calf that had been draining her now swimming, spouting and throwing its flukes into the air, then leaving its swirling "footprints" on the surface of the water alongside. Her breath exploded like a cow elephant's, communicating her peremptory pleasure in the ease of this glorious midsummer's day. We weren't harassing them yet in the Zodiacs, so there didn't seem to be a complaining or protesting tone to it, just a jumbo emphasis upon how independent, vigorous, and good she felt—a booming exhalation nearly on a par with the distant avalanches and the glaciers that we heard noisily splitting.

When we did start following the two, their movements, though not frightened, became constrained. The blowing lost its sense of jubilation. Luckily, before we'd chased them far, two leopard seals began to investigate us, which afforded our twenty photographers a worthy distraction. These "polar bears of the South," eight-hundred-pounders, ten feet long, trailed and examined us, rolling closely under the boats, then rising slowly out of the water at arm's length, head to head, even more predatory than we were. With their leopard-spotted chests and grimly primitive heads, as huge-mouthed and simple in configuration as the python I keep at home (only, a hundred times heavier than he is), they re-examined and inspected us further. Under the boats and up, again under and up, and swiveling to face us in a lithe, leisurely, whimsically unbrotherly fashion, these penguin seizers that slap and shake a bird clear out of its skin before swallowing it gave us a thorough once-over before going their merry way. We were uncommonly silent.

We left the whales and seals to visit another abandoned British survey-team hut and, after passing a German research vessel, the *Polar Star,* steamed for three hours down Gerlache Strait and Neumayer Channel to Port Lockroy, a former whaling station in a sheltered inlet on Wiencke Island, where several 1940s structures remain. Also, somebody had assembled a composite humpback whale skeleton from scattered vertebrae and other bones. We posed for a group photo in front of this. Thousands of dowdy, pretty gentoos were nesting vociferously in the vicinity, and a few blue-eyed shags—pointy-beaked, fast-flying, and infinitely trimmer birds with eyes like tiny bull's-eye targets—were feeding fish to their young in the hyperalert manner of other cormorants, although hugging the fringe of the fussy gentoos' site for the relative safety this offered their own nests against the skuas' attacks.

On Jougla Point the penguins wobbling down to the sea to obtain a meal for their hollering chicks were squeezed into a narrow aisle between the rocks that we were sitting on and the rocks that were their nesting ground. I felt sorry for them, especially when some of our photographers spilled into their three-foot passageway for close-ups and a hungry leopard seal appeared at the beach end, looping and somersaulting in the water, barely bothering to conceal his presence as he waited impatiently for the poor penguins to run our gauntlet and reach him. The jostling in the colony above us, too, was threatening to knock a couple of chicks off their nests and into oblivion. Every twenty minutes or so an avalanche on the mainland would roar, and the gusts of wind kicked up quite cold, as if to remind us where we really were. Fog was moving in, with a nice "fogbow"—a yellow arc like a rainbow—just parting enough to remind us that black cliffs lay all around.

The tension broke when one of our number, a computer guy who had touched me from the start in his dorky isolation, which sometimes reminded me of myself, got sprayed with penguin feces by a nervous mother, and suddenly became everybody else's pent-up butt. People who had never expressed the slightest ridicule of him now howled at his plight and thus made him yet more frantic to wash it off. So he got his clothing wet in the icy ocean while trying to. It was purgative. We cleared out of the penguins' navigating space, and everyone got washed clean of their own geekiness for the time being.

Suppering as we passed the end of Anvers Island, Chuck said he and Lynn keep a van all stocked with sleeping bags, a stove, and food so that they can take right off from the office in California for camping trips. He said it was no good believing that opposites attract; he'd tried that in a previous marriage. Lynn added, however, that soon after they had started dating he'd gone off for a month and a half, guiding a climb of Aconcagua, and lost so much weight that when he came back, he had a different body to get used to. With a barometer strapped to his wrist, and orange and yellow triangles dramatically marking his parka for rescue aircraft to home in on—lurchy, abrupt, electric, compulsive—he seemed to want to launch projects beyond our paltry capacities. Oldish folk, desk jockeys, we irritated *me* too.

On past Doumer Island, we reached Lemaire Channel, between Booth Island and the mainland, at sixty-five degrees, six minutes (the Antarctic Circle, again, is sixty-six and one-half degrees). This was farther south than we had gotten in the Weddell Sea, and it was gorgelike enough to take your breath away. Toothy nunataks stuck up out of the cascading ice on Booth Island, which rose more than sixty-five hundred feet above the water on our starboard side, while just to port the mainland mountains went higher, above vertiginous chutes and endless carpets of snow.

I was at the bow a lot, no longer afraid of jumping over. I was too happy, and besides, such incongruous, gratuitous self-absorption would have struck me as absurd. People do kill themselves in beautiful settings, like the Golden Gate Bridge, but they probably have more compelling reasons and the place itself becomes a kind of still life or stage setting for gruesome self-dramatization. This was not San Francisco Bay, arty and softly lit for amateur theatricals. This was a primeval grindstone, as grand as Genesis, or Genesis in reverse.

Death loses part of its sting, and therefore interest, when I am outdoors. But my wife, raised in the city, had been quite frightened in the out-of-doors. She was an indoor person—it was of course part of our problem. Even on her brief visits to our country place, she seldom stepped outside. Talk was her life's blood, scintillating and warm of heart, so that our lack of a phone there, which was a plus to me, was a hardship from her standpoint. And indeed when I think of other friends I miss and mourn, it wasn't nature they drew their faith from, it was great music and classic literature, or an Irish effusion of friendship. It was the pleasure of lazing and lovemaking, schmoozing and eating, a webwork of arcane loyalties. Curiosity and a bracing cynicism sustained some of them, or love of work, love of family, or the hope of love and sex and fame and money. I haven't seen the peace which passeth understanding prevail in many people after they've been told that they should prepare to die. Instead they naturally feel a tearful, gnawing frustration—their youngest child not yet out of college, their best books, perhaps, not yet written; and to both the precious child and in the projected book, *so much left unsaid!* My former wife, a writer, had been one of these.

Nature doesn't speak for you afterward, if you haven't had your say in the world. But nature, if you place your faith in it, dilutes that compulsion and other vanities. The wiggling gleam of flowing water, the romantic disk of the moon, the soothing enigma of starlight, the sight of wind-blown grass, whirling leaves, and large-crowned trees, the smell of woods soil, the extraordinary comfort, both emotional and physical, delivered by the sun, are free. We may have different enthusiasms. I like to look at animals without attempting to shoot them, for instance, and prefer to look up at mountains, not down from their summits. I love the densest cities—believing nature also encompasses human nature in Cairo, New York, or Bombay—whereas you may think great cities are an eczema. But these distinctions are as immaterial to nature as whether or not you carry a swagger stick. What matters is how long you're alive to what's going on.

Lemaire Channel was our destination, a fitting turnaround. The channel funneled narrower, plushly implacable, till you might think a little fishing boat would be a safer vehicle. Winding through such savage scenery, I was mesmerized. My eyes glissaded down extravagant piled-up choked snowdrifts, ivory ice, jagged ebony rock in giddy outcroppings, and a silence whose match I might never know again. A hardy band of us, mostly women, stood a long while at the bow despite the cold: the Boston banker with the wonderfully muscular arms and legs and a tough-love mouth who had compared our trip to a space voyage; my friend the sales clerk from Chicago, with a taste for swashbuckling men and desperate romance; the video packager with the haunting, thwarted-looking beauty; and the slight, grizzled Bayer engineer from Cologne who had been in sixty countries and taken fifteen thousand color slides. I knew this was an isolation I would never see equaled in my lifetime, not in the wildest inhabited place.

At a pocket in the channel between the cliffs of ice, the *Professor Molchanov* most carefully turned around, though our passage toward the Shangri-la of ultimate coldness could have continued if we had wished to take it. I'd thought daily of the professor, in handcuffs and leg shackles, painfully hungry, dying of a pistol shot from a countryman in the cruel snow within sight of his beloved St. Petersburg, and the contrasting fact that the danger I had feared in signing up for this jaunt to Antarctica was not of sinking or freezing or catching pneumonia or any other old-fashioned natural danger but the silly, self-hexing squirrel trap of suicide, which seemed to exemplify the diminishment of our self-indulgent age. Cascades of ice, the bottomless ocean, and two skeletons of rock to hang the ice from on each side were all we had, but the honeycomb of frigid fjords and inlets, the aeolian solitude, and our sense of traveling on the brink of borrowed time lent glory to the procession of recapitulated sights.

There was a saying in the nineteenth century, when people returned from a gold rush or a war or some arresting sortie along the edge of the frontier: *I have seen the Elephant.* It is, of course, a paler time. We have fewer "elephants," and try to synthesize a great many faux ones for each that really exists. Many of us have logged more mileage than Captain Cook in a mathematical sense, and childhood has no wondrous centerpiece, such as a glimpse of a one-ring-circus elephant by torchlight at the county seat must have been. Yet even so, and even on a package tour, the traveler does retain the final initiative in the privacy of his mind. You *can* see Antarctica and allow it to register. I'm not sure how much I succeeded at this. Like everything now, it's a matter of subtle ambiguity, of silence and cacophony. But I stayed outside, both for the joy I felt and to give my mind a chance, until we had left Lemaire again.

(1995)

A Peaceable Kingdom

It's too good to be true, I've always thought, for the past thirty years, when spring rolls around once again and I drive up to my warm-weather home, now the only occupied house on a four-mile stretch of dirt road that crosses a mountain notch in northeastern Vermont. A two-story frame dwelling, painted blue-gray and nearly a hundred years old, it was built by the first family who cleared these spare fields. They had forty acres, ten or twelve cows, and three other families for neighbors, two living in log cabins that have since fallen in—enough kids altogether for a one-room school, which later was moved next door as a shell, when *that* family's original house burned and they needed a new one.

My predecessors, too, had thrown together a log cabin at first; a barge-shaped depression in the woods still marks where it stood. Then when they decided to stay, they dug a cellar hole here with a horse-drawn scoop, split some granite boulders at the base of the cliff for blocks of stone to line it with, and set up a little sawmill to cut floorboards of spruce. Sand from the stream was used for the plastering, and they planted apple trees and a black cherry tree, and four oaks, now nice and big, in front.

The farming ceased about forty years ago. The man I bought the house from was supporting himself by brewing corn whiskey and bathtub beer and shooting deer out of season for meat. He died too soon from drinking too much, and his British war-bride wife afterward, though she was a favorite person of mine and planted many of the flower beds I continue to enjoy. The lack of electric and phone lines had made them eager to move, and indeed explains why this mountain road has never been as unpopulated as it is now, and why beyond my house it is being abandoned "to the Indians," as the town authorities say.

What I do when I arrive here is air and sweep the house, load the wood stove, turn the water pipe on (it runs by gravity from a cistern uphill), browse my bookshelves for a glimpse of old friends, and check to see if the local ermine has spent the winter inside, clearing the place of the few pairs of white-footed mice that otherwise might have chewed my socks. I prefer to find her hairy little twists of dung over anybody else's. Chipmunks, when they wake from semi-hibernation, may have sought entry, too.

I open the four bird boxes that hang on trees to clear out squirrel nests (if any red squirrels have sheltered there through the snowy months), hoping that now tree swallows will come instead, and climb into the hayloft of the barn to see if a bear slept out the season in the mounds of hay, or merely some raccoons. I also look for the phoebes, early arrivals that nest under my eaves, then listen for white-throated sparrows, ovenbirds, yellowthroats, wood thrushes, robins, winter wrens, rose-breasted grosbeaks, chestnut-sided warblers, mourning warblers, and black-throated green, black-throated blue, and black-and-white warblers. Cedar waxwings, indigo buntings, flickers, and goldfinches will be arriving. A certain apple-tree limb is where the hummingbirds will nest.

If the large mother coon has survived the winter, she will probably be using the hollow maple as a den tree. By putting my ear next to it, I may hear her kits. The ermine (now an ordinary brown weasel) that protected my woolens has meanwhile moved from the house to nest among the timbers of the barn. Investigating clues perhaps left by the adolescent bear in the hayloft, I'll hear her burbling expressions of alarm. The mother woodchuck hibernates under the chicken coop and reappears as soon as the grass does; and if I'm lucky, I'll see a migrating trio of black ducks sneak in at dusk for a night's rest—out of the hurly-burly of the lakes nearby—in my high-up, hidden frog pond. They'll eat some water greens at dawn, and then be gone. Bears will have already clipped off the young spring sedges at water level. Sedges are among the first foods bears taste; or they trudge to the fir woods a few hundred yards downhill, where some deer have generally wintered, to find out if any died. I look for antlers the living bucks have dropped, but bears sniff for a carcass they can eat, though they will gobble deer droppings, too, in this hungry time, and search for last fall's sprouted beechnuts on the ground.

The lawn under my oaks, mossy and mushroomy, doesn't need much mowing. The apple trees mainly feed the wildlife, and I bush-hog the fields only often enough to keep them open. The stream was dammed seventy-five years ago for homegrown experiments with water power, but flows just as it wishes now, and moose, deer, and coyotes drink from it instead of cows. I sometimes do, too, or kingfishers, ravens, or woodcock make use of it, and a great blue heron hunts mice and frogs alongside. I had the frog pond dug, hiring a bulldozer for the purpose of filling the air with song. Spring peepers and wood frogs start up in April. Then tree frogs, green frogs, pickerel frogs, and of course toads—my favorite serenaders of all—join in. As the lush orchard grass and the thick raspberry patch sloping away from the old barn have lost their soil nutrients from half a century's worth of cow manure from the animals that were stabled there, fireweed and other hardscrabble plants replaced them and what had been a teeming colony of earthworms became scarcer. This was tough on the colony of garter snakes living underneath my house, which had fed on them. But the frogs, increasing tenfold, took up some of the slack as a food source.

These garter snakes, just twenty miles short of Canada, are blacker than the same species in southern Vermont because they need to absorb as much heat as possible during the brief summer season in order to digest what they eat; the sun is their engine. The woodchucks are blacker, too, not to accumulate heat but as camouflage: In these northern forests dark fur shows up less. The bears are black, the moose are black, the porcupines dark. The deer in their red summer coats look quite odd, as in fact they should because they followed the white men north.

In the house, I load the flashlights, put candles around, fill the kerosene lamps, and look to see if anything has been pilfered over the winter—pipe wrenches, a fire extinguisher, boots, blankets, or possibly my ax? Secondhand books sell hereabouts for a dollar a box, so no one steals books, though somebody once purloined the magnifying glass that went with my *Oxford English Dictionary*. And, once, my field glasses were lifted just before hunting season started, yet then were left on my woodpile during December. The next year, when it happened again, they weren't returned—this being such an impoverished area that woodpiles, too, are sometimes stolen. A furniture factory is the principal local employer, using the yellow birch and rock maple that people log around here when they aren't cutting pulpwood. Unemployment is so high it keeps wages low. Other people truck milk to Massachusetts, or cattle to the hamburger slaughterhouses down there. Where you see goshawks, red-tailed and broad-winged hawks, and peregrine falcons, you don't notice ads in the paper saying "Help Wanted."

My windows and rooms are small, as befits the cold climate most of the year. On some of the richest days, when a moose stalks by or a bear is blueberrying or munching hazelnuts outside, I think of my house as a bathysphere suspended in the wilderness. Nevertheless, it's comfortable—the floors painted russet, the furniture homey, the walls nearly covered with pictures I've taped up over the last quarter century. I'm partly surrounded by an eight-thousand-acre state forest, to which I'm leaving my land as a minor addition, except for the house, which will belong to my daughter. Big Valley Brook, Stillwater Swamp, May Pond, Boiling Spring, and Moose Mountain are spectacles that live in my head, yet I can walk to. If the weather muscles in, I chop four hours' worth of wood. I hear an owl; I hear the ravens; I hear a redstart.

Gardeners and trout fishermen got busy outdoors around mid-April this year, when the high water permitted; and the kids in town started shagging fungoes or fishing Kids' Brook, a stretch of stream

near the fairgrounds so easy that it's lent to them. For me, spring had
begun a month earlier, when a big male bobcat's tracks looped down
off Moose Mountain into my wooded notch and intersected in a romancing scrawl with the solitary lady bobcat who shares the area with
me. When the snow is gone, of course, her movements become more
of a mystery, but my dog has treed her. On other rare occasions I notice her prints beside the pond or hear a rabbit scream at night, utterly
suddenly, caught from ambush.

Then on the last day of March a bear that dens near my house left
her little cave to enjoy what was perhaps her first drink in four
months. Going a hundred feet so she could lap the trickling meltwater in a brook, her tracks showed that she made an immediate return
trip to sleep some more. On Tax Day she was still in her den, her
head protruding dozily, but the next day she descended a quarter
mile to a patch of swamp to eat some cattails, with yearling-sized
tracks accompanying her. The presence of the grown cub meant that,
in the bearish biennial ritual, a male would probably come visit us in
June so she could have new cubs next winter.

Among certain Indian tribes, a family used to inherit a given cluster of bear dens and the winter nutrition to be gained by killing the
occupants in prudent rotation. Though I avail myself of the local supermarket, I'm just as protective: Don't mess with my bears. And the
dog doesn't. Wally is a sheepdog and patrols the meadow aggressively
but regards the forest as foreign territory. On the other hand, when
the county airstrip comes to life and low-flying Cessnas angle over, he
is inspired to defend the perimeter of our empty field from these
roaring eagles with a pell-mell frenzy, as if we had a bevy of lambs
that they might grab. Then after chasing a plane away, he'll cock his
leg and pee triumphantly against a tree, the same as when his adver-
sary has been a wandering fox or coyote, so it will know next time
who it must reckon with.

He'll also mark a rabbit's trail, a squirrel's roost, a mouse's nest for
later reference when he hunts, although I doubt he is one-tenth as efficient at that occupation as a fox. In June, I'll lie in the field at dusk
and listen to a vixen's hectic rustle as she gleans a stomachful of
meadow mice, deer mice, shrews, moles, night crawlers, and such to

take back to her burrow and vomit for her pups. And I remember how quickly a woodchuck that had grown feisty from taunting Wally at the mouth of its hole fell prey to a lank coyote that rambled through. The coyote began to carry the body off, but stopped, dropped it, and performed an unexpected sort of victory dance, stiff-legged, around the corpse.

"Joy walking" is what deerhunters call what I do in the woods because I bring no gun. For Wally, as well, our outings are a matter of glee, not necessity. He'd rather simply haul home a dehorned head or a gut pile a poacher has left than hunt for more than a few minutes himself. Carrion tastes, I suspect, a bit winy, cheesy, anchovy and green olivey, Béarnaise and sour-creamy (which may be why we late primates try so hard to approximate the piquancy of fermentation with sauces). Wally drinks from muddy puddles and nibbles green sprouts as a further change from piped-in water and dog kibble before curling at my head as a sentinel when we camp out.

Wally celebrated spring around Tax Day by running down to the pond alone for his first swim: this when the wood frogs and song sparrows had just started to sing. I was lolling in a patch of sunny grass, watching a pair of robins, listening to a kinglet and a phoebe, but, lest my delight seem unadulterated, also picking off my first tick of the season. Instead of forest lore, Wally has become adept at reading human beings (hunters are the only predators he flees), such as the precise moment every morning when he can jump on my bed without waking and angering me—or the extraordinary value I place on the welfare of the goofy parrot in the kitchen, versus the crows in the garden, which he is encouraged to chase. They fly up into the basswood tree and razz him, then look for a hawk they can mob and mistreat.

(1997)

Earth's Eye

Water is our birthplace. We need and love it. In a bathtub, or by a lake or at the sea, we go to it for rest, refreshment, and solace. "I'm going to the water," people say when August comes and they crave a break. The sea is a democracy, so big it's free of access, often a bus or subway ride away, a meritocracy, sink or swim, and yet a swallower of grief because of its boundless scale—beyond the horizon, the home of icebergs, islands, whales. Tears alone are a mysterious, magisterial solvent that bring a smile, a softening of hard thoughts, lend us a merciful and inexpensive respite, almost like half an hour at the beach. In any landscape, in fact, a pond or creek catches and centers our attention as magnetically as if it were, in Thoreau's phrase, "earth's eye."

Lying on your back in deep meadow grass facing a bottomless sky is less focusing, but worth a drive of many hours, as weekend traffic will attest. Yet the very dimensions of the sky, which are unfathomable after the early surge of pleasure that they carry, cause most of us to mitigate their power with preoccupations such as golf or sunbathing as soon as we get outdoors. That sense of first principles can be unnerving, whereas the ground against our backs—if we lie gazing up into the starry night or a piebald day—is seething with groping roots and sprouting seeds, and feels like home, as the friendliest dappled clouds can't be. Beyond the prettiest azure blue is black, as nightfall will remind us, and when the day ends, cold is the temperature of black.

A pond, though, is a gentle spot (unless you are Ophelia). Amber or pewter-colored, it's a drinking fountain for scurrying raccoons and mincing deer, a water bugs' and minnows' arena for hunting insect larvae, a holding pen for rain that may coalesce into ocean waves next year. Mine flows into the St. Lawrence River. I live in Vermont and spent a hundred dollars once to bulldoze a tadpole pond next to my little stretch of stream. A silent great blue heron, as tall as a Christmas tree, and a castanet-rattling kingfisher, a faster flier and brighter blue, showed up to forage for amphibians the next year. Garter snakes also benefited from the occasional meal of a frog, and a red-tailed hawk, cruising by, might grab a snake or frog. More exciting, a bull moose began using it as a hot-weather wallow, soaking for half an hour, mouthing algae, munching sedges, and browsing on the willows that lean from the bank. A beaver cut down some poplar saplings to gnaw and stitch into a dam for creating a proper flow, but the depth remained insufficient to withstand a New England winter, so he retreated downstream to a wetland in my woods.

I bought this land for eighty-five dollars an acre in 1969, and today a comparable hideaway would probably still cost no more than about the price of a good car. We're not talking luxury: As with so much of life, your priorities are what count, and what you wish to protect and pay attention to. I've been a sinner in other ways, but not in this respect.

Remoteness bestows the amenity of uninterrupted sleep. No telephone or electric line runs by, and the hikers and pickups are gone by sunset. When the season of extravagant daylight shortens so I can't simply sleep from dusk to dawn, I light candles or kerosene, but in balmy weather I can nap with equal ease at any hour in the meadow, too, or watch the swallows and dragonflies hawk after midges, as the breezes finger me and a yellowthroat hops in the bushes to eat a daddy longlegs. At dark the bats hawk for bugs instead, or an owl hunts, all wings, slow and mothlike, till it sees a rodent. The trees hang over a swimming hole nearby, with a dovish or a moonlit sky showing beyond the leaves like a kind of vastly enlarged swimming hole, until I feel I was born floating in both the water and the air. It's a hammock all the more beguiling because if you relax too much while swimming and let yourself sink, you might conceivably drown. Similarly, in the meadow, if you lazed too late into the fall, woolgathering, snow could fill your mouth.

Nature is not sentimental. The scenery that recruits our spirits in temperate weather may turn unforgiving in the winter. It doesn't care whether we love it and pay the property taxes to save it from development, having walked over it yard by yard in clement conditions. When the birds flee south and other creatures, from bears to beetles, have crawled underground to wait out the cold, we who remain have either got to fish or cut bait: burn some energy in those summer-lazy muscles cutting wood, or take some money out of the bank.

A mountain can be like that all at once. Summer at the bottom, winter at the top; and you climb through all the climates of the year as you scramble up. In the past half century I've climbed Mount Jefferson in Oregon (a cousin died there in a fall soon afterward), and Mount Washington in New Hampshire; Mount Katahdin in Maine, and Mount Etna in Sicily. I've clambered a bit in Wyoming's Wind Rivers and in the Absaroka Range; also in British Columbia and North Yemen; in the Western Ghats in southern India and the Alpes Maritimes in the south of France; and have scrambled modestly in the High Sierras, Alaska's Brooks Range, and on the lower slopes of Mount Kinyeti in the Imatong Massif in the southern Sudan. More particularly I climbed all of Vermont's fire-tower mountains, back when Vermont still used towers to locate fires, instead of planes.

This feast of variety is part of a writer's life, the coin of the realm you inhabit if you sacrifice the security Americans used to think they'd have if they weren't free-lance in their working lives. In reality, everybody winds up being free-lance, but mountains telescope the experience. During a weekend you climb from flowery summer glades to the tundra above tree line, slipping on patches of ice, trudging through snowdrifts; the rain turns to sleet. The view is rarefied until a bellying, bruise-colored sky turns formidable, not pretty. Like climbing combers in a strong surf, there's no indemnity if you come to grief. You labor upward not for money, but for joy, or to have *been somewhere*, closer to the mysteries, during your life. Finding a hidden alpine col, a bowl of fragile grassy beauty, you aren't just gleeful; you are linked differently.

Leaving aside specific dangers like riptides, vertigo, or terrific cold, I found I was comfortable on mountainsides or in seawater or in caves or wilderness swatches. In other words, I was fearful of danger but not of nature. I didn't harbor notions of any special dispensation, only that I too was part of it. I'd fought forest fires in the Santa Ana Mountains of southern California when I was twenty and had discovered that moderate hardship energized yet tempered me, as it does many people, just like the natural sorties for which one puts on hiking shoes and ventures where barefoot peoples used to go. In central Africa I've walked a little with tribesmen like the Acholi and the Didinga, who still tend to be comfortable when nearly naked, and have seen that the gap between us seems not of temperament or of intuitions, but only acculturation.

As virtual reality captures our time and obsessive attention, some of the pressures that are killing nature may begin to relent. Not the primary one of overpopulation, which is strangling the tropics; but as people peer more and more into computer screens and at television, the outdoors, in affluent countries, may be left in relative peace. This won't stop the wholesale extinction of species, the mauling of the ocean, or other tragedies, but close to home may give a respite to what's left of nature.

Where I live alone each summer, four families lived year-round eighty years ago. The other new landowners don't choose to occupy their holdings even in warm weather because of the absence of electricity. An unusual case, yet I think indicative, and supported by the recent return of numbers of adaptive sorts of wildlife, like moose and fisher, to New England—though, in contrast, along the lake a few miles downhill, cottages perch atop one another, motorboats and water-skiers buzz around, and trollers use radar fish-finders to trace the final sanctuaries of the schools that the lake still holds.

Just as habitat is the central factor in whether birds and animals can survive, what *we* are able to do in the woods will be determined by land regulation or taxing policy and public purchases. Maine's private timberlands have remained unpopulated because of America's lavish need for toilet paper—as Vermont's trees, too, make paper, cottonmill bobbins, cedar fencing, and yellow-birch or maple dowels that become furniture legs. Any day, I watch truckloads of pulpwood go by. And in the California Sierras above Lake Tahoe, or on the pristine sea island of Ossabaw, off Savannah, Georgia, I've devoted lovely, utterly timeless hours to exploring refuges that seem quite empty of people, but are actually allotted in careful fashion by state or federal agencies for intensive recreational use. The animals hide while the sun is up and feed when it's down. This is the way it will have to work. Levels of life on the same acreage. Or else it won't work at all.

I can be as jubilant indoors, listening to Schubert or Scott Joplin, as when sauntering underneath a mackerel sky on a day striped yellow, red, and green. Indeed, the density of sensations in which we live is such that one can do both—enjoy a virtuoso pianist through a headset outside. We live two lives or more in one nowadays, with our scads of travel, absurd excesses of unread informational material, the barrage of Internet and TV screens, wallpaper-music, the serializing of polygamy and the elongation of youth blurring old age. A sort of mental gridlock sometimes blocks out the amber pond, the mackerel sky, the seething leaves in a fresh breeze up in a canopy of trees, and the Walkman's lavish outpouring of genius, too. Even when we just go for a walk, the data jams.

Verisimilitude, on computer screens or in pictorial simulation, is carrying us we don't entirely know where. I need my months each year without electricity and a telephone, living by the sun and looking down the hill a hundred times a day at the little pond. The toads sing passionately when breeding, observing a hiatus only at midmorning when the moose descends from the woods for his therapeutic wallow, or when a heron sails in for a meal. I see these things so clearly I think our ears have possibly changed more than our eyes under the impact of civilization—both the level of noise and subtleties of sound are so different from hunter-gatherer whisperings. I'm a worrier, if not a Luddite. The gluttonies that are devouring nature are remorseless, and the imbalances within the human family give me vertigo. The lovely old idea that human life is sacred, each soul immortal, is in the throes of a grand mal seizure; overpopulation is doing it in. I didn't believe that, anyway, but did adhere to the transcendental idea that heaven is right here on earth, if we perceive and insist on it. And this faith is also becoming harder to sustain.

"Religion is what the individual does with his own solitariness," as A. N. Whitehead said. ("Thus religion is solitariness; and if you are never solitary, you are never religious," he added.) I fall back on elemental pleasures like my love of ponds, or how my first sight of any river invariably leaves me grinning. And the sheen of rain water on a bare, black field in March. The thump of surf, combed in the wind and foaming, glistening, yet humping up again like a dinosaur. Yet fish don't touch me as much as animals, perhaps because they never leave the water. Frogs *do;* and I seem to like frog songs even more than bird songs, maybe because they're two-legged like us but can't fly either and were the first vertebrate singers. But I especially respond to them because they live a good deal more than we do in the water.

Frogs are disappearing worldwide in a drastic fashion, perhaps because of ultraviolet rays or acid rain; and I may finally cease to believe that heaven is on earth, if they do. Water without dolphins, frogs, pelicans, cormorants will not mean much to me. But in the meantime I like to search out springs in the high woods where brooks begin—a shallow sink in the ground, perpetually filling. If you carefully lift away the bottom covering of waterlogged leaves, you'll see the penny-sized or pencil-point sources of the groundwater welling up, where it all originates—the brook, the pond, the stream, the lake, the river, and the ocean, till rain brings it back again.

(1999)

Natural Light

Loving the city didn't prevent me from needing some country. So in 1969, when my daughter was seven months old (and at the same time as I'd begun to write essays), I took another plunge and bought an eight-room house on forty acres near Barton, in northeastern Vermont, plus an old Volkswagon Beetle to get to it.

Marion and I dug out the gravity spring up the hill, where our water flowed from, put in a heater to make it hot, a bathtub, and a little gas furnace to supplement the 1921 cast-iron wood stove. We hired a carpenter to jack up the sills and resettle them (the price of the house had been $5,000), a mason to rebuild the chimney, and a roofer. We filled the woodshed from the discard heap at a dowelmill down the road, bought more lily bulbs and cultivated the roses, the rhubarb and horseradish, limed the worn old lawn, and spread ashes on the lilac beds, rented a P.O. box, and acquired a library card.

The place, of course, snowballed in importance for me during the next three decades. I wrote about it frequently as I gained familiarity, and in the 1980s dictated a good number of *New York Times* nature editorials from the nearest pay phone, six miles downhill, because our road had no electric or phone lines. We kept chickens, goats, dogs, and Molly grew up with memories of kerosene light in the evening for at least a part of every year, and the sight of deer and the occasional bear, of foxes hunting woodchucks and killdeer soaring, woodcock diving, and snipe wheeling in lariat loops. It was an eight-hour drive from New York to Wheeler Mountain, which curved around in front of us and the house of our only neighbors, Karl and Dorothy Wheeler, but seemed farther because the cliffs looked more like Idaho than Vermont. Bobcats had colonized them, ravens nested on them, and people came from Montreal and Burlington to climb them.

While house-hunting, I'd found that the real estate agent I was looking for in town was married to the owner of the gas station where I stopped to ask directions (which, passed from father to son, was still in the same family at the millennium, as were Barton's other principal businesses; and the village still had about a thousand people). Avis Harper took me along a few back roads where a guy might step out on the porch with a shotgun to see what we wanted; then passed me on to Em Hebard, who had kept a general store, served as a Republican state legislator, and later wound up as Vermont's treasurer. Em had enjoyed, however, a secret, early "socialist" period in Washington, D.C., and Greenwich Village—a job in the Agriculture Department at the tail end of the New Deal, and then a sublet over a jazz club in New York City, where he could sit out on the roof and listen to jam sessions all night. So, whether just through luck, or else insightful fellow-feeling, he brought me straight to the raw corner of Caledonia County where I fell in love.

The Wheelers, though almost eighty, weren't selling their land. Karl had been stationed in Brownsville, Texas, during World War I—and his only child, Hilda, was there. Then after the army, he was employed as a railroad fireman near home, until the Depression derailed that job, and he took over his father's farm, under the twenty-four-hundred-foot mountain that bore their name. Unlike Dorothy, he had plenty of kith and kin around, who, like Dorothy herself, gradually became my friends. Dorothy had grown up in the Shaker colony in Canterbury, New Hampshire, where her father was the handyman after her mother's death from TB (and she took an unsentimental view of those crabby Shakers). Making do with Karl, she had sold cottage cheese and buttermilk, cream and pies, eggs and cakes to the summer folk on Willoughby Lake, going the five or ten miles by horse and wagon, and had boarded a few of the jitterier single ones in her spare room, when that sort of arrangement flourished as a custom in New England. Best, she'd liked writing a weekly column for a newspaper during their salad days while Karl was on the railroad. Now, the big cow barn had fallen down, as well as the sugarhouse. Even their "Wind Charger" windmill for sporadic battery power had broken. But they were comfortable on the old place and called Karl's nephew at suppertime at 5:15 each afternoon on a CB radio to tell him they were okay.

Next door to the Wheelers, in the only other house on this four-mile stretch of dirt road—and no road paralleled it in either direction for at least another four—lived the Basfords, who *did*, however, want to sell. Donald was a housepainter seasonally and otherwise made a poor living brewing corn whiskey that he sold for $1.50 a pint, and bathtub beer for 35 cents, if you supplied the bottle. Kay, the humorous English war bride whom he had brought home a quarter-century before, cleaned house for the pharmacist's family downtown, and warned me in all fairness that in the wintertime it got so cold here that their rabbit-dog would jump into the oven in the morning when she first lit the stove. Also that the man who had built the house, around 1900, had shot his mother-in-law and, a few hours later, himself. She pointed to the bullet holes and said, not her, but other people suspected the presence of a ghost.

Kay was eager to achieve the benefits of electricity. They had given up their couple of cows, and an attempt at Christmas tree and ginseng farming, and did subsistence vegetable growing and ate deer meat. In the family Bible Kay kept a clipping from the *Caledonia-Record* of the time when Donald had caught a $65 bobcat skin. I got to know them pretty well after they had ceded their house so gladly to me; and their story is a sad one. Donald beat her; she fled one midnight, hitchhiked to safety, and returned to Britain for three years; then came back to nurse him through his strokes and decline. Donald was a saturnine, unrelenting iconoclast, a north country agin'er from the get-go—about politics, religion, social norms, and what-have-you.

Unlike Karl's relatives—sometime hunters and trappers who also ate raccoon or bear or bobcat meat—Donald didn't maintain a wider net in the community than that which bootlegging provided him. *They* paid their taxes much quicker, worked at the high school, served on the Rescue Squad, joined the American Legion. Nevertheless, an acidulousness like Donald's raffish outlawry is a kind of shirttail cousin to the cynicism that goes with lawyering or writing. And Donald benefited for a while from (besides mine) the powerful friendship of our most distinguished citizen in Barton, Lee Emerson, Vermont's "last balanced-budget governor." If the snowplow hadn't pushed up Wheeler Mountain Road for a week or more, despite Kay and Donald's standard bribe of a glass of apple cider and a deer meat sandwich for the driver, Lee would leave his office over the bank and walk across the hall to the Town Clerk's office, or place a potent phone call to the Town Garage, and the truck would be there in an hour: and no sandwich necessary. Donald used to paint Lee's big house on Park Street, with the mansard roof and distinctive turret.

An unfortunate feud with the Wheelers had begun when Donald accused Karl of molesting Donald's stepdaughter, Mickie, while dandling her on his knee during her visits just up the road (accurately, Karl's wife Dorothy said). Karl thereupon cut off Kay and Donald's access to the original spring that the two houses had shared for fifty years, and for a while they had no running water. Mickie herself became a friend of mine briefly, years later, after her parents' deaths, and before her own from alcoholism. And her bitterness was directed at Donald, no one else. She'd seen him hold a meat fork to her mother's throat and rape her on the living room floor, next to where we were sitting as we talked. Or force the two of them, with a pistol at their backs, to face the wall for hours on a Saturday night, his "English whore and her little bastard." Mickie had escaped through marriage after high school, but she had picked a crook, who earned her a year in jail as an accessory to one of his burglaries. (Hiring a lawyer, he got out sooner.) She said her favorite husband had been the one who beat the shit out of Donald once on a visit home, and left him hog-tied on the floor, after Donald had bloodied Kay, and told Kay to burn the house down when they were gone—which was a tried-and-true method of dealing with unwanted relatives in Old Vermont.

Mickie was a blowsy, commonsensical, attractive sort of woman with a drinking problem, visiting her mother's grave before she stopped to chat with me, with a young son in tow, or her new fiancé (a guy twenty years older than her and missing some teeth, whose chief charm seemed to be his social security check, but certainly quite ga-ga over his good luck), and worried about her children. She had returned to Barton, her hometown, after another shipwreck. But the children's switch in schools was being blighted by the memory people had of Mickie's return another time—one August maybe twenty years before—when, as if to spite her parents, she had danced naked on the stage of a girlie tent-show at the County Fair. Her kids needed to fight with other kids every day in order to defend her name. She told me her drinking had started when she was nine or ten, a "little waitress" carrying glasses of bathtub beer downstairs to the customers and secretly sipping from each one.

Kay Basford used to tell me that she had had "two daughters," the bad and the good, but I didn't realize at first that both were poor Mickie. Mickie had been so loved by boys as a girl that two separate fiftyish men stopped in, the year of her death, to revisit the house where they had felt her spell. Her worst early experience, she said, was when Donald had sold a darling, cast-off horse that he'd picked up for her a few months before. Sold it to the local mink rancher for drinking money: and hadn't warned her. She happened to be standing in the schoolyard at recess when she saw it rolling by—her precious Blacky—tied in the back of the knacker's truck. She screamed and screamed, but there was no way she could rescue it, even by jumping on her bike.

I mention all of this as a prelude to the ambiguity of driving around Vermont. I found Donald himself companionably amusing and irreverent in an axe-swinging sort of way, and Kay flirtatious, tasteful, rather wise, until Donald stopped me one noontime outside the drugstore and told me he was going to kill me because his wife had just run off to England and I must have helped her because how else could she have gotten the money? Actually, from the pharmacist's wife—yet he couldn't prove it, and didn't kill her either, but moved into a trailer down the highway with a woman who was rumored to have killed her husband (ruled a suicide, though supposedly the pistol was left out of reach), until Kay came home and Donald had his several strokes and lay abed, cursing at his helplessness.

We had a district attorney, elected by the county at around that time, who was not an attorney; he had to hire a green law school graduate to do the lawyering for him. And our postmistress referred to almost anybody with a foreign accent as an Eye-talian. Not more than a few years back, nightriders from the next town had shot into the house of a black minister, a newcomer, and driven him out—a spasm of violence that was condoned by the state police who investigated it, as well as by our county newspaper. More recently, the local sheriff lost his bid for re-election after being accused of sleeping with the game warden's wife. . . . It was that kind of place; and when Neil Armstrong and Buzz Aldrin walked on the moon, Marion and I went to the Hotel Barton to watch the spectacle in the lobby (plus take baths for a dollar a pop—we hadn't hot water yet). Though the sight was breathtaking, at dusk the clerk turned off the TV set and went upstairs to bed at his regular hour—sent us home laughing. But this lovely, rambling, three-story, eighty-year-old white building with a wrap-around porch burned on the night before Thanksgiving a couple of years later, when the interstate highway construction crew was bunking there, and probably lonely: the price of progress.

Other "flatlanders," "from away," besides us were showing up, but they were mostly of the generation ten or fifteen years younger than Marion and me, the so-called hippies of the baby boom, born during the hyper-sexual years of World War II, not in the depths of the Depression, and thus less cautious and skeptical, more communal and programmatic, settling year-round on other hundred-dollar-an-acre abandoned farms, with the secondary aim of trying to change the world. I wanted the world changed, too (and Lyndon Johnson, on our honeymoon-weekend at the Plaza in New York, had renounced his candidacy for re-election because of the debacle in Vietnam), and so have remained fascinated ever since by the flower-child experiments of some of these Boomers, and the complicated fallout.

A leading edge at the moment was the commune movement here along the Canadian border, near the sources of the Connecticut River and in the watershed of the St. Lawrence. It had been Rogers' Rangers raiding territory during the French and Indian War, and of disaffection during the American Revolution and the Civil War. Disaffection, insurrection, slave- and alien-smuggling, draft-dodging (one of my current friends was regularly guiding draft resisters into Canada about now)—so why not a bit of pot-growing and free love in the name of brotherhood? Although North Country folk were often offended by this new counterculture, they tended not to go and snitch to the narcs. Their grandpas had outraced Customs men in low-slung roadsters during Prohibition, or hidden the dudes that did. And thus one of Barton's leading businessmen, after hearing confidentially from the local state trooper that a certain single mom who had shown up wearing a peasant blouse, earthy skirt, a glassy look, and windblown hair, was really a federal plant, tipped off her neighbors, so that she fished in vain for information from them for a whole year.

As a New Yorker, I disliked what drugs were doing to the city, and the hippies' notion that shuttling the stuff down there was a romantic livelihood and a lark. But I was in the mountains for the wildness; and one of the commune leaders joined me for a forty-mile walk through the forests (twice as far as I went with an official Fish & Wildlife biologist) and became a dear pal. Another dropped in unexpectedly on me at Wheeler Mountain with three cohorts to check my bona fides, but thereafter allowed me a free run at his Farm, where some of the women gardened bare-breasted because they thought it helped the veggies grow. And another let me watch him snort cocaine, if I chanced to be around—though a dealer from the city who was making a pickup told me that if word got out, I would be tied up, put in a bathtub, and the hot water turned on. The only law I knew of that was being broken which seriously angered me was when some hippie hunters would shoot a moose—of the first, protected few that were wandering in from the faunal reservoir of the

Maine woods, where they had survived the nineteenth-century slaughter—and hold a barbecue.

Life sports a Janus face, spendthrift and yet miserly, with both a grin and grimace underneath. We often weep in seizures of intense happiness, for instance, and smile in grief: just as, in my stint in the army, working at the hospital morgue, I'd noticed how commonly the dead had managed at the last moment a benign or temperate sort of smile. This circularity is neither alarming nor incongruous, but rather seems to make things whole and complete. In the summer, dancing butterflies of pretty colors will congregate where I've gone outside to piss in the grass. The glint of tiger yellow or cobalt blue in their beautiful wings may be enhanced by the minerals that they so crave and that my body has declared surplus. And if a nesting phoebe soon grabs one, she is going to profit also—which is a foretaste of the myriad uses that more extensive portions of me will be put to eventually.

As during my three trips to northern British Columbia in the 1960s, I was in the country to take risks and seek linkage, in a place where the very reason that change is slow is because of those many links and risks. My neighboring writers, Wallace Stegner and Howard Mosher, doubtless felt the same. Stegner, whose literary and teaching careers were in the West, willed that his ashes be scattered in a bed of ferns at his half-century old summer house in Greensboro, Vermont, because he said it had been altered less destructively during his lifetime. And Mosher has constructed, over several decades, a "Kingdom County" in his fiction from Vermont's Northeast Kingdom's ligaments and legends. We would go around, Mosher and me, sometimes together, scribbling at a hot-rod race or a cattle sale; and I ceded the old-timers mostly to him (after my British Columbia book, which had been entirely about old-timers), just as he left the counterculture, and the mud-wrestlers at the county fair, and most wildlife to me. When the British Columbia book came out and got few reviews and skimpy sales, however, I found myself vomiting blood, because I thought it might be the best I'd ever write. But the doctor in town headed off an ulcer for his standard charge of three dollars for an office visit, and I walked over Moose Mountain, behind my house, into Big Valley, camping in a flyweight tent, with my brown hiking goat named Higgins, and Bimbo, a savvy white collie who had lived with the Basfords.

To recapitulate the stages of my education in Barton is difficult because the biota itself has been evolving; the people and land values changed. Vermonters began playing golf, traveling like summer people, and voting like Oregonians. And the moose and coyotes—which are such players on the scene now—came in after I did. The Wheelers' pastures grew up to woods, changing the populace of birds. Winter wrens, hermit thrushes, and ovenbirds supplanted the meadowlarks and field sparrows and bobolinks. Fishers (having been all trapped out, for the fur market in "sable") were reintroduced to the state about the same time that I was, primarily so they could control the oversupply of porcupines, which had no other natural enemies. I'd had to shoot nine porcupines—which were gnawing at my house for the salts porcupines seek in their diet—in the first year alone. But in another dozen, the "hedgehogs" and the "fisher cats," as people call the two species, were back in balance. Meanwhile, warming winters brought wild turkeys, as well as turkey vultures, north from gentler climates—right up to the Canadian border, to shake hands with boreal birds, like blackpoll warblers, three-toed woodpeckers, and spruce grouse. My Connecticut woods and circus days and British Columbia trips of course connected as a preparation. I'd live-trapped weasels, seeded baby turtles in different ponds, kept gopher snakes and homing pigeons at the age of ten or twelve, then had cared for menagerie tigers, and wandered in grizzly territory. So, meeting a black bear in a beech wood or a gawky moose in a cattail glade was not an unprecedented experience. And the pairs of barn swallows, chimney swifts, the green-and-yellow garter snakes, the flickers, pewees, and chipping sparrows that Kay Basford had protected (the one cruelty of Donald's that I witnessed was when while painting my house, he caught a snake and painted it red), were already friends of mine from boyhood.

I've now accumulated more than thirty years of close observation of the matriarchal colonies of garter snakes that live under my house, not to mention underneath the Wheelers' (which was next inherited by Dorothy's niece). Though not big, they are relics, to me, of the dinosaurs, and superb survivors, more anatomically advanced than pythons, for example. Through having caught and released them by the many dozen, I've known individuals for long periods—old blackened males that finally needed some help with the special exertion of shedding their skins, or perhaps a week of in-the-house heat in order to digest a last meal in September, after a lean dry summer, before going underground to hibernate all winter. These snakes breed in May, immediately after emerging, but a pregnant female will fast for a month or two, as her womb swells by August, displacing her stomach. And so, when she ages, she will live and breed for a few extra years if you capture her and feed her earthworms during the crucial couple of weeks in early autumn, between when her babies are born and when hibernation must start in such a rugged climate. Otherwise, in her exhausted condition, she may not be able to muster the energy to locate, grab, subdue, swallow, and digest enough prey to put on fat for those eight months of suspended animation (and wriggle out of her old skin). Though by now she is a confident hunter, she may get caught, still engorged, by a shift in the weather—a freeze, a snowfall. If the sun that is the engine of her metabolism loses heat before her innards process that last meal, it will rot inside her during hibernation and burst and poison her.

I've watched many births and seen the twenty or so babies distribute themselves afterward in little (I think, same-sex) yearling bands. Also the later confrontational hostility between garter snakes from different maternal colonies, and especially between the mothers themselves, if they are suddenly caged together—although the crisis of captivity dissolves their belligerence after a day or two, and they'll coil amicably, just as they hibernate every winter balled in a common mass together under the wood bin in the Wheelers' basement, or under the Basfords' old milk cooler, buried in the ground outside my garage. Each house had had two colonies for a long while, until Dorothy's niece decided that she wanted to rent the Wheeler house to summer people and asked me to transplant her snakes to mine. *Four* breeding females and their individual colonies now established around my house and chicken coop and barn have made for inevitable complications.

The bears I've known—because of the eight thousand acres of state-owned forestland close around—seem to have been able to maintain a continuity of vastly larger, but possibly somewhat comparable arrangements. Five to fifteen square miles is said, by those who study bears, to fill each breeding female's needs; and I would guess that in the broad vicinity of this notch I've kept aware of the resident sow's biennial birthing of her cubs, and then eviction of them the following year, when a series of males revisit her in June and the baffled yearlings begin blundering about in search of footing for themselves, except for a daughter from that or a previous pair who will remain within her mother's territory, as a sort of understudy. I've watched the amorous, rangy, burly males, and the disowned, panicky cubs, at that summer juncture when the world turns upside down for them. The physiology of bears' hibernation, their method of breeding and parturition, and later nursing and nurturing, are obviously different from a snake's methodology. Yet she defends her boundaries and food sources as punctiliously. I've lain on the ground in many cherry seasons and listened to a feeding trio—the mother and her cubs—munch fruit close to my house after dark has settled down. Though they were well aware of me, the old female knew I was harmless, and was only intent on warning off other bears—who wished to descend from the ridgeline of Wheeler Mountain to my chokecherry bushes and apple trees to fatten for their winter's sleep—with deeply directed growls. The clocking of her seasons and her years, her shifts from cave to cave for different winters or different pregnancies, her quarrels with my dogs, and nattering vocalisms while educating successive pairs of cubs (and bathing in the Wheelers' tablewater spring, until the niece's husband fenced it in), have engrossed me as much as the coyotes' more recent advent—who howl so personally in July, once their pups are mobile, from the vicinity of their den on the slope above my house.

Constancy is what we want—the snipe and the woodcock whickering in lariat loops every spring during their mating flights; and killdeer even earlier. Barred owls and white-throated sparrows also making themselves heard, about then; and "a ton of" robins landing from the south, flocks desiring to beat the crowd—fifty, ahead of the next fifty, and foraging in a skirmish line. Wood thrushes, mourning warblers, waxwings. And the later sharing of the land, by which my local doe deer delivered a fawn in mid-June in the waving grass and full-leaved willow trees alongside the same stretch of stream, a hundred yards in front of my door, where the coyote pair had flirted and bred repeatedly for a couple of hours, till sunrise, four months earlier—coyotes that would have nourished their two-month-old pups with the newborn fawn if they had known. So would the bear have eaten it, if she had been alert to the matter and not perhaps distracted by a June-moon suiter. More meaty was the moose calf born the last week of May in a glade three or four hundred yards from my house, and closer to the coyotes' den. But the succulent plant life right there permitted the cow moose (as big as a horse) to stay close for a while, and neither the coyotes nor the bear would have been fool enough to mess with her.

Life is flux, but habitat in Vermont has lately been turning somersaults, when it's not state-owned, as everyone tries to make his mark with a chain saw, skidder, bulldozer, or fancy landscaping—or simply double his money by buying and splitting up a bunch of acreage. Given an opportunity, the red-tailed hawks are likely to return to the same nesting tree, if it's not cut; and blue goshawks will drop by every fall to try for the adolescent snowshoe rabbits that no bobcat has ambushed. The years that you live on your place acquire a bounce because you know that the wood frogs will sing again in the snowmelt, and spring peepers right after them, when the red squirrels are nibbling maple twigs for the sweet sap, and song sparrows get back— once the zero nights are well past, when you had puffed your own feathers like a nuthatch and sat mute. Red-winged blackbirds, yellow-bellied sapsuckers, rose-breasted grosbeaks, scarlet tanagers, yellow warblers, indigo buntings, yellowthroats: this is wild plumage, not civilian, and the names speak to the effect that spring has, as birds materialize variously in migratory pulses, and the sow bear rummages in the swamp by Wheeler Pond for jack-in-the-pulpit and fern roots and sedges, and the waterthrushes strut, the tree frogs climb the poplars, and ovenbirds make the woods ring with *teacher-teacher-teacher*, just as teachers like me feel that the term may end.

My life was bifurcated between New York and Wheeler Mountain—*that* carbonation, and these still mineral waters. I loved the kerosene lamps, and then the city's electricity, in six-month bouts. And my marriage provided me with a solid flooring to write essays, because employing the pronoun "I" appeared to take more assurance than working anonymously as a novelist. (In 1970 not a lot of writers were using it.) The problematic part, however, was that Marion could never learn to drive; and although she gladly gave our daughter over to the life of the country every summer and did enjoy being in a small town, I doubt in twenty years she ever walked more than two hundred feet beyond our house except on the road. She was a city person, as was I; but she was so wholeheartedly a metropolitan New Yorker that half of my life, half of what I loved, we couldn't share. The country, with its mysteries, frightened her—its tracklessness and shifting skies, night cries and octopus-armed vegetation. We were good company indoors in Barton, as well as in New York: affectionately amused that her endearing mother, Peshka, when she came north to visit, was reminded of the *shtetl* in Russia, Semiatych, that she had left at twenty. For *these* cramped rooms and oil-burning lamps Peshka had crossed to the New World!

We'd married for the backup we provided one another—the layers of enthusiasms, authors, historical perspectives that we filled in for or lent to each other—besides the sexual chemistry and limber parrying of marriage. Marion had never dropped a fallen friend, and hadn't a pennyweight of New York brutality. Had been so loyal to that high school, Evander Childs, in the Bronx, that she'd refused the transfer to the much flossier Hunter College High, near midtown in Manhattan. But Marion's alternative to New York (and most New Yorkers do need one, whether it's Nova Scotia or a charter boat in Jamaica Bay), was Tel Aviv, rather than anywhere to the north, west, or south. Her heart was there; and over time, like two Roman riders—with legs spread, each of us straddling two galloping horses as though around a circus ring—we drifted apart, because only one of our plunging horses was shared.

I never went to the country to leave the cruelties of the modern world behind. Like Marion, I loved New York and didn't stop considering myself a New Yorker (nor did Marion regard herself as an Israeli) or think the rural matrix kinder. In Barton we had a wild, cruel county fair with cunnilingual girlie shows—three dollars for a lick—

famous among carnie types as far south as Alabama, and that the Quebecois poured across the border by the thousands to pay to see. The
director employed prisoners as cheap labor at his cedar sawmill and
limped, it was said, because he had been shot in the foot as a kid by a
farmer he'd stolen a turkey from. His son was one of the men who
had driven the black minister out of Vermont. And our dog-catcher
once shot a stray dog in his own living room in front of his small, crying children, according to a friend of mine who was drinking with him
at the time. I could go on with tales of the spiritual penury and hard-
scrabble misery in these ice-rasped hills. But I wasn't in Vermont for a
respite. I'd experienced mostly kindness in my own life anyway,
whether on the highway with strangers, or a long-distance pay phone,
when trying to place a collect call home in the pre-touch-tone 1950s,
with four or five or six operators, plus their supervisor, hanging on the
line attempting to decipher the numerals I was struggling to say. In
prep school I'd sometimes been made fun of as a "commie" because
my politics were liberal, or a "fairy" for wanting to write novels, but
never for my handicap.

Under Wheeler Mountain, I peered out my windows as if in a bathysphere, watching birds of passage or random mammals—a stalky
bobcat, a sinuous fisher—and the wide, ancient, homely cliffs that
towered up with cracks across them like the pentimento of a thin-
lipped grin, and two slightly mounded, snoutlike nostrils near the
top. The rock itself was not a monochromatic granite, but striped
with dark. And stunted spruces clung to precarious indentations, like
green brushstrokes along the face, except where recent avalanches
had marred the visage, stripping it of hard-won soil, like a vertical
palsy after a stroke. As I'd done as a boy, I transplanted nesting turtles
to different ponds when I found them egg-laying on a sandy road in
June, or the hatchlings in September. My pace on a moose trail was
city-quick, like the accommodation to congested agendas and scrambled viewpoints you make in a metropolis—but not so unlike a countryman's improvisations either, except in tempo. Then, during a rain
shower, I'd duck under a tree, where city-time stood still. The canopy
of leaves deflected most of the falling water; and I'd wool-gather, or
watch a mink twist underneath a boulder after a salamander, and no-

tice beyond it—where a stretch of soggy ground had drowned an aisle of trees—a vista opening toward a concave facet of the cliff that I'd never seen in all my previous walks.

I might become aware, also, of a scent from quite another sort of prehistory: a personage whose black hairs had rubbed off against the bark over my head, and who had left macho claw marks reaching idiosyncratically here and there above where I was sitting as a message not to me but other beings. Strolling on between rain squalls, I'd find perhaps another kind of bear tree, a nursery birch with two cubs hunkering in the upper branches while their mother fed in a swale a mile away—or an ample, large, old, nutting beech, smooth-skinned, that generations of bears had climbed, impatient to consume its fruits even before they fell. It was claw-scarred wherever bears had shinnied up, ten, twenty years ago, as though with archeo-handprints that had fossilized. These spoke to me, like the moose tooth-furrows that had stripped the bark in a poplar copse, or a buck-banged willow trunk by a stream's ravine.

The "ledge hawks," as Dorothy Wheeler used to call the peregrine falcons that nested on the mountain before pesticides wiped them out, are reappearing in a tentative fashion—already well established on Mount Pisgah nearby. But raven pairs have been thriving way up there throughout, hollering like howler monkeys as they school each annual quartet of chicks—flying them down off their fledgling ledge into the maple trees and firs, the butternuts and basswoods, the orchards and meadows—all of the complexities of humor and food. Hazelnuts and carrion, squirming or pouncing things, berries and bugs. The parents instruct their young in eating a shrew: and then the mouse that the shrew had been eating; then a spider on the apple that the mouse had been gnawing; and the apple itself. Hearing a coyote bark, they all flap over and spot her gobbling grasshoppers in a hayfield, and gobble lots of those, while staying out of her reach. Seeing a bittern from the air that has been fishing in a marsh and is poised with a perch crosswise in his beak, they stoop and startle him, bully him, and lift it when he drops it, take the fish to a tree, and make a little meal of *that*. In the pasture above the bittern's pool, a cow has been giving birth. So, wait with patience on a branch until she finishes. Then seize the afterbirth before a fox that's circling, sniffing the prize, feels brave enough to dart close and grab part of it—beating out a turkey vulture, too—vultures being more instinct-ridden and slow, like a roadkill bird.

The ravens' acrobatics enable them to finesse some of the mincing of habitat that is under way below, as people shop about for patches of property like new habiliments that they can try to construct another persona from. Having done mergers and acquisitions, or worked in malls or cyberspace, they hope raw land may be a new costume to get comfortable in, plus a hole in which to park some money, and a keepsake to leave to the children, if nature ever becomes their bag. When I chat at the soda fountain in the drugstore with a new guy for a while, it can become like watching amateur theatrics. Landed gentry, or Natty Bumppo—*How'm I doing?* he asks. Or I may learn that he had won a dismissal on embezzlement charges in a previous domicile. One aging neighbor of mine roamed through the woods in a killing fever, shooting any bird or animal on sight, as if their deaths could postpone his own. Quite the opposite, is a friend I have, beached here by divorce, who is a former Green Beret and has quit killing. He confronts poachers on my land with his AK-47 and asks if they want a duel. Or else, in a more suicidal mood, he'll spread his arms and tell them to blow him away—"I want to die." He sometimes fantasizes that the CIA has posted snipers on the cliffs of Wheeler Mountain to wipe him out because of the villages in Vietnam that he saw flayed. Another friend, with memories of combat as a marine in South Korea to exorcise, will blacken his face before dawn and creep into the woods, sneak behind a poacher, and put a chokehold on his neck. Up the road, however, is a fourth-generation farm family whose daughter is studying to be an opera singer, and who, when they notice that the mother bear whose territory we share is hanging out with her cubs, just witness her activities without wanting to make her into a rug.

A quiltwork, if not a crazy quilt, of landowners has spread across the old farmsteads that other families jettisoned. A gentleman not far beyond them, who was both a Seventh-Day Adventist and a psychiatrist, was raising llamas, but died taking off in his homebuilt airplane.

We still do have an elk farmer, growing antlers for the Chinese medicinal trade. And a man I know produces South American parrots and Central American king snakes for pet wholesalers in what used to be a dairy barn. Rain forest birds and reptiles, even when replicated in ski-climate Vermont, coincidentally may come in designer colors because in the course of eons the jungle endowed them with striking tints of camouflage that are flamboyant when removed from the surroundings that germinated them. The hues and tints, although perhaps originally intended to conceal the creature, now become a drawing card (like the comedy of a "talking" bird) and appeal to our jaded and disoriented optic nerves because the russet, emerald, brick, or blue has been mediated through eternity by a logic that inseminated us, as well. The snake's lovely colors—in a sort of contradance with its slither—fetch us back to the emotional content of Creation, when alarm and delight were marbled together.

Across the road from this former hippie, breeding tropical parrots and serpents, lives another flower child, who bid goodbye to his commune's disintegration by setting off alone on his stallion, Ace, and rode from Vermont to Oregon. But after that heroic effort, he didn't stay; just visited his mother and trucked Ace east again to use for logging and plowing right where they'd started. Similarly, a woman who crewed a couple of years on a yacht in the South Seas returned to work on a weekly newspaper. And a man and woman who had established modern dance careers as a touring duo came back to build their studio and base themselves in the Northeast Kingdom.

To feel at home is the essence of adulthood. And when I poked around with Bimbo, my white collie, looming like Sancho Panza in the backseat window, I'd drive for an hour or so and park where some back road ended, scramble across a beaver dam, a moosey bog, and then up to the top of West Mountain (which is actually east of East Mountain), or one of several others, tuck my sleeping bag under a white ash tree (for its quiet rustle), boil a pot of rice-and-something in spring water over a wisp of fire, and gaze at the roll of the forest and sky. The wind's seethe was soothing to dream in, once I'd caught my breath and eaten. Notch Pond, South America Pond, Seneca Mountain, Bull Mountain, Ferdinand Bog, Unknown Pond, and the spread between, without houses, barns, cabins, or pavement in any direction as far as you could see. Only a gaudy lightning storm in a menagerie of clouds—or the cerulean blue that we know the physics of, but not the more significant explanation for why it evokes such a sense of equanimity in us, and peace and glee. I'd lie and look and almost seem to join the sky, as water vapor is sucked up. What I like to call serene turmoil—or the Brownian motion undergirding life—is not dispiriting, because it never stops. If the seas did quit sloshing, the moon tilting its crescent, clouds scrimmaging, leaves falling and sprouting, we would promptly wish to bury ourselves.

And human nature being nature, I've often found the effect not different to walk ten miles in the city. The moil there also produces a serenity in me because underlying the swarm of sights is the same sensation of enlargement, though it may tire me more and not last as long, for lack of (let's say) bandwidth. But the equanimity and, cumulatively, the jubilation are quite the same. Although each of us wants to be unique and important, a deeper satisfaction arises from yearnings that seem the opposite, and make a city different from a suburb or a grid of summer cottages. To be a mote, to blend into a vast and celebrative mass, as part of a collective voice, with bells ringing—whether in Saint Peter's Square at Eastertime or Times Square on Victory Day—linked and swaying, not only with blood kin but other people, including and especially strangers, is exhilarating. It's why hymns sung by a congregation have a collective, ethereal sweetness surpassing the voice of any individual parishioner's, or those particularly glorious days when you are glad that everybody is in Central Park, not just you, and that life isn't crimped and measly: not for them, and therefore in the largest, deepest sense, not for you. Mobs, of course, don't engender our best instincts, but crowds occasionally parallel, I believe, our intricately wild and teeming beginnings. And—taking advantage of the calendar in some of these climactic fests at the turning of the year or midsummer Independence Day—we gather confidence, amidst the anonymity of numbers, to reclaim our birthright of hopefulness, and rub shoulders not against but *with* other people, as the seat of the brain that we call the heart wants to anyway.

I had a friend who lived in a busted trailer by the lake in Barton on his old-age check and from the trotline that he kept rigged for fish and the nightcrawlers that he raised and sold to day-trippers who put their boats into the water at the public-access point near him. He owned no car, but, come October, would hail a Greyhound bus on the highway and go to Florida on his fish-worm money, living in a roominghouse a few blocks from the ocean, and (as slim and funny as he was) dodge proposals from the widows there. Though born in Vermont, he had the open gaze that vastness lends—the bigger sky, huge spaces he had encountered when he went west as a kid in the 1920s and home-steaded on the Alberta prairie, in the grand mix of Indians, Métis, Mounties, outlaws, and railroadmen. He was a blithe man when death took him.

Another neighbor is a former dairyman, a practicing Christian, share-and-share-alike. If somebody robs his house, he'll say they needed the stuff they took more than he did. He used to try to con-vert me to accepting the Lord, but lately seems to recognize that our ideas of what is sacred aren't so incompatible, and equally under siege. He sees things as Creation, as I do, but, perhaps fearful of being disillusioned, is less interested in the biological details, and—again, like me—foresees the end of the world we love, or else unnerv-ing alternatives. I sometimes attend the evening services of his Solid Rock Assembly of God Church for the hymns and tears and general hugging, which can be a mild catharsis for me too, at least at lonely moments and mostly watching others do it. We both know that true religion is not teary for long, but ebullient, even in the face of unnerv-ing alternatives: that Brownian motion (to use my metaphor) will override the changes.

My friend, having retired from milk testing, tracks the headwa-ters of every nearby stream, the movements of our moose herd, be-sides going fishing, and fulfilling his paternal duties to five grown children caught in the current venal whirl. Being a Bible believer, he envisions a God more immutable than mine. Immutable, how-ever, in what way?—mercifully, implacably? Like the endgame of the new technology, that remains a mystery. We're less bewildered than suspended in a state of dread. Our faith itself makes us more

427

vulnerable than a cynic or an atheist. We are ebulliently in dread and under siege.

The other friend—that combat veteran who gets a chokehold on some of the poachers who hunt my land—once held a buddy's severed head in his arms all night, lying hiding on the ground while a Korean "gook" patrol searched for him also. When staying in my house, he's been known to shoot a hole through the woodshed because a woodpecker had tapped on it and he thought the knock might be an intruder. Like the ex-Green Beret who imagined CIA snipers on the cliffs who wished to terminate him for what he did for America in Vietnam, he's in the woods partly for his wounds. But he says that he was injured more during his childhood, before he ever joined the marines, when his father threw his mother down the cellar stairs and nailed him underneath the back-porch stoop to improvise a cage. The Green Beret came home, bought a piece of pretty land and put a trailer on it, but then the man he'd bought it from shot another man and the sale dissolved in legal riddles. For relief, I've seen him shoot his crossbow at a straw target. A Navy Seal I know was forced by his mother to lick her spittle off the floor, when he was small: and now is a commando.

In other words, it doesn't end. Yet that is how the West was won, the frontier settled—by wounded folk like us. And the regularity of the arboreal and faunal cycles, the rolling weather so dependably unpredictable that it jounces you as air pockets do a plane and you can't go on autopilot—and the bronco-ing landscapes, pummeled not just by recent glaciers but, in the case of Wheeler, a three-hundred-million-year time frame—medicates us. I prefer a house that looks upward at a natural panorama, instead of down, as if you'd conquered everything you see (which will soon be webbed with roadworks, anyway). Gazing up at fastnessess that the clouds, in a mime show of animalia, alter almost hourly, I watch the mountain go from being a sperm whale's broad profile, to an immense, snouty sphinx, and then a pubic travesty of a vulva-and-bush, four hundred feet in height. Or just a surf wall of rock, a breaking, gray comber taller than that.

The solidity of the town I'd chosen, Barton, lay in its long-time grocery-and-meats family, the Comstocks, and the Harper family, whose garage likewise went from father to son, as did E. M. Brown's feed and hardware store, which mixed its own grain formulas from freight-carloads at the Canadian Pacific Railway siding, and constituted an anchor for the dairy farms for twenty miles around. Almost everyone in the village ate at the counter of the Ruggles' drugstore once in a while (also a business that passed from father to son); and when Lee Emerson retired, his law practice, in the brick bank building, was taken over by Bill May, from one of the town's oldest families. Since the 1860s, there had been water-powered mills and little factories alongside the tumbling falls at the outlet of Crystal Lake, manufacturing tables, rockers, toilet seats and water tanks, piano sounding-boards, Peerless ladies' underwear, and wagons, buggies, butter tubs. Also a woolen mill, a gristmill, an iron foundry. The water-closet seats were fashioned out of oak or cherry to look like mahogany; and the carriage-maker was equally classy. This considerable commercial history underpinned Barton's middle-class pretensions, although by now the only factory of any size was Ethan Allen's furniture operation in the next village, Orleans. Dairy farming and pulp-logging for the New Hampshire paper industry were Barton's other economic mainstay; or cutting yellow birch and rock maple for Ethan Allen, or cedars for making fencing, tamaracks for railroad ties and barn floorboards, or sawmill spruce and pine. Real estate wasn't much of a factor in 1969; you simply went to the agent's home and drove with him to look at hundred-dollar acres. Or insurance: I insured my home through a retired shop teacher who told me on his front porch how—as an infantryman in an advanced platoon in northern Italy in 1945—he had watched Benito Mussolini being hustled away from his last mountain hideout at Salo by German soldiers, before the partisans seized him at Lake Como and strung him upside down. And how twice, as a good buddy died, he "gave him his (morphine) shot."

The suburb of my boyhood, New Canaan, had been a regular Connecticut town in transition toward becoming a high-end bedroom community, when we moved there in 1941. It still had a two-story Checkerboard feed store to supply the relic farms around; a rinky-dink railroad station on a trolleylike spur line; volunteer firemen who responded from their homes to a code of whistles blown at the firehouse that told them where to go; and a local tackle-football team that grown men played on in games against the neighboring towns. The golf course was a modest nine holes (though I remember watching Babe Didrikson Zaharias swatting an exhibition round, and Don Budge and Bill Tilden once on the tennis courts). The genteel scramble began in earnest after the war, with titans such as Thomas J. Watson, the founder of IBM, occupying dachas, Philip Johnson building his glass house (much ridiculed at the time), and narrow roads named after real Siwanoy Indians—Ponus, Oenoke, Wahackme—becoming grandiose. My father, in fact, wrote an article for the historical society about "Indian Rocks," a traditional campground a mile or two from us, where corn had been pounded in hollows in the stone. It soon became a forcing-bed for advertising, technophile, and banking wealth of the postwar decades, however; and as a small boy I used to walk the putting greens of The Club with my father and a few proto-captains of the new industries. He occupied a middle level in the pecking order of all this ferment, so before puberty I learned to recognize some of the ethology on display.

Barton, by contrast, didn't get a golf course until twenty years after I arrived. Instead, town softball teams played on a diamond on the river bottom behind the drugstore, as a main event all summer long—and not just the Little League, and then the Babe Ruth League for teenagers, but the Frontier League, or Northern Vermont League, for adults. There are still some local games between teams sponsored by nostalgic merchants who buy the uniforms, but fewer; and the men's basketball league is gone. The funeral director, on Church Street, was a charitable man who had wanted to be a priest when he was young. He used to put on movies for the kids in the Town Hall, at cost, on Friday and Saturday nights, and make popcorn. But that is over. A friend of mine bought coon skins and other furs to sell to New York dealers, but he is dead. Next to nobody traps. The mink are doing so well that they prowl right into the sporting-goods shop in the basement of the drugstore and eat the bait fish, kept alive in a tank there, waiting to be sold to day-trippers.

The fluctuations in how land and the houses on it are employed puzzle many people (being occupied intensively for two months; then not for ten), and require considerable elasticity from the wildlife, too. New cottages spring up, but the owners live like suburbanites, in their cars, if not indoors; and the mammals and birds will form concentric circles of minihabitat around each dwelling—robins and flycatchers exploiting the lawn, wood warblers and woodpeckers out beyond the fringe. Foxes hunt and den closer to a house than the coyotes (who will eat a fox) normally choose; and deer feed and bed down closer than a moose. Although accordioned into ever smaller parcels, the land can yet retain a certain stubborn ecological value if it's manhandled less: if, that is, the people are away somewhere, or mostly on the Internet, or else in front of the TV, instead of being out sugaring, or driving cows around, cutting hay and corn and firewood, trapping bears, and shooting owls and "chickenhawks." Wild critters can swing right into a summer person's dooryard in the early fall and grab whatever rabbits, squirrels, and the like that have been sheltering there. Or when the snow flies, you'll see a bobcat's tracks go into the cellar and out again, and mouse nests demolished. The people bought the cabin to kick back in, watch the wrens, keep a boat, a diary, and entertain eccentric thoughts, dodge extraneous conversations—plus possess the inestimable privilege of merely thinking about it when gridlocked in the city.

The woods become a proscenium for many folk to strut their stuff in particular roles they may have picked: whether as a sandaled Gandhian; or a "beaver-trapper" clumping about with a full beard, green wool pants, and mud boots; a Mafia don with a pistol in an ankle holster and a cultivated manner of menace; or an old-time fiddler, hirsute and picky, with a yoke of oxen, to boot. In the 1970s, cropped-headed women and Prince Valiant men hilled potatoes, home-schooled their kids, argued at public meetings, and bid for a grain-sack full of laying hens at Souliere's Tuesday-night animal auctions. I was chameleon enough myself that I hung out more with these heterodox hippies than with either the middle-class pillars of Barton society or the guys who turned dowels into table legs and stained furniture for Ethan Allen.

Now, newcomers tend to try to dilute the character of any place they move so that it won't seem unsettlingly different from where they left. But the hippies only sought to alter Vermont's morals, not its wider mores, and for years put quite a brake on change. They burned stovewood, plowed with horses, maintained numerous farmstands,

helped or bartered with their neighbors, and disdained pecuniary os-
tentation. But, having few fixed rules and private spaces, there also
was a trickster, totem-pole quality, a sliding variability to some of
these communes. The faces and personalities were often tiered, as if
piggyback, until, next week, the arrangement switched. Scouting up
a humpy road to reach one of them, you never knew what you'd
stumble on, a buttermilk picnic or a bad acid trip. Would they build
their New Jerusalem or piss it away? Eventually they did piss it away,
for the most part, in six-pack binges and false starts; left dozens of
jerry-built dwellings abandoned in the woods. But all this took at
least a decade of merriness and angst. And some tough nuts did hang
on, such as the friend I'd bushwhacked the forty miles of forest with.
A Bronx boy and Coast Guard veteran, Al had run Dorothy Day's
Catholic Worker soup kitchen near the Bowery in New York and was
a committed idealist, though more of a loner than a leader. The leaders crashed.

I had my dog and sleeping bag, so I could stay over if it suited.
But usually I wouldn't, because I liked to be at home at work when
the sun rose. There were anomalies in several of these Brigadoons,
such as the medieval enthusiast who had floated in on the tide of
Heads yet was said to be sleeping with his own daughters to tutor
them in sex, because that's what the thanes supposedly had advo-
cated. And some lesbians were reported to have fertilized themselves
with a turkey baster from a wooden bowl that a few men had volun-
teered to jerk off into, so none could later claim paternity and the
women might bear their kids in simultaneous solidarity. But in general, a commune visit was cheery—the ballooning conversation and
the good salads. And the hippies blended with the locals better than
contemporary uplink people, with their bicoastal assets and cyberspace income. The hippies and the farmhands, or an assembler from
Ethan Allen, might meet in a beer joint and begin to trade car parts,
or else ice-fish and do a little redneck pot together. They could all
use a chain saw, pound nails, drive a bread truck, or kick cow shit. In
both cultures, all work was regarded as of equal dignity and futility,
and a night's mischief (if not the underlying alienation) was fairly
similar—the junker cars and woodpile winters, the beer runs and di-
sheveled children.

Now that everybody wants a "place" somewhere, people bump into each other with far less rhyme or reason. The guy training a pair of coonhounds on the weekend to clear his lungs of the reek of furniture stain, and a matron walking in the woods with a cell phone and a mushroom guide—who has a chalet down on the lake but winters in Arizona—are gingerly when they meet at a foot-log across my stream. Ours is a town where three bank robbers used simply their deer rifles for the stick-up (directing traffic outside the bank as if the barrels were batons), and then perhaps put the money in a boxcar that rattled into Canada, while the cops were tipped off to search through several manure piles. And who knows if the showoffs who scattered play-money in front of the grandstand at the next demolition derby—from a jalopy painted THANK YOU, HOWARD BANK—were really them? Around the same time, the grandstand roared to life when the then-governor of Vermont was officially introduced to the crowd by the master of ceremonies, before giving a speech, as "a Porky Flat-lander." Our *later* bank robbers, on the other hand, were just three vacationers from New Jersey, doing it (as they told a friend of mine, who saved their newspaper clippings for them, after they had got away) "for the rush."

If farmers live by the weather's vagaries, the hippies were directed by their daily shifts in mood, and saw the cycle as rather analogous, drawing on food stamps and other poverty programs—if not a trust fund—in the meantime. Thus, the self-proclaimed "Wood-chuck" type of Vermonters, who hibernated as much as they could through a frigid winter, weren't so unlike this dogged class of hippie, who slept in their long johns in a yurt or a tepee, a geodesic dome, or a remodeled cowshed, in January (not just during the summer), and pulled on bib overalls in the morning and went and kicked the ice out of the pigs' and chickens' water dishes, and bundled their children off to school. It wasn't much like bohemianism in the East Village in New York, where the city's jitters percolated and, for example, the genius of the Abstract Expressionists lay along the edge—where people slept less and knew that life was short. Here, they might just bliss out for the rest of the day, once the kids were fed and in snowsuits and the basic carpentry of winterizing the sleeping-loft was done. Yet the hippies' suspicion of the mercenary economy they had fled from dovetailed nicely with many farm families' poignant reluctance to shatter their traditional long view of the value of land and simply cash out to a summer person, run to Florida, and watch TV programs. A hustler in our county was going around to impoverished elderly couples, speaking French to the ethnic Canadians, and carrying a bottle of whiskey, a suitcase full of stacked money, and the paperwork all filled out. But by and large, the entire state's resistance to cheapshot change was reinforced by the counterculture's choice of Vermont as a real focal point: while the sexual promiscuity they also brought with them was a national tide that was rolling in upon New England anyway.

The hippies were anti-bookish, in the main. Even the college graduates soft-pedaled the idea of education in favor of what they could prove or accomplish with their hands. This, like their lack of interest in money, made them unintimidating. Herbert Marcuse had had some philosophical influence: but the sandaled marginalia was what had fostered Gandhi, Buddha, Christ, not the buttoned-down, bought-off universities, with their rich endowments and literary/scientific canon. Nor was *Midtown* where anything was at. Midtown was where the Vietnam War was hatched, and Nelson Rockefeller's savage state-trooper riot at Attica Prison in 1971, in which forty-three people died, and where investment bankers swaggered down the sidewalk. If you were a Green Mountain hillbilly who had never set foot in a city except maybe delivering a load of Christmas trees, you had nothing to fear from chumming around with the hippies. They wouldn't embarrass you by suggesting you'd missed anything—just tuck ten pounds of pot in the back of your truck next time, underneath the wreaths.

That's changed. Divorce, job-hunting, the interstate, and electronic thruways have inoculated nearly everybody against an Appalachian sort of localism. Even bear hunting is done by radio-collaring the dogs and driving around in a pickup according to where the signals turn; then punishing the dogs with electronic shocks to the neck if they mess up. My own reaction is to pull in, be more private than I used to be: as, indeed, most people are, with their online aliases and faceless e-mail. It was fun the old way, dropping in on people who had no phone and what-you-see-is-what-you-get. I was fortyish and therefore spared the sort of juddering blunders I might have stumbled into during this fevered period, even as an onlooker, otherwise. The herpes, smuggled from Brooklyn, that some of my friends caught; the bar fights with cue sticks in the Osborne Hotel in Island Pond (a guy laying his pistol down next to his drink); the rollovers in vehicles that other friends of mine kept suffering, or near-death episodes from pneumonia in fireless cabins. The "Smash Monogamy" hippies, the "Free Vermont" people, the "New Morning" individuals, and the "Weather People" stayed downstate, like the Red Clover and Red Mountain and Pie-In-the-Sky communes, and others who preferred a more political, less offstage stance—though some Yippies from Berkeley did establish an anarchic, populous commune called "Earth People's Park" right on the Quebec border, with a "Ho Chi Minh Trail," where drugs could be backpacked across.

It's a wonder that I can only think of a couple of young people who were murdered in the Northeast Kingdom probably over drug deals that went awry; and one aging man who overdosed on boron in a weird kind of potency health craze. And I remember only the suicide of a boy who lived in a treehouse at Mad Brook Farm: after a spell of riding the rooftree of the main farmhouse on nice days, and hollering a lot. People from the age of twenty to thirty were trying to hack free of extraneous edicts and restraints, surmount their own makeup, and retune the rest of the world; and the remarkable thing was how few of them met with a train wreck. Mostly, they lost half a dozen years or so, and some laps in the race, lamed their children a bit, and were sidelined. But the booming American economy carried them along without desperate consequences. They got boozy, sheepish, lunky—as the fallen often do—but were soon not noticeable as a bloc anymore. Summer people swamped them. Golfers outnumbered them. Gun nuts enlisted a few of them; or the fad for organic gardening, which meant that they could sell their vegetables at a farmers' market to the leisure class and maybe venture inside some rich Stowe housewife's pants. From disillusion, a person can slip into the notion that all life is a con; and as the hippies lost much of their enthusiasm for the showy, frenetic promiscuity that had aroused widespread disapproval in the towns around, they saw Vermonters themselves begin going overboard with divorces, live-ins, love swaps, bed-hopping (or "jumping the fence," Vermonters call it), gender-bending, toke-puffing, and other longhair stuff.

What didn't catch on during the 1980s and 1990s was the hippies' fastidious disdain for money: which is the only thing they were fastidious about. For example, although they were nominally pacifists, in my thirty years of writing about Vermont, the only person who has ever threatened to burn down my house because of what I'd said was a hippie, not a regular old-fashioned, hawkish, crew-cut Vermonter. Unmercenary communitarianism has never been adopted much in America (it's not a hallmark of the Mormons' signal success); and so the hippies who didn't morph into go-getters were stranded, delivering newspapers, laying flagstones for patios, and pounding studs and plasterboard, as if their gambit had fizzled. Nor did they believe they'd actually proved anything, because they lost faith in the 1960s' mantra that all work is of equal dignity, honor, and fascination. They'd gotten sick of life underneath-the-house or underneath-the-car, fixing the plumbing or the transmission and differential in freezing weather, when you're existing on a minimum wage and fighting off the flu and the multiple lovers somehow haven't added up to one true partner. Now they worked just to eat. Work was another con.

My curiosity faltered when the experiment collapsed, although I remained sympathetic to my hippie friends who seemed as baffled as dolphins suffering after running up on a beach. The 1960s had been like the 1930s for an earlier generation: a failed revolution in many ways, but which did leave a sea change in the culture, despite its know-nothing dimensions. The Vietnam War—like the stock market Crash of 1929—had magnified and helped delineate a national emergency. In throttling the war and passing civil rights legislation—as with the New Deal's social security, welfare, and Fair Labor laws—the country as a whole had been upended in unforeseen, ancillary respects, its hierarchies mutated. Transience and egalitarianism were boosted; dress codes and lifestyles changed. So, when I go to hippie reunions nowadays, I remember the wistful men I saw hanging out in Union Square in New York City in the middle 1950s. Twenty years had passed, by then, since those grunts from the trenches of the proletarian revolt had had their heyday during the Depression, and they, too, had wilted. Mainstream culture had digested what it wanted of their innovations in union-organizing and the rest, and spit them out.

The hippies' aims struck me as more nebulous because, in keeping with their dropout stance, they seldom participated in politics. On the communes, they practiced women's liberation, consensus government, legalized marijuana, and nonmercenary self-help, but thought that corruption imbued "the system" so pervasively, you should live separately. Just by being there, however, they liberalized the interior of New England, when formerly there had been a disjunction between the working-class, manufacturing towns and rock-ribbed, rural viewpoints. They could plow snow, chop a log, sew clothes, hold up one end of a reasonable discussion, and cook "American chop suey," just like a "Woodchuck." The differences, of course, lay in their imported sense of an emergency, whereas the local families had lasted in these tough hills through the Civil War, two world wars, and various economic recessions, when land might be worth a dollar an acre or a hundred an acre, yet provided a steady living and would anchor you to the nth generation.

The hippies admired *that* idea, but the farmers, too, were eclipsed not long after them, and partly by the money scramble. Money had been a scrimmage before—in 1900, 1925, 1950, or whenever—without dissolving so many family farms. Not everyone had joined the gold rush or gone to the big city, and land values way out in the sticks were not in play as asset management. Nor did people hop about in lifestyle phases or via electronics, as they do now. The hippies, though building on the grungier kinetics of the fifties city Beatniks—that low-rent nihilism, combined with social rebellion and impromptu, circular travel—had added a cleansing, country dimension: a place for women and for Gaea, the Earth Mother, for multicultural music, a green thumb, and an egalitarian self-sufficiency that dropped out of ordinary society not as an end but as a means. ("God is dead" disappeared as a mantra.) Hippie women weren't supine. They cooked and hugged and marched in protests the way Neal Cassady drove, and didn't value unhappiness as a spiritual talisman the way the fifties groupies had. They believed in the virtue of other people, in other words. And yet it was a thin Buddhism, and they bathed in the elixir of nature without much thought for its survival. Not a total solipsism, like the Beats' had been, or the Yuppies' that followed: but living by the day was their motto, with a little help from Mary Jane to bend the mind.

Continuity. How fast the poplars grow; and how slow the oaks. The staunch white pine that I still can't see the top of when I am standing underneath, although a forester told me it would be all but dead of blister-rust disease a quarter-century ago. The barn and house have new metal roofs that ought to last them much longer than that. My marriage didn't last, yet the place somehow did. The continuity of reddish-sided jumping mice and white-throated sparrows, two-lined salamanders and blue goshawks, shorttail weasels and starnose moles. The smell of the cedars, and the joe-pye weed (like vanilla ice cream), while a nighthawk dashes softly overhead, and a mink frog brusquely calls. A toad starts singing; and a big green frog—and one of the cliff's pair of ravens seems to mimic the green frog. A male bear descended steeply from his den overlooking my house in late April for a stillborn calf that had been left for him, while the resident fe-male roamed sideways separately on a gentler gradient that her cubs could handle from *hers* (catty-corner in the V of this mountain notch from his wintering spot) to find the one left in order to get her off to a well-nourished start.

Thirty-some years of yellowthroat song from the apple tree and raspberry patch in back of my house, and a Nashville warbler in front. Spotted sandpipers out by the pond, and a pair of young beavers try-ing to colonize that stretch of stream, but beaten back by shallow water every fall, though they may have pooled enough for a king-fisher to hunt. Two moose, heading there, slanted across my back field last evening as I finished this. But they would have been deer, looking toward my window, when I came to Vermont.

(2000)

III
People

In Praise of John Muir

We must go halfway with John Muir. He was more of an explorer than a writer, more confident of his abilities in botany and geology than of what he could do with the eagle-quill pens he liked to use (while encouraging a friend's year-old baby to clamber about the floor, lending liveliness to the tedium of a writer's room). He was a student of glaciers, cloud shapes, and skyscapes—a lover of Sitka spruce one hundred fifty feet tall, of big sequoias, tiny woods orchids, and great waterfalls. He put together his books late in life—he was fifty-six before *The Mountains of California*, his first book, was published—from magazine articles, most of which had themselves been reconstructed well after the events described, from notes jotted down in the field with wildfire enthusiasm but little thought of eventually publishing them. Though he was a wonderful talker, he was never entirely respectful of the written word and was surprised to find that there was an audience willing to read him, amazed he could earn a living by writing. Being one of those people "who give the freest and most buoyant portion of their lives to climbing and seeing for themselves," he doubtless wished that more of his readers preferred to hike on their own two feet into the fastnesses he had described.

Henry Thoreau lived to write, but Muir lived to hike. "I will touch naked God," he wrote once, while glacier climbing. And, on another jaunt, lunching on his customary dry crust of bread: "To dine with a glacier on a sunny day is a glorious thing and makes common feasts of meat and wine ridiculous. The glacier eats hills and sunbeams." Although he lacked the coherent artistic passion of a professional writer, he was Emersonianism personified. There is a time freeze, a time warp to a river of ice, as if God had been caught still alive, in the act and at work, and because Muir's passions were religious and political instead of artistic, Muir—unlike Thoreau, who in comfortable Concord only speculated that his Transcendental intuitions were right—put his life and his legs on the line in continual tests of faith in the arduous wilderness of the High Sierras. He believed that if his intuitions were wrong, he would fall, but he didn't ask himself many questions about what was happening, as Thoreau would have done, and didn't believe such exalted experiences could be conveyed to the page anyway.

Thoreau welded together one of the enduring prose styles of the nineteenth century. He may be America's paramount stylist and also established in his spare time a famously disobedient stance toward the institutionalized cruelties of the world, which later was to help Gandhi and, through Gandhi, Martin Luther King in formulating mass-movement nonviolent campaigns, before dying of TB at only forty-four, in 1862. Of course, Thoreau was in addition what we would call a conservationist, but not a militant, innovative one like Muir. Muir (1838–1914) was the founding president of the Sierra Club and the chief protector of Yosemite Park. Thoreau, on the other hand, anathematized American imperial conduct in the Mexican War and got still more exercised about slavery, angrily championing the early "terrorist" John Brown. Muir—who was all in all a more conventional soul in his politics—even after the end of the Civil War commented approvingly during a trek through Georgia that "the Negroes here have been well-trained and are extremely polite. When they come in sight of a white man on the road, off go their hats, even at a distance of forty or fifty yards, and they walk bare-headed until he is out of sight."

It's important to recognize that such contrasts were not merely due to the fact that Muir was born twenty-one years after Thoreau and thus lived through the ambiguities of Reconstruction. Thoreau sought out the company of Indians on his trips to Maine and respectfully studied their customs, whereas Muir generally disparaged the Indians of California as ignoramuses and children, dirty and cultureless wretches. Not until his adventurous travels to Alaska in middle age—he took three trips during his forties, three in his fifties, and one tour to the Bering Sea by steamer at sixty-one—did he admit a semblance of tolerance into his view of Indians. And though as a conservationist he was highly "advanced," a Vermonter named George Perkins Marsh, born back in 1801, proved to have sounded as modernist a tocsin as Muir's in a widely read book called *Man and Nature*, which came out in 1864. Thirty years before *The Mountains of California*, Marsh counterposed to the biblical theory that nature was a wilderness mankind should "subdue and rule" the idea that

> Man has too long forgotten that the earth was given to him for usufruct alone, not for consumption, still less for profligate waste.... We are, even now, breaking up the floor and wainscoting and doors and window frames of our dwelling.... The earth is fast becoming an unfit home for its noblest inhabitant, and another era of equal human crime and human improvidence ... would reduce it to such a condition of impoverished productiveness ... as to threaten the depravation, barbarism, and perhaps even extinction of the species.

Marsh was a complex personality, who served four terms in Congress and twenty years as U.S. ambassador to Italy, but he was a quiet visionary and public servant in the style of a New England Brahmin—not a public figure, not the man of mounting celebrity that Muir became. Muir as lecturer, as Westerner, as "John o' the Mountains," learned, like Walt Whitman and Longfellow, to wear a public sort of beard. Living to the ripe old age of seventy-six, he enjoyed three active decades that were denied to Thoreau and changed a good deal during the course of them. Although a far "wilder" naturalist, he had lived nearly as celibately as Thoreau for nearly as long. However, with no undue enthusiasm, he did marry, a week short of being forty-two. He then had two daughters—whom he deeply loved—and turned himself into a substantial, successful landowner and grape farmer as well as a well-known writer and a force to be reckoned with in Sacramento and occasionally in Washington, D.C. International lecture tours, friendship with Teddy Roosevelt, honorary degrees from Harvard and Yale—in these extra years he knew rewards that Thoreau had never aspired to, yet remained an adventurer to the end, traveling to Africa, South America, and Asia late in life. Only Jack London and John James Audubon among American artists come to mind as adventurers with a spirit to compare with his, and for both of them adventuring was more closely tied to ambition.

Thoreau, less and less a thinker and more and more a naturalist after he turned forty, was also changing in personality before he died. Supporting himself as a professional surveyor and by reorganizing his family's pencil business, he was making elaborate mathematical calculations in his journal and sending zoological specimens to Louis Agassiz. But though he didn't know it, he was already on the point of winning a considerable readership. Being in a small way a professional lecturer too, he might have capitalized on that development eventually, just as Muir did. In his last year he traveled to Minnesota to try to repair his health; and with the love that he felt for the big woods of Maine, Thoreau might well have given up his previous insistence that it was enough to have "traveled a good deal in Concord" if he'd lived on. Perhaps his best work was behind him, but there would have been some interesting darkening of the tints and rounding of the details if he had blossomed as a generalist and an essayist again.

It's doubtful, nevertheless, that Thoreau, given another thirty years, would have become as touching an individual as Muir. He was always a less personal man—less vulnerable, vociferous, strenuous, emotional. He would never have married; and not having gone through a childhood as miserable, a youth as risky and floundering as Muir's, he wouldn't have burgeoned in such an effusion of relief when fame and financial security blessed him.

Yet, really, no amount of worldly acclaim made Muir half as happy as being in remote places. Muir is touching just because he was so immensely gleeful in wild country—happier than Thoreau, Audubon,

London, Whitman, Mark Twain, James Fenimore Cooper, Francis Parkman, and other figures one thinks of as being happy out of doors. He was a genteel and ordinary man in most of his opinions, and his method of lobbying politically for his beloved Yosemite was to ally himself with rich men, such as the railroad magnate E. H. Harriman, who had the power to sway events their way if the whim seized them. He was no nay-sayer on social questions and never would have conceived of putting himself in jail overnight to register a protest, as Thoreau had done. He would have agreed with Thoreau's now famous phrase "In Wilderness is the preservation of the world," but Muir emphasized a wilderness of joy. And that, after all, is what the 1872 law creating Yellowstone—the first of the national parks—had stipulated: "The region is hereby . . . set aside as a public park and pleasuring ground for the enjoyment of the people. . . ."

Muir was not a hypocrite, and he once let Harriman hear of his saying to some scientist friends that he didn't regard Harriman as truly rich: "He has not as much money as I have. I have all I want and Mr. Harriman has not." Muir, indeed, devoted only seven years of his life to the primary aim of making money. ("The seven lost years," his wife called them, when he was managing full time the fruit ranch she inherited from her father.) But he valued money and respectability and held few views on any subject to alarm a "bully" president like Roosevelt or a tycoon like Harriman. Like Audubon, Muir was proud of being foreign-born. He nurtured the strong streak of business acumen, the religious if disputatious temperament, the Spartan understatement and resilience, and the excellent mechanical aptitudes that he considered to be part of his Scottish heritage. His mix of idealism and innocence with the hard-mannered Scotch burr—a familiar, respected accent in the immigrant stream of a hundred years ago—charmed at the same time as it reassured such men. ("Frenchiness" would not have been nearly as useful.)

Although Mr. Harriman's Southern Pacific Railroad had no stake in what happened to Yosemite Valley, he responded charitably and fancifully to Muir's pleas for help in 1905, when the valley's fate was being decided in the state senate, with a confidential telegram to his chief agent in San Francisco. The vote was whisker close, but to the astonishment of the logging and livestock industries, nine legislators that Southern Pacific "owned" suddenly swung their votes behind a bill to give this spectacular scenery to the federal government. The next year, Harriman wrote with the same potent effect to the Speaker of the U.S. House, and to Senate leaders, to have Yosemite included in a national park. And after Teddy Roosevelt's presidency had ended, Muir's odd appeal also worked upon William Howard Taft, a much tougher nut among presidents.

Muir as an advocate was a Johnny-one-note, but oh, that note! "When California was wild, it was one sweet bee-garden throughout its entire length," he wrote with yearning. "Wherever a bee might fly within the bounds of this virgin wilderness . . . throughout every belt and section of climate up to the timber line, bee-flowers bloomed in lavish abundance." Wistfully he proposed that all of the state might be developed into a single vast flower palace and honey hive to the continent, its principal industry the keeping, herding, and pasturing of bees.

When California was wild! Luckily, he'd seen it then. He had arrived by ship seven years after Mark Twain appeared by stagecoach in Nevada, on the other side of the Sierras, to transcribe the experiences of *Roughing It.* Both Muir and Twain originally had harbored the hope of lighting out for the Amazon, but Twain got sidetracked into piloting Mississippi riverboats and Muir got seriously sick in Florida and Cuba en route to South America. Muir—who had reveled in one of the best adventures in his life in walking south from Louisville to Georgia—sailed to New York City to recuperate. However, disliking the city, he caught a packet immediately for San Francisco, landing in March of 1868, a month before his thirtieth birthday.

Unlike Twain, Muir hadn't gone west as a writer; not till he was thirty-seven did he resolve to be one. This was "the wild side of the continent," he said, which was reason enough. Yet he invariably soft-pedaled its dangers and hardships. Twain, quite the opposite, and quintessentially "American," celebrated the badmen and primitive conditions in marvelously exploitative tall tales, boasting of how his knees knocked. Twain used the mountains as a theatrical prop, having abandoned his career manqué as a silver miner as soon as he obtained a job as a newspaperman in Virginia City. The mountains themselves had small fascination for him, and he sought companionship with writerly acquisitiveness at every opportunity, whereas Muir at that time was grasping at solitude, avoiding "the tyrant of creation," as Audubon had once described mankind.

But the reason Muir so seldom speaks about the cold rains, the ice bite and exhaustion he met with in the mountains, the terror of an avalanche, of breaking through ice in crossing a waterway, or about the many deer he must have observed starving to skin and bones after a series of snows, is not simply Scottish diffidence and asceticism. He loved most of nature's violence—"the jubilee of waters," as he called one particular winter storm. In the earthquake of 1872, "disregarding the hard fist of fear in his stomach, he ran out into the moonlit meadows," according to Linnie Marsh Wolfe, his biographer. "Eagle Rock, high on the south wall of the valley, was toppling. . . . All fear forgotten, he bounded toward the descending mass," shouting exuberantly in the shower of dust and falling fragments, leaping among the new boulders before they had finished settling into their resting places on the valley floor.

Besides, when he got around to organizing the journals of his early wanderings, he had become sharply political. He had been jotting plant identifications and geological evidence of glaciation but now was gleaning memories from the same pages, meaning to write to save the wilderness from obliteration—and not just by the timber and mining companies. More pervasive a threat at the turn of the century was the injunction in Genesis that any wilderness was a wasteland until tilled, that man was made in the likeness of God and in opposition to wilderness and its multitudinous creatures, which were not. This seems a very old pronouncement; yet it had been the revolutionary edict of a new religion attacking established spiritual values—monotheism on the offensive against polytheism, which revered or at least incorporated the realities of the wilderness. Furthermore, later texts and preachers went beyond the objection that certain mountains, forests, springs, and animal races had been considered gods, to decry the wilderness as actually devil-ridden, inimical to the salvation of man.

Muir, like the eastern Transcendentalists, was not advocating polytheism. Nor was he secular. He believed that wilderness, like man, was an expression of one God; that man was part of nature; that nature, fount of the world, remained man's natural home, under one God. Like Emerson and Thoreau—and like Twain and Whitman and Melville and Hawthorne—Muir had found Christianity to be a stingy religion in matters vital to him. In his case, it wasn't the church's vapid response to the issue of slavery or to the mysterious ambiguities of evil or the imperatives of love that swung him toward the perilous experiment of inventing his own religion (for Twain, this became atheism). Polytheism was long dead, yet the wilderness was still perceived as inimical, and so Muir didn't want to increase by even a little the lore that had contributed to such a misreading.

His father had been a free-lance Presbyterian preacher, when not working on their Wisconsin farm—a hellfire Presbyterian, fierce with the one flock given into his care, who were his children. The family had immigrated to America when John was eleven, and from then on he worked like an adult, dawn to dusk in the summer, with many beatings. At fifteen, he was set the task of digging a well in sandstone by the light of a candle. Daily for months, except on Sundays, he was lowered alone in a bucket, and once, at the eighty-foot level, passed out from lack of oxygen. Though he was rescued only just in time, two mornings later his father punctually lowered him to the bottom all over again. Not till he was ninety feet down did he hit water.

This amok Presbyterianism helped to estrange Muir from Christianity, but not from religion, and paradoxically made him gentler toward everyone but himself. He had encountered kinder treatment from some of the neighbors and, despite his deficiencies in schooling, was welcomed to the University of Wisconsin in Madison, where a science professor and Emerson and Agassiz disciple named Ezra Carr, and especially Mrs. Carr, drew him into their household like a son. His education was so hard won that he seems to have gotten more out of his two and a half years of college in terms of friendships and influences than Thoreau did at Harvard, though both learned to keep an assiduous notebook and to insist that America had a great intellectual role to play in the world.

Muir was one of those people who believe in the rapture of life but who must struggle to find it. He wasn't always blissful in the woods. During the Civil War, when he was twenty-six, he fled to Canada, partly in order to evade the draft, and wandered the environs of the Great Lakes for eight months in intermittent torment. He had already aspired to be a doctor, then had leaned toward natural science, had exhibited a phenomenal knack for inventing machine tools and implements—the kind of talent that has founded family dynasties—and had won his independence from his father without bruising his mother and sisters and brothers unduly. He had had fine friends, had been in love; yet still he wanted to leave "the doleful chambers of civilization, the beaten charts," and search for "the Law that governs relations between human beings and Nature." There was one indispensable lesson he had gained from the brutal schedule of labors of his boyhood. When it was essential during the next couple of decades that he explore, laze, gaze, loaf, muse, listen, climb, and nose about, he was free of any puritan compulsion to "work." After the north-woods sojourn, he put in another two years as a millwright and inventor for wages (not drudgery, because he enjoyed it), before a frightening injury to his right eye in the carriage factory where he worked bore in upon him the realization that life was short.

Once, finding himself in the metropolis of Chicago, he had passed the five hours between trains by botanizing in vacant lots; and now, as he struck off like one of his heroes, Alexander von Humboldt, for the valley of the Amazon, he set a compass course directly through Louisville so as not to notice the city too much. Beginning this, his earliest journal extant, he signed himself, with ecstatic curlicues, "John Muir, Earth-planet, Universe." Later on, in California, he would set off into the radiant high country of "the Range of Light"—as he called the Sierra Nevadas—with his blanket roll and some bread and tea thrown into a sack tossed over his shoulder like "a squirrel's tail." He might scramble up a Douglas fir in spiked boots in a gale to cling to it and ride the wind "like a bobolink on a reed," smelling the flower fields far away and the salt of the sea. "Heaven bless you all," he exclaimed, in his first summer journal from the Sierras—meaning all California's citizenry, including its lizards, grasshoppers, ants, bighorn sheep, grizzly bears, bluebottle flies (who "make all dead flesh fly"): "our horizontal brothers," as he was apt to describe the animal kingdom.

On the giddy cliffs and knife edges he was not out to test his courage, like the ordinary outdoorsman, but was set upon proving the beneficence of God. More than Thoreau, though less than Emerson, he skewed the evidence. God was in the mountains, as he knew from his own sense of joy; and as he gradually discovered that his intuitions were tied in with compass directions, storms brewing, the migration of ice, and the movements of bears, he was preparing to preach the goodness of God to us as well as himself. In even the mildest Christian theology, nature was simply handed over in servitude to man, and the Transcendentalists were trying to bypass not only this destructive anthropocentrism, as they perceived it, but also the emphasis Christianity placed upon an afterlife at the expense of what seemed a proper reverence for life on earth. Such stress upon salvation appeared to isolate people from one another as well, because each person's fate was to be adjudicated separately. Transcendentalists believed in universal links and, while never denying the possibilities of an afterlife, chose to emphasize the miraculous character, the healing divinity, of life here and now.

Emerson admired and communed with Muir during a visit to Yosemite and afterward encouraged him by correspondence. Other intellectual doyens—Asa Gray, Agassiz, Joseph Le Conte—took up his banner, and he was offered professorships in science in California and Massachusetts, which he turned down. From the start he had seemed a marked man. Like his father's neighbors, his college instructors, and factory mentors, Muir's first employer in the Sierras, a sheep owner named Mr. Delaney, predicted that he was going to be famous and "facilitated and encouraged" his explorations, Muir said. Some of the Mormons, too, appear to have noticed him favorably when he descended from the Wasatch Range on one of his larks to hobnob a bit near Salt Lake City. Ardent, outspoken, eloquent in conversation, he wore his heart on his sleeve throughout his life, but although more driven, more energetic than Thoreau, he lacked Thoreau's extraordinary gift of self-containment and single-mindedness. He had more friendships—an intricacy of involvements—and was a "problem solver," as we say nowadays, a geyser of inventiveness. The trajectory of his career carried him finally to the winsome, wise figure leading day hikes for the Sierra Club, or posed on his ample front porch in vest and watch fob with his high-collared daughters and black-garbed wife; to the Muir quarreling publicly and condescendingly with the Hudson River naturalist John Burroughs, and Muir as a visiting fireman in London, or elected to the American Academy of Arts and Letters in 1909. Yet for all these amenities, and the freedom he won to do as he liked in the world, he never achieved anything like Thoreau's feeling of mastery over it—that easy-wheeling liberty to analyze, criticize, anatomize, and summarize society's failings with roosterly pleasure: "the mass of men lead lives of quiet desperation." Compared to Thoreau's spiky commentaries on his neighbors and other townsfolk, on politics, culture, labor, industry, civilization, "Boston," Muir's admonitory remarks sound aloof, stiff, and hostile, as if directed at targets with which he had no firsthand familiarity. For despite all his friendships, Muir sought the glory of God far from other people; and just as he had had to reinvent Transcendentalism for himself way out on a kind of rim of the world, he devised his own brand of glaciology to explain the land-forms of Yosemite—notions at first ridiculed by the academic geologists, then vindicated, though Muir had taken no account of previous or contemporaneous studies, mainly because he was unacquainted with them. We need to remember that one reason he roamed so high and far was to measure living glaciers and inspect virgin evidence, but he was both too religious and too idiosyncratic to rightly pursue a scientific career, and so he moved on to become a rhapsodist, a polemicist, and a grandfather whitebeard.

He had seen the last of the Wisconsin, Appalachian, and California frontiers. Like twenty-two-year-old Francis Parkman on the Oregon Trail in 1846, like twenty-six-year-old Sam Clemens jolting into Fort Bridger in 1861, he had gone west for adventure. But he stayed in the West, stayed exhilarated, witnessing nature on a scale never presented on the Atlantic seaboard: volcanoes, landslides, calving glaciers, oceans of flowers, forests of devil's-club and Alaskan hemlock. He was thick-skinned to criticism, like Mark Twain, but more personally peaceable, as exuberant in Alaska as Jack London but indifferent to gold rushes and desperadoes. His favorite bird was the water ouzel—an agile, inoffensive creature living in mountain watercourses—not the golden eagle; and his favorite animals were squirrels.

> The Douglas squirrel is by far the most interesting and influential of the California *sciuridae*, surpassing every other species in force of character. . . . Though only a few inches long, so intense is his fiery vigor and restlessness, he stirs every grove with wild life, and makes himself more important than even the huge bears that shuffle through the tangled underbrush beneath him. Every wind is fretted by his voice, almost every bole and branch feels the sting of his sharp feet. How much the growth of the trees is stimulated by this means is not easy to learn, but . . . Nature has made him master forester and committed most of her coniferous crops to his paws. . . .

This is not the author of *White Fang* talking.

Like Audubon, Muir was often painfully lonely in wild places and was later pursued by rumors of romantic misconduct. With regard to sex, our nature writers tend to be damned if they do and damned if they don't. A special prurience attaches to inquiries as to whether Thoreau really fell in love with Emerson's wife, or why Audubon was abruptly exiled from Oakley Plantation in West Feliciana Parish, Louisiana, where he had been tutoring "my lovely Miss Pirrie," or whether poor Mrs. Hutchings, wife of Muir's sawmill employer in Yosemite Valley, left her husband as a result of her winter's companionship with Muir when her husband went east. Furthermore, *did* Muir sleep with the Honorable Mrs. Thérèse Yelverton, a divorcée celebrity who visited Yosemite in 1870 and made him the hero of a novel? Or Mrs. Jeanne Carr, his early benefactress at the University of Wisconsin? Still, it's true that most of our preeminent nature interpreters did not recognize that the nexus of the sexes could become a natural adjunct of what is lately called "the wilderness experience," and something faintly ludicrous attaches to their infirmity. They differed in this respect from he-men like London, from the internationally minded Audubon, and from certain British explorers, like Sir Richard Burton and Sir Samuel Baker (not to mention innumerable mountainmen-squawmen).

As seems to be the case with many wounded hearts who make a decisive leap away from wherever they were wounded, joy eventually became Muir's strong suit. His joy in the bee meadows under sun-shot granite and ice, in the fir trees and river willows, the tiny water ouzels diving into cold rapids and running on the bottom after insects, ruddering themselves amid the currents with their half-open wings, was so tactile that he repeatedly experienced episodes of mental telepathy. He lived recklessly and efficiently enough to have done as much scrambling, ambling, trekking, and roaming as he sensibly could have, but at the age of seventy still had published just two books. His most delicious volumes—*A Thousand Mile Walk to the Gulf* and *My First Summer in the Sierra*—were reconstructed from his youthful journals only after that: journals by then forty years old. His true story of the brave loyal mongrel "Stickeen," which may be the best of all dog stories, took seventeen years to see print in a magazine after the night that they shared on a glacier. And he postponed work on what might have been his finest book, *Travels in Alaska*, until the last year of his life, when his energies were not up to the task. He died of pneumonia in a Los Angeles hospital with his Alaska notes beside his bed. A collaborator had to finish jiggling them into narrative form.

Although Muir helped to invent the conservation movement, he was a tender soul, not merely a battling activist, and lived with the conviction that God was in the sky. Yet the Transcendalists, in revering the spark of life wherever it occurred, were groping toward a revolutionary concept of survival for Western man: that we must live together with the rest of nature or we will die together with the rest of nature. Centrist churchmen over the years had issued apologias for inquisitions, wars of racial and sectarian extermination, slavery, child labor, and so on, and their ethics were proving inadequate once again. And because Muir is such an endearing individual, to grow to care for him is all the sadder because the crusade failed. We lead a scorched-earth existence; so much of what he loved about the world is nearly gone. Naturalists themselves are turning into potted plants, and mankind is re-creating itself quite in the way of a born-again fundamentalist, who once went to school and learned some smattering of geology, biology, and human history, but who abruptly shuts all that out of his mind, transfixed instead by the idea that the earth is only six thousand years old, that practically every species that ever lived is right here with us now for our present service and entertainment. So it is with our preternatural assumption that the world was invented by Thomas Edison and Alexander Graham Bell.

Thoreau's optimism is out of fashion, but not Thoreauvian combativeness and iconoclasm. The whole theater of orchards, ponds, back fields, short woods, short walks in which *Walden* was staged remains accessible to anyone who wants to recapitulate the particulars of what Thoreau saw and did. Muir, however, is not the same. Less thoughtful, less balanced to begin with, he hooked himself to the wide world of wilderness for support, and now that that world is shattering all around, it's hard to imagine where he would tie his lifeline. Except as a tactician and a man of goodwill, he has no current solutions to offer us. More than Thoreau, in other words, he is a sort of historical embodiment, like some knight of chivalry, or a leader of the Wobblies from 1919. Frank Norris employed him as the mystic Vanamee in his 1901 novel, *The Octopus,* opposed to unbridled industrial power.

"Instinct with deity" was how Muir described the elements of nobility that he recognized among the Tlingits of southeastern Alaska, who were the only Indians he ever took to. His own "instinct with deity" was gushier, vaguer, more isolated in character, being linked to no central traditions, no hereditary culture, no creation myths or great-grandfather tales. Muir, not born to it, blundering and fumbling as he sought to create a religion in reaction to his savage foe from childhood, Presbyterianism, left out a lot that the Indians put in. There were no carrion smells beneath his landslides, no half-eaten elk in his glacial basins, no parched nestlings fallen from his spruce trees and aspens. More than Thoreau, he let his philosophy dictate which observations he wrote down. But though his embrace of nature is not to be confused with the more intimate and inherent conjugality that animist tribal peoples on all continents have had, his was sufficiently headlong that we would find it almost impossible to duplicate now.

We have disacknowledged our animalness. Not just American Indians spoke affectionately to turtles, ravens, eagles, and bears as "Uncle" and "Grandfather," but our ancestors as well. The instant cousinhood our children feel for animals, the way they go toward them directly, with all-out curiosity, is a holdover from this. Even now, to visit the Tlingit villages on Admiralty, Chichagof, and other islands of the Alexander Archipelago, where Muir kayaked and boated, is to meet with a thicket of animal life—whales in the channels, bears ashore—from which the native clans trace their origins and which therefore were seldom hunted. Bears still have territorial spheres of influence on these islands, which are accepted, and the roofs in the villages belong to the ravens as much as the streets do to the people, while eagles bank as closely as seagulls overhead.

In looking on my bookshelves for a contemporary writer who has the same earthy empathy and easy knowledgeability for what is going on out of doors as Muir did, the nearest kindred spirits I could find were the Craighead brothers, Frank and John, who are old hawk, owl, and grizzly experts, and the coauthors of a field guide to Rocky Mountain wildflowers, which was first published thirty years ago. It's too unorthodox and informal a book to be particularly popular now, but I love thumbing through it. The fact that brothers wrote it is appealing. Like the Murie brothers, Olaus and Adolph, who ten years earlier had studied elk and wolves, waterfowl and wildlife tracking, the Craigheads possess an old-fashioned air of blood alliance and clannish loyalty. And writing about the Rockies, whose climatic zones vary too much for ecological cycles to be described simply by dates on a calendar, they say that wild violets come into bloom when wood ducks are building nests and crows are brooding their eggs; that vetch vines flower at the same time that moose are having calves; that chokecherries blossom when prairie falcons are about to fledge, fireweed when bald eagles are making their first flights from the nest, and primroses when young goshawks leave for good. Coyote pups depart from their dens at about the time blueberry plants have fully bloomed. Bearberries start to flower when tree swallows return from the south, are in full blossom when Canada goose eggs begin to hatch, and the berries themselves, although still green, have formed by the time young chipmunks are to be seen scampering about. The life schedules of wild licorice and lodgepole lupine are linked to the flight lessons of ruffed grouse; meadowsweet to long-eared owls; balsamroot and serviceberries to bighorn ewes; harebells and silverweed to mallard ducklings; long-plumed avens to bison calves and Swainson's hawks.

On and on these virtuosos go. Since the book is about flowers, they are limited to events of the spring and summer, but we know that this inventory of lore could spin around the larger cycle of the year as no ecologist of a younger generation would conceive of trying to do. The Craigheads and the Muries did not age into crusaders on the order of John Muir, and they were too late to enjoy Muir's faith in God. But in their various modest books the same joy is there—and the feeling of an encyclopedic synthesis of experience and observation on a scope and scale Muir had and few outdoorsmen will ever be permitted again.

(1984)

About H. D. Thoreau

It is a pleasure to sink into the personality of a masterpiece and enjoy its company at one's own pace. And like *Robinson Crusoe* or *Oliver Twist, Huckleberry Finn* or *Moby Dick*, Thoreau's *Walden* has a succinct motif that, along with its personality, has helped to carry it down through the decades since its publication in 1854. Not a castaway or a waif, not a raftsman or a whale fisherman, Thoreau (1817–1862) was a Harvard graduate, the son of a mildly successful pencil manufacturer in Concord, Massachusetts, who, after floundering a bit, at the age of twenty-seven built himself a ten-by-fifteen-foot cabin of pine logs and secondhand boards beside Walden Pond and lived there alone for twenty-six months, raising much of his own food. This was not then a cliché, though twentieth-century back-to-the-landers have some- times threatened to make it seem so. Like George Orwell, the great English essayist, a hundred years later—an Eton boy who chose an urban form of self-denial while "down and out in Paris and Lon- don"—Thoreau was seeking special insight from a stripped-down ex- istence. Both men were radicals, but Thoreau was after rapture, not social realism. Both were essayists, but Thoreau in his rash and roost- erly optimism is quintessentially American.

Walden is not fiction, yet, during the seven-year period when he drafted and revised it, Thoreau shaped his experiences for careful effect, almost as if he were composing a novel. He compressed two years' events into one, for example, and left out many elements of his life which didn't fit his purpose, such as the grief that he still felt for his brother, John, who had died in his arms of lockjaw in 1842, or his guilt at having accidentally set fire to three hundred acres of Concord's woods, for a loss of more than two thousand dollars, in 1844. (Here was a nature lover who entitled his first chapter "Economy" and boasted of having spent only twenty-eight dollars in building his house.) He left out his past failures in love and at the profession of schoolteaching too, as well as scarcely mentioning the night he voluntarily spent in jail in 1846, at about the midpoint of his sojourn at the pond, by which he fostered the concept of civil disobedience for later figures like Gandhi and Martin Luther King. He was protesting the government's continuing tolerance of slavery and America's invasion of Mexico that year, which he considered imperialistic. What he did for his brother, of course, was to write a separate book about a boating trip the two of them had taken on the Concord and Merrimack rivers, and then he wrote a separate essay, called "Resistance to Civil Government" (later, "Civil Disobedience").

A book on serenity is necessarily also about its absence, and Thoreau starts *Walden* in quite a feisty tone, ridiculing the notion of private property—young men "whose misfortune it is to have inherited farms, houses, barns . . . Why should they begin digging their graves as soon as they are born?" The mass of men lead lives of quiet desperation. Six weeks of work in a year should suffice, he says. By sauntering, "hooking" apples, watering the red huckleberry, living "like a dolphin," he gets more genuine profit from Concord's farms than the owners do. "What my neighbors call good I believe in my soul to be bad, and if I repent of anything, it is very likely to be my good behavior," he says. "There are nowadays professors of philosophy, but not philosophers."

He turned his face to the woods to transact some private business with the fewest obstacles, he adds. He was a man of impulse, excursions, independence, nonconformity, who roamed the woodlots several hours a day. Walkers should be a sort of "fourth estate," outside of Church or Government or the People. True walking "of which I speak has nothing in it akin to taking exercise," he writes in another essay, and, in *Walden*, "men of ideas instead of legs" are intellectual centipedes. He ended up keeping a two-million-word journal from which he stitched his books, including two fine travel meditations, *Cape Cod* and *The Maine Woods*, edited by his sister Sophia and a close friend, Ellery Channing, and published posthumously.

Thoreau had good friends, was never bereft of supporters, but Nathaniel Hawthorne, who, like Ralph Waldo Emerson, Thoreau's principal mentor, also lived in Concord, probably spoke for many of his acquaintances when he described Thoreau as "a young man with much of wild original nature still remaining in him. . . . He is as ugly as sin, long-nosed, queer-mouthed, and with uncouth and somewhat rustic, although courteous manners. . . . He has repudiated all regular modes of getting a living, and seems inclined to lead a sort of Indian life among civilized men." Even Emerson, though more sympathetic—it was Emerson who bought and then loaned Thoreau the land on which he built his hut—was occasionally alarmed by his extremism. When he spent the night in jail protesting slavery, Emerson complained to a friend that it was a "mean and skulking" act "and in bad taste," and wrote in his journal: "Don't run amuck against the world. . . . The prison is one step to suicide." But Emerson housed and nurtured Thoreau during his shaky periods as a young man, eulogized him after his death from tuberculosis (Orwell, too, died of TB in his forties), and lent Thoreau books and ideas during his gradual progression from blundering nature lover to visionary, rhapsodist, and social critic ripe with the most supple specificity. He recognized that his protégé was the "American Scholar" he had called for in a famous essay that was delivered first, coincidentally, as an address at Thoreau's graduation—a writer who rubbed shoulders with Irish ice cutters and French-Canadian wood-choppers, an inspector of snowstorms, a man who studied bean fields and bread-making as well as the *Bhagavad Gita*, Ovid, Milton, and Homer.

In winter, the whooping ice was Thoreau's bedfellow, and a red squirrel was his alarm clock, "as if sent out of the woods for this purpose." "A man is rich in proportion to the number of things which he can afford to let alone," he wrote. And, "I would rather sit on a pumpkin and have it all to myself, then be crowded on a velvet cushion." As for the railroad that ran by the pond and embodied industrialization: "We do not ride on the railroad; it rides upon us." (He also thinks humorously of the fish feeling its rumble.)

Some sounds of the town—church bells and roosters—he enjoys in the woods, however. Sauntering is what he does—from *à la Sainte Terre*, "to the Holy Land," as he says elsewhere—and his genius, he brags, "is a very crooked one." He never knew "a worse man than myself." What he means is not some form of depravity, but complexity and paradox. Emerson, in his essay "Self-Reliance," had written the clarion adage "A foolish consistency is the hobgoblin of little minds." And Walt Whitman, Thoreau's contemporary, whose *Leaves of Grass* first came out a year after *Walden* ("I loafe and invite my soul,/I lean and loafe at my ease . . . I think I could turn and live with animals, they are so placid and self-contain'd"), wrote in the same vein. "Do I contradict myself?/Very well then I contradict myself/(I am large, I contain multitudes.)" Thoreau's way of saying the same thing was "I love a broad margin to my life."

The first summer he preferred hoeing beans even to reading, except for those mornings when he sat in his doorway from sunrise till noon, "rapt in revery, amidst the pines and hickories and sumachs, in undisturbed solitude and stillness." He had planted a couple of acres of beans but allowed the woodchucks to eat part of the patch, stopped cultivating much of the rest, and exchanged some of the twelve bushels that he harvested for rice, which he preferred. The second year he planted just a third of an acre, not wishing to be indentured to his crops, as he suggested that dairymen are to their herds. Considering the importance of a man's soul, he believed "that that was doing better than any farmer in Concord." Life is a long haul for many people, but Thoreau was "anxious to improve the nick of time . . . to stand on the meeting of two eternities, the past and future." Fishing for horned pout in the moonlight on the pond, he thinks of casting his line upward into the air for ideas and thus catching "two fishes as it were with one hook." And with amusement, at other times, he strikes his paddle on the side of his boat, eliciting an echoing growl from the woods. The pickerel are gold and emerald, fabulous, as "foreign as Arabia to our Concord life." He even bends over with his head between his legs to capture an upside-down glimpse of his beloved Walden ("earth's eye") and its skimming swallows; or sounds and maps its 61½ acres, 102 feet deep; or creeps out onto its thin black ice, prone "like a skater insect," to study the bottom shallows, giving a disquisition upon bubbles. The thawing sand in a railroad cut looks like leopards' paws, birds' feet, coral. An outlandish spotted salamander reminds him of the Nile, though he had never been to the Old World.

Transcendent is the word. Transcendentalism for these New England enthusiasts was a borrowed garment, from German or English figures such as Kant, Goethe, Coleridge, Carlyle, and Wordsworth. But the idea that intuition has divine authority, that there is an "Over-Soul," in Emerson's term, within which every person's particular being is subsumed, was especially suited to an optimistic new country experimenting with democracy. "No man ever followed his genius till it misled him," Thoreau says. Flattered for a moment that he thinks we *have* genius, we nearly believe this unfashionable idea. The most vivid expression of Transcendentalism ever written is *Walden*'s "Conclusion," ending with the sentences "Only that day dawns to which we are awake. There is more day to dawn. The sun is but a morning star." We can still thrill to it, but after two world wars and the twin juggernauts of Marxism and Capitalism, we wouldn't pay attention to such upbeat faith if Thoreau hadn't more to him.

"I love the wild not less than the good," he says. And elsewhere, in his essay on walking, "In Wilderness is the preservation of the World." About the Flints (or "skin-flints," as he calls them), who own the shores of a neighboring pond, he suggests that they "loved better the reflecting surface of a dollar, or a bright cent," than the miraculous water. To farm right there is to raise potatoes in a churchyard. Farmers were then burghers, not an endangered species, and, like other people of a certain wealth, weren't so much an offense against philanthropy, in Thoreau's individualistic view, as slaves to their own avarice. He was a revolutionary.

We Americans tend to forget that our country was born in sedition, subversion, and violent dissent. Protest, if not Protestantism, was our founding creed and helped foment revolutions around the world. For every immigrant who sailed here to get rich quick, another may have come to get away from money grubbing, tenant grinding, and flag waving. Thoreau speaks of the distended "vast abdomens" of imperial nations. "Patriotism is a maggot in their heads," he says of people whose loyalty is all external. Explore thyself; the defeated and deserters from *this* battle go to war, he says. The only conflict he's ever watched was between ants, and the martial fuss of July 4 wafting on the breeze gives him "a vague sense all the day of some sort of itching and disease in the horizon. . . . But sometimes it was a really noble and inspiring strain. . . . I felt as if I could spit a Mexican with a good relish . . . and looked round for a woodchuck or a skunk to exercise my chivalry upon."

Rebelliousness is appealing and keeps Thoreau fresh for younger readers, generation by generation. But it's also an American note, common to Walt Whitman, Herman Melville, Mark Twain—the yawp of the New World—sounded by Abraham Lincoln as well, in a speech to the U.S. House of Representatives in 1848, protesting the conduct of the Mexican War, while Thoreau, his fellow protester, was working on *Walden*. "Any people anywhere . . . have the *right* to rise up, and shake off the existing government, and form a new one that suits them better. This is a most valuable,—a most sacred right—a right, which we hope and believe, is to liberate the world," said Lincoln. It's the line of thinking of the revolutionist Thomas Jefferson, too, in 1776, in the Declaration of Independence. "We hold these Truths to be self-evident . . . ," wrote Jefferson, beginning his explanation to the rest of the world for the American Revolution. It's what you'd sort of better say when you are saying something new. All men are created equal, endowed by their creator with certain inalienable rights, among them life, liberty, and the pursuit of happiness. With aplomb, with serenity, Jefferson announced that these ideas are "truths" and are "self-evident!" *Where?* a conservative with a law library might have asked.

This aplomb in announcing impious, outrageous ideas is notable in *Walden,* in Whitman's *Leaves of Grass* ("I celebrate myself . . . ,/And what I assume you shall assume,/For every atom belonging to me as good belongs to you," it commences. *Really?* a Tory would have asked), as well as in Melville's *Moby-Dick*—each of which was composed during the nation's anguished and tumultuous buildup to the Civil War.

But we don't read Thoreau simply for his pronouncement that the mass of men lead lives of quiet desperation, or as a protoconservationist either, or as an eremitical Tom Paine. It is his glee that wins us over. Glee is rarer than outrage, at least in books, and whether he is house building, boiling hasty pudding, going a-chestnuting, a-berrying, a-fishing, or looking into a partridge chick's intelligent eye ("coeval with the sky"), his happiness is catching. "I rejoice that there are owls," he tells us—and otters, bullfrogs, whippoorwills on his ridgepole, moles in his cellar, and a nighthawk wheeling like a mote in the eye of the sky. "This is a delicious evening." A friend leaves him a note penciled on a walnut leaf. But mystery is never far. On the bottom of White Pond are sunken logs like huge water snakes perpetually in motion.

In *Walden* Thoreau doesn't write about a dachshund or a tabby cat, the way so many modern essayists do who take up the subject of nature. But it's important to remember that nothing he did is beyond our means. During a summer in New England I regularly see deer, moose, bear, and wild turkeys—animals that were no longer part of Concord's woods and that Thoreau mourned for, though they are on an upsurge now. He felt the woods diminished by this loss; yet he didn't head for the Rocky Mountains, where there were grizzlies, buffalo, and all. He made his masterpiece out of modest materials, deliberately choosing a setting where the issue was to subdue and cultivate not a wilderness but "a few cubic feet of flesh" instead. (And his serenity would be less interesting if we did not also sense his edginess.)

Walden's shore was "as much Asia or Africa as New England. I have, as it were, my own sun and moon and stars." Advance confidently toward your dreams, and the world will accommodate you, he said. As you simplify your circumstances, your surroundings will appear less tangled, "and solitude will not be solitude, nor poverty poverty, nor weakness weakness." What faith!—and to imagine, when you have so far won an audience of nil, that you can speak to the ages and catch "the broad, flapping American ear" is as extravagant. Almost by definition, essayists are teachers, reformers, gadflies, and contrarians who look against the grain of prevailing attitudes to point out paradoxes, follies. The farmer plowing behind his ox tells Thoreau he can't believe in vegetarianism because it's got "nothing to make bones with"—the ox's vegetarian bones meanwhile are jerking both plow and farmer along. But in Thoreau, besides the New England ag'iner, there is the lilt of advocacy. "I wish to speak a word for Nature, for absolute freedom and wildness," he says in an essay on walking. "I wish to make an extreme statement." Sounds like great fun: except extremism cuts both ways. In *Walden* he argues that "all sensuality is one." Not even a singing kettle stands between him and nature. Sex, wine, luxurious food, "sensual" sleeping, go by the boards. The spring water from Brister's Hill, or raisins in his bread, were enough of a treat for him. His senses are so clarified that he can sniff the pipe smoke of a passerby at better than three hundred yards.

He was a critic of society but not antisocial, and wanted "so to love wisdom as to live . . . a life of simplicity, independence, magnanimity, and trust." This is not mere iconoclasm, and his book does become gentler, fonder, more good-humored, less adversarial, as it goes on, detailing the struggling lives of freed slaves who had lived in squatters' cabins near Walden Pond, welcoming a more heterogeneous set of visitors to his own lodging than the "poets" who had come before—even an occasional farmer, whom once he might have said knew "Nature but as a robber." Nature after all extends from "the quiet parlor of the fishes" underneath the ice "even into the plains of the ether." Nature after dark does sometimes discomfit him with what he calls "questions," which he then tries to discount by suggesting that nature isn't really nature until the morning.

He says he left the woods for as good a reason as he went there. He had other lives to lead. But he doesn't tell us whether he became lonelier or exasperated or assailed by doubts; whether he burned the midnight oil and paced his tiny cabin in his long johns talking to himself and suffering insomnia and sexual fantasies. Like Henry Adams, that other saliently American memoirist—whose *Education* never mentions the suicide of his wife, Marian Adams—Thoreau didn't think a reader ought to know the author's messy personalia. Excavations a century later revealed that he had bent and spoiled hundreds of nails with his bad aim in putting up his hut, not a frustration that he ever mentions, incidentally. But who knows what berserk streak a more precipitous excavation might have uncovered: Emerson's hint of a leaning toward "suicide," for instance? Thoreau required considerable nurturing from his friends, boarding with the Emersons for months on end, and more than once suffered a nervous collapse, in particular after his brother's death and after the hanging of John Brown, the abolitionist, whom he revered.

The Transcendental idea that people are innately good until tainted by civilization is out of fashion, as is Thoreau's personal asceticism and literary discretion. But we don't need confessions from every author. ("Every generation laughs at the old fashions, but follows religiously the new," he says.) His skepticism about regimentation, industrialism, and materialism, the liberties he took with public authority, his anguish over the skinning of the land, all ring a popular chord. Like his contemporary Karl Marx, he wanted to stop Capitalism in its tracks, but from an opposite angle. He also wanted to lure a generation of hothouse intellectuals outdoors, to lend them courage and confidence in their own surroundings, and to wean them a little more, as Emerson and Whitman were doing, from Europe and the superstition of European superiority. By his middle thirties he had written his best work and become more of a natural scientist than a moral philosopher. He was a radical in politics but a social conservative, like so many of the conservationists who have succeeded him, and he died unmarried but in the bosom of his family, muttering the words "moose" and "Indian," still true to his youthful enthusiasms, and a minority of one.

"I did not wish to take a cabin passage, but rather to go before the mast and on the deck of the world" to see the moonlight on the mountains, he wrote in *Walden*. And, "We should come home from far, from adventures, and perils, and discoveries every day," and not breathe our own breath over and over. For such visions we read him, and for his playful exactitude: the horsehair rabbit snares he finds, tended by "some cow-boy," the pines that under the snow's weight sharpen their silhouettes until they look like firs, and the squirrels whose motions "imply spectators as much as those of a dancing girl."

In closing, Thoreau claims with splendid extravagance that "a tide rises and falls behind every man which can float the British Empire like a chip," if it were ever summoned. How charming a rhetorical flight of fancy, his scanty band of admirers must have thought (and what humbug, to his detractors). Who, in the mid-nineteenth century, could have supposed that this quaint man, whose books at the time of his death were either out of print or not yet published, would easily outlive the British Empire? And, beyond that, who could have imagined that by helping to inspire Gandhi, Thoreau would prove to be in on certain pivotal events of that very feat of flotation a hundred years later?

(1991)

Abbey's Road

Edward Abbey, who died in March 1989, at sixty-two, seemed, at his best, like the nonpareil "nature writer" of recent decades. It was a term he came to detest, a term used to pigeonhole and marginalize some of the more intriguing American writers alive, who are dealing with matters central to us, yet it can be a ticket to oblivion in the review media. Joyce Carol Oates, for instance, in a slapdash though interesting essay called "Against Nature," speaks of nature writers' "painfully limited set of responses . . . REVERENCE, AWE, PIETY, MYSTICAL ONENESS." She must never have read Mr. Abbey; yet it was characteristic of him that for an hour or two, he might have agreed.

He wrote with exceptional exactitude and an uncommonly honest and logical understanding of causes and consequences, but he also loved argument, churlishness, and exaggeration. Personally, he was a labyrinth of anger and generosity, shy but arresting because of his mixture of hillbilly with cowboy qualities, and even when silent, appeared bigger than life. He had hitchhiked west from Appalachia for the first time at seventeen, for what became an immediate love match, and, I'm sure, slept out more nights under the stars than all of his current competitors combined. He was uneven, self-indulgent as a writer, and sometimes scanted his talent by working too fast. But he had about him an authenticity that springs from the page and is beloved by a rising generation of readers who have enabled his early collection of rambles, *Desert Solitaire* (1968), to run through eighteen printings in mass-market paperback and his fine comic novel, *The Monkey Wrench Gang* (1975), to sell half a million copies. Both books, indeed, have inspired a new eco-guerrilla environmental organization called Earth First!, whose other patron saint is Ned Ludd (from whom the Luddites took their name), though it's perhaps no more radical than John Muir's Sierra Club appeared to be in 1892, when that group was formed.

Like many good writers, Abbey dreamed of producing "The Fat Masterpiece," as he called the "nuvvle" he had worked on for the last dozen years, which was supposed to boil everything down to a thousand pages. When edited in half, it came out in 1988 as *The Fool's Progress*, an autobiographical yarn that lunges cross-country several times, full of apt descriptions and antic fun—*Ginger Man* stuff—though not with the coherence or poignancy he had hoped for. A couple of his other novels hold up fairly well too: *Black Sun* and *The Brave Cowboy*, which came out in movie form, starring Kirk Douglas and Walter Matthau, in 1962 (*Lonely Are the Brave*) and brought Abbey a munificent $7,500.

I do think he wrote masterpieces, but they were more slender: the essays in *Desert Solitaire* and an equivalent sampler that you might put together from subsequent collections like *Down the River, Beyond the Wall,* and *The Journey Home.* His rarest strength was in being concise, because he really knew what he thought and cared for. He loved the desert—"red mountains like mangled iron"—liked people in smallish clusters, and didn't mince words in saying that industrial rapine, glitz malls, and tract sprawl were an abomination heralding more devastating events. While writing as handsomely as others do, he never lost sight of the fact that much of Creation is rapidly being destroyed. "Growth for the sake of growth is the ideology of the cancer cell," he wrote. And he adopted for a motto Walt Whitman's line: "Resist much, obey little." Another was Thoreau's summary in

Walden: "If I repent of anything, it is very likely to be my good behavior. What demon possessed me that I behaved so well?"

Abbey traveled less than some writers do, but it is not necessary to go dithering around our suffering planet, visiting the Amazon, Indonesia, Bhutan, and East Africa. The crisis is plain in anyone's neck of the woods, and the exoticism of globe-trotting may only blur one's vision. Nor do we need to become mystical Transcendentalists and commune with God. ("One Life at a Time, Please" is another of Abbey's titles. On his hundreds of camping trips he tended to observe and enjoy the wilds rather than submerge his soul.) What is needed is honesty, a pair of eyes, and a further dollop of fortitude to spit the truth out, not genuflecting to "Emersonian" optimism, or journalistic traditions of staying deadpan, or the saccharine pressures of magazine editors who want their readers to feel good. Emerson would be roaring with heartbreak and Thoreau would be raging with grief in these 1990s. *Where were you when the world burned? Get mad, for a change, for heaven's sake!* I believe they would say to milder colleagues.

Abbey didn't sell to the big book clubs or reach best-sellerdom or collect major prizes. When, at sixty, he was offered a smallish one by the American Academy of Arts and Letters, he rejected it with a fanfare of rhetoric, probably because it had come too late. War-horse that he was, he did not find a ready market in mainstream publications of any stripe and was relegated through most of his career by the publicity arm of publishing to the death trap of "naturalist" stuff. So the success, wholly word-of-mouth, of *The Monkey Wrench Gang* in paperback pleased him more than anything else, and he delighted in telling friends who the real-life counterparts were for its characters, Seldom Seen Smith, Bonnie Abbzug, and George Washington Hayduke. They, too, had torn down billboards, yanked up survey stakes, poured sand into bulldozer gas tanks, and sabotaged "certain monstrosities" in fragilely scenic regions that shouldn't need free-lance protection in the first place, as "Seldom Seen" says, still taciturn now, when you call him up.

"Abbzug" speaks of how Abbey in real life would go through three (used) cars a year, bouncing across the Sonoran desert on his pleasure jaunts, peeling the plates off of each as it died. And when they got fooling, he would laugh till he had to come up for air, then laugh some more, even once when they'd broken down a great many miles from water and thought they were doomed, with only a bottle of wine to live on. Most good writers are walkers, but Abbey was something different, ranging the Southwest afoot or river running with somewhat the scope of John Muir in the High Sierras. It was the building of Hetch Hetchy Dam in Yosemite National Park (now thought to have been unnecessary for San Francisco's water needs) that finally embittered Muir; and the unfinished business of "monkeywrenching" in *The Monkey Wrench Gang* is to blow up Glen Canyon Dam, a structure that, before Abbey's eyes, had drowned a whole stretch of the Colorado River's most pristine, precious canyons.

Robinson Jeffers, another regionalist of fluctuating popularity, who made of the close examination of his home country at Big Sur in California a prism to look at the rest of the world, concluded in several poems that mankind had turned into "a sick microbe," a "deformed ape," "a botched experiment that has run wild and ought to be stopped." In "The Broken Balance" (1929) he spoke for Abbey's anger as well:

> *The beautiful places killed like rabbits to make a*
>   *city,*
> *The spreading fungus, the slime-threads*
> *And spores . . . I remember the farther*
> *Future, and the last man dying*
> *Without succession under the confident eyes of the*
>   *stars.*

"Let's keep things the way they were," Abbey liked to say. Yet he was a bold, complex man who had had five wives and five children by the end of his life; and although he spilled too much energy into feuds with his allies and friends, he was often a jubilant writer, a regular gleeman, not just a threnodist, and wanted to be remembered as a writer of "that letter which is never finished"—literature—such as Desert Solitaire is.

We corresponded occasionally for twenty years, wanting to go for a lengthy sail on the Sea of Cortez or go camping somewhere in the hundred-mile Air Force gunnery range which for its isolation eventually became another favorite redoubt of his. I hoped we could drift down the Yukon River together and compile a dual diary. ("Is that dual or *duel?*" he asked once.) He had lived in Hoboken, New Jersey, for a couple of years while unhappily married, with the "Vampire State Building" on the skyline—also in Scotland and Italy—and responded to Manhattan's incomparably gaudy parade of faces as a cosmopolitan, though marked, himself, as an outlander by his uncut grayish beard, slow speech, earnest eyes, red-dog-road shuffle, raw height and build, and jean jacket or shabby brown tweed. On his way home to Oracle, Arizona, he'd usually stop in the Alleghenies, after conferring in New York City with editors, to visit his mother, Mildred, a Woman's Christian Temperance Union veteran, and his father, Paul Revere Abbey, a registered Socialist and old Wobbly organizer, who'd met Eugene V. Debs in his youth and has toured Cuba and still cuts hickory fence posts in the woods for a living.

Abbey was a writer who liked to play poker with cowboys, while continuing to ridicule the ranch owners who overgraze the West's ravaged grasslands. The memorial picnic for him in Saguaro National Monument outside Tucson went on for twelve hours; and besides readings performed with rock-bottom affection, there was beer drinking, lovemaking, gunfire, and music, much as he had hoped. The potluck stew was from two "slow elk," as he liked to call beef cattle poached from particularly greedy entrepreneurs on the public's wildlands. He was an "egalitarian," he said—by which he meant that all wildlife and the full panoply of natural vegetation have a right to live equal to man's—and these beeves had belonged to a cowman who specialized in hounding Arizona's scarce mountain lions.

Abbey died of internal bleeding from a circulatory disorder, with a few weeks' notice of how sick he was. Two days before the event, he decided to leave the hospital, wishing to die in the desert, and at sunup had himself disconnected from the tubes and machinery. His wife, Clarke, and three friends drove him out of town as far as his condition allowed. They built a campfire for him to look at, until, feeling death at hand, he crawled into his sleeping bag with Clarke. But by noon, finding he was still alive and possibly better, he asked to be taken home and placed on a mattress on the floor of his writing cabin. There he said his gentle goodbyes.

His written instructions were that he should be "transported in the bed of a pickup truck" deep into the desert and buried anonymously, wrapped in his sleeping bag, in a beautiful spot where his grave would never be found, with "lots of rocks" piled on top to keep the coyotes off. Abbey of course loved coyotes (and, for that matter, buzzards) and had played the flute to answer their howls during the many years he had earned his living watching for fires from government towers on the Grand Canyon's North Rim, on Aztec Peak in Tonto National Forest, and in Glacier National Park, before he finally won tenure as a "Fool Professor" at the University of Arizona. His friend who was the model for G. W. Hayduke in *The Monkey Wrench Gang* was squatting beside him on the floor as his life ebbed away—"Hayduke," under a real-life name, is a legend in his own right in parts of the West, a contemporary mountain man who returned to Tucson as to a "calving ground" several years ago when he wanted to have children—and the last smile that crossed Abbey's face was when "Hayduke" told him where he would be put.

The place is, inevitably, a location where mountain lions, antelope, bighorn sheep, deer, and javelinas leave tracks, where owls, poor-wills, and coyotes hoot, rattlesnakes crawl, and cacomistles scratch, with a range of stiff terrain overhead, and greasewood, rabbitbush, ocotillo, and noble old cactuses about. First seven, then ten buzzards gathered while the grave was being dug; but, as he had wished, it *was* a rocky spot. "Hayduke" jumped into the hole to be sure it felt O.K. before laying Abbey in, and afterward, in a kind of reprise of the antic spirit that animates *The Monkey Wrench Gang* (and that should make anybody but a developer laugh out loud), went around heaping up false rock piles at ideal grave sites throughout the Southwest, because this last peaceful act of outlawry on Abbey's part was the gesture of legend, and there will be seekers for years.

The stuff of legend: like Thoreau's serene passage from life muttering the words "moose" and "Indian," and Muir's thousand-mile walks to Georgia, or in the Sierras, "the Range of Light." Can he be compared to them? Muir, after all, bullied the Catskills naturalist John Burroughs from sheer orneriness, as Abbey, the controversialist, regularly blistered his colleagues with vitriol through the mails, and

Thoreau—a stark individual in his own way—orated vehemently on behalf of the reviled "terrorist" John Brown. (That Thoreau of witticisms such as what a pearl was: "the hardened tear of a diseased clam, murdered in its old age.") A magazine published Abbey's last account of a trip by horseback through Utah's slick-rock canyons, and it's got a hop like a knuckle ball's on it, unmistakably Abbey, as briny with personality as his heyday essays. Nor had twenty years changed him. Thoreau, by contrast, in a swift incandescent burst of work, vaulted from the relatively conventional *Week on the Concord and Merrimack Rivers* to the vision of *Walden,* but soon fell back into dutiful natural science. And Muir went from being a lone-wolf botanist and geologist to a passionate advocate, skillfully lobbying Teddy Roosevelt and William Howard Taft on behalf of Yosemite National Park, until, late in life, when he was finished with localism, he wandered rather disconsolately to Africa, Asia, and South America in celebrity guise.

Abbey was consistent but, unlike Thoreau, was not self-contained; some compulsive agenda unknown to him blunted his efforts to surpass himself. And his ambitions were confined to truth telling, rhapsody, and the lambasting of villains. As an essayist he did not aspire to the grandeur of versatility, or try hard to turn into a man of letters either—his novels can seem flat or foreshortened next to Peter Matthiessen's, for example, and his literary pronouncements were scattershot, bilious, or cursory. Like most conservationists, he was a political radical but a social conservative, going so far as to aver the old-fashioned idea that there are two sexes, not simply one, which, expressed with his customary crowing, abrasive overstatement, offended people. (Yet he wrote in a love letter to a woman friend after a breakup, "If you ever need me in any way I will cross continents and oceans to help you," a sentiment that even his favorite *bête noire,* Gloria Steinem, might have appreciated.) Speaking of various sins of omission of his personal life, he would sometimes describe himself as a coward—as being a neglectful father to his sons and a passive witness to his second wife's death by cancer, in particular.

There's a saying that life gets better once you have outlived the bastards, which would certainly be true except that as you do, you are also outliving your friends. I miss him. Sitting in silence in restaurants as our twinned melancholy groped for expression, or talking with him of hoodoo stone pillars and red-rock canyons, I've seldom felt closer to anybody. Honesty is a key to essay writing: not just "a room of one's own" but a view of one's own. The lack of it sinks more talented people into chatterbox hack-work than anything else. And Abbey aspired to speak for himself in all honesty—*X: His Mark*—and died telling friends he had done what he could and was ready. He didn't buzz off to Antarctica or the Galápagos Islands, yet no one will ever wonder what he really saw as the world burned. He said it; didn't sweeten it or blink at it or water it down or hope the web of catastrophes might just go away. He felt homesick for the desert when he went to Alaska, and turned back, yet if you travel much there, it is Abbey's words you will see tacked on the wall again and again in remote homestead cabins in the Brooks Range or in offices in Juneau, because he had already written of greed, of human brutality and howling despair, better than writers who write books on Alaska.

Last year a paean to Abbey's work in *National Review* finished with a quote from a passage in Faulkner: *"Oleh, Chief. Grandfather."* To which we can add Amen. But instead let's close with a bit of Ed Abbey, from a minor book called *Appalachian Wilderness* (1970), which foretold why he chose that lost grave where he lies:

> How strange and wonderful is our home, our earth, with its swirling vaporous atmosphere, its flowing and frozen liquids, its trembling plants, its creeping, crawling, climbing creatures, the croaking things with wings that hang on rocks and soar through fog, the furry grass, the scaly seas . . . how utterly rich and wild. . . . Yet some among us have the nerve, the insolence, the brass, the gall to whine about the limitations of our earthbound fate and yearn for some more perfect world beyond the sky. We are none of us good enough for the world we have.

(1989)

Ansel Adams at 100

The synchronies of nature, such as the way a bestiary of clouds will seem to stream overhead like a narrative across the expanse of the sky, while a rock face almost bubbles on a mountainside in compressed geologic time, are all around us if we choose to make the mental leap. And it will be a better one if we don't bend what we see to our preconceptions: as, for example, the clouds to a specifically zoological bestiary. But the Great Bear and Big Dipper in the firmament have anchored tribal peoples for longer than we'll know, and the linkage of a bestiary with the ontogeny of our dreams may have a power that abstract expressionism lacks. Shamans presumably knew both, and perceived the grim ballet in the twists that old, much-punished trees have undergone in order to accommodate the wind or heal after a lightning strike, somewhat in the way *we* do, even before ballet could serve them as a metaphor. Out-of-doors, geometry, like intuition, is always curved.

And with landscapes, the intensity of our response to the nuances of beauty and drama argues for a grace that is more than mathematical or anthropological. That is, we grew up as a species climbing trees and on the veldt; yet we respond quite as intrinsically to surf. And flowers court insects, but also move *us*—as can clouds wreathing a massif by happenstance, or long, sheeny grass growing as tightly as sun and soil permit, when it undulates with the wind: though we don't eat flowers or wild grasses or snow peaks or clouds in the wind, or mate with them. They don't warm our bodies or save our lives. Nor do songbirds, rainbows, or a rippling, glistering lake. There is a slow-fuse, out-of-body ecstasy at the doorstep, if we have the eyes and ears for it. Rain or frost on the windowpane, glacial chatter marks, snowflake shapes, oak and aspen leaves. We all have retinas, but some very few of us may have a sense of juxtaposition that enhances the Half Dome of Yosemite with opulently fragile cottonwoods in the picture, or a moonrise with cemetery crosses, or makes the tumult of stratification of the Grand Canyon practically bosomy.

Raddled buttes, defunct stumps, and waterfalls exploding had speaking parts in Ansel Adams's work; and his photographs may suggest a continuum embroiling in its trajectory not just death but an aftermath. Thoreau had described Concord's pond as "earth's eye," for instance, and you can see that perfection in Adams, too, although as a Californian he was more of a mountain man. John Muir's "Range of Light," the High Sierra, was Adams's main hangout. He tended to picture it more austerely than Muir, however, because half a century of development had changed the natural equations on the West Coast. But simultaneously he aspired to know "the minute detail of the grasses, the clusters of sand shifting in the wind, the small flotsam of the forest," as he once put it. The world is either chaos, entropy, and Brownian motion, or has been authored with a sort of eloquence that we don't simply invent, but respond to. And Adams, like Muir and Thoreau, was in the Transcendental line of Emersonian rhapsodists. Yet even Emerson opened his beloved first wife Ellen's tomb after a year or so to see what burial had done to her. They were not wimps, these guys, and Adams often photographed doomsday artifacts, such as sea rocks or dead trees that had been battered as if beyond bearing. He climbed vertiginously to seek out major mountain shapes—sometimes choosing not the most majestic side, but a more pummeled, poignant slope, and by what he called "previsualization" imposed darker tonalities with a red filter.

Adams's pictures "are about the way that light dissolves weight," John Szarkowski writes in his introduction to *Ansel Adams at 100* (comparing him to the more sculptural landscapist, Edward Weston), and says they embody an incomparable "tenseness—an edgy, nervous vitality—that is only barely contained." Elsewhere, he calls him "an electric charge in the form of a man." Adams, as a child, had been so jittery he couldn't attend school after the age of twelve without plunging into hysteria, interrupting the class with yells. Nowadays he would be given Ritalin but, then, his patient father presented him with a yearlong pass to the San Francisco World's Fair of 1915 (he had been born in the same year as Charles A. Lindbergh), where he no doubt roamed to good purpose.

Adams wanted to be a musician at first, and, being plausibly talented, didn't veer to photography for keeps until his late twenties. Recognition and financial security came rather slowly, in part because he was patronized during the 1930s and 1940s, even by colleagues, as a mere scenic portraitist reveling in the rocks and clouds. Thus he was not germane to the terrible social struggles of the Great Depression, as were the likes of Dorothea Lange, or the suffering and action of World War II, like Robert Capa. When eventually the conservation movement came of age and became the rage, though, he was designated an icon—a single-minded advocate with springy legs who had scrambled to the spirit-places to record their aspects in all light and weather, and who had led a life essentially of love and reverence.

Szarkowski, a template of excellence, writes in a limber, lucent prose, describing different photos as "flickering in space like the aurora borealis," or "all elbow and jostle," or "like the chattering of a windigo's teeth during the starvation moon." But we have in Adams's vision a world that already seems scarcely accessible—in altitude, in solitude—to most of us, when blinders are generally required now to find a setting anywhere that's free of clutter. So he arouses in us a haunting yearning for vistas that might well have spoken as directly to our spirits too, and that we could have loved. Looking, we can catch a hint of the spell that animist religions cast, as strongly as the anthropocentric monotheism that followed and supplanted them. The ominous, the radiant: if you wonder how a sixteenth-century

American Indian felt at times, just gaze at the tattered, castellated cirques and avalanched watershed ridges overhanging mountain passes that he might have crossed in anxious haste, if at all, because they didn't really belong to people, or to grizzly bears, but to Bigfoot and to wraiths and ghosts—places that could ambush you with more grim fore-knowledge than you could ever use or want.

It can be argued that we impose an imaginary order upon nature that isn't there by seeing beauty in what is actually a random, mechanistic geometry; that we imagine that birds sing with pleasure, and rain is "merciful," and lofty mountains exert a mystic pull. But in Adams one feels an orgy of perspective—meteorological, geological, botanical, and watery. I've been to a number of sights in California, Canada, Alaska, Texas, and Wyoming that are pictured here, but never saw them so emotionally. I don't mean that I wasn't inspired by El Capitan in Yosemite, or by Santa Elena Canyon at Big Bend. My intuitions were, but my eyes didn't ground my intuitions as solidly in the complexity of reality. Incidentally, unlike Mr. Szarkowski, I prefer the more detailed, trenchant, and grieving or "pessimistic" interpretation Adams gave to an old negative of Mount McKinley late in his life, which is reproduced in the book alongside the clear-sailing version of thirty years before. It's not because I'm yet convinced that man has become analogous to a skin cancer or fungus on the face of the earth—as Adams's friend Robinson Jeffers sometimes said—but because I am reluctantly beginning to be.

Adams (1902–1984) must have been staggered by the changes in landscape that he saw. Jeffers's (and my friend Edward Abbey's) view was that nature would survive and endure—wind and sand and cliff and waterfall—after the asphalt and electric wiring were gone, and that the shapes they clove to, in the mountains, in the desert, would remain the same with no human eyes admiring them. Therefore, at least in a rather briny sense, it's a hopeful experience to plunge into an Adams retrospective. Although we are losing the wide-angle ecstasy and grandeur he saw—the waterfalls that almost ejaculate, and sphinxy peaks that can't quite "peak" because it is too brutal up there—they will return to center stage again.

(2002)

Selborne's Sage

Nature writing, as we know it now, has evolved from the late eighteenth century, when Gilbert White, an English curate living in the village of Selborne—about fifty miles southwest of London—invented the naturalist's essay with a series of 110 formal but endearingly observant "letters" addressed to two knowledgeable friends. Interestingly enough, this was a couple of hundred years after Montaigne had fathered the form of the essay itself. Montaigne's *Essais* had been published in 1580; *The Natural History of Selborne* came out in 1789. It seems to have taken that long for writers to conclude that, once ecclesiastical domination and medieval superstition had been thrown off, the proper study of mankind need not be limited to man, and among scientists, the emphasis upon rationality had made a fetish of taxonomy. Nothing but dissecting dead creatures counted.

Meanwhile, in North America, Gilbert White's contemporary, William Bartram, a botanist from Philadelphia exploring for specimens through the primeval South, didn't just bring back leaves and seeds. He composed his magnificently vivid *Travels through North and South Carolina, Georgia, East and West Florida, the Cherokee Country, the Extensive Territories of the Muscogulges, or the Creek Confederacy, and the*

Country of the Chactaws, which appeared in 1791 and, like *The Natural History of Selborne*, excited a host of other writers, such as Samuel Taylor Coleridge and William Wordsworth. Modern science entered the picture when brilliant generalists like Charles Darwin and his colleague and rival, Alfred Russel Wallace, wrote still-fresh accounts of their separate journeys around the world in search of evidence or inspiration, while gradually fathoming evolution in the latitudes of South America and beyond. Wallace, always more intuitive, achieved his central flash of understanding during a feverish bout with malaria on the island of Halmahera (part of Indonesia) in February 1858. He drafted his theory of the survival of the fittest in three nights, and as soon as he could, mailed it off to Darwin. Darwin had been working methodically for two decades, marshalling proof after deducing a similar concept. But this double-pronged approach of intuition assisting evidence has radiated to more recent figures such as Loren Eiseley (*The Immense Journey*), Claude Lévi-Strauss (*Tristes Tropiques*), and Edward O. Wilson (*Biophilia*). "The Sad Tropics" was, of course, a prescient title, as the holocaust of species extinctions since Lévi-Strauss's travels in Brazil during the 1930s has proved.

Gilbert White (1720–1793) was a Church of England cleric, an Oxford graduate, and one-time don, and in no way a nonconformist except in the self-effacing but important sense that he avoided priestly advancement in order to stay close to home and pursue his studies as a "faunist" into "the life and conversation of animals," as he put it: Quite a revolutionary phrase. Animals had conversations in native mythologies in every clime, but not in taxonomy or Anglicanism. Science was not yet in conflict with organized religion, however, as it would be when, for instance, in 1860 "Darwin's bulldog," Thomas Huxley (who also coined the word *agnostic*), debated and demolished Bishop Samuel Wilberforce at Oxford. And then another century would pass before late visionary nature writers like Robinson Jeffers and Edward Abbey would conceive of human beings as having become a cancer or fungus afflicting the skin of the earth.

White's predecessor, John Ray (1627–1705), who is regarded as the founder of English natural history, as well as of taxonomy before Linnaeus because he established species as the ultimate unit of classification, used to say, "Divinity is my profession." A Cambridge man, Ray titled his most popular book *The Wisdom of God Manifested in the Works of the Creation* (1691); and White, a hundred years later, might have done the same. White's favorite creatures—the swallows he so loved and referred to so frequently and the swifts that harvested flying insects even higher in the vault of the sky—epitomize the devout joy that seems to have energized him.

But White wrote discursively like an essayist, not systematically like John Ray. And although detailed descriptions of natural phenomena had ornamented the Age of Enlightenment (whose British avatar was Isaac Newton), a cold analysis or mechanistic, bean-counter mentality was in vogue, attuned more to geometry than divinity. Nature, unblinkered by episcopal dogma, was to be viewed without empathy or intuition. *Biophilia,* as we call it now—an innate emotional affiliation with other creatures—would have seemed like backsliding, except perhaps in nature poetry, whose long traditions included rhapsody and fervor, wit or dread. White's sweetness of voice, yet clarity of focus, as flexible as a letter, therefore bridged the gap to the romanticism that was to come, and even to us.

Nature writing has gradually grown into a literature of love and requiem from, first, the biblical viewpoint of fear and loathing of the chaos of the wilderness; and then dry inventories that sought to tame or eviscerate it. By and by these did tame it, except for gloomier novelists like Thomas Hardy or Herman Melville and Joseph Conrad, for whom the ocean would continue to encompass awesome ambiguities, exalted and exuberant though they sometimes felt when they were afloat upon it. Explorers such as Lewis and Clark, George Catlin, and John James Audubon provided Americans with a graphic portrait of their continent when it was still limitless and raw, an ocean of forest and grass. And nobody knew—not the wisest witness, like Thomas Jefferson, who thought "a hundred generations" would be required to fill the West with settlers—how soon a requiem might be appropriate.

But the Reverend White, located as an observer of tidy constancy in his very birthplace in the hamlet of Selborne, much as Henry Thoreau would be—writing a voluminous journal in *his* birthplace of Concord, Massachusetts, in the mid-nineteenth century—was in a different position from Audubon, Catlin, Lewis and Clark, Melville, Conrad, Darwin, Henry Bates, Richard Spruce, Henry Stanley, John Muir, Rudyard Kipling, Mungo Park, W. H. Hudson, and other authors whom we look to for a view of nature before the impact of industrialism. White, like Thoreau, was writing of a spot no wilder than where I live now, and which reportedly is little changed. I, too, see larks and owls and swallows, turn up field mice in the meadow, hike a daily round, value cherry and basswood trees, keep a tortoise whose activities intrigue and touch me, and watch some of my neighbors eventually join their mothers and fathers in the graveyard. White is not merely historical. Like the evergreen Thoreau, he tells us things we can still recapitulate or do.

His was also an era of discovery and the puzzles of existence absorb him—where birds go in the winter—but not the behindhand reasons, not the whys. He knows *God* is, though not a missionary or evangelist on behalf of churchly certainties. Unlike Thoreau, who was an equally devout, committed man, he is not quarreling with us as we read along, telling us how we ought to reform our lives. Both men were lifelong bachelors, probably virgins, who filled their need for companionship partly by close attachments to their families, though White had the advantage in the number of brothers and sisters he had—who gave him cause to boast of sixty-two nieces and nephews by the time he died. Their journal-keeping, their good educations and yet their stubborn decision to eschew conventionally ambitious careers, and the daily zeal with which they walked the countryside instead, are similar. And White enjoyed his saddle horse so much that his best friend, John Mulso, called him "the Huzzar Parson" for the zest with which he rode. Unlike Thoreau, he was a passionate flower gardener, and raised cantaloupes in a "melonry," as well as many other vegetables and had a herb garden on the seven acres that he cultivated intensively, behind a ha-ha, lovely tree plantings, and other landscaped subtleties.

He was a gentleman by design—not prickly like Thoreau—and did not employ the inspiration of natural history to try to reconfigure society. The English pattern of nature lovers, anyway, was that they were landed, leisured Tories, beneficiaries of the ancient hierarchies. They were likely to feel as White did in a church report in 1783, where he was pleased to write that "for more than a century past there does not appear to have been one Papist or any Protestant dissenter of any denomination" in Selborne. Six years later, as Parisians stormed the Bastille and British workers joined together in Jacobin clubs, he wrote a friend:

> You cannot abhor the dangerous doctrines of levellers & republicans more than I do! I was born & bred a Gentleman, & hope I shall be allowed to die such. The reason you have so many bad neighbours is your nearness to a great factious manufacturing town. Our common people are more simple-minded & know nothing of Jacobin clubs.

The contrast with Americans like Thoreau and Emerson, down to contemporary nature writers, prominently associated with radical politics like Edward Abbey and Peter Matthiessen, couldn't be more stark. If there were exceptions in the New World, they were apt to be artists foreign born, like Audubon and Muir, who had more feel for caste and ceremony even when they were poor, and who didn't particularly bridle at the sight of slavery or Jim Crow. When Gilbert White refers to one of his informants, Thomas Knight, in a letter and in his journal as "a sober hind," it's startling to a reader accustomed to Thoreau. But it fits the popular 1848 British hymn,

> All things bright and beautiful,
> All creatures great and small,
> All things wise and wonderful,
> The Lord God made them all.
> The rich man in his castle,
> The poor man at his gate.
> God made them, high or lowly,
> And order'd their estate.

Emerson and Thoreau hated slavery. Thoreau harbored runaways, championed John Brown, and went to jail for a night in 1846 as a gesture of civil disobedience—inspiring Gandhi a hundred years later and Martin Luther King. In *Walden* (1854), he ridiculed the notion of inheritance and private property, and, like Bartram and Catlin, he was profoundly, precociously interested in Indian customs. Emerson's liberal spirit extended to these issues as well, plus women's suffrage. And the frontier belonged to everyone with such an abundance of nature to share, first come, first served. Though gold rushes and land rushes were distasteful to Thoreau because of the greed that was displayed, they defined the young democracy and delighted another master nature writer, Mark Twain, whose river rhapsodies about the Mississippi are twinned in *Huckleberry Finn* with quite a radical interpretation of society. We see again today what an extraordinary combination it is when a naturalist's high gusto is allied with political radicalism, in the great contemporary New World novel—Gabriel García Márquez's *One Hundred Years of Solitude*. And in Russia, perhaps the most sublime depiction of nature in all of literature, Ivan Turgenev's *A Sportsman's Notebook*, may also have been the most potent book of European fiction in its political effects. Turgenev's harrowing portrait of serfdom, published in 1852 (which brought him nineteen months of internal exile), is said to have eventually helped persuade Czar Alexander to emancipate the serfs. Even as domestic a nature writer as John Burroughs—who was about as serene as the Americans *got*—showed his true colors by his tirelessly affectionate advocacy of Walt Whitman in print and in person, over the course of thirty years.

Walt Whitman, the ultimate American-style democrat, and Gilbert White had in common, however, a singular sense that human nature was part of all nature. White appears to have held up the publication of *The Natural History of Selborne* in order to complete what he thought of as its companion, *The Antiquities of Selborne*, which is an inferior compilation of human activities. We can be surprised at his Blimpish reactions to the "Lop and Top Riot" near Selborne in 1784, when hard-pressed peasants sought firewood from the limbs and tops of a thousand oak trees that a certain Lord Stawel had logged. (White wrote that "these folks, especially the females, are very abusive, and set my Lord at defiance.") But when he discusses crickets, for example, in Letters XLVI–XLVIII to Daines Barrington, the kindly, distinguished barrister and naturalist who in 1767 had first given him a diary of blank pages to fill with observations, White jumps at least to our century. Humane and dedicated, paying exceptional attention, he escapes his time frame. He could be Rachel Carson or Annie Dillard or someone not yet born making a "humble attempt to promote a more minute inquiry into . . . the life and conversation of animals." The "conversation" of animals! Not since paganism had a solid citizen employed such a term.

Undulant as wing beats, the book scuds along, not fretful or self-preening as so much nature-y scribbling is now. The drama of house martins plastering mud onto their nests with their chins, "moving their heads with a quick vibratory motion;" the "quick and glancing evolutions" of swallows who then "twitter in a pretty inward soft manner in their nests;" the skylark's versus the titlark's song in flight; the vigorous instincts of baby vipers; the value of earthworms, "hermaphrodites, and much addicted to venery," to a farmer; a report that most owls hoot on a note of B-flat; the anatomy of a new species of bat; the structure of a peacock's tail. He devotes a letter to a sow that mothered three hundred piglets; and another to the bizarre hardihood of gypsies; a friendship between a horse and hen; a rabbit nursed by a cat, like Romulus and Remus suckled by a wolf; and an idiot boy obsessed with bees. He does not dwell much on the gypsies or the idiot boy, but dissects a cuckoo and a nightjar to see if there are structural reasons that compel the former bird to lay its eggs in the nest of the latter, and not vice versa.

Audubon's first published writing, in the 1820s, also was concerned with swallows, with their nesting and the vexing question of whether they migrated or somehow hibernated. And John Muir, up in the Sierras of California in the late 1800s, delighted in and saluted the dipper, or water ouzel, which might be described as a kind of underwater swallow in its agility at navigating mountain streams. White's heart-felt love of swallows chimes with anybody's who responds to sprightly grace. He is meticulous yet gleeful, but not a complex witness like Richard Jefferies of Wiltshire (1848–1887), who may be White's closest kin among the British of the next century. Jefferies began as a Tory country essayist of shaky, small-holder social rank, often callous or flippant in describing laborers. But he was luminous and confidently exact in his knowledge and affection for surviving pockets of nature ("A Brook—A London Trout"), and as he fought a painful losing battle against tuberculosis, amid the Grub Street necessities of earning a living in London, his eye and memories shifted toward the poignant dignities of life and people in the country. Like

William Cobbett, an earlier, astutely feisty, peripatetic, nineteenth-century outdoor English chronicler (*Rural Rides*), whose politics carry us a bit toward the present connotations of "Green," Jefferies became more of a modernist, an angry young man hustling a living—at first lashing out at his origins but at the same time permanently smitten with them.

White felt no such conflicts. Grandson of a vicar, son of a retired barrister, he never needed to go off to London to win his fortune in the world. Oxford politics were sufficient for him, and, losing his bid to be provost of his college at thirty-six, he was not all that skillful at those. In England, unlike America, wealth was sometimes used to protect nature, not obliterate it. Nor were other forms of disillusion appropriate to his cast of mind. Like most of us, he would not have believed in T. S. Eliot's theorem that "April is the cruellest month," or Thoreau's that "the mass of men lead lives of quiet desperation," or otherwise climb out on a limb that marked him as a writer of a particular age and slant. And he didn't use the backdrop of nature for great hortatory adventures, like Lemuel Gulliver's or Robinson Crusoe's, or a transcendental embrace of all humanity, black and white and red, like Whitman's, or sharp, Frostian metaphors. Observing the darting swifts or the slow antediluvian antics of Timothy, the seven-pound tortoise he inherited from his aunt, Rebecca Snooke, he simply exercised his god-given eyes. He was not attempting to be comprehensive, like Hardy or like *Middlemarch*. He is one of those light-irradiated artists who just see what they see and do what they do, waking up in the morning and looking outside, and later somehow energized Coleridge, Wordsworth, Darwin, Virginia Woolf, W. H. Auden, and on and on.

White's was the cheerful era of Thomas Jefferson, Hector St. John Crèvecoeur, Peter Kalm, and the Quakerishly gargantuan Bartram, and other frontier enthusiasts in America, and of the free-lance free spirit, Jean-Jacques Rousseau, elucidator of the natural man, in France. The eighteenth century's currents had legitimized the role of nature in revealing God's essence, as well as the sufficiency of individual responses to it, whether as inspiration, dissent or merely factual observation. Facts were valued, and though the Church of England had not been the leverage behind this shift, it was—like most state religions—institutionally loose and confident in its static liturgy, not onerous in the demands it made upon a curate whose sustained light-heartedness, signalized by his love of swallows, lent him wings.

Echoes occupy him; as do hedgehogs' methods of gnawing roots; gossamer spider webs that rain from the wind; the different heights at which large and little bats, or swifts and swallows, feed; the drowning of two witches in 1751 in the village of Tring; and various birds that wash themselves with water, versus those that "dust," like "a strict Mussulman" in the desert. He speculates on the importance of eating fresh vegetables and meat; visits a dead captive moose before it putrefies; says that he would ride forty miles to see a tree full of herons' nests; and mentions a raven that loyally died with her nesting tree, rather than abandon her eggs.

Not encyclopedic like Buffon or reclusive like Fabre, not spiky like Thoreau, evangelical on behalf of scenery like John Muir, or a doomsayer like Jeffers, he was the mildest of revolutionaries. And the energy of his observations (see Letter XLII to Mr. Barrington!), un-knotted with controversy, and of his avid, even-tempered empathy for nature helped as much as anybody to unravel the earlier conception of wildness as chaos. What Mark Van Doren wrote in a revival of William Bartram's work in 1928 could be applied equally to White. He combined "in his very pleasing disposition a gentle and passionate love of nature with a zeal for study and report." Bartram, White's fellow visionary, wrote for his part:

> I am known to be an advocate or vindicator of the benevolent and peaceable disposition of animal creation in general, not only toward mankind, whom they seem to venerate, but always toward one another, except where hunger or the rational and necessary provocations of the sensual appetite interfere.

White would probably have signed on to this, a conclusion that in a lifetime spent watching animals I've also reached, but that remains quite novel or heretical unless you go clear back to hunter-gatherer mythology, where it is commonplace. White, Bartram, Thoreau, and later writers did not pay more attention to nature than soothsayers and ordinary native hunters had done. They simply paid as much, which for a thousand years in Europe had ceased to be the case.

William Bartram was the son of John Bartram, the King's own botanist in the American colonies, and had the good fortune of traveling extensively on wilderness expeditions as a young man. And Thoreau's great stroke of luck was to have had Ralph Waldo Emerson as a neighbor, a cheering section, and a formative patron in the literary hub of Concord (also Nathaniel Hawthorne's home). Emerson was then America's chief essayist, a leading magazine editor, and an international intellectual, as well as the avatar of transcendentalism, which had lent nature lovers a new cachet. Banned from Harvard's speaking platforms for thirty years because of his apostasy from Unitarian orthodoxy, Emerson as a friend and freethinker was incalculably beneficial to Thoreau.

But White—born a hundred years earlier than Thoreau—lived in a backwater, the roads hardly even passable during the winter. Though he had rubbed shoulders with Oxford dons and for a few years had been one, he wrote in 1767 to Thomas Pennant:

> It has been my misfortune never to have had any neighbours whose studies have led them towards the pursuit of natural knowledge; so that, for want of a companion to quicken my industry and sharpen my attention, I have made but slender progress in a kind of information to which I have been attached from my childhood.

That he devoted some eighteen years to fitfully working on *The Natural History of Selborne*, and didn't begin till he was ten years past the age at which Thoreau died, is surely attributable to this isolation. If Selborne had boasted an equivalent figure to Emerson in Concord—if, say, Samuel Johnson, a generous spirit who was White's contemporary, had happened to put in some years there—it's hard to doubt that White would have written and published quicker and perhaps in a more elegant form. "Letters" (and almost half the text of White's did not actually pass through the mails) are a primitive sort of essay, much as the epistolary novels like *Pamela* and *Humphrey Clinker* that appeared in the eighteenth century were an experimental start on storytelling of a new and extended kind. But the essay as a device for expression, if we date its origins from Montaigne, was already farther along.

It seems odd to transpose the mature and celebrated Samuel Johnson from London to Selborne as a counterpart to Emerson in Concord, because nature in British literature was relatively marginal—not, as in America, a geophysical force. From early on in America, nature pervaded the books of Edgar Allen Poe, James Fenimore Cooper, and Washington Irving. Then it continued as a central motif for Thoreau, Emerson, Melville, and Twain, on through Sherwood Anderson and Willa Cather, to William Faulkner and Ernest Hemingway—who both were born in an era when it was still commonplace that they should have known Indians and deep primeval woods as they were growing up, and thus wrote familiarly about the wilderness in several of their best books. The British, instead, became great travelers to the Nile, the Amazon, the Himalayas: Richard Spruce, Henry Bates, David Livingstone, Sir Samuel Baker, Sir Richard Burton, Evelyn Waugh, Graham Greene, Joyce Cary, George Orwell, Wilfrid Thesiger, Bruce Chatwin, Colin Thubron, and on and on. Travel writing became a triumphant British specialty, whereas adventurous American aristocrats like Francis Parkman, Clarence King, or Theodore Roosevelt, and restless soldiers like Meriwether Lewis, William Clark, and John Wesley Powell didn't need to catch a ship—just strike west from their front doors to find aboriginal peoples and dangerous terrain where a career might be made.

So Gilbert White, eschewing foreign travel much as Thoreau in America stubbornly stayed east, was pioneering on an original tack, as a bridgehead from eighteenth century rationalism to nineteenth-century romanticism. He was bestowing a new emphasis upon home-town nature while jiggery-poking journal entries of different dates and consolidating into one "letter" for publication observations that had first been addressed to another recipient. The chalk hills of the Sussex Downs were White's version of Thoreau's Maine woods, furnishing him with more room than he had time or strength to properly roam, and the three-hundred-foot "Hanger" or bluff behind his house gave him endless domesticated wildness and amusement, with its zigzag path laboriously constructed up through the beech groves, and a "Hermitage" for picnics on top. His brother Benjamin White, a London bookseller and publisher, was his main link to literary life and introduced him to both correspondents who nominally helped to frame his book. Pennant, who was a famous zoologist of the time, a hard-driving professional man, naturally hoped to use White's data in his own work, whereas Barrington, whose livelihood lay in practicing law, was a more disinterested friend. White's letters to him are more numerous, supple, and intimate, Barrington, in 1767, having proffered him the diary of blank pages in which he had begun his book.

But *The Natural History of Selborne* hasn't run through two hundred editions from lack of elegance. Constancy is one of its virtues. It is a distillation of how to live if your senses are alive to what's outside, and brought the study of nature from the museums into the field. "Larkers," "bat-fowlers," "warreners," viper-catchers and others of the poaching peasantry who made their living netting bird and beast probably knew more about ecology than the scientists did. White himself discovered the harvest mouse, the noctule bat, and delineated three species of willow warbler, but of course his much more significant contribution was the eccentrically equal play he seemed to give to people and animals, not putting either ahead of the other: This during the eighteenth century, which is extraordinary enough, but in the same year that William Blake, a younger sky watcher and visionary, published *Songs of Innocence*.

We see again such rapt impartiality in Mikhail Prishvin (1873–1954), a Russian writer of scintillating gifts who survived Stalin's purges by his honest focus upon the out-of-doors, as in *Nature's Diary*, or in the "naturalist's trance," as Edward O. Wilson describes it, of writers like Wilson, Donald Culross Peattie, and John Fowles, who can fall into complete absorption watching a tree, a beetle or an ant. Nature writing brings the quintessential tool of civilization to bear on the questions of wilderness—which we understand now is not chaos but intricately ordered, and indeed laddered into the very structure of our minds. It's no coincidence that we first read nature writing in conjunction with children's literature, woven into Aesop or Kipling, *The Wind in the Willows* or E. B. White, and other authors' books that became classics partly because they fed an appetite that was already there, stitched into our responses virtually from birth. And later we keep reading it to be reminded of a peace which passeth understanding, and of the ultimate tests of mettle that are provided when we're underneath the sky—not only of stoicism and endurance but also of our equanimity, serenity, and undergirding of joy—that "green man" John Fowles speaks about, who inhabits each of us until he has been smothered.

Nature writing has always been a literary stepchild or poor relation, however. The illustrious tradition of landscape painting, filling art museums with the work of geniuses from many settings across the centuries, has no good counterpart in literature. Maybe readers, writers, reviewers, and editors are congenitally just too bookish; but the result has been too little contemporary protest as nature has been destroyed. The coming claustrophobic death of wildlife on his narrow island and elsewhere of course hadn't yet pinched White, though he mildly mourned Selborne's loss of black grouse and red deer. His brother John, a chaplain on Gibraltar, stood at the brink of Africa, conveying to him the limitless mysteries beyond. Even Ireland, White recommends to "some future faunist" as "a country little known to the naturalist." (And "the manners of the wild natives . . . their sordid way of life, will extort from him many useful reflections.") Not the storming of the Bastille in the same year that his book came out, but World War I finally accomplished the real social leveling of his England that he'd feared. Though he was a genial, charitable, and dutiful pastor by repute, the weddings, christenings, and funerals of his parishioners are remarkably absent from his diaries. Thoreau's are much ampler, by contrast, including more generosity on the human side.

But White has a Mozartian (*another* contemporary, and beneficiary of Daines Barrington's unusually kindly energies)—a Mozartian sort of precision and gaiety that seems pristine nowadays. And this is not just because such faith in amateur observation was eclipsed by a long epoch of pouter-pigeon professionalism. Like nouveaux riches, learned people in White's rationalist age hated to admit there might be any animate puzzles beyond their ken, such as migration, by which dumb animals like birds demonstrated powers of navigation far surpassing man's. They preferred to think that swallows hibernated, for instance. Linnaeus too. White cogitated a lot about the question as well, but White's loving open-mindedness and pellucid transparency wears better over time than the triumphalists. Similarly, one might compare Thoreau's adaptability to the new concept of Evolution in the mid-nineteenth century to his panjandrum contemporary, Louis Agassiz, whose dogmatic, prejudiced rejection of it stalled the study of biology at Harvard by at least a generation. Agassiz, a trenchant classifier, was the Linnaeus of Thoreau's time. Or we might possibly leap ahead to compare the amazing reluctance of many prominent scientists of our own day, such as Stephen Jay Gould, to forgo momentarily the fascinations of paleontology, and get involved in the fight against the current holocaust of extinctions, with the passionate commitment to living creatures of contemporary nature writers like Edward Abbey and Peter Matthiessen, whose eyes were open to the catastrophic tragedy all along.

Oftener than not, the steamroller of destruction, fueled by economic factors, was abetted, not mitigated by science. And Gilbert White, after all the hullabaloo of the two centuries following his death, has a kind of harpsichord purity and simplicity. Not a piano, like the wider-ranging Thoreau, or the orchestral ambiguities of the great nineteenth-century nature novelists—but the never-stale, never-tripping harpsichord. And what has happened is that we have recently realized that half of all the species on earth may be extinguished within a single person's life span, most never examined by a scientist at all. This is a staggering state of affairs. It capsizes the mind. People years from now will be flabbergasted, not as much that it occurred as how unaccountably little the community of intellectuals of our half-century did to raise the alarm.

Provincialism, egoism, careerism, myopia—whatever the combination of causes, maybe more of Gilbert White was needed. More reverence, catholicity and delight: an unpaid, untenured, unsleeping attentiveness and less varnishing of epaulettes. White, living in the hamlet of Selborne from the age of ten, believed that men who undertake a study of "only one district are much more likely to advance natural knowledge than those that grasp at more than they can possibly be acquainted with . . ." Like Thoreau in Concord, he set himself against the grain. He didn't ransack the huge red stretches on maps of the world that denoted the British Empire because, like Blake or Thoreau, he knew that heaven was in a wildflower. "The methods of Providence" were what he wished to discover. And that didn't require a trip.

(1997)

SHORT STORIES

"Cowboys," *The Noble Savage*, No. 1, February 1960
"The Last Irish Fighter," *Esquire*, August 1960
"The Witness," *The Paris Review*, Summer-Fall 1967
"The Colonel's Power," *New American Review*, No. 2, January 1968
"Kwan's Coney Island," *New American Review*, No. 5, January 1969
"A Fable of Mammas," *Transatlantic Review*, No. 32, Summer 1969
"The Final Fate of the Alligators," *The New Yorker*, October 18, 1969
"Seven Rivers West," *Esquire*, July 1986
"The Mind's Eye," *The Nature of Nature*, (ed. Wm. Shore), Harcourt, 1994

ESSAYS

"The Big Cats," *Esquire*, April 1961
"The Draft Card Gesture," *Commentary*, February 1968
"Notes from the Century Before," *The Paris Review*, Winter 1968
"On Not Being a Jew," *Commentary*, April 1968
"The Threshold and the Jolt of Pain," *The Village Voice*, October 17, 1968
"The Courage of Turtles," *The Village Voice*, December 12, 1968
"The Elephant Trainer and the Man on Stilts," *The Village Voice*, April 17, 1969
"Why this Extra Violence," *The Village Voice*, May 8, 1969
"Knights and Squires: For Love of the Tugs," *The Village Voice*, May 29, 1969
"The Problem of the Golden Rule," *Commentary*, August 1969
"Blitzes and Holding Actions," *The Village Voice*, October 16, 1969
"Books, Movies, the News," *Book World*, November 9, 1969
"Home is Two Places," *Commentary*, February 1970
"The Circus in 1970," *The Village Voice*, April 9, 1970
"The Moose on the Wall," *New American Review*, No. 9, April 1970
"Americana by the Acre," *Harper's*, October 1970
"Meatcutters Are a Funny Bunch," *The Village Voice*, December 17, 1970
"The Portland Freight Run," *The Atlantic*, February 1971
"The War in the Woods," *Harper's*, February 1971
"Splendid, with Trumpets," *The Village Voice*, April 8, 1971
"Two Clowns," *Life*, April 25, 1971
"The Assassination Impulse," *The Village Voice*, May 27, 1971

"Of Cows and Cambodia," *The Atlantic*, July 1971

"The Soul of the Tiger," *Esquire*, July 1971

"Hailing the Elusory Mountain Lion," *The New Yorker*, August 7, 1971

"Jane Street's Samurai," *The Village Voice*, November 25, 1971

"Nobody Writes Stories about Unicorns," *The Village Voice*, December 16, 1971

"Passions and Tensions," *The Village Voice*, February 2, 1972

"On the Question of Dogs," *The Village Voice*, March 30, 1972

"City Rat," *Audience*, March-April 1972

"Women Aflame," *The Village Voice*, April 27, 1972

"Marriage, Fame, Power, Success," *The Village Voice*, May 18, 1972

"In the Toils of the Law," *The Atlantic*, June 1972

"Looking for Wilderness," *The Atlantic*, August 1972

"Thoughts on Returning to the Mountain . . ." *The Village Voice*, November 1972

"Heart's Desire," *Audience*, November-December 1972

"Howling Back at the Wolves," *Saturday Review*, December 1972

"Wall Maps and Woodpeckers," *The Village Voice*, January 25, 1973

"Fred King on the Allagash," *Audience*, January-February 1973

"Mountain Towers," *The Village Voice*, February 15, 1973

"At Pinkham Notch," *The Village Voice*, March 15, 1973

"Wildlands in Vermont," *The Village Voice*, March 22, 1973

"In a Lair with a Bear," *Sports Illustrated*, March 26, 1973

"Tricks, Innocence, Pathos, Perfection," *The Village Voice*, May 10, 1973

"The Young Must Do the Healing," *The New York Times Magazine*, June 10, 1973

"Other Lives," *Harper's*, July 1973

"A Run of Bad Luck," *Newsweek*, July 30, 1973

"Writing Wild," *The New York Times Book Review*, September 23, 1973

"That Gorgeous Great Novelist," *The Village Voice*, November 15, 1973

"But Where Is Home," *The New York Times Book Review*, December 23, 1973

"A Mountain with a Wolf on It," *Sports Illustrated*, January 14, 1974

"Where Have All the Heroes Gone," *The New York Times Book Magazine*, March 10, 1974

"Where the Action Is," *The New York Times Book Review*, October 13, 1974

"Nine Home Truths about Writing," *The Village Voice*, January 20, 1975

"The Tug of Life at the End of the Leash," *Harper's*, February 1975

"Big Frog, Very Small Pond," *Sports Illustrated*, March 3, 1975

"City Walking," *The New York Times Book Review*, June 1, 1975

"The Survival of the Newt," *The New York Times Book Magazine*, July 27, 1975

"Apocalypse Enough," *Not Man Apart*, July 1975

"A Paradox among Us," *Harper's*, January 1976

"Southern Mansions," *Travel & Leisure*, February 1976

"What I Think, What I Am," *The New York Times Book Review*, June 27, 1976

"Cairo Observed," *Harper's*, June 1976

"At Large in East Africa," *Harper's*, August 1976

"The Fragile Writer," *The New York Times Book Review*, December 12, 1976

"The Ridge-Slope Fox and the Knife-Thrower," *Harper's*, January 1977

"Do Writers Stay Home," *The New York Times Book Review*, May 22, 1977

"Without American Express," *The New York Times Book Review*, June 4, 1978

"Into Eritrea: Africa's Red Sea War," *Harper's*, July 1978
"Unsilent Spring," *The Nation*, May 26, 1979
"Gabriel, Who Wanted to Know," *The New England Review*, Summer 1979
"Being Between Books," *The New York Times Book Review*, October 28, 1979
"Tugs," *Harper's*, December 1979
"Johnny Appleseed," *American Heritage*, December 1979
"December Song," *The Nation*, December 6, 1980
"Mountain Notch," Sierra Club's 1981 Wilderness Calendar
"America Was Promises (Still)," *The Nation*, February 21, 1981
"Making of a Writer," *The New York Times Book Review*, October 4, 1981
"Gods, Masks, and Horses," *Vanity Fair*, July 1983
"Anchorage," *Vanity Fair*, October 1983
"Up the Black to Chalkyitsik," *House & Garden*, June 1984
"Hail the Anhinga," *The Nation*, June 9, 1984
"Memories of Circuses Past," *The Nation*, March 9, 1985
"In Okefenokee," *National Geographic Traveler*, Spring 1985
"Nectar Feeding," *The Nation*, July 20, 1985
"In Praise of John Muir," *Antaeus*, Autumn 1986
"Three Trains Across Canada," *Travel & Leisure*, March 1987
"Up With Spring," *The Nation*, June 6, 1987
"Treasured Places," *Life*, July 1987
"Summer Skunks," *The Nation*, August 29, 1987
"Christmases Past," *The Nation*, December 26, 1987
"Heaven and Nature," *Harper's*, March 1988
"Arabia Felix," *Interview* magazine, May 1988
"The Indispensable Thoreau," *American Heritage*, July 1988
"Learning to Eat Soup," *Antaeus*, Autumn 1988
"The Hunger in Manhattan Life," *Harper's*, June 1989
"Jubilant Spring," *The Nation*, June 19, 1989
"A World Worth Saving," *Life*, October 1989
"O Wyoming," *Outside*, October 1989
"Tolstoyan Tide," *The Nation*, May 14, 1990
"Shh, Our Writers Are Sleeping," *Esquire*, July 1990
"On Betting One's Footing" (reprinted from "Anxious Dreams," *Manchester Guardian*, January 20, 1990), *Harper's*, August 1990
"Roadless Regions," *Literary Outtakes*, September 1990
"Passing Views," *Harper's*, January 1991
"Good Trips, Bad Trips," *Outside*, April 1991
"The Best Idea," *Life*, May 1991
"Spring Medley," *The Nation*, June 10, 1991
"Holy Fools," *The Nation*, September 16, 1991
"Everybody Comes to Belize," *Outside*, February 1992
"Meat for the Old Man," *Outside*, May 1992
"Christmas Observed," *The New York Times Magazine*, December 20, 1992
"To the Point," *Harper's*, March 1993
"Skin and Bones," *The Nation*, May 3, 1993

An Edward Hoagland Checklist

"The Unknown Thoreau," *The Nation*, June 7, 1993

"Nature's Seesaw," *Vermont*, May 1994 (also in Land's End Catalogue, September 1993)

"All This Good World," *Manoa*, June 1994

"Strange Perfume," *Esquire*, June 1994

"The View from 61," *The New York Times Magazine*, November 27, 1994

"Brightness Visible," *Harper's*, January 1995

"Surge Time at the Bottom of the Earth," *Outside*, March 1995

"Scenes from a Forty-Year War," *The Nation*, April 10, 1995

"Like a Saul Bellow Character," *Salmagundi*, Spring 1995

"Stepping Back," *The New York Times Magazine*, November 12, 1995

"Books that Need Authors," *The Nation*, November 13, 1995

"The Daring Art of Rockwell Kent," *Civilization*, January 1996

"Dying Argots," *Harper's*, January 1996

"Running Mates," *Hungry Mind Review*, November 1996 (also Spring 1999)

"Generational Pioneer," *The New York Times Magazine*, December 8, 1996

"A Last Look Around," *Civilization*, February 1997

"A Peaceable Kingdom," *Preservation*, March 1997 (also in *Vermont*, June 1999)

"Wild Things," *Granta*, Spring 1997

"Samos, Reflections on Love, and Love Lost," *Islands*, June 1997

"Henry James and Porky Pig," *The Nation*, June 30, 1997

"The Sage of Selborne," *The Yale Review*, July 1997

"Spring Comes to the Kingdom," *Vermont Woodlands*, Spring 1998

"I Can See," *Granta*, Summer 1998

"India," *River City*, Summer 1998

"Vermont Journal," *The American Scholar*, Summer 1998

"Vermont: Suite of Seasons," *National Geographic*, September 1998

"Lost Between Burma and Tibet," *Outside*, October 1998

"On the Lure of Water," *Sierra*, May 1999

"Writers Afoot," *The American Scholar*, Summer 1999 (also in "Writers Afoot," *Harper's*, October 1999)

"Earth's Eye," *Northern Woodlands*, Autumn 1999

"That Sense of Falling," *Preservation*, October 1999

"Calliope Times," *The New Yorker*, May 22, 2000

"Natural Excursions," *Orion*, Summer 2000

"Fire," *The American Scholar*, Autumn 2000

"Natural Light," *Harper's*, October 2000

"Vermont's Civil Union," *The Washington Post*, late October 2000

"Secrets of the Stutter," *U.S. News and World Report*, April 2, 2001

"Smirko, Smirko, Smirko!" *Yankee Magazine*, June 2001

"Two Kinds of People," *Worth*, November 2001

"Circus Music," *Harper's*, February 2002

"Ansel Adams at 100," *Aperture*, Spring 2002

"John Muir's Alaskan Rhapsody," *The American Scholar*, Spring 2002

"Blind Faith," *Food & Wine*, April 2002

"1776 and All That," *The Nation*, July 22, 2002

"Diaries," *The Paris Review,* Summer 2002
"The Circus of Dr. Lao," *Post Road,* Fall 2002
"Not Even the Giant Squid," *Harper's,* November 2002
"Sex and the River Styx," *Harper's,* January 2003

OTHER ESSAYS

Commencing from March 12, 1979, fifty-plus unsigned editorials in *The New York Times:*
    "The Price of Fur," "In the Spring," "Hang-ups," "Mountain House," etc., to 1989
Anchorage Daily News, June 28, 1992
The Manchester Guardian, January 20, 1990; August 12, 1990; March 31, 1991
Manoa, June 1999
New England Monthly, May 1987
The New York Times, January 11, 1986; June 15, 1991; October 5, 1993; May 13, 1995
Pequod, Winter 1986
Portland Magazine (Oregon), Summer 1996; Winter 1996; Winter 1997; Spring 2002
Rolling Stone, May 28, 1998
Vermont, June 1994
Yankee Homes, September 1989

BOOK REVIEWS

In *The New York Times Book Review,* May 9, 1971; June 13, 1971; February 6, 1972;
    October 7, 1973; October 21, 1973; December 2, 1973; April 14, 1974;
    May 19, 1974; June 22, 1975; November 9, 1975; December 7, 1975;
    April 11, 1976; April 18, 1976; May 9, 1976; August 15, 1976; September 5, 1976;
    November 14, 1976; January 9, 1977; June 19, 1977; August 14, 1977;
    September 11, 1977; November 27, 1977; December 11, 1977;
    November 19, 1978; November 26, 1978; January 21, 1979; February 4, 1979;
    June 24, 1979; July 22, 1979; March 23, 1980; March 30, 1980; June 8, 1980;
    August 17, 1980; March 15, 1981; November 8, 1981; June 6, 1982;
    August 29, 1982; October 17, 1982; November 21, 1982; June 12, 1983;
    January 22, 1984; October 1984; February 16, 1986; July 19, 1987;
    September 11, 1988; January 8, 1989; May 7, 1989; March 18, 1990;
    November 25, 1990; July 2, 2000
In *The Boston Herald,* December 20, 1970
In *The Village Voice,* December 30, 1971; October 24, 1974; October 1982
In *The Chicago Daily News,* December 1, 1974
In *Life,* October 14, 1971; April 21, 1972; October 27, 1972
In *Harper's Book Letter,* May 12, 1975
In *Harper's,* July 1977; May 1985; January 1986; February 1989
In *Saturday Review,* April 28, 1979, December 1980
In *New York* magazine, May 28, 1979
In *The New Republic,* October 20, 1979; March 1, 1980
In *Washington Post Book World,* April 12, 1970; June 6, 1970; October 30, 1972; June
    15, 1980; October 11, 1981; August 2, 1987

In *Inside Sports*, November 1980
In *Science Digest*, October 1981
In *Chicago Tribune*, November 6, 1988
In *Wigwag*, October–December 1989
In *USA Today*, October 23, 1992; November 13, 1992; January 21, 1994
In *The Boston Globe*, November 19, 1995; April 19, 1998
In *Los Angeles Times*, September 22, 1996
In *Civilization*, November 1994; March 1995; July 1995; October 1997

OTHER WORK

General editor of the Penguin Nature Library; later called the Penguin Nature
   Classics series: thirty volumes in total, at its height; 1985 on.

Introductions written for:

The Mountains of California, by John Muir, Penguin, 1985
The Maine Woods, by Henry David Thoreau, Penguin, 1988
Vanishing Arctic, by T. M. Watkins, Aperture Books, 1988
The Pushcart Prize XVI, Best of the Small Presses, edited by Bill Henderson, 1991
Walden, by Henry David Thoreau, Vintage, 1991
The Circus of Dr. Lao, by Charles G. Finney, Vintage, 1993
Steep Trails, by John Muir, Sierra Club Books, 1994
Land of Rivers, by Peter Mancall, Cornell University Press, 1996
N by E, by Rockwell Kent, Wesleyan University Press, 1996
The Natural History of Selborne, by Gilbert White, Penguin, 1997
The Best American Essays 1999, edited by Edward Hoagland, Houghton Mifflin
Elevating Ourselves, by Henry David Thoreau, Houghton Mifflin, 1999
Our Like Will Not Be There Again, by Lawrence Millman, Ruminator Books, 2001
The Shameless Diary of an Explorer, by Robert Dunn, Modern Library, 2001
Shooting Blind, by Visually Impaired Collective, Aperture Books, 2002
Step Right This Way, by Edward J. Kelty, Barnes & Noble Books, 2002
Travels in Alaska, by John Muir, Modern Library, 2002

Contributor to large-format books:

Our World's Heritage, National Geographic Society, 1987
Paths Less Traveled, Atheneum, 1988
Favorite Places, a Travel & Leisure Book, 1989
Heart of a Nation, National Geographic Society, 2000